Death and Dying
Challenge and Change

Death and Dying
Challenge and Change

Edited by
Robert Fulton
Eric Markusen
Greg Owen
Jane L. Scheiber

Courses by Newspaper
A project of University Extension
University of California, San Diego
Funded by The National Endowment for the Humanities

Addison-Wesley Publishing Company
Reading, Massachusetts • Menlo Park, California
London • Amsterdam • Don Mills, Ontario • Sydney

Courses by Newspaper
Death and Dying: Challenge and Change

ACKNOWLEDGMENTS

Articles

1.
Death and Dying: The Issues Today

Robert L. Fulton, *On the Dying of Death,* from *Explaining Death to Children,* ed. by Earl A. Grollman. Copyright © 1967 by Earl A. Grollman. Reprinted by permission of Beacon Press.

Melvin Maddocks, *Life and Death in the USA,* reprinted by permission from *Encounter,* December, 1974

Edwin S. Shneidman, *National Survey of Attitudes toward Death,* from "You and Death," by Edwin S. Shneidman. Reprinted from *Psychology Today Magazine,* June 1971, Copyright © 1971, Ziff-Davis Publishing Company.

Samuel Vaisrub, *Dying Is Worked to Death,* from *The Journal of the American Medical Association* 229 (14), September 30, 1974, pp. 1909–1910. Copyright 1974, American Medical Association. Reprinted by permission.

Ronald Jay Cohen, *Is Dying Being Worked to Death?* from *The American Journal of Psychiatry,* vol. 133, pp. 575–577, 1976. Copyright 1976, The American Psychiatric Association. Reprinted with permission of Ronald Jay Cohen, Ph.D., and the American Psychiatric Association.

2.
Historical Perspectives on Death

David E. Stannard, *The Puritan Way of Death,* abridged from *The Puritan Way of Death: A Study in Religion, Culture and Social Change.* Copyright © 1977 by Oxford University Press, Inc. Used by permission.

Stanley French, *The Cemetery as Cultural Institution,* from *Death in America,* ed. by David E. Stannard. Copyright © 1975 by American Quarterly. Reprinted by permission.

Philippe Ariès, *The Reversal of Death,* translation of "La mort inversée. Le changement des attitudes devant la mort dans les societés occidentales," *Archives Européennes de Sociologie* 8 (1967). From *Death in America,* ed. by David E. Stannard. Copyright © 1975 by American Quarterly. Reprinted by permission.

3.
Death in Popular Culture

Michael J. Arlen, *The Air: The Cold, Bright Charms of Immortality,* from "The Cold, Bright Charms of Immortality" from *The View from Highway 1* by Michael J. Arlen. Copyright © 1975, 1976 by Michael J. Arlen. Reprinted with the permission of Farrar, Straus & Giroux, Inc. This selection appeared originally in *The New Yorker.*

Alexander Walker, *The Case of the Vanishing Bloodstains,* reprinted by permission from *Encounter,* March 1973.

Geoffrey Gorer, *The Pornography of Death,* portions of "The Pornography of Death" from *Death, Grief and Mourning* by Geoffrey Gorer. Copyright © 1965 by Geoffrey Gorer. Reprinted by permission of Doubleday & Co., Inc.

4.
Demography of Death

Monroe Lerner, *When, Why, and Where People Die,* excerpted from "When, Why, and Where People Die," in *The Dying Patient,* ed. by Orville G. Brim, Jr., et al., © 1970 Russell Sage Foundation, New York.

Robert Blauner, *Death and Social Structure,* excerpted from "Death and Social Structure," *Psychiatry* (1966) 29:378–394. Copyright © 1966 by the William Alanson White Psychiatric Foundation, Inc. Reprinted by special permission of the William Alanson White Psychiatric Foundation, Inc.

Calvin Goldscheider, *The Social Inequality of Death,* from *Population, Modernization, and Social Structure,* Little, Brown & Co. Copyright 1971 by Calvin Goldscheider. Reprinted by permission of the author.

5.
Death and Social Change

Stanislav Grof, *The Changing Face of Death,* from *The Human Encounters with Death* by Stanislav Grof and Joan Halifax. Copyright © 1977 by Stanislav Grof and Joan Halifax. Reprinted by permission of the publishers, E. P. Dutton.

Ivan Illich, *Death against Death,* from *Medical Nemesis* by Ivan Illich. Copyright © 1975 by Ivan Illich. © 1976 by Random House, Inc. Reprinted by permission of Pantheon Books, a division of Random House, Inc.

Eric J. Cassell, *Dying in a Technological Society,* from *Death Inside Out,* ed. by Peter Steinfels and Robert M. Veatch. Copyright © 1975 by Eric Cassell. Reprinted by permission of the author.

6.

Life after Death:
Old and New Meanings

Eric Markusen, *Religious Conceptions of Afterlife,* adapted from a book review of S. G. F. Brandon's *The Judgment of the Dead,* in *Omega,* vol. 2, 1970. Copyright 1970 by *Omega.* Reprinted by permission.

Rosalind Heywood, *Death and Psychical Research,* from *Man's Concern with Death* by Arnold Toynbee, et al., copyright © 1968 by Arnold Toynbee, A. Keith Mant, Ninian Smart, John Hinton, Cicely Yudkin, Eric Rhode, Rosalind Heywood, H. H. Price. Reprinted with permission of the publisher, Hodder & Stoughton Limited.

Raymond Moody, *Cities of Light,* excerpted from *Reflections on Life after Life,* © 1977 by Raymond A. Moody, Jr. All rights reserved. Reprinted by permission of the publishers, Mockingbird Books.

Peggy Taylor and Rick Ingrasci, *Out of the Body: An Interview with Elisabeth Kübler-Ross,* excerpted from "Out of the Body." *New Age* (32 Station St., Brookline, MA 02146), November 1977.

Samuel Vaisrub, *Afterthoughts on Afterlife,* from *Archives of Internal Medicine,* February 1977, p. 150, Copyright 1977, American Medical Association.

Bertrand Russell, *Do We Survive Death?* from *Why I Am Not a Christian* by Bertrand Russell. Reprinted by permission of George Allen & Unwin Ltd., publishers.

7.

The Dying Patient

Claire F. Ryder and Diane M. Ross, *Terminal Care: Issues and Alternatives,* from *Public Health Reports,* 92 (1), January–February 1977. Reprinted by permission of Diane M. Ross, Director of Health Education, Family Health Services, Inc.

Roberta Lyder Paige and Jane Finkbiner Looney, *Hospice Care for the Adult,* copyright © 1977, The American Journal of Nursing Company. Reprinted from *American Journal of Nursing,* November, Vol. 77, No. 11.

Cicely Saunders, *Should a Patient Know?* from *Nursing Times,* July 15, 1976. Reprinted with permission.

Thomas Powers, *Learning to Die,* from *Harper's,* June 1971. Copyright © 1971 by Thomas Powers. Published by permission of Karen Hitzig, agent.

Edwin S. Shneidman, *Death Work and the Stages of Dying,* copyright © 1973 by Edwin S. Shneidman. Reprinted by permission of Quadrangle/Times Books from *Deaths of Man* by Edwin S. Shneidman.

Elisabeth Kübler-Ross, *Interview with a Seventeen-Year-Old Girl,* reprinted with permission from *On Death and Dying* by Elisabeth Kübler-Ross. Copyright © 1969 by Elisabeth Kübler-Ross.

Stewart Alsop, *Stay of Execution,* from *Saturday Review/World,* December 18, 1973. Copyright © Saturday Review, 1973. All rights reserved.

Avery Weisman, *An Appropriate Death,* from *On Dying and Denying: A Psychiatric Study of Terminality* by Avery D. Weisman. Copyright © 1972 by Behavioral Publications, Inc., New York. Reprinted by permission of Human Sciences Press and the author.

8.

Death and the Child

Edgar Jackson, *When to Talk about Death,* from *Telling a Child about Death* by Edgar Jackson. Copyright © 1965 by Edgar N. Jackson. By permission of Hawthorn Books, Inc.

Robert Kastenbaum, *The Kingdom Where Nobody Dies,* from *Saturday Review/Science,* - January 1973. Copyright © 1973 Saturday Review.

Earl Grollman, *How Does a Child Experience Grief?* from *Explaining Death to Children,* ed.

by Earl A. Grollman. Copyright © 1967 by Earl A. Grollman. Reprinted by permission of Beacon Press.

9.
Grief

Erich Lindemann, *Symptomatology and Management of Acute Grief,* from *The American Journal of Psychiatry,* vol. 101, pp. 141–148, 1944. Copyright 1944.

Philippe Ariès, *The Denial of Mourning,* from "The Reversal of Death: Changes in Attitudes toward Death in Western Societies," translation of "La Mort inversee. Le changement des attitudes devant la mort dans les societes occidentales," *Archives Europeennes de Sociologie* 8 (1967). From *Death in America,* ed. by David E. Stannard. Copyright © 1975 by American Quarterly. Reprinted by permission.

Geoffrey Gorer, *Death, Grief, and Mourning,* from *Death, Grief and Mourning.* Reprinted by permission of Doubleday & Company, Inc.

Colin Murray Parkes, *The Broken Heart,* reprinted from *Bereavement* by C. Murray Parkes. By permission of International Universities Press, Inc. Copyright 1972 by International Universities Press.

Robert L. Fulton, *Anticipatory Grief, Stress, and the Surrogate Griever,* from *Cancer, Stress and Death,* ed. by Tache, Selye and Day. Reprinted by permission of Plenum Publishing Corporation.

10.
Widowhood

Helena Z. Lopata, *Living through Widowhood,* reprinted from *Psychology Today Magazine,* July 1973. Copyright © 1973, Ziff-Davis Publishing Company.

Lynn Caine, *Widow,* abridgement of chapters "Breaking the Silence," "The Lonely Goose," "Like a Penis in the Bank," "You'll Get Married Again," pp. 221–222, and Obituary for Martin J. Caine from *Widow* by Lynn Caine. Copyright © 1974 by Lynn Caine. By permission of William Morrow & Company, Inc.

Arnold Toynbee, *Man's Concern with Death: Epilogue,* from "The Relationship between Life and Death" from *Man's Concern with Death* by Arnold Toynbee et al., copyright © 1968 by Arnold Toynbee. Reprinted with the permission of the publisher, Hodder & Stoughton Limited.

11.
The Funeral

Vanderlyn Pine, *The Care of the Dead: A Historical Portrait,* from *Caretaker of the Dead: The American Funeral Director* by Vanderlyn Pine. © 1975 by Irvington Publishers, Inc. Reprinted by permission.

Ruth Mulvey Harmer, *Funerals, Fantasy, and Flight,* from *Omega,* Vol. 2, 1971. Copyright 1971 by Ruth Mulvey Harmer. Reprinted by permission.

Howard C. Raether, *The Place of the Funeral: The Role of the Funeral Director in Contemporary Society,* from *Omega,* vol. 2, 1971. Copyright 1971 by *Omega.* Reprinted by permission.

12.
Morality and Mortality in Modern Society

Elizabeth Hall with Paul Cameron, *Our Failing Reverence for Life,* from *Psychology Today Magazine,* April 1976. Copyright © 1976, Ziff-Davis Publishing Company.

Daniel C. Maguire, *Death, Legal and Illegal,* portion of "Death, Legal and Illegal" from *Death by Choice* by Daniel C. Maguire. Copyright © 1973 by Daniel C. Maguire. First appeared in *Atlantic Magazine.* Reprinted by permission of Doubleday & Company, Inc.

Robert M. Veatch, *The Legislative Options,* from *The Hastings Center Report,* October 1977. © Institute of Society, Ethics and the Life Sciences, 360 Broadway, Hastings-on-Hudson, NY 10706.

Sonya Rudikoff, *The Problem of Euthanasia,* reprinted from *Commentary,* by permission; copyright © 1974 by the American Jewish Committee.

Robert White and H. Tristram Engelhardt, Jr., *A Demand to Die,* from *The Hastings Center Report,* June 1975. © Institute of Society, Ethics and the Life Sciences, 360 Broadway, Hastings-on-Hudson, NY 10706. Reprinted by permission.

13.
Suicide

14.
Death, War, and the Human Condition

15.
The Death System:
Review and Prospectus

Poetry

Corporation. Reprinted by permission of New Directions Publishing Corporation.

J. V. Cunningham, "Epitaph for Someone or Other" reprinted from *The Collected Poems and Epigrams* © 1971 by J. V. Cunningham, by permission of The Swallow Press, Chicago.

Nahuatl poem, "I Have Wept for You."

Martin Buber, "The Deaf Man," reprinted by permission of Shocken Books Inc. from *Tales of the Hasidim: The Early Masters* by Martin Buber. Copyright © 1947, 1975 by Shocken Books Inc.

James Weldon Johnson, from "Go Down Death" from *God's Trombones* by James Weldon Johnson. Copyright 1927 by the Viking Press Inc. Copyright © renewed by Grace Nail Johnson.

William Shakespeare, from *Hamlet.*

Emily Dickinson, "The Heart Asks Pleasure First."

Martin Buber, "The Fear of Death" from *Tales of the Hasidim: The Later Masters* by Martin Buber. Reprinted by permission of Shocken Books Inc. Copyright © 1948, 1975 by Shocken Books Inc.

Kahlil Gibran, "Parting," from *A Tear and A Smile* by Kahlil Gibran. © 1950 by Alfred A. Knopf, Inc. Reprinted by permission of the publisher.

Karl Shapiro, "Auto Wreck." © 1942, renewed 1970 by Karl Shapiro. From *Selected Poems by Karl Shapiro*. Reprinted by permission of Random House, Inc.

Dylan Thomas, "Do Not Go Gentle into That Good Night," from the *Poems of Dylan Thomas,* © 1952 by Dylan Thomas, reprints by permission of New Directions and Dent & Sons, Ltd.

Euripides, from *Hippolytus,* translated by Gilbert Murray.

William Butler Yeats, "The Second Coming."

Morton Leeds, "Old Man 3" from "Poems" by Morton Leeds, *Omega,* vol. 3, no. 3. Copyright © 1972 by *Omega*. Reprinted by permission.

"A Speech Made by a Losaala Youth from Lawra at His Friend's Funeral." Reprinted from *Death, Property, and the Ancestors* by Jack Goody with the permission of the publishers, Stanford University Press. © 1962 by John R. Goody.

Emily Dickinson, "I Felt a Funeral in My Brain."

Ted Rosenthal, from *How Could I Not Be among You?* reprinted with the permission of the publisher, George Braziller, Inc. © 1973 by Ted Rosenthal.

"At Fifteen I Went to War," from the *Yüeh-Fu* from *Chinese Poetry* by Wai-Lim Yip. Reprinted by permission of the University of California Press.

Martin Buber, "How the Rabbi of Sasov Learned to Love," from *Tales of the Hasidim: The Early Masters* by Martin Buber. Copyright © 1947, 1975 by Shocken Books Inc.

Edna St. Vincent Millay, "Lament," from *Second April,* © 1950 and 1956 by Harper & Row, used with permission of Norma Millay Ellis.

William Shakespeare, "Sonnet 64."

Yosa Buson, "I Felt a Sudden Chill."

Emily Dickinson, "Because I Could Not Stop for Death."

Psalm 23

Eskimo poem, "Dead Man's Song."

A. E. Housman. "I Counsel You Beware."

The Oath of Hippocrates

Walt Whitman, from "The Wound Dresser," in *Leaves of Grass.*

Robinson Jeffers, from "Suicide's Stone," © 1924, renewed 1952 by Robinson Jeffers from *Selected Poetry of Robinson Jeffers*. Reprinted by permission of Random House, Inc.

Anonymous, from "A Dispute Over Suicide," from *A Comparative Study of the Literature of Egypt, Palestine, and Mesopotamia* by T. Eric Peet (Schweich Lecture 1931) by permission of Oxford University Press.

Sylvia Plath, "Suicide Off Egg Rock." © 1960 by Sylvia Plath from *The Colossus and Other Poems*. Reprinted by permission of Alfred A. Knopf, Inc.

from the *Shih Ching,* from *Chinese Poetry* by Wai-Lim Yip. Reprinted by permission of the University of California Press.

Robinson Jeffers, "The Beautiful Captive" from *The Beginning and the End and Other Poems* by Robinson Jeffers. © 1963 by Garth Jeffers and Donnan Jeffers. Reprinted by permission of Random House, Inc.

Carl Sandburg, "Grass," from *Cornhuskers,* Copyright 1918 by Holt, Rinehart and Winston, Inc. Copyright © 1946 by Carl Sandburg. Reprinted by permission of Harcourt, Brace, Jovanovich, Inc.

Wilfred Owen, "Dulce et Decorum Est," from *Collected Poems.* Copyright © 1946, 1963 by Chatto & Windus, Ltd. Reprinted by permission of New Directions.

Photographs

Tim Carlson, Stock, Boston, page 5
Harry Wilks, Stock, Boston, page 39
Jeff Albertson, Stock, Boston, page 58
Mimi Forsyth, page 81
Josef Koudelka, Magnum, page 103
Jeff Albertson, Stock, Boston, page 127
Bernie Wisneski, St. Luke's Hospital, page 160
Ken Heyman, page 195
Constantine Manos, Magnum, page 216
Ken Heyman, 246
Eve Arnold, Magnum, page 267
David Powers, Jeroboam, page 302
Charles Gatewood, Stock, Boston, page 337
Philip Jones Griffith, Magnum, page 362
Wide World, page 390

Illustrations

LeRoy H. Appleton, *American Indian Design and Decoration,* © 1950, 1971 by LeRoy H. Appleton. Used by permission of the publisher, Dover Publications, Inc. Pages i, 12, 67, 105, 108, 122, 150, 155, 174, 180, 214, 220, 225, 234, 298, 306, 330, 358, 375, 380.

Edmund Vincent Gillon, Jr., *Early New England Gravestone Rubbings,* © 1966 by Dover Publications, Inc. Used by permission of Dover Publications, Inc. Pages 2, 8, 19, 38, 44, 51, 52, 62, 74, 120, 130, 147, 178, 182, 197, 249, 257, 266, 292, 310, 323, 344, 356, 370, 389, 392, 398, 408.

Barbara Jones, *Designs for Death,* © 1967 by Barbara Jones. Published by Andre Deutsch Ltd. Used by permission. Pages 32, 83, 159, 200, 215, 271, 275, 315.

Ernst and Johanna Lehner, *Devils, Demons, Death and Damnation,* © 1971 by Dover Publications, Inc. Used by permission of Dover Publications, Inc. Pages xix, 3, 4, 28, 35, 41, 78, 87, 96, 115, 135, 141, 164, 187, 190, 194, 240, 263, 301, 334, 339, 350, 365, 386, 405.

Death and Dying
Challenge and Change

CONTENTS

PART TWO
The Experience of Death

PART THREE
Survivors of Death

PART FOUR

Dilemmas of Death

PREFACE

This is the tenth in a series of books developed for Courses by Newspaper (CbN). A national program originated and administered by University Extension, University of California, San Diego, and funded by the National Endowment for the Humanities, Courses by Newspaper develops materials for college-level courses that are presented to the general public through the nationwide cooperation of newspapers and participating colleges and universities.

The program offers three levels of participation: interested readers can follow a series of newspaper articles comprising the course "lectures"; they can pursue the subjects further with a supplementary anthology (the Reader), study guide, and audio cassettes; and they can enroll for credit at any of three hundred participating colleges or universities or through the Division of Independent Study at the University of California, Berkeley. In addition, many community organizations offer local forums and discussion groups based on the Courses by Newspaper series.

This Reader supplements the fifteen articles written for the course, "Death and Dying: Challenge and Change," published weekly in newspapers across the country in winter and spring 1979. It is divided into four parts: (1) Changing Meanings of Death and Dying; (2) The Experience of Death; (3) Survivors of Death; and (4) Dilemmas of Death.

The selections within each of the parts supplement and amplify the different issues discussed by the newspaper faculty.

As editors of this Reader, we have endeavored to provide a comprehensive and balanced analysis of the issues and challenges posed by death and dying in modern society. Four objectives have guided the organization of this book and the selection of articles. First, we wanted to cover a broad time spectrum, thereby examining present realities in the light of past circumstances and future possibilities. Second, we have considered death and dying from a variety of perspectives, including the individual, the family, and the society. Third, we have included diverse academic disciplines, from history and sociology through medicine and psychology to literature and ethics. Fourth, we have presented several points of view on such controversial topics as life after death, care of the dying patient, funerals, and moral and ethical dilemmas.

No single book can hope to treat definitively the complex issues relating to death and dying. Of necessity, we had to be highly selective in choosing from the burgeoning materials in this field. Moreover, many of these issues are multifaceted. In particular, the moral and ethical dilemmas of death and dying could easily fill an entire book, rather than a single section. It is our hope, however, that these selections will offer the reader a basic understanding of the key issues and points of view.

This Reader contains extensive editorial commentary—in the prologue and epilogue, introductions to the major parts, introductory essays for each section, and headnotes for each article. This commentary is an integral part of the Reader. It contains material not found in the selections and indicates important points and issues. Supplementary bibliographies are included to facilitate further study.

To keep the book within manageable length, sentences, paragraphs, and, on occasion, whole sections of the original articles have been deleted. The editors made every effort, however, to keep the spirit of a piece if the letter itself could not be retained. We hope no real violence was done to the respective contributions as we strove to meet the challenge of the materials as well as the needs of our readers within the space available. We thank the contributors to this volume and their publishers for permission to reprint their essays and for any liberties we took with their articles.

Both this book of readings and the Courses by Newspaper for which it was prepared are designed to encourage private thought as well as public discussion of the issues relating to death and dying in contemporary society. For it is only in open forum that we are best able to assess their impact upon our collective and private lives.

The efforts of many people and organizations make Courses by Newspaper possible. We should like to acknowledge them here. Hundreds of newspaper editors and publishers across the country have contributed valuable newspaper space to bring the specially prepared articles to their readers. The faculties and administrations of colleges and universities participating in the program have cooperated to make credit available to students throughout the nation.

Deserving special mention at the University of California, San Diego, are Paul D. Saltman, vice chancellor for academic affairs and professor of biology, who has chaired the faculty committee and guided the project since its inception and served as the first academic coordinator in 1973; Caleb A. Lewis of the University Extension, who originated the idea of Courses by Newspaper; and the faculty committee, who contributed to the conception of this course. The authors also wish to thank Dr. George A. Colburn, project director of Courses by Newspaper, for his support throughout the preparation of this volume. Vital to the success of this year's program were the dedicated members of the Courses by Newspaper staff: Cecilia Solis, Yvonne Hancher, Stephanie Giel, and Jacqué JoNess of the University of California, San Diego. Elliot Wager and Moreen Hirsch need to be specially recognized for their material efforts on our behalf. Julie Fulton and Susan Rains from the Center for Death Education and Research, University of Minnesota, gave generously of their time and talents to this undertaking..

We also wish to thank the authors of the newspaper articles for their efforts on behalf of the series and their individual contributions to this anthology—Eric Cassell, Edgar Jackson, Robert Kastenbaum, Monroe Lerner, Robert Lifton, Helena Lopata, Colin Murray Parkes, Vanderlyn Pine, Edwin Shneidman, David Stannard, Robert Veatch, Avery Weisman, and George Williams.

Finally, we wish to express our gratitude to the National Endowment for the Humanities for funding Courses by Newspaper. The Endowment, a federal agency created in 1965 to further education, research, and public activity in the humanities, has generously supported this nationwide program from its beginning. In this regard, we wish particularly to acknowledge the support and advice of James Kraft, the Endowment's Director of Special Projects.

Although Courses by Newspaper is a project of University Extension, University of California, San Diego, and is supported by the National Endowment for the Humanities, the views expressed in this course and the accompanying articles are those of the authors only and do not necessarily reflect those of the Endowment or of the University of California.

PROLOGUE

In his life philosophy of individualism, industry, and independence and in his genius for tinkering, technology, and organization, Henry Ford, Sr., the founder of the Ford Motor Company, probably symbolized American society better than anyone else. Aldous Huxley recognized this in *Brave New World* when he proposed that Americans calculate time not according to the "year of our Lord" but according to the "year of our Ford." What Huxley meant by that remark was that Ford brought into our world new principles of organization, such as the division of labor and the assembly line, that maximized specialization. In so doing Ford caused a radical shift in both our private philosophies and our world views. He profoundly changed our beliefs about the next world as well as this one, and he was instrumental in transforming America from an agricultural to an industrial society, from rural to urban, and from an extended family system to a nuclear lifestyle.

Not much more than two generations ago, the extended family in rural America lived much as the ancient Greeks and Romans or medieval people throughout the world once lived. People in a direct and immediate way were compelled to go to the fields, the forests, or the lakes and rivers for their livelihood. They lived by fate, chance or belief in divine intervention and prayer. There was always the question of where tomorrow's meal would come from, whether a child would be born alive, whether a cow would calve, or whether fire or drought or hail or other natural calamities would destroy the work of a person, a family, a whole community, or a generation. Man's increasing control of the environment has profoundly changed our social patterns in a multiplicity of ways, reducing dependency upon, as well as fear of, nature.

One such change brought about fifty years ago by the industrialization of America was that the family gave up its dead and turned the responsibility for them over to a paid functionary. This does not mean that we had no funeral directors before World War I. Burial of the dead goes back many thousands of years. In Egypt, Europe, and Africa there have always been people who have assisted in laying out the dead or disposing of the body. But the general extension of this service in America occurred approximately fifty years ago.

The custom that is probably as old as humankind—the practice of family members being immediately and directly responsible for the laying out of their dead—changed in America. The principle of specialization was adopted by the undertaker. When American families moved from relatively spacious homes in rural areas to small quarters in cities across the United States, as they did in great numbers at the time of World War I, there wasn't always room for traditional rural family practices. Some family members moved to the city singly and began to live solitary and isolated lives. The loss of relatives, loss of neighbors, loss of community, the rush of city life, the time-oriented character of factory life—these factors and others made the family assign their private dead to the man with the public parlor.

By World War II, Ford's industrial principles had also been adopted by medical science. War put such a demand on medical resources that the all-inclusive public hospital became a material necessity. It no longer was practical or efficient for the physician to make house calls. Hospitals offered what the solitary physician could not: competent specialists in a variety of fields; modern, sophisticated

1

medical equipment; blood banks; a nursing staff; and clean beds. And people went to the hospitals. In 1925, hospital bed occupancy of at least twenty-four hours totalled seven million. In 1970 it totalled more than thirty-two million, while the national population only doubled and this year, over seven out of ten persons who die will do so in an institution.

With the relatively recent rise of the nursing home industry, we can observe the culmination of a process whereby in less than fifty years the dead have been removed from the home and from the direct responsibility of the family to a funeral home; the seriously and chronically-ill have been removed to the hospital; and more and more of the elderly have been removed to a nursing home—all under the supervision of specialists who in effect, are strangers paid to take care of those among us who are elderly, chronically ill, moribund, or dead.

Industrialization, however, transformed not only our ways of caring for the dead and the dying, but also our ways of inflicting death. And while it is a great leap from the fateful silence of a hospital room to the ominous quiet of a nuclear silo, that is our inheritance. The succeeding pages of this book take up the issues that confront us.

Changing Meanings of Death and Dying

The first part of this book, "Changing Meanings of Death and Dying," serves as an introduction as well as a vehicle for bringing into social and historical perspective the parts that follow. The initial part is divided into six sections: (1) Current Issues in Death and Dying; (2) Historical Perspectives on Death; (3) Death in Popular Culture; (4) Demography of Death; (5) Death and Social Change; and (6) Life after Death: Old and New Meanings. Each section addresses itself to an issue that helps to inform the whole.

In Section 1, "Death and Dying: The Issues Today," the authors take up the question of the recent interest that has been expressed in the subject of death, and they explore and debate its meaning. Social and cultural factors that are presumed to be instrumental in this resurgence of attention are analyzed, while contemporary attitudes on a variety of death-related topics are examined.

In Section 2, "Historical Perspectives on Death," an attempt is made to place the contemporary scene as it relates to death and dying within a historical framework. "The child is father of the man" no less so in the matter of death than in life. Our European roots, our Puritan traditions, and our Victorian practices are held up to our view and serve to instruct us as to the nature and content of our social and cultural inheritance.

Section 3, "Death in Popular Culture," addresses itself to the manner in which the mass media depict and interpret death for the "now" generation. Television and the cinema are examined for the content as well as the impact of their message upon the American mind. The "medium is the message," McLuhan observed.

And we might add that it is also a messenger; and it reports a tale of violence and death.

Section 4, "The Demography of Death," examines the significance of changing mortality rates upon our society, our institutions, and ourselves. In doing so, it permits us to understand better the subtle but powerful forces that are locked within the "who," "where," "when," and "why" of death.

Section 5, "Death and Social Change," explores the manner in which our health care institutions and our changing medical philosophies, procedures, and practices have affected our ways of thinking and dealing with dying and death. The "medicalization" of death, Illich warns, may in itself fly in the face of the Hippocratic injunction, *primus non nocere* (above all do no harm).

Section 6, "Life after Death: Old and New Meanings," deals with an important new development in the area of dying and death. Under the imprimatur of the noted psychiatrist Dr. Elisabeth Kübler-Ross, a body of literature has appeared purporting to report scientific evidence of life after death. The significance of these claims for each and every one of us, our society, and indeed the world, is without parallel and deserves the careful study and analysis that is herein reported.

Death and Dying: The Issues Today

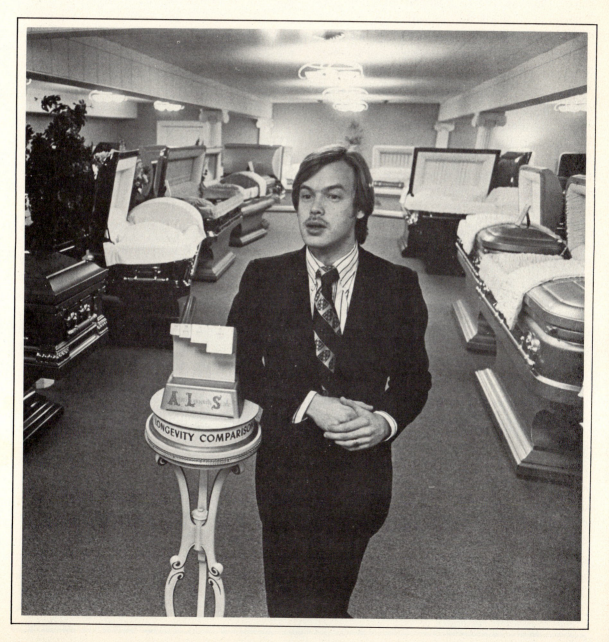

Experience with death in modern urban America has changed significantly over the past few decades. It is barely forty years since Thomas Eliot, a social psychologist, attempted to draw our attention to the problems associated with mortality. His plea for a systematic study of bereavement, in order that we might heighten our awareness and enhance our understanding of the impact of separation and loss upon our lives, went unheeded. In the 1930s and indeed until well after the Second World War, death in America was taboo. It was a subject to be avoided or disguised. Linguistically, a person did not "die" but "passed away," while a body "lay in state" in the "slumber room" of a funeral home awaiting the call "home." Clergymen, teachers, life insurance salesmen, as well as parents and funeral directors, studiously attempted until recently to protect children from direct contact with and observations of death and the dead.

How times change! Today we are certain that Eliot would jump out of his skin if he knew that educators were now jumping out of caskets in the name of death education, and in all likelihood he would have left the dead to bury the dead if he could have anticipated the living burying the living under a mountain of books, articles, and other communications. As Maddocks observes in his article "Life and Death in the USA," grief therapy, grief counseling, "build-it-yourself" caskets (cum coffee tables, cum wine racks), "play dead" encounter groups, grief simulation workshops, and other innovative enterprises in this new growth industry are further glaring testimony to contemporary America's rediscovery of death, if not indeed to the American genius for doing well while ostensibly doing good.

Parallel to such activity, as well as a stimulus to it, has been the concomitant introduction of death-related courses in high schools, colleges, and universities across the country. It has been estimated recently that there are well over two thousand courses at the college and university level alone, of which 90 percent have been in existence for less than five years.

In the Minneapolis-St. Paul area, for instance, thirty-six high schools offer a course in death education. A recent study shows, however, that seven out of ten instructors are under forty years of age, 75 percent have had no formal education in the subject, and only half report having any direct personal experience with death.

What is happening to the American psyche: what clarion call of death has caused people to behave so? As Vaisrub wryly reminds us, "death and dying have always been with us." Indeed, academic interest in the subject began even prior to Eliot's work in the 1930s and has been uninterrupted, albeit circumscribed, ever since. This can be seen in the writings of such scholars as Scott, Hall, Eissler, Feifel, Strauss, Sudnow, Fulton, and others, to say nothing of numerous anthropological studies or the intermittent forays against American mortuary practices, such as Jessica Mitford's now-famous ambush of the American funeral in 1963, *The American Way of Death.*

Why then the current interest and concern? What explains the intensive and extensive literature on death and dying, on the hows and whys of attending to our dying citizens and their grieving survivors?

The recent upsurge of interest in the subject can be said to have begun in 1959 with Herman Feifel's book, *The Meaning of Death*. The floodgates were breached, however, in 1969 with Elisabeth Kübler-Ross' book *On Death and Dying*. The book crystallized for the hospital nurse the problems she or he faced in attempting to deal with the private issues of death in a public setting. In short, Dr. Kübler-Ross said that we must attend to the death of another with our hearts as well as with our minds. The death of a fellow human being cannot take place ignominiously in the obscurity of back wards and darkened rooms, without such deaths casting dark shadows across the lives of us all.

Her important and timely message to critical care nurses and other caregivers across the country also reached the public's ears as it touched their hearts, and its effect was electrifying. Her book appeared, moreover, at the time when the outraged reaction of Americans toward the Vietnam war was at its zenith and when the cold, mechanistic attitude of the Administration toward the war and its victims was being publicly scrutinized. The government's denigration of life and depersonalization of death as reported in the daily news did much to galvanize public sentiment and lift up private emotions.

Vaisrub, in his article in this section, "Dying is Worked to Death," however, questions this interpretation. Is not, he asks, our recently enhanced attention to death the result of a universal fear of death that flares up in the human psyche during times of national or global crises rather than of any increased concern for our fragile human condition? To that

question, Shneidman would demur. In his national survey of attitudes toward death, which originally appeared in *Psychology Today*, Shneidman found that over half his respondents reported that their lives had been influenced by the threat of nuclear war. On the other hand, Vaisrub is in all likelihood correct, given the findings of two earlier studies by Fulton and Feifel, when he observes that for the most part the individual is generally oblivious to his own death, and that of the two certitudes, death and taxes, it is the latter that will command his greater attention.

Fulton, however, in his article "On the Dying of Death," while agreeing that there has been a major change in death attitudes, nevertheless attributes the observed shift to a convergence of social and cultural factors rather than to an unconscious fear of death or to the singular threat of nuclear extinction. For Fulton, long and often imperceptible social changes need to be considered in any discussion of causation. He proposes such factors as the rise of secularism and the halting decline in the strength of traditional religious beliefs, the general increase in life expectancy and the consequent burgeoning of an elderly population, the physical and social mobility of the American public, the shift to the hospital as a place to die, the deritualization of death and mourning, and the general insularity of the young from death. These and other social and cultural factors, he states, have served to rend us from our traditional philosophical and religious mold and to bring us to our present state.

With what consequence? For Vaisrub the present interest and commotion concerning such issues as the dying patient and nuclear extermination is essentially superficial and reflects more the ease with which people can write about death than any true comprehension or fundamental concern with it. He reminds us pointedly that "words alone cannot bridge the infinite chasm of eternity."

Cohen, however, disagrees with the view that Vaisrub holds. He argues instead, in his article "Is Dying Being Worked to Death?" that, no matter what the ultimate cause of the current preoccupation with our "brother death," the attention expended has been on balance beneficial. Not only have the media been of general value and perhaps of some cathartic value, he observes, but scholarly research into the area has served to advance our understanding of mankind's most problematic experience—to die.

Fulton concurs. It is his observation that the effect of twentieth-century trends has been to segregate the aged from the rest of the community at the time of their dying and simultaneously to isolate our children from any direct experience with death. The consequence of such a development is to rob both child and adult of a significant human experience that is as important as it is inevitable. Moreover, he says, the deritualization of death and the suppression of grief and mourning that are observed in contemporary society also serve to aggravate the isolation among generations. Thus he cautions us that the repudiation and social denial of grief not only may be associated with the rising tide of vandalism and violence among the young, but that death avoidance and suppression also leave the survivor grievously alone and ill-equipped to cope with the myriad social and personal difficulties that arise when those we love die.

Then Almitra spoke, saying, We would ask now of Death.
And he said:
You would know the secret of death.
But how shall you find it unless you seek it in the heart of life?
The owl whose night-bound eyes are blind unto the day cannot
    unveil the mystery of light.
If you would indeed behold the spirit of death, open your heart
    wide unto the body of life.
For life and death are one, even as the river and the sea are one.

Kahlil Gibran
The Prophet

Robert Fulton

On the Dying of Death

The following essay by Robert Fulton, a pioneer in the sociology of death, examines several important trends and issues relating to death and dying. Fulton shows how broad social and cultural changes have rendered traditional religious meanings of death obsolete; yet, contemporary meanings are often confused and contradictory. While death is denied by a variety of means in daily life, disturbingly violent and dehumanized images of death are staple fare on our entertainment media. The care of the dying and the dead has been assigned to such specialized functionaries as physicians and funeral directors. Rituals and customs that have traditionally facilitated social support for the bereaved are being questioned and rejected. Such trends strongly affect particularly the elderly persons in our society. The aged are placed in double jeopardy: they are surrounded by numerous demeaning and discriminatory stereotypes on the one hand, while their proximity to death often arouses anxiety in younger persons on the other. Their social isolation is further intensified by the trend toward highly mobile, two-generation families with neither room in their homes nor desire in their hearts to care for grandmothers and grandfathers.

These sweeping changes have made their presence felt also upon the generation born after World War II. This generation, according to Fulton, has been more "death-insulated" than any in history. Ironically, however, this death-insulated generation has inherited from its parents the legacy of nuclear weapons which increasingly threaten our civilization with total annihilation. It would be the final irony to have rediscovered and confronted death in our personal lives at the moment in history when we collectively kill not only ourselves, but our pasts and futures as well.

Death is the great rupturer. Since man first appeared on earth, death has been his constant companion and ultimate threat. The question "Why should man die?" has traditionally been answered in Western society within the framework of sacred doctrine. Man, according to this doctrine, was God's creature, and his death, no less than his life, was an act of Divine will. Death, for Western man, was a personal matter between God and himself. He believed, moreover, that the very purposefulness of his death placed him at the center of existence and elevated him above all other creatures as the principal subject of creation. As part of a Divine plan, death was confronted openly, spoken of freely, and regarded as an inevitable event. Shakespeare expressed this idea succinctly when, in *Henry IV,* he said, "We owe God a death." For Western man, the recognition of death was a prime requisite for life as well as an integral dimension of his personal identity.

In contemporary American society, a profound shift can be observed in man's attitudes toward death. An increasing number of Americans no longer view death as the result of Divine displeasure or as the price of moral trespass: rather, in our modern, secular society death is coming to be seen as the result of personal negligence or of an unforeseen accident. Death is now a temporal matter that man treats much as he would an avoidable illness or physical stigma. Like syphilis or some other infectious disease it is a personal embarrassment to be discussed only reluctantly with a physician. Death, like a noxious disease, has become a taboo subject in American society and as such it is the object of much avoidance, denial, and disguise.

The significance of the mass media for depicting our attitudes toward death as well as for molding them cannot be minimized. If we look for a moment at the way the films characteristically have dealt with death, and at the way films do so today, we can perhaps catch something of the change in attitude that we have attempted to describe.

Early film classics such as *Frankenstein* and *Dracula* clearly portrayed the traditional polarities within Christian theology, i.e., the polarity between spirit and flesh, good and evil, and life and death. Within the dramatic structure of these films, death was understood as the justifiable punishment for those who trespassed against the moral order or as a ritual of purification for those who died championing it.

The struggle between these polarities could also be seen in our traditional western movie with great clarity. The hero, chaste, courageous, and God-fearing, was confronted with the appearance of evil in the form of cattle-stealing Indians, land-stealing foreigners, or gold-stealing bankers. Without compromise the hero righted wrong, as an instrument of justice he restored law and order, and as a servant of God, he reaffirmed the principle of faith.

The world in which good struggled against evil, and the spirit vied with the flesh, finds itself today forced to give way to a different definition of the order of things, and is compelled to retreat before the advances of what might be termed relativistic secularism.

In the new genre of film entertainment offered American society, epitomized by the James Bond thriller, the hierarchical world of Christian transtemporalism is no longer described; rather what is presented is an existential world in which good and evil reside in both friend and foe alike.

The image of modern existential man portrayed on the screen today is that of a rational, intelligent, youthful man—a man who is functioning within an environment but who is not a part of it. His values are pragmatic and relativistic. His loyalties are to a group, movement, or state. Oftentimes he works in the employ of someone as little known to him and possibly as hostile toward him as his unknown adversary. For a cause that transcends one's individual self our modern hero is expendable, as are those persons with whom he struggles. His claim to life—and it is a life abundant with power, wealth, and sexual pleasures—is made existentially dramatic by the fact that at any given moment he may have to give it up. Carelessness or expediency may cause him to receive a fatal thrust from his enemy or a deadly push from a "friend." Life for our contemporary hero in such a world is relative, immediate, sensual, and lonely, while his death is irrelevant. In contrast to traditional conceptions of social reality this emerging functional secularism offers us a new vision for man and the promise of a new social order.

When we turn our gaze away from the reflected image of the screen to the object of its illumination, contemporary America, it can be seen that sometimes entertainment as well as art mirrors life.

Historically, it has been a basic proposition in American society that every man had the same claim to life. Equality of life has served as a fundamental underpinning to the structure of our society. The new ethic emerging in

America, however, threatens to negate this proposition. The invention of the kidney machine in Seattle, Washington, [in 1954] raised the question of who should benefit from this machine.

Initially, only one machine was available and its use, of necessity, was limited to a few patients. How were they to be chosen? Our religious and political philosophy would argue for a democratic selection; each man would have the same chance to life. However, the criteria that were initially established contradicted this traditional philosophy and said in effect that some men have a greater claim to life than others. Of course, it has always been true that wealthy persons could afford better medical care than the poor, but it has never been an official medical proposition that a person of wealth had a greater claim to life than any other person. Now it has been established by an anonymous committee of seven, known portentously as the "Life and Death Committee," that one's right to a life-sustaining machine is a function of his potential or actual contribution to society. The young academic, the young doctor, the young lawyer, the executive on the way up, it is implied, have a greater claim to life than the unskilled, the unemployed, or the unwanted.

Death in our society is no longer the wages of sin. Today it is seen as something that does not have to happen. Furthermore, the idea is being entertained that it is remotely conceivable that for a very significant minority, that death eventually won't need to happen at all. In this connection it should be noted that more than a dozen bodies have been frozen following death in order that they may later benefit from future advances in medical technology and thereby be restored to life and good health.

One strategy that has emerged in contemporary society to cope with the dying and death of our aging members in a more immediate way is the retirement city movement. This movement encourages the segregation and isolation of those most likely to die before they actually do so. Such a development in modern life allows us for the first time to avoid death almost entirely and to mute the grief and anguish of bereavement. Time and separation loosen family and friendship ties. Once an older person is emotionally separated from the members of his family or group his death will register but lightly upon them, if at all.

Another movement in American society that augurs for the privatization of death is the memorial society movement. This author surveyed members of eleven such memorial societies (or funeral reform societies, as they are called) across the United States. Highly educated, and relatively low in traditional religious affiliation, and reporting an annual income twice that of the average American family, members of memorial societies could well represent the vanguard of future Americans. The study showed that this group desired to eliminate the body from the funeral, avoided funerals more often than the average American, and showed a greater reluctance than the average person to permit their children to attend a funeral ceremony. This last finding is of particular interest. Typically, families of the social, professional, and intellectual level of these respondents attempt to deal realistically with their children. They characteristically discourage such fantasies as ghosts, hobgoblins, Santa Claus, and the bogies of sex. Nevertheless, where death is concerned, they appear to behave contrary to form and seek to shield the ultimate truth from their children.

It would appear that temporal-mindedness and scientific skepticism are coterminous with death suppression. Complementing the memorial society members' expressed desire to shield their children from the dead is the practice in medical hospitals of shielding children from the dying. In two separate studies, [Herman] Feifel and this writer have shown that the dying person often wishes to be surrounded by family and friends. Hospitals, nevertheless, typically prohibit children from visiting patients. When permitted to do so children are allowed only in specific areas and at designated times.

Today in the United States more than twenty-one million persons are now 65 years of age or older. Never before in our history have we had such an aged population. Moreover, by 1985 their numbers will total more than twenty-five million persons. But what of this group and of those members who are, or presently will be, dying? And what of the dy-

ing person himself? How is he to view his death in the face of a society that increasingly seeks to deny the reality of his existence and at the same time attempts to avoid the reality of his death? How will American youth, brought up in a society that seeks to disguise death, greet the death of its elders?

These questions cannot be answered easily nor can the problems they present to us be solved readily. Medicare, increased Social Security, nursing programs, emerging terminal hospital facilities, modern medical technology, and new techniques for the utilization of body parts all suggest new attitudes toward dying and death as well as ways of coping with life different from what we have ever known before.

Franz Borkenau, a distinguished historian, has characterized our modern era as post-Christian. With the disintegration of belief in immortality, Borkenau saw modern society prepared to embrace a nihilistic philosophy of despair and denial. He believed that modern secularism would ultimately deny the relevance of self so that death itself, finally, would be defeated. It was Borkenau's conviction that modern man yearned for some unity of identity beyond himself and that to avoid existential extinction he would abandon himself to some temporal absolute such as a racial, social, or national group.

Borkenau's thoughts have relevance and immediacy for our society. The specter of statism in Russia and China, of racism in the Union of South Africa and Rhodesia, in which the individual is subordinated to the needs and aspirations of the society, cannot readily be dismissed. Nor are we necessarily free from the urge toward a collective identity for self here in the United States. The ultimate significance of the late President Kennedy's statement, "Ask not what your country can do for you—ask what you can do for your country," can only be judged by history. It does not appear, however, to be in the general political tradition of the primacy of the individual upon which the political institutions of this society were founded. Nor does it follow a much older conception of man's relationship to the state which has also served as the cornerstone of American political and religious life, namely, the directive, "Render therefore to Caesar the things that are Caesar's; and to God the things that are God's." It would seem that, politically, at least, the conception that a man is a unique entity, prior to the state, and having recourse ultimately to an authority beyond the state is in danger of being lost in America.

Perhaps in no other era have the gods played such cruel games with youth. While this present generation in America can be said to be the first "death-insulated" generation in the history of the world, i.e., the average young person can reach adulthood without experiencing a death in the family, the prospect of sudden mass extermination by a nuclear attack hangs threateningly over their heads. Contempt for authority and impatience with the older generation reflect their hostile attitude toward this bittersweet inheritance. In such a world that has known two intercontinental wars within this century and presently contemplates a third, the question of a meaningless life is made more poignant for those who must at the same time contemplate what is for many of them a meaningless death.

Thus we can see in contemporary society the emergence of different strategies and techniques designed ultimately to avoid a direct confrontation with death. Simultaneously we also can observe a nascent conception of the individual which would equate his worth as a man with his value to society. It is within this context that death must be viewed. Moreover,

it is within this social environment that strives to achieve the death of death itself that its meaning in our lives must come to be understood. And finally, it is within such a context that we must articulate the modern meaning of life and death to our children....

The problems associated with death are beginning to polarize at two different points within the social structure. The first area of concern is the disengagement of the aged from a society that is becoming less interested in them as individuals or as functionaries within the social system. The second area of concern centers around children who in a nuclear family setting have the burden of coping with an irreplaceable loss through death—a loss made greater by the reduced number of significant persons in his immediate family. While these two issues are not unrelated, they do seem to constitute two foci around which the major problems of death, grief, and bereavement cluster.

Deritualization of mourning and the suppression of grief are growing apace in America. The death crisis that survivors must face, given the pattern of modern living, can be greater or more profoundly disruptive emotionally, if not socially, than ever before.

The recent reform movement in America that proposes we cope with death by immediate nonpublic disposal of the dead, and that we manage our grief by stoically denying it, is in sharp contrast with our social past as well as with our present knowledge regarding the dynamics of personal, irreparable loss. But, on the other hand, a ceremony that no longer appropriately symbolizes the understood meaning of a death, or fails correctly to dramatize the change that has overtaken the living and the dead, can create only confusion, if not anger and frustration, on the part of the bereaved. Some young couples today, for example, see their lives as a private affair and choose a civil or nonpublic wedding as a result. Reasons of practicality or economy can only partially explain this choice. We must recognize that such a restricted ceremony serves to dramatize for them their place in the world and their perception of that world. The same can be said in the case of the funeral. A funeral that attempts to represent relationships, ideas, or values which the individual no longer believes in or holds true may serve to thwart and anger him rather than achieve its intended end.

Though death may indeed be dying in the United States, nevertheless we are still confronted with those who must die. In a society which has a lessened evaluation of death there is a strong tendency for many to respond to the death of another by turning away. Like the divorced person of several decades ago, ostracized and neglected, many bereaved individuals today are to a large extent without traditional religious resources or community support and often lack the skills necessary to deal adequately with their loss.

If we view the question of death from the standpoint of personal loss, what we see is the imminent threat of increasing disruption of family life and other social relations by death in a society which increasingly is unable either to accept or to explain it. The problem is further intensified moreover by the fact that we have as yet no scientific way of demonstrating whether or not the patterns of behavior we observe in attempting to cope with the death crisis are functionally relevant. However, in the light of research the wise management of grief in children as well as in adults revolves around two major factors: one, the encouragement and facilitation of the normal mourning process, and two, the prevention of delayed and/or distorted grief responses.

In our society the funeral possesses the potential to compel the individual to acknowledge his loss. The ritual of the funeral when it is responsive to the social and psychological needs of the survivors, can facilitate what Lindemann has called normal grief work.

The presence of a child at a funeral permits the child to recognize that death has occurred. He sees that he is only one among several who are experiencing the loss. Further, depending upon his relationship to the deceased, he may receive comfort. support, and expressions of love and affection from relatives and friends who normally would not be so demonstrative toward him. Moreover, the law of Talion may also be operative. The child may fear his own involvement in the death. The responses of the others can serve to assure him that he is not culpable. The child, by the nature of his inexperience with death, has a crisis to work through.

Children, the evidence would suggest, are little aided in this crisis by their well-intended parents or their friends who advise that they not participate in the celebration of a death. To the contrary, such a decision may be interpreted by the child as an expression of wrongdoing on his part. When the funeral is over, the mourners return home sad and depressed. At this juncture the child is ignored. His tentative questions are brusquely answered or quickly silenced. Rather than being embraced and taken into the sorrowing group, he is sent away to ponder alone what has occurred.

There are those in America who would withhold from children, particularly, a knowledge of, or experience with, death. It would appear to be in the best interest of children, however, that such ideas be resisted for it seems that the evidence compels us to recognize the fact that death is too personal an event to be left a private matter.

Melvin Maddocks

Life and Death in the USA

Like the social surgeon that he is, Melvin Maddocks in this delightfully acerbic essay "Life and Death in the USA," carefully vivisects for our edification and enjoyment the present day preoccupation with mortality. After taking note of the dramatic reversal in our posture before death from fearful prey to willing lover, Maddocks concludes that the present day excitement and activity surrounding the topic suggest all the earmarks of a social revolution. "It is," he observes, "the ultimate civil rights course"—a public protest to death's infringement upon our right to life, liberty, and the pursuit of happiness.

If death is un-American, our response to it, however, is characteristically American—we form a committee. The politics of death is no exception and Maddocks identifies three familiar American archetypes: the death pragmatist, the death optimist, and the death existentialist.

Death as an issue, for Maddocks, is not a caprice, another fruit to be found in the garden of human delights, but rather an actuality that has forcibly imposed itself upon both the American conscience and consciousness.

Mr Barlow, you are afraid of death."
"No, I assure you."
"It is a natural instinct, Mr Barlow, to shrink from the unknown."

Evelyn Waugh
The Loved One (1948)

Evelyn Waugh's novella *The Loved One* seemed to crystallize to malicious perfection the American posture towards death. Or rather, against death, for the posture surely was one of aversion. Death was judged to be an obscenity, and like all obscenities, required its fig leaves. One did not discuss death even at funerals—especially at funerals. One spoke of "passing on" rather than dying. One spoke of the "leave-taking," not the burial. The corpse, or rather, the "loved one," was painted back to health by cosmetic applications that might make a street-walker blush. No matter how horribly or prematurely the "loved one" died, these iron-willed words summed up the subject: "It's for the best"—the signal for a general stampede back to daily life on the part of the graveside survivors because: "He (she) would have wanted it that way."

Who could have predicted twenty years ago that the death-shy American (like the sex-shy American of fifty years ago) would metamorphose from one caricature into the opposite? As recently as 1967 that wise observer of native anxieties, Erik Erikson, listed only one index under "Death" in *Youth: Identity and Crisis*—and that referred to Arthur Miller's play, *Death of a Salesman*. Yet today the fear that supposedly dared not speak its name is being discussed by the young, the middle-aged, and the old to the point of obsession.

If death was once dismissed as un-American, nothing could be more American than its sudden discovery. Death has grown into a knowledge industry with its own institutions (e.g., the Center for Thanatological Studies, University of Minnesota) and its own press (e.g., see *Omega,* an international journal for the psychological study of dying, bereavement, suicide, and other lethal behaviors). The "death course," as it is known, has become a glamorous elective in American college catalogues. A typical undergraduate listing reads:

Death: Events, Ritual, Decision. Personal/professional/social decisions regarding life and death—abortion, capital punishment, suicide, war.

"Field assignments" are promised but not specified. A typical graduate course listing reads:

Death and Suicide. Partial death; megadeath; lethality; the psychological autopsy.

Still another breed of specialist has appeared in the world of specialists: the death expert. What exquisitely cruel sport Waugh might have made of the American Association of Suicidology, whose members conducted their annual convention last year at a Texas motel, listening to papers with titles like *Methodological Problems in the Development of a Post-Hospital Suicide Prediction Scale.*

Nor has death become merely the latest subdiscipline of scholars. The fascination with death is broad and popular. A "death questionnaire" sponsored by the magazine *Psychology Today* elicited thirty thousand responses from readers, as compared to twenty thousand for the "sex questionnaire," the pre-

vious record-holder. Another general magazine, *Human Behavior,* has instituted a department called "Death." A whole genre has developed that might be dubbed *death lit.;* and here is the smallest random sampling of recent titles, with description by author or publisher.

The Art of Dying "introduces a series of mental exercises which help the individual face his own death with a sense of ease instead of panic, fear, or the thought of pain. To accept the death of others that we love as part of the rhythm of life."

Suicide: The Gamble with Death "reveals how such factors as age, sex, race, and alcohol and drug use affect suicide and actual completions"—not to mention correlations with marital status, the state of the economy, and the weather.

Deaths of Man "examines in detail, and from a number of points of view, what the actual dying process is like. Above all, it stresses the ways in which a person may be helped to die a *more appropriate death.*"

The Immortality Factor reports that, "as fantastic as it seems, science is now at the threshold of achieving control over death" and asks: "What does this mean for life on earth as we know it?"

Last Rights: A Case for the Good Death "sets forth the belief that every human being should be able to choose the manner of his dying: in dignity."

What do these books and other death lit. books share in common? Judged by content, they have the sort of distant-cousin relationship that justifies (but barely) still another reader's packaging service—say, the Thanatology Book Club. The genre even spills across other publishing boundaries. For instance, books about abortion can be grouped as a women's liberation lit. subdivision. Essays on cryogenics—the freeze-now, thaw-later program of installment mortality—constitute a kind of science nonfiction. Where death lit.

books do resemble one another is in their approach.

Never has death been treated as so practical a matter. *Do something about it!* is the reflexive cry-from-the-heart. Death lit. books qualify as manuals, handbooks, or the latest in *how-to* guides. (One such self-help text is devoted to How to be a Widow.) Americans have an impulse to politicize—as the modish verb has it—even the most philosophical issue, and death is no exception. At their most ambitious, death lit. books are manifestos: pamphlets for a movement that already exists or ought to. Death, to be a little crude, has become the radical's newest revolution, the reformer's ultimate civil rights cause.

The politics of death might be illustrated by the topics of abortion or suicide. But euthanasia, at the moment, appears to be *the* issue; and as a case study of that peculiarly native phenomenon—hard-sell idealism—euthanasia knows no peer. The Euthanasia Council[1] (twenty-five thousand members) supplies "Right-to-Die" educational kits to schools, for children down to the age of twelve. With death as with sex (as once with God), the theory is that one cannot indoctrinate too early. A fifty-six-minute film depicting (in color) the so-called "good death" may be rented for $55.

The tenets of euthanasia are forever being stated and restated, as if for the pleasure of authors listening to the sounds of their own convictions.... [A] recent rehearsal of the credo was sponsored by the magazine *The Humanist*. The cover of the July–August [1974] issue is designed in the shape of a Declaration of Independence scroll, but the redundant heading reads: *"A Plea for Beneficent Euthanasia."* "We, the undersigned..." the familiar rhetoric begins, going on to "appeal to an enlightened public opinion to transcend traditional taboos and to move in the direction of a compassionate view toward needless suffering in dying." The signers endorse not only "passive euthanasia"—i.e., "the withdrawal of extraordinary life-prolonging techniques, such as intraveneous feeding and resuscitation." They are also for "active euthanasia," i.e., "the administration of increasing dosages of drugs (such as morphine) to relieve suffering, until the dosage, of necessity, reaches the lethal stage."

How does one recognize the precise point at which the "good death" becomes preferable to a "bad life" for this newly defined "loved one": the patient *in extremis?* A professor of Biomedical Ethics at the University of Virginia, Joseph Fletcher, has proposed "Indicators of Humanhood" as the criteria. Fetuses, comatose persons, and those scoring lower than a 40 I.Q. are among the candidates who fail to qualify for "humanhood" on the Fletcher scale.[2] The patient still passing his "humanhood" test but nervous about his grades may or may not be reassured by a Professor Emeritus of Psychology at Western Maryland College, O. Ruth Russell, who is sure that a "comprehensive euthanasia law" would "meet a broad spectrum of needs and provide adequate safeguards for every case." To guarantee himself a "good death," however, the sensible "loved one" is advised to draw up a contract known as

---

1. Editor's note: The Euthanasia Council has been renamed "Concern for Dying."

2. Dr. Fletcher also seems to have a scale ("Indicators of Subversionhood" perhaps?) for those who oppose him: "I will wager any amount that the Wallaces and Maddoxes, who defended Lieutenant Calley and hail him as a hero, are devout and pious opponents of euthanasia and abortion probably." In fairness to Dr. Fletcher, his enemies are quite prepared to call him a neo-Nazi greasing the "slippery slope" to genocide. Understatement is no problem in the Great American Death Debate.

the "Living Will," which has proved to be euthanasia's *pièce de résistance* with the public. When "Dear Abby," the Miss Lonely-hearts columnist, printed a description of a "Living Will," fifty thousand readers wrote to the Euthanasia Council for copies. Marya Mannes, a novelist and essayist, has published her own "Living Will" with this uncompromis-ing codicil:

> I do not wish to survive a stroke that impairs my ability to speak or move, nor any accident or disease resulting in vision too impaired to see or read or in total deafness.
> A world without beauty heard or seen is no world for me.
> A life without freedom and movement is no life for me.

Alas, the politics of death, like a lot of Ameri-can politics, has a tendency to escalate into evangelism. If the dominant notion of the American used to be that death is nonexistent, the *idée fixe* of the 1970s threatens to be that death can be beautiful—not merely a controlled disaster (how to say it?)—but a success story.

Consider just the subtopic of dying last-words. A grudging "So be it" might once have been about the most that could be expected. Today serenity is the least that will be con-doned; gusto is preferred. "My cup runneth over" may be the most enthusiastic quote recorded so far in death lit., but who knows what will follow? A scrutiny of texts discloses that death is counted upon to be not only "gen-tle and easy" but marked by "dignity" and the same sense of "purpose" required of life. One clergyman has declared that dying should be an "adventure." *The Art of Dying* assigns among its exercises for readers: "Write fifty words of wonder about your own death" and ends with the wish: "May you always be sur-prised by your own dying and living." Death,

in fact, ought to be "beautiful," according to the Council for Christian Action of the United Church of Christ. In its policy statement on euthanasia, the Council affirm "Death for an older person should be a beautiful event," arguing "What's more beautiful than...the beautiful brightly colored autumn leaves gliding gracefully to the ground?" Dr. Walter W. Sackett, Jr., a Florida legislator who spon-sored a *"Death with Dignity"* statute, has pro-mised: "Death, like birth, is glorious."

To the familiar American archetypes of the Death Pragmatist *(Do something about it)* and the Death Optimist *(It could be the best thing that ever happened to you)* must be add-ed the Death Existentialist. Conspicuously neither a pragmatist nor an optimist, the Death Existentialist is recruited principally from the native anti-Americans known and feared as The Young. "Melancholy has been a privilege granted to 'solitary eminences,'" Günter Grass once observed. "As a social attitude, however, it has seldom been legalized"—least of all in the United States. There is one exception: American adolescents (who may be as near to "solitary eminences" as the United States can boast) are allowed, in-deed expected, to be melancholy; and in this particular they seldom let their elders down. There are no pessimists like the children of optimists.

Death and madness (see R. D. Laing) have become the high grounds on which the young stage their great refusal of the "plastic life" and "crazy normalcy" of late twentieth-century America. Like volleys they hail down apt quotes from Albert Camus ("A mass death sentence defines the human condition"), Her-mann Hesse ("The whole world seemed des-troyed and poisoned; there seemed to be no joy, no more innocence, no more love on earth"), and Sylvia Plath ("Dying is an art, like everything else. I do it exceptionally well").

One honours suffering, case by case; one cannot help wondering about *The Sorrows of Werther* as a popular epidemic. According to one of those ubiquitous polls that topics like death give steady employment to, no less than 50 percent of the students at the University of Maine said they had "considered, threatened, or actually attempted suicide." Has death become the supreme authenticator for a generation that craves more than anything to be authenticated? In his superb black comedy *The Suicide Academy*, the novelist Daniel Stern formulates this logic for "the kind that all their lives would not take yes for an answer"—"I die, therefore I am."

There is even a suspicion that the new pre-occupation with death may have originated with the first Nuclear Era children. Edwin Shneidman, director of the Laboratory for the Study of Life-Threatening Behavior at the University of California at Los Angeles, has wondered if "the current generation might not be termed psychological *Hibakusha* [the Japanese word for the "explosion-affected" survivors of Hiroshima]. At the least they are Atomic Bomb Age children." Dr Shneidman provides a collection of statements written by students in his "death courses" at UCLA and Harvard:

> "I think my whole generation has grown up and been tremendously influenced by the imminent threat of death."
> "Death is part of my life."
> "The constant threat of nuclear war, the arms race, and the continual reminder of this threat on television makes me acutely aware that death could happen at any time."

Apocalypse is the operative word—or is it?

For a case may be submitted that Viet Nam rather than Hiroshima is the historical episode that spells "death" to a '70s American. "Mega-death," a term that seems to spread like a mushroom, conveys a Doomsday sense of

Xerxes the great did die
And so must you and I.

The New England Primer

quantity, of "body count." But "wasted," the term that came out of Viet Nam, carries an even more terrible message: meaninglessness; the bitter taste of power at its most destructive (and most impotent); first-hand, irrevocable knowledge of the word "defeat."

America's youthfulness is its oldest tradition, Oscar Wilde remarked—it's been going on for almost three hundred years; and it went on for another half-century after Wilde's quip. In Viet Nam did America arrive at last at middle-age? These novel and dismaying sensations were experienced: a sudden faltering of the will, describable as Manifest-Destiny fatigue; an inclination to refer to the "American Dream" in quotes (and with sarcasm), followed by the unheard-of question, "Is it all worth it?"; an unprecedented attack of self-doubt about the purity of one's motives. *America can die*—the American has admitted this heresy to himself for the first time, and the traumatic effect has yet to be fully measured. But one thing is certain. Watergate, double-digit inflation—the catastrophes that have beset the United States since Viet Nam—are now read in the perspective of potentially mortal symptoms.

Death, then, is not an arbitrary topic, confronted by '70s *avant-gardistes* in order to break a conspiracy of silence, "a stink of hypocrisy," as one put it. Death has imposed itself upon the reluctant American with a painfulness, an *actuality* he could not ignore if he wanted to. A historical montage of the past decade or so seems to play through the collective American memory as a sequence of deaths: two Kennedys gunned down; the bodies of three civil rights workers buried in Mississippi; booby-trapped GI corpses in rice paddies; Marilyn Monroe. The Death Prag-

matists and Optimists might like to reduce death to a managed event. The Death Existentialists might like to turn it into a trip, a mind-blowing *idea*. But already the subject of death is proving harder to contain than it used to be to overlook. Death is like Moby Dick: once one sticks in the harpoon, the quarry takes the initiative, and the presumed hunter becomes a passenger at the end of the line. Here are a couple of guesses as to where the white whale might tow Americans next.

SCENARIO NO. 1: THE ANTI-DEATH MACHINE   Five years ago the brilliant novelist and maverick philosopher Alan Harrington blurted out in a passionate, book-long diatribe, *The Immortalist,* the radical pragmatism, the all-or-nothing optimism that may still—even in post–Viet Nam middle age—be the only truth an American knows in his bones. "Death," Harington declared flatly, "is an imposition on the human race, and no longer acceptable." (How languid the nineteenth-century liberalism of euthanasia propaganda sounds by comparison!) The modern soul's final and absolute discontentment with mortality, Harrington submitted, was the malaise behind all the other discontentments of the 1960s: Angst and alienation; drugs and this-or-that revolution. "Good death" to Harrington was a contradiction in terms. He stood with Renan ("I find death loathsome, hateful, and senseless") and Herbert Marcuse, who, in a comment on the "strange masochism" of death-welcoming, wrote indignantly: "A brute, biological fact, permeated with pain, horror, and despair, is transformed into an existential privilege."

A new and bizarre little encyclopaedia called *The Best,* half put-on, half serious—the sort of book that could happen only in America—devotes one of its sections to "The Best Way to

Stay Alive," summing up: "It may be possible to finesse the whole problem [mortality] by growing whole new bodies, twins identical to the originals save for memory, from the genetic information contained within single cells." Something like this is what Harrington had in mind when he proposed that "an 'Immortality Program' would not be nearly as expensive as the atomic energy and space projects."

The limited objective, the merely reasonable expectation, has never been the American style. Is Harrington—a spaced-out Job, asking his anguished "Why?", then his desperately cocky "Why not?"—voicing what Americans still feel today but are too sophisticated or too tired to say? This scenario predicates that Americans might recover their notorious energy and their fine old touch of native fanaticism to go all-out—to play the Great Gatsby— one more time. "Gatsby believed in the green light, the orgiastic future that year by year recedes before us," Scott Fitzgerald wrote of his American Everyman. "It eluded us then, but that's no matter—tomorrow we will run faster, stretch out our arms farther...And one fine morning..."—Immortality!

SCENARIO NO. 2: THE AGE OF COMPASSION If Waugh's Mr. Barlow were to return to America today, he would be pressed by a new question. At almost every turn of American life (and now death) a voice modulated to a perfect pitch of consideration asks: "Why must you suffer? Why must anybody suffer? Let me help you to exercise the latest amendment to the Bill of Rights: 'Each man has a natural right to be treated kindly.'"

"Compassion" is replacing "competitiveness" as the American *beau idéal.* In the August [1974] issue of *Reader's Digest* Mrs. Norman Vincent Peale pronounced *Compassion* together with *Self-Confidence* and *En-*

thusiasm to be the qualities Americans most desire in their children. But what exactly is this *caring,* a word that American writers so regularly italicize, as if to make it mean more than it means? Is compassion the descendant of "charity" of *I Corinthians: 13*—a habit of *Imitation of Christ* that post-Christians have inherited in spite of themselves, a matter of half-playing Jesus, half-playing a Good Joe? Is compassion the final proof to an American that he has ceased to be a Puritan—has stopped believing at last that suffering and punishment build character?

Compassion, according to Scenario No. 2, will become the one virtue that can make an American feel in the right even when he is in the wrong. And without it, he will feel wrong even if he is right. Certainly compassion will be—if it is not already—the correct, the almost compulsory posture towards death, as diplomatic nonrecognition once was. But this will not be death as one used to know it—a business of gasp, rattle, and agony: the enemy himself. This will be death surrounded by adjectives ("good," "dignified," "timely") and buried under statistics. This will be death hidden beneath new euphemisms like "terminal living" that seem no improvement over "passing on." This will be death as an abstraction, a mask of itself: as profound an evasion as reticence ever was.

A worthy but negative purpose—*not* to suffer—will become the primary purpose of life. Anger, humour, piety—the emotions that sprang from the heart of the race and once made dying a human experience of an inhumane event—will disappear into a general blandness. Death, if that is possible, will become banal. For compassion is a bureaucrat's emotion finally—duty aspiring to be love. As bureaucracy continues to grow, it will turn death into a social ill, like unemployment. There ought to be a government agency for this sort of death, and there probably will be.

In fact, Scenario No. 2 may not be a scenario at all but a work-in-progress. The only obstacle to its fulfillment appears to lie in the answer to the question: How many Savages are left? If Waugh was the supreme commentator on death in the Age of the Great Ignoral, Aldous Huxley, surely, has been its prophet for the Age of Compassion, insisting more than forty years ago that to discount what is intolerable about dying would mean to discount what is most precious about living. Here is the Controller, Mustapha Mond (talking to that vain, possibly fraudulent, yet curiously appealing romantic known as the Savage in *Brave New World*):

> "We prefer to do things comfortably."
> "But I don't want comfort. I want God, I want poetry. I want real danger, I want freedom, I want goodness. I want sin."
> "In fact," said Mustapha Mond, "you're claiming the right to be unhappy."
> "All right then," said the Savage defiantly, "I'm claiming the right to be unhappy."
> "Not to mention the right to grow old and ugly and impotent; the right to have syphilis and cancer; the right to have too little to eat; the right to be lousy; the right to live in constant apprehension of what may happen tomorrow; the right to catch typhoid; the right to be tortured by unspeakable pains of every kind."
> There was a long silence.
> "I claim them all," said the Savage at last.
> Mustapha Mond shrugged his shoulders. "You're welcome," he said.

The American Savage, of course, has been the artist. One may even claim (like Leslie Fiedler in *Love and Death in the American Novel*) that the native Muse is Death. For a sweeping generalization, how specifically it proves itself! Thorton Wilder's *Our Town*,

Edgar Lee Masters' *Spoon River Anthology* literally begin in the graveyard. What are the works of America's best playwright (Eugene O'Neill) about, from start to finish, except death? From Hawthorne to Hemingway, from Poe to Faulkner, the grinning skull has been the imprimatur, as it were, of the American author, mocking the lives of the death-evading countrymen he has written about and for.

So the specter has been at the back of the American mind since the beginning. The veritable babble about death today represents a frantic game of cultural catch-up—the children and grandchildren of Babbitt ready, at last, to learn what their benignly neglected poets could have told them all along. If we are diligent at our overdue homework, we may eventually know (Scenario No. 3?) what Emily Dickinson knew when she wrote:

> That short—potential stir
> That each can make but once—
> That Bustle so illustrious
> 'Tis almost Consequence—
>
> Is the éclat of Death—
> Oh thou unknown Renown
> That not a Beggar would accept
> Had he the power to spurn—

But now such merciless accuracy, such bitter intensity—such accustomed "quiet nonchalance of death"—are beyond our final comprehension as readers, to say nothing of our reach as writers. Late starters at a difficult calling, we can just about handle, it seems, the alphabet verses of *The New England Primer*—those elementary stark facts that every Puritan child knew as soon as he learned his X and Y:

> Xerxes the great did die
> And so must you and I.
>
> Youth forward slips,
> Death soonest nips.

Edwin S. Shneidman

National Survey of Attitudes toward Death

It would appear that the overwhelming response to a survey on death attitudes that Shneidman conducted through the pages of *Psychology Today* bears witness to Gorer's observation that death has replaced sex as the national obsession. Shneidman, an internationally renowned psychologist and co-founder of the suicide prevention centers in the United States, reports that more than thirty thousand highly educated young people responded to his seventy-five-item questionnaire, a three to two margin of response over an earlier *Psychology Today* sex survey. The death questionnaire dealt with such issues as childhood experiences and attitudes toward death, beliefs about afterlife, thoughts about one's own life, funerals, the disposition of one's body, and suicide.

While the respondents generally were from a narrow band of middle-class lifestyles within the social structure, their responses to the survey nevertheless are important. This is so for several reasons. First, these young respondents occupy a potentially important position in the age structure; they will be the parents and decision-makers of tomorrow. Second, the nature and degree of the responses to many of the questions are appreciably different from today's typical attitudes and practices. There can be no doubt that this group of respondents constitutes a critical minority in our society and may well be the harbinger of traditional attitudes to come.

Sigmund Freud said that death was the goal of all life, and Peter Pan saw it as an awfully big adventure. Socrates thought it might be the greatest of all human blessings.

Readers of *Psychology Today* apparently feel that it is more important than sex; the single biggest surprise in the result of the *P. T.* death questionnaire was the sheer volume of response. More than thirty thousand readers returned the research questionnaires, and more than two thousand of them sent substantial letters with their replies. This broke the record set by the *P. T.* sex questionnaire, which fetched somewhat over twenty thousand replies.

It was almost as though thousands of persons had been waiting for a legitimate occasion to unburden themselves about death and then felt somehow cleansed after writing their unspoken thoughts. Several letters said as much, indicating how grateful the respondents were and how meaningful the exercise had been to them.

These letters, clippings, quotations, and such—multipaged autobiographical accounts and philosophical treatises—helped to flush out the inescapable two-dimensional quality of the questionnaire "You and Death" (*P. T.*, August 1970). In these writings one could see the key forces of life at work: the unconscious facets of the mind, luminescent between the lines of often poignant text.

Spectrum. There were seventy-five items in the questionnaire. The first section explored childhood experience of and attitudes toward death, including first-person involvement and family discussions, then influences—such as books, religion, or actual events—that might have affected early attitudes and current ones. Other questions dealt with beliefs and wishes about afterlife and with thoughts about one's own death (including the aspect that seemed most distasteful), and with feelings about the disposition of one's body. Several questions probed the problem of suicide, asking about past tries and probability of future attempts. Wills, funerals, and other death rituals also came under scrutiny.

Like other *P.T.* surveys—on sex, on law and crime, on drugs, on the cities—"Death and You" reflects the *Psychology Today* audience rather than the general American public—and in some ways it does not even totally reflect that group. While, according to recent subscriber surveys, 53 percent of the subscribers are women, women contributed 63 percent of all replies. Students also answered out of proportion to their numbers: 33 percent of all replies came from students, who make up 17 percent of the *P.T.* readership.

Profile. The typical respondent to the death questionnaire is a twenty- to twenty-four-year-old single, Caucasian Protestant ("somewhat religious"), politically independent ("somewhat liberal") female. She has had some college education, earns between $10,000 and $15,000 a year, lives in the Midwest, and comes from a small family (one sibling). She is in "very good" (but not "excellent") physical and mental health, and she states that there is little probability of her committing suicide.

The reader might keep in mind that responses from a young and highly educated group of people—perhaps a critical minority, a cutting edge—may reveal where the rest of society is heading.

Urgency. The size of the response is of more than passing interest. Both the editors of *Psychology Today* and I believe that it is more than simply the habituation of *Psychology Today* readers to questionnaires as such. We believe that this volume reflects an urgency to talk about death—not only the permissiveness to talk about it. Indeed, the major debate in this country swirls around the algebra of death: Do we save more lives in a hypothetical long run by killing x number of persons today?

For many, the major result of the death questionnaire likely was that the respondent could remove death from his list of taboo topics. Death is something that most decent persons do not know how to discuss, especially with an aged or dying person. The introduction of death into such conversations usually results in embarrassment, evasion, or pretense. Along with our urgent need to discuss death, we apparently have an equally strong counterphobic reaction to it. Taken together, attraction and repulsion constitute a basic ambivalent theme that threads its way through the questionnaire. Some of our readers are quite aware of their own ambivalence.

"Reflecting upon the way I live," wrote one male student, "I know that there are things I do that make me take chances with death. The way I cross the street, the way I drive a car, the way I ski too fast, the way I sleep too little. I realize also that much of the way is in fact partly an acting out of my ambivalent feelings about life." So forbidden has death been in our culture that a third of the respondents could not recall from childhood a single instance of discussion of death within the family circle. In more than one-third of the families, it was mentioned with discomfort, and in only 30 percent was death talked about openly.

Split. Indeed, America's current attitude

toward death is deeply ambivalent: awe of death and an attraction toward death; risking death and loving life; wanting happiness and behaving in self-destructive ways; regarding death as taboo and insisting on a new permissiveness to talk about it; an obsession with the Bomb and a deep concern with spiritual rebirth. We live in a death-conscious time in which man, the center of his own world, boldly asserts that he is not psychologically degradable.

Man's view of death has undergone radical change in the last few generations—perhaps the first major radical changes since the seventeenth century of Descartes. The Cartesian view of death is tied to a view of man as essentially a biological vessel, subject to the whims of fate or fortune. Death is one such whim. The Cartesian philosophic spirit necessarily implies a fatalistic view of life.

The results of the death questionnaire unequivocally demonstrate the demise of fatalism. Our reader—and perhaps most of twentieth-century men—has made himself the center of his own universe and has put himself back into his own death. He recognizes death and dying as aspects of living. Thanks primarily to Freud, he sees man as playing conscious and unconscious roles in his own fate. Most *P.T.* readers believe in the possible influence of psychological factors on man's death; 92 percent either "firmly believe" or "tend to believe" that psychological factors can influence or even cause death. But while they opt strongly for the possibility of mind over matter, half of the respondents believe that events over which individuals have no control cause most deaths. A sizable group (43 percent) believe that most persons participate consciously or unconsciously in their own deaths. Men and women generally agree in these beliefs.

Witness. Many things go into shaping a person's view of life and death and the part he plays in either by his own volition. The usual experiences with death in America have changed dramatically over the last two generations. It used to be that almost everyone, by the time he was an adolescent, had personally witnessed a death, usually at home, of some loved one—a baby brother or sister, a mother or father. Today most dying is done in hospitals, largely out of sight and almost always under formal institutional regimen.

Many respondents (43 percent) had their first personal involvements with death when their grandparents died. Over half first became aware of death after they were five but before they were ten, and 35 percent say that their present attitudes toward death came about from the interior—primarily from introspection and meditation.

Faith. The interface between religion and death is especially fascinating. Numerous studies have shown that nominal religious affiliation is not meaningful in understanding religious conviction. But we asked for "religious background," which allowed us to see that one's religious environment, whether he accepts or rejects the tenets of his faith, whether he stays with the church of his fathers or leaves it, certainly affects many of his attitudes toward death. Ten percent of the respondents checked "other" rather than Protestant, Catholic, or Jewish to describe their religious backgrounds. The "other" category runs the gamut from atheism to Islam, and must include Buddhists, Hindus, Confucians, Unitarians, and complete absence of religion in the respondent's home.

Important in most current attitudes toward death is the reader's own estimate of his degree of religiosity. The "very religious" slightly outnumber the "antireligious" in our sample; roughly one out of ten *P. T.* readers falls into each group. Almost a fourth of the respondents are "not at all religious," while over half see themselves as "slightly" or "somewhat" religious. Women are more likely to be religious than men....

TABLE 1 How religious do you consider yourself to be?

Very religious	11%
Somewhat religious	32
Slightly religious	23
Not at all religious	24
Antireligious	9

Hell. Religious background makes a difference on a number of attitudes. Jews are less likely to be religious than are Christians—53 percent of respondents with Jewish backgrounds are either "antireligious" or "not at all religious," while only 2 percent are "very religious." Jews are also the least likely of any group to have believed in heaven and hell when they were very young. Eleven percent of those with Jewish backgrounds believed in heaven-hell concepts, while 44 percent of Protestants and 73 percent of Roman Catholics believed in them.

As adults, 18 percent of Jews "tend to believe" or "strongly believe" in afterlife, and 65 percent of them are either convinced that there is no afterlife or "tend to doubt it." Forty-two percent of Protestants and 55 percent of Roman Catholics, on the other hand, either believe or tend to believe in a hereafter, while 38 percent of Protestants and 25 percent of Roman Catholics doubt or do not believe in the existence of life after death. In every category, there were more persons who wished there were an afterlife than there were who

believed or tended to believe in one. Generally, the more religious one is, the more likely he is to wish for an afterlife, but 9 percent of the "very religious" and 36 percent of those whose attitudes toward death were significantly shaped by religion prefer that there be no life after death....

TABLE 2 To what extent do you believe in a life after death?

Strongly believe in it	23%
Tend to believe in it	20
Uncertain	19
Tend to doubt it	22
Convinced it does not exist	16

Regardless of your belief about life after death, what is your wish about it?

I strongly wish there were a life after death	55%
I am indifferent	34
I definitely prefer that there not be a life after death	11

View. As one would expect, religion played a very significant role in the attitudes on death of an overwhelming majority of the "very religious" (77 percent). While most of the antireligious say that religion played little part in their own attitudes, a substantial number report that religion indeed had significant roles for them, apparently pushing them away from the traditional religious outlooks on death. Readers who consider themselves "not at all religious"—i.e., nonbelievers but not hostile to organized religion—are less likely than the antireligious to attribute a very significant role to religion.

Both Roman Catholics and Protestants report that religion played a greater role in their attitudes toward death than did other groups. Fifty-three percent of the Catholics and 44 percent of Protestants say that religion played a "very significant" or a "rather significant" role in their attitudes toward death. Only 16 percent of the Jews agree; 71 percent say that it played "no role at all" or only a "minor role." Among those who never belonged to one of the major U.S. religious groups, 24 percent say that the role of religion in their own attitudes was significant, while 61 percent say its role was nonexistent or only minor.

TABLE 3 How much of a role has religion played in the development of your attitude toward death?

	No role	Rather significant	Very significant
Very religious	2%	14%	77%
Not at all religious	25	7	6
Antireligious	39	4	15

TABLE 4 How much of a role has religion played in the development of your attitude toward death? (all respondents)

A very significant role	22%
A rather significant role	20
Somewhat influential, but not a major role	23
A relatively minor role	23
No role at all	12

Influence. If religion did not play a significant role in forming attitudes toward death, what, in this secular age, did? Introspection and meditation, say over a third of the respondents. Given another choice and asked to apply the influences to their own deaths, more than a third reinforced their first choice by selecting existential philosophy.

Men are more likely to be existentialists than women are: 38 percent of male respondents chose existential philosophy, while only

TABLE 5 Which of the following most influenced your present attitudes toward death?

Death of someone close	19%
Specific reading	11
Religious upbringing	15
Introspection and meditation	35
Ritual (e.g., funerals)	5
TV, radio, or motion pictures	3
Longevity of my family	3
My health or physical condition	2
Other	8

28 percent of the women cast their lots with Sartre or Kierkegaard. The existentialists are as likely to be religious as they are to be atheists.

Books. Asked what books or authors had had the most effect on their attitudes toward death, 41 percent of our respondents reply that no books or authors had influencd them. (Thirty-five percent of our existential respondents are nonreaders. But before McLuhanites take too much satisfaction in these statistics, they should consider that while 11 percent say that reading had been the most important influence on their attitudes, only 3 percent credit TV, radio, or motion pictures.)

After the Bible, which influenced 23 percent, the most influential works were those of Albert Camus, Hermann Hesse, and Shakespeare. James Agee influenced only 1 percent, as did Thomas Mann. Eighteen percent specify books or authors not listed on the questionnaire, and 20 percent of the existentialists are among those influenced by other writers. Among twenty-year-olds, Camus' *The Stranger* and Hesse's *Steppenwolf, Demian,* and *Siddhartha* are mentioned again and again. Nearly two-thirds of the Camus and

Hesse readers also chose existential philosophy as most influential.

Existential despair does not weigh heavily on our existentialists. They report themselves no more likely than other respondents to attempt suicide; 81 percent of them feel good, cheerful, wonderful, or on top of the world; they are more likely than the average respondent to consider death as the final process of life; they are more likely than the other respondents to feel resolved when they consider their own mortality.

Bomb. Since 1945 man has faced the possibility of destruction on a scale that he has never known before: the Bomb. More than half the respondents have been influenced to some degree by the threat of nuclear war. One young man put his fear into words: "I am part of the nuclear generation. The hippie's interest in Eastern religions and emphasis on self rather than social change is in the same vein as this persistent threat of death. Philosophies are undoubtedly influenced by the atomic age and I am a product of that age."

TABLE 6   To what extent has the possibility of massive human destruction by nuclear war influenced your present attitudes toward death or life?

Enormously	5%
To a fairly large extent	14
Moderately	18
Somewhat	15
Very little	25
Not at all	23

Drugs.   Fifteen percent of all twenty- to twenty-four-year-olds who returned the questionnaire report that narcotic or hallucinogenic drugs have affected their attitudes toward death; thus one out of every seven persons in this age group has had a significant death-and-drug experience. Drugs appear to be confined mainly to the young; only scattered returns came in from drug users over thirty-five. When all respondents are taken into consideration, men are more likely to have taken drugs than women are. Forty percent of men and 31 percent of the women have used narcotic or hallucinogenic drugs.

Religious background affects one's use of drugs. The ghostly fingers of puritanism appear to restrain Protestants, but only to a slight degree; 32 percent of them have taken drugs, and only 5 percent have been affected by their use. Among Roman Catholics, 34 percent have taken drugs, but 11 percent have had drugs affect their attitudes toward death. More Jews (44 percent) than non-Jews have tried drugs, but fewer have been affected. Only 4 percent have experienced changes in attitudes toward death after drug use. "Others" are more susceptible: 41 percent have taken drugs, but 18 percent of this group—one out of every six—say that drugs have affected their attitudes toward death. Religiosity also helps predict drug use. The more religious one says he is, the less likely he is to have taken drugs.

TABLE 7 Have your attitudes toward death ever been influenced by narcotic or hallucinogenic drugs?

	Under 20	20-24	25-29	30-34
Yes	9%	15%	4%	4%
I have taken drugs but my attitudes toward death have never been affected by them	28	34	25	24
I have never taken drugs	63	52	71	72

Age. If we put together attitudes at various ages in reference to beliefs, we find—with no great surprise—that questionnaire results show that attitudes toward death change as one matures. Typically, religious beliefs become phenomenological or secular or scientized. One then sees death simply as the end of life. The typical childhood conception of death is in terms of an afterlife, which for most involves ideas of heaven and hell (57 percent). But by adulthood, the percentage of individuals who believe in an afterlife as their primary view of death has been cut almost in half, to 30 percent.

TABLE 8 What does death mean to you?

The end; the final process of life	35%
The beginning of a life after death; a transition, a new beginning	13
A joining of the spirit with a universal cosmic consciousness	12
A kind of endless sleep; rest and peace	9
Termination of this life but with survival of the spirit	17
Don't know	10
Other	4

From late adolescence on, the largest single percentage group sees death simply as the final process of life (35 percent). Among adults, beliefs about death seem to be in terms of eternal loss of consciousness—the absolute end of one's mental (including spiritual) existence. In this belief, there are no remarkable sex differences, but the older one is, the more likely he is to be convinced that there is no life after death. . . .

Thought. All these results point to one of the main findings of the questionnaire, namely that—over the past generation or two—there has been a tremendous secularization of death. Nowadays people die ascetically in aseptic hospitals rather than aesthetically in their homes. The physician has replaced the priest; the doctor is today's magician who has the power to extend life, our new escort from this vale of tears. The funeral industry directs the molds of mourning, ushering us from burial to bereavement.

The average respondent thinks about his own death "occasionally," and the thought is likely to make him feel resolved in relation to life or to take pleasure in being alive.

There are no significant sex differences, although men are slightly more likely to feel pleasure in being alive or to be resolved, while women more often tend to be fearful. There seem to be no particular age trends in regard to this feeling, except that members of the 25-29 age group are more fearful than any other group; 30 percent say that fear is their response to thoughts of death. Perhaps it is at about this age that a person first begins to recognize his own mortality. But when respondents were asked at what age they thought other people were most afraid of death, their answers spread across the spectrum. Women, however, are a bit more likely

TABLE 9   How often do you think about your own death?

Very frequently (at least once a day)	5%
Frequently	17
Occasionally	57
Rarely (no more than once a year)	15
Very rarely or never	6

When you think of your own death (or when circumstances make you realize your own mortality), how do you feel?

Fearful	19%
Discouraged	5
Depressed	11
Purposeless	5
Resolved in relation to life	26
Pleasure in being alive	25
Other	9

than men to say that children under twelve are most afraid, perhaps because of their closer contact with young children. Both men and women place the time of least fear in the years over seventy, but women are almost as likely to say that the thirties are least haunted by the specter of death....

Respondents would prefer quiet and dignified deaths, sudden but not violent. Eight out

TABLE 10   If you had a choice, what kind of death would you prefer?

Tragic, violent death	1%
Sudden, but not violent death	38
Quiet, dignified death	30
Death in the line of duty	1
Death after a great achievement	6
Suicide	2
Homicidal victim	0
There is no "appropriate" kind of death	16
Other	6

of ten would not, even if it were possible, want to know the exact date on which they are going to die, but if they had a terminal disease, seven out of ten would want their physicians to tell them so. Men are more likely than women to want to know the exact date of their deaths.

Further, if they had a terminal disease and limited time to live, nearly half would either shift their concerns to others or finish projects and tie up loose ends. Even though over a third formed their basic attitudes toward death through contemplation and introspection, only one in twenty would spend his remaining days contemplating or praying. Twenty percent would make no change in lifestyle, and 19 percent would satisfy hedonistic needs through travel, sex, or drugs.

Facing. Perhaps because so many men have seen combat in this war-torn century, more men than women have been in situations in which they seriously thought they might die. Seventy-nine percent of the men and 70 percent of the women have faced death at least once, and 28 percent of the men as compared to 20 percent of the women have faced death "several" or "many" times.

Only 16 percent hold life so dear that they would not sacrifice it for any reason. More men than women report themselves willing to sacrifice their lives for an idea or a moral principle; women are more likely to say they would sacrifice their lives for loved ones. Age also affects one's attitude. Respondents under twenty are least eager to sacrifice their lives for those they love, but are more willing than most other groups to die for an idea or in combat. Respondents from thirty-five to thirty-nine value their own lives more highly than members of any other age group; 30 percent would not give their lives for any reason. As Mark Twain said, "Each person is born to one possession which out-values all others—his last breath."

TABLE 11 For whom or what might you be willing to sacrifice your life?

For a loved one	58%
For an idea or a moral principle	15
In combat or a grave emergency where a life could be saved	11
Not for any reason	16

Two. Arnold Toynbee has written that death is essentially a two-person affair, involving both the survivor and the decedent. He further asserts that if a married person truly loves the spouse, that person will wish the spouse to die first, so the spouse will be spared the anguish of bereavement. Respondents to the death questionnaire divide on this issue, an equal percentage (23 percent) saying yes and no; most persons (54 percent) cannot make up their minds. But when we ignore the undecided, we find a definite split between the sexes. Among the men, 33 percent want to outlive their wives, while 18 percent of the women want to outlive their husbands. Eleven percent of the men and 30 percent of the women would like to die first. Housewives have made up their minds; only 38 percent are undecided, and 35 percent would prefer to outlive their husbands—twice as many as women readers on the average. Only the business managers and the executives are as likely to want to survive their spouses. Readers over thirty are more likely to say they wish to outlive their spouses. The reasons they give for "yes" and "no" responses are themselves equally divided between selfish and selfless reasons. One is reminded of what Lord Nelson is reported to have said as he lay dying aboard the *Victory:* "The pain is so great that one might wish one-

self dead, but one would like to live a little longer too." As ambivalence is the keystone of life, so is it a characteristic of death....

Almost a quarter of those who answered report that they contemplate suicide "once in a while" or "very often," and women are twice as likely as men to think frequently of killing themselves (8 percent of the women compared with 4 percent of the men). Respondents under twenty are more likely than average (11 percent as compared to 6 percent) to contemplate suicide "very often." One-third of *P. T.* readers are sure that they would never commit suicide; another 41 percent doubt that there is any possibility that they would; and 81 percent are sure that they will not commit suicide in the near future. But 3 percent are afraid that they might kill themselves and 1 percent plan to commit suicide someday.

TABLE 12 Has there been a time in your life when you wanted to die?

Yes, mainly because of great physical pain	2%
Yes, mainly because of great emotional upset	37
Yes, mainly to escape an intolerable social or interpersonal situation	18
Yes, mainly because of great embarrassment	1
Yes, for a reason other than above	3
No	40

Motive. What might drive a *P. T.* reader to suicide? Loneliness, illness, or physical pain, say 55 percent. Only 2 percent say they would kill themselves to get even or hurt someone. Women are more likely than men to give loneliness, the loss of a loved one, or atomic war as a motive for suicide, while men are more likely to say they might kill themselves because of failure or disgrace or to avoid sickness or physical pain. One wonders about the courage of the stronger sex when 33 percent of the male readers say that physical illness or pain could drive them to commit suicide. Only 19 percent of the women say they might kill themselves for that reason. Anticipated pain may be more frightening than actual pain; only 2 percent of respondents say they have ever wished for death as escape from physical pain. The older one is, the more likely he is to say that illness or pain could motivate his suicide....

Rites. Their attitudes about funerals are quite definite and echo Jessica Mitford's *The American Way of Death*. Most (80 percent) believe that funerals are "very much overpriced," and 62 percent believe that funerals should cost less than $300. Only 2 percent consider a price in excess of $600 to be a "reasonable" charge.

Only 2 percent would like formal funerals—"as large as possible"—and a third of *P. T.* readers want no funerals of any kind. Large, formal funerals are rejected unanimously by respondents who are antireligious, who want no part of any afterlife, or who have religious backgrounds that are neither Jewish, Catholic, nor Protestant. The less religious one is, the less likely he is to want a funeral. Among the very religious, 20 percent do not want funerals; the prejudice against these rites climbs steadily through the categories of religiosity, with 63 percent of the antireligious saying they do not want funerals. Readers believe that rituals such as funerals and wakes are rather important for the survivors (47 percent) although almost a fifth (18 percent) say that such rituals are not important at all. Readers with Jewish backgrounds are more likely than members of any other group to say that whatever their survivors want is fine with them.

Almost no one (6 percent) approves of lying in state at his own funeral. One-fourth of all respondents dissociate themselves from their bodies and say they just "don't care." But a substantial majority (70 percent) definitely do not want to lie in open caskets. Women tend to feel more strongly against lying in open caskets than do men. Antireligious readers register overwhelming disapproval (91 percent) against the display of their corpses, and Roman Catholics are most likely to approve than any other group (12 percent).

Bodies. If it were entirely up to them, nearly a third (32 percent) of the respondents would donate their bodies to medical schools or to science. There is a very slight tendency among those who believe or tend to believe in reincarnation to be readier than average to donate their bodies to science. This tendency also ex-

Death, be not proud, though some have called thee
Mighty and dreadful, for thou art not so:
For those whom thou think'st thou dost overthrow
Die not, poor Death; nor yet canst thou kill me.

John Donne [1573–1631]
Holy Sonnets

ists among people who prefer that there be no afterlife.

Most respondents are willing to donate their hearts for transplantation; 82 percent would—after their own deaths—donate their hearts to anyone, and another 3 percent would donate their hearts to friends or relatives. While 15 percent of all readers would decline to make their hearts available, the very religious are most likely to refuse to give their hearts (25 percent).

Among readers who do not wish to donate their bodies to science, there are more who choose cremation than there are who select burial. But the antireligious are overwhelmingly against burial; only 2 percent would allow their bodies to be interred in caskets, and over half (52 percent) would like to be cremated. Religious background plays a part in one's choice. A third of all readers with Jewish or Roman Catholic backgrounds want to be buried, while only 13 percent of the Protestants would agree with them. Protestants are likelier to donate their bodies or to choose cremation than either Jews or Roman Catholics.

Most approve of autopsies; 83 percent either approve of them or have no strong feelings against having autopsies performed on their own bodies. There is a slight tendency for men to be more in favor of autopsies than for women to approve them. One's wish for an afterlife affects one's feeling toward autopsies.

TABLE 13   If it were entirely up to you, how would you like to have your body disposed of after you have died?

Burial	22%
Cremation	31
Donation to medical school or science	32
I am indifferent	16

The less one wishes for an afterlife, the more likely he is to approve of autopsies. While 79 percent of those who strongly wish for a hereafter do not object to autopsies, 93 percent of those who want the grave to be the end have no strong feelings against them.

Respondents to the death questionnaire furnish a few clues for our heightened preoccupation with death today. A sizable percentage (45 percent) attribute the increase in concern within the last twenty-five years to wars and to the prescence of the Bomb. This is not the place to dwell on the complicated morality of the war in Indochina, but perhaps even more important is the mushroom cloud of death represented by the omnipresent threat of nuclear war. The largest single factor relating to death in the 1970s may well be the threat of atomic bombs, and in a chain reaction, it might be that this heightened concern with atomic deaths accounts in part for our outwardly disdainful attitude toward life itself: excessive risk-taking, burning out with drugs, daring authority, flouting tradition, and the many other inimical and destructive forms of behavior toward ourselves and toward our institutions and traditions. One young college woman wrote: "I can't say that I think this or do such and such because we all may die tomorrow, but I'm convinced that in all our minds there's an underlying nagging fear that the world could blow up, a fear which today is more silent than in the bomb-shelter era of a few years ago but perhaps even more strongly felt and exhibited in minute, imperceptible ways."

But we human beings, especially the young ones, fight on. Another twenty-year-old wrote about this questionnaire: "If I pass this test do I get immortal life as a prize? Think what a bummer that would be. Fear of death puts a little excitement into life. R.I.P."

Samuel Vaisrub

Dying Is Worked to Death

In his brief but trenchant editorial "Dying Is Worked to Death," Samuel Vaisrub, senior editor of the *Journal of the American Medical Association,* expresses his concern that the recent flood tide of literature on the subject of death and dying may be ultimately counter-productive, serving more to obscure rather than to illuminate the issues to which it is addressed. Moreover, he observes that in the wish "to do good" by the patient, the physician is often maligned while the family of the patient is exonerated.

How sincere is the present concern of ours for the terminally ill patient? How substantial is our interest? Is ours a knee-jerk response to some subterranean fear of death to which we are all captive, or does this increased activity and effort on behalf of our moribund citizens reflect a heightened awareness of our common predicament and an acceptance on our part to share and care? We shall see.

•

We are now witnessing an extraordinary influx of essays, editorials, even books and specialized journals, on the subject of death and dying. The tide, no longer limited to the medical literature, overflows into lay publications and other communication media.

Death and dying have been always with us. Why then the current preoccupation? Even if we allow for some ethical and legal problems created by recent technological advances in life support—problems that are sufficiently new to merit comment—how do we account for the extensive writing on the "why's" and the "how's" of looking after a dying patient and his family? Has there been a recent change in attitudes toward death?

Some authorities claim that this is indeed the case. They contend that because the belief in afterlife is no longer as firm as it was in the past, death assumes the terrifying nondimension of nothingness. "Tell me your secret," pleads the protagonist of Ingmar Bergman's *The Seventh Seal,* who made a pact with Death. "I have no secrets," replies Death, "I am nothing."

This explanation may seem plausible, but it collapses when we read the chronicles of medieval plague epidemics, or when we look at their contemporaneous paintings portraying death as a grim-faced rider wielding a scythe, a haggard woman roaming the streets of Baghdad, or a grotesque skeleton cavorting in a *danse macabre.*[1]

Clearly, death was no more attractive then than it is now. After all, afterlife did not necessarily mean the Kingdom of Heaven. Even religious martyrs must have had apprehensions about arriving at a much less desirable destination.

There also exists a widespread impression that both the physician and the family have

---

1. Editor's note: Dance of death. See p. 112 for discussion of the *danse macabre.*

been neglecting the dying. The physician avoids the moribund patients because he feels frustrated and helpless. After all, he has been trained to cure, not to comfort; to relieve pain, not to dispel dread. The family has abdicated much responsibility by letting the patient die in a hospital rather than at home.

Without denying that this impression may have some basis in fact, it is possible to argue that our neglect of the dying has been exaggerated. Even a cursory glance at a hospital ward will show that the chairs at the bedside of the dying patient are rarely empty. At times it would seem that the family did not move the dying patient from home, but rather moved the home to the patient. And, as to the doctor, has anyone actually timed his visits, or quantitated his spirit-sustaining contribution?

Fear of death is, of course, not confined to the dying. We all feel that death is peering over our shoulders. Many psychiatrists think that the dread of extinction is central to the human psyche. Some think that this fear becomes intense in times of national or global crises. For instance, at the height of the cold war, the threat of atomic warfare hung like a pall over the individual, causing anxiety and neurosis. Perhaps this universal fear of death is responsible for the proliferating literature that relates to it.

How true are these theories? Do we often think of death? Have we lost any sleep over the possibility of nuclear catastrophes? It could easily be argued that a mysterious protective reflex keeps the individual oblivious to the certainty of this death. Of the two certitudes—death and taxes—it is the latter that is likely to be the dominant worry.

It is much too easy to write about death. There is no need for statistical evidence and for lengthy references. And no one can claim to have more direct information on the subject from high-up. Perhaps because it is so easy to write about dying, so much is written about it without saying anything new. Words cannot bridge the infinite chasm of eternity.

Ronald J. Cohen

Is Dying Being Worked to Death?

Ronald J. Cohen, senior psychologist, Department of Psychiatry, New York University, in this brief communication from the *American Journal of Psychiatry,* replies to those who question the value of the proliferation of the literature on dying and death. Cohen acknowledges the concern of the critics that death has taken on many of the attributes of a fad and that it is in danger of becoming a bandwagon for easy riders. He asks, however, that we not pass judgment prematurely. Evaluating the various approaches to the death and dying literature, he found seven overlapping categories of interest and concern. These range from the care of the patient *in extremis;* demographic and legal, ethical and moral issues; to introspective accounts on life and death by aged individuals. From this survey, Cohen concludes that whatever the reason might be for this current preoccupation with death, the attempt to amplify our understanding and quantify our observations more than justifies the cacaphony of sounds emanating from the bandwagon.

The trend in the popularity of death as an area of scientific inquiry could be described as having gone from "warmed-over" to "hot." In an editorial in the *Journal of the American Medical Association* questioning the utility and value of the burgeoning literature on death, Vaisrub noted that "we are now witnessing an extraordinary influx of essays, editorials, even books and specialized journals, on the subject of death and dying."

Others have observed that "death is one of the current fads" and that "it is incongruous to envisage death as a bandwagon but this is what it seems likely to become." A coup de grace is dealt to the would-be writer in this area by those who argue that everything that could possibly be said on the topic has been said already.

> It is much too easy to write about death. There is no need for statistical evidence and for lengthy references. And no one can claim to have more direct information on the subject from high-up. Perhaps because it is so easy to write about dying, so much is written about it without saying anything new. [Vaisrub]

EVALUATION OF THE LITERATURE
Rather than indicting en masse the literature in this multifaceted area, it would seem reasonable to independently evaluate the contributions of the various approaches. Broadly speaking, seven overlapping categories can be distinguished. One is concerned with the care and treatment of the patient in extremis. Publications included here range from research reports and case histories to "do-it-yourself" primers. Closely related is the category in which phenomena associated with death and dying are examined from a developmental/psychopathological perspective. Representative publications in this category deal with the death-related anxiety of various populations,

the distinction between affective fear of and cognitive preoccupation with death, and the elucidation of bereavement processes, with special reference to the question of normal versus pathological grief.

Demographic and epidemiological approaches comprise a third category of papers. Amid the seeming plethora of statistical studies included here are many insightful and compelling findings such as those linking psychosocial variables with the occurrence of either death or suicidal attempts. Another classification includes publications that expound the numerous sociocultural aspects of death and dying. A fifth category is reserved for the discussion of legal, ethical, and philosophical issues. This literature ranges from the presentation of guidelines for research to debate over current and increasingly complex clinical issues (e.g., "active" versus "passive" euthanasia and "Patients' Bill of Rights").

The sixth category is comprised of theses that are concerned only coincidentally with death-related issues. Descriptions of the testing of hypotheses derived from such notions as achievement motivation, locus of control, and other formulations would be included here. A final category is reserved for those papers whose primary contribution is to supplement discussion in any of the other six areas by providing stimulating reports amenable to scientific inference. Nonevaluative transcripts of aged individuals' introspections and heuristic experimental findings open to interpretation are representative samples.

DISCUSSION   If the media accurately reflect popular concerns, then the wide appeal of Kübler-Ross's *On Death and Dying,* the extensive coverage given the Quinlan case, and the box-office success of sundry films (e.g., *Love and Death* and *Death Wish*) may be taken as evidence that death-related concerns are not confined to professional journals. How is this heightened general interest in death-related phenomena to be explained? Some may argue that it is the threat of world war and the specter of nuclear annihilation that have compelled individuals to intellectually confront the inevitable. Others de-emphasize international concerns to underscore intranational ones such as the recent rise in cancer-related deaths, the alarming increase in street crime, and the unprecedented increment of political bombings and other terrorist activities in this country. Theologians may point to the decline of the Church and the subsequent unrest stemming from ambivalence attendant on the relinquishment of sacred notions such as the belief in an afterlife. Humanists may argue that the growing literature on death is indicative of a rebellion against cold scientific inquiry and a reawakening of awareness that the dying person is, first of all, a person. There is no shortage of explanations, and those which are put forth are likely to vary within and between academic discipline as well as medical specialty.

Allowing for discussion of ethical and legal issues raised by medical advances, Vaisrub's question concerning the reason for the "current preoccupation" is a cogent one. But whatever the reason for the apparent Zeitgeist, scholarly attempts to amplify, quantify, and reify phenomena related to death and dying have generally had the effect of richly enhancing psychological theorizing and complementing extant dynamic and behavioral intervention strategies. Even the lay media's treatment of this topic has been of educational and perhaps cathartic value.

Is dying being worked to death? I think not. It seems unfair to demean the proliferation of death-related literature as a "bandwagon" if this literature is useful in disseminating the raw data with which behavioral theories and life-supportive psychotherapies can be constructed and/or evaluated. The literature sampled in the seven categories conceptualized herein is only minutely representative of the many recent *novel* contributions to man's appreciation of his mortal dilemma. Untimely deaths have been defined as those that are premature, unexpected, and calamitous. In an era when the psychiatric community will increasingly be called upon to consult with moribund patients and their families, a call for a moratorium on death-related publishing would indeed be "untimely."

What has this bugbear Death to frighten man,
If souls can die, as well as bodies can?...

So, when our mortal frame shall be disjoin'd,
The lifeless lump uncoupled from the mind,
From sense of grief and pain we shall be free;
We shall not *feel,* because we shall not *be*....

As last, suppose great Nature's voice should call
To thee, or me, or any of us all,
"What dost thou mean, ungrateful wretch, thou vain,
Thou mortal thing, thus idly to complain,
And sigh and sob, that thou shalt be no more?
For if thy life were pleasant heretofore,
If all the bounteous blessings, I could give,
Thou hast enjoy'd, if thou hast known to live,
And pleasure not leak'd through thee like a sieve;
Why dost thou not give thanks as at a plenteous feast,
Cramm'd to the throat with life, and rise and take thy rest?
But if my blessings thou hast thrown away,
If undigested joys pass'd through, and would not stay,
Why dost thou wish for more to squander still?
If life be grown a load, a real ill,
And I would all thy cares and labors end,
Lay down thy burden, fool, and know thy friend."

Lucretius
On the Nature of Things, Book III
translated by John Dryden

2.

Historical Perspectives on Death

Death has been a constant throughout history: every society has had to cope with the inevitability of death. But attitudes toward death and dying have been as variable as the civilizations and cultures in which they developed.

Archeological evidence shows that even in very early prehistoric times—more than sixty thousand years ago—humans attached great significance to death and had established elaborate rituals for burying their dead. Both the ornaments found in these early graves and the fetal positions of the bodies suggest that prehistoric peoples believed in some form of life after death.

Written records and the artifacts of a later period, of course, give a much more precise idea of man's beliefs regarding death. These beliefs shaped not only attitudes toward death and dying, but attitudes toward life as well. The ancient Mesopotamians, for example, believed that all human beings, regardless of their moral worth or worldly status, were condemned to an afterlife in a dark, miserable underworld. The ancient Egyptians, on the other hand, developed the idea of divine judgment after death: different fates awaited those who had led a moral life and those who had sinned. In both cultures death was something to be feared; but the certainty of misery after death led the ancient Mesopotamians to indulge themselves in the pleasures of life, while the uncertainty of one's fate after death led the ancient Egyptians to be concerned about sin.

Some two thousand years later, Christianity elaborated on the idea of divine judgment, damnation, and salvation. Emphases changed within Christianity over the centuries: opti-mism about the heavenly rewards of the afterlife alternated with pessimism about the tortures of hell; belief in salvation through good works alternated with belief in predestination and the innate depravity of all human beings. The belief in immortality and life after death remained constant, but the fear of death fluctuated with shifts in theological emphases. Such were the traditional Western attitudes toward death that the first settlers brought with them to America.

Attitudes toward death, of course, are shaped not only by religious beliefs but by the physical world as well. Throughout most of history, that was a world of hardship, poverty, disease, and starvation. As will be seen more fully in Section 4, while infant mortality was high, death was a common occurrence among all ages, even in the absence of the epidemics and plagues that periodically decimated the population. As a result, death was very much a part of everyday life, a fact with which even the youngest child was familiar and one for which everyone had to be prepared. In America, until well into the nineteenth century, even burial was among the living—on farms, in town commons, as well as in churchyards.

Also important in shaping attitudes toward dying and death are social and economic institutions. Community, family, church, interacting with technological developments and increasing industrialization and commercialism, all have affected our perspectives toward death and our ways of dying.

Our historical attitudes toward death and dying have been shaped by the interrelationships among religious and philosophic beliefs, physical realities, and social and economic organization, as can be seen in the selections in this section. David Stannard traces the evolution of American attitudes toward death from the Puritans, who lived in terror of eternal hell, through the Romantics and Victorians of the late eighteenth and nineteenth centuries, for whom death was a sweet passage to a heavenly reunion with loved ones. These changes, according to Stannard, reflected not only a shift in religious beliefs, but also a change in the social and economic climate of the growing nation.

Stanley French's article further develops a theme touched upon in the Stannard selection—the rural cemetery movement of the 1830s and 1840s that both reflected and helped to develop new attitudes toward death.

Expanding the consideration of attitudes toward death from the American scene to the Western historical tradition, Philippe Ariès focuses on the dying man and the individual's role in life and death. He maintains that the development of the family as the central institution in modern society has combined with medical advances to deprive the dying person of control over his death and the circumstances surrounding it. The result, according to Ariès, has been the denial of death that Fulton has noted and that has, until the last few years, prevailed in contemporary society.

David E. Stannard

The Puritan Way of Death

The Puritans who came to America in the first half of the seventeenth century brought with them a strong sense of community and a strong belief in Calvinist doctrine. The former guided them as they sought to establish in the wilderness a "City upon a Hill" that would serve as an example to the rest of the world. The latter, with its tenets of predestination and salvation through divine grace alone, meant that they lived in fear of death, for no one could be sure whether he or she was among the small group of elect who would be saved. Clergymen such as Increase Mather exhorted their congregations, and particularly the children, to contemplate the horrors of hell. In the following account, Yale historian David Stannard explains how the Puritan vision of death gave way to Romantic notions, as later generations sought in the afterlife the sense of community that no longer existed in an increasingly commercial world.

Mather's most determined and terrifying words were reserved for the youngest and most vulnerable members of the congregation, as well as for those of more discretion and understanding. It was for this more inclusive group that the specter of parental and ministerial separation and betrayal was merged with the promise of death and damnation. "Beg as for your lives that the God of your fathers would pour his spirit upon you," Mather exhorted them.

> Go into secret corners and plead it with God.... If you dy and be not first new Creatures, better you had never been born: you will be left without excuse before the Lord, terrible witnesses shall rise up against you at the last day. Your godly Parents will testifie against you before the Son of God at that day: And the Ministers of Christ will also be called in as witnesses against you for your condemnation, if you dy in your sins....

If there is one thing on which modern psychologists have agreed concerning the fear of death in young children, it is that such fear is generally rooted in the anticipation of separation from their parents. Time and again experimental studies have shown that, as one writer puts it, "the most persistent of fears associated with death is that of separation— and the one which is most likely to be basic, independent of cultural, religious, or social background." "In children," this writer adds, "dread of separation seems to be basic."

There are, to be sure, ways that children seem to have of defending against separation anxiety resulting from the anticipation of death. One of these—one that has inspired poets down through the ages—is the expectation of reunion in death, a defense that makes separation a temporary matter. But this was a defense denied the Puritan child. As if addressing this question directly, Increase Mather in 1711 remarked on

> what a dismal thing it will be when a Child shall see his Father at the right Hand of Christ in the day of Judgment, but himself at His left Hand:

And when his Father shall joyn with Christ in passing a Sentence of Eternal Death upon him, saying, Amen O Lord, thou art Righteous in thus *Judging:* And when after the Judgment, children shall see their Father going with Christ to Heaven, but themselves going away into Everlasting Punishment!...

Another common defense against childhood fear of separation and death that is mentioned (though proscribed) in the psychological literature is the parental interjection that only old people die, not children. Puritan children met precisely the opposite advice....

James Janeway's *A Token for Children,* a book designed for reading to and by children, had as its sole purpose to remind children of the ever-nearness of death and its possible consequences. It may have been exceeded in popularity only by the *New England Primer;* but even as they learned the alphabet from this latter book, Puritan children were instructed with such rhymes as: "G—As runs the *Glass/* Mans life doth pass"; "T—*Time* cuts down all/Both great and small"; "X—*Xerxes* the great did die, / And so must you & I"; "Y—*Youth* forward slips / Death soonest nips." And Cotton Mather, once again, in words directed to the "many children: the *Small People*" in his congregation, including both those who had and those who had not achieved a certain "Forwardness at the *Grammar School,*" advised that they "Go into Burying-Place, CHILDREN; you will there see *Graves* as short as your selves. Yea, you may be at *Play* one Hour; *Dead, Dead* the next."...

Like the Puritan child, the child of the Romantic and Victorian eras was instructed to spend a good deal of time thinking about death. But the similarity between the Puritan child and the child of the nineteenth century, at least as far as death was concerned, ends there. The child of the Puritan was told to "think how it will be on a deathbed"; to consider the terror of certain separation from, and even betrayal by, parents and loved ones; and to imagine what his well-deserved torments in Hell would be like. The instruction of the nineteenth-century child involved the precise reversal of all this: the child was rarely told to contemplate the physical act of dying, and whenever he was, it was because the transformation thus effected was seen as a peaceful and beautiful deliverance—the releasing of a butterfly from a cocoon; instead of separation from or betrayal by parents and loved ones, eternal and heavenly *reunion* was stressed; and instead of visions of Hell and damnation, the nineteenth-century child was told to contemplate the sweet glory of salvation. Indeed, in place of death a new *life* was emphasized—death as a lonely finality or a grim eternity of torment was simply willed out of existence.

Even in its physical aspects, death to the Romantics, at least as it concerned young women dying of consumption, was often celebrated for its beauty. There is of course a very long historical tradition for viewing death as personified by Harlequin, a dark and mysterious lover. But with the rise of Romanticism this tradition reached new heights. "In fact," notes Mario Praz, "to such an extent were Beauty and Death looked upon as sisters by the Romantics that they became fused into a sort of two-faced herm, filled with corruption and melancholy and fatal in its beauty—a beauty of which, the more bitter the taste, the more abundant the enjoyment." Praz points to Poe and other literary figures as American examples of this association, but the roots were imbedded in American culture even more deeply than that. As a New York state schoolteacher, self-described as a "pennyless unattractive girl," observed in her diary upon the death of her younger sister:

> the broad snowy brow grew more & more fair
> her eyes beamed with almost unearthly lustre &
> the bright crimson spot upon her cheek rendered
> her even more beautiful than when in her usual
> health consumption *seems to delight to deck its
> victims* just as they are to be hid in the tomb.

Earlier...it was noted that the first New England primers contained numerous references to death, even when the child was simply to be mechanically learning the alphabet. Schoolbooks of the nineteenth century also contained frequent references to it—of twenty-nine "Poetical Lessons" in McGuffey's *Fourth Eclectic Reader* at least sixteen involve themes of death—but they were a far cry from the earlier primers' solemn warnings. The following poem, "What is Death?" is a fair example of McGuffey's treatment:

> *Child.* Mother, how still the baby lies!
>   I can not hear his breath;
>   I can not see his laughing eyes;
>   They tell me this is death.

> So shalt thou rest, and what if thou withdraw
> In silence from the living, and no friend
> Take note of thy departure? All that breathe
> Will share thy destiny. The gay will laugh
> When thou art gone, the solemn brood of care
> Plod on, and each one as before will chase
> His favorite phantom; yet all these shall leave
> Their mirth and their employments, and shall come
> And make their bed with thee. As the long train
> Of ages glide away, the sons of men,
> The youth in life's green spring, and he who goes
> In the full strength of years, matron and maid,
> The speechless babe, and the gray-headed man—
> Shall one by one be gathered to thy side,
> By those who in their turn shall follow them.

> William Cullen Bryant
> *Thanatopsis*

They say that he again will rise,
  More beautiful than now;
That God will bless him in the skies;
  O mother, tell me how!

Mother. Daughter, do you remember, dear,
    The cold, dark thing you brought,
  And laid upon the casement here?
    A withered worm, you thought.

  Look at that chrysalis, my love;
    An empty shell it lies;
  Now raise your wondering glance above,
    To where yon insect flies!

Child. O mother! now I know full well,
    If God that worm can change,
  And draw it from this broken cell,
    On golden wings to range;

  How beautiful will brother be
    When God shall give him wings,
  Above this dying world to flee,
    And live with heavenly things!

The same themes can be found over and over again in other school- and popular books, with frequent reference to the child in question as "Little Nellie," "Little William," "Little Georgie," and so on....

Although verse and prose of this type were widely circulated during the nineteenth century, the fact that they often appear in cemetery literature...is of special significance. At the same time that this literary romanticization of death was emerging, the plans for various new "rural" cemeteries were being laid. In place of the dreary, decaying burial grounds that had scarred the landscape after the collapse of Puritanism, the new cemeteries—Boston's Mount Auburn in 1831, Philadelphia's Laurel Hill in 1836, Brooklyn's Greenwood in 1838, and many others to follow—were monuments to a lush and idealized pastoralism; they were, in the words of one popular tract, "Gardens of Graves."...

But it is in the newer cemeteries that the social tensions that gave rise to this mood can be most clearly seen. At the same time that the rural cemetery was being celebrated as the eventual home or "dormitory" for everyone, as the epitome of the close community that was but a fast-receding memory of the recent past, the realities of the present were closing in. Such cemeteries were turning out to be enormously profitable investment ventures—the value of the land on which Mount Auburn was situated, for example, increased in value *eighty* times in just a few short years—and more and more they were coming to be the distinctive resting places of the nation's wealthy and rapidly coalescing merchant classes. By the late 1840s so many families had erected iron railings to fence off their plots that people once again began complaining about the appearance of the cemeteries....There was, it seems, a contradictory pull being felt between the individualistic forces of commerce and acquisitiveness and the communitarian forces attempting to find in the graveyard the sense of fraternity and fellowship that had marked the past....

This is not to say, of course, that the dominant American attitude toward death in the nineteenth century, as I have described it, was shared by all urban Americans; nor is it to say that it was *not* shared by many rural Americans. What does seem clear, however, is that in the period from the birth of the new nation at least until the time when Americans were recovering from the Civil War, the overriding national treatment of death was shaped by a reaction to the dual forces of social and commercial expansion and specialization, and cultural romanticism. In large measure, if not entirely in response to the growing individual anonymity brought on by changes in their social world, Americans sought a return to their lost sense of community in the graveyard and the heavenly world of the dead; in the process, paradoxically, they effectively banished the reality of death from their lives by a spiritualistic and sentimentalized embracing of it.

But if the frankness and simplicity of much of rural America's approach to death was increasingly overwhelmed by the romanticization of it in the swelling ranks of the country's urban population, the nature of that romanticization itself would, by the end of the century, be succumbing to still other emerging forces. . . .

By 1884 the poetry on death that had filled the cemetery and consolation literature of an earlier day, and that was still being reproduced in elementary school readers, was being satirized by Mark Twain in his second "boy's book," *The Adventures of Huckleberry Finn.* Young Emmeline Grangerford, Twain wrote, was an untiring poetic recorder of the deaths of all who passed her way. "She warn't particular," Huck reports, "she could write about anything you choose to give her to write about just so it was sadful. Every time a man died, or a woman died, or a child died, she would be on hand with her 'tribute' before he was cold." The example of her verse "quoted" by Twain—"Ode to Stephen Dowling Bots, Dec'd"—is one of the more humorous passages in the novel to most modern readers; but few modern readers have probably realized how closely the tone and mood of the poem resemble much of the serious verse penned in America only a few years earlier.

At the same time that such sentimentalization was giving way to the cynicism of people like Twain and to the more realistic cultural climate of the late nineteenth century, the ever-rising tide of "progress" and commercialism was working its way into the nation's treatment of death—and in its own way was filling some of the space left behind by the Romantic Era. Embalming of the dead was steadily becoming the norm in postmortem preparations, and even coffin design underwent enormous change. Literally hundreds of patents were taken out between 1850 and 1880 for new and elaborate casings for the dead, as the simple traditional coffin metamorphosed into the more aesthetically pleasing (and expensive) "casket"—the word quite consciously adopted because of its original meaning, a jewel box. By the 1880s the undertaker was becoming a "funeral director" and began joining national professional associations, attending conventions, and reading and contributing to "in-house" publications with names like *Mortuary Management, Sunnyside, Shadyside,* and *The Casket.* If a single example of the change taking place in the new profession can be pointed to as most indicative of the times, perhaps it might be the contest announced in *Sunnyside* in 1885 in which a $1,000 prize was offered for the funeral director exhibiting the "best appearing" corpse after a lapse of sixty days between embalming and examination.

With the dawning of the nineteenth century, then, a number of interconnected developments in American social life—all related in one way or another to a fading sense of community purpose and to changes that had begun to beset the world of the Puritan before the middle of the eighteenth century—contributed to the emergence of new attitudes and responses to death and dying. But by the time the nineteenth century was drawing to a close the speed and force with which these new cultural values were entering the society became more than the structure of Romantic culture could bear: sentimentality began giving way to realism and even secularism. The effects on the American way of death were dramatic. . . .

Stanley French

The Cemetery as Cultural Institution
The Establishment of Mount Auburn and the "Rural Cemetery" Movement

Burial of the dead is an ancient practice among human beings. From the sixty-thousand-year-old gravesite at Shanidar, Iraq, to the garden cemetery of Hollywood's well-publicized Forest Lawn, people the world over have regarded death with solemnity and ceremony.

Like every other social institution, however, the cemetery, the earthly repository of the dead, comes to reflect the vagaries and shifts in a community's beliefs, sentiments, and values. In the nineteenth century, death took on a new meaning for American society. The idea of perdition and the pit gave way to the promise of resurrection and reunion. Death as punishment in the eigthteenth century became reward in the nineteenth.

This shift in America's vision of death over these two centuries is captured by French in his account of the cemetery as a cultural institution. In the stone sculpture and spacious gardens of Boston's Mt. Auburn cemetery, he finds the new sentimentalized view of death that characterized that time.

I n her account of her tour of the United States in the late 1840s Lady Emmeline Wortley wrote that the first time she went to Cambridge, Massachusetts, she visited the family of President Edward Everett of Harvard College, and that for her first sight-seeing excursion in the area the Everetts took her on a carriage ride through nearby Mount Auburn Cemetery. After an enthusiastic description of the cemetery she mentioned that next "we went to see a little of the colleges." For most Americans today this ordering of events is a curious inversion of

priorities, if they would consider conducting a visitor through the local cemetery at all. Yet the statement reflects the prominence given to Mount Auburn at the time. From its beginnings in 1831 Mount Auburn ranked as one of the major points of interest in the Boston area. It was proudly displayed to foreign and native visitors in the decades before the Civil War when Americans were still self-consciously trying to disprove Sydney Smith's famous taunt in the *Edinburgh Review* [of 1820] that America was a cultural wasteland.

Only two years after Mount Auburn's establishment the English actress Fanny Kemble reported that it was already "one of the lions" of the area, and that "for its beauty Mount Auburn might seem a pleasure garden instead of a place of graves." About the same time a Swedish visitor was so enchanted with Mount Auburn that he declared, "a glance at this beautiful cemetery almost excites a wish to die." Lady Amelia Murray after her visit to Mount Auburn thought that "in feeling and taste it is really perfect. No crowding up in disgusting heaps like our own graveyards." She hoped that Mount Auburn would soon be copied in the vicinity of London. The Boston entrepreneur Amos Lawrence bought a large family plot to which "he continually resorted," and he purchased adjacent plots for his living friends and for reinterring dead friends. Forty-five years after its founding James Russell Lowell sardonically commented that the people of Boston seemed to have only two ideas of hospitality: a boring dinner party followed by a ride in Mount Auburn—"Your memory of the dinner is expected to reconcile you to the prospect of the graveyard." These are but a sampling of comments about Mount Auburn from the middle decades of the nineteenth century. Clearly the cemetery was a significant institution.

The creation of Mount Auburn marked a change in prevailing attitudes about death and burial. It was a new type of burial place designed not only to be a decent place of interment, but to serve as a cultural institution as well. Because of its influence the traditional generic terms "graveyard" and "burial-ground" were replaced by the word "cemetery." And the example of Mount Auburn became the prototype of the "rural cemetery" which was extensively duplicated throughout the country. The term "garden cemetery" would be a less misleading and more apt description, but since "rural cemetery" was the common term at the time it will be used in this paper.

Since the beginnings of settlement in New England the standard places of burial had been amid the living—in the middle of towns, in churchyards or in churches, a practice which in England dated back to the eighth century. In New England town commons were also frequently employed as graveyards. It is obvious from the dearth of comments about early New England graveyards, from the nature of the comments that do exist, and from the grim symbolism of the period's monuments, that graveyards were treated simply as unattractive necessities to be avoided as much as much as possible by the living. This attitude continued from the beginnings of settlement into the early years of the nineteenth century.

The Rev. William Bentley, the voluminous diarist of Salem, Massachusetts, perhaps spoke for many New Englanders at the turn of the nineteenth century: "I have a most settled enmity to all ceremonies for the dead. Let their memories live but let their ashes be forgotten." His description of a graveyard in Portsmouth, New Hampshire, illustrates the social effects of this prevalent attitude. "Grave point has an antient [sic] graveyard in the greatest confusion and tho' the monuments of the best families are to be found in it they are in the utmost neglect." Timothy Dwight, in his *Travels in New England and New York,* mentions the subject of graveyards several times and describes the one at Guilford, Connecticut, as being a typical town graveyard. It was simply an unenclosed, unkempt section of the town common where the graves and fallen markers were daily trampled upon by people and cattle. In "The Burial Place" (1818) William Cullen Bryant explained that the Puritans did not bring to the New World the old English customs of decorating graves and adorning graveyards with vegetation:

> ...Naked rows of graves
> And melancholy ranks of monuments
> Are seen instead, where the coarse grass, between
> Shoots up its dull spikes, and in the wind
> Hisses, and the neglected bramble nigh,
> Offers its berries to the schoolboy's hand....

The neglected graveyard was characteristic not only of New England but was common throughout the other colonies and states. In Philadelphia until the 1820s, for instance, sites for graveyards were simply temporarily vacant lots to serve the needs of the day which were soon obliterated by the expanding city as if they had never existed. The condition of burial grounds in the South was frequently worse because the decentralization of the population had, except in the few more settled areas, led to a general replacement of community burial grounds by individual family plots on private land. Many such family plots did not survive a change in land ownership.

The attitude of indifference concerning burial places was not limited to the colonial or early national period of the United States, but was prevalent throughout Western Europe. This Western attitude was reflected in, and probably augmented by, the international vogue for the poetic theme of melancholy and the "graveyard school" of poets during the eighteenth century. In the English-speaking world the beginnings of the elegiac form can be traced back to the 1640s, but the main works appeared in the first half of the next century. The most important of these were: Thomas Parnell, "Night-Piece on Death" (1722); Edward Young, "Night Thoughts..." (1742); Robert Blair, "The Grave" (1743); and Thomas Gray, "Elegy in a Country Churchyard" (1751). These poems stressed the finality of death and the horrors of decomposition, while making only scant reference, if any, to the comforting hopes of Christianity. The general tenor of these poems is well illustrated by Blair's "The Grave" which starts:

> ...the task be mine,
> To paint the gloomy horrors of the tomb;
> ...The Grave, dread thing!
> Men shiver when thou'rt named: Nature appal'd
> Shakes off her wonted firmness. Ah! how dark
> Thy long-extended realms, and rueful wastes!
> Where nought but silence reigns, and night,
>   dark night,
> ...The sickley taper,
> By glimmering through thy low-browed misty
>   vaults
> (Furred round with mouldy damps, and ropey
>   slime),
> Lets fall a supernumerary horror,
> And only serves to make the night more irksome.

In America the funeral elegy initially appeared at about the same time as it did in England, but it was confined to the Puritan culture of New England, where it continued as a strong tradition into the nineteenth century. In the Revolutionary era the elegiac form became more generally accepted in America and poets as diverse as John Trumbull and Philip Freneau wrote elegies.

In the early years of the nineteenth century attitudes about death and burial began to change. People started to complain about the frequently revolting state of burial places. Timothy Dwight, for instance, continued his discussion of the Guilford, Connecticut, graveyard by declaring:

> Both remains and the memorials of the dead are presented to the mind in circumstances so gross and indicative of so little respect in the living as to eradicate every emotion naturally excited by the remembrance of the deceased, and to give to those which remain a coarseness and commonness destructive of all moral influence. Nor is it unreasonable to suppose that the proximity of these sepulchral fields to human habitation is injurious to health.

During his visit to Westminster Abbey in the 1820s Washington Irving was disgusted by a French sculptor's recent work, a memorial to a Mrs. Nightingale, which stressed the finality of death in a grisly manner. He exclaimed:

> Why should we thus seek to clothe death with unnecessary terrors.... The grave should be surrounded by everything that might inspire tenderness and veneration for the dead, or that might win the living to virtue.

The old gloomy poetic attitude toward melancholy and death culminated in America with Bryant's great poem "Thanatopsis" (1817). In Great Britain such poems as Robert Pollack's "The Course of Time" and Thomas Hood's "Ode to Melancholy," both published in 1827, seemed to mark the end of the "invocation to melancholy" and the graveyard-school approach to the subject. Thereafter, that poetic tradition seemed to die out about the same time that the rural cemetery movement began. Bryant's later poems concerning death and burial differ markedly from his "Thanatopsis." Such poems as "The Lapse of Time" (1825), "The Two Graves" (1826), and "The Past" (1828) generally stress the naturalness of death, its appropriateness as part of the life cycle and its moralizing influences.

A new attitude toward death and burial can also be seen in the mourning picture which was a popular genre of folk art in America during the first four decades of the nineteenth century. The graves and memorials depicted were not in crowded weedy fields, but were set amid beautiful foliage in rustic surroundings. The actual basis of the mourning picture was probably the family burial plots of the Southern plantation country. Certainly, the idea of the private cemetery was extant in the South long before it existed in the more settled Northern areas. Thomas Jefferson wrote up his plans for a private garden burial place for Monticello in 1771. His specifications describe the content of a typical mourning picture. Probably the general idea of a rustic setting for burial received a great impetus from the popularity of the artistic motif of George Washington's grave—a typical private garden burial scene of the plantation country.

By the beginning of the nineteenth century there were pressing social reasons for changes in burial customs. Because of the rapidly increasing population the old graveyards became so crowded that they were frequently little more than stinking quagmires—chronically offensive and occasionally serious public health hazards.

In New York City the problem was such that the Board of Health appointed a special committee to investigate the situation. The committee recommended that "intramural" (inner city) interments be prohibited, and it suggested that the existing city cemeteries be converted into parks "instead of remaining receptacles of putrefying matter and hot-beds of miasmata." No effective legislation came from this report and the problem was allowed to ride until a yellow fever epidemic carried off sixteen thousand in the city in 1822. Since the disease was particularly virulent in the vicinity of Trinity Church burying ground the whole issue of intramural interments was revived. A couple of pamphlets strongly urging the closing of city graveyards appeared in 1822 and 1823, but again the city took no effective action. The problem was finally rendered less acute by the creation of a "rural cemetery" in Brooklyn in 1838....

With the establishment of Mount Auburn, the conception of the cemetery as an instructional institution and inculcator of morality became a more common theme in the contemporary discussions of the purpose of a rural cemetery than arguments concerning overcrowded facilities and health hazards. Time and again, the belief that "a rural cemetery is a school of both religion and philosophy" was reiterated....

In the new type of cemetery the plenitude and beauties of nature...combined with art would convert the graveyard from a shunned place of horror into an enchanting place of succor and instruction. The world of nature would inculcate primarily the lessons of natural theology. The fullness of nature in the rural cemetery...would enable people to see death in perspective so that they might realize that "in the mighty system of the universe, not a single step of the destroyer, Time, but is made subservient to some ulterior purpose of reproduction, and the circle of creation and destruction is eternal." In a lesson reminiscent of Gray's "Elegy" another moralist [Nehemiah Adams] stated that if in our wanderings through the grounds we come across some flower blooming unseen in a remote spot we should experience "a feeling of the spontaneous goodness of God" and from this example: "Man should learn from Him, to be the same everywhere that he would choose to be in the sight of his fellows, and to have all his actions proceed from a deep, uncompromising convic- tion of duty, and love of what is right, rather than from a hope of reward." Even the winds in the trees of the cemetery "represent the vicissitudes of life: but they inculcate the lesson that there is no adversity that is not followed by a better day." . . .

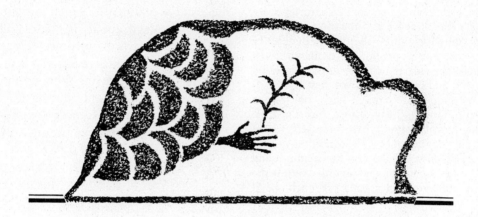

She was dead. No sleep so beautiful and calm, so free from trace of pain, so fair to look upon. She seemed a creature fresh from the hand of God, and waiting for the breath of life; not one who had lived, and suffered death. Her couch was dressed with here and there some winter berries and green leaves, gathered in a spot she had been used to favor. "When I die, put near me something that has loved the light, and had the sky above it always." Those were her words. . . .

She was dead. Dear, gentle, patient, noble Nell was dead. Where were the traces of her early cares, her sufferings, and fatigues? All gone. Sorrow was dead, indeed, in her; but peace and perfect happiness were born, imaged, in her tranquil beauty and profound repose. . . .

Along the crowded path they bore her now, pure as the newly fallen snow that covered it, whose day on earth had been as fleeting. Under that porch where she had sat, when Heaven, in its mercy, brought her to that peaceful spot, she passed again, and the old church received her in its quiet shade.

Charles Dickens
"The Death of Little Nell"

Philippe Ariès

The Reversal of Death

Changes in Attitudes Toward Death in Western Societies

If the seventeenth and eighteenth centuries were marked by a fear of death and the nineteenth century by its romanticization, the twentieth century has been marked by its denial. Increasingly, death occurs among the elderly, who are already isolated in our society, and in hospitals, with few in attendance but the immediate family. Thus, not only is death kept from most of the society, but it is often kept hidden from the dying person himself, whose questions and doubts about his condition go unanswered. The effect of such avoidance and denial on the individual seeking a meaningful death is the focus of the following selection by French social historian Philippe Ariès.

Also noteworthy is Ariès' discussion of the role of the social sciences in exploring new meanings of death not only in America but throughout Western Europe.

It is strange how the human sciences, so outspoken regarding family, work, politics, leisure, religion, and sex, have been so reserved on the subject of death. Scholars have kept silent, acting like the men that they are and like the men that they study. Their silence is only a part of this great silence that has settled on the subject of death in the twentieth century. Although literature has continued its discourse on death, with, for example, Sartre's or Genet's *"mort sale,"* ordinary men have become mute and behave as though death no longer existed. The chasm between the discussion of death in books, which is still prolific, and actual death, which is shameful and not to be talked about, is one of the strange but sigificant signs of our times. This silence is the main subject of this essay. As is usually the case with silence, it has gone unnoticed and therefore unknown; only during the past few years has it been the subject of discussion.

A history of death was begun with Alberto Tenenti's two books, *La vie et la mort à travers l'art du XVᵉ siècle,* which appeared in 1952, one year after Edgar Morin's essay, and *Il senso della morte e l'amore della vita nel Rinascimento.*

A sociology of death was begun in 1955 with Geoffrey Gorer's comprehensive article, "The Pornography of Death."[1] Next came the collection of interdisciplinary studies (anthropology, art, literature, medicine, philosophy, psychiatry, religion, etc.), edited by Herman Feifel under the title *The Meaning of Death,* which had been presented at a colloquium organized by the American Psychological Association in 1956. The mere idea of a colloquium on death testifies to the awakening interest in this hitherto forbidden topic. Indeed it seems that, with regard to the forbidden topic of death, today's sociologists are following the example of Freud concerning the forbidden topic of sex. Thus it is that the current taboo regarding death is being threatened in an indirect way by social scientists. Literature

1. Editor's note: See below, p. 77.

remains conservative and continues with the old themes, even when it take the form of their opposites.

On the other hand, sociology and psychology are supplying the first signs that contemporary man is rediscovering death. And far from suppressing these scholarly works, newspapers and popular weekly magazines have given them a great deal of attention. A literature of social criticism has followed, which first became popular with Jessica Mitford's book *The American Way of Death*. Today hardly a month passes without the French, British, or American press reporting on a book concerned with death, or some observed curiosity regarding it. Death is now becoming what it had ceased to be since the very end of the Romantic era, the subject of an inexhaustible supply of anecdotes—a fact which would lead one to suspect that the newspaper-reading public is becoming interested in death, perhaps initially because of its seemingly forbidden and somewhat obscene nature.

The new sociology of death, then, marks not only the beginning of a scientific bibliography on death, but very likely also a turning point in the history of attitudes toward death. Sociology, however, is not very conscious of history: Edgard Morin was led to treat the death of philosophers as history, because his philosophic and literary documents were already a part of history—for a long time of the history of ideas, for only a few decades, of social history. On the other hand, common attitudes toward death, such as are being discovered today by sociologists, psychologists, and doctors, seem so unprecedented, so bewildering, that as yet it has been impossible for observers to take them out of their modern context and put them into historical perspective. Nevertheless, that is what this article proposes to do....

THE DYING MAN IS DEPRIVED OF HIS DEATH For thousands of years man was lord and master of his death, and the circumstances surrounding it. Today this has ceased to be so.

It used to be understood and accepted that a man knew when he was dying, whether he became spontaneously aware of the fact or whether he had to be told. It seemed reasonable to our old storytellers that, as the plowman in La Fontaine says, man would feel his approaching death. In those days death was rarely sudden, even in the case of an accident or a war, and sudden death was much feared, not only because there was no time for repentance, but because it deprived a man of the experience of death. Thus death was almost always presaged, especially since even minor illnesses often turned out to be fatal. One would have had to be mad not to see the signs, and moralists and satirists made it their job to ridicule those foolish enough to deny the evidence. Roland "feels that death is taking all of him," Tristam "felt that his life was draining away, he realized that he was dying." Tolstoy's peasant replied to the goodwoman who asked him if he were all right: "Death is here"; for Tolstoy's peasants died like Tristam or like La Fontaine's plowman, having the same resigned, comfortable attitude toward it. This is not to say that the attitude toward death was the same throughout all this long period of time, but that it survived in some social strata from one generation to the next despite competition from other styles of death.

When the person involved was not the first to become aware of his fate, others were expected to warn him. A papal document of the Middle Ages made this a task of the doctor, a task he for a long time carried out unflinchingly. We find him at Don Quixote's bedside: "He took his pulse, and was not happy with

the results. He therefore told him that whatever he did, he should think of saving his soul,
as his body was in grave danger." The *artes
moriendi*[2] of the fifteenth century also charged
with this task the "spiritual" friend (as opposed
to "carnal" friends), who went by the
name—so repugnant to our modern fas-
tidiousness—of *nuncius mortis*.[3]

As man progressed through time, the higher
up the social and urban ladder he climbed, the
less he himself was aware of his approaching
death, and the more he had to be prepared for
it; consequently, the more he had to depend
on those around him. The doctor renounced
the role that for so long had been his, probably
in the eighteenth century. In the nineteenth
century he spoke only when questioned, and
then somewhat reticently. Friends no longer
had to intervene, as in the time of Gerson or
even Cervantes, because from the seventeenth
century on, it was the family that took care of
this—a sign of development in family feeling.
An example of this can be seen in the de La
Ferronnays' household in 1848. Mme. de La
Ferronnays had fallen ill. The doctor announced that her condition was dangerous,
and "one hour later, hopeless." Her daughter
wrote: "When she came out of the bath...she
suddenly said to me, while I was thinking of a
good way to tell her what the doctor thought:
'but I can't see anything any more, I think I'm
going to die.' She immediately recited an
ejaculatory prayer, 'Oh Jesus.'" The daughter
then remarked, "what a strange joy I felt from
those calm words at such a terrible time." She
was relieved because she had been spared the
distress of making a nevertheless indispensable
disclosure. The relief is a modern characteristic, the necessity to disclose the truth is ancient.

Not only was the dying man not to be deprived of his death, he also had to preside over
it. As people were born in public, so did they
die in public, and not only the king, as is well
known from Saint-Simon's famous pages on
the death of Louis XIV, but everyone. Countless engravings and paintings depict that scene
for us. As soon as someone "was helplessly sick
in bed," his room filled with people—parents,
children, friends, neighbors, fellow guild
members. The windows and shutters were
closed. Candles were lit. When passersby in
the streets met a priest carrying the *viaticum,*
custom and piety demanded that they follow
him into the dying man's room, even if he was
a stranger. The approach of death transformed
the room of a dying man into a sort of public
place. Pascal's[4] remark, "man will die alone,"
which has lost much of its impact on us since
today man almost always dies alone, can only
be understood in this context. For what Pascal
meant was that in spite of all the people crowded around his bed, the dying man was alone.
The enlightened doctors of the end of the
eighteenth century, who believed in the
qualities of fresh air, complained a great deal
about this bad habit of crowding into the
rooms of sick people. They tried to have the
windows opened, the candles snuffed, and the
crowd of people turned out.

We should not make the mistake of thinking
that to be present at these last moments was a
devout custom prescribed by the Church. The
enlightened or reformed priests had tried, long
before the doctors, to do away with this crowd
so that they could better prepare the sick person for a virtuous end. As early as the *artes
moriendi* of the fifteenth century it had been
recommended that the dying man be left alone
with God so that he should not be distracted

2. "The art of dying." The term refers to fifteenth century literature on this subject.
3. Editor's note: messenger of death.

4. Editor's note: Blaise Pascal (1623–1662), French
philosopher and mathematician.

from the care of his soul. And again, in the nineteenth century, it sometimes happened that very pious people, after yielding to the custom, asked the numerous onlookers to leave the room, all except the priest, so that nothing would disturb their private conversation with God. But these were rare examples of extreme devotion. Custom prescribed that death was to be marked by a ritual ceremony in which the priest would have his place, but only as one of many participants. The leading role went to the dying man himself. He presided over the affair with hardly a misstep, for he knew how to conduct himself, having previously witnessed so many similar scenes. He called to him one by one his relatives, his friends, his servants, "even down to the lowliest," Saint-Simon said, describing the death of Mme. de Montespan. He said farewell to them, asked their pardon, gave them his blessing. Invested with sovereign authority by the approach of death, especially in the eighteenth and nineteenth centuries, the dying person gave orders and advice, even when this dying person was a very young girl, almost a child.

Today nothing remains either of the sense that everyone has or should have of his impending death, or of the public solemnity surrounding the moment of death. What used to be appreciated is now hidden; what used to be solemn is now avoided.

It is understood that the primary duty of the family and the doctor is to conceal the seriousness of his condition from the person who is to die. The sick person must no longer ever know (except in very rare cases) that his end is near. The new custom dictates that he die in ignorance. This is not merely a habit that has innocently crept into the customs—it has become a moral requirement. Vladimir Jankélévitch confirmed this unequivocally during a [1966] colloquium of doctors on this subject: "Should

we lie to the patient?" "The liar," he stated, "is the one who tells the truth....I am against the truth, passionately against the truth....For me, the most important law of all is the law of love and charity." Was this quality then lacking prior to the twentieth century, since ethics made it obligatory to inform the patient? In such opposition we see the extent of this extraordinary reversal of feelings, and then of ideas. How did this come about? It would be too hasty to say that in a society of happiness and well-being there is no longer any room for suffering, sadness, and death. To say this is to mistake the result for the cause.

It is strange that this change is linked to the development in family feelings, and to the emotional centrality of the family in our world. In fact, the cause for the change must be sought in the relationship between a sick person and his family. The family has no longer been able to tolerate the blow it had to deal to a loved one, and the blow it also had to deal to itself, in bringing death closer and making it more certain, in forbidding all deception and illusion. How many times have we heard it said of a spouse or a parent: "At least I had the satisfaction of knowing that he never felt he was dying"? *This "not feeling oneself dying" has in our everyday language replaced the "feeling one's impending death" of the seventeenth century.*

In point of fact, it must happen quite often— but the dead never tell—that the sick person knows quite well what is happening, and pretends not to know for the sake of those around him. For if the family has loathed to play *nuncius mortis,* a role which in the Middle Ages and at the beginning of modern times it was not asked to play, the main actor has also abdicated. Through fear of death? But death has always existed. Only it used to be laughed at—"What haste you are in, O cruel goddess!"—while society compelled the terrified dying man nevertheless to act out the great scene of farewells and departure. Some say this fear is innate, but its suppression is equally innate. The fear of death does not explain why the dying man turns his back on his own death. Again we must seek for the explanation in the history of the family.

The man of the late Middle Ages and the Renaissance (as opposed to the man of the early Middle Ages, like Roland, who still lives in Tolstoy's peasants) insisted on participating in his own death, because he saw in his death the moment when his individuality received its ultimate form. He was master over his life only insofar as he was master over his death. His death was his, and his alone. However, beginning with the seventeenth century he no longer had sole sovereignty over his own life and, consequently, over his death. He shared his death with his family, whereas previously his family

had been isolated from the serious decisions he, and he alone, had to make regarding his death.

Last wills and testaments are a case in point. From the fourteenth century to the beginning of the eighteenth century, the will was one way for each person to express himself freely while at the same time it was a token of defiance—or lack of confidence—with regard to his family. Thus, when in the eighteenth century family affection triumphed over the traditional mistrust by the testator of his inheritors, the last will and testament lost its character of moral necessity and personal warm testimony. This was, on the contrary, replaced by such an absolute trust that there was no longer any need for writen wills. The last spoken wishes became at long last sacred to the survivors, and they considered themselves to be committed from then on to respect these wishes to the letter. For his part, the dy-

---

...I have given my name and my day-clothes up to the nurses
And my history to the anaesthetist and my body to surgeons.

They have propped my head between the pillow and the sheet-cuff
Like an eye between two white lids that will not shut.
Stupid pupil, it has to take everything in.
The nurses pass and pass, they are no trouble.
They pass the way gulls pass inland in their white caps,
Doing things with their hands, one just the same as another,
So it is impossible to tell how many there are.

My body is a pebble to them, they tend it as water
Tends to the pebbles it must run over, smoothing them gently.
They bring me numbness in their bright needles, they bring me sleep.
Now I have lost myself I am sick of baggage—
My patent leather overnight case like a black pillbox,
My husband and child smiling out of the family photo;
Their smiles catch onto my skin, little smiling hoops.

Sylvia Plath
Tulips

ing man was satisfied that he could rest in peace on the word of his close ones. This trust that began in the seventeenth and eighteenth centuries and was developed in the nineteenth century has, in the twentieth century, turned into alienation." As soon as serious danger threatens one member of a family, the family immediately conspires to deprive him of information and thus his freedom. The patient then becomes a minor, like a child or a mental defective, to be taken into charge and separated from the rest of the world by his spouse or parents. They know better than he what he should do and know. He is deprived of his rights, specifically the formerly essential right of knowing about his death, of preparing for it, of organizing it. And he lets this happen because he is convinced that it is for his own good. He relies on the affection of his family. If, in spite of everything, he does guess the truth, he will pretend to not know it. Death used to be a tragedy—often comic—acted out for the benefit of a man who was about to die. Today, death is a comedy—always tragic— acted out for the benefit of a man who does not know he is about to die.

Without the progress of medicine the pressure of family feeling would probably not have been sufficient to make death disappear so quickly and so completely. Not so much because of the real conquests made by medicine as because, as a result of medicine, in the mind of the sick man death has been replaced by illness. This substitution first appeared in the second half of the nineteenth century. When the dying peasant in Tolstoy's *Three Deaths* (1859) was asked where he hurt, he replied: "I hurt all over, death is here; that's what it is." On the other hand Ivan Ilych (1886), after overhearing a conversation that could leave him in no doubt, continues to think obstinately of his floating kidney, of his infected appendix, which can be cured by the doctor or the surgeon. The illness has become the focus of illusion. His wife treats him like a child who is disobeying the doctor's orders: he is not taking his medicine properly, that is why he is not getting better.

Moreover, it is clear that, with the advancements in therapeutics and surgery, it has become increasingly more difficult to be certain that a serious illness is fatal; the chances of recovering from it have increased so much. Even with diminished capacities, one can still live. Thus, in our world where everyone acts as though medicine is the answer to everything—where even though Caesar must die one day, there is absolutely no reason for oneself to die—incurable diseases, particularly cancer, have taken on the hideous, terrifying aspects of the old representations of death. More than the skeleton or mummy of the *macabres* of the fourteenth and fifteenth centuries, more than the leper with his bell, cancer today is death. However, the disease must be incurable (or thought to be so) in order for death to be allowed to come forward and take on its name. The anguish this releases forces society to hurriedly intensify its customary demands of silence, and thus to bring this overly dramatic situation to the banal level of an afternoon walk.

People die, then, in secret—more alone than Pascal ever imagined. This secrecy results from refusing to admit the imminent death of a loved one by concealing it beneath the veil of a persistent disease. There is another aspect of this secrecy that American sociologists have succeeded in interpreting. What we have been inclined to view as avoidance, they have shown to be the empirical establishment of a style of dying in which discretion appears as the modern form of dignity....

3.

Death in Popular Culture

Every society must teach its members the meanings, values, and behaviors necessary for participation in social life. That which is taught or passed on from past generations to succeeding ones is called culture. Culture includes spoken and written language; systems of thought, like religion and philosophy; values and beliefs about what is right and wrong, good and evil; forms of creative expression like art, music, and literature; guidelines for social living, such as etiquette, law, and political systems; and the myriad material objects that surround us. Students of culture note that it both reflects and affects our attitudes and lifestyles. Culture, like the societies whose members teach, learn, and create it, is continuously changing as traditions of the past give way to new inventions, beliefs, and practices.

The meanings of death are vital aspects of our cultural heritage that influence the way we live and die. For example, if we learn to believe that death represents a transition to a supernatural realm, we are likely to lead different lives than we would if we believed that death results in absolute termination. A cultural tradition that death in defense of one's nation is noble supports both the kamikaze pilot and the Medal of Honor recipient. Cultural traditions like mourning customs and funeral rituals afford solace and support for the bereaved. Their absence or attenuation, however, can make the task of recovering from the death of a significant person considerably more difficult. Material aspects of culture also reflect and affect the meanings of death for a society and its members. The invention of embalming in ancient Egypt facilitated the elaborate

memorialization of the dead, and the belief in a post-death existence impelled the construction of such monuments as the Great Pyramids and the Taj Mahal. In our own time, the invention of ever more effective weapons of mass destruction has conversely altered our conception of life and death.

In this section, we will focus on one aspect of culture that is particularly relevant in modern societies—popular culture. Some controversy surrounds the definition of popular culture. Baseball cards, hula hoops, movie and rock and roll stars, television shows, popular heroes ranging from astronauts like John Glenn to television personalities like Johnny Carson—all can be thought of as part of our popular culture. For our purposes, popular culture will be defined in terms of two features: pervasiveness—the extent to which the cultural content is disseminated throughout the society, and power—the influence of cultural content on the attitudes and behavior of the society's members. Three forms of popular culture that are both extremely pervasive and powerful in our society are the mass media of television, movies, and popular music.

Television is a particularly powerful and pervasive medium for the transmission of popular culture. More than 90 percent of the homes in America have at least one set. One study of television viewing patterns found that one-third of the adults in our society watch an average of four hours each day, while the typical ten-year-old spends more time watching television each week than attending class. Television has become so central a feature of our lives that some analysts refer to it as "the glass teat" and "the flickering blue parent." According to some critics, television has seriously encroached upon family, school, and church as the basic sources of cultural learning.

An examination of the depiction of death and dying in these mass media provides a glimpse into the contemporary meanings of death in our society and may shed some light on the dilemmas of death considered in this anthology.

Such an examination, however, discloses an intriguing paradox: whereas the reality of death has been assiduously denied and avoided in our daily lives, death is not only quite prevalent in the mass media, it is also depicted in grossly discrepant ways.

The avoidance of death in our daily lives is accomplished by relegating the dying and dead to specialists. Dying persons are segregated in medical institutions, and professional funeral directors display cosmeticized "loved ones" in "slumber rooms." Trained grief counselors offer help to the bereaved; and the very old, whose proximity to death mocks our desire to deny it, are increasingly separated from the young. Until quite recently, death was a taboo topic in the schools. Modern churches are more concerned with dwindling congregations than with interpreting the mystery of death. On a mundane level, the local butcher kills our animals for meat, while the veterinarian "puts to sleep" our aging or ailing pets.

Yet while we fastidiously avoid actual death, we find it is fun fare in the mass media. A child who has never attended a funeral or seen a corpse has quite likely witnessed thousands of killings on television and watched live news coverage of battlefield casualties and the removal of mutilated bodies from the scene of an airplane crash or natural disaster. Teenagers who would find a serious discussion of death and dying unpleasantly morbid or simply irrelevant eagerly flock to concerts where Alice Cooper assaults a female mannequin and sings "I Love the Dead." Adults who feel at an uncomfortable loss for words at the funeral of a family member or colleague are amused by such death-filled movies as *The Godfather* and *Jaws*.

In the real world, the overwhelming majority of deaths involve elderly people succumbing to degenerative diseases in medical institutions. The process of dying is frequently prolonged for weeks, months, and even years by the use of medicines and life-maintaining machines. When death does occur, it is an intensely meaningful experience for everyone involved—the dying person, family and friends, and, often, the medical staff. The impact of grief, for example, can be so severe as to actually shorten the remaining lives of the bereaved, as will be shown in Section 9. However, as the articles in this section indicate, death as depicted in the mass media tends to be both violent and impersonal.

Arlen examines the treatment of death on what is perhaps our most powerful medium—television. He finds that fictional treatment of death commonly entails the violent killing of people whose human qualities are portrayed very superficially. The victims are either "bad guys" who deserve what they get, or hapless individuals whose deaths are but passing incidents in an action-filled plot. The human drama of their own dying and its effect on their survivors is largely ignored. The violent act overshadows the humanity of the victim. When the deaths of actual people are reported on television news, violence is also a prime element. Mass deaths from violent causes—natural disasters, airplane crashes, terrorism, and war—are particularly newsworthy. The focus is on the body count; the human meaning of the deaths is submerged in the fascination for the nature and extent of the violence. Such deaths are further dehumanized when they are casually sandwiched between items of mundane interest and commercial breaks.

Walker's analysis of death in contemporary movies also notes the popularity of violence and the dehumanization of the victims. Movie censors have tended to be far more lenient with the depiction of violence than with sex, and Walker indicates that movies are becoming progressively more explicit in showing violent deaths and, at the same time, both killers and victims are shown as less humane and human. The killers are unemotional and the victims are trivial. The act of destruction is the focus. One might add to Walker's analysis the observation that death in movies is often treated humorously. *Harold and Maude* share a mischievous voyeurism at the funerals of strangers; Woody Allen in *Love and Death* cuts up against a background of war and revolution; Agent 007's enemies tend to be dispatched in a ludicrous manner. Even the real possibility of unprecedented violent, mass death from a nuclear war is satirized in *Dr. Strangelove*.

Such a peculiar contradiction—to fear and avoid actual, natural death while finding it entertaining in distorted depictions in the mass media—has prompted Gorer, in "The Pornography of Death," to suggest that natural death has become "smothered in prudery" while violence has replaced sex as the primary pornographic topic of our time. It is a stunning testimony to the vagaries of the human psyche, as well as to the ingenuity of cultural expression, that people who fear actual death will pay money to be entertained by pornographic death.

The implications of this disjunction between real and media death are complex and controversial. Defenders of current programming argue the producers are simply providing what audiences want, and that the depiction of violence provides vicarious release of violent inclinations in viewers, thus actually promoting a peaceful society. Critics of violence on the media—particularly television, which is accessible to children—fear that violence on the screen may lead to violent behavior. They cite incidents like the recent Zamora case, in which a teenage boy committed a murder virtually identical to one he had observed on an installment of "Ironside" on television. Critics also cite studies that suggest that frequent television viewers tend to overestimate the amount of violence in the real world because of the disproportionate amount on the media. Moreover, some findings suggest that a regular diet of television violence may desensitize viewers to violence in the outside world. Such densensitization could have catastrophic consequences if it hinders people from taking actual violence seriously, both on a personal scale, as when a young woman named Kitty Genovese was stabbed repeatedly to death while dozens of neighbors listened passively to her screams without even telephoning the police, and on a societal scale, as when people are able to laugh at the image of a crazed cowboy in *Dr. Strangelove* straddling an atomic bomb as it drops through the air.

It is difficult to document conclusively the precise effects of so much violent and impersonal death in the media. One thing seems clear, however: a society that has been characterized by the inability to treat death as a normal and meaningful aspect of life is likely to suffer some deleterious consequences when its popular culture complicates the situation by treating it in an unrealistic and dehumanizing fashion.

On the other hand, the mass media do have the potential for providing responsible death education that can counteract the denial in everyday life and the distortion in the media themselves. TV programs like "Brian's Song" and movies like *Madame Rosa* can teach audiences much about the human realities of death and dying. Nonfictional accounts like John Gunther's moving portrait of his dying son in "Death Be Not Proud" and the recent public television production of "Dying," in which three dying persons are filmed and interviewed, can take death "out of the closet" and provide information that can help viewers cope when death intrudes on their lives.

The problems and potential of the mass media for transmitting the cultural meanings of death were highlights in the controversy surrounding the recent production of "Holocaust" on prime time television. "Holocaust," which traced both a Jewish family and a young SS officer through the systematic extermination of Jews and other "undesirables" by the Nazis in World War II, exposed millions of viewers—especially the post-War generation—to one final consequence of depersonalization and mass violence. Defenders of the show argued that television provided a means of reaching more people with a more dramatic statement than would have been possible with any other form of cultural expression. Critics noted that the constraints of television scheduling and censorship necessitated a presentation which, as horrifying as it was, did not fully reveal the extent of the horrors nor the causative forces in the society that perpetrated them. Further, they argued, the story was demeaned, and its lessons weakened, by the frequent interruptions for commercials that stridently advertised facial preparations and mouthwash.

The mass media, in summary, can either distort the realities of death and further erode our ability to live and die meaningfully, or they can be extremely valuable transmitters of our vital cultural meanings of life and death. In a society where attitudes toward death are likely to come from the mass media rather than from direct confrontation with the dying, this is a matter of no little concern.

Michael J. Arlen

The Air

The Cold, Bright Charms of Immortality

Michael Arlen, a critic for *The New Yorker* magazine, examines the treatment of death on television in this selection. Death on the media tends to be violent and impersonal—the human dimensions of the victims are eclipsed by a fascination for the manner of their demise and the scale of destruction. Since television is an extremely important medium of cultural transmission, one cannot help but wonder at the implications of such depiction for a generation of children for whom television has become a parent-teacher surrogate. While television violence may not necessarily inspire violent behaviors in its young audience, there is a danger that children may become desensitized to violence and less able to take it seriously or respond to it in real life. Living as we do under the shadow of nuclear annihilation, we can ill afford to lose touch with the realities of violent and impersonal death as a result of becoming overfamiliar and comfortable with their fictional portrayal on the screen.

In our modern world, death breaks into our lives suddenly—as it were, by surprise—even though it remains a fact that most men and women in the country still die in their beds of what used to be called old age. A death occurs in the family! Long-distance telephone calls crisscross through the night. The survivors—uneasy with a sense of uniqueness, their separate grief imprisoned in their separate civilities—stand about in suits and overcoats while tiny explosions detonate inside their heads, and then start for home.

The Sioux, I'm told, placed their dead on platforms up in the branches of trees along the Platte River—companionable treefuls of dead Sioux. The Crow made sure to show their grief by cutting off part of a finger. The Arapaho acknowledged death's imminence by singing a song to it; an abandoned warrior, dying, would brace himself against a rock and sing the Death Song until he died. Generally, nowadays, we do things differently.

An uncle of mine died a few weeks ago—a kind and modest man whom I much cared about; he had been seventy-three at the time of his heart attack, which, as my sister asserted, had come "out of nowhere." His dying naturally made me think of death—at first, in the usual manner, whereby for a while after the death of a close friend or relative harsh winds of mortality gust with a sudden, temporary significance through the heads of those remaining. Then, perhaps because he had been such a calm, methodical, gently purposive man, and there had been something calm, methodical, and—yes—gently purposive about his death and the manner of its arrival, I found myself feeling the moment quite differently. For an instant, death itself seemed almost like a modest, commonplace event—perhaps like what it was. In his fine book *The Lives of a Cell,* Dr. Lewis Thomas has written, "There are three billion of us on the earth, and all three billion must be dead, on a schedule, within this lifetime." Just then, from inside one's modern, individual isolation, one could nearly sense the dim, communal, ordinary idea of mortality that was beyond us, and that human beings sometimes reached for—without attaining. And so afterward, mindful of this individual community, I thought of television, and wondered what—were I to watch it steadily for a while—I might find that this pervasive communicator was telling us, or not telling us, about this mass, ongoing, collective activity; about death.

I picked a definite period of one week to study, and I watched, with reasonable fidelity, for ten or twelve hours each day. I wrote down only references to death or dying, and they appear as follows:

Friday. In "The Edge of Night," there were two references to the earlier murder of a young woman named Taffy Simms. In "Days of Our Lives," Bob said, "Phyllis, you almost died." From the NBC local news: "A mine disaster in northern France has claimed forty-one lives." And "Eighteen persons were killed in Brazil this morning as a train crashed into a bus." And "Fifteen died today in Portugal when two passenger trains collided outside a railroad station in Lisbon." And "Eighteen people were reported strangled in the Ethiopian city of Asmara. This brings the total number of deaths by strangulation to forty-five." The death of Jack Benny was reported, accompanied by a photograph of Benny during his early days on radio, when he worked for NBC, and prominently displaying the NBC microphone. There was a film from Darwin, Australia, that briefly showed a dead victim of the Darwin cyclone being carried away on a stretcher, and also presented an interview with a survivor. "What happened to your wife?" the

reporter asked. "My wife was killed," the survivor said. The CBS network news mentioned the forty-one mine-explosion deaths in France and the fifteen Portuguese who had been killed this morning in a train crash "just outside Lisbon's main railroad station." There was an item about Jack Benny: "Benny Kubelsky, better known as Jack Benny, died in his home today of cancer. For half a century, Jack Benny made people laugh by laughing at himself." In "Kolchak," a score of people were murdered by a vampire. In the movie *The Last Run,* a man fell to his death; another man was shot and then burned up in a car; two men were killed in a gunfight. In "Police Woman," the dead body of a man was found in a car trunk, and four men were killed in a gunfight.

Saturday. There were no deaths in any of the entertainment programs. From the NBC network news: "In recent months, more than twenty thousand people have died of starvation" in Bangladesh. And "Doctors have said that more tests will be needed to determine the cause of the fall last evening which resulted in the death of columnist Amy Vanderbilt. Miss Vanderbilt was an authority and author of several books on etiquette." In an ABC documentary, "Crashes: The Illusion of Safety," there were references to numerous plane crashes, in which a total of forty-eight hundred people had died. On the NBC late news, there was an item about a retired policeman who had been shot and killed. And "There still appears to be some mystery surrounding the death of columnist Amy Vanderbilt. Police have indicated the possibility of suicide, although her husband has said he knows of nothing to indicate that motivation."

Sunday. In "World of Survival," a reef crab was killed by an octopus. "A very sad day for the crab," said the announcer. From the CBS local news: "Pakistani authorities have estimated that over three hundred people have been killed in an earthquake in northern Pakistan." And "Nicaraguan guerrillas killed three guards yesterday." And "Three persons were killed in a four-car accident at the corner of Barlow and a Hundred and Thirty-ninth Street." CBS News (whose parent company, CBS, had hired Benny away from NBC) provided an hour-long "Tribute to Jack Benny." There were brief scenes of Hollywood celebrities arriving in cars. "This was the day of his [Jack Benny's] funeral, and all of Hollywood was there," said correspondent Charles Kuralt. A 1967 CBS tape showed the late Ed Sullivan. "It's true that Jack Benny spoke his first words on the air on an Ed Sullivan radio show," said Mr. Kuralt. Benny's former CBS announcer, Don Wilson, said, "Jack, above all, was a great human being.... Jack was a very normal person.... He never went to a psychiatrist—he never had to." There was a tape of Benny's recent appearance with Dinah Shore on CBS's "Dinah!" "One of the last times he made us laugh was just this fall, when the première of the new Dinah Shore program had a walk-on guest," said Charles Kuralt. Milton Berle said, "We've lost an institution....It's like the sinking of the Statue of Liberty." CBS board chairman William Paley was interviewed and spoke of Benny's "professionalism that was unique and outstanding." There was a tape of Benny doing a skit with his violin. "The violin is stilled," said Mr. Kuralt. In "Kojak," an old man was shot to death by gangsters, and two men were killed in a gunfight. In "Columbo," one woman was strangled to death, and another woman was drowned in her bathtub.

Monday. In "The Edge of Night," there were two references to the murder of Taffy Simms. In a "Popeye" cartoon, a bully was pushed off a tall building and fell into an open coffin, which was hammered closed. From the ABC local news: "A sniper, armed with a rifle, has killed three people in the town of Olean, New York." And "The dead are still being counted at the scene of the massive earthquake in northern Pakistan." From the ABC network news: "Authorities in northwest Pakistan say the death toll from an earthquake there has reached four thousand seven hundred, and is likely to go higher." In "Gunsmoke," two men were killed in a gunfight. In "Born Free," a man was killed by a leopard. In "Frankenstein: The True Story," seven corpses were disinterred.

Tuesday. From the CBS local news: "Twelve fishermen are feared drowned after two boats capsized in heavy seas" off the coast of southern Italy. And "An Israeli patrol reportedly shot and killed three guerrillas as they were spotted crossing the border." In "Hawaii Five-O," a man was murdered with a hara-kiri knife, and another man was shot and killed in a gunfight. In "Barnaby Jones," a man was killed in a gunfight.

Wednesday. From the NBC local and network news: "Twenty-three persons were feared dead as a busload of holiday skiers plunged into a lake near the town of Omachi, north of Tokyo." And "Two policemen were killed this afternoon in an auto accident as they were driving in response to an emergency call." In "Cannon," one man was killed in an overturned car, and another man was shot to death by a rifle. In "The Manhunter," one man was killed by being pushed out of a tall building, and another man was killed by a pistol shot.

Thursday. In "The Edge of Night," a character referred to "the tragic death of Taffy Simms." Three bandits were blown up by dynamite in a "Popeye" cartoon. From the ABC local news: "Word from the National Safety Council is that this year's Christmas holiday death toll is down by 20 percent." From the ABC network news: "Four Arab civilians were killed by Israelis in a raid across the border early this morning." In "Ironside," a judge shot to death a man who was trying to kill him. In "Harry O," an unknown man was shot to death; a woman was beaten to death; another man was shot to death, and the man who shot him was killed. From the ABC late news: "Fire killed a two-year-old girl and injured several members of her family. Indications are that the victim, Carmen Allen, had been playing with matches."

It's hard to know what a "survey" of this kind proves, beyond the obvious, which in this case is that we are a violent people—seemingly entranced by violence—and have no serious regard for death. Also, I'm not at all sure what can be conveyed truly—by writing—of watching television for its acknowledgments of death. Twelve hours or so of television for seven days adds up to roughly eighty-four hours of more or less continuous broadcasting—the equivalent of around a half million words. How to convey the absence of death—real death—from this daily torrent of supposedly realistic narrative and imagery?

On the whole, a study of death on television turns up few surface surprises. After all, it should be no surprise by now that half of American network prime-time entertainment programming seems to be crime-oriented, and employs death by murder or in gunfights casually and routinely, as a simple plot device. (In fact, in most detective programs nowadays—as if they were following a prescribed ritual—there is usually a key murder of an unknown but significant figure within the first five minutes; there is sometimes a throwaway murder of a secondary character in the middle; and there is invariably a gunfight, which kills off one or two secondary or unknown characters, within the last five minutes.) Nor, in the area of news reporting, should it be much of a surprise that the detached and captionlike quality of the networks' regular news coverage is generally carried over into their accounts of death in the nation and across the world. Thus, snippets of information about the death of Brazilians in a bus crash or of Frenchmen in a mine disaster are blithely transmitted between snippets of information about factory layoffs in Detroit or gold speculation in London.

Perhaps, in the end, the surprise is that one is so little surprised. We accept the fact that death is mentioned so rarely on television—and usually in such a relentlessly offhand and stylized manner—because we apparently accept the idea that, as a nation, we have no wish to confront death, or deal with it, except by euphemism and avoidance. Doubtless, to a considerable extent this is true. It doesn't seem to be true of most of the rest of the world, especially of the poorer and less advanced countries, where—despite enormous populations, and the contrary expectations of many Western military experts—people appear to care hugely about human life and death, but perhaps it is more true of technologically progressive countries, or, at any rate, it is becoming true. Still, even here in America—with our Forest Lawns and pet cemeteries—our proverbial avoidance of or uncaringness about death often seems illusory or skin-deep. In private lives, for example, there are surely myriad explosions of grief, incomprehension, and deep human response—taking place literally all the time in the isolation of families where death occurs. And in public America—though the surface appears impervious to death—it was, ironically, television that, some time ago, on the occasions of the deaths of the two Kennedy brothers and Dr. Martin Luther King, helped the American people break through their apparent fear of death and death's imagery, and assisted in creating a nearly national rite of passage.

To be sure, the deaths of the two Kennedys and of Dr. King were extraordinary events—touched not only by public and private loss but also by high drama and by a kind of national guilt. (That is, if we had been more aware and sensible of death, we might have been less bland in letting these three notable, high-profile men walk prematurely into theirs.) One might, then, say that television respects death only in the famous. But this misses the point. First, if it were generally true that television (or our public society) respected death only in the famous, that would be at worst a commonplace of life; art alone, which can draw a Sancho Panza as vividly as a knight of La Mancha, seems consistently to skirt class differences. But, for the most part, even when

THE DEATH OF LITTLE NELL

The child who had been her little friend, came there, almost as soon as it was day, with an offering of dried flowers, which he begged them to lay upon her breast. He told them of his dream again, and that it was of her being restored to them, just as she used to be. He begged hard to see her: saying, that he would be very quiet, and that they need not fear his being alarmed for he had sat alone by his younger brother all day long when he was dead, and he had felt glad to be so near him. They let him have his wish; and, indeed, he kept his word, and was, in his childish way, a lesson to them all.

Charles Dickens
in McGuffey's *New Sixth Reader*

television attempts to deal with the death of famous persons what it commonly does is to attend briskly and meretriciously to the *famousness* of the departed, and to leave the death, and everything that humanly has to do with death, at arm's length. Thus, at the death of Jack Benny—a man who had clearly been much liked in his lifetime, and whose dying had doubtless produced many true feelings of loss and change—the texture of his leaving us was somehow cleaned up for television. No grief appeared on camera. The chairman of the CBS "family" spoke about "professionalism." Taped highlights were shown of a man who had existed ten or twenty years before. As for the death of the less famous Miss Vanderbilt, her accident popped in and out of the news for a day and a half not as the real death of a real woman but as hoked-up "mystery."

The point seems to be that television—this great communicating force—has settled into a role of largely ignoring the reality of death. It does this in part by simply not mentioning it, as if, despite the fact that folktales since ancient times have been filled with the reality of human death, it had lately become—for our "mass audience"—an irrelevant subject. And it does this, perhaps inadvertently, by asserting that the whole reality of death is violence. In entertainment programs, for example, a woman is matter-of-factly drowned in a bathtub; two unknown men are killed in a gun battle; a character—possessed of no past, present, or future—is shot to death by fleeing burglars. In almost no instances of fictional death on television do the dead victims, or their deaths, have any depth or meaning—or, sometimes, even identity—for the audience. (Indeed, one could state it almost as an axiom that no one in a popular television drama who has a fully developed character ever dies.) And when

death occurs it arrives invariably through violence, though it is usally a casual, spurious, stage violence, unconnected to personality or feeling, either among the characters or in the audience—a ubiquitous, toy violence. On the news programs, where deaths are regularly announced, these, too, are generally the result of violence or catastrophe, are similarly anonymous, and take place in the unconnected remoteness either of a brief factual caption or of a distant, meaningless locale. In a sense, one might say that the standard news broadcasts, with their nightly accounts of the deaths of fifteen identity-less Portuguese in a train crash, or of a dozen persona-less Italian fishermen in a shipwreck, come close to representing the actual scattered randomness of death as it occurs on this planet. But, once again, these real deaths are treated as if they had no meaning—except as the statistical byproduct of some disaster. Death is usually reported to us in the sterility of numbers—"body counts"— and on the few occasions when a person has been found who is humanly connected to real death (as with the two-sentence interview of the man who had lost his wife in Darwin), the cameras, or editors, move gingerly in their treatment of the situation, compressing or squeezing out the humanity and skipping quickly on.

The matter of violence on television has been much discussed recently, though its connection with death seems mainly to be a specious and distorting one. Certainly there has been a plenitude of violent action in commercial broadcasting, and, quite plausibly, there have been a number of surveys, studies, and pronouncements dealing with the subject. Critics, on the whole, have said that there is too much violence on the airwaves, and that violent entertainment tends to breed violent citizens. Telefilm producers have replied that the citizens were violent to begin with, and that everyone knows that detective or Western programs are only fiction, and that, besides, the audience loves a good gunfight. Probably this is a situation in which both sides are more or less right, and the problem will somehow sort itself out in due course. Clearly, there is an oversupply of violence, and, also clearly, the majority of the viewers don't take the stuff very seriously. The trouble is that death is not the same as violence. Death is not inseparable from violence. It's true that crimes of violence have increased in this country in recent years, as it's true that the reporting and communicating of crimes of violence have increased in recent years, but in most of its occurrences in the world and in America death is (how else to say it?) *itself:* supremely ordinary, supremely deep. Each week, across the seven continents of the earth, roughly a million human beings die, and most of them die from a classic confluence of age and state of health and the vagaries of life. In other words, to shy away from death because it has been glibly associated with violence—and with stage violence, at that—is like throwing out *King Lear* along with the proverbial bathwater of trivial detective stories. For example, I've read approving comments lately from consumer groups and certain network executives on the decline in the "level of violence" on children's programs, and, basically, this is bound to be an improvement. On the other hand, in the entire week of television that I watched I never once saw death appear in human form on a children's program. (I discount "Popeye," which seems in this regard no worse and no better than "Hawaii Five-O.") Childhood is the time in life when we first become aware of death—when we try to open our eyes to it, have bad dreams, and ask strange, tactless questions. It seems regrettable, at the least—

especially considering the frequent presence of death in the great stories for children—that our television fathers and families just won't talk about death to young people.

But it's not only children in our society who are isolated from death by our communications organizations. Virtually all the rest of us have been left to shift for ourselves in dealing with this great, commonplace matter—have been made enemies of death, terrified and stricken by its seeming uniqueness, frozen at gravesides into our separate overcoats. One has heard it said that everyone must deal with death on his own, and perhaps that's true in terms of the physical act of one human being's dying. But for much of history both the dying and the survivors (soon to be the dying) have devised systems—tribal custom or religion—whereby it was possible to place death where it belonged, as part of the continuous, collective cycle of human life. In our era, television has pushed its way into the void left by the fading presence of religion and tribal authority. Television is, if not a formal system, at any rate a huge, cool authority, and also a kind of family, and juggling act, and troupe of players—and priesthood. Indeed, once, with the Kennedy deaths and the death of Martin Luther King, it showed what it could do in incorporating into the community not just a particular or famous death but *death*. Since then, however, it has been mainly silent on the subject. We do not die, apparently, except in numbers, or in Rangoon, or with blank faces in a gunfight. The institution of television often claims to be a mirror reflecting our society, and often many of us are agreeable to thinking that this is so. Perhaps it's more and more worth realizing that it's a mirror that reflects only a part of us. Our deaths, at least—that mass collective act—are not yet part of the reflection.

Alexander Walker

The Case of the Vanishing Bloodstains

Alexander Walker, in this review from *Encounter* magazine, analyzes the depiction of death and killing in several popular movies. Stating that "the world's escalating violence finds its most vivid metaphor in the movies . . . ," he concludes that a preoccupation with the minute details of violent death and destruction is increasing, while concern with sensitively portraying the human qualities of both killers and victims is declining. In other words, the audience tolerance level for violence is rising—so producers are compelled to purvey ever more graphic and ingenious methods of killing— but the moral and human meanings of such violence are becoming irrelevant. Of course, violent deaths have always made good entertainment, from the days of the gladiatorial battles in the Roman Coliseum to the public executions in European countries. But in past societies, death was a common experience in daily life. The gory spectacles amplified daily reality. In our own society, death is avoided and denied whenever possible. The mass media thus become powerful sources of death education both by default and by design.

Holmes bent over this grotesque frieze for some minutes and then suddenly sprang to his feet with an exclamation of surprise and dismay. His face was haggard with anxiety.

"We have let this affair go far enough," said he.

Arthur Conan-Doyle
The Dancing Men

About [ten] years ago a change came over the character of death on the cinema screen. What came into being has been called "medical materialism," a phrase I owe to Dr. Jonathan Miller. By this he meant that death, which had hitherto been a fairly ritual affair, was turning into an anatomy lesson, or, rather, an autopsy.

Previously the gun barked, the victim jackknifed, a token bloodstain welled up on his shirt front, another public enemy lay down and died. The damage was more sartorial than arterial; and the censor's work was correspondingly simplified, since deserving justice had been seen to be done and there was really no mess to speak of. It is curious considering the high place that *ciné-verité* techniques occupy in the screen's approach to life that the film which probably did more than any other to change this approach to death has been overlooked, in spite of being seen by more people in the world than any other American movie.

Let me momentarily conceal the event it recorded, as well as the names of the parties at the center of it, and quote instead from a synopsis written some time afterwards but very like the "continuity" script that's put together from the completely edited film:

The [car] continues to slow down. The interior is a place of horror. The last bullet has torn through [his] cerebellum, the lower part of his brain. Leaning towards her husband [she] has seen a piece of his skull detach itself. At first there is no blood. And then, in the very next instant, there is nothing but blood spattering him. . . . Gobs of blood as thick as a man's hand are soaking the floor of the back seat, [his] clothes are steeped in it, the roses are drenched, [his] body is lurching soundlessly towards his wife, and Motor Cycle Police Officer Hargis, two feet from her, is doused in the face by a red sheet. To Kellerman it appears that the air is full of moist sawdust.[1]

Those who have read William Manchester's landmark piece of investigative reporting, *The Death of a President,* will hardly need to be told by now that what this describes is the assassination of President Kennedy in Dallas in November 1963.

But what makes it relevant to this enquiry into the contemporary cinema's approach to death is the way that Manchester duplicates the effect of a camera's eye seeing in slow motion, and thereby giving itself the *time* to see, the bloody havoc accompanying the onset of sudden and extremely public death. As well as the eye-witnesses he names, Manchester had indeed the supplementary evidence of a camera's eye—the one with the famous Zoomar lens being wielded by Abe Zapruder, the garment manufacturer and amateur cinematographer who happened to be filming the Presidential motorcade at the precise moment of the assassination. In the 8.3 seconds which it took the color film to register it on 152 frames the most notorious piece of "medical materialism" was recorded to be later relayed throughout the world during one of the most deeply shared periods of grief in history.

It is odd how this reproduction of an event dramatically heightens it. As the narrator in Stanley Kubrick's *A Clockwork Orange* says, "The colors of the real world only seem really real when you viddy them on the screen. . . ." Not that the Zapruder film recorded the anatomical detail of the Manchester "scenario,"

although once the posthumous event is treated to an "action replay"—as it was, countless times in the course of the subsequent enquiries, lay and official—one seems to be seeing it broken down into the fractions of time in a slow-motion version. Over the years it has assumed an iconographic vividness irresistible to any film-maker disposed to draw his inspiration from a historical and moral shock of its magnitude.

So one is not at all surprised to find this confirmed in an Arthur Penn interview in *Les Cahiers du Cinema,* four years after Kennedy's assassination, in which the director of *Bonnie and Clyde* explicitly refers to the earlier event when speaking of the fusillade of eighty-seven bullets fired at the end of his film into the eponymous hero and heroine. "We put on the bullet holes," says Penn, "and there's even a piece of Warren's [Beatty's] head that comes off, like that famous photograph of Kennedy." In fact if one turns to the screenplay of *Bonnie and Clyde,* written by David Newman and Robert Benton, what one finds is an eerie echo of the precise, present-tense tone of the Manchester "scenario" which came out in the same year as the film, 1967:

> We see alternately the bodies of Clyde and Bonnie twisting, shaking, horribly distorted; much of the action is in slow motion. Clyde is on the ground, his body arching and rolling from the impact of the bullets. Bonnie is still in her seat; her body jerking and swaying as the bullets thud relentlessly into her and the framework of the car.
>
> *Exterior the car on the verge.* Bonnie's body slews out sideways, head first. A final burst and her head and shoulders drop down on to the running board. Clyde's body rolls over and over on the ground and then lies still. The firing stops.[2]

1. William Manchester, *The Death of a President* (1967), p. 196.

2. *The Bonnie and Clyde Book,* compiled and edited by Sandra Wake and Nicola Hayden. Simon & Schuster, New York; Lorrimer, London, pp. 162-4.

The reason Penn used a slow-motion technique at this point in the film was to get what he called "the spasm of death," and a most sophisticated technique it was. It involved no fewer than four cameras shooting at twenty-four, forty-eight, seventy-two, and ninety-six frames a second "so that I could cut to get the shock and at the same time the ballet of death. There's a moment in death when the body no longer functions, when it becomes an object and has a certain kind of detached ugly beauty. . . ."

Now anyone who talks of the "beauty" of death is treading in a grey area of aesthetics; yet can anyone doubt that Penn acquitted himself responsibly in *Bonnie and Clyde*? Freely admitting to the fascination he found in rendering the kinetic effects of violence, which is what makes it so dangerously appealing where most spectators of events real or imaginary are concerned, he nevertheless saves himself from the charge of mortuary gloating by what one can only call an act of charity towards his victims. While slow motion gives us the time to see them die by protracting the moment of death into an eternity, it nevertheless withholds the full destructive force of the medical materialism which eighty-seven bullets ripping into two people would have conveyed to us. They would have literally been torn apart. What really horrifies us is the "overkill" nature of the lawmen, almost believing that their victims had charmed lives and must be filled with their own weight of lead. All the same their outlines are intact as they lie there, like effigies. What Penn has done is extinguish the life but preserve the legend.

When we next saw slow-motion used to record the violent rhythms of death it was in a far more materialistic cause. Sam Peckinpah's film *The Wild Bunch* also derived from the Kennedy assassination, more precisely from the debate on the role of the gun in American life which in the aftermath of this event and the deaths of Robert Kennedy and Martin Luther King, looked like ushering in far tighter curbs on the sale and ownership of firearms in a society traditionally based on a man's right to bear and use them.

Peckinpah's film celebrated the power of the gun by showing it in action, which meant showing the bloody destruction contained in one split second. Blood spurts like a drinking fountain from a burst artery in the opening massacre, a body bumps up off the ground like a rubber toy, dust rises in slow motion, a limb trails out at a ghastly angle as if in a state of weightlessness and the corpse settles down with a spasm that has the effect in slow motion of a small avalanche. *The Wild Bunch* always keeps returning to the gun. It is the hero if anything is, far more so than the human beings, a bunch of aging cowboys feeling their obsolescence, whereas their guns will go marching on into the new century, coming out in ever improving models. The brand-new machine-gun that goes off like a fractious baby in the arms of the ignorant peon cuddling it is a quantum leap into totalitarian destructiveness.

But what is the film saying to us? This is more difficult to answer and even after a prudent second viewing I am driven to conclude that it *says* nothing for the very reason that it *shows* everything. The end doesn't simply justify the means, as it always does in a Peckinpah film; the end is the means in the way (remember?) that the medium is the message.

Now this should have put us on our guard. I know that some people were; but to me, reviewing the film at the time, its bloody excesses seemed justified as a response to the contemporary wave of revulsion against violence. I am far less certain of this now, especially after Peckinpah's *Straw Dogs*.... In any case there were other omens we should have read about the cinema's attitude to the new violence. As Pauline Kael put it once, "immediately something enters mass culture, it travels fast." Which in this case meant not only the new presentation of death, but the film industry's hope of new life for itself. What we're apt to forget is that it isn't really a creative industry: it is an imitative one in which only a few creative people at any time are tolerated. Commercial opportunism which can present an honest face to the world by the opportunities it gives an artist frequently shows a cruder and truer side in the way it sells his work. The lyrical spell of *Bonnie and Clyde,* presented as "Lovers" on the posters at the film's opening, swiftly dissolved into a keener pitch for the audience's emotions once they moved into the hinterland and became "Killers."

Over the last few years one has witnessed a whole arsenal of death-dealing weapons coming to dominate the cinema posters, in Britain anyhow, as the central, selling feature of the film and irresistibly recalling the swollen organs of potency commonplace in every porn book. (A prospective Ph.D. would find richly rewarding territory to research in the psychopathology of cinema advertising.) Of course every true craftsman is vulnerable to exploitation by the trade he works in; but the film industry's sense of where the appeal lies is shown to be fairly accurate by the box-office success which is being enjoyed to a phenomenal degree by the quantum leap into human physical destruction and violent death.

A frieze of death has stretched across the screen since *Bonnie and Clyde* and *The Wild Bunch* initiated the "action autopsy" approach

to it or, in Joseph Morgenstern's phrase, tried "to explore the nature of life with the aesthetics of death." To follow the trail of bloodstains makes a profoundly disquieting pursuit. And when the perplexed Watson reaches the point where he cries, "There are no more bloodstains," one must sympathize with the inevitable reply from Holmes, "Yes, that is the most disquieting thing of all."

I don't think it was accidental that the curve of violence in films began its steep rise just about the time one would expect the new Hollywood films, which had profited from the 1965–66 revision of the Production Code to deal with sex more and more candidly, began to face the problem of their subsequent sale to television. Sex undressed is patently sex; violence on the other hand can be dressed up as many things. Moreover, the motion-picture code, reflecting the taboos of the early Legion of Decency and the Roman Catholic Church as well as the truisms at the center of the American historical experience, was basically more tolerant to the depiction of violence than sex. One has also to reckon with a number of film-makers, all men whose forte lay in the harsh-grained action film, now finding that the dangerous but exhilarating tide of fashion was running with them and even propelling their ingrained aggressiveness along almost faster than they could keep up with it.

The world's escalating violence finds its most vivid metaphor in the movies; which is not to say that the movies predispose us to add to the violence. But as the power of certain films proves so strong that we tend to conceptualize real events in their terms I think that it may predispose us to tolerate violence, or at least its latest form when it is succeeded by some new and awful escalation. The imitative pressures of the industry drive its film-makers to let themselves rip on a spiraling ascent into new levels of death and destruction until it "peaks" in some explosive display of psychopathy. . . .

But as one moves along the bloodstained trail to *The Godfather* one enters some extremely dark territory. By late August [1972], when Francis Ford Coppola's film opened in Britain, the censor had finally screwed himself to the sticking place where he was now prepared to pass the Warhol/Morrissey movie, *Trash,* which had languished for nearly a year, with an "*X*" Certificate as well as substantial cuts. (An "*X*" in Britain excludes any person under eighteen years of age.) He reached

---

I LOVE THE DEAD

I love the dead before they're cold,
They're bluing flesh for me to hold.
Cadaver eyes upon me see nothing.
I love the dead before they rise,
No farewells, no goodbyes.
I never even knew your rotting face.
While friends and lovers mourn your silly
  grave.
I have other uses for you, Darling.
We love the dead,
We love the dead, Yeah.

Alice Cooper

---

a decision over *The Godfather* with far less moral wrestling, giving it an "*X*" Certificate, too, but insisting on the smallest imaginable cut, namely a nine-second trim towards the end of the scene where "Sonny" has run into the vendetta at the toll-gate and been slaughtered by the rival Mafia. The censor thought it inadvisable to show one of the gang kicking the inert body: on the old British principle, I suppose, that you should never kick a man when he's down, even if he's dead.

Now the feast of death that *The Godfather* provides is so well known that I may be spared running through the obits. I only observe that the garrottings, assassinations, and serial slayings have their appeal deftly enhanced by the care taken never to repeat the slaughter in quite the same way twice. It is the principle of pornography, too. In contrast, what the censor advised should be cut out of *Trash,* in order to give it an "*X*" Certificate, was almost entirely sexual and included a fellatio scene (shortened) and a moment when a beer bottle was put to an unusual use to obtain an orgasm (though as the self-pleasurer was a male-in-drag it remains a mystery what arcane technique the censor ascribed to him/her) The interpretation is irresistible—that the film censor deplores violence, but what he cuts is sex.

For anyone operating on this double standard *The Godfather* is a gift. For in spite of being one of the most continuously violent films ever made, it contains absolutely no sex—none at all. This has escaped general notice, perhaps by its very obviousness. It was brought home to me by the satisfaction with which a rather staid friend, who had frequently deplored the growing permissiveness of the movies, expressed his pleasure to me that here at last was a film to which he could take his wife without embarrassment. No distressing full frontals, you see, at least not where sex was concerned. I think he might have been more appalled, or maybe his wife would have been, if one of the early victims whose gun hand is skewered to the bar with a knife while his throat is garrotted had been in a state of nudity at the time.

A film cannot be estimated to earn 150 million dollars world-wide without this layman's opinion of what is decent for him and his wife to see being shared by the majority of those who will go to *The Godfather*. Indeed the audience reaction is interesting. I saw the film several times, having had to take along friends from backward countries, lands where *The Godfather* hadn't been opened, and on each occasion the audience sat dumbly through the plethora of Mafia killings. When they did react audibly it was only once, a low collective whistle of shock at the end when the "godson" deliberately lies to his wife. Seeing death at its most anatomically violent on the screen had apparently lost its power to repel: lying to your wife, on the other hand, is still something that goes home to the heart of the petit bourgeoisie. Nothing else has so sharply indicated to me how the tolerance-level of violence is rising.

I don't ascribe the fact that the film fails to shock or outrage to the nice-safe feeling it paradoxically generates—keeping death inside the family, so to speak. Of course these Mafia bosses are "golden oldies"—the slaughter of '46 out of the summer of '42. But distance lending security to the viewer doesn't satisfactorily explain its appeal. As I see it, we are witnessing a far more frightening phenomenon than the deaths on the screen; we are witnessing nothing less than the death of people's humanity. We have been so raped by violence that we are like the daughter heeding her mother's injunction as she leaves on a dubious date: that if you can't resist it, lie back and enjoy it. And even this residual pleasure is

losing its savor. It is drying up the way the emotions are on the screen. Death no longer has any humanity, so it can offer no purgative satisfaction. Not even our pity is solicited. Man-made monsters once had hearts, which broke even as they crushed their makers. Now all they exhibit is the coolness of successful psychopaths—no emotions whatsoever. There is scarcely a gangster film out of the 1930s which hadn't some particle of humanity embedded in it, besides the slugs of rivals for the South Side, even if it was only misguided mother-love for Jimmy Cagney.

In the second half of *The Godfather* an extraordinary change comes over Al Pacino which is relevant to this. At the start of the film it is almost as if Paramount were making him into a 1940s *Love Story* figure, with his air of diminished cuddliness as he nibbles his courtship on the fringe of the family. When he takes over power (and the story) he reverts to a much earlier decade than the 1940s: he affects the glossy, brushed-back hair-style and close-fitting wardrobe of the 1930s. He appears a stereotype companion to Humphrey Bogart and George Raft except in one vital respect. The movie still assigns to him the arid, passionless, mechanistic ethos which is its own attitude to all human life in the 1970s. Its nostalgia only goes back so far: when it comes to the killing, it is bang up to date.

The *Mechanic* may look like a freelance *Godfather,* operating exogamously against any target he is paid to eliminate. In Michael Winner's film, as in *The Godfather,* one is overwhelmed by the same emotionally drained attitude to death. But whereas the "godson" reminds his doubting girl friend that "everybody kills today, the Army, the Government, Big Business," the professional assassin in *The Mechanic* takes this acceptance of the world as it is to its logical conclusion and propagandizes that anybody has the right to kill anybody. The same refrain was heard from the acolytes of Charles Manson. It is language being used as an instrument of murder. *The Mechanic* in fact takes it a stage beyond Manson. Charles Bronson's assassin doesn't kill for the thrill of it all; to him, it is simply "the Job," carried out dispassionately upon receipt of a registered envelope of instructions. Whom he kills, much less why, we are never told. What does it matter, since the act of killing is all that counts? We have come a long way in the few years from the pathetic dimension of the massacre in which Bonnie and Clyde died and made us care to the almost bloodless killings of *The Mechanic* in which we don't know who dies and couldn't care less.

There are literally "clean" killings. The only scene in which I can recall blood actually flowing and lingered over is the one in which the jilted girl friend of the mechanic's young male apprentice deliberately severs her wrists with a razor blade as the two men sit looking on.

Her pitiful gesture is an attempt to move at least one of them into emotional involvement with her; they simply regard her suicide as the test of how "cool" they can remain. Such men are smooth operators; but their essence is their refusal to sympathize, to become involved. It is the black side of Kennedy's avowal of "grace under pressure"—"coolness under stress." The essay on *The White Negro* which Norman Mailer wrote in 1957 praising the "psychopathic brilliance" of the hip style that models itself on the Black experience has been brought to life in *The Mechanic*—if "life" is the word for a mode of existence dedicated to keeping on top by extinguishing all human feelings and maintaining one's mechanistic responses in trim for taking human life.

In an earlier script, I am told, the liaison in *The Mechanic* between both men was homosexual as well as homicidal. Even that has been siphoned out of them, leaving only their mutual boast that in a society which is actually no better than they are, the psychopath is king.

Even this is not the film's most ominous feature. The way it has been *accepted* is highly unsettling. Far from being given a British "X" Certificate, putting it on the same shelf beside *The Godfather,* it has drawn a straight "*AA*" Certificate, a much milder rating allowing fourteen-year-old children to see it. This view is presumably based on the belief that in its externals it differs little from a standard gangster drama of the 1930s. There could scarcely be a more dangerous misreading of its essential significance. In it as in other films we are being asked to accept the ascendancy of the Psychopath, the man who has no doubts, knows no fears, experiences no guilt, feels no humanity, but simply acts in the only way he believes gives meaning to a society in which the rejection of restraints has become epidemic. He kills.

From the addition of medical materialism to its repertoire, the cinema has passed on to the celebration of moral anarchy. And it has us staring at the panorama as ambiguously as the Mechanic himself stares at the reproduction of the Bosch painting known alternatively as *Earthly Pleasures* or as *Lust,* depicting a carnival of hideous fantasies, which hangs on his living room wall. Is it a foretaste of Hell that he draws from it? Or is it fresh inspiration? And is there any difference?

The bloodstains we've been following have given out: in the moral void in which much of the contemporary screen exists and flourishes, the only guide is our own fears.

Geoffrey Gorer

The Pornography of Death

Geoffrey Gorer, a British sociologist whose book *Death, Grief, and Mourning* stimulated widespread interest in the problems of grief in contemporary European and North American society, examines the discrepancy between natural death and the violent depiction of death in mass media in this classic essay. Gorer notes that while our society strives to avoid and deny actual death, we find violent death entertaining. Death, he argues, has replaced sex as a primary topic of pornographic interest.

Birth, and copulation, and death.
That's all the facts when you come to brass tacks:
Birth, and copulation, and death.

T. S. Eliot
Sweeney Agonistes

Pornography is, no doubt, the opposite face, the shadow of prudery, whereas obscenity is an aspect of seemliness. No society has been recorded which has not its rules of seemliness, of words or actions which arouse discomfort and embarrassment in some contexts, though they are essential in others. The people before whom one must maintain a watchful seemliness vary from society to society: all people of the opposite sex, or all juniors, or all elders, or one's parents-in-law, or one's social superiors or inferiors, or one's grandchildren have been selected in different societies as groups in whose presence the employment of certain words or the performance of certain actions would be considered offensive; and then these words or actions become charged with effect. There is a tendency for these words or actions to be related to sex and excretion but this is neither necessary nor universal; according to [anthropologist] Malinowski, the Trobrianders surround eating with as much shame as excretion; and in other societies personal names or aspects of ritual come under the same taboos.

Rules of seemliness are apparently universal; and the nonobservance of these rules, or anecdotes which involve the breaking of the rules, provoke that peculiar type of laughter which seems identical the world over; however little one may know about a strange society, however little one may know about the functions of laughter in that society (and these can be very various), one can immediately tell when people are laughing at an obscene joke. The topper of the joke may be "And then he ate the whole meal in front of them!" or "She used her husband's name in the presence of his mother!" but the laughter is the same; the taboos of seemliness have been broken and the result is hilarious. Typically, such laughter is confined to one sex group and is more general with the young, just entering into the complexities of adult life.

Obscenity then is a universal, an aspect of man and woman living in society; everywhere and at all times there are words and actions which, when misplaced, can produce shock, social embarrassment, and laughter. Pornography, on the other hand—the description of tabooed activities to produce hallucination or delusion—seems to be a very much rarer phenomenon. It probably can arise only in literate societies, and we certainly have no records of it for nonliterate ones; for whereas the enjoyment of obscenity is predominantly social, the enjoyment of pornography is predominantly private. The fantasies from which pornography derives could, of course, be generated in any society; but it seems doubtful whether they would ever be communicated without the intermediary of literacy....

Traditionally, and in the lexicographic meaning of the term, pornography has been concerned with sexuality. For the greater part of the last two hundred years copulation and (at least in the mid-Victorian decades) birth were the "unmentionables" of the triad of basic human experiences which "are all the facts when you come to brass tacks," around which so much private fantasy and semiclandestine pornography were erected. During most of this period death was no mystery, except in the sense that death is always a mystery. Children were encouraged to think about death, their own deaths and the edifying or cautionary deathbeds of others. It must have been a rare individual who, in the nineteenth century with its high mortality, had not witnessed at least one actual dying, as well as paid his respects to "beautiful corpses"; funerals were the occasion for the greatest display, for working class, middle class, and aristocrat. The cemetery was the center of every old-established village, and they were prominent in most towns. It was fairly late in the nineteenth century before the execution of criminals ceased to be a public holiday as well as a public warning....

In the twentieth century, however, there seems to have been an unremarked shift in prudery; whereas copulation has become more and more "mentionable," particularly in Anglo-Saxon societies, death has become more and more "unmentionable" *as a natural process*. I cannot recollect a novel or play of the last twenty years or so which has a "death-

---

TELEVISION WAS A BABY CRAWLING TOWARD THAT DEATH CHAMBER

... Six thousand movietheaters, 100,000,000 television sets, a billion radios, wires and wireless criscrossing hemispheres, semaphore lights and morse, all telephones ringing at once to connect every mind by its ears to one vast consciousness at This Time's Apocalpyse ...

Allen Ginsberg

bed scene" that describes in any detail the death "from natural causes" of a major character; this topic was a set piece for most of the eminent Victorian and Edwardian writers, evoking their finest prose and their most elaborate technical effects to produce the greatest amount of pathos or edification.

One of the reasons, I imagine, for this plethora of deathbed scenes—apart from their intrinsic emotional and religious content—was that it was one of the relatively few experiences that an author could be fairly sure would have been shared by the vast majority of his readers. Questioning my old acquaintances, I cannot find one over the age of sixty who did not witness the last agony of at least one near relative; I do not think I know a single person under the age of thirty who has had a similar experience. Of course, my acquaintance is neither very extensive nor particularly representative; but in this instance I do think it is typical of the change of attitude and "exposure."

The natural process of corruption and decay has become disgusting, as disgusting as the natural processes of copulation and birth were a century ago; preoccupation with such processes is (or was) morbid and unhealthy, to be discouraged in all and punished in the young. Our great-grandparents were told that babies were found under gooseberry bushes or cabbages; our children are likely to be told that those who have passed on (fie! on the gross Anglo-Saxon monosyllable) are changed into flowers or lie at rest in lovely gardens. The ugly facts are relentlessly hidden; the art of the embalmers is an art of complete denial.

It seems possible to trace a connection between the shift of taboos and the shift in religious beliefs. In the nineteenth century most of the inhabitants of Protestant countries seem to have subscribed to the Pauline beliefs in the sinfulness of the body and the certainty of the afterlife. "So also is the resurrection of the dead. It is sown in corruption; it is raised in incorruption: It is sown in dishonor; it is raised in glory...." It was possible to insist on the corruption of the dead body, and the dishonor of its begetting, while there was a living belief in the incorruption and the glory of the immortal part. But in England, at any rate, belief in the future life as taught in Christian doctrine is very uncommon today, even in the minority who make church-going or prayer a consistent part of their lives; and without some such belief, natural death and physical decomposition have become too horrible to contemplate or to discuss. It seems symptomatic that the contemporary sect of Christian Science should deny the fact of physical death, even to the extent (so it is said) of refusing to allow the word to be printed in the *Christian Science Monitor.*

During the last half century public health measures and improved preventive medicine have made natural death among the younger members of the population much more uncommon than it was in earlier periods, so that a death in the family, save in the fullness of time, became a relatively uncommon incident in home life; and simultaneously, violent death increased in a manner unparalleled in human history. Wars and revolutions, concentration camps, and gang feuds were the most publicized of the causes for these violent deaths; but the diffusion of the automobile, with its constant and unnoticed toll of fatal accidents, may well have been most influential in bringing the possibility of violent death into the expectations of law-abiding people in time of peace. While natural death became more and more smothered in prudery, violent death has played an ever growing part in the fantasies offered to mass audiences—detective stories, thrillers, Westerns, war stories, spy stories, science fiction, and, eventually, horror comics.

There seem to be a number of parallels between the fantasies which titillate our curiosity about the mystery of sex and those which titillate our curiosity about the mystery of death. In both types of fantasy the emotions which are typically concomitant to the acts—love or grief—are paid little or no attention, while the sensations are enhanced as much as a customary poverty of language permits. If marital intercourse be considered the natural expression of sex for most of humanity most of the time, then "natural sex" plays as small a role as "natural death" (the ham-fisted attempts of D. H. Lawrence and Jules Romains to describe "natural sex" realistically but high-mindedly prove the rule). Neither type of fantasy can have any real development, for once the protagonist has done something, he or she must proceed to do something else, with or to somebody else, more refined, more complicated or more sensational. This somebody else is not a person; it is either a set of genitals, with or without secondary sexual characteristics, or a body, perhaps capable of suffering pain as well as death. Since most languages are relatively poor in words or constructs to express intense pleasure or intense pain, the written portions of both types of fantasy abound in onomatopoeic conglomerations of letters meant to evoke the sighs, gasps, groans, screams, and rattles concomitant to the described actions. Both types of fantasy rely heavily on adjectives and similes. Both types of fantasy are completely unrealistic, since they ignore all physical, social, or legal limitations; and both types have complete hallucination of the reader or viewer as their object.

There seems little question that the instinct of those censorious busybodies preoccupied with other people's morals was correct when they linked the pornography of death with the pornography of sex. This, however, seems to be their only correct deduction or attempted action. There is no valid evidence to suppose that either type of pornography is an incitement to action; rather are they substitute gratifications. The belief that such hallucinatory works would incite their readers to copy the actions depicted would seem to be indirect homage to the late Oscar Wilde, who described such a process in *The Picture of Dorian Gray;* I know of no authenticated parallels in real life, though investigators and magistrates with bees in their bonnets can usually persuade juvenile delinquents to admit to exposure to whatever medium of mass communication they are choosing to make a scapegoat.

Despite some gifted precursors, such as... Edgar Allan Poe, most works in both pornographies are aesthetically objectionable; but it is questionable whether, from the purely aesthetic point of view, there is much more to be said for the greater part of the more anodyne fare provided by contemporary mass media of communication. Psychological utopians tend to condemn substitute gratifications as such, at least where copulation is involved; they have so far been chary in dealing with death.

Nevertheless people have come to terms with the basic facts of birth, copulation, and death, and somehow accept their implications; if social prudery prevents this being done in an open and dignified fashion, then it will be done surreptitiously. If we dislike the modern pornography of death, then we must give back to death—natural death—its parade and publicity, readmit grief and mourning. If we make death unmentionable in polite society—"not before the children"—we almost insure the continuation of the "horror comic." No censorship has ever been really effective.

4.

Demography of Death

Demography is the study of the facts and figures of human populations—their composition in terms of sex ratios, age, and racial and ethnic categories, and the changes in these and other factors over time. The facts of death in a society—who dies when, of what causes, and where—are also important topics for study. By examining such facts of death, demographers can shed valuable light on the way we live.

The articles in this section examine several aspects of the demography of death. Lerner demonstrates that the average length of life has been dramatically extended. Whereas the ancient Greeks were fortunate to live into their thirties, and in our own country by the time of World War I the average life expectancy was under fifty-five years, most of us alive now can expect to live into our seventies. Women, however, tend to live longer than men, although the exact reasons for this difference have not been conclusively identified. The causes of death have also changed. Communicable diseases like influenza and tuberculosis have been largely controlled, and chronic degenerative diseases, like heart disease and cancer, have become major causes of death.

These trends have many implications for our present lifestyles. Elderly people form a considerably larger proportion of our population than ever before in history. Many of these persons are retired and live on fixed incomes from Social Security and private pensions. Moreover, they require increasing medical care as they get older. Medical care not only has the potential to keep the elderly alive longer, but it also possesses the capability of stretching out the dying process: persons who might have succumbed to a stroke can be maintained indefinitely with modern life support technology. As medical costs rise and inflation continues to erode spending power, the economic burdens on the elderly are likely to increase. Women who outlive their husbands are particularly likely to suffer from economic insufficiency. The problems faced by widows generally involve financial difficulties as well as grief and social isolation.

Most deaths in modern societies occur among the elderly. But as Blauner points out in considering the social impact of individual deaths, these people tend to be occupationally and socially disengaged from the important functions of the society. Their deaths, therefore, do not disrupt society generally. The slight social impact of their deaths is further reduced by what Blauner refers to as "the bureaucratization of death." Not only do the aged tend to live apart from the more active members of the society—they go to medical institutions to die. However, we must bear in mind that what is expedient or efficient for the society may be very difficult for the individual elderly patient, who must face death removed from familiar relationships and surrounded by strange persons and machines. Moreover, elderly Americans are vigorously resisting their disengagement from our society and lobbying to end mandatory retirement, to improve their housing, and to increase retirement benefits and health coverage. If such groups as the Gray Panthers and the American Association of Retired Persons are successful in obtaining their expressed goals, we may witness yet more major changes in the ways we both live and die.

Goldscheider's article on "The Social Inequality of Death" reminds us that just as people do not have equal standards of living or incomes, neither does death confront us on an egalitarian basis. Quite simply, poorer people tend to die younger than people of greater means. Mortality rates tend to go up as income level goes down. Furthermore, people with greater income have better health and greater access to health care than poorer people. As the costs of health care continue to skyrocket, one may well see such differences increase unless, of course, changes are made in lifestyles, the distribution of income in the society, and/or the delivery of health care to the population.

As for man, his days are like grass;
　　he flourishes like a flower of the field;
for the wind passes over it, and it is gone,
　　and its place knows it no more.
But the steadfast love of the Lord is from
　　everlasting to everlasting upon those
　　who fear him, and his righteousness to children's children,
to those who keep his covenant
　　and remember to do his commandments.

Psalm 103

When, Why, and Where People Die

This selection by Monroe Lerner, an authority on both demography and health care at Johns Hopkins University, presents some important facts of death in our society that have significant implications for our lifestyles. Longer lives, lower death rates for women than men, and changing causes of death are reflected in a burgeoning elderly population in our country composed largely of widows who are increasingly dependent on medical care as they get older. Rising costs of health care and intractable inflation aggravate the financial difficulties of our elderly citizens, while outmoded stereotypes of the aged in a youth-oriented society create social isolation.

Perhaps one of man's greatest achievements in his endless quest to extend the limits of his control over nature has been his success in increasing the average duration of his lifetime. This success has been particularly substantial in the modern era, beginning with the mid-seventeenth century, and during the second third of the twentieth century it extended even to the far corners of the globe. During this period, and possibly for the first time in human history, the lifetimes of a substantial proportion of the world's population have been extended well beyond even the economically productive years, so that most people can now reasonably expect to survive at least into their retirement period.

The ability to do this has always been highly valued, at least as an ideal, and perhaps especially in those societies able at best to struggle along only at the subsistence margin and with almost no economic surplus to support life during the barren years. But even in other circumstances, more than one conception of the "good society" has had a component notion that survival beyond the productive years could be within the realm of possibility for all. Nevertheless, only in the technologically advanced Western nations of today does the *average* duration of life reach, and even in some instances exceed, the famous Biblical standard of threescore and ten. If the average duration of life—life expectancy, to use the technical term of statisticians and actuaries—is conceived of as an important indicator of man's control over nature and at the same time also as a crucial element in the moral evaluation of society, then surely man's difficult journey down the long paths of history may be described as social progress rather than merely as evolution.

In any case, whether progress or evolution, man certainly has extended his average lifetime. This [selection] first traces that process, as much as it is possible to do so from the inadequate historical data, and only in the most general terms, from prehistory down to the present situation in the United States. Life expectancy, however, is in one sense simply a refined measure of mortality, and for some purposes it is more useful to deal with mortality rates rather than with life expectancy. Mortality, then, becomes the focus of the remainder of the present discussion.

Later, mortality trends in the United States are traced from 1900 to the present, for the total population and separately by age and sex. Young people—infants, children, and young adults—and females at all ages have clearly been the chief beneficiaries of this process, although other segments of the population have also gained substantially. The major communicable diseases—tuberculosis, influenza and pneumonia, gastritis and duodenitis, the communicable diseases of childhood, and so on—have declined as leading causes of death, to be replaced by the "degenerative" diseases, that is, diseases associated with the aging process—heart disease, cancer, and stroke—and by accidental injury.

Populations may be perceived not only as consisting of sex and age groups, but also as individuals and families ranged along a multidimensional, socioeconomic continuum. The problem then becomes: How do people at various points or in various sections of this continuum fare with regard to mortality risk or, in a more literal meaning of the term than was intended by the German sociologist Max Weber who coined it, what are their life-chances?

Perhaps the most meaningful way of dealing with this question, if the objective is to identify large groups or strata in the population who actually do experience gross or at least identifiable differences in mortality risk, is to assume the existence of three major socioeconomic strata in this country, each characterized by a distinctive and unique life-style—the white-collar middle class, the blue-collar working class, and the poverty population. Various structural factors in the life-styles of

these populations are conducive to different outcomes in mortality risk. In general, the poverty population experiences relatively high mortality rates at the younger ages and from the communicable diseases, while the white-collar middle class, especially its male members, experiences relatively high mortality rates at mid-life and in the older ages, from the "degenerative" diseases. The blue-collar working class, to the extent that it avoids both types of disabilities, appears for the moment at least to be experiencing the lowest mortality rates among the three strata.

Finally, the place where death occurs—that is, in an institution, at home, or elsewhere—has long been a neglected area of mortality statistics. From national data..., it seems clear that the proportion of all deaths in this country occurring in institutions has been rising steadily, at least for the last two decades and probably for much longer than that. It may now be as high as, or higher than, two-thirds of all deaths. Almost 50 percent of all deaths occurring outside an institution in 1958 were due to heart disease, and especially to the major component of this cause-of-death category, arteriosclerotic heart disease, including coronary disease, which accounted for 37 percent of the total. Cancer, stroke, and accidents comprised the remaining major components of the total, accounting for another 30 percent of the out-of-institution deaths.

HISTORY AND THE DURATION OF HUMAN LIFE

Scholars can only estimate, in the absence of direct data, what the average duration of life must have been during prehistory. Such estimates have been made, however, and they appear to be roughly consistent with the fragmentary data available from the few surviving contemporary primitive groups, in Africa and elsewhere, whose conditions of life resemble those of our remote ancestors at least in some of their major relevant aspects. Prehistoric man lived, according to these estimates, on the average about eighteen years; life during prehistory was, in the Hobbesian sense, indeed nasty, short, and brutish. Violence was the usual cause of death, at least judging from the many skulls found with marks of blows, and man's major preoccupation was clearly with satisfying his elemental need for survival in the face of a hostile environment including wild beasts and other men perhaps just as wild. Survivorship in those days was very seldom beyond the age of forty. Persons who reached their mid-twenties and more rarely their early thirties were *ipso facto* considered to have demonstrated their wisdom and were, as a result, often treated as sages.

With the rise of the early civilizations and the consequent improvements in living conditions, longevity must surely have risen, reaching perhaps 20 years in ancient Greece and perhaps 22 in ancient Rome. Life expectancy is estimated to have been about 33 years in England during the Middle Ages, about 35 in the Massachusetts Bay Colony of North America, about 41 in England and Wales during the nineteenth century, and 47.3 in the death-registration states of the United States in 1900.[1] Thus a definite upward progression in life expectancy has been evident in the Western world throughout its history, and this progression is, furthermore, one in which the pace has clearly accelerated with the passage of time.

1. All life expectancy and mortality figures presented in this chapter pertaining to the U.S. in 1900 or subsequent years, unless otherwise specified, are based on various published reports of the National Vital Statistics Division of the National Center for Health Statistics (formerly the National Office of Vital Statistics), U.S. Public Health Service.

The upward progression has continued during the twentieth century and, at least in the United States, its rate of increase has accelerated even further. Thus, life expectancy continued to rise in this country after 1900, even if somewhat erratically; by 1915 it had reached a temporary peak at 54.5 years. The 1918 influenza epidemic caused a sharp drop in life expectancy, to just below 40 years, a level probably typical of "normal" conditions in the United States during the first half of the nineteenth century. But thereafter the upward trend in life expectancy resumed and, between 1937 and 1945 and following the development of the sulfa drugs and the introduction of penicillin during World War II, its increase was extraordinarily rapid. From 1946 to 1954, however, although life expectancy in this country continued upward, the *rate* of increase tapered off. And from 1954, when life expectancy was 69.6 years, to 1967[2] when it had reached only to 70.2, the gain was at a snail's pace compared to what it had been during the earlier period.

In broader perspective, that is, during the first two-thirds of the twentieth century that we have now experienced, life expectancy rose by almost twenty-three years, an average annual gain of about one-third of a year. This is a breathtaking pace compared to any period of human history prior to this century, and it clearly could not be sustained over a long period of time without enormous social disruption. In line with this, however, life expectancy in the country may now have reached a plateau at, or just above, seventy years.

Where does the United States stand in life expectancy compared with other nations, and

2. All 1966 and 1977 figures shown in this [selection] are provisional. Based on past experience, however, the provisional rates are likely to be identical, or nearly so, to the final rates.

what can we anticipate as the reasonable upper limit, or goal, that this country *should* be able to attain in the present state of the arts? Although international comparisons of this type appear to be a hazardous undertaking, in large part because of the substantial obstacles to comparability, a number of other nations clearly have higher life expectancies than we do, and at least in some instances the differences are fairly substantial. Even cursory observation of a recent international compendium of demographic statistics (United Nations, 1967) reveals, for example, that in Australia, Denmark, The Netherlands, New Zealand, Norway, and Sweden life expectancy may be as much as two to three years higher than the comparable figure in the United States. Countries such as Belgium, France, East Germany, the Federal Republic of Germany, Switzerland, England and Wales, and many others, also exceed us in life expectancy, but not by so wide a margin.

Surely this country should at least be able to reach the level of those listed above, if not to exceed them. It is possible that these countries may be nearing an upper limit, however, one that may persist unless some major medical breakthrough occurs. Returning to our own country, future projections of life expectancy and mortality made prior to 1954 now appear to have been much too conservative; on the other hand, those made subsequent to 1954 were clearly too optimistic. [James] Tarver (1959), for example, projected a life expectancy of about 73.5 years in 1970, but it now appears that we may be a long time in reaching this goal.

Life expectancy by definition is equivalent to the average duration of life. But how are the numbers obtained for this measure? Starting with a hypothetical cohort of one hundred thousand persons at birth, the mortality rates by age and by sex of a given population in a given year are applied to this cohort as it ages and moves through its life cycle, reducing it in number until no survivors of the original cohort remain. The number of years lived by the *average* person in this cohort is termed the given population's life expectancy. Clearly then, the life-expectancy figure thus obtained is simply the inverse of mortality experience; it depends entirely upon age-and-sex-specific mortality rates. Employment of the measure "life expectancy" as an indicator of the mortality experience of a population is useful for comparison purposes both currently and across time. This is especially true because this measure eliminates the disturbing influence on the mortality rate of variation in the age-and-sex composition of populations. It is precisely because of this characteristic that life expectancy was used in the preceding discussion to make comparisons across the long span of history. For discussion of the immediate past and current situations, however, it is perhaps best to shift the locus of the discussion from life expectancy to mortality.

MORTALITY IN THE UNITED STATES, 1900 TO 1967: *Trends and Differentials, Overall and by Age and Sex*   Paralleling inversely the increase in life expectancy from 1900 to the present, the mortality rate (deaths per 1,000 population) of the United States population has declined sharply during this century. Thus in 1900 the mortality rate was 17.2 per 1,000 population, but by 1954 it had dropped to 9.2 per 1,000, the lowest ever recorded in the United States. Since that time it has fluctuated between 9.3 and 9.6, and in 1967 the rate was 9.4, representing a decline of about 45 percent since 1900. These figures understate the extent of the "true" decline, however, primarily because the age composition of the United States population has

changed drastically since 1900. This change has generally been in the direction of increasing the high-mortality-risk age segments of the population as a proportion of the total and at the expense of the low. With age composition held constant, that is, using the 1940 age composition of the United States population as a standard, the hypothetical "age-adjusted" death rate in this country declined between 1900 and 1967 from 17.8 to 7.2 per 1,000, a drop of about 60 percent.

AGE AND SEX   The pattern of mortality rates by age in this country during 1900 was generally similar to that prevailing today (see Table 1). Thus in 1900 the mortality rate was high during infancy, 162.4 per 1,000, in comparison to the rates at other ages; it dropped to the lowest point for the entire life cycle, 3.9, at ages 5–14; but thereafter it rose steadily with increasing age until at ages 85 and over the

TABLE 1   Mortality Rates per 1,000 Population by Age and Sex, United States, 1900 and 1966

Age (in years)	1900			1966		
	Both sexes	Males	Females	Both sexes	Males	Females
All ages	17.2	17.9	16.5	9.5	11.0	8.1
Under 1	162.4	179.1	145.4	23.1	25.7	20.4
1–4	19.8	20.5	19.1	1.0	1.0	0.9
5–14	3.9	3.8	3.9	0.4	0.5	0.4
15–24	5.9	5.9	5.8	1.2	1.7	0.6
25–34	8.2	8.2	8.2	1.5	2.0	1.0
35–44	10.2	10.7	9.8	3.1	3.9	2.3
45–54	15.0	15.7	14.2	7.3	9.7	5.1
55–64	27.2	28.7	25.8	17.2	23.6	11.2
65–74	56.4	59.3	53.6	38.8	52.0	28.1
75–84	123.3	128.3	118.8	81.6	98.5	69.5
85 +	260.9	268.8	255.2	202.0	213.6	194.9

mortality rate was 260.9 per 1,000 population. In 1966 the comparable rate was only 23.1 per 1,000 during infancy; the low point was 0.4 at ages 5-14; and again the rates rose steadily with increasing age, to 202 per 1,000 at ages 85 and over. Between 1900 and 1966 the largest *relative* declines in the mortality rates took place at the younger ages, especially during infancy and childhood. Although the declines at the older ages are less impressive percentages, they are, nevertheless, very substantial in absolute numbers. For example, at ages 85 and over the mortality rate dropped by about 59 deaths per 1,000 population, that is, from 261 to 202 per 1,000.

Although the mortality rates for both males and females in the United States population declined substantially since 1900, the *rate* of decline was much sharper for females. Thus the mortality rate for females dropped from 16.5 in 1900 to 8.1 in 1966, a decline of 51 percent. For males the corresponding drop was from 17.9 to 11.0, or by 39 percent. The male death rate has been significantly higher than the female death rate in this country throughout the twentieth century, but the relative excess of male over female rates has increased over the years, from 8.5 percent in 1900 to 36 percent in 1966. When these rates are age-adjusted to a standard population, the excess of male over female rates in 1966 is considerably larger, about 70 percent.

In 1900, the relative excess of male over female mortality rates by age was largest during infancy, at 23 percent. At ages 5-14, the mortality rates for males were actually slightly lower than the comparable rates for females; at ages 15-34, rates were about the same for each sex; and in each of the age groups at 35 and over, the mortality rates for males exceeded the comparable rates for females only by a relatively slight amount, that is, by from 5 to 11 percent. By 1966, however, although the mortality rates at each age were lower for each sex than the comparable rates in 1900, the decline in almost all cases was larger for females. As a result, the percentage excess of male mortality rates over female rates was larger in most age groups during 1966 than it had been during 1900. It was largest (an excess of almost 200 percent in 1966), at ages 15-24.

MORTALITY IN THE UNITED STATES, 1900 TO 1967: *Trends and Differentials by Cause of Death*

One of the most significant changes in the mortality experience of this country since 1900 has been the decline in the major communicable diseases as leading causes of death and the consequent increase *in relative importance* of the so-called chronic degenerative diseases, that is, diseases occurring mainly later in life and generally thought to be associated in some way with the aging process. Accidents, especially motor vehicle accidents, have also risen in relative importance as causes of death during this period, but mortality during infancy and maternal mortality, that is, mortality associated with childbearing, have declined sharply.

THE COMMUNICABLE DISEASES. The leading cause of death in 1900 was the category: "influenza and pneumonia, except pneumonia of the newborn." This major communicable disease category was listed as the cause of 202.2 deaths per 100,000 population in 1900 (see Table 2), and it accounted for 11.8 percent of all deaths in that year. By 1966, however, the mortality rate for this category was down to 32.8, it ranked fifth among the leading causes of death, and it now accounted for only 3.4 percent of all deaths during the year.

Tuberculosis (all forms) and the gastritis

grouping, second and third leading causes of death, respectively, in 1900, were both reduced so significantly and to such low rates during the course of this century that neither category was listed among the ten leading causes of death in 1966. Tuberculosis had caused 194.4 deaths per 100,000 in 1900, or 11.3 percent of all deaths, while the gastritis grouping, with 142.7 deaths per 100,000, had accounted for 8.3 percent of the total. By 1966

the comparable rates for these two categories were 3.9 and 3.3, respectively, with each accounting for substantially less than one-half of 1 percent of all deaths in that year. The percentage declines for each from 1900 to 1966 were by 98 percent.

Diphtheria had been listed as tenth leading cause of death in 1900, with 40.3 deaths per 100,000 population. In 1966 this condition accounted for only forty deaths all told in this

TABLE 2   The Ten Leading Causes of Death, by Rank, United States, 1900 and 1966

Rank	Cause of death	Deaths per 100,000 population	Percent of all deaths
1900	All causes	1,719.1	100.0%
1	Influenza and pneumonia	202.2	11.8
2	Tuberculosis (all forms)	194.4	11.3
3	Gastritis, duodenitis, enteritis, etc.	142.7	8.3
4	Diseases of the heart	137.4	8.0
5	Vascular lesions affecting the central nervous system	106.9	6.2
6	Chronic nephritis	81.0	4.7
7	All accidents	72.3	4.2
8	Malignant neoplasms (cancer)	64.0	3.7
9	Certain diseases of early infancy	62.6	3.6
10	Diphtheria	40.3	2.3
1966	All causes	954.2	100.0%
1	Diseases of the heart	375.1	39.3
2	Malignant neoplasms (cancer)	154.8	16.2
3	Vascular lesions affecting the central nervous system	104.6	11.0
4	All accidents	57.3	6.0
5	Influenza and pneumonia	32.8	3.4
6	Certain diseases of early infancy	26.1	2.7
7	General arteriosclerosis	19.5	2.0
8	Diabetes mellitus	18.1	1.9
9	Cirrhosis of the liver	13.5	1.4
10	Suicide	10.3	1.1

country, that is, considering the entire United States population as at risk, so that the death rate was about one death per five million persons. Other major communicable diseases with impressive declines in mortality were some of the other communicable diseases of childhood, such as whooping cough, measles, scarlet fever, and streptococcal sore throat, and syphilis, typhoid and paratyphoid fevers, rheumatic fever, and typhus.

[George A.] Hillery *et al.* (1968), comparing recent mortality data from forty-one countries, have shown that the communicable diseases ("infectious diseases" in their terminology) as causes of death decline significantly as a proportion of all deaths in each country as these countries move "up" in the demographic transition, that is, as their birth and death rates decline, and as they concomitantly become at least presumably more "advanced" technologically and socially. Thus, in the "transitional" countries (low death rates but high birth rates), communicable diseases account for about one-third of all deaths on the average, while in the demographically "mature" countries (both death rates and birth rates low), the comparable proportion is about one in twelve of all deaths. This finding is generally in conformity with past experience in this country and elsewhere.

THE DEGENERATIVE DISEASES "Diseases of the heart" ranked fourth among the leading causes of death in this country during 1900; this category caused 137.4 deaths per 100,000 and accounted for 8.0 percent of all deaths. By 1966, however, it had risen so far in importance that it had become the leading cause of death, far outranking all others. Its mortality rate had risen to 375.1 deaths per 100,000 population, and it accounted for nearly 40 percent of all deaths in that year. Between 1900 and 1966 the unadjusted death rate from this disease rose by 173 percent; the rise was much less if the age-adjusted rates for these two years are compared, but even this rise was very substantial.

The pattern of increase for malignant neoplasms (cancer) as a cause of death was generally quite similar. This disease ranked eighth among the leading causes of death in 1900. It accounted for 64 deaths per 100,000 population and less than 4 percent of all deaths. By 1966, however, its rank among the leading causes had risen to second, its rate per 100,000 to 154.8, and its proportion of the total of all deaths exceeded 16 percent. Vascular lesions of the central nervous system, although remaining relatively stable in number of deaths per 100,000 (106.9 in 1900 and 104.6 in 1966), nevertheless rose in rank (fifth to third) and as a proportion of all deaths (6 to 11 percent).

How can we account for the increases, in both absolute and relative terms, in these "degenerative" diseases as causes of death? As the classification implies, these are diseases occurring later in life and closely associated with the aging process. Whereas formerly people died on the average much earlier in life, victims primarily of the communicable diseases, they survive today to a much later age, only to succumb in due time to the degenerative conditions. Hillery and his associates (1968) in their interesting study have generalized this trend also. Thus in their demographically transitional countries (low death rates but high birth rates) the degenerative diseases account for less than one-third of all deaths, whereas in their demographically mature countries (both death rates and birth rates low) these diseases account for just under two-thirds of the total. The net overall gain has clearly been an extension of life by many years.

Robert Blauner

Death and Social Structure

The effect upon the society of the deaths of individual members is analyzed in this selection by Robert Blauner, a prominent American sociologist. In complex and populous modern societies, the death of an individual—typically an elderly person disengaged from an active role in his or her community— generally causes negligible disruption in the ongoing equilibrium of the society. Moreover, the bureaucratization of death and dying further reduces any possible disturbance in the social system. However, what may be functional for the society as a whole may have dysfunctional consequences for individual members as they face their own deaths or the loss of others. Blauner observes that segregation of the dying in medical institutions, deritualization of funerals, and attenuation of mourning customs may generate problems of adjustment on the individual and family level, at the same time as they facilitate the smooth, uninterrupted operation of society.

Mortality and its impact are not constants. In general, the demographic structure of preindustrial societies results in an exposure to death that appears enormous by the standards of modern Western life. [The anthropologist Branislaw] Malinowski, writing of the Trobriand Islanders and other natives of Eastern New Guinea, states that "death . . . causes a great and permanent disturbance in the equilibrium of tribal life." The great impact of mortality and the vividness of death as a theme in life emerge clearly from [Jack] Goody's account of the LoDagaa of West Africa. Jules Henry's study of the Kaingang "jungle people" of the Brazil highlands depicts a tribe whose members are in daily contact with death and greatly obsessed with it. Kingsley Davis speculates that many characteristics of Indian life, such as the high birth rate, the stress on kinship and joint households, and the religious emphasis, may be attributed to the nearness to death that follows from the conditions of that subcontinent. The relatively small scale of communities in most preindustrial societies compounds death's impact. Its regular occurrence— especially through the not infrequent catastrophes of war, famine, and epidemics— involves more serious losses to a society of small scale, a point that has been made forcibly by Krzywicki:

Let us take, for instance, one of the average Australian tribes (usually numbering 300–600 members). The simultaneous loss of ten persons is there an event which quantitatively considered, would have the same significance as the simultaneous death of from 630,000 to 850,000 inhabitants in the present Polish state. And such catastrophes, diminishing an Australian tribe by some ten persons, might, of course, occur not infrequently. An unfortunate war expedition, a victorious night attack by an enemy, a sudden flood, or any of a host of other events might easily cause the death of such a number of tribesmen; in addition, there were famines, such as that which forced the Birria, for instance, to devour all their children, or the epidemics which probably occurred from time to time even in primitive communities. And, what is most important, conditions of primitive life sometimes created such situations that there was a simultaneous loss of about a dozen or a score of persons of the same sex and approximately the same age. Then such a misfortune affecting a community assumed the dimensions of a tribal disaster.[1]

This is not to suggest that a continuous encounter with mortality is equally prevalent in all preindustrial societies. Variations among primitive and peasant societies are as impressive as common patterns; I simply want to make the point that *many* nonmodern societies must organize themselves around death's recurrent presence. Modern societies, on the other hand, have largely succeeded in containing mortality and its social disruptiveness. Yet the impact of mortality on a society is not a simple matter of such demographic considerations as death rates and the size of the group. Also central is the manner in which a society is organized, the way it manages the death crisis, and how its death practices and mortuary institutions are linked to the social structure.

LIFE EXPECTANCY, ENGAGEMENT, AND THE SOCIAL RELEVANCE OF THE DEAD   Death disrupts the dynamic equilibrium of social life because a number of its actual or potential consequences create problems for a society. One of these potential consequences is a social vacuum. A member of

1. Ludwik Krzywicki: *Primitive Society and Its Vital Statistics.* London: Macmillan, 1934, p. 292. The very scale of modern societies is thus an important element of their control of mortality; unlike the situation in a remote village of India or the jungle highlands of Brazil, it would require the ultimate in catastrophic mortality, all-out nuclear war, for death to threaten societal survival.

society and its constituent groups and relationships is lost, and some kind of gap in institutional functioning results. The extent of this vacuum depends upon how deeply engaged the deceased has been in the life of the society and its groups. The system is more disrupted by the death of a leader than by that of a common man; families and work groups are typically more affected by the loss of those in middle years than by the death of children or old people. Thus a key determinant of the impact of mortality is the age and social situation of those who die, since death will be more disruptive when it frequently strikes those who are most relevant for the functional activities and the moral outlook of the social order.

In modern Western societies, mortality statistics are more and more made up of the very old. The causes are obvious: The virtual elimination of infant and child mortality and the increasing control over the diseases of youth and middle life. Almost one million American males died in 1960. Eight percent were younger than fifteen years. Fifty-five percent were sixty-five or older (29 percent were past seventy-five), and another 18 percent were between fifty-five and sixty-four. The middle years, between fifteen and fifty-four, claimed the remaining 19 percent of the deaths. As death in modern society becomes increasingly a phenomenon of the old, who are usually retired from work and finished with their parental responsibilities, mortality in modern society rarely interrupts the business of life. Death is uncommon during the highly engaged middle years, and the elderly are more and more segregated into communities and institutions for their age group.

Although accurate vital statistics for contemporary preindustrial societies are rare, the available data indicate that the primary concentration of death is at the opposite end of the life span, in the years of infancy and childhood. For example, among the Sakai of the Malay Peninsula, approximately 50 percent of the babies born die before the age of three; among the Kurnai tribe of Australia 40 to 50 percent die before the age of ten. Fifty-nine percent of the 1956 male deaths in Nigeria among the "indigenous" blacks were children who had not reached their fifth birthday. Thirty-five percent of an Indian male cohort born in the 1940s died before the age of ten. The same concentration of mortality in the early years was apparently also true of historical preindustrial societies.

Aside from this high infant and child mortality, there is no common pattern in the age composition of death in preindustrial societies. In some, there appears to be a secondary concentration in old age, suggesting that when mortality in the early years is very high, the majority of those who survive may be hardy enough to withstand the perils of middle life and reach old age. . . .

In other societies and historical periods, conditions are such that mortality remains heavy in the middle years, and few people reach the end of a normal life span. Thus calculations of age at death taken from gravestones erected during the early Roman empire (this method is notoriously unreliable, but the figures are suggestive) typically find that 30 to 40 percent of the deceased were in their twenties and thirties; the proportion who died past the age of fifty was only about 20 percent. The life table of the primitive Cocos also illustrates this pattern. Only 16 percent of the deaths are in the old-age group (past fifty-five years), since mortality continues high for that minority of the population that survives childhood. The contrast in death frequency during the middle years is suggested by the data shown in Table 1 on mortality rates for specific age periods for four countries.

The demographic pattern where mortality is high in the middle years probably results in the most disruption of ongoing life. Procedures for the reallocation of the socially necessary roles, rights, and responsibilities of the deceased must be institutionalized. This is most essential when the roles and responsibilities are deemed important and when there is a tight integration of the society's groups and institutions. Such is the situation among the LoDagaa of West Africa, where many men die who are young and middle-aged. Since the

TABLE 1   Number of Deaths During Specified Year of Age per 1,000 Males Alive at Beginning of Age Period

Country	Age				
	20–25	25–30	30–35	35–40	40–45
Congo, 1950–1952	54	49	68	82	98
Mexico, 1940	46	53	62	71	84
United States, 1959	9	9	10	14	23
Canada, 1950–1952	2	2	2	2	3

From United Nations: *Demographic Yearbook,* 13th edition. New York: Department of Economic and Social Affairs, 1961, p. 360. Decimals have been rounded off to the nearest integer.

kinship structure is highly elaborated, these deaths implicate the whole community, particularly the kinship group of the bereaved spouses. The future rights to these now unattached women, still sexually active and capable of childbearing, emerge as an issue that must be worked out in the funeral ceremonies through a transfer to new husbands. In contrast, in modern Western societies, the death of a husband typically involves only the fragmented conjugal family; from the point of view of the social order as a whole, it makes little difference whether a widow replaces her deceased husband, because of the loose integration of the nuclear family into wider kinship, economic, and political spheres.

Another way of containing the impact of mortality is to reduce the real or ideal importance of those who die. Primitive societies, hard hit by infant and child mortality, characteristically do not recognize infants and children as people; until a certain age they are considered as still belonging to the spirit world from which they came. Therefore, their death is often not accorded ritual recognition—no funeral is held. Ariès has noted that French children were neither valued nor recognized in terms of their individuality during the long period of high infant mortality:

> No one thought of keeping a picture of a child if that child had . . . died in infancy . . . it was thought that the little thing which had disappeared so soon in life was not worthy of remembrance.... Nobody thought, as we ordinarily think today, that every child already contained a man's personality. Too many of them died.

One of the consequences of the devaluation of the old in modern society is the minimization of the disruption and moral shock death ordinarily brings about. . . .

BUREAUCRATIZATION OF MODERN DEATH CONTROL ...Modern societies control death through bureaucratization, our characteristic form of social structure. Max Weber has described how bureaucratization in the West proceeded by removing social functions from the family and the household and implanting them in specialized institutions autonomous of kinship considerations. Early manufacturing and entrepreneurship took place in or close to the home; modern industry and corporate bureaucracies are based on the separation of the workplace from the household. Similarly, only a few generations ago most people in the United States either died at home, or were brought into the home if they had died elsewhere. It was the responsibility of the family to lay out the corpse—that is, to prepare the body for the funeral. Today, of course, the hospital cares for the terminally ill and manages the crisis of dying; the mortuary industry (whose establishments are usually called "homes" in deference to past tradition) prepares the body for burial and makes many of the funeral arrangements. A study in Philadelphia found that about 90 percent of funerals started out from the funeral parlor, rather than from the home, as was customary in the past. This separation of the handling of illness and death from the family minimizes the average person's exposure to death and its disruption of the social process. When the dying are segregated among specialists for whom contact with death has become routine and even somewhat impersonal, neither their presence while alive nor as corpses interferes greatly with the mainstream of life.

Another principle of bureaucracy is the ordering of regularly occurring, as well as extraordinary, events into predictable and routinized procedures. In addition to treating the ill and isolating them from the rest of society, the modern hospital as an organization is committed to the routinization of the handling of death. Its distinctive competence is to contain through isolation and reduce through orderly procedures the disturbance and disruption that are associated with the death crisis. The decline in the authority of religion, as well as shifts in the functions of the family, underlies this fact. With the growth of the secular and rational outlook, hegemony in the affairs of death has been transferred from the church to science and its representatives—the medical profession and the rationally organized hospital.

Death in the modern hospital has been the subject of two sociological studies: Sudnow has focused on the handling of death and the dead in a county hospital catering to charity patients; Glaser and Strauss have concentrated on the dying situation in a number of hospitals of varying status.[2] The county hospital well illustrates various trends in modern death. Three-quarters of its patients are over sixty years old. Of the two hundred and fifty deaths Sudnow observed, only a handful involved people younger than forty. This hospital is a setting for the concentration of death. There are one thousand deaths a year; thus approximately three die daily, of the three hundred and thirty patients typically in residence. But death is even more concentrated in the four wards of the critically ill; here roughly 75 percent of all mortality occurs, and one in twenty-five persons will die each day.

Hospitals are organized to hide the facts of dying and death from patients as well as from visitors. Sudnow quotes a major text in hospital administration: "The hospital morgue is best located on the ground floor and placed in an area inaccessible to the general public. It is important that the unit have a suitable exit leading onto a private loading platform which is concealed from hospital patients and the public." Personnel in the high-mortality wards use a number of techniques to render death invisible. To protect relatives, bodies are not to be removed during visiting hours. To protect other inmates, the patient is moved to a private room when the end is foreseen. But some deaths are unexpected and may be noticed by roommates before the hospital staff is aware of them. These are considered troublesome because elaborate procedures are required to remove the corpse without offending the living.

The rationalization of death in the hospital takes place through standard procedures of covering the corpse, removing the body, identifying the deceased, informing relatives, and completing the death certificate and autopsy permit. Within the value hierarchy of the hospital, handling the corpse is "dirty work"; when possible, attendants will leave a body to be processed by the next work shift. As with so many of the unpleasant jobs in our society, hospital morgue attendants and orderlies are

2. David N. Sudnow, "Passing On: The Social Organization of Dying in the County Hospital," unpublished Ph.D. thesis, University of California, Berkeley, 1965. Barney G. Glaser and Anselm L. Strauss, *Awareness of Dying* (Chicago, 1965).

often Negroes. Personnel become routinized to death and are easily able to pass from mention of the daily toll to other topics; new staff members stop counting after the first half-dozen deaths witnessed.

Standard operating procedures have even routinized the most charismatic and personal of relations, that between the priest and the dying patient. It is not that the church neglects charity patients. The chaplain at the county hospital daily goes through a file of the critically ill for the names of all known Catholic patients, then enters their rooms and administers extreme unction. After completing his round on each ward, he stamps the index card of the patient with a rubber stamp that reads: "Last Rites Administered. Date_____ Clergyman_____." Each day he consults the files to see if new patients have been admitted or put on the critical list. As Sudnow notes, this rubber stamp prevents him from performing the rites twice on the same patient. This example highlights the trend toward the depersonalization of modern death and is certainly the antithesis of the historic Catholic notion of "the good death."

In the hospitals studied by Glaser and Strauss, depersonalization is less advanced. Fewer of the dying are comatose, and as paying patients with higher social status they are in a better position to negotiate certain aspects of their terminal situation. Yet nurses and doctors view death as an inconvenience and manage interaction so as to minimize emotional reactions and fuss. They attempt to avoid announcing unexpected deaths because relatives break down too emotionally; they prefer to let the family members know that the patient has taken "a turn for the worse," so that they will be able to modulate their response in keeping with the hospital's need for order. And drugs are sometimes ad-ministered to a dying patient to minimize the disruptiveness of his passing—even when there is no reason for this in terms of treatment or the reduction of pain.

The dying patient in the hospital is subject to the kinds of alienation experienced by persons in other situations in bureaucratic organizations. Because doctors avoid the terminally ill and nurses and relatives are rarely able to talk about death, he suffers psychic isolation. He experiences a sense of meaninglessness because he is typically kept unaware of the course of his disease and his impending fate and is not in a position to understand the medical and other routines carried out in his behalf. He is powerless in that the medical staff and the hospital organization tend to program his death in keeping with their organizational and professional needs; control over one's death seems to be even more difficult to achieve than control over one's life in our society. Thus the modern hospital, devoted to the preservation of life and the reduction of pain, tends to become a "mass reduction" system, undermining the subjecthood of its dying patients.

The rationalization of modern death control cannot be fully achieved, however, because of an inevitable tension between death—as an event, a crisis, an experience laden with great emotionality—and bureaucracy, which must deal with routines rather than events and is committed to the smoothing out of affect and emotion. Although there was almost no interaction between dying patients and the staff in the county hospital studied by Sudnow, many nurses in the other hospitals became personally involved with their patients and experienced grief when they died. Despite these limits to the general trend, our society has gone far in containing the disruptive possibilities of mortality through its bureaucratized death control.

Calvin Goldscheider

The Social Inequality of Death

Calvin Goldscheider, a demographer at Hebrew University in Jerusalem, documents the fact that the social inequality of death mirrors inequalities prevailing in the society. A long, healthy life—as the following selection indicates—is increasingly dependent upon medical care. However, as medical care grows more expensive, one may well expect the disparity between rich and poor in terms of mortality rates and health status to widen. Many of the problems of death and dying that are examined in this book are affected by the politics and economics of health care.

S OCIOECONOMIC STATUS AND MORTALITY   On April 14, 1912, the maiden voyage of the *Titanic* met with disaster. However, not all the passengers died at sea. The official casualty lists revealed that only 4 first-class female passengers (3 voluntarily chose to stay on the sinking ship) of 143 were lost; among second-class passengers, 15 of 93 females drowned; among third-class female passengers, 51 out of 179 died. The social class selectivity among females on the *Titanic*—from 3 percent to 45 percent who died—dramatically illustrates the general inequality in death associated with social class levels.

The unequal distribution of death for various social classes has been observed regularly since the turn of the twentieth century. Sir Arthur Newsholme wrote in 1910 about England that "no fact is better established than that the death rate, and especially the death rate among children, is high in inverse proportion to the social status of the population." In a review of infant mortality conditions in the United States during the first quarter of this century, Woodbury notes that low socioeconomic status, particularly low-income earnings, is the "primary cause" of excess mortality.

Let us review briefly the relationship between social class and mortality for several European countries, where data have been more accurate and more readily available for a longer period of time, and for the United States. The countries to be considered include Scotland, England and Wales, the Netherlands, Denmark, and the United States....

In Scotland, infant and fetal mortality rates for all social classes (defined by father's occupation) have declined over the last three decades, but the mortality differential between the lowest and highest social class has widened. In 1939, the fetal death rate of the lowest occupation class was one and one-quarter times as high as that of the highest occupational class grouping; in 1963, it was two and one-third times as high. Similarly, in 1939, the highest social class had a neonatal mortality rate of 30 per 1,000 live births, whereas the lowest social class had a neonatal mortality rate of 40 per 1,000 live births; in 1963, the gap widened with the highest social class having a neonatal mortality rate of 9.5, and the lowest social class a rate of 22.3. Moreover, the gap between these two class extremes was most evident in the postneonatal period, where socioeconomic environmental conditions clearly outweigh biological factors. In 1939, postneonatal deaths in the lowest occupational class were six times that of the highest occupational class, whereas in 1963, the differential more than doubled, and postneonatal death rates were more than thirteen times as great among the lowest than among the highest social classes.

Since 1911, British statistics have repeatedly shown this same inverse relationship between parental social class (father's occupation) and infant mortality. Although significant declines in infant mortality *within* each social class during the first half of the twentieth century have been reported, the relative differences *between* classes have not decreased. The gap is indeed large: mortality among infants born into families of unskilled laborers is two and one-half times that of infants born into families of professionals and rates of infant deaths among the lowest class lag thirty years behind infant death rates among the highest class. This has occurred in Britain and Scotland even when medical care is readily available to the entire population and where maternity hospital accommodations are ample. Moreover, some evidence shows that the steep mortality gradient from the highest to the lowest occupational class has widened in England and Wales, as in Scotland, precisely during the same period when the gap between the incomes of these class extremes has decreased.

The Danish evidence reveals the same pattern of considerable mortality differences from one occupation group to another. In a 1967 report, data derived in 1954–1955 show that two and one-half times as many children of "domestic workers" (lowest occupational rank) died in their first year of life when compared to the children of self-employed persons in professional services. The widening of class inequalities in life chances, particularly between the highest and lowest social classes, has also been observed for Denmark.

The Netherlands data provide an interesting confirmation of the persistence of inequality in death rates between social classes. Infant mortality in the Netherlands (15 per 1,000 live births in 1964) is one of the lowest recorded in the world (second only to Sweden) and probably one of the lowest recorded in world history. After World War II, the Netherlands became one of the Western European welfare states characterized by social security for the great masses, moderate wages increasing with the living standard, relatively little unemployment, and no real poverty. Yet, despite the fact that infant loss has reached low levels, the classic rule still prevails: unfavorable social conditions increase perinatal and postnatal mortality. Mortality is lowest in the highest social class and increases more or less progressively with decreases in social class. Data for 1961–1962 show a wide mortality range by social class in the Netherlands. Neonatal and postneonatal mortality among children with parents in the highest occupational class was about 20 percent below the averages for the country as a whole, whereas in the lowest occupational class, the mortality rates were 10 percent above the national average. The influence of father's occupation on infant mortality is unmistakable. Infant mortality in the lowest social class shows a lag of about seven years in reaching the level attained by the highest social class. The lag would be even greater if the highest income group included in the highest occupational class were compared with the lowest income group in the lowest occupational class. The decline in infant mortality has been fairly uniform for all occupational groups and, at least over the last decade, no appreciable increase in the gap between the highest and lowest class has been observed.

Most European data available on social class differences in general mortality are based on the occupation of father. For overall mortality, it is difficult to separate deaths associated with the "risks" or hazards of various occupations from deaths due to the social and economic implications of life styles associated with occupational class. But the data on infant mortality classified by the occupation of father unmistakably reflect lifestyle and social class factors. In addition, information in England on social class differentials in mortality of women classified by the occupation of their husbands show the same mortality gradient by social class. In these cases, the relationship found could only be a function of differential social and economic lifestyles indicated by occupational groupings.

Comparable data on socioeconomic class differences in mortality are unavailable for the United States. The several community, ecological studies (ranking census tracts by some measure of socioeconomic status and correlating census tract mortality measures), direct studies for New York State and California, and preliminary national estimates based on death record-census matching of 1960 have all noted the inverse relationship of social class indicators and mortality. These findings, based on various methodologies, gain in reliability not only because of the consistency of results but because of the overall similarity with the European evidence, which is based on more accurate data for a longer period of time. Several United States studies

illustrate similar findings using the three methodologies cited.

First, one of the most carefully executed ecological-correlation studies, of Providence, Rhode Island, found infant mortality to be less a sensitive indicator of socioeconomic status as it was in the past. However, when neonatal mortality was separated from postneonatal mortality, i.e., where the major causes of death are farther removed from the physiological processes of gestation and birth, the findings point clearly to an inverse relationship between postneonatal mortality and socioeconomic status.

In a 1961–1963 special study of health problems associated with poverty in New York City, sixteen poverty areas were identified by low income and high frequency of social problems. In 1961–1963, infant mortality in New York City was 26 per 1,000 live births, but in the sixteen poverty areas the rate was 35 per 1,000. The maternal mortality rate for the sixteen poverty areas was almost two and one-half times that of the rest of New York City. When health districts were grouped by housing quality in New York City, districts with poor housing had an infant mortality rate over twice that of districts with good housing and a maternal mortality rate almost four times as high.

Studies of upstate New York, for the 1950–1952 period, reaffirm the inverse relationship between level of father's occupation and infant deaths. Neonatal mortality ranged from 14 per 1,000 births among the children of professionals to 20 per 1,000 among the children of laborers; postneonatal mortality (28 days to 11 months per 1,000 survivors to 28 days among births) ranged from 3.5 to 3.7 among professionals and managers to 9.6 among nonfarm laborers.

Finally, carefully matched death and census

records (350,000) in the United States resulted in the following estimates of mortality (twenty-five years of age and older) by years of school completed and family income.

1. Among white males with no schooling, mortality was about 10 percent higher than among the college educated; among females mortality was about 50 percent higher among those with no schooling than among those with some college education. The inverse gradient characterizes both sexes and most age groups.

2. Among white males with family incomes below $2,000 a year, mortality was over 50 percent higher than among males with incomes $10,000 a year or more; among females mortality was slightly less than 50 percent greater among those with the lowest family incomes than among those with the highest family incomes.

3. A strong inverse relationship between mortality and level of educational attainment was found for the 1960 nonwhite population. Among nonwhite males, from twenty-five to sixty-four years of age, mortality was 31 percent higher for those with less than five years of schooling when compared to males with some high school or college education. Poorly educated nonwhite females from twenty-five to sixty-four years of age had mortality rates 70 percent higher than better educated nonwhite females.

Health can be measured not only by length of life but also by positive elements of good health. Information from the United States

---

THE WIDOW'S LAMENT IN SPRINGTIME

Sorrow is my own yard
where the new grass
flames as it has flamed
often before but not
with the cold fire
that closes round me this year.
Thirtyfive years
I lived with my husband.
The plumtree is white today
with masses of flowers.
Masses of flowers
load the cherry branches
and color some bushes
yellow and some red

but the grief in my heart
is stronger than they
for though they were my joy
formerly, today I notice them
and turned away forgetting.
Today my son told me
that in the meadows,
at the edge of they heavy woods
in the distance, he saw
trees of white flowers.
I feel that I would like
to go there
and fall into those flowers
and sink into the marsh near them.

William Carlos Williams

National Health Survey clearly confirms the generally accepted positive relationship between poor health and low income. People in families with a total income of less than $2,000 a year (in 1961) had twenty-nine restricted days of activities per year, per person; for those with family incomes of $2,000 to $4,000 a year, disability days dropped to eighteen, and in families with incomes of $4,000 a year and over the number was thirteen. To some extent income may be low because of greater illness just as illness may be low because of higher incomes—but it is clear that the two misfortunes exist together.

The National Health Survey in the United States further reveals that lower income persons, despite their increased level of illness and greater need for health care, receive fewer health services than people with higher incomes. Information gathered between 1963 and 1964 shows that 59 percent with family incomes below $2,000 a year consulted a physician at least once during the preceding year, compared with 66 percent of those with annual incomes between $4,000 and $7,000 a year and 73 percent of those with annual incomes of $10,000 a year. Finally, twice as many of those with higher incomes ($7,000 a year or more) avail themselves of medical specialists when compared to those with the lowest income status (below $2,000 a year).

In sum, the evidence from several European countries and the United States points consistently to the social inequality of death for members of different social strata. Some evidence, by no means universal or documented fully, also indicates an increased mortality discrepancy between the highest and lowest classes since World War II, paralleling the findings for racial mortality differentials in the United States and South Africa. Sufficient materials are not yet available to account for these increased mortality discrepancies, if they do in fact exist. Two points of conjecture are worthy of intense and rigorous testing. First, social class mobility may result in the movement out of the lower classes of persons who are healthier and more motivated to achieve a positive state of health. In the process, the lower classes, over time, may become composed of social and physical "rejects," whose mortality patterns may be consequently higher. This selective upward mobility may have increased after World War II, and, in part, may account for increased discrepancies between the lowest and higher classes. A second possibility relates to processes of urbanization and changing environmental densities since the end of World War II. The increasing urbanization of the lower classes, especially Negroes, as a result of rural-to-urban and interurban mobility, and the increasing concentration of urban residents among the poor in substandard housing and deprived social environments, may have increased mortality rates between classes and races. Although static areal measures show lower mortality rates in overall urban areas, more refined measures that subdivide urban areas into homogeneous socioeconomic sections are needed. A contributing and interrelated factor beyond the changing social-environment situation of millions of poor persons relates to the differential availability of health and medical facilities and services and, more significantly perhaps, differential motivation to utilize services when they are available. Whether these motivational elements have changed in the last decades requires careful research. These suggestions for research may illuminate the specific problem of the social inequality of death, its persistence and increase, and in the process may suggest alternative solutions for diminishing such inequalities.

5.

Death and Social Change

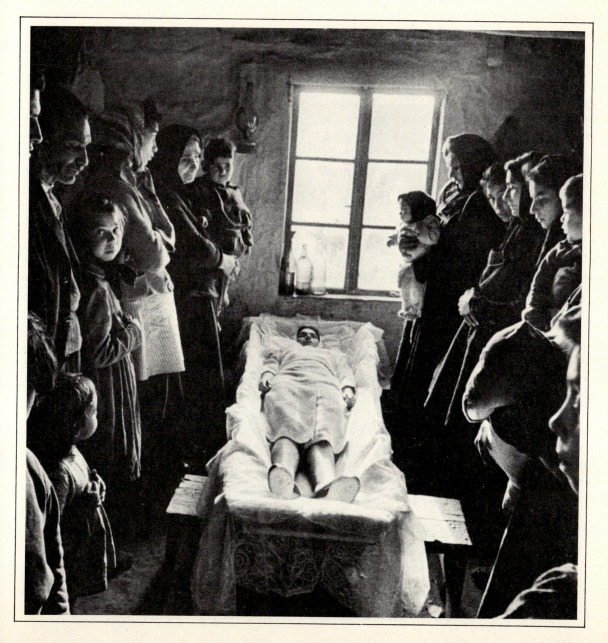

Death is certainly one of the most basic facts of life. Yet, by its very nature, death is as mysterious as it is inevitable. Since the dawn of history, human beings have endeavored to give meanings to this ultimate mystery. However, we are born with no inherent understanding of death: it becomes meaningful only as we learn the concepts, values, and practices that prevail in our society. When society undergoes profound changes, however, so do the meanings and experiences relating to death. As will be seen in this section, many of the problems surrounding death and dying in modern society reflect broad changes in the social order and cultural milieu.

Students of social change have discerned important trends that are germane to our discussion. Alvin Toffler, in *Future Shock*, argues that the rate of social change is rapidly accelerating, and speculates that people will have increasing difficulty coping with such a bewildering pace. William Ogburn noted early in the twentieth century that material and technological change tended to outpace cultural values and social practices. A frightening example is the invention of nuclear weapons, which are proliferating despite disarmament negotiations by international organizations. Similarly, the creation of machines that can maintain breathing and circulation of blood in a body after the brain has been irreversibly injured has precipitated as yet unresolved dilemmas concerning the use of such devices.

The articles in this section analyze several areas of social change in terms of their impact on death and dying. A common theme is the growing importance of science and technology and the concomitant decline in the relevance of traditional religious orientations. The invention of the scientific method and its technological application have enabled people to manipulate the environment with far greater effectiveness than was afforded by either magical incantation or religious invocation.

Science, with its focus on material and observable phenomena, has changed our thinking about death and its mysteries. Spiritual meanings have, for many, been eclipsed by a preoccupation with the biological facts of death. Rather than a gateway to an afterlife, death is seen as absolute cessation—when the brain and mind die, so does the person. Such a perspective offers little comfort for either a dying person or those who must live on in his or her absence. Hence, as we have seen, modern society exhibits an attitude of massive denial of death. Death has been removed from daily life and thought: for the present generation of young people, actual death is seldom observed, and instead, the media are replete with either fictional or distant death, both of which are, in a sense, unreal.

As death has been removed from the realm of everyday experience, it has been relocated in the province of modern medicine. As Ivan Illich points out, we have witnessed the "medicalization" of death. Death is no longer an important mystery to be fathomed, but is instead viewed as a disease to be cured. Medical doctors have replaced religious leaders. This development has been a mixed blessing. The very tools and techniques that permit us to avoid and delay death can also depersonalize our dying and make death meaningless.

As science and technology have supplanted religion as the basic orientation towards life and death, we have gained longer lives and mastery over nature. But, according to some thinkers, we have also lost much of our sense of the meaningfulness of death and its relation to life. Religious orientations provided detailed explanations of the nature and purpose of death. Generally, death was viewed as a transition from life on this earth into life in a supernatural realm. Thus, religion could comfort the dying person with the prospect of survival and the bereaved with the hope of eventual reunion. Moreover, religion furnished detailed guidance for the conduct of earthly life, in terms of both day-to-day morality and preparation for the afterlife.

One result of these changes is that dying and bereaved persons receive scant social support and spiritual solace when facing the inevitable confrontation with death. It comes as little surprise, therefore, that people today are experiencing new problems as they face a timeless experience. Grof's article in this section provides a perspective on these problems by reviewing some of the differences between non-Western orientations towards death and those prevailing in the modern Western world. Illich provides a detailed history of the medicalization of death from the fourteenth century to the present. Death, he observes, has shifted in meaning from a personal destiny with which we figuratively danced throughout our lives from the moment of birth until the day of our death, into a diagnosable disease entity to be combatted by modern medicine. Cassell amplifies these themes and concludes that technological responses cannot fully resolve moral dilemmas. Scientific medicine can increase our control over when, where, and of what we shall die, but it cannot furnish answers to the meaning of life or death.

EPITAPH

When I shall be without regret
And shall mortality forget,
When I shall die who lived for this,
I shall not miss the things I miss.
And you who notice where I lie
Ask not my name. It is not I.

J. V. Cunningham

The Changing Face of Death

Stanislav Grof, professor of medicine at the University of Maryland, examines the growing obsolescence of traditional religious orientations in modern societies that popularly deny the reality of death while relegating the dying to health care institutions. The religious belief in life after death is being replaced by the pragmatic assumption that the death of the body and the mind results in absolute and final termination. There is no place for a soul in the domain of empirical science. Hence, modern persons are simultaneously being bereft of comforting beliefs in postdeath survival and placed to die in technological societies where they are depersonalized into disease entities. In such a context, many of the problems of death and dying that will be considered in this book are more understandable. It is ironic that technological and social change has enhanced our abilities to prolong physical life while threatening the quality of our spiritual life.

Death is one of the few universal experiences of human existence. It is the most predictable event in our lives, one that is to be expected with absolute certainty. Yet the nature of death is immersed in deep mystery. Since time immemorial the fact of our mortality has stimulated human fantasy and found incredibly varied expression in the realms of religion, art, mythology, philosophy, and folklore. Many extraordinary works of architecture throughout the world have been inspired by the mystery of death: the monumental pyramids and sphinxes of Egypt and its magnificent tombs and necropolises; the mausoleum in Halicarnassus;[1] the pre-Columbian pyramids and temples of the Aztecs, Olmecs, and Mayans; and the famous tombs of the great Moghuls, such as the Taj Mahal and the Monument of Akbar the Great. According to recent research, even the legendary Minoan palace in Crete was not a royal residence but, rather, a gigantic necropolis.[2]

The enigmatic nature of death opens a wide range of possibilities for individual and collective imagination. To take only a few examples from Western culture, people have seen death as the Grim Reaper, Terrible Devourer, Abominable Horseman, Senseless Automaton, Implacable Punisher, Gay Deceiver, Pas-

1. The mausoleum of Halicarnassus was the tomb of Mausolus of Caria, a provincial governor of the Persian Empire who died in the year 353 B.C. It was built by a group of sculptors at the request of his devoted sister and widow, Artemisia, and became one of the seven wonders of the ancient world because of its unusual form, rich decoration, and exquisite finish. The mausoleum consisted of thirty-six columns resting on a high base and supporting a marble pyramid capped by a four-horse chariot.

2. According to Dr. Hans Georg Wunderlich, professor of geology and paleontology from Stuttgart, the palace of King Minos at Knossos had never been intended for the living but was a necropolis where a powerful sect practiced elaborate burial rites, sacrifices, and ritual games. Wunderlich expounded his provocative theory in his book, *The Secret of Crete.*

sionate Lover, Sweet Pacifier, and Great Unifier. The emotions associated with these images cover a broad spectrum, from a profound sense of horror to feelings of ecstatic rapture.

Different concepts of death and associated beliefs have a deep influence not only on the psychological state of dying people but also on the specific circumstances under which they leave this world and on the attitudes of their survivors. As a result of this, dying and death can be understood and experienced in many different ways. From this point of view it is interesting to compare the situation of a person facing death in contemporary Western civilization with that of individuals in ancient cultures or from preindustrial countries.

Most non-Western cultures have religious and philosophical systems, cosmologies, ritual practices, and certain elements of social organization that make it easier for their members to accept and experience death. These cultures generally do not see death as the absolute termination of existence; they believe that consciousness or life in some form continues beyond the point of physiological demise. Whatever specific concepts of afterlife prevail in different cultures, death is typically regarded as a transition or transfiguration, and not as the final annihilation of the individual. Mythological systems have not only detailed descriptions of various afterlife realms, but frequently also complex cartographies to guide souls on their difficult posthumous journeys.

The intensity of this belief in the postmortem journey found its expression in a variety of funeral rites. Most researchers interested in death customs emphasize that the common denominators of these procedures seem to be the basic ambivalence of the survivors toward the dead and the belief in an afterlife. Many aspects of funeral rites represent an effort to facilitate and hasten the transition of the deceased to the spirit world. However, the opposite tendency can be observed with almost equal frequency—namely, the ceremonial establishment of the relationship between the quick and the dead to obtain safety and protection. Specific aspects of many rituals conducted after death can be simultaneously interpreted in terms of helping the dead in their posthumous journeys as well as preventing them from returning.

A special variation of the belief in the continuation of existence after death is the concept of reincarnation. In addition to the element of disembodied existence following the death of an individual, it also involves an eventual return to material existence in a different form in the phenomenal world as we know it. The belief in reincarnation occurs in such diverse cultural and religious frameworks as philosophies and religions of India, cosmologies of various North American Indian tribes, Platonic and Neoplatonic philosophy, the Orphic cult and other mystery religions of ancient Greece, and early Christianity.[3] In Hinduism, Buddhism, and Jainism this belief is connected with the law of karma, according to

3. Since it is generally assumed that the belief in reincarnation is incompatible with Christianity and alien to it, it seems appropriate to elaborate on the above statement. The concept of reincarnation existed in Christianity until it was attacked in 543 A.D. by the Byzantine emperor, Justinian, together with other teachings of the learned father, Origen, and finally condemned by the Second Council in Constantinople in 553 A.D. Origen, considered the most prominent of all Church Fathers with the exception of Augustine, stated explicitly in his work, *De Principiis:* "The soul has neither beginning nor end. . . . Every soul comes to this world strengthened by the victories or weakened by the defeats of its previous life. Its place in this world as a vessel appointed to honor or dishonor is determined by its previous merits or demerits. Its work in this world determines its place in the world which is to follow this."

which the quality of individual incarnations is specifically determined by the person's merits and debits from preceding lifetimes.

It is not difficult to understand that a firm conviction concerning the continuity of consciousness or life beyond the framework of an individual's biological existence—or even an open-minded attitude toward such a possibility—can alter the experience of aging, the concept of death, and the experience of dying itself. In the extreme, the relative values attributed to life and death can be completely reversed in comparison with prevailing Western concepts. The process of dying can then appear to be even more important than living. This is true, for example, in the case of some of the philosophical or religious systems that involve a belief in reincarnation. Here, the period of dying can be of paramount significance, because the attitude of the dying individual determines the quality of the entire future incarnation, and the nature and course of the next existence is an actualization of the manner of death. In other systems, life is experienced as a state of separation, a prison of the spirit, and death is a reunion, liberation, or return home. Thus for the Hindu death is an awakening from the world of illusion (*maya*) and an opportunity for the individual self (*jiva*) to realize and experience its divine nature (Atman-Brahman). According to Buddhist scriptures, suffering is an intrinsic aspect of biological existence; its deepest cause is the force that is responsible for the life process itself. The goal of the spiritual path is to extinguish the fire of life and leave the wheel of death and rebirth.

In some cultures dying means moving a step up the social or cosmological hierarchy into the world of ancestors, powerful spirits, or demigods. In others it is a transition into a blissful existence in the solar realms or in the presence of gods. More frequently, the afterlife is clearly dichotomized; it involves hells and purgatories as well as heavens. The posthumous journey of the soul to a desirable destination is fraught with perils and ordeals of various kinds. It is essential, for a successful completion of the journey, to be familiar with the geography and rules of the other world. Thus many of the cultures that believe in an afterlife have developed complicated and elaborate procedures that familiarize the individual with the experience of dying.

I have wept for you
and now know you no more;
I remain behind
sad that you have gone—
gone to your homes
and left me on earth.

Nahuatl poem

In all ages and in many different cultures, ritual events have existed in which individuals have experienced a powerful symbolic encounter with death. This confrontation is the core event in the rites of passage of temple initiations, mystery religions, and secret societies, as well as in various ecstatic religions. According to the descriptions in historical sources and anthropological literature, such profound experiences of symbolic death result not only in an overwhelming realization of the impermanence of biological existence but also in an illuminating insight into the transcendent and eternal spiritual nature intrinsic to human consciousness. Rituals of this kind combine two important functions: On the one hand, they mediate a deep process of transformation in the initiate who then discovers a different way of experiencing the world; on the other hand, they serve as preparation for actual physical death.

In several places specific manuals were developed to guide individuals through the encounter with death, whether experienced on a symbolic level within the framework of spiritual practices or associated with the physical destruction of the biological vehicle. The so-called *Tibetan Book of the Dead (Bardo Thödol)*, the collection of funeral texts usually referred to as the *Egyptian Book of the Dead (Pert Em Hru)*, and the literature from medieval Europe known as *The Art of Dying (Ars Moriendi)* are the best known examples of this kind.

Anthropological literature abounds in descriptions of those rites of passage conducted in various cultures at the time of important life transitions such as birth, puberty, marriage, birth of one's child, change in life, and dying. In the elaborate rituals enacted on these occasions, individuals learn to experience transitions from one stage in life to the next, to die in one role and be born and incorporated into another. In many rites of passage, with the help of psychedelic substances or powerful nondrug techniques, initiates undergo an experience of death and rebirth comparable to those occurring in ancient temple mysteries. All of the encounters with dying, death, and transcendence experienced in the rites of passage during the lifetime of an individual can be seen as profound psychological and experiential training for the ultimate transition at the time of death.

In many preliterate societies, the homogeneous, intimate, and ultimately sacred nature of the human community is the weave within which the dying individual finds him or herself. Here, the consciousness of the clan, tribe, or kingdom is more important than the distinct consciousness of the individual. It is this very factor that can make the loss of individuality experienced in dying less painful than in those cultures where ego attachment is great. On the other hand, the loss of an individual from the social fabric can have profound consequences for the living if the community is a homogeneous collective. Dying and death in the situation of *communitas* allows for both group support of the dying individual and for the expression of grief and anger on the part of survivors, who have lost an essential person in the mystically bonded social group.

Many Westerners find that some of these approaches to death are alien to their value system. Elaborate ritual enactments revolving around death and the emphasis on impermanence in many religious practices seem to indicate a morbid preoccupation with the macabre and are frequently interpreted in the West as manifestations of social psychopathology. A sophisticated Westerner tends to consider the belief in an afterlife and the concept of the posthumous journey of the soul as products of primitive fears of individuals who have been denied the privilege of scientific knowledge. In this context the preponderance of tribal consciousness over that of the individual appears to be a sign of psychological immaturity. However, a closer look at our own culture shows that we have moved toward the other extreme—massive denial and neglect of all the issues related to death. There are very few situations in human life that are of such paramount significance as dying and death. Every single individual has to face during his or her lifetime the deaths of close relatives and, eventually, confront the issue of his or her own impermanence and biological demise. In view of the utmost relevance of death, the avoidance and denial of the problems related to this area are truly astounding. Aging, fatal disease, and dying are not seen as a part of the life process but as the ultimate defeat and a painful reminder of the limits of our ability to master nature. With our pragmatic philosophy emphasizing achievement and success, the dying person is a loser in life's race. People in our culture are only beginning to realize that there is a lesson to be learned from an encounter with aging and dying individuals.

The contemporary medical approach to a dying person is dominated by a determined effort to conquer death and delay its advent by all means possible. In this struggle for mechanical prolongation of life at any cost, very little attention is paid to the quality of an individual's remaining days. The companions of many dying individuals are infusion bottles and tubes, oxygen tanks, electric pacemakers, artificial kidneys, and monitors of vital functions. In an effort to hide from the dying the reality of their situations, medical personnel and family members often play complicated games that obscure relevant issues and instill false hope. This further deepens the feelings of isolation and despair experienced by the dying, many of whom intuitively sense the dishonesty surrounding them.

Religion, which can be of great help for the dying, has lost much of its significance for the average Westerner. A pragmatic life orientation and philosophical materialism have replaced religious fervor. With some exceptions Western religions have lost their function as vital forces in life. They have been reduced to formal rituals and ceremonies divested of their original meanings.

The scientific world-view based on philosophical materialism further confirms the grimness of the situation that dying individuals are facing. According to this view there is no reality outside of that occurring in the material world. To perceive reality one has to be a living organism with functioning organs of perception. Consciousness itself is seen as a product of the brain, and is thus critically dependent on its integrity and normal functioning. The physical destruction of the body and brain is the irrevocable end of human life.

There is little that our contemporary social structure, or our philosophy, religion, and medical science, has to offer at present to ease the psychological suffering of the dying. Many persons in this situation are thus facing a profound crisis that is basic and total, since it affects simultaneously biological, emotional, philosophical, and spiritual aspects of the human being. Yet psychiatrists, psychologists, and other members of the helping professions who have otherwise developed systems for crisis intervention in various difficult life situations surprisingly have not until recently identified this area as one where sensitive help is urgently needed.

Ivan Illich

Death against Death

Ivan Illich, founder of the Center for Intercultural Documentation in Cuernavaca, Mexico, documents the fact that different cultures in different historical epochs have widely varying images and experiences of death. In his survey of historical developments relating to death and dying from the fourteenth century into the present era, Illich observes a general expansion of the realm of the technical and scientific and, in particular, the tendency for death to be regarded as a problem for medicine and health professionals. As the proficiency of medicine steadily improved, physicians usurped the position of theologians as arbiters of life and death dilemmas. Increasingly, the good life was viewed as the long and healthy life, and it could be purchased from purveyors of scientific medicine and health care. As persons became patients, the social and political power of the medical profession steadily increased. Such progress, however, is not without its price, as will be revealed in succeeding sections of this Reader.

In every society the dominant image of death determines the prevalent concept of health. Such an image, the culturally conditioned anticipation of a certain event at an uncertain date, is shaped by institutional structures, deep-seated myths, and the social character which predominates. A society's image of death reveals the level of independence of its people, their personal relatedness, self-reliance and aliveness. Wherever the metropolitan medical civilization has penetrated, a novel image of death has been transplanted. Insofar as this image depends on the new techniques and their corresponding ethos, it is supranational in character. But these very techniques are not culturally neutral; they assumed concrete shape within Western cultures and expressed a Western ethos. The white man's image of death has spread with medical civilization and has been a major force in cultural colonization.

The image of a "natural death," a death which ought to come under medical care and find us in good health and old age, is a quite recent ideal. In five hundred years it has evolved through five distinct stages, and is now ready for a sixth mutation. Each stage has found its iconographic expression: (1) the fourteenth-century "dance of the dead"; (2) the Renaissance dance at the bidding of the skeleton man, the so-called "Dance of Death"; (3) the bedroom scene of the aging lecher under the *Ancien Régime;* (4) the nineteenth-century doctor in his struggle against the roaming phantoms of consumption and pestilence; (5) mid-twentieth-century doctors who step between the patient and his death; and (6) death under intensive hospital care. At each stage of its evolution the image of natural death has elicited a new set of responses that increasingly acquired a medical character. The history of natural death is the history of the medicalization of the struggle against death.

THE DEVOTIONAL DANCE OF THE DEAD   From the fourth century onwards, the Church had been struggling against the pagan tradition of crowds dancing in cemeteries: naked, frenzied, and brandishing swords. Nevertheless, the frequency of ecclesiastical prohibitions testifies that they were of little avail, and for a thousand years Christian churches and cemeteries remained dance floors. Death was an occasion for the renewal of life. The dance with the dead over their tombs was an occasion for affirming the joy of being alive and a source of many erotic songs and poems. By the late fourteenth century, the sense of these dances seems to have changed: from an encounter between the living and those who were already dead, it was transformed into a meditative, introspective experience. In 1424 the first Dance of the Dead was painted on a cemetery wall in Paris. The original of the "Cimetière des Innocents" is lost, but good copies allow us to reconstruct it: king, peasant, pope, scribe, and maiden each dance with a corpse. Each partner is a mirror image of the other in dress and feature. In the shape of his body Everyman carries his own death with him and dances with it through his life. During the late Middle Ages, indwelling death faces man; each death comes with the symbol of rank corresponding to his victim: for the king a crown, for the peasant a pitchfork. After dancing with dead ancestors over their graves, people turned to representing a world in which everyone dances through life embracing his own mortality. Death was not represented as an anthropomorphic figure but as a macabre self-consciousness, a constant awareness of the gaping grave. It is not yet the skeleton man of the next century to whose music men and women will soon dance through the autumn of the Middle Ages, but rather each one's own aging and rotting self.

At this time the mirror becomes important in everyday life, and in the grip of the "mirror of death" life acquires a hallucinating poignancy. With Chaucer and Villon death becomes as intimate and sensual as pleasure and pain....

THE DANSE MACABRE   In the morality plays, death appears in a new costume and role. By the end of the fifteenth century, no longer just a mirror image, he assumes the leading role among the "last four things," preceding judgment, heaven, and hell. Nor is he any longer just one of the four apocalyptic riders from Romanesque reliefs, or the bat-like Maegera who picks up souls from the cemetery of Pisa, or a mere messenger executing the orders of God. Death has become an independent figure who calls each man, woman, and child, first as a messenger from God but soon insisting on his own sovereign rights. By 1538 Hans Holbein the Younger had published the first picture book of death, which was to become a best-seller: woodcuts on the *Danse Macabre*. The dance partners have shed their putrid flesh and turned into naked skeletons. The representation of each man entwined with his own mortality has turned into a frenzied exhaustion in the grip of a force of nature. The intimate mirror image colored by the "new devotion" of the German mystics has been replaced by an egalitarian force of nature, the executioner of a law that whirls everyone along and then mows them down. From a life-long encounter, death has turned into the event of a moment.

Death here becomes the point at which linear clock-time ends and eternity meets man, whereas during the Middle Ages eternity had been, together with God's presence, immanent in history. The world has ceased to be a sacrament of this presence; with Luther it became the place of corruption that God saves. The proliferation of clocks symbolizes this change in consciousness. With the predominance of serial time, concern for its exact measurement and the recognition of the simultaneity of events, a new framework for the recognition of personal identity is manufactured. The identity of the person is sought in reference to a sequence of events rather than in the completeness of one's life span. Death ceases to be the end of a whole and becomes an interruption in the sequence.

Skeleton men predominate on the title pages of the first fifty years of the woodcut, as naked women now predominate on magazine covers. Death holds the hour glass or strikes the tower clock. Many a bell clapper was shaped like a bone. The new machine, which can make time of equal length, day and night, also puts all people under the same law. By the time of the Reformation, post-mortem survival has ceased to be a transfigured continuation of life here below, and has become either a frightful punishment in the form of hell or a totally unmerited gift from God in heaven. Indwelling grace had been turned into justification by faith alone. Thus during the sixteenth century, death ceases to be conceived of primarily as a transition into the next world, and the accent is placed on the end of this life. The open grave looms much larger than the doors of heaven or hell and the encounter with death has become more certain than immortality, more just than king, pope, or even God. Rather than life's aim, it has become the end of life.

The finality, immanence, and intimacy of personal death was not only part of the new sense of time, but also of the emergence of a new sense of individuality. On the pilgrim's path from the Church Militant on earth to the Church Triumphant in heaven, death was experienced very much as an event that concerned both communities. Now each man faced his own and final death. Of course, once death had become such a natural force, people wanted to master it by learning the art or the skill of dying. *Ars Moriendi*,[1] one of the first printed do-it-yourself manuals on the market, remained a best seller in various versions for the next two hundred years. Many people learned to read by deciphering it. Solicitous to provide guidance for the "complete gentleman," Caxton published the *Art and Craft to Knowe ye Well to Dye* in 1491 at the Westminster Press....

In popular devotion a new kind of curiosity about the afterlife developed. Fantastic horror stories about dead bodies and artistic representations of purgatory both multiplied. The grotesque concern of the seventeenth century with ghosts and souls underscores the growing anxiety of a culture faced with the call of death rather than the judgment of God....

Simultaneously medical folk practices multiplied, all designed to help people to meet their death with dignity as individuals. New superstitious devices were developed so that one might recognize whether one's sickness required the acceptance of approaching death or some kind of treatment. If the flower thrown into the fountain of the sanctuary drowned, it was useless to spend money on remedies. People tried to be ready when death came, to have the steps well learnt for the last dance. Remedies against a painful agony multiplied, but most of them were still to be performed under the conscious direction of the dying who played a new role and played it consciously. Children could help a mother or father to die, but only if they did not hold them back by crying. A person was supposed to indicate when he wanted to be lowered from his bed onto the

---

1. Editor's note: *The Art of Dying.*

earth which would soon engulf him, and when the prayers were to start. But bystanders knew that they were to keep the doors open to make it easy for death to come, to avoid noise so as not to frighten death away, and finally to turn their eyes respectfully away from the dying man in order to leave him alone during this most personal event.

Neither priest nor doctor were expected to assist the poor man in typical fifteenth- and sixteenth-century death. In principle, medical writers recognized two opposite services the physician could perform. He could either assist healing or help the coming of an easy and speedy death. It was his duty to recognize the "facies Hippocratica," the special traits which indicated that the patient was already in the grip of death. In healing, as in withdrawal, the doctor was anxious to work hand in glove with nature. The question as to whether medicine ever could "prolong" life was heatedly disputed in the medical schools of Palermo, Fez, and even Paris. Many Arab and Jewish doctors denied this power outright, and declared such an attempt to interfere with the order of nature to be blasphemous....

The new image of death helped to reduce the human body to an object. Up to this time, the corpse had been considered as something quite unlike other things: it was treated almost like a person. The law recognized its standing: the dead could sue and be sued by the living, and criminal proceedings against the dead were common. Pope Urban VIII, poisoned by his successor, was dug up, solemnly judged a simonist, had his right hand cut off, and was thrown into the Tiber. After being hanged as a thief, a man might still have his head cut off for being a traitor. The dead could also be called to witness. The widow could still repudiate her husband by putting the keys and his purse on his casket. Even today the executor acts in the name of the dead, and we still speak of the "desecration" of a grave or the secularization of a public cemetery when it is turned into a park. The appearance of natural death was necessary for the corpse to be deprived of much of its legal standing.

The arrival of natural death also prepared the way for new attitudes towards death and disease, which became common in the late seventeenth century. During the Middle Ages, the human body had been sacred; now the physician's scalpel had access to the corpse itself. Its dissection had been considered by the humanist Gerson to be "a sacrilegious profanation, a useless cruelty exercised by the living against the dead." But at the same time that Everyman's Death began to emerge in person in the morality plays, the corpse first appears as a teaching object in the amphitheater of the Renaissance university. When the first authorized public dissection took place in Montpellier in 1375, this new learned activity was declared obscene, and the performance could not be repeated for several years. A generation later, permission was given for one corpse a year to be dissected within the borders of the German empire. At the University of Bologna, also, one body was dissected each year just before Christmas, and the ceremony was inaugurated by a procession, accompanied by exorcisms, and took three days.... Attitudes changed so rapidly that by 1561 the Venetian Senate ordered the hangman to take instruction from Dr. Fallopius in order to provide him with corpses well suited for "anatomizing." Rembrandt painted "Dr. Tulp's Lesson" in 1632. Public dissection became a favored subject for paintings and, in the Netherlands, a common event at carnivals. The first step towards surgery on TV and in the movies had been taken. The physician had advanced his knowledge of anatomy and his power to exhibit his skill; but both were disproportionate to an advance in his ability to heal. Medical rituals helped to orient, repress, or allay the fear and anguish generated by a death that had become macabre. The anatomy of Vesalius rivalled Holbein's *Danse Macabre* somewhat as scientific sex-guides now rival *Playboy* and *Penthouse* magazines.

BOURGEOIS DEATH   Baroque death counterpointed an aristocratically organized heaven. The church vault might depict a last judgment with separate spaces reserved for savages, commoners, and nobles, but the Dance of Death beneath depicted the mower, who used his scythe regardless of post or rank. Precisely because macabre equality belittled worldly privilege, it also made it more legitimate. However, with the rise of the bourgeois family, equality in death came to an end: those who could afford it began to pay to keep death away.

Francis Bacon was the first to speak about the prolongation of life as a new task for physicians. He divided medicine into three offices: "First, the preservation of health, second, the cure of disease, and third, the prolongation of life," and extolled the "third part of medicine, regarding the prolongation of life: this is a new part, and deficient, although the most noble of all." The medical profession did not even consider facing this task, until, some one hundred and fifty years later, there appeared a host of clients who were anxious to pay them to try. This was a new type of rich man who refused to die in retirement and insisted on being carried away by death from natural exhaustion while still on the job. He refused to accept death unless he was in good health in an active old age. Montaigne had already ridiculed such people as exceptionally conceited: "'Tis the

THE DEAF MAN

Rabbi Moshe Hayyim Efraim, the Baal Shem's grandson told, "I heard this from my grandfather: Once a fiddler played so sweetly that all who heard him began to dance, and whoever came near enough to hear, joined in the dance. Then a deaf man who knew nothing of music, happened along, and to him all he saw seemed the action of madmen—senseless and in bad taste."

Martin Buber
Tales of the Hasidim: Early Masters

last and extreme form of dying...what an idle conceit is it to expect to die of a decay of strength which is the effect of the extremest age, and to propose to ourselves no shorter lease on life...as if it were contrary to nature to see a man break his neck with a fall, be drowned by shipwreck, be snatched away with pleurisy or the plague...we ought to call natural death that which is general, common and universal." Such people were few in his time; by 1830 their numbers had increased. The preacher expecting to go to heaven, the philosopher denying the existence of the soul, and the merchant wanting to see his capital double once more, were all in agreement that the only death that accorded with nature was one which would overtake them at their desks....

Formerly, only King and Pope had been under an obligation to remain in command until the day of their deaths. They alone consulted the faculties: the Arabs from Salerno in the Middle Ages, or the Renaissance men from Padua or Montpellier. Kings kept court physicians to do what barbers did for the commoner: bleed them and purge them, and in addition, protect them from poisons. Kings neither set out to live longer than others, nor expected their personal physicians to give special dignity to their declining years. In contrast, the new class of old men saw in death the absolute price for absolute economic value. The aging accountant wanted a doctor who would drive away death; when the end approached, he wanted to be formally "given up" by his doctor and be served his last repast with the special bottle reserved for the occasion. The role of the valetudinarian was thereby created and, with it, the economic power of the contemporary physician.

The ability to survive longer, the refusal to retire before death, and the demand for medical assistance in an incurable condition had joined forces to give rise to a new concept of sickness: the type of health to which old age could aspire. In the years just before the French Revolution this had become the health of the rich and the powerful; within a generation chronic disease became fashionable for the young and pretentious, consumptive features the sign of premature wisdom, and the need for travel into warm climates a claim to genius. Medical care for protracted ailments, even though they might lead to untimely death, had become a mark of distinction.

By contrast, a reverse judgment now could be made on the ailments of the poor, and the ills from which they had always died could be defined as untreated sickness. It did not matter at all if the treatment doctors could provide for these ills had any effect on the progress of the sickness; the lack of such treatment began to mean that they were condemned to die an unnatural death, an idea that fitted the bourgeois' image of the poor as uneducated and unproductive. From now on the ability to die a "natural" death was reserved to one social class: those who could afford to die as patients.

Health became the privilege of waiting for timely death, no matter what medical service was needed for this purpose. In an earlier epoch, death had carried the hour glass. In woodcuts, both skeleton and onlooker grin when the victim refuses death. Now the middle class seized the clock and employed doctors to tell death when to strike. The Enlightenment attributed a new power to the doctor, without being able to verify whether or not he had acquired any new influence over the outcome of dangerous sickness.

CLINICAL DEATH   The French Revolution marked a short interruption in the medicalization of death. Its ideologues believed that untimely death would not strike in a society built on its triple ideal. But the opening of the doctor's clinical eye caused him to look at death in a new perspective. Whereas the merchants of the eighteenth century had determined the outlook on death with the help of the charlatans they employed and paid, now the clinicians began to shape the public's vision. We have seen death turn from God's call into a "natural" event and later into a "force of nature"; in a further mutation it is now turned into an "untimely" event unless coming to those who were both unhealthy and old. Now it had become the outcome of specific diseases certified by the doctor.

Death has paled into a metaphorical figure, and killer diseases have taken his place. The general force of nature that had been celebrated as "death" turned into a host of specific causations of clinical demise. Many "deaths" now roam the world. A number of book plates from private libraries of late nineteenth-century physicians show the doctor battling with personified diseases at the bedside of his patient. The hope of doctors to control the outcome of specific diseases gave rise to the myth that they had power over death. The new powers attributed to the profession gave rise to the new status of the clinician....

TRADE UNION CLAIMS TO A NATURAL DEATH In our century, a valetudinarian's death while undergoing treatment by clinically trained doctors came to be perceived, for the first time, as a civil right. Old age medical care was written into union contracts. The capitalist privilege of natural extinction from exhaustion in a director's chair gave way to the proletarian demand for health services during retirement. The bourgeois hope of continuing as a dirty old man in the office was ousted by

the dream of an active sex life on social security in a retirement village. Lifelong care for every clinical condition soon became a peremptory demand for access to a natural death. Lifelong institutional medical care had become a service that society owed all its members.

"Natural death" now appeared in dictionaries. One major German encyclopedia published in 1909 defines it by means of contrast: "abnormal death is opposed to natural death because it results from sickness, violence, or mechanical and chronic disturbances." A reputable dictionary of philosophical concepts states that "natural death comes without previous sickness, without definable specific cause." It was this macabre yet hallucinating death-concept that became intertwined with the concept of social progress. Legally valid claims to equality in clinical death disseminated the contradictions of bourgeois individualism among the working class. The right to a natural death was formulated as a claim to equal consumption of medical services, rather than as a freedom from the evils of industrial work or as new liberties and powers for self-care. This unionized concept of an "equal clinical death" is thus the inverse of the ideal proposed in the National Assembly of Paris in 1792: it is a deeply medicalized ideal....

Our new image of death also befits the industrial ethos. The good death has irrevocably become that of the standard consumer of medical care. Just as at the turn of the century all men were defined as pupils, born into original stupidity and standing in need of eight years of schooling before they could enter productive life, today they are stamped from birth as patients who need all kinds of treatment if they want to lead life the right way. Just as compulsory educational consumption came to be used as a device to discriminate at work, so medical consumption became a device to alleviate unhealthy work, dirty cities, and nerve-racking transportation. What need is there to worry about a less murderous environment when doctors are industrially equipped to act as life savers!

Finally, "death under compulsory care" encourages the re-emergence of the most primitive delusions about the causes of death.... Among them, death always requires a supernatural explanation, somebody to blame: the curse of an enemy, the spell of a magician, the breaking of the yarn in the hands of the Parsee, or God dispatching his angel of death. In the dance with his mirror image, European death emerged as an event independent of another's will, an inexorable force of nature that all had to face on their own. The imminence of death was an exquisite and constant reminder of the fragility and tenderness of life. During the late Middle Ages, the discovery of "natural" death became one of the mainsprings of European lyric and drama. But the same imminence of death, once perceived as an extrinsic threat coming from nature, became a major challenge for the emerging engineer. If the civil engineer had learned to manage earth, and the pedagogue-become-educator to manage knowledge, why should the biologist-physician not manage death? When the doctor contrived to step between humanity and death, the latter lost the immediacy and intimacy he had gained four hundred years earlier.

The change in the doctor-death relationship can be well illustrated by following the iconographic treatment of this theme. In the age of the Dance of Death, the physician is rare; in the only picture I have located in which death treats the doctor as a colleague, he has taken an old man by one hand, while in the other he carries a glass of urine, and seems to be asking the physician to confirm his diagnosis. In the age of the Dance of Death, the skeleton man makes the doctor the main butt of his jokes. In the earlier period, while death still wore some flesh, he asks the doctor to confirm in the latter's own mirror image what he thought he knew about man's innards. Later, as a fleshless skeleton, he teases the doctor about his impotence, jokes about or rejects his honoraria, offers medicine as pernicious as that which the physician dispensed, and treats the doctor as just one more common mortal by snatching him into the dance. Baroque death seems to intrude constantly into the doctor's activities, making fun of him while he sells his wares at a fair, interrupting his consultations, transforming his medicine bottles into hour glasses, or taking the doctor's place on a visit to the pesthouse. In the eighteenth century a new motif appears: teasing the physician because of his pessimistic diagnosis, death seems to enjoy abandoning those sick persons whom the doctor has condemned. Until the nineteenth century, death deals always with the doctor or with the sick, usually taking the initiative in the action. The contestants are at opposite ends of the sick bed. Only after clinical sickness and clinical death had developed considerably do we find the first pictures in which the doctor assumes the initiative and interposes himself between his patient and death. We have to wait until after World War I before we see physicians wrangling with the skeleton, tearing a young woman from its embrace, and wresting the scythe from death's hand. By 1930 a smiling white-coated man is rushing against a whimpering skeleton and crushing it like a fly with two volumes of Marle's *Lexicon of Therapy*. In other pictures, the doctor raises one hand and bans death while holding up the arms of a young woman whom death grips by the feet. Max Klinger represents the physician clipping the feathers of a winged giant. Others show the physician locking the skeleton into prison or even kicking its bony bottom. Now the doctor rather than the patient struggles with death. As in primitive cultures, somebody can again be blamed when death triumphs; again, this somebody has no face, but he does hold a charter: the person is not a person but a class....

DEATH UNDER INTENSIVE CARE   We cannot fully understand the deeply rooted structure of our social organization unless we see in it a multifaceted exorcism of all forms of evil death. Our major institutions constitute a gigantic defense program waging war on behalf of "humanity" against death-dealing agencies and classes. This is a total war. Not only medicine but also welfare, international relief, and development programs are enlisted in this struggle. Ideologial bureaucracies of all colors join the crusade. Revolution, repression, and even civil and international wars are justified in order to defeat the dictators or capitalists who can be blamed for the wanton creation and tolerance of sickness and death.

Curiously, death became the enemy to be defeated at precisely the moment in which mega-death comes upon the scene. Not only the image of "unnecessary" death is new, but also our image of the end of the world. Death, the end of *my* world, and apocalypse, the end of *the* world, are intimately related; our attitude towards both has clearly been deeply affected by the atomic situation. The apocalypse has ceased to be just a mythological conjecture and has become a real contingency. Instead of being due to the will of God, or man's guilt, or the laws of nature, Armageddon has become a possible consequence of man's direct decision.

An uncanny analogy exists between atomic and cobalt bombs: both are deemed necessary for the good of mankind, both are effective in providing man with power over the end. Medicalized social rituals represent one aspect of social control by means of the self-frustrating war against death....

The dominance of industry has disrupted and often dissolved most traditional bonds of solidarity. The impersonal rituals of Industrialized Medicine create an ersatz unity of mankind. They relate all its members to an identical pattern of "desirable" death by proposing hospital death as the goal of economic development. The myth of progress of all people towards the same kind of death diminishes the feeling of guilt on the part of the "haves" by transforming the ugly deaths of which "have nots" die into the result of present underdevelopment, which ought to be remedied by further expansion of medical institutions.

Of course, medicalized death has a different function in highly industrialized societies than it has in mainly rural nations. Within an industrial society, medical intervention in everyday life does not change the prevailing image of health and death, but rather caters to it. It diffuses the death image of the medicalized elite to the masses and reproduces it for future generations. But when "death prevention" is applied outside of a cultural context in which consumers religiously prepare themselves for hospital deaths, the growth of hospital-based medicine inevitably constitutes a form of imperialist intervention. A sociopolitical image of death is imposed; people are deprived of their traditional vision of what constitutes health and death. The self-image that gives cohesion to their culture is dissolved, and atomized individuals can be incorporated into an international mass of highly "socialized" health consumers. The expectation of medicalized death hooks the rich on unlimited insurance payments and lures the poor into a gilded deathtrap. The contradictions of bourgeois individualism are corroborated by the inability of people to die with any possibility of a realistic attitude towards death. The Customs man guarding the frontier of Upper Volta with Mali explained to me this importance of death in relation to health. I wanted to know from him how people along the Niger could understand each other, though almost each village spoke a different tongue. For him this had nothing to do with language: "As long as people cut the prepuce of their boys the way we do, and die our death, we can understand them well."

In many a village in Mexico I have seen what happens when social security arrives. For a generation people continue in their traditional beliefs; they know how to deal with death, dying, and grief. The new nurse and the doctor, thinking they know better, teach them about a Pantheon of evil clinical deaths, each one of which can be banned, at a price. Instead of modernizing people's skills for self-care, they preach the ideal of hospital death. By their ministration they urge the peasants to an unending search for the good death of international description, a search which will keep them consumers for ever....

Through the medicalization of death, health care has become a monolithic world religion whose tenets are taught in compulsory schools and whose ethical rules are applied to a bureaucratic restructuring of the environment:

sex became a subject in the syllabus and sharing one's spoon is discouraged for the sake of hygiene. The struggle against death, which dominates the lifestyle of the rich, is translated by development agencies into a set of rules by which the poor of the earth shall be forced to conduct themselves.

Only a culture that evolved in highly industrialized societies could possibly have called forth the commercialization of the death image that I have just described. In its extreme form, "natural death" is now that point at which the human organism refuses any further input of treatment. People die when the electroencephalogram indicates that their brainwaves have flattened out: they do not take a last breath, or die beause their heart stops. Socially approved death happens when man has become useless not only as a producer but also as a consumer. It is the point at which a consumer, trained at great expense, must finally be written off as a total loss. Death has become the ultimate form of consumer resistance.

Traditionally the person best protected from death was the one whom society had condemned to die. Society felt threatened that the man on Death Row might use his tie to hang himself. Authority might be challenged if he took his life before the appointed hour. Today, the man best protected against setting the stage for his own dying is the sick person in critical condition. Society, acting through the medical system, decides when and after what indignities and mutilations he shall die. The medicalization of society has brought the epoch of natural death to an end. Western man has lost the right to preside at his act of dying. Health, or the autonomous power to cope, has been expropriated down to the last breath. Technical death has won its victory over dying. Mechanical death has conquered and destroyed all other deaths.

Eric J. Cassell

Dying in a Technological Society

Eric J. Cassell, clinical professor of Public Health at Cornell University Medical College, analyzes death and social change in terms of the shift of death from the moral to the technical order. Traditionally, death was conceived in terms of sentiment, conscience, and morality—questions about the meaning of death were phrased in terms of good and evil, right and wrong. In modern societies, however, such questions have been largely replaced by issues of practicality and expediency. The rise of the scientific ethos has purchased longer, healthier lives at the price of less meaningful, depersonalized deaths. While the mechanical events involved in the death of a physical organism can be explained by technical concepts, questions of the value of life cannot. Unless a balance is found between the moral and technical orders, we can anticipate that many of the problems of the dying person and the bereaved will remain unresolved.

The care of the terminally ill in the United States has changed as the business of dying has shifted from the moral to the technical order. The moral order has been used to describe those bonds between men based in sentiment, morality, or conscience, that describe what is right. The technical order rests on the usefulness of things, based in necessity or expediency, and not founded in conceptions of the right. The change of death from a moral to a technical matter has come about for many reasons based in social evolu-tion and technical advance, and the effects on the dying have been profound.

One reason for the change has been the success of modern medicine in combatting death. For most, in the United States, premature death is no longer imminent. The death of infants is unusual, the death of children rare, and the death of young adults so improbable that it must be removed from the realistic possibilities of young life. Further, the nature of death has also changed. The degenerative diseases and cancer have become predominant. Lingering sickness in the aged is a less common event because medicine is able to combat the complications of chronic disease that so often in the past kept the sick person from functioning. Accompanying these changes brought about by technical advances, there has been a change in the place where death occurs. Death has moved from the home into institutions—hospitals, medical centers, chronic care facilities, and nursing homes.

FROM THE MORAL TO THE TECHNICAL
There are other reasons for the shift of death in the United States from the moral to the technical order. One is the wide-spread acceptance of technical success itself. Because life expectancy has increased, the dying are old now. But, life expectancy is not an individual term, it is a statistical term. For individuals, what has changed is their death expectancy;

...And Death heard the summons,
And he leaped on his fastest horse,
Pale as a sheet in the moonlight.
Up the golden street Death galloped,
And the hoofs of his horse struck fire
  from the gold,
But they didn't make no sound.
Up Death rode to the Great White Throne,
And waited for God's command.

And God said: Go down, Death, go down,
Go down to Savannah, Georgia,
Down in Yamacraw,
And find Sister Caroline.
She's borne the burden and heat of the day,
She's labored long in my vineyard,
And she's tired—
She's weary—
Go down, Death, and bring her to me....

While we were watching round her bed,
She turned her eyes and looked away,
She saw what we couldn't see;
She saw Old Death. She saw Old Death
Coming like a falling star.

But Death didn't frighten Sister Caroline;
He looked to her like a welcome friend.
And she whispered to us: I'm going home,
And she smiled and closed her eyes.

And Death took her up like a baby,
And she lay in his icy arms,
But she didn't feel no chill.
And Death began to ride again—
Up beyond the evening star,
Out beyond the morning star,
Into the glittering light of glory,
On to the Great White Throne.
And there he laid Sister Caroline
On the loving breast of Jesus.
And Jesus took his own hand
  and wiped away her tears,
And he smoothed the furrows from her face,
And the angels sang a little song,
And Jesus rocked her in his arms,
And kept a-saying: Take your rest,
Take your rest, take your rest.

Weep not—weep not,
She is not dead;
She's resting in the bosom of Jesus.

James Weldon Johnson
Go Down Death—A Funeral Sermon

they do not expect to die. They may use fantasies of early death or fears of death for personal or psychological reasons, but the reality belief is that death need not occur in the foreseeable future, that death is a reversible event. That belief in the reversibility of death, rooted in the common American experience of modern medicine, begins to move death out of the moral order. Death is a technical matter, a failure of technology in rescuing the body from a threat to its functioning and integrity. For the moment, it does not matter that the death of a person cannot be removed from the moral order by the very nature of personhood; what matters is the mythology of the society. The widespread mythology that things essentially moral can be made technical is reinforced by the effect of technology in altering other events besides death; for example, birth, birth defects, or abortion.

The fact that technology can be seen so often as altering fate nurtures an illusion that is basic to the mythology of American society—that fate can be defeated.

FROM THE FAMILY TO THE HOSPITAL
Another reason why death has moved away from the moral order lies in the changes in family structure that have occurred over the past decades in the United States. The family remains the basic unit of moral and personal life, but with the passing of functionally meaningful extended families have come changes directly related to the care of the dying. The old, both the repository of knowledge about what is right and the major recipients of moral obligation, have left the family group. For many reasons, not the least their desire for continued independence in the years when previously material dependency would have been their lot, the aged frequently live alone.

In retirement they may live far from their roots or their children, associating largely with others of their own age. An age-graded way of life has emerged that depends again on technical success and public responsibility (such as old age benefits) to solve problems for the aged that previously would have been the primary concern of the family. There is the belief, reinforced by the advantages of the change in family structure and geographic mobility, that essentially moral problems—obligations to parents, for example—have become part of the technical order amenable to administrative or technical solutions.

On the other hand, in his search for continued independence and comfortable retirement, the old person has allowed his family to separate, allowed the young to achieve their independence. In previous times and in other cultures, the mantle passed to the next generation only with the death of the old. Here it is voluntary. But, a problem is created for the dying patient. The old person who is going to die is already out of the family. To die amidst his family he must return to them—reenter the structure in order to leave it. Reenter it in denial of all the reasons he gave himself and his children for separation, reasons equally important to them in their pursuit of privacy and individual striving and in their inherent denial of aging, death, and fate.

Thus, by reason of technological success and changes in family structure that are rooted in the basic mythology of America, death has moved from the moral order to the technical and from the family to the hospital. . . .

MECHANICAL EVENTS IN THE MORAL SPHERE
In the process of the shift of death from the moral to the technical a basic confusion arises that confounds the usefulness of

technical solutions in what are essentially moral problems. The mechanical events involved in a body becoming dead, which occur in the technical sphere, are confused with the process of dying, which occurs in the moral sphere. It is a natural error but one that we do not frequently make in health. That is to say that while we are aware that the mechanical event that is a beating heart is essential to life, we do not confuse ourselves with our heartbeat. As a matter of fact if someone becomes too conscious of his heartbeat, we consider it a symptom, or neurosis. But in the sick or the dying the confusion is rampant. There are two distinct things happening in the terminally ill, the death of the body and the passing of the person. The death of the body is a physical phenomenon, a series of measurable events that are the province of physicians. The passing of the individual is a nonphysical process, poorly defined, largely unmeasurable, and closely connected to the nature of the dying person. It is the process by which he leaves the group and during which we take leave of him. Indeed, in the manner in which many act towards the newly dead body—as though it still contained some part of the person—the passing of the individual, at least for the onlooker, may not end with death. It is obvious that in sudden death, a person may pass away who was never dying; or conversely, in the depressed, the person may be dying with no evidence of impending death.

The passing of the individual is also part of the work of physicians, but of more importance, it is the province of family, friends, and clergymen—indeed the entire group. But in a technical era, the passing of the person, since it is unmeasurable and does not fit the technical schema, is not a legitimate subject for public discourse.

Those feelings within that relate to the dying person are difficult to organize, to deal with, or to speak about. The social rituals that previously enabled those confused meanings and feelings to spend themselves appropriately have diminished or disappeared along with the extended family. In the moral order, time slows down for those around the dying; but in the world of things, of necessity or expediency, time moves on relentlessly, making its case for those around the dying to return to that world. Furthermore, with decreasing practice in moral matters, even when social forms remain, the content becomes increasingly sterile. Men obscure the moral content of the passing of the person by using the facts and artifacts of the death of the body as the vehicle for their interchanges—much as talk about the weather or sports draws the sting on other occasions.

The confusion of the mechanical events of the death of the body with the personal and social nature of the passing of the person confounds attempts to solve the essentially moral problems of the dying—problems of sentiment, conscience, or the knowledge of what is right. Thus, in matters such as when the respirators should be turned off, and by whom, essentially moral questions, the mechanical events loom so large that attention is diverted away from the moral, back to the technical. And this is the corollary problem to that raised earlier: the context of death no longer gives weight to the values of the dying person and forces a resort to legal or administrative protection of his rights.

DEPERSONALIZATION OF CARE   The confusion of mechanical events for moral processes creates the further problem of depersonalization of care. And it is seen in the greater attention paid to diseases than to people by doctors and their institutions—a common complaint about physicians and particularly about physicians in their care of the dying. Frequently we explain this depersonalization by saying that it is the physician's psychological defense against the emotional burden imposed by the care of the dying. Though that may be true, it is only part of the truth. We have seen how the whole society has shifted its public focus from moral to technical in many areas of life: doctors are no exception to the trend. The problem cannot solely lie among physicians, or the society would not let them get away with it. Social forces would drive doctors back towards a more holistic view of their patients. Indeed, such a change is beginning to occur in response to the increasingly vocal dissatisfaction with medical care.

Because depersonalization is so much a part of the technical order, not only in medicine, and so antithetical to the values of personhood, let us further examine how depersonalization takes place. Each dying patient is not only a person, but also the container of the process or events by which his body is dying. By definition, since he is dying, these processes or events cannot be controlled by existing technology. Because of the inability of the technology to control such things—and cancer or heart failure are examples—they acquire independent meaning apart from the person containing them. From the viewpoint of caring for the terminally ill, such depersonalization may be justly deplored. But from the viewpoint of medical science the pursuit of the meaning of the resistant body process, apart from the person containing it, is a legitimate end in itself. That is to say, the heart as an abstraction, as a pump, an electrical system or what have you, is a proper object of technical concern and quite distinct from the fact that human hearts are found only in humans. Further, it is the nature of any system of abstract or formal thought not to be content with

mystery, but to continue operating on any problem until understanding results. Mystery is a threat to the adequacy of the system of thought itself. Consequently, the disease process must be probed and probed, not only because of its relevance to the care of the sick and dying, but also because lack of a solution poses a threat to the entire logical construct of which the body process is thought to be a part. Thus, the depersonalization and abstraction of body mechanics is both necessary and legitimate within the framework of science, and understanding of the body-as-machine is impeded by consideration of human values.

The problem of depersonalization depends in part on the degree to which the dying person's disease process is understood. For example, in the care of the patient with bacterial pneumonia, easily treated with antibiotics, depersonalization poses little difficulty. The abstractions necessary for understanding microbes, antibiotics, and so forth, are so much a part of the physician's thinking that he or she is able to integrate them back into a total concept of man, patients, etc. Withdrawal and depersonalization are not frequent, I think, when experienced doctors and nurses care for the dying, if the cause of death is something acceptably inevitable, such as pneumonia in the very old, or stroke. If it is correct that persons dying of a poorly understood process are more likely to be depersonalized by their physicians, we can better understand why the accusation of depersonalization is most often brought against young physicians. To the inexperienced doctor almost everything about the dying person is unfamiliar or poorly understood thus requiring the abstraction that leads to depersonalization. Effective integration of the learned technical material with human needs, values, and desires comes only at a later stage of learning.

TEMPLES OF THE TECHNICAL ORDER

In the United States, the modern medical center is the very temple of the technical order, revered both by medicine and the public. As medical science, in its effort towards understanding, has taken the body apart system by system, it has departmentalized the intellectual structure of the hospital. By that I mean not only the well known division of medicine into specialties, but the further subdivisions that represent specific body functions. The corridors of any American medical center reveal rooms whose doors bear titles such as pulmonary function laboratory, cardiographics laboratory, nuclear medicine, sonography, and so forth. Each of these specialized functions has contributed immeasurably to the diagnostic and therapeutic power of the modern physician, and no doctor who has grown accustomed to their use will feel wholly comfortable in their absence. They are unlike the traditional clinical or research laboratory which when examining a function of the patient's body takes the whole patient along; it is not his blood or urine that goes to the laboratory, it is the patient. But it is not the person who holds the interest for the specialized laboratory; instead the interest centers on the person's lungs, or heart, or whatever. A good coronary arteriogram is not necessarily a good patient or even good for the patient, it is merely a technically good example of coronary arteriograms. Patients are usually not aware or interested in those distinctions and all too frequently, but in an opposite sense, neither is the physician who performed the test. One can see the hospital, thus compartmentalized, as the concrete expression of the depersonalization resulting from the abstract analytic thought of medical science. Thus, the dying patient in the modern hospital is in an environment ideally suited for the pursuit of knowledge and cure, but representing in its technology and idealized representative—the young doctor—technical values virtually antithetical to the holistic concept of person. This does not imply that the most personal and humane care cannot be and is not given in such hospitals, but rather that those who do give such care must struggle against their technical depersonalized thinking about the body, and against the structure of the hospital that such thought has produced....

A BALANCE OF THE MORAL AND TECHNICAL

We have seen that the problem is larger than widespread insensitivity which might be corrected by new educational programs. Rather, there has been a shift of death from within the moral order to the technical order. The technical, the expedient, the utilitarian that has worked so well in so many material ways seemed to promise easier solutions to the problems previously seen as matters of conscience, sentiment, or obligations between men. But the promise has not been fulfilled; not in the United States nor elsewhere where the technical order spreads its dominance.

Even if it were possible, the solution is not a return of American society to technical innocence. I do not believe that men were inherently more moral in the past when the moral order predominated over the technical. The path seems to lie in the direction of a more systematic understanding of the moral order to restore its balance with the technical. Understanding the body has not made it less wonderful, and the systematic exploration of the moral nature of man will not destroy that nature but rather increase its influence. In the care of the dying, it may give back to the living the meaning of death.

6.

Life after Death
Old and New Meanings

The belief in life after death is as ancient as the history of the human race and as contemporary as the morning newspaper. Archeological evidence indicates that the earliest human beings ceremonially painted the bodies of the dead in anticipation of some form of continued survival. Modern news media carry numerous accounts of people who "died" on the operating table, only to be revived and return from their close encounters with death with remarkably uniform reports of peaceful feelings and bright lights.

Traditionally, religions have expressed the belief in the immortality of the human soul. As Markusen's article indicates, conceptions of life after death in the major religions assume a variety of forms; taken collectively, however, their centrality in most religious orientations suggests a very strong human need to believe in some form of continued existence following physical death. By the same token, the wide variation among the specific depictions of post-mortem life underscores the capacity of human beings to live and die within the context of diverse belief systems.

A recurrent theme in this anthology has been the replacement of religion by science as the dominant perspective on life and death in modern societies. Science is based upon observation of tangible phenomena or processes, and within its domain there is virtually no room for such intangible concepts as spirits or souls. Of course, this does not prove that souls do not, in fact, exist. It means, rather, that it is unlikely that the existence of immortal souls will be "proved" through the application of science. Belief in the soul will have to rest, as it traditionally has, on faith, although as faith is popularly discredited in favor of scientific evidence, the security of such beliefs will be precarious.

The decline in the power and pervasiveness of religion notwithstanding, belief in the survival of the soul or spirit after physical death is still widespread in our society. Of course, there are still millions of persons for whom religion is still a very viable and meaningful part of their lives. For them, there is little question of the existence of life after death. However, to judge from the burgeoning sales of such books as Raymond Moody's *Life after Life* as well as the rising popular interest in astrology, the occult, and mysticism, there are many people who are not firmly integrated into a traditional religious orientation but who nevertheless want to believe in the reality of post-mortem existence. Many of these persons who are yearning for confirmation of their beliefs, but for whom religion is not sufficiently credible, are finding it in an interesting blend of scientific research, medical developments, and rather old-fashioned faith.

The Heywood article discusses the accumulating evidence of the existence of such paranormal phenomena as telepathy (the ability to communicate thoughts with no apparent physical transmission) and precognition (the ability to forecast the future). Such phenomena are being conscientiously researched under scientific conditions at several reputable universities in the United States and Europe. While considerable controversy surrounds the findings, there is little doubt that the capacities of the human organism, and the brain in particular, are far more complex than was thought previously. This realization is being corroborated in medical centers around the world, where neurologists are rapidly expanding our understanding of the marvels of the human mind. In fact, the discoveries of neurology are similar to those in astronomy and subatomic physics—the more we learn, the more we realize how little we actually do know or understand. Indicative of the adventurous open-mindedness in medical research on the frontiers of the mind is a recent article in the highly respected *Journal of Nervous and Mental Diseases*. The article reviewed the existing evidence on survival after death. However, as Heywood concludes, the existence of paranormal phenomena does not prove that any aspect of the person or mind does in fact survive death. She adds that many researchers are still on the fence, and stepping off in either the direction of belief in survival or disbelief "entails an act of faith."

Raymond Moody and Elisabeth Kübler-Ross are two physicians whose names are immediately associated today with the life-after-death debate. Moody's best-selling book, *Life after Life,* presented several case studies of persons who had ostensibly "died" or at least been very "near death" and who survived to tell of their experiences. The consistency with which they described wondrous, peaceful feelings and glowing vistas captured the imaginations and interests of millions of readers. Kübler-Ross, whose book *On Death and Dying* has been justly credited with focusing attention on the human needs of dying patients, has recently publicized her own paranormal experiences as well as her conviction that the spirit survives after physical death. It is probably not insignificant that

neither Moody nor Kübler-Ross is a representative of an established religious orientation and that both are scientifically trained medical doctors. It is perhaps a sign of our secular times that physicians now threaten to usurp the role of theologians as guides to the beyond.

Moody's selection reports several "near death" experiences that persons who were later revived were able to recall vividly. Images of total knowledge, of cities of light, and of perfect peace and contentment are likely to warm the heart of the believer, or would-be believer, in life after death. The "realm of bewildered spirits" he describes, however, is rather less pleasant, but at least the prospect of leaving it remains open. As Vaisrub points out, however, one must never forget in reading such case studies that none of the persons actually died. We therefore cannot assume that these reports tell us anything about what actually comes after death. But it is perhaps another sign of the times that readers are willing to suspend their ordinary judgment in order to read and enjoy such accounts by a medical doctor.

Taylor and Ingrasci's interview with Kübler-Ross included in this section contains a detailed account of her own out-of-body experience. Kübler-Ross matter-of-factly talks of patients who had clinically died and "came back to life telling what they experienced." Again, one must note that "clinical death," that is, the temporary cessation of heartbeat and breathing that is afterwards restored through resuscitative efforts, is not *death*. Death of the body is irreversible. If the body is revived, then death *per se* has not occurred. While this fact does not disprove the survival of the spirit, it reminds us that "near death" experiences most certainly do not prove it.

Vaisrub, a senior editor of the *Journal of the American Medical Association*, suggests that the current spate of reports of "near death" experiences might have a darker side. So far, most reports of the "next life" have been very pleasant and appealing. For persons plagued with difficult lives or painful diseases, "cities of light" might have a strong appeal. However, Vaisrub notes the possibility of some experiences being horrifying and miserable. One is reminded that many traditional religious perspectives envisioned not only an afterworld of peace and bliss, but also a place of misery and torment. Reopening the door to the realm of spirits in our modern age may let in demons as well as angels. Caution, as well as compassion, is called for.

The final selection by Bertrand Russell argues that our scientific research has shown that that which is distinctively human resides in the marvelous organ of the human brain. When the brain is destroyed, our humanness is destroyed as well. Russell asserts that our fear of death and our egotism compel us to believe in survival after death. Furthermore, when he examines carefully the history of humankind, he questions whether he would want to see very many people from the past living forever —how would Attila the Hun and Adolf Hitler fit into a celestial city of light?

...To die, to sleep;
To sleep: perchance to dream: ay, there's the rub;
For in that sleep of death what dreams may come
When we have shuffled off this mortal coil,
Must give us pause....

William Shakespeare
Hamlet

Eric Markusen

Religious Conceptions of Afterlife

This selection by Eric Markusen, a co-editor of this Reader and staff member of the Center for Death Education and Research of the University of Minnesota, is based on a book review of *The Judgment of the Dead,* S. G. F. Brandon's survey of beliefs in post-death existence held by the major religions of the world. As one appreciates the significance of such beliefs throughout history, the implications of the growing secularization of modern societies become more important and disquieting. Conceptions of post-mortem existence have significantly influenced both the lifestyles and deathstyles of countless millions. Both Karl Marx and Sigmund Freud stated that such beliefs are socially and psychologically necessary for people to function in society. In terming religion "the opiate of the masses," Marx noted that the hope of salvation in the next world enabled people to endure the injustices of this one. Freud, in *The Future of an Illusion*, theorized that beliefs in an omnipotent deity provide human beings with essential emotional support in the face of unfathomable and uncontrollable forces and events. If there is any truth in these formulations, then one wonders how future generations, in the absence of theological interpretations of death, will be able to attach meaning to it.

A survey of the major world religions indicates that conceptions of post-mortem existence have been basic to virtually all of them. Therefore, we can assume that a sizeable portion of the billions of human beings who have inhabited this planet, have grown up learning some cultural tradition of survival after death.

Out of the array of beliefs about life after death, S. G. F. Brandon, in *The Judgment of the Dead,* has discerned three broad patterns. First we see that several religions—notably the ancient Mesopotamians, the early Jews, and the Homeric Greeks—depicted the hereafter as a bleak underground place to which everyone, regardless of his earthly merit, was consigned. Hence the issue of post-mortem judgment was irrelevant.

The second pattern appears in those religions whose deities play an active part in man's ultimate fate. This pattern is found in the religions of the ancient Egyptians, later Jews, Christians, and Muslims. Conformity to dogma is the criterion which distinguishes the saved from the damned. Belief in post-mortem judgment is necessary for such theodicies in which the faithful suffer and often die unvindicated. Belief in a hereafter serves, for those religions, to reconcile man's experience with his hopes.

The third pattern of belief about life after death is seen in Hinduism and Buddhism, two religions without a strong theistic perspective. Instead of teaching, as the other religions do, that man has only one earthly life which death terminates, they teach that man undergoes a potentially endless series of reincarnations. Between reincarnations, the individual either goes to a place of reward or retribution, depending on his actions, or karma, in the previous life. Karma also determined the conditions of subsequent reincarnations. If his previous life was characterized by evil karma, he is reincarnated as a degraded human or in some sub-human form. In contrast to the theistic religions, karma, which determines post-mortem fate, is not conceived as an omniscient deity, but as an impersonal process, which no amount of ritual or intercession can influence.

Although there are diverse ideas regarding the fate of man after death and the nature of the judgment process, Brandon notes a remarkable uniformity in the imagery used to present ideas symbolically. The image of the judging of the soul after death, for example, appears in the eschatological artifacts of the ancient Egyptians, Greeks, Christians, Muslims, Hindus, Buddhists, and Japanese. Depictions of heaven and hell in the various religions also show much in common. Whereas heaven is customarily depicted with relatively vague symbolic allusions, hell has inspired horrifically detailed descriptions and paintings, ranging from the "Dooms" on Christian churches to the Japanese scrolls in which specific tortures for given crimes are painstakingly portrayed.

The historical pervasiveness and cultural impact of such belief systems stimulate speculation on the well-documented attenuation of religious orientations in modern, industrialized nations. Religions have traditionally been the primary sources for interpretations of death and its relation to life. Science, however, which has progressively challenged the relevance and influence of religion, is inherently unable to shed light on the ineffable mysteries of the grave and beyond. It is possible that beliefs in post-mortem existence and judgment, which archaeological evidence indicates date back to the Paleolithic era, are simply unnecessary and irrelevant. It is also possible, however, that age-old beliefs and yearnings will find their expression in new forms. Perhaps, the resurgence of interest in the occult, mysticism, and what are erroneously called "near death" experiences all testify to the desire for tangible information about one of life's central experiences in a society whose secular lifestyle denies its existence while its belief system is incapable of considering its presence.

Rosalind Heywood

Death and Psychical Research

Heywood, a prominent English authority on psychical research, that is, studies of paranormal phenomena, examines the implications of accumulating evidence for the existence of such paranormal phenomena as these relate to the concept of survival of the spirit after death. She mentions that numerous people have experienced what appeared to be contact with the spirit of a dead person and questions how they should feel. Should they try to forget such experiences, discarding them as illusions? Should they doubt their sanity? As more people feel able to share such experiences, they may become more "normal"; in turn, others who had been afraid or ashamed to report similar experiences may be encouraged to "go public." Such disclosures will fan the flames of interest in the idea of survival and perhaps stimulate further research that will someday permit more conclusive findings. Until then, many researchers will probably remain "on the fence," neither firmly believing nor disbelieving.

From the point of view of the investigator, then, the findings of psychical research in relation to death seem to amount to something like this. On the one hand the apparent potentialities of ESP make it hard to conceive what kind of evidence could give coercive proof of survival—evidence that could not at a pinch be ascribed to some combination of telepathy, clairvoyance, precognition or retrocognition in relation to events in this world. As against this, the more we learn about the range of these capacities, about

man's apparent power to transcend the limitations of the known senses and of time and space as presented to him by those senses, the less inconceivable it may be that the early researchers were on the right track in surmising that there could be something in him— what Professor C. D. Broad discreetly calls some psi component—which might be able to function independently of a physical body.

In a book concerned with attitudes to death some reference should perhaps be made not only to the attitude of the scientific researcher as regards the possibility of survival, but also to those of people who have themselves had ESP-type experiences connected with death. It may be guessed that most actively religious Christians who have such experiences accept them for what they appear to be, and that a number of the non-Christians who have them join some group, such as the theosophists or spiritualists, into whose beliefs their experiences will fit, for this gives them peace of mind. But how many people are there like the flight lieutenant, who appeared to talk quite normally with his dead fellow pilot and yet had no framework of belief which would hold his experience? Judging from the many cases sent to Dr. Louisa Rhine and to other writers of seriously-intentioned books on psi, there must be an appreciable number, and owing to the present orthodox belief that death is the end, it looks as if some of them dare not mention such experiences for fear of being thought out of their minds. Some even wonder, could that perhaps be true? "Can you possibly explain this?" they write, "I have never dared ask anyone before. Do you think I could be mad?"

The experiences most often reported, incidentally, as with most of the authenticated cases in the annals of psychical research, are far removed from the headless, chain-clanking "ghosties and ghoulies" of fiction and Christmas Numbers. Apart from the apparently aimless haunting type, modern "ghosts" usually seem to want to help, or warn, or merely to appear to a loved friend or relative. And sometimes they are not distinguished from living persons until they vanish.

For those of us, then, who are conditioned by the widespread belief that mind and body die together, and who yet have apparent contacts with the purposeful discarnate, what is our rational attitude towards those contacts, especially as they are admittedly sporadic, fleeting, and not to be repeated to order? Perhaps I may be forgiven a personal summarized illustration of this dilemma, since it is not easy to describe other people's experiences as if from the inside.

In the 1950s the expected death occurred of an inventor friend, with whom, as we both accepted that death was the end, I had shortly before agreed regretfully that he would never be able to bring to fruition the many ideas still seething in his brain. About ten days after his death I was astounded and delighted to "meet," quite naturally, his apparently living personality, and to be assured with emphasis that we had been quite mistaken; he now had scope and opportunity beyond his wildest dreams. In some imageless way I seemed able to participate in his awareness of scope and opportunity and I was rejoicing in this when it

flashed across my mind that I ought to ask for evidence of his splendid liberation. But the reply he made was, "I can't give you any evidence. You have no concepts for these conditions.[1] I can only give you poetic images." Which he did. But quite soon I realized that I could not hold the state into which, unexpectedly, my consciousness had switched, so I said, "Goodbye, I must drop now." And I "dropped" at once to ordinary awareness of mundane surroundings.

Although this experience does not appear to be very exceptional, there is not a shred of evidence to support my account of it, and investigators will therefore—and quite rightly—feel it their duty to dismiss it as a mere anecdote. But again, what is the rational attitude for the people who have such experiences, sometimes repeatedly? Should we discard them all as illusions, in obedience to orthodoxy? Should we even suspect our own sanity? (I asked two eminent psychiatrists to check on mine and they both gave me a clean bill of health. But one did say sadly, "I'm *afraid* you're quite sane.") Or should we defy the voice of contemporary science and bet on the reality of our own experiences, however fleeting and unpredictable?

On one thing, perhaps, the psi-experiencing agnostic can afford to bet—that were the whole of humanity to have experiences similar to his own, of the occasional momentary, purposeful presence of discarnate persons he had

---

1. In an article in *The New Scientist* for August 30th, 1962, Dr. Richard Gregory has suggested that travellers in space might be faced with a similar problem. "Suppose," he says, "we were to meet something really odd—say a new life form—could we see it properly? The perceptual system is a computer, programmed by evolutionary experience and by our own personal experience of the world. A new kind of object requires the perceptual computer to solve a new problem with an old program, which may be neither adequate nor appropriate."

known in life, it would not occur to them, however mistaken they might be in fact, to doubt the reality of survival. As things are, however, the only place where his reason can feel at ease and honest is on the fence. And there he will at least be encouraged to find a number of distinguished scholars who have thought it worthwhile to study the evidence for survival for many years. This is how [two] among them summed up their conclusions in the 1960s. First, the well-known American psychologist Professor Gardner Murphy.

> Where then do I stand? To this the reply is: what happens when an irresistible force strikes an immovable object? To me the evidence cannot be bypassed, nor, on the other hand, can conviction be achieved. . . . Trained as a psychologist and now in my sixties, I do not actually anticipate finding myself in existence after physical death. If this is the answer the reader wants, he can have it. But if this means that in a serious philosophical argument I would plead the antisurvival case, the conclusion is erroneous. I linger because I cannot cross the stream. We need far more evidence; we need new perspectives; perhaps we need more courageous minds.[2]

And [secondly,] Professor C. D. Broad, sometime Knightbridge Professor of Moral Philosophy at Cambridge. He, incidentally, does not hide the fact that he does not want to survive.

2. *Challenge of Psychical Research,* Harpers, New York, 1961, p. 273.

The position as I see it is this. In the known relevant normal and abnormal facts there is nothing to suggest and much to countersuggest, the possibility of any kind of persistence of the psychical aspect of a human being after the death of his body. On the other hand, there are many quite well-attested *paranormal* phenomena which strongly suggest such persistence, and a few which strongly suggest the fullblown survival of a human personality. Most people manage to turn a blind eye to one or the other of these two relevant sets of data, but it is part of the business of a professional philosopher to try to envisage steadily both of them together. The result is naturally a state of hesitation and skepticism (in the correct as opposed to the popular sense of that word). I think I may say that for my part I should be slightly more annoyed than surprised if I should find myself in some sense persisting immediately after the death of my present body. One can only wait and see, or alternatively (which is no less likely) wait and not see.[3]

It looks then as if at the present time to step off the fence on either side as regards survival entails an act of faith. On one side we can believe—but cannot prove—that men of science already know enough about the nature of things to be able to assert with safety that it is impossible; on the other we can believe—but equally cannot prove—that certain phenomena demonstrate that it is a fact.

3. *Lectures on Psychical Research,* International Library of Philosophy and Scientific Method, Routledge and Kegan Paul, 1962, p. 430.

Cities of Light

Raymond Moody, M.D., author of *Life after Life*, presents several intriguing reports from persons who have undergone "near death" experiences. Such reports, especially insofar as they are uplifting and pleasant, exercise a powerful appeal for many people who seek greater meaning for both life and death. One must remember, however, that "near death" is not *death*; as such, these reports cannot be taken as providing scientific evidence of post-mortem survival. Their popularity, on the other hand, testifies to the yearning for greater meaning on the parts of millions of people.

In the process of studying the large number of accounts of near-death experiences which I have collected since the completion of Life After Life, I have encountered several new elements which were not included there. Each of the elements that I will be discussing here has been reported to me by more than one person, but they are far from being as common as the original fifteen. With the exception of the "supernatural rescues," all of these unusual elements occurred exclusively in the reports of subjects who had near-death encounters of extreme duration.

THE VISION OF KNOWLEDGE *Several people have told me that during their encounters with "death," they got brief glimpses of an entire separate realm of existence in* which all knowledge—whether of past, present, or future—seemed to co-exist in a sort of timeless state. Alternately, this has been described as a moment of enlightenment in which the subject seemed to have complete knowledge. In trying to talk about this aspect of their experience, all have commented that this experience was ultimately inexpressible. Also, all agree that this feeling of complete knowledge did not persist after their return; that they did not bring back any sort of omniscience. They agree that this vision did not discourage them from trying to learn in this life, but, rather, encouraged them to do so.

The experience has been compared, in various accounts, to a flash of universal insight, institutions of higher learning, a "school," and a "library." Everyone emphasizes, however, that the words they are using to describe this experience are at best only dim reflections of the reality they are trying to express. It is my own feeling that there may be one underlying state of consciousness which is at the root of all these different accounts.

One woman who had "died" gave the following report during an extended interview.

You mentioned earlier that you seemed to have "a vision of knowledge," if I could call it that. Could you tell me about it?

This seems to have taken place after I had seen my life pass before me. It seemed that all of a sudden, all knowledge—of all that had started from the very beginning, that would go on without end—that for a second I knew all the secrets of all ages, all the meaning of the universe, the stars, the moon—of everything. But after I chose to return, this knowledge escaped, and I can't remember any of it: It seems that when I made the decision [to return] I was told that I would not retain the knowledge. But I kept being called back by my children....

This all-powerful knowledge opened before me. It seemed that I was being told that I was going to remain sick for quite a while and that I would have other close calls. And I did have several close calls after that. They said some of it would be to erase this all-knowing knowledge that I had picked up...that I had been granted the universal secrets and that I would have to undergo time to forget that knowledge. But I do have the memory of once knowing everything, that it did happen, but that it was not a gift that I would keep if I returned. But I chose to return to my children.... The memory of all these things that happened has remained clear, all except for that fleeting moment of knowledge. And that feeling of all knowledge disappeared when I returned to my body.

It sounds silly! Well, it does when you say it out loud...or it does to me, because I've never been able to sit and talk to someone else about it.

I don't know how to explain it, but I knew.... As the Bible says, "To you all things will be revealed." For a minute, there was no question that didn't have an answer. How long I knew it, I couldn't say. It wasn't in earthly time, anyway.

In what form did this knowledge seem to be presented to you? Was it in words or pictures?

It was in all forms of communication, sights, sounds, thoughts. It was any- and everything. It was as if there was nothing that wasn't known. All knowledge was there, not just of one field, but everything.

One thing I wonder. I've spent a lot of my life seeking knowledge, learning. If this happens, isn't that sort of thing rather pointless?

No! You still want to seek knowledge even after you come back here. I'm still seeking knowledge.... It's not silly to try to get the answers here. I sort of felt that it was part of our purpose. . .but that it wasn't just for one person, but that it was to be used for all mankind. We're always reaching out to help others with what we know....

I am impressed by the similarity between this concept and one which was expressed—in an admittedly metaphorical and poetic way—by Plato in his telling of the story of Er, a warrior who came back to life on the funeral pyre, after having been believed dead. Er is said to have seen many things in the afterlife, but he was told that he must return to physical life to tell others what death is like. Just before he returned, he saw souls which were being prepared to be born into life:

They all journeyed to the Plain of Oblivion, through a terrible and stifling heat, for it was bare of trees and all plants, and there they camped at eventide by the River of Forgetfulness, whose waters no vessel can contain. They were all required to drink a measure of the water, and those who were not saved by their good sense drank more than the measure, and each one as he drank forgot all things. And after they had fallen asleep and it was the middle of the night, there was a sound of thunder and a quaking of the earth, and they were suddenly wafted thence, one this way, one that, upward to their birth like shooting stars. Er himself, he said, was not allowed to drink of the water, yet how and in what way he returned to the body he said he did not know, but suddenly recovering his sight he saw himself at dawn lying on the funeral pyre.

The basic theme being presented here, that before returning to life a certain kind of "forgetting" of knowledge one has in the eternal state must take place, is similar in the two cases.

During another interview, a young man told me this:

Now, I was in a school...and it was real. It was not imaginary. If I were not absolutely sure, I would say, "Well, there is a possibility that I was in this place." But it *was* real. It was like a school, and there was no one there, and yet there were a lot of people there. Because if you looked around, you would see nothing...but if you paid attention, you would feel, sense, the presence of other beings around.... It's as if there were lessons coming at me and they would keep coming at me....

> That's interesting. Another man told me that he went into what he called "libraries" and "institutions of higher learning." Is that anything like what you're trying to tell me?

Exactly! You see, hearing what you say he said about it, it's like I know exactly what he means, that I know he's been through this same thing I have. And yet...the words I would use are different, because there really

are no words...I cannot describe it. You could not compare it to anything here. The terms I'm using to describe it are so far from the thing, but it's the best I can do.... Because this is a place where the *place* is knowledge.... Knowledge and information are readily available—all knowledge....You absorb knowledge.... You all of a sudden know the answers....

I go on seeking knowledge: "Seek and ye shall find." You can get the knowledge for yourself. But I *pray* for wisdom, wisdom more than all....

A middle-aged lady described it this way:

There was a moment in this thing—well, there isn't any way to describe it—but it was like I knew all things.... For a moment, there, it was like communication wasn't necessary. I thought whatever I wanted to know could be known.

CITIES OF LIGHT   *I stated in* Life after Life *that I had not found any cases in which a "heaven"—at least in a certain traditional portrayal of that place—was described. However, I have now talked with numerous individuals who tell with remarkable consistency of catching glimpses of other realms of being which might well be termed "heavenly." It is interesting to me that in several of these accounts a single phrase—"a city of light"—occurs. In this and several other respects the imagery in which these scenes are described seems to be reminiscent of what is found in the Bible.*

One middle-aged man who had a cardiac arrest related:

I had heart failure and clinically died.... I remember everything perfectly vividly....

Suddenly I felt numb. Sounds began sounding a little distant.... All this time I was perfectly conscious of everything that was going on. I heard the heart monitor go off. I saw the nurse come into the room and dial the telephone, and the doctors, nurses, and attendants came in.

As things began to fade there was a sound I can't describe; it was like the beat of a snare drum, very rapid, a rushing sound, like a stream rushing through a gorge. And I rose up and I was a few feet up looking down on my body. There I was, with people working on me. I had no fear. No pain. Just peace. After just probably a second or two, I seemed to turn over and go up. It was dark—you could call it a hole or a tunnel—and there was the bright light. It got brighter and brighter. And I seemed to go *through* it.

All of a sudden I was just somewhere else. There was a gold-looking light, everywhere. Beautiful. I couldn't find a source anywhere. It was just all around, coming from everywhere. There was music. And I seemed to be in a countryside with streams, grass, and trees, mountains. But when I looked around—if you want to put it that way—there were not trees and things like we know them to be. The strangest thing to me about it was that there were people there. Not in any kind of form or body as we know it; they were just there.

There was a sense of perfect peace and contentment; love. It was like I was part of it. That experience could have lasted the whole night or just a second. . .I don't know.

Here's the way one woman described it:

There was a vibration of some sort. The vibration was surrounding me, all around my body. It was like the body vibrating, and where the vibration came from, I don't know. But when it vibrated, I became separated. I could then see my body.... I stayed around for a while and watched the doctor and nurses working on my body, wondering what would happen.... I was at the head of the bed, looking at them and my body, and at one time one nurse reached up to the wall over the bed to get the oxygen mask that was there and as she did she reached *through* my neck....

And after I floated up, I went through this dark tunnel...I went into the black tunnel and came out into brilliant light.... A little bit later on I was there with my grandparents and my father and my brother, who had died.... There was the most beautiful, brilliant light all around. And this was a beautiful place. There were colors—bright colors—not like here on earth, but just indescribable. There were people there, happy people.... People were around, some of them gathered in groups. Some of them were learning....

Off in the distance...I could see a city. There were buildings—separate buildings. They were gleaming, bright. People were happy in there. There was sparkling water, fountains...a city of light I guess would be the way to say it.... It was wonderful. There was beautiful music. Everything was just glowing, wonderful.... But if I had entered into this, I think I would never have returned.... I was told that if I went there I couldn't go back...that the decision was mine....

A REALM OF BEWILDERED SPIRITS
Several people have reported to me that at some point they glimpsed other beings who seemed to be "trapped" in an apparently most unfortunate state of existence. Those who described seeing these confused beings are in agreement on several points. First, they state

that these beings seemed to be, in effect, unable to surrender their attachments to the physical world. One man recounted that the spirits he saw apparently "couldn't progress on the other side because their God is still living here." That is, they seemed bound to some particular object, person, or habit. Second, all have remarked that these beings appeared "dulled," that their consciousness seemed somehow limited in contrast with that of others. Third, they say it appeared that these "dulled spirits" were to be there only until they solved whatever problem or difficulty was keeping them in that perplexed state.

These points of agreement came across in the following segment of an interview with one woman who was believed "dead" for some fifteen minutes.

> You mentioned seeing these people—spirits who seemed very confused. Could you tell me more about them?

These bewildered people? I don't know exactly where I saw them.... But as I was going by, there was this area that was dull—this is the contrast to all the brilliant light. The figures were more humanized than the rest of them were, if you stop to think of it in that respect, but neither were they in quite human form as we are.

What you would think of as their head was bent downward; they had sad, depressed looks; they seemed to shuffle, as someone would on a chain gang. I don't know why I say this because I don't remember noticing feet. I don't know what they were, but they looked washed out, dull, gray. And they seemed to be forever shuffling and moving around, not knowing where they were going, not knowing who to follow, or what to look for.

As I went by they didn't even raise their heads to see what was happening. They seemed to be thinking, "Well, it's all over with. What am I doing? What's it all about?" Just this absolute, crushed, hopeless demeanor—not knowing what to do or where to go or who they were or anything else.

They seemed to be forever moving, rather than just sitting, but in no special direction. They would start straight, then veer to the left and take a few steps and veer back to the right. And absolutely nothing to do. Searching, but for what they were searching I don't know.

> Did they seem to be aware of the physical world?

They didn't seem to be aware of anything—not the physical world or the spiritual world. They seemed to be caught in between somewhere. It's neither spiritual nor physical. It's on a level somewhere between the two—or it appeared so to me. They may have some contact with the physical world. Something is tying them down, because they all seemed to be bent over and looking downward, maybe into the physical world...maybe watching something they hadn't done or should do. They couldn't make up their minds what to do, because they all had the most woebegone expressions; there was no color of life.

> So they seemed to be bewildered?

Very bewildered; not knowing who they are or what they are. It looks like they have lost any knowledge of who they are, what they are —no identity whatsoever.

> Would you say they were in between the physical world and what you were in?

In my memory, what I saw was after I left the physical hospital. As I said, I felt I rose upward and it was between, it was *before* I actually entered this tunnel—as I referred to it— and before I entered the spiritual world where there is so much brilliant sunlight—well, not sunlight, but the brilliant light that surrounded everything and was brighter than sunlight, but it didn't hurt like the sunlight can hurt your eyes, no glare to it. But in this particular place there was the dullest, drab gray. Now, I have a friend who is color blind and I've heard him say that the world to him is just shades and tones of gray. But to me, I'm full of color —and this was something that was maybe like a black and white movie. Just the different tones of gray—dingy, washed out.

They were not aware of me. They showed no sign of being aware that I was there. It was quite depressing.

They seemed to be trying to decide; they were looking back; they didn't know whether to go on or to return to the bodies where they were. They did seem to hover; they kept looking downward and never upward. They didn't want to go on to see what was awaiting them; they also reminded me of what I have read of as descriptions of ghosts; they would be mainly the see-through type of thing. There seems to have been a great huge array of them around.

Some persons who have seen this phenomenon have noticed certain of these beings apparently trying unsuccessfully to communicate with persons who were still physically alive. One man related many instances he observed while he was "dead" for an extended period of time. For example, he told how he saw an ordinary man walking, unaware, down the street while one of these dulled spirits hovered above him. He said he had the feeling that this spirit had been, while alive, the man's mother,

and, still unable to give up her earthly role, was trying to tell her son what to do. . . .

SUPERNATURAL RESCUES *In several accounts I have collected, persons say that they had near-death experiences through which they were saved from physical death by the interposition of some spiritual agent or being. In each case, the person involved found himself (knowingly or unknowingly) in a potentially fatal accident or set of circumstances from which it was beyond his own powers to escape. He may even have given up and prepared himself to die. However, at this point a voice or a light manifested itself and rescued him from the brink of death. Persons undergoing this relate that afterward their lives were changed, that they came to feel they were saved from death for a purpose. They have all reported that their religious beliefs were strengthened.*

One experience of this type which has become quite well known is that related in the

The Heart asks Pleasure—first—
And then—Excuse from Pain—
And then—those little Anodynes
That deaden suffering—

And then—to go to sleep—
And then—if it should be
The will of its Inquisitor
The privilege to die—

Emily Dickinson

book A Man Called Peter, by Catherine Marshall. She describes how, during his boyhood in Scotland, Peter Marshall was saved from falling to his death over a cliff in the fog by a voice which called to him from behind. This experience affected him greatly, and he went on to become a minister.

Here is a part of one interview in which a "rescue" of this type is reported. A man told me of being involved in an industrial accident in which he was trapped in a huge vat, into which a stream of very hot acid and steam was being pumped under high pressure. He recalled:

The heat of all this was terrific. I yelled, "Let me out of here. I'm getting trapped." I had gotten as far as I could into a corner, and put my face into the corner, but the stuff was so hot that it was burning me through my clothing. So, at that time I realized that in just a matter of minutes I would be scalded to death.

I guess it was in my weakness or whatever that I gave up. To myself, I just said, "This is it. I'm a goner." I could not see, and the heat was so intense that I could not open my eyes. I had my eyes closed the whole time. But it seemed that the whole area lit up with a glow. And a verse of Scripture that I had heard all my life, that had never meant too much to me, "Lo, I am with thee always," came from a direction which later turned out to be the only way out.

I couldn't stand to open my eyes, but I could still see that light, so I followed it. I know that my eyes were closed the whole time, though. The doctor didn't even treat my eyes later. No acid got in them....

Did this change your life in any way?

After I got back to work, some of the people who work there were talking about how calm I was after the whole thing had happened. I'm not that brave a man; I don't have that much courage. The fact that I was led by an unseen hand out of the danger was the source of my courage, was the calmness they saw. It was not in me. The voice that led me out was the same voice that gave me that courage.

I know that the hand of Jesus Christ reached down and got me out of that place. I think it's not a matter of think, it's a matter of know that it was God's will that my life be spared— for what reason, I don't know. At that time I was not living as close to God as I should have. I have been drawn closer to him by this. I still have problems. I know that a God that can step in and save a man in a moment of crisis can handle anything. So I have learned to depend on him.

When you heard the voice, was it just like a normal physical voice?

No. It was as if it was magnified, amplified. There was no question that I heard. There was no question as to the direction it came from. If it had come from my right or from my left, and I had followed it. I would have been instantly killed, The fact that it came from the direction it came from and that I followed the voice was why I came out alive.... Never would I have stepped out into that heat myself. I knew what I was in for.

[This voice] was a commanding voice—not "Will you come this way?" The first thing that popped into my mind was "Here I am down here by myself and I'm going to die." And when I heard that voice, there was no doubt in my mind, I knew that within myself I had no way to get out.

How long did this last?

It seemed like an eternity. In other words if you are crawling some forty or fifty feet through acid, each time you make a move you know you are moving at top speed. I would say the whole thing happened in a matter of a couple or three minutes after I saw that I was trapped, but it seemed like an eternity.

Did this seem like a normal physical light?

No. It was nothing like I had ever seen before. It was what you might see if you looked up into the sunlight. And this was a dark place where I was trapped. It was a big bright light and a voice. I didn't see a figure or anything like that. I followed the light the whole way.

Did the light seem to hurt your eyes? Was it uncomfortable to look into it?

No. Not in any way.

Did it seem to have any particular color?

No. Nothing other than just a bright white light. It was like the sun—like looking into the sun....

Finally, here is the account of one woman who was extremely ill with an infection. Note that in this example the patient seems to have been instructed and guided in her own resuscitation.

The doctors had all given up on me. They said I was dying.... I got to the point where I was feeling the life going out of my body.... I could still hear what everyone was saying, though I couldn't see anything. I wished I could live to raise my children and to play a part in their lives....

That's when I heard God's voice talking to me. He had the most loving gentle voice.... I know I wasn't out of my head, as some people might think.... I could hear the voices of the others in the room, in the background...but I could sense his voice, too, and it was so overwhelming. He told me that if I wanted to live, I was going to have to breathe...and so I did, and when I took that one breath, I started to come back. Then he told me to breathe again, and I was able to take another breath, and life came back into my body....

The doctors were amazed. They had all given me up, and naturally they hadn't heard the voice I had. They couldn't understand what happened.

I will close by reminding the reader that these are by no means common accounts of near-death experiences. However, they have occurred in a sizeable number of my cases and each of them is connected, within the context of the particular experience, with the elements which were reported earlier. For example, in the first interview quoted under "The Vision of Knowledge" above, the subject also described being out of her body, going through a dark tunnel, seeing the events of her life in review, and many other of the common elements. Similarly, note that the passage through a dark tunnel and being out of the body are prominently reported in two of the interviews quoted above in "Cities of Light." In each case, these new features—like the ones with which I have previously dealt—were described to me by ordinary people, who were not seeking these experiences, who had no previous interest in or knowledge of such matters, and yet who, afterward, had absolutely no doubt about the reality of what they had seen.

Peggy Taylor
Rick Ingrasci

Out of the Body
An Interview with
Elisabeth Kübler-Ross

Elisabeth Kübler-Ross, M.D., is perhaps the person most prominently identified with current interest in dying and death. In fact, so great is her following on the lecture circuit, that she is usually given extended standing ovations before she even begins to speak. Therefore, when she publicizes her own beliefs in survival after death, as well as her personal out-of-body experiences, one can expect that many people will take heed. Her message of a continued existence affords comfort and solace for countless individuals. However, there are hazards. What if the afterlife proves to be unpleasant or downright hellish? What might happen if several survivors of "near death" reported "bad trips"? When she states that "the dying process can be a very beautiful experience for children..." we must not forget that it can also be miserable, meaningless, and painful both for the child whose life is being cut short prematurely as well as for the family. Belief in the realm of the spirits can be a two-edged sword—it behooves us to explore it with caution and care. The interview with Dr. Kübler-Ross appeared in *New Age* magazine.

New Age. At the San Diego Holistic Health Conference last year you gave a talk titled "Death Does Not Exist." How did you come to that conclusion?

I have found that there are many, many phenomena that you cannot understand with the present-day scientific thinking. I think my first personal experience was when I had a spontaneous out-of-body experience.

New Age. When was that?

Oh, about three years ago. And I didn't know what an OOB experience was. I'd never heard of that.

It was at the end of one of my one-week workshops which I give for about sixty or seventy people. We work from eight in the morning to two or three in the morning for five days and five nights. There are about ten ill patients in a group and maybe ten parents of dying children and maybe ten people who have just lost somebody—a mother or a father or a brother or a lover. The other people come from a variety of backgrounds—physicians, nurses, clergy, social workers, counselors, philosophers, yogis, and once in a while we get a psychic or poet.

We'd had an incredible cross-section of people in this workshop, and by the end, on the last night, I was very pooped. During the week people get in touch with their negativity and their fears, or the shame and guilt, and all the unfinished business they've been carrying with them their whole life long. And then on the last evening of workshops we always have a party; it's a ritual.

We present the workshops in such a way that you really go through the stages of dying. People come and can't believe that they can open up with people. We call the first day Baloney Day. Everybody presents their life's role: "I have a Ph.D. in this and a degree in that"—all the formalities and other nonsense. Then I ask each of them individually why they came to this death and life transition workshop. They say "Oh, to become a better rabbi, a better priest, a better doctor...." We call it Baloney Day because it's not why they're there.

The first night—usually after midnight, when people are tired from the long trip and beginning to open up—it's almost always a dying patient who gets just sick and tired of the baloney: "Listen, we only have five days, and I may have only two months to live, and I'm sick and tired of this crap." They really cut through the baloney, and then they share their experiences—how they were told about their illness or *not* told, how they reacted, and all the painful experiences they've had to keep inside to play the game. And that triggers a chain reaction; all the other dying patients or the parents of dying children start pitching in.

The second day there's an incredible sharing of the deepest stuff you could possibly imagine, and anybody who gets in touch with anything negative—whether it's fear or anger or resentment or guilt over not having been at the bedside of a dying father or something like that—we work through right there and then in front of the whole group of seventy people. There's an incredible amount of crying and weeping and going through emotions—it's a form of psychodrama, but one that leads you right through the whole thing.

And then Wednesday is Angry Day. It's almost as if they're mad at me for having stripped them in public, for having shown their real selves. They deal with a lot of anger—an old kind of anger.

And Thursday night, when everything's put together, we talk about life after death: what life is all about, what death is all about. By Thursday night everybody has to have found a pinecone. They put into the pinecone that negative part of themselves which they're willing to give up permanently. They have to really think about that—they have to take it very seriously.

And then the last night we have a fire outdoors. We all sit around in a circle and sing all night. Whenever one person is ready, they go through a lot of emotion and trepidation and concerns whether they are really able to make this kind of commitment, and then they get up and throw the pinecone in the fire... and then another person, until usually all seventy participate. After that we have a party. We have wine and we bake our own bread, and we make a whole ritual with bread and wine.

Anyway, it was about five in the morning, and I was almost ready to go to sleep and I still had one day ahead of me. Then a terminally ill woman wanted me to sit at her bedside and hold her hand. She really acted out—she just couldn't let go. I told her I'd sit with her for fifteen minutes—that that was her lesson, that she had to learn to let go. By about five-thirty I was in my room, about to sleep for an hour and a half, and the minute I lay down on my bed, a girl dashed into the room and said, "Elisabeth, I wanted you to watch the sunrise and celebrate my birthday with me!" I said, "I didn't even know it was your birthday. Happy birthday!" And she said, "Well, it's not my birthday, but symbolically it is my birthday, because I'm really starting a whole new life and I want to celebrate this with you." And I said, "Well, you can celebrate your birthday at the window. Watch the sunrise for me and with me, but I'm going to sleep for an hour and a half. You can sit right here and watch the sunrise, and I'll be with you in spirit, but my body will sleep." I stayed on the bed and in about two minutes—I really have no time concept—I was out of my body and I was gone. I had an incredible experience, as if there were a lot of beings who took all the tired parts out of me and replaced them with new parts. I'm not terribly car-oriented, but I felt as if somebody brought the car to the shop, and ten people, a dozen people worked on it, and everybody worked on one part so that within a very short time every rusty part was replaced with a new one.

It was an incredible experience—everybody worked on this machine, on me, and I was just floating and taken care of. An hour and a half later I woke up and felt as if I were twenty years old—no tiredness, no fatigue. I felt super-healthy, and I had no idea what had happened to me—it was the first experience of my life of this kind. And this woman sat there with her mouth open. She said, "You know, anybody who walked into this room would have been absolutely convinced that you were dead. There was no respiration, no breathing, no pulse. You were warm, but there was nothing. If I hadn't known that this could be an out-of-body experience, I would have really been worried." I said, "A what?" She tried to explain to me what all this is about. Later I went to look it up. I read the books about out-of-body and learned that one part of you can separate from the body. That was my first experience.

Then our patients who had clinically died and come back to life started telling us what they experienced when they were declared dead. This was often after accidental death: sudden deaths where they had no preparation, they couldn't go through what we call the stages of dying. They told us that at the moment of death they had an incredible experience where they just left their bodies.

In a car accident, say, they can see the scene of the accident: they see the rescue team, they see the people who try to get them out of the car with blow torches, and they look as if they're in terrible pain and agony and going through a dreadful nightmare. Meanwhile, though, they are floating above the wreck, having a beautiful sense of peace and equanimity. They watch what's going on with a detached kind of observer's point of view, but without any of the effect, except peace and sudden surprise when they realize that that person is really them, and sometimes there's some confusion about that.

That's only true in sudden deaths. In deaths of cancer, or with people who have been ill, there is no confusion, and they always have this guide (or what Christians would call a guardian angel), who is present and helps them in this transition as well as the people they loved dearly who preceded them in death. They are always very reluctant to come back, because there is no pain, no fear, no panic, no anxiety, and there is a total physical wholeness. That means that people who have been blind can see, and you can imagine their joy. I had one multiple sclerosis patient whom I worked with for quite a while, who had been paralyzed for years; he was almost blind and couldn't speak anymore—he was really handicapped. And the moment he had this death experience, he could dance and sing, and he said he was just dancing and singing in the presence of this loving being, and then he was very, very disappointed when he was brought back to life. Here he is again, blind and unable to speak. So people who have been there are more often than not unhappy that we make them come back. It changes their values in life fantastically. They are no longer what you would call materialistically oriented. Those things are not important anymore.

New Age: Most people become more spiritually oriented?

All of them. And not one of them has ever been afraid of death since.

New Age: What has been your experience working with dying children? Do they go through the five stages of dying you describe in your books?

It depends on whether you have two-year-olds or twelve-year-olds, and how long they've been ill. Children die much more easily than grownups. They are much more open and honest— they're not yet as badly programmed as grownups are. The dying process can be a very beautiful experience for children who have not been overly conditioned. The difficulty working with children is the grownups, not the children—and not the parents so much, but other adults who influence them. The parents have a problem because there is probably no pain bigger than losing a child. They go through a lot of agony, and pain, and anguish, and tears, and sometimes have trouble communicating with children about it. But if children have someone near who works with the dying they'll be okay.

I'll give you an example of what might be a problem with children. We had an adorable twelve-year-old girl, Liz, who was full of cancer. She was from a very beautiful family— Catholic, very close-knit, good family. The mother was able to communicate beautifully with the child; she could even talk about death and dying. It was very open, very comfortable. The father was totally nonverbal—he was an introvert, he could not speak about anything —but he showed his love: he would bring red roses home and put them on her night table without a word. He was just the kind of man who doesn't talk, but he showed his love in a million other ways. It was very beautiful, very touching.

They thought that the other children didn't know—they were six, ten, and eleven. I didn't believe it, because children know it before

THE FEAR OF DEATH

The rabbi of Ger once said, "Why is man afraid of dying? For does he not then go to his Father! What man fears is the moment he will survey from the other world everything he has experienced on this earth."

Martin Buber
Tales of the Hasidim: Later Masters

grownups. So I asked for permission to be at their house when the children came home one day from school. I wanted to lock the living room and not allow the grownups to come in. They gave me permission to do that. I used my technique with drawings. I asked them to draw me a picture of just anything that came into their minds, and they drew incredible pictures.

It was the six-year-old, naturally, who was the easiest to do it with. I looked at the picture and said, "Tell me a little bit about what's what." It was very clear that it was his sister. I said, "It seems to me that she's terribly sick." By then they had already given up on her in the hospital. We had taken her home and made a bed for her in the den on a kind of cot. She had a big protruding belly and was skin and bones. And the six-year-old said, "Well, she's very sick," and I said, "How sick?" He said, "Well, she's very, very sick." Grownups beat around the bush like this, but children don't. So I said something like "Let's be open" and he said, "Well, she might die." I said, "She *might* die or she is dying?" He looked at me and said, "Is that okay?" and I said "Yes, that's okay because she *is* going to die."

Then the ten- and eleven-year-old pitched in. We had a marvelous session, and I asked them what bugged them about their sister. The six-year-old said, "Well, sometimes I'm so sick and tired of her, I wish she would die already. Since she's here we can't watch television anymore, we can't slam doors, and I can't bring any friends home." That seemed to me like a very normal reaction and I told them that this is terribly normal, that all children feel this way and very few have the guts to say so, and that this was the time when we could have the guts to say anything and *boy* did they pour it out! It was terrific.

So before we opened the door again, I said to all three of them, "If you have anything that bugs you about her or something nice you want to say to her, since she could die in a day or two, let's go now and each of us tell her what we feel like telling her. If you don't feel like doing it now, you can do it this evening. But do it today, not tomorrow." The six-year-old went in and said, "You know, Liz, I really have to tell you that sometimes I've just hated that you're in here. We can't slam the doors, I can't bring in my friends, I can't watch television." And Liz was so happy that they had finally stopped playing games, they were all hugging one another. It was delightful.

And then everything was finished: the parents were prepared, the children were prepared. But the child couldn't die: she was just hanging in there. One day I told the mother, "She should have died at least a week ago. She's ready, she wants to go, she can let go, but there's something that prevents her." The mother was getting to a point where she just couldn't take it anymore, twenty-four hours a day, and I said, "If you don't mind, I'm going to go in there and ask her right out, but I want you to be present so that you are not frightened by what I might say, so you are there to hear it." So I went into the room and said, "Liz, you can't die?" She said, "No." I said, "Why?" She said, "Because I can't get to heaven." I said, "You *what*?" You have a very strong gut reaction to things like that. She said, "I can't get to heaven." They are very strong Catholics and I was just ready to say, "Who told you this?" But I stopped myself. The hardest thing in this counseling is that you try to help people and you end up knocking somebody. It's very hard not to, because you are faced with so much quackery, so much crap, and so much fear-producing nonsense that people are told, that is so negative that I even have trouble not becoming negative myself. So I controlled myself and said, "Who told you *that*?" By the way you say it, you say it anyway. And she said the priests and the sisters who would come and visit her had told her many, many times, even before she was sick, that you don't go to heaven unless you have loved God more than anybody else in the whole wide world. Then she leaned up and whispered in my ear so God wouldn't hear. She said, "You know, I love my mommy and daddy better than anyone in the whole wide world." Oh, I was ready to cry.

The problem is that we do not train staff what to do at this point—you know, to take that guilt away. So what would you do? What would you say? I was very tempted to say to heck with this kind of teaching, that this is wrong, God could not possibly be this way. And then I remembered I've gone around telling people not to knock other people, only to help them. I said, "You know, I won't get into this argument at all. I think we should just leave this. Why don't we talk together the way we have always talked? We've talked about school many times. Your biggest dream was to become a schoolteacher, wasn't it?" She said, "Yes." And I said, "You were very very superbright in school, and that was the dream of your life. And the saddest I've ever seen you was in September, when school started again after Labor Day." She had suddenly realized, then, for the first time that she would never go back to her beloved school, because by then she had just started to metastasize. And she'd been told the month before that she was cured, so she never had to deal with it. I said, "That was the saddest day of your life, wasn't it?" and she said, "Yes." I said, "I want you to answer me one question. Your teacher sometimes gives some children in the class some very tough special assignments. All I want to hear from you is, does she give these

supertough assignments to the stupidest kids in the class, does she give it to just anybody in the whole classroom, or does she give it to only very few of the super-special kids in her class?" And her face lit up—I'd never seen anything like it. She said, "Oh, she gives it to only a very few of us." She was in what is called the honors class and she was very proud. "Well," I said, "in my opinion God is also a teacher. Do you think He gave you a tough assignment or did He give you an assignment He could give to just any kid?"

And then something very moving happened. She was lying flat on her back and her belly was like nine months pregnant, really protruding, and her arms and legs were just sticks. She looked at her really ugly body and there was a happy smile on her face. She said, "I don't think God could give a tougher assignment to any child." I didn't even have to say, "Now what do you think he thinks of you?"

I call this symbolic language—that's something we teach the people who work with our patients, and it's a marvelous way of getting at the very thing without knocking somebody else. I guess you would call it parables. I think it's our biggest strength—using this kind of symbolic language. It's the language our patients use when they can't talk directly about death and dying. It's like learning a foreign language and they talk like this the longest time.

I visited Liz one more time and the first thing she did when I walked in the room was look at her ugly body. She had a big happy smile on her face and we never had to talk about it again. She died about three or four days later.

So it is not just the grownups, it's what we *do* to our children. It's the stupid conditioning that uses fear and threats indirectly to teach people. If they only knew that God is all love

PARTING

Now I am come to the mountaintop,
And my spirit soars in the upper regions of freedom and release.
I am become far, far away, sons of my mother,
And the hill's face is hidden from mine eyes beyond the mist.
The emptiness of the valley is submerged in a sea of silence,
And the ways and passes erased by fingers of forgetfulness.
The meadows and the forest are concealed behind phantoms, white
   like clouds in spring,
And yellow as the sun's rays,
Red as the cloak of evening.

The song of the sea waves is stilled,
The music of the brooks in the fields grows faint,
And voices rising from the multitude are silenced.
I hear not any more save the hymn of Eternity,
Merging with the soul's desire....

Return you to your dwelling places
And there shall you find that which Death cannot take
From you and me.
Leave now this place.
Whom you seek is gone far from this world.

Kahlil Gibran
A Tear and a Smile

and that only humans are judgmental and discriminating, I think we could avoid a lot of fear, not only in dying children, but in dying grownups too. I have ninety-year-old women who can't die because they are afraid they'll go to hell. If they only knew that this doesn't exist, it only exists in yourself. But you have to somehow convey that gently, and those who use the power of fear to intimidate people, you understand that they are very upset when they hear statements like this. So it's like putting your hands in a wasp's nest. But after a while you get immune to the stings.

New Age: You've said that you feel the future depends on raising the children, the next generation, in a better way.

Yes, we have started a healing center in this in Escondido, California. . . .

New Age: You now use out-of-body techniques?

We've used it very sparingly with Vietnam victims, some quadraplegics. We have a good method and technique now to teach it. But it is not our greatest strength. There is a group in Virginia that is very good at teaching this: we let them do the teaching. My strength is much more in helping people to get rid of their negativity so that they can all do the things they do best. And my best field is working with handicapped and dying patients—children, grownups, and families. And this healing center, which we call Shanti Nilaya, will also be a place where healthy people can come and learn how to live in such a way that they will never again be afraid to die and can get rid of all their negativity.

New Age: What does *Shanti Nilaya* mean?

I'll tell you where this name comes from because it was probably the highlight of my life. Two years ago, on July 4th, I heard about Robert Monroe's group in Virginia where they teach these OOB techniques. . . . We were lying on this waterbed in a small cubbyhole, totally isolated from sound and everything. We were hooked up on a polygraph, and you get then this audio feedback into your ear, through earphones. I was dying to see if it was really possible to induce OOB experiences. . . .

The second I was hooked up, I gave myself the command: I'm going to go faster than the speed of light and I'm going to go further than any human being has ever been. That was my command to myself and no sooner did he get going, I took off with the speed of light until it dawned on me that I'm going *this* way—I'm going horizontally! My God, by then I had gone a few hundred thousand miles and the second I realized I was going horizontally and that's wrong—just the thought—I turned at a right angle and went vertically. Stuff like this excites me! And I went so far and so fast that nobody could ever catch up with me. I felt very safe: nobody could find me. I was really where nobody had ever been and from then on I have no recollection. I knew I had probably gone where nobody had ever been. I felt super.

When I came back and we met again in this group of scientists, everybody stared at me and said I had a total glow around me. I felt young and healthy and almost as if it weren't me—I probably hadn't felt this way since I was sixteen years old. I felt super-healthy. They were all just dying to know where I'd been and what I had experienced, and I couldn't remember one single thing except that they were chanting "Shanti Nilaya." No one in the group knew what that meant, except they all knew that *Shanti* means "peace." And you can imagine how the scientists tried to figure it out, tried to bring my recall back—but nothing worked. I'm sure I didn't want to remember. It was much too sacred to share with these strangers. I had to digest it myself first....

Then the second night, after I had had the experience with "Shanti Nilaya," as I walked up the forest to this lonely house, I went through terrible trepidations over whether I had not gone too far. And I didn't know what that meant—all I knew is that I thought I had gone too far and the question came whether I should go to the motel where all those scientists were staying or ask Monroe whether I could come to the main house and use the guest room there, or whether I maybe should have the guts to go and face whatever it was that was coming. I somehow preconsciously knew that something was brewing, and I think my conclusion was that having gone that far, I had to go all the way now. I had to face it, because if I didn't face it then, it would happen later on.

So I ended up in this house at about one-thirty in the morning. I didn't even bother locking the doors anymore, but I kept a night light on and the porch light on. I went to bed and it was the most incredible night of my entire life. I tried to sleep but I couldn't—I remember tossing back and forth. It was like in a fever: I was delirious, fighting to sleep, wanting to sleep, but knowing that I couldn't fight it much longer—that kind of a turmoil. And then it hit me like lightning—the whole experience. To describe it in words is. . . What happened is that I went through every single death of every single one of my thousands of patients that I had seen by then. And when I say I went through their death processes, I mean this literally—I had every experience every patient ever had and the bleeding and the pain and the agony and the

cramps and incredible pains and tears and loneliness and isolation—every negative aspect of every patient's death. And this repeated itself a thousand times— always in a different version but with the same agony. And during this endless incredible agony (which was physically very real: I couldn't breathe, I couldn't catch my breath, I couldn't even finish a thought because it would hit me again —a cramp, bleeding, or shortness of breath), somewhere in the middle I was able to say one sentence, and I asked for a shoulder to lean on. I was very specific: it had to be a man's left shoulder where I could put my head. And I thought if I had a shoulder, a man's shoulder to lean on, I could bear it. And the minute I finished this thought—this prayer perhaps, to give me a shoulder to lean on—this incredible voice came from everywhere: "You shall not be given." Those words: "You shall not be given." And then I did not have time even to think why not or anything, because I was in much too much agony. Then an eternity later I asked for a hand to hold—by then I was much less choosy. I didn't ask for a man's hand—just a hand. But I expected this hand to come up, and I could hold on to it, like when you're in bed and you want something to hold on to. And this voice came again: "You shall not be given." My last request, which I contemplated but didn't make, was for a fingertip. The purpose of the fingertip was full knowledge—very conscious knowledge. You cannot hold on to a fingertip, but you're aware of the presence of another human being. And then—typically me—I said, "Damn it, if I can't get one hand, I don't want the damn fingertip either." And that was my final conclusion. Even I deserve a bare minimum, and my bare minimum is one anonymous hand: the fingertip is not acceptable. It was like my bargaining and my anguish was all put into this thought. Then I went through a lot more agony, thinking, "I have held so many hands when people were alone and desperate and dying, why don't I get a hand? Am I bad? Am I a bad person?"

Then I realized that this is something that I had to do alone—not even in the presence of a fingertip. And the moment I said yes to that, like "Yes, I'm willing to take that. Give me whatever you have in store, and I can take it alone" (there were no thoughts then like this—it was just simply saying yes to it), the *second* I said yes to it, the whole agony stopped, in a split second.

What followed cannot be put into words. I was lying on my back. The room was illuminated by the night light. My abdominal walls started to vibrate at a very very high speed—it was going super, super fast—and I looked at my belly and what I saw was anatomically impossible. (I felt this scientifically even while I was going through it. It was as if I had an observing ego watching the whole thing.) And every time I watched a part of my body, it started to follow, vibrating. And then I looked at the closet, and it started to vibrate. And the walls started to vibrate, and the whole world...I had a vision of the whole universe, everything vibrating. And in front of me something opened. It was a visual image. At first I thought it was a vagina. The moment that I focused on it, it turned into a lotus flower bud. It had the most incredible colors—beauty that I cannot put into words. I watched this and the vibrations going on in the whole room. Behind this flower bud came something like a sunrise—an incredible light. And this bud opened up into the most fantastic lotus flower. I looked at all this in utter awe. There were sounds and colors and visions beyond description.

The moment the light was at the peak and the flower was wide open, all the vibrations stopped and all the million molecules (it's as if somebody put a million pieces of a puzzle into one—that's the best way I can describe it) became one and I was part of that one. I really cannot describe this experience.

After everything was together, it became totally still, totally quiet, and I fell asleep. I must have slept for about an hour. I needed to be up at sunrise. I wanted to walk down the hill and I wanted Bob to be in front of his house, sitting on the bench and looking at me and knowing everything so I would never have to talk about it—it was like too sacred to talk about it. So I got up and walked down this steep path to Monroe's house and it was an experience that most people would probably think is crazy. I was in love with every leaf, with every bird and every grasshopper and cloud, even the pebbles that I stepped on. Except I didn't step on the pebbles—I walked half an inch above them down that path.

Later in Berkeley I shared this experience for the first time. There were a lot of Buddhist monks and people from India around—you know, typical Berkeley population—and I thought that would be a place where I could talk about it, because I needed to understand what it was all about. And they told me that this was called cosmic consciousness and that *Shanti Nilaya* in Sanskrit means "the ultimate home of peace," which we find when we have gone through the turmoil and have given up our need for a shoulder or a hand to lean on and have learned to give up those needs and take on the burden of the pain and work through it. That is the ultimate gift we receive when we have been able to go through all the negativity and take other people's negativity onto ourselves, and that is the ultimate gift that we will receive.

Samuel Vaisrub

Afterthoughts on Afterlife

Samuel Vaisrub is a physician who takes a more skeptical view of the burgeoning reports of "near death" experiences than either Moody or Kübler-Ross. He reminds us that, quite simply, resuscitation is not resurrection, and he alludes to the possibility of people returning with dark and troubling visions.

Reporting on experiences described by patients who had been resuscitated after cardiac arrest, Burch et al[1] wrote as follows:

At the onset of cardiac arrest most patients experience a pleasant feeling as though they were entering a peaceful sleep. There was no fear or anxiety. They became unconscious and were completely unaware of the activities around them. If resuscitative procedures had not been undertaken, all would have ended in an "eternal sleep" after the initial pleasant beginning. However, with resuscitation before serious cerebral damage had occurred, consciousness was regained after variable periods of time. At this time many patients felt pleasant again and were pleased to know they were still alive.

That was 1968. It should have been obvious even then that the report was too true to be good. It lacked excitement. More vividly imaginative accounts were bound to come.

And come they did—articles, books, televised testimonials with accompanying com-

ments by recognized authorities on death and dying—all related to experiences of life after death. These experiences conformed to a pattern: detachment of the spirit from the body, swift unreeling of important past events, passage through a dark tunnel, warm welcome by friends or saintly persons, and eventual emergence into brilliant light. The picture is not unfamiliar to those who have seen similar representations of the hereafter in filmed Hollywood fantasies, which, unlike the testimonials, made no claim to scientific validity.

Without casting doubts on the veracity of the witnesses or imputing base motives to those who publicize their testimony, one is compelled to take issue with any attempt to present these tales as scientific evidence for the existence and the nature of afterlife. Aside from the general unreliability of testimonials (cf, UFO, the Sasquatch Bigfoot, and the Loch Ness monster), the particular experiences of resuscitated patients do not relate to death. Resuscitation is not resurrection. These patients were neither biologically nor legally dead. Their hearts may have stopped beating for a minute or more, but their brains remained alive. There is nothing extraordinary, let alone supernatural, in seeing dream-like visions, as consciousness returns to normal.

It may seem cruel to demolish the dream, to deprive millions of a vision that would sustain

1. Burch, G. E., DePasquale, N. P., Phillipes, J. H.: What death is like. *Am. Heart J* 76:438-439, 1968.

their belief in a better world awaiting them after death. On the other hand, it would be equally unkind to leave the dream be, only to see it contradicted by other resuscitands who may yet come up with a darker, drearier vision that is more consistent with their memories and past experiences.

It would be similarly inconsiderate to foist a particular pattern of the hereafter on a staunch believer in the soul's immortality, whether his belief rests on traditional faith or inner conviction. His private vision of the world to come may not be a skyscape of dazzling psychedelic, but a quiet abode of the spirit. And his conviction does not require testimonials or scientific evidence. If anything, these sources of proof would tend to trivialize the awesome mystery that has tantalized mankind since the dawn of intelligence.

AUTO WRECK

Its quick soft silver bell beating, beating,
And down the dark one ruby flare
Pulsing out red light like an artery,
The ambulance at top speed floating down
Past beacons and illuminated clocks
Wings in a heavy curve, dips down,
And brakes speed, entering the crowd.
The doors leap open, emptying light;
Stretchers are laid out, the mangled lifted
And stowed into the little hospital.
Then the bell, breaking the hush, tolls once,
And the ambulance with its terrible cargo
Rocking, slightly rocking, moves away,
As the doors, an afterthought, are closed.

We are deranged, walking among the cops
Who sweep glass and are large and
   composed.
One is still making notes under the light.
One with a bucket douches ponds of blood
Into the street and gutter.
One hangs lanterns on the wrecks that cling,
Empty husks of locusts, to iron poles.

Our throats were tight as tournaquets,
Our feet were bound with splints, but now,
Like convalescents intimate and gauche,
We speak through sickly smiles and warn
With the stubborn saw of common sense,
The grim joke and the banal resolution.
The traffic moves around with care,
But we remain, touching a wound
That opens to our richest horror.
Already old, the question Who shall die?
Becomes unspoken Who is innocent?
For death in war is done by hands;
Suicide has cause and stillbirth, logic;
And cancer, simple as a flower, blooms.
But this invites the occult mind,
Cancels our physics with a sneer,
And spatters all we knew of denouement
Across the expedient and wicked stones.

Karl Shapiro

Bertrand Russell

Do We Survive Death?

Bertrand Russell, the famous philosopher, argues pithily that our life as we know it consists of our memories, thoughts, and habits. These, in turn, reside in the brain. At death, the brain is irreversibly destroyed. Hence, Russell reasons, there is no rational basis for belief in life after death. Emotionally, however, we seek such beliefs because of our egotism and our fears of death. Written in 1936, Russell's definition of life as primarily psychological anticipated the current controversies surrounding the definition of death—and brain death in particular—which are examined in Section 13 on moral-ethical issues.

Before we can profitably discuss whether we shall continue to exist after death, it is well to be clear as to the sense in which a man is the same person as he was yesterday. Philosophers used to think that there were definite substances, the soul and the body, that each lasted on from day to day, that a soul, once created, continued to exist throughout all future time, whereas a body ceased temporarily from death till the resurrection of the body.

The part of this doctrine which concerns the present life is pretty certainly false. The matter of the body is continually changing by processes of nutriment and wastage. Even if it were not, atoms in physics are no longer supposed to have continuous existence; there is no sense in saying: this is the same atom as the one that existed a few minutes ago. The continuity of a human body is a matter of appearance and behavior, not of substance.

The same thing applies to the mind. We think and feel and act, but there is not, in addition to thoughts and feelings and actions, a bare entity, the mind or the soul, which does or suffers these occurrences. The mental continuity of a person is a continuity of habit and memory: there was yesterday one person whose feelings I can remember, and that person I regard as myself of yesterday; but, in fact, myself of yesterday was only certain mental occurrences which are now remembered and are regarded as part of the person who now recollects them. All that constitutes a person is a series of experiences connected by memory and by certain similarities of the sort we call habit.

If, therefore, we are to believe that a person survives death, we must believe that the memories and habits which constitute the person will continue to be exhibited in a new set of occurrences.

No one can prove that this will not happen. But it is easy to see that it is very unlikely. Our memories and habits are bound up with the structure of the brain, in much the same way in which a river is connected with the riverbed. The water in the river is always changing, but it keeps to the same course because previous rains have worn a channel. In like manner, previous events have worn a channel in the brain, and our thoughts flow along this channel. This is the cause of memory and mental habits. But the brain, as a structure, is dissolved at death, and memory therefore may be expected to be also dissolved. There is no more reason to think otherwise than to expect a river to persist in its old course after an earthquake has raised a mountain where a valley used to be.

All memory, and therefore (one may say) all minds, depend upon a property which is very noticeable in certain kinds of material structures but exists little if at all in other kinds. This is the property of forming habits as a result of frequent similar occurrences. For example: a bright light makes the pupils of the eyes contract; and if you repeatedly flash a light in a man's eyes and beat a gong at the same time, the gong alone will, in the end, cause his pupils to contract. This is a fact about the brain and nervous sytem—that is to say, about a certain material structure. It will be found that exactly similar facts explain our response to language and our use of it, our memories and the emotions they arouse, our moral or immoral habits of behavior, and indeed everything that constitutes our mental personality, except the part determined by heredity. The part determined by heredity is handed on to our posterity but cannot, in the individual, survive the disintegration of the body. Thus both the hereditary and the acquired parts of a personality are, so far as our experience goes, bound up with the characteristics of certain bodily structures. We all know that memory may be obliterated by an injury to the brain, that a virtuous person may be rendered vicious by encephalitis lethargica, and that a clever child can be turned into an idiot by lack of iodine. In view of such familiar facts, it seems scarcely probable that the mind

survives the total destruction of brain structure which occurs at death.

It is not rational arguments but emotions that cause belief in a future life.

The most important of these emotions is fear of death, which is instinctive and biologically useful. If we genuinely and wholeheartedly believed in the future life, we should cease completely to fear death. The effects would be curious, and probably such as most of us would deplore. But our human and subhuman ancestors have fought and exterminated their enemies throughout many geological ages and have profited by courage; it is therefore an advantage to the victors in the struggle for life to be able, on occasion, to overcome the natural fear of death. Among animals and savages, instinctive pugnacity suffices for this purpose; but at a certain stage of development, as the Mohammedans first proved, belief in Paradise has considerable military value as reinforcing natural pugnacity. We should therefore admit that militarists are wise in encouraging the belief in immortality, always supposing that this belief does not become so profound as to produce indifference to the affairs of the world.

Another emotion which encourages the belief in survival is admiration of the excellence of man. As the Bishop of Birmingham says, "His mind is a far finer instrument than anything that had appeared earlier—he knows right and wrong. He can build Westminster Abbey. He can make an airplane. He can calculate the distance of the sun.... Shall, then, man at death perish utterly? Does that incomparable instrument, his mind, vanish when life ceases?"

The Bishop proceeds to argue that "the universe has been shaped and is governed by an intelligent purpose," and that it would have been unintelligent, having made man, to let him perish.

To this argument there are many answers. In the first place, it has been found, in the scientific investigation of nature, that the intrusion of moral or aesthetic values has always been an obstacle to discovery. It used to be thought that the heavenly bodies must move in circles because the circle is the most perfect curve, that species must be immutable because God would only create what was perfect and what therefore stood in no need of improvement, that it was useless to combat epidemics except by repentance because they were sent as a punishment for sin, and so on. It has been found, however, that, so far as we can discover, nature is indifferent to our values and can only be understood by ignoring our notions of good and bad. The Universe may have a purpose, but nothing that we know suggests that, if so, this purpose has any similarity to ours.

Nor is there in this anything surprising. Dr. Barnes tells us that man "knows right and wrong." But, in fact, as anthropology shows, men's views of right and wrong have varied to such an extent that no single item has been permanent. We cannot say, therefore, that man knows right and wrong, but only that some men do. Which men? Nietzsche argued in favor of an ethic profoundly different from Christ's, and some powerful governments have accepted his teaching. If knowledge of right and wrong is to be an argument for immortality, we must first settle whether to believe Christ or Nietzsche, and then argue that Christians are immortal, but Hitler and Mussolini are not, or vice versa. The decision will obviously be made on the battlefield, not in the study. Those who have the best poison gas will have the ethic of the future and will therefore be the immortal ones.

Our feelings and beliefs on the subject of good and evil are, like everything else about us, natural facts, developed in the struggle for existence and not having any divine or supernatural origin. In one of Aesop's fables, a lion is shown pictures of huntsmen catching lions and remarks that, if he had painted them, they would have shown lions catching huntsmen. Man, says Dr. Barnes, is a fine fellow because he can make airplanes. A little while ago there was a popular song about the cleverness of flies in walking upside down on the ceiling, with the chorus: "Could Lloyd George do it? Could Mr. Baldwin do it? Could Ramsay Mac do it? Why, NO."[1] On this basis a very telling argument could be constructed by a theologically minded fly, which no doubt the other flies would find most convincing.

Moreover, it is only when we think abstractly that we have such a high opinion of man. Of men in the concrete, most of us think the vast majority very bad. Civilized states spend more than half their revenue on killing each other's citizens. Consider the long history of the activities inspired by moral fervor: human sacrifices, persecutions of heretics, witch-hunts, pogroms leading up to wholesale extermination by poison gases, which one at least of Dr. Barnes's episcopal colleagues must be supposed to favor, since he holds pacifism to be un-Christian. Are these abominations, and the ethical doctrines by which they are prompted, really evidence of an intelligent Creator? And can we really wish that the men who practiced them should live forever? The world in which we live can be understood as a result of muddle and accident; but if it is the outcome of deliberate purpose, the purpose must have been that of a fiend. For my part, I find accident a less painful and more plausible hypothesis.

1. Editor's note: David Lloyd George, Stanley Baldwin, and James Ramsay MacDonald were prime ministers of Great Britain from World War I to the 1930s.

PART TWO

The Experience of Death

This part, "The Experience of Death," takes up two subjects that are both poignant and painful for us all: the dying patient, and death and the child.

In Section 7 we come to know the world of the dying patient and the conditions, issues, and concerns that envelop him and his family as well as those who minister to him. And we come to learn, too, that the humane care of the dying is not only a noble ideal to be pursued, but, as Dr. Elisabeth Kübler-Ross has brought forcibly to our attention in her book, *On Death and Dying,* it is an urgent need also.

Section 8 brings us to the child's discovery of death, an exploration that begins with the game of peek-a-boo and ends in the permanent, irreversible experience of separation through the loss of a parent, friend, or pet. It is in the process of living that we learn about death, just as in our dreams and fantasies we have a glimpse of immortality.

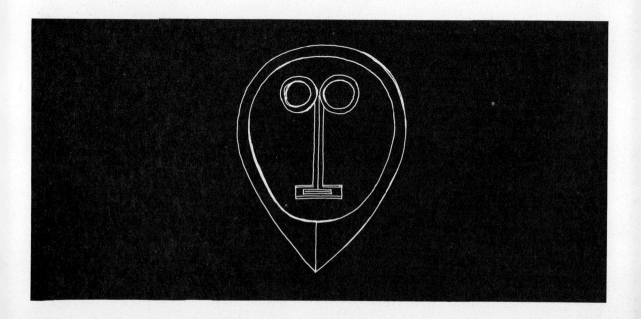

7.

The Dying Patient

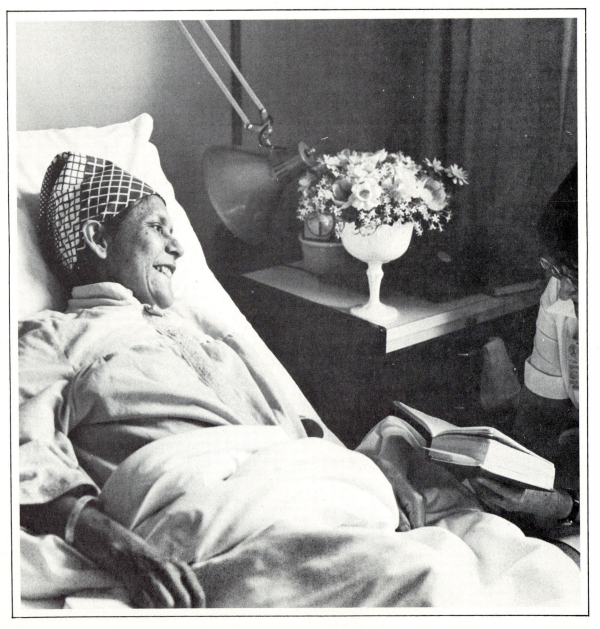

We all know that eventually each of us must die. It has been said that each person's death is uniquely individual, just as each life is different from any other. However, the personal experience of dying is also influenced by factors over which the individual often has little or no control: causes of death, prevailing social and cultural values that give meaning to life and death, and attitudes and behavior of other people all have a decisive impact on the dying person. As we have seen in earlier sections, the causes of death, the ages at which most people die, and the places where they die have changed dramatically since the industrial revolution. Most people in developed societies die of degenerative disease at advanced ages in hospitals. Hence, most dying persons are also dying patients.

The personal needs of dying patients were not widely appreciated until 1969, when Elisabeth Kübler-Ross published *On Death and Dying,* a book based on her extensive interactions with dying patients. Dr. Kübler-Ross publicized the dying patient's need for honest, caring communication from both family and staff. She also identified several stages of adjustment through which many patients progress from the time when they learn they are going to die until death occurs. Her book has stimulated dedicated efforts on the part of health-care professionals to create circumstances in which persons can die with dignity and meaning.

But the goal of providing personalized, dignified care of the dying is often not easily attained. Death and dying are topics that, until quite recently, people in our society have tended to avoid and deny. Patients frequently have difficulty accepting their impending deaths and are additionally burdened by the discomfort of both symptoms and treatments, as well as by a range of emotions which include despair, fear, and resentment.

Family and friends, likewise, experience many contradictory emotions—a desire to provide care and support is often interwoven with a wish to deny the fact of impending loss; resentment and guilt are often felt but seldom expressed; concern with the spiritual dimensions of death alternates with anxiety over the financial costs of hospitalization and loss of earnings. And medical caregivers—trained to regard patients in terms of diseases to be cured and death as an enemy to be conquered—experience difficulty in finding a balance between detached professionalism and personalized care.

Humane care of the dying is also complicated by the setting in which it occurs: general hospitals may be excellent places for restoring health, saving lives, and conducting research, but they are often seen as bewildering, mechanical, and impersonal by patients and their visitors. The personal needs and preferences of the dying patient must fit into the policies and procedures of a large bureaucratic organization. Patients are often hooked up to feeding tubes, catheters, and machines that monitor their vital signs. It is little wonder that they are inclined to feel a loss of individual identity. Moreover, the efforts of the medical staff—particularly the nursing personnel who attend the patients on eight-hour shifts—to provide personalized care can be hampered by the exigencies of hospital routine. A heavy workload can preclude spending sufficient time with a patient to become familiar with his or her individual feelings and fears. And, as we shall see in the section on grief, caregivers must protect themselves against becoming overinvolved with a person who will die. To experience too much grief as a result of personal involvement with one patient or family could impair effective care of others.

Largely as a result of such problems, several alternative settings have emerged for the care of the dying, including hospices (which are examined in this section), hospice wards in general hospitals with special routines and staff, and home care for dying persons supervised by hospital-based medical staff. Hospices, in particular, are being established as attempts to provide humane, individualized care for dying persons. Pilot hospice programs in Marin County, California; New Haven, Connecticut; and Seattle, Washington testify to the growing consciousness of the indignities of dying in many conventional medical settings.

The future of the hospice movement, however, is questionable. Novel ideas and dedicated caregivers are challenged by ingrained traditions as well as financial contingencies. Many health professionals question the establishment of places reserved primarily for the dying. Such specialization could degenerate into segregation. Also, there are very real concerns involving the psychological hazards of staff working exclusively with patients who are terminally ill and dying. Financially, the relative costs of conventional hospital care and hospice care are still being evaluated. Moreover, many traditional health insurance programs do not cover the type of palliative care that hospices provide. If insurance companies won't pay for the hospice care, few people may be able to afford their services; on the other hand, expanded insurance coverage would be reflected in higher premiums. If hospices are able to combine personalized care with a reduced cost-per-patient figure, their future seems assured. If, on the contrary, further experience indicates that it may be costlier to provide a separate facility for the dying, the hospice movement may meet an untimely demise. Perhaps, a workable compromise may be effected by the development of hospice-type wards within conventional medical settings. The selection by Paige and Looney in this section describes the focus on personalized care given by staff on such a specialized ward in a hospital.

In addition to addressing the needs of dying patients, the articles in this section explore both problems in providing care for the dying as well as possibilities for improving it. Ryder and Ross discuss tendencies in modern medicine that lead to a focus on the person as a patient with a particular disease, rather than as a whole person. They also examine the idea that patients can die as social beings before their physical death occurs. Finally, they describe St. Christopher's Hospice—a special facility in London for the care of the dying. Paige and Looney consider the importance of genuine, sensitive care on the part of medical staff—a very strong theme in current nursing literature, thanks largely to the pioneering work of Kübler-Ross. Cicely Saunders, the director of St. Christopher's Hospice, addresses the issue of the patient's right and need to know the facts of his or her condition.

She maintains that the communication of imminent death must be accompanied by honesty and sincere caring for the patient.

The selections by Powers and Shneidman examine the patient's adaptation to dying and death. Powers describes the five stages of denial, anger, bargaining, depression, and acceptance that have been identified by Kübler-Ross. Shneidman, who has also had extensive experience in counseling dying patients, presents an alternative view. These selections underscore the need to remember that each death, like each life, is both similar to others and highly unique.

Kübler-Ross' interview with a seventeen-year-old girl dying of a blood disease and Alsop's account of his own hospitalization for inoperable cancer provide glimpses into the thoughts and feelings of persons who are facing impending death in medical settings. The teenager, facing such an untimely death, is sustained by her religious faith and comforted by open communication with family and staff. Alsop, facing death in the ripeness of life and career, feels demeaned by the technological appurtenances to which he must be connected and muses on how, for one who is sick unto death, death loses some of its fearsome qualities.

Weisman's article on "An Appropriate Death" concludes this section with the reminder that the dying person is still very much alive. His concept also underscores the importance of treating the dying patient as an individual and trying, wherever possible, to allow the patient to make his or her own decisions. The participants in the dying, moreover, must not allow their own fears of death to interfere with their sensitive care of the dying patient.

Special mention should be made of the unique circumstances surrounding the dying child. The death of a child in modern society is tragic and untimely. Since the turn of the century, mortality rates in infancy and childhood have declined significantly. When a child dies today, either as a result of an accident or a fatal disease, the persons involved are often surprised or shocked as well as hurt. Although many of the problems involving the dying child are similar to those faced by adults, the dying child faces additional difficulties. The death of an elderly person at least contains an element of timeliness—the person has lived a long life and death is appropriate and normal. The terminally ill child, on the other hand, is facing death at a very inappropriate time in life. The untimely death offends our values and sense of meaning. The older person facing death can look back on a lifetime of experience, whereas the dying child must face the premature termination of a future. The sense of "wrongness" can create additional anger and resentment, both for the child and for those who care for him or her.

The dying adult, moreover, can understand the nature of the disease and treatments, at least if the medical staff are open and communicative. The child, however, has limited ability to make sense of what is happening. It becomes very important that the child be surrounded by people who can take the time to discuss and explain everything possible. Family and caregivers must be extremely sensitive to the child's unspoken needs as well.

As modern medicine is able to save the lives

of many children who would formerly have died and to prolong the lives of others, more and more children have entered hospitals when facing imminent death. Hospital staffs, in turn, have developed greater sensitivity to the needs of the child and family—special wards have been arranged in which ordinary hospital visiting rules do not apply and trained counselors are available to facilitate communication and adjustment. Also, some caregivers, like Ida Martinson and her nursing colleagues at the University of Minnesota, are experimenting with home care arrangements whereby critically ill children can spend longer periods of time at home under care of visiting nurses.

Humane care of the dying is both an urgent need and a noble ideal. The circumstances of death and dying and the meanings of life and death in our society are undergoing bewildering changes. The persons who are dying during such a period bear the brunt of these changes. Today's elderly patient grew up in a vastly different world than the one in which he or she is dying. It is essential that the issues surrounding the dying person continue to have high priority among our many concerns. It is very likely that each of us will face death as a dying patient; it is therefore in our own best interests, as well as that of the society as a whole, to promote humane standards of care and facilities capable of providing it.

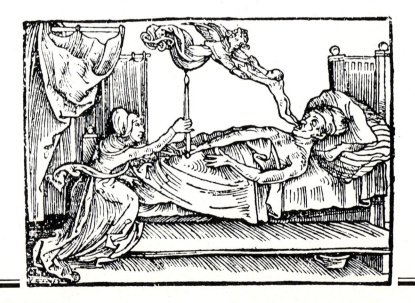

Claire F. Ryder
Diane M. Ross

Terminal Care

Issues and Alternatives

Several important issues concerning care of the dying patient are examined in this article by two public health professionals, Claire Ryder and Diane Ross. The shift from home to hospital as the usual setting for dying has created new dilemmas and challenges. Patient, family, and staff have differing perspectives on the impending death with which they are all involved. Hence, communication is often as difficult as it is important. The patient's desire to be regarded as a unique individual can clash with the staff's inclination to maintain a clinical detachment. Families not only face the anticipated loss of a member, but also must watch the dying occur in a bewildering world of machines, medicines, and strangers in white uniforms. Hospitals, which originated as institutions to cure sick people and save lives, are often not designed to provide optimal care to patients who will not recover. In response to growing recognition of the problems of terminal care in conventional hospitals, however, several alternatives have emerged. Foremost among them is St. Christopher's Hospice in London, which Ryder and Ross discuss in some detail.

PROFESSIONAL ATTITUDES TO-WARD DEATH AND DYING   The present orientation of the medical profession is not in caring for patients afflicted with degenerative diseases but in curing them. Technological breakthroughs in medicine have perpetuated a phenomenon found among health professionals as well as in the society at large, a phenomenon referred to as "death denying." Until recently, this attitude was reflected in the training of physicians and nurses. Recurrent in the medical student's education was the idea that "every death corresponds to a failure, either of the individual physician, or more commonly, of medicine, as a whole." The student becomes desensitized to death symbols—blood, bone, corpses, and the characteristic stench—and through transference may become desensitized to death itself. In his dedication to the ideals of the scientific community, the physician responds with "vigorous application of laboratory diagnostic tests, technological gadgetry, and heroic therapy in order to prolong life."[1] Therefore, whereas fifty years ago the physician was considered a member of a consolatory profession, science has now given him omnipotent powers to keep the vital functions of a body operative by artificial means long after the natural course of disease has vitiated these functions.

Thus, the new orientation of physicians reduces the crux of the problem to the question: When does death occur? Much of the current literature deals with ethical and legal questions surrounding the point of death and delineates problems that occur when the prolongation of life past its natural point preempts

1. D. Rabin and L. Rabin, "Consequences of Death for Physicians, Nurses, and Hospitals," *The Dying Patient* (New York, 1970).

death as a natural process. We are now at the point where considerations of quality of life are secondary to concern about the length of life. Quality of life is a subjective assessment, but when applied to the terminal patient as primary to the length of survival, it takes on specific meaning. One can debate whether survival amid tubes and respirators is life at all.

WHERE PEOPLE DIE   The home no longer provides a person with an extensive support system. In light of this, it is not surprising that the death rate in institutions has risen considerably over the past decades. Although national statistical studies pertaining to deaths in institutions as opposed to deaths at home are scarce, some state and local data are available. From 1949 to 1958, a 10 percent national increase occurred in institutional deaths, including those in general hospitals, mental hospitals, and nursing homes. New York City statistics reveal an increase from 53,746 institutional deaths in 1955 to 64,083 in 1967, representing a 7 percent increase, and a 7 percent decrease in deaths at home, from 25,598 in 1955 to 21,222 in 1967. Furthermore, there is evidence that this latter figure has decreased rapidly in more recent years. . . .

Since 70 percent of institutionalization for the terminally ill pertains to the general hospital, the burden of care is placed largely on the hospital staff. However, the organizational structure of the hospital makes care routinized rather than individualized, and is, therefore, frequently inappropriate to the needs of the dying patient. The large teaching hospital's primary functions are diagnosis and treatment of patients with acute illnesses. In contrast, the chronic illness hospital or wing, which houses a large population of dying patients, is generally relegated a lower social status, and thereby has difficulty in attracting

funding and quality staff. The hierarchy for patient care in a general hospital is (a) acute illness, (b) chronic illness, and (c) terminal illness.

The medical staff adheres to this hierarchy in its orientation toward care. As more demands of physical care of those with acute curable illnesses are met, the psychological and emotional needs of the incurable are more often neglected. Physicians tend to view cure as their triumph and death as their failure; they therefore attend to dying patients only as prescribed by duty. Nurses tend to "pull away" from dying patients and to focus more on the diagnostic and curative aspects that are implicit in their trained professional approach to patients. . . .

Patients suffering from cancer are often shuttled from one specialist to another, which results in further fragmentation of care rather than an integration of services emcompassing the physical, social, and emotional needs of the patient.

Pain is singularized as physiological pain that can be easily treated with the use of psychopharmacological* agents. These agents often replace staff contact, which, in the case of the dying patient, is already minimized. The psychological experience of the patient and family "is deadened by the use of narcotic and analgesic drugs which reinforce the collusion of avoidance rather than enhance the experience of death."[2] The drugs aid in meeting the goal of patient manageability, essential in a busy hospital.

Terminal patients also die in nursing or convalescent homes, many of which are classified as skilled nursing facilities. These facilities are

*Editor's note: Drugs that act on the mind.
2. G.L. Klerman, "Drugs and the Dying Patient," *Psychopharmacological Agents for the Terminally Ill and Bereaved* (New York, 1973), p. 15.

often not oriented to meet the needs of the dying patient, focusing on physical rehabilitation or restoration rather than on the total needs of the patient. In a 1975 survey of 77 nursing homes, a majority indicated that they removed deceased patients as clandestinely as possible so as not to disturb the other residents—a practice that seeks to deny death by making it a covert issue.

SOCIAL DEATH VERSUS BIOLOGICAL DEATH

The result of the institutionalization of dying patients is a phenomenon of "social death" prior to biological death, which incorporates "the process of mutual disengagement and rejection by which 'organization man'—more precisely, the human being as a member of society—seems prone to take his leave from the land of the living." Once the patient has been labeled terminal and the physician has given up hope for recovery, the institution treats the patient as a dying body with little concern for his individuality or humanness. Sudnow, in his study of a county hospital, observed:

> When a physician abandons hope for a patient's survival, the nurses establish what they refer to as a "death watch," a fairly severe form of social death in which they keep track of relevant facts concerning the gradual recession of clinical life signs. As death approaches, the patient's status as a body becomes more evident from the manner in which he is discussed, treated, and moved about. Attention shifts from concern about his life, possible discomforts, and the administration of medically prescribed treatments to the mere activity of the events of biological leave-taking.
> In a patient who has not yet passed into a death coma, suctioning the nasal passages, propping up pillows, changing bed sheets, and the like occur as part of the normal nursing routine. As blood pressure drops, and signs of imminent death appear, these traditional nurs-

ing practices are regarded as less important; the major items of interest become the number of heartbeats and changing condition of the eyes. On many occasions nurses' aides in the county hospital were observed to cease administering oral medications when death was expected within the hour.[3]

When social death precedes biological death in this manner, the needs of the dying patient essentially become secondary to institutional routine. What are these unique needs and how are they met? Hospice, Inc., New Haven, Conn., in a study of cancer deaths between 1969 and 1971 in the South Central Health Planning Region in Connecticut summarized these needs:

> (1) the noxious symptoms of the illness, (2) the need to be with family and friends in familiar surroundings, (3) involvement in decision-making, (4) honest and frequent communication, (5) a need to maintain one's identity and role, (6) freedom from heroic measures which become more of an obstacle to the quality of life than even the disease, (7) need for a staff which understands and helps the patient work through anger and depression in coming to terms with dying, and (8) unattended bereavement which results in physical and/or psychological impairment to the survivors.[4]

In a 1975 symposium on the terminally ill, Dr. Balfour Mount, medical director of the Royal Victoria Hospital's terminal patient ward in Montreal, Canada, noted that each need is interconnected and that all needs essentially signify relief from pain. Although all else is secondary to physical pain which must be dealt with before any other consideration, a hospital environment often limits the

3. Sudnow, "Dying in a Public Hospital," *The Dying Patient* (New York, 1970).
4. R. J. Nelson, "Hospice: An Alternative Solution to the Problem of Caring for the Dying Patient." Colloquy, March, 1974.

definition of pain to somatic. An expanded definition would include mental, financial, interpersonal, and spiritual aspects of pain. The dying patient may experience a sense of isolation, especially in a hospital setting, because of a lack of comfort and communication with medical personnel and family. Physicians, in avoiding the reality of death and projecting their fears onto the patient, often choose not to disclose the prognosis of impending death to the patient. Hence, an aura of deceit and covertness hampers the patient's ability to cope with his situation and to take care of unfinished business.

COPING WITH DYING AND DEATH   The coping process involves several stages, the transition from one to another being facilitated by a neutral uninvolved party, be it physician, nurse, social worker, professional counselor, member of the clergy, or understanding volunteer. The stages, as outlined by [Elisabeth Kübler-] Ross are (a) denial, (b) anger, (c) bargaining, and (d) acceptance, each with its unique reactions and communication patterns. The patient experiences these various emotions in regard to his finiteness, successes, failures, family, all tied together into a package of fear, guilt, and an intense desire, on the part of many, to remain independent. The concerns of dying patients, of course, vary with age—the young girl feeling alienated from companions, the mother worried about the burden on her family and the safety of her children, the successful businessman concerned about his finances—all essentially emphasizing the need to retain a unique identity. This realization of individuality is in conflict with the treatment of only the physical discomfort of the deteriorating body rather than the whole human being with a past and a present.

The mental anguish of a person approaching death is intrinsically bound to interpersonal communication with those who are close to him, usually the family. In actuality, the needs of the family are so closely interwoven with the patient's needs, that to deny the former is to hinder the patient's process of acceptance. Indeed, often the family must experience the same mental stages as the patient's. Communication is enhanced by a realistic, honest expression of feeling through which both the patient and family are relieved of guilt. Often a "game" is played between spouses that consists of hiding knowledge of impending death from each other. Until both parties can communicate and share this knowledge, progress toward mutual acceptance of the inevitable is halted. Again, each patient and family unit's problems and the manner in which they are most appropriately handled are unique.

Financial considerations are an undeniable aspect of the problems of coping with terminal illness. According to a Department of Health, Education, and Welfare Report of the Task Force on Medicaid and Related Programs, "the catastrophically ill are at almost any income level where insurance benefits (including the most liberal major medical coverage) do not cover the cost of sustaining expensive, long-term illnesses." Generally, those under sixty-five years of age are not eligible for Medicare and those above a certain income level (specified by each State) are not covered by Medicaid. A study by Cancer Care, Inc., in 1973, revealed that the median cost incurred by the families of cancer patients was $19,055, which is two and two-thirds times more than the median family income of $8,000. Such universal inability to meet the high cost of hospitalization, surgery, and other treatment strikes hard at the nerve of the patient's guilt, as he may feel personally responsible for the foregone education of a child or the general depletion of the family funds for the future. Financial difficulties may trigger maladjustments as family members may be forced to adopt new roles; for example, housewife turned sole supporter.

Of course, the spiritual needs of a patient are an individual matter. Each person copes with religion or the absence of religion in his own way. Although some attempt to deal with death as the cessation of existence of the mind and body, many patients need to view their death in a religious context, either in relation to a deity or to nature, or both. There are as many perceptions of death as there are people, including concepts such as an indestructible soul, continuation with nature, reunion with Christ, or continuity through survivors. Each patient should be encouraged to express his feelings about death.

The ultimate culmination of a dying person's needs is dignity of personhood in living and in death. It may be argued as to the definition of "death with dignity," some attesting that this implies accepting death, others claiming that this implies dying in the fashion in which one lived; for example, a hostile person would die with the grudge he carried with him through life. Nevertheless, the crux of dying with dignity is in retaining one's individuality, be that in acceptance or denial, anger or serenity, without the humiliation of unnecessary life-prolonging machines.

Although the concerns of the patient cease with the end of his life, the problems of the family linger; in fact, they often intensify with the patient's death. The length and pattern of bereavement is contingent upon the relationship of the survivor to the deceased and the degree to which communication channels were open during the dying process of the patient, relating to identification with the patient, working through ambivalent feelings, and the satisfaction of mutual dependency needs. Hospital environments seldom are conducive to laying the groundwork for a normal bereavement period as relatives are rushed in and out at prescribed visiting hours, children are not allowed to visit patients, and there are incidents of the family being pushed into the hallways while the patient is pronounced dead by a hurried physician who is not capable of dealing with the emotional reaction of the family.

Do not go gentle into that good night,
Old age should burn and rave at close of day;
Rage, rage against the dying of the light.

Though wise men at their end know dark is right,
Because their words had forked no lightning they
Do not go gentle into that good night.

Good men, the last wave by, crying how bright
Their frail deeds might have danced in a green
 bay,
Rage, rage against the dying of the light.

Wild men who caught and sang the sun in flight,
And learn, too late, they grieved it on its way,
Do not go gentle into that good night.

Grave men, near death, who see with blinding
 sight
Blind eyes could blaze like meteors and be gay,
Rage, rage against the dying of the light.

And you, my father, there on the sad height,
Curse, bless, me now with your fierce tears,
 I pray.
Do not go gentle into that good night.
Rage, rage against the dying of the light.

                                        Dylan Thomas

THE HOSPICE CONCEPT   In attempts to deal with all these very special needs of the dying patient and his family, various plans in the United States and Canada have adopted the paradigm of caring for the total patient and family needs with the ideals set forth in the hospice concept. This concept is used in two British facilities which serve as prototypes. Saunders, medical director of the largest of these models, St. Christopher's Hospice in London, speaks of the goals of this concept as individualization of death and relief of distress:

> The name hospice, "a resting place for travelers or pilgrims," was chosen because this will be something between a hospital and a home, with the skills of the one and the hospitality, warmth, and the time available of the other and beds without invisible parking meters beside them. We aim, above all, to recognize the interest and importance of the individual who must be helped to *live* until he dies and who, as he does so in his own way, will find his "own" death with quietness and acceptance. A staff who recognize this as their criterion of success will not find this work negative or discouraging and will know that it is important, both in its own right and also in all the implications it holds for the rest of medicine and, indeed, the rest of life.[5]

St. Christopher's Hospice is a fifty-four-bed inpatient facility for people who are in the advanced stages of neurological and malignant diseases. The foremost concern is the relief of the symptoms that often become so closely interwoven with mental anguish. Common problems in addition to pain are nausea and vomiting, constipation, diarrhea, anorexia, and anticholinergic effects. It is essential that the patient be as symptom-free as possible, so that the dying does not derive from the symptoms rather than the disease. Tension and anxiety can result from the common practice of withholding medication until the pain has become incapacitating. Furthermore, this may cause the patient to become dependent, not only on the drug but on the person who administers it. St. Christopher's Hospice makes a practice of giving a fixed dosage continually in anticipation of the pain so that the patient never knows the severe potential of the pain. A common pain killer used for this purpose is Bromtom's mixture, a concoction of heroin, cocaine, alcohol, and fruit syrup—understandably, the possibility of addiction is not of concern. In addition, steroids are used to enhance the sense of well-being, to improve the appetite, to relieve pain and lower the narcotic dose, to reduce inflammation, and to alleviate weakness. In short, great care is given to the relief of pain and, in turn, to relieve mental anguish and to facilitate awareness of the experience of living until death.

The importance of living until death as a positive fulfillment necessitates an interdisciplinary staff. Each aspect of care is essential to meet the goal of total patient and family unity, including physical, mental, interpersonal, and spiritual elements. As the primary evaluator and prescriber of a medication regimen, the physician is an essential member of the hospice team. His concern for the patient's mental and physical comfort moves him to open channels of communication. As Cotter observes:

> In ways unique to the relationship with each individual patient, caring enables the doctor to discern the patient's desire to discuss the future course of his illness, the nearness of his death, and the circumstances which may surround it, as well as the ways in which his family may best be supported in bearing this knowledge.[6]

5. C. Saunders, "Terminal Patient Care," *Geriatrics*, 21 (Dec., 1966), 70.

6. Z.M. Cotter, "Institutional Care of the Terminally Ill," Hosp. Prog. 52 (June, 1971).

This sharing allows both the patient and family to discuss matters openly and permits them to "say goodbye," which studies have revealed as important. The physician is essentially in an omnipotent position to help this exchange or to "inflict wounds by his own thoughtlessness or need to hurry away from something that is very hard to witness."[7]

In the hospice, the nursing staff must be sensitive to the elements of human dignity. They must be aware of individual differences and responses in personal care because many patients have become quite helpless, and the nurses must convey feelings of compassion and understanding for the person's integrity and retention of uniqueness. The nurses must relay any changes in the patient's condition to the physician, so that appropriate adjustments may be made in medication as well as to the patient's daily needs for food and fluid intake, oral hygiene, and body positioning. Cotter points this out:

> Taking time to explain procedures, to honor preferences, to respect privacy and modesty, to consult with the patient concerning his feelings and his needs, to involve him in social and recreational activities and in small celebrations reflect the nurse's recognition of the patient's personal worth and convey to him the certainty that he still matters, that he has not been "written off" as finished.

The emphasis on religion in this therapeutic community takes on a new meaning of the spiritual. At St. Christopher's, a church-based institution, there is an involvement of clergy and other church-based personnel whose vocation is founded in such work. . . .

Although substantial attention is given to inpatient care within the physical structure of St. Christopher's, where four hundred pa-

tients die each year, 10 to 15 percent of the patients are discharged home for a period of time before death. The staff realizes the value of home care by allowing the patient to feel a part of his family and to return to a relative degree of normalcy, however limited and temporary.

In essence, St. Christopher's Hospice has successfully combined the art of medicine with its value and judgment, with the science of medicine to assuage the pains of patients as they approach death, and with help for their families. The prevailing ideology is succinctly summed up in Saunders' assessment: "There is a stage when the treatment of a hemorrhage is not another transfusion; but adequate sedation, or someone who will not go away but will stay and hold a hand.". . .

SUMMARY   The most desired goal for patients and concerned health professionals is home care for the terminally ill. The familiar surroundings and faces help to relieve the psychological suffering encountered in the dying process and allow freer communication channels between patient and family. However, it is apparent that during some point in the last weeks of life the patient may require closer medical supervision for pain relief, or the family may not be able to continue care once the patient has reached a certain phase, thereby warranting some type of institutionalization. The present choices are, basically, acute-care hospital or nursing home, but, as presently structured, these settings are too often inappropriate to satisfying needs of the terminal patient and family unit. An innovative, yet long-awaited alternative is the use of the hospice concept, which aims at anticipatory pain relief, as well as the psychological and comforting aspects of terminal care. . . .

7. C. Saunders, *"The Management of Terminal Illness"* (London, 1967).

Roberta Lyder Paige
Jane Finkbiner Looney

Hospice Care for the Adult

In this selection, two nurses who specialize in working with terminally ill patients illustrate the emphasis placed on sensitive, personalized care in the hospice program of a medical center. Control of symptoms, especially pain, is a key aspect of the program, but the main focus is on caring. The nurse must become sufficiently close to the patient to be attuned to his or her unspoken feelings. Such caring can be of great value to the dying patient and family. However, there may be emotional hazards in becoming so personally involved with patients who are dying—nurses are as susceptible to grief as other associates of the patient, particularly if a prolonged dying process has resulted in an especially close relationship. This issue will be examined in Fulton's article on "Anticipatory Grief, Stress, and the Surrogate Griever" in Part Three.

Controlling a patient's symptoms is only a part of Hospice care. Caring is really the chief ingredient in what we do. Caring is an attitude reflected in a person's character and in his behavior toward another. It is shown by a willingness to take action regarding a patient's concern no matter how minor it seems.

Caring requires a commitment and a willingness to do the unlovely. Neither education nor experience quite prepare you for doing the unlovely. The disoriented patient who is incontinent of feces can be a challenge to any nursing staff. Keeping him clean is difficult on a number of levels. He most likely will not express his appreciation for what you have done nor will anyone else.

A Hospice patient who weighed three hundred pounds developed decubitus ulcers with an odor so bad that the nurses became queasy while giving care. The ulcers were treated, and odor control was accomplished by sprinkling spirits of peppermint on the bed linen and by the use of room deodorizers. The patient's main wish was to get out of bed. We accomplished this with the help of a Hoyer lift and extra staff.

Sitting with someone who is having a fatal hemorrhage is also difficult. A stimulating conversation with an oriented verbal patient can seem much more satisfying and can somehow appear to be a more therapeutic use of one's time. But keeping a patient clean or staying with a hemorrhaging patient may be the most caring thing to do.

Caring also means extending your concern beyond the patient to the environment. Is the bedside area neat and clean? Even if it is, could something be added to make the environment seem less institutional? Flowers can be a source of color and a symbol of life. At Hospice, a volunteer donates two plants every week and these are given to selected patients to brighten their rooms.

We encourage patients to wear colorful robes and to have familiar objects by the bedside. The staff on one unit joined together to buy a bright colored afghan for a patient's birthday. Both the family (including young children) and the staff shared in the bedside birthday party as the patient could not be moved.

We have found that patients' spirits are lifted by a change in environment. Some patients are taken to porches, solariums, the gift shop, the chapel, or the garden adjoining the hospital. One patient's desire to live was rekindled by a walk around the block and a stop to buy a hot dog from a vendor.

Relieving emotional pain is another aspect of caring. Since man is an integrated whole, unmet physical, social, and spiritual needs can affect his emotional well-being. Continued physical deterioration, in light of the knowledge that one has a terminal disease, takes a tremendous toll on emotions. Often a patient's anger over his increasing helplessness and dependence on others is directed at the staff or the "horrible food." Realizing this and not personalizing the anger directed at you can be a tremendous help to you and the patient in keeping open lines of communication and understanding.

Caring demands listening and observing with your whole person. The patient's chief concern determines our initial point of focus. Our need might be to explore with the patient his concept of death and to make sure the patient understands that he is dying. But the patient might want to be shaved or to go home or have his bowels move or his nausea stop or to talk about places he has visited. The caring person is sensitive to what the patient wants to discuss and responds to his cues.

Listening without having to give answers or a "cure" will allow the patient, if he is able, to continue expressing emotional conflicts and turmoil. Recognizing this also reduces the listener's burden that she must do something. Empathy is needed—not sympathy. Empathy is the ability to enter into the feelings and struggle of a patient as if you were the patient, without losing the "as if" quality. Once a care giver loses the "as if" quality, he sympathizes and identifies so closely with the patient that he becomes an additional burden for the patient. Then the patient can no longer freely share because he must try to protect or not upset the nurse. A caregiver should share her humor and seriousness, not her personal burdens.

To care means to be trustworthy. If we promise to return with pain medication, we return. At least one team member sees the patient, as promised, in the clinic after discharge. Continuity of care and the commitment of the staff increase the patient's sense of security and decrease his fear of abandonment as he approaches death. The more secure a patient feels, the more certain he is that his hope of a comfortable death will be realized.

To care is to be available to family members or the patient's close friends. When he nears death, his social contacts are usually limited to close family and a few friends, each of them coping differently with feelings of helplessness and impending loss. A nurse who has learned to listen and to be at ease with these uncomfortable feelings can be a great help.

A nurse needs to be realistic in assessing relationships that can either cause social pain or bring comfort, depending on their long-standing nature. In the months before death, it is unrealistic to try to change years of strained relationships and poor communication. Small efforts, though, can be helpful. A nurse can tell relatives that hearing still remains even though the patient may be semicomatose. This allows a close relative to share previously unexpressed feelings or last meaningful words.

Caring includes being aware of patients' spiritual needs. A nurse can offer support in this area, apart from and in addition to what the minister, priest, or rabbi offers. We have found that patients who freely talk about their diagnosis and prognosis also tend to talk more freely about their faith in God, or god as they perceive it. Patients seem to grow less concerned with their church or religious affiliation and more concerned with their faith in God and their need of God's help as death approaches. Each person is somewhere along a continuum of no faith to great faith in God (a god).

Stallwood and Stoll define spiritual needs as "any factors necessary to establish and maintain a person's dynamic personal relationship with God (as defined by that individual)." To assess spiritual needs, ask the patient about his perception of God in relation to his illness. Some patients believe that illness is a punishment from God, and others believe that God is trying to get their attention. Symptoms of a spiritual need are reflected in comments by the patient that indicate a desire for love, forgiveness, and acceptance by God.

The nurse's responses should stem from the patient's need and not from any wish to impose her faith on the patient. By offering to bring a Bible or to pray with him, the nurse may encourage the patient to share with her his spiritual needs. When the patient can no longer read, the nurse may read his favorite Bible scripture or meditation booklet. Praying with a patient for his realistic requests decreases his sense of isolation and gives him hope. Anointing services conducted by the chaplain with nursing staff and family present are deeply meaningful to all.

Caring is costly. It takes a great amount of physical, emotional, and spiritual energy. Allowing time to be good to one's self is important. To maintain a healthy perspective on life, the caregiver needs exposure to beauty and to whatever she enjoys. To be responsive to the needs of the dying and to reach out and care, the caregiver, too, must have a support system, peer support in the work situation and outside support from people who care for her.

A caregiver needs to be aware of her own limitations, strengths, and weaknesses. Knowing one's self is a safeguard against the trap of playing "savior" or of having to be perfect. The caregiver herself cannot escape death, a fact that forces her to reassess her philosophy, to consider what is ultimately significant in life. Her answer to this question cannot help but influence her comfortableness in caring for the dying.

Oh, pain were better than tending pain!
For that were single, and this is twain.

Euripides
Hippolytus
translated by Gilbert Murray

Cicely Saunders

Should a Patient Know?

A central theme in literature on the dying patient is the importance of open, caring communication. Interviews with patients reveal that all too often they are not given information on their condition, or else are told of their terminality in a brusque, unfeeling manner. In a society that has avoided the topic of death, confrontation with one's own mortality is apt to be especially difficult and lonely. Cicely Saunders, director of St. Christopher's Hospice in England, examines the question of the patient's knowledge from several points of view. Two points deserve special mention: first, the patient is often able to handle the news of impending death better than the family and, second, nurses often inherit the responsibility of facing the patient's questions when the physician avoids the issue. Finally, the role of hope—both false and realistic—in the patient's remaining life is considered.

This title from the 1959 edition might perhaps be rewritten "Does a patient know. . .?" This knowledge depends not only on what he is told but also on what he has found out for himself by watching people around him, from their silences and their reassurances as much as from their anxiety and grief. He learns from his past memories of illness among family and friends and from what is happening in his own body.

Too often, all around persuade themselves that he is being protected from a truth that they find so hard or cannot even face. He is then left alone with the very truth from which they believe he is being sheltered. But there has been a considerable change in medical and nursing opinion over these years as we have learned from various writers such as John Hinton (1963, 1974), Elisabeth Kübler-Ross (1970), Avery Weisman (1972), and from a more forthright generation of medical and nursing students. Perhaps we are at last becoming more confident in the courage and common sense of our patients.

Although the climate may be changing, this question is still discussed frequently by nurses and doctors and also by a patient's friends and relations. It is wrong to be dogmatic and it is impossible to suggest a general rule, but we do need to consider some basic principles on the subject if we are not to be caught unawares and make decisions based on little more than our own feelings of the moment. . . .

ACCEPTANCE AND PEACE   It is [essential] to notice when a patient needs to talk and to help her bring her fears to the surface gradually. We see how the lies which are intended to shield from fear may in fact add to distress, and that a patient must be allowed to take the initiative. She may well know her real need much better than we do. We see that the problem may not be solved by one person alone but by several who, while keeping the patient's confidence, may yet help each other to make their individual contributions. . . .

A RIGHT TO OUR COOPERATION   Relatives vary as patients do in their desire for the truth and many ask that the patient should not be told, and prefer to try to keep up normal relationships. Some do this "successfully" to the end. Others may need to be restrained from over-acting or helped to see when the patient really wants to be honest with them. One patient was greatly distressed because as she gradually realized she was dying her husband remained apparently cheerful and oblivious. When he was told what was happening he was able at last to show her how much he cared.

The first reaction of many patients on being told how ill they are is frequently, "Does my husband know?" or even, "I will have to tell my husband." They have not realized that their relatives will almost certainly have been told already. This is common practice—perhaps we should question it. The patient may be the strongest member of the group and the one most able to assume leadership in dealing with the situation. Sometimes perhaps we should tell the patient rather more and the family rather less, as a man suggested to me, when he had finally discovered what had caused his feeling of separation from his wife. Because she knew and he did not there was a chasm between them and, as he said, he could not think what had happened to his marriage.

When a patient is admitted families tell us more if we ask, "What sort of way has he been talking about his illness?" than if we say, "Does he know what he's got?" "Does he know how ill he is?" In telling us they may also understand better what has been happening.

Some families are afraid that when the truth is finally open the patient will blame them for their deception. They can be reassured; few patients will blame them, for most of them will realize that they would probably have acted in the same way themselves. "But suppose it had been the other way round. . .?" has been a helpful phrase on this and similar occasions.

It is difficult to know what another man needs. The responsibility for "telling" lies with the doctor, but so often we still seem to fail. In hospital the problem often devolves upon the houseman and the ward sister who may receive a lead from the consultant. The ward sister often knows the patient and his needs best, but feels it is not her job; the houseman is inexperienced and he is often perplexed by the situation.

Very often it is the nurse doing the blanket-bath who gets the direct question. It is not her responsibility and she cannot answer directly. But that may be the very reason why the patient feels safe enough to talk to her. Because she cannot answer, she can keep listening and then be able to pass this question on to someone more senior.

She is likely to be nearest to the patient in his distress and able not only to support him as he faces what is happening but also to enlighten others as they try to understand him.

TRUTH IS NOT IN WORDS   It is not right in principle to set out deliberately to deceive and truth must not be lightly disposed of in any situation. I do not, however, think it is essential for every patient to know he is dying. Trust and faith in life and death are not two different things but come from the same basic attitude. The most important principle is love; not sentimentality, but compassion and understanding. Those who establish close contact with their patients will best be able to decide whether they want or need to be enlightened and will approach as friends with courtesy and kindness. In this setting those who want to know can accept reality and find the strength to face it.

In my own experience I find that the truth

dawns gradually on many, even most, of the dying even when they do not ask and are not told. They accept it quietly and often gratefully, but some may not wish to discuss it and we must respect their reticence. Others take the initiative and ask, or tell us that they already know, at an earlier stage—but they will not ask unless they believe they will receive a considered and kindly answer. If they do ask I believe they should be told. I think it is often wrong for us to take the initiative, and even when we are asked we must sometimes hedge and prevaricate where we judge the patient to be unready as yet to face the full knowledge. But then we must return, for this may need a whole series of exchanges. I do not pretend that it is ever easy either to decide or to carry out our decision, nor that we will not have regrets.

WHAT IS HOPE?   Most of us have been told, "We must never take away hope" but we do not always consider carefully enough what happens to someone when hope—presented always in terms of getting better—becomes more and more obviously false. There are realistic and creative hopes for those whom we tell that their sight will never return, and we tell them because we want them to step out with them. There are also better hopes for the mortally sick and the progressively disabled than reaching out for the mirage of a miracle cure.

One of the continual surprises for those entering this field of care is the joy and reality of life at this stage. It can still be full of good expectations. People tell you of their hopes and say such things as, "I hope I will be able to help my family to make plans, see my friends again, hold my new grandchild, get things tidied up." So many women I have known have had their hair permed during their last weeks and I have always thought this was a gesture of some kind of hope in the future. We also hear of the little hopes, "I hope my wife comes today," "that I get that weekend at home"; I remember one patient who said, "I just want to see the trees come out," and another, "I do want to see Easter." Their wishes were granted and they were content.

Hope grows as we try to meet the challenges that face us as honestly as we can—in dying as well as in living. It springs out of reality and from facing and tackling a situation, however bleak it may be.

Paula was blonde and beautiful, still young but already bedridden with advanced disease. She was facing the certain outcome like the tough and realistic person she was. She had always lived her life day by day—it had been that sort of life—and she still did so without much thought of anything beyond the world of her immediate surroundings and with a wry self-centeredness. When she said, "I try not to moan," she added, "I just don't want people to remember me as a nasty person." We remember her all right. And all the clutter she accumulated around her bed, *and* the horny little red devil she had placed in the wall niche where a small cross had been. . . looking at us sideways to see if we had noticed and taken the point.

All the time she was with us she used to join in our teaching rounds. We would bring groups of students to her room (with her permission) and, first startling them by announcing that she knew she had terminal cancer, she used to show them that what really mattered was what someone was like—not how ill they might be.

Her appearance mattered a lot to her and she was always immaculate, even on the days when things nearly got on top of her. She was demanding of our time and interest but took an equal interest in our doings in her turn, an entertainer and a good friend to the end. She was concerned with the general doings of the Hospice (though not too much with the other patients) and we used to discuss all sorts of things with her.

On her last night I was sitting in her room for an evening gossip when she suddenly said, "All I hope is that I can sit in that chair and watch the nurses making this bed. . .but I wonder. . . ." During the night she became much iller. But first she had a long talk with the night sister, asking her what she believed was the meaning of life and if there was anything beyond it. At the end Paula said, "I can't say I believe like that. . .would it be all right if I just said that I hoped?" With that she took off her false eyelashes and, asking sister to put them away, said, "I won't need them any more. . . ." Within a day she had died, keeping us all at her beck and call to the end.

Hope means being vulnerable and ready to take off masks and pretense, ready to reach out trustfully without even knowing what is the truth for which you long. It also means being able, as night sister was, to speak simply of the truth as you see it. Her hope, which was in Jesus Christ, met Paula's longing and helped her to make the simple gesture of being

just herself and to reach out into the darkness of death and not be afraid.

Hope for Paula at the end of her short life meant being vulnerable, open and ready to take the next step, trusting in the unknown, good news from a far country. Such a meeting comes out of one's own belief and experience. Much help of this kind is best offered indirectly and in a way that makes it easy for the unwilling or uninterested patient to refuse it. Harm may be done by unwelcome discussion and we should never impose our own beliefs on another person, most of all on those for whom we care.

SPIRITUAL HELP   The care of the dying is preeminently the time for doctor, nurse, and chaplain to cooperate. In practice at the moment, many people are so out of touch with the Church that they find it hard to respond to the visit of a clergyman at this stage. Moreover, as Worcester (1935) points out, "The dying do not always recognize the difference between the clerical and medical professions and are also unable to distinguish between the need of physical relief and that of consolation."

Doctors and nurses who have time and heart to listen will have all types of problems, mental, moral, and spiritual, brought to them. They will refer their patients to a clergyman if appropriate, but it is important that he should not just be called in at the last moment. In many hospitals the chaplain's visit is a routine, but it is a great help to him if he is told as soon as possible of anyone who is in special need. While we are waiting for the opportunity to call in someone else we have a responsibility to do the best we can for the people who turn to us, for it may be that someone who has been helping the patient with his physical needs has the key to his confidence and the first opening to help him in this way.

Learning to Die

Perhaps no individual has shed more light on the needs of the dying patient than Elisabeth Kübler-Ross. Her landmark book, *On Death and Dying,* is a manifesto calling for recognition that the dying patient is still very much alive and needs open communication and humane care. In her book, she presents her famous, and controversial, "stage theory" of the adaptation to impending death. In this selection, journalist Thomas Powers summarizes the five stages of denial, anger, bargaining, depression, and acceptance, which provide a guide for understanding the feelings and experiences of the terminally ill. The final stage, acceptance, which Powers mentions only in passing, is the most difficult to describe in ordinary language. Many, but not all, patients eventually attain a calm, serene readiness to face their deaths. Reaching this state of acceptance, however, can be greatly facilitated by sensitive care and support on the part of family, friends, and medical staff.

When patients finally do realize they are dying, a pattern of behavior often follows which was first described in detail by Dr. Kübler-Ross. Based on interviews with hundreds of dying patients over the past five years, she divides the reaction to knowledge of impending death into five distinctive stages.

The first stage is one of denial, even when a patient has suspected the worst and fought to determine the truth. All his life he has casually accepted the fact that "we all have to go." He is stunned to realize that now *he* has to go.

After the discovery, patients often retreat into a self-imposed isolation, remaining silent with friends or relatives or even refusing to see them, while they get used to the fact that no mistake has been made, that they are *now* in the process of dying. Dr. Kübler-Ross believes that the dying never completely lose hope that a cure for their disease will be discovered at the last minute or that an outright miracle will occur ("the Scripture says that nothing is impossible with God"). This hope remains a deep-seated thing, and for practical purposes, such as writing wills and settling their affairs, the dying generally accept the fact they are dying once they have been told, directly or indirectly, that it is truly so.

The second stage is one of anger, especially when the dying individual is young. The anger can be released in any direction: at the doctors for doing nothing, at relatives because they are going to live, at other patients for not being quite so ill, at nurses for being young and healthy, at God for being unjust. In 1603, when Queen Elizabeth was told by her physician, Sir Robert Cecil, that she was seriously ill and must go to bed, she flared back, "*Must!* Is *must* a word to be addressed to princes? Little man, little man! Thy father, were he alive, durst not have used that word." Her mood quickly shifted to gloomy self-pity. "Thou art so presumptuous," she said, "because thou knowest that I shall die."

Eventually the anger subsides and the dying patient enters a curious stage in which he tries to bargain for his life. He begins to talk about all the things he has failed to do but will undertake if he recovers. He laments the fact he spent so much time earning a living and so little with his family, promising to alter his priorities if he gets home again. The most explicit bargains, generally proposed to God, are usually kept a secret. They are often legally precise, offering regular church attendance and sincere belief in return for a few more years. The bargains tend to be selfless, for the dying person knows he is about to lose himself altogether. Bargains can be offered for almost anything, for the chance to attend a son's wedding or to see another spring, but they all have one element in common: they are *never* kept. If the dying person actually does live until

spring he immediately proposes another bargain.

Religious individuals often insist they submit themselves happily to God's pleasure ("Thy will be done") but are prepared to propose a reasonable compromise. St. Anselm, the Archbishop of Canterbury, dying in 1109, told fellow clerics gathered about his deathbed, "I shall gladly obey His call. Yet I should also feel grateful if He would grant me a little longer time with you, and if I could be permitted to solve a question—the origin of the soul." God did not accept the offer, and St. Anselm shortly died, but if He had, Dr. Kübler-Ross suggests that St. Anselm would quickly have proposed another bargain.

The fourth stage is one of altogether reasonable depression, part of the process doctors refer to as "anticipatory grief." In effect, the dying patient is grieving for himself before the fact of death, since he is about to lose everything he loves. It is this grieving which is probably most feared by doctors and relatives. It is painful to witness a death, and doubly painful when the dying person reacts in a fearful or hysterical manner. This is exceedingly rare, and yet doctors and relatives, perhaps unsure what their own reactions would be, fear the possibility so greatly that they put off discussion of death as long as possible and sometimes, as mentioned above, deny the truth until the end. In every other circumstance of life, no matter how bleak, some consolation can be genuinely offered; with those who know they are dying, there is nothing to say. Dr. Kübler-Ross has found, however, that the grieving patient will often come out of his depression and face the prospect of death more calmly for having been through it.

The final stage, not always reached, is one of acceptance. . . .

Edwin S. Shneidman

Death Work and the Stages of Dying

An alternative to Kübler-Ross' stage theory of the dying patient's adjustment to impending death is presented in this selection by Edwin Shneidman. Rather than a clear progression through five stages, Shneidman has observed in his own clinical experience with dying patients a complex alternation between acceptance and denial. This difference of professional opinion underscores the importance of realizing that dying, like living, is a highly individual phenomenon. To the extent that people die of similar diseases in similar hospital settings, there are likely to be consistencies in the patterns of dying from one person to another. However, it is unwise to expect each patient to undergo the same series of experiences or stages. Such formulations as Kübler-Ross' and Shneidman's are valuable insofar as they sensitize us to what the patient is undergoing and furnish us with guides to facilitating his or her adjustment, reminding us that the dying patient is first and foremost a yet living person.

Dr. Elisabeth Kübler-Ross has delineated five psychological stages in the process of dying, based on her work with terminally ill patients in a Chicago hospital. Her deep concern with their welfare is evident; her book *On Death and Dying* (1969) is a clear manifesto of care for those who are benighted by the shadow of death. At the least, it stands as an antidote to some of the callous conventional hospital procedures surrounding the dying patient, described so well by Sudnow in *Passing On* (1967) and by Glaser and Strauss in *Awareness of Dying* (1965) and *Time for Dying* (1968).

Her book grew out of an interdisciplinary seminar at the University of Chicago, in the course of which dying patients were interviewed, or more accurately, were invited to speak of their fears and hopes, dreams and nightmares. The results of this unexampled open discussion were strikingly salutary for both the stressed dying person and the stressed hospital personnel. The interviews often have an evocative and haunting quality, resonating deep within one and stirring buried aspirations and fears. One cannot help being moved by the great human spirit in the voices of these dying fellow beings.

Kübler-Ross explicates five psychological stages of dying, or sets of reactions to one's awareness of imminent death. Categorized primarily "in terms of coping mechanisms at the time of a terminal illness," these stages are defined as: (1) denial and isolation ("No, not me; it can't be true!"); (2) anger-rage, envy, resentment ("Why me?"); (3) bargaining ("If you'll . . . then I'll . . ."); (4) depression ("What's the use?"); and (5) acceptance (the final rest before the long journey). According to her analysis, "the one thing that persists through all these stages [is] hope" ("I will not die"). . . .

Dr. Kübler-Ross does not tell us what percentages of the dying patients lived through each of these five stages or what the consequences were if any were cut off before they achieved the last stage. One key question is how one makes the transition from the negative affective states (which characterize the first four stages) to a state of acceptance. . . .

My own limited work has not led me to conclusions identical with those of Kübler-Ross. Indeed, while I have seen in dying persons isolation, envy, bargaining, depression, and acceptance, I do not believe that these are necessarily "stages" of the dying process, and I am not at all convinced that they are lived through in that order, or, for that matter, in any universal order. What I do see is a complicated clustering of intellectual and affective states, some fleeting, lasting for a moment or a day or a week, set, not unexpectedly, against the backdrop of that person's total personality, his "philosophy of life" (whether an essential optimism and gratitude to life or a pervasive pessimism and dour or suspicious orientation to life).

Philosophers—all but the twentieth-century analytic so-called philosophers—have traditionally taken life and death as their core topics. In relation to death and philosophy, the interested reader can turn to [Jacques] Choron's *Death and Western Thought* (1963) for a résumé of what major philosophers have thought about death. As to the tie between philosophic reflection and easing the burden of one's own death, I know of nothing more illuminating than Pepper's crisp and insightful essay, "Can a Philosophy Make One Philosophical?" (1967).

What of that nexus of emotions manifested by the dying person? Rather than the five definite stages discussed above, my experience leads me to posit a hive of affect, in which there is a constant coming and going. The emotional stages seem to include a constant interplay between disbelief and hope and, against these as background, a waxing and waning of anguish, terror, acquiescence and surrender, rage and envy, disinterest and ennui, pretense, taunting and daring, and even yearning for death—all these in the context of bewilderment and pain.

One does not find a unidirectional movement through progressive stages so much as an alternation between acceptance and denial. Denial is a most interesting psychodynamic phenomenon. For a few consecutive days a dying person is capable of shocking a listener with the breathtaking candor of his profound acceptance of imminent death and the next day shock that listener with unrealistic talk of leaving the hospital and going on a trip. This interplay between acceptance and denial, between understanding what is happening and magically disbelieving its reality, may reflect a deeper dialogue of the total mind, involving different layers of conscious awareness of "knowing" and of needing not to know. . . .

Interview with a Seventeen-Year-Old Girl

The following selection affords a poignant glimpse into the mind of a young woman facing an untimely death from an incurable blood disease. Her interview with Elisabeth Kübler-Ross reveals several insights that are germane to our understanding of dying patients. Foremost is the importance of caring communication and support from family and staff. The young woman greatly appreciates the opportunity to share her feelings in an atmosphere of trust and concern. Also, her acceptance of her condition is facilitated by religious beliefs, which include a conviction of God's purpose as well as her own spiritual survival after physical death.

The following is an interview of a seventeen-year-old girl with aplastic anemia, who asked to be seen in the presence of the students. An interview with her mother took place immediately afterwards, followed by a discussion among the medical students, attending physician, and nursing staff of her ward.

Doctor: I think I'll make it a little easy on you, okay, and let us know please if you get too tired or are in pain. Do you want to tell the group how long you have been ill and when it all started?

Well, it just came on me.

Doctor: And how did it come on?

Well, we were at a church rally in X, a small town from where we live, and I had gone to all the meetings. We had gone over to the school to have dinner and I got my plate and sat down. I got real cold, got the chills and started shaking and got a real sharp pain in my left side. So they took me to the minister's home and put me to bed. The pain kept getting worse and I just kept getting colder and colder. So this minister called his family doctor and he came over and said that I had an appendicitis attack. They took me to the hospital and it seemed like the pain kind of went away; it just kind of disappeared by itself. They took a lot of tests and found that it wasn't my appendix so they sent me home with the rest of the people. Everything was okay for a couple of weeks and I went back to school.

Student: What did you think you had?

Well, I did not know. I went to school for a couple of weeks and then I got real sick one day and fell down the stairs and felt real weak and was blacking out. They called my home doctor and he came and told me that I was anemic. He put me in the hospital and gave me three pints of blood. Then I started getting these pains in here. They were bad and they thought maybe it was my spleen. They were going to take it out. They took a whole bunch of X-rays and everything. I kept having a lot of trouble and they didn't know what to do. Dr. Y. was consulted and I came up here for a checkup and they put me in the hospital for ten days. They ran a whole bunch of tests and that's when they found out that I was aplastic.

Student: When was this?

That was about the middle of May.

Doctor: What did this mean to you?

Well, I wanted to be sure it was too, because I was missing so much school. The pain hurt quite a bit and then, you know, just to find out what it was. So I stayed in the hospital for ten days and they ran all kinds of tests and then they told me what I had. They said it was not terrible. They didn't have any idea what had caused it.

Doctor: They told you that it was not terrible?

Well, they told my parents. My parents asked me if I wanted to know everything, and I told them yes, I wanted to know everything. So they told me.

Student: How did you take that?

Well, at first I didn't know and then I kind of figured that it was God's purpose that I got sick because it had happened all at once and I had never been sick before. And I figured that it was God's purpose that I got sick and that I was in his care and he would take care of me so I didn't have to worry. And I've just gone on like that ever since and I think that's what kept me alive, knowing that.

Student: Ever get depressed about it?

No.

Student: Do you think others might?

Oh, someone might get real, real sick. I feel that, you know, there's no reassuring thing,

but I think everybody who gets sick feels that way once in a while.

Student: Do you wish at times that it was not your parents that had told you about the condition—you wish maybe the doctors had told you about it, had come to you?

No, I like my parents to tell me better. Oh, I guess it was all right that they had told me, but I would have kind of enjoyed that so much. . . if the doctor had shared it with me.[1]

Student: The people that have been working around you, the doctors, and nurses, do you think they have been avoiding the issue?

They never tell me anything, you know, just mostly my parents. They have to tell me.

Student: Do you think you've changed your feelings about the outcome of this disease since the first time you heard about it?

No, I still feel the same.

Student: Have you thought about it long?

Uh huh.

Student: And this hasn't changed your feelings?

No, I went through the trouble, they can't find veins on me now. They give me so many other things like that with all these other problems, but we just have to keep our faith now.

Student: Do you think you've got more faith during this time?

Uh huh. I really do.

Student: Do you think this would be one way that you've changed? Your faith is the most important thing then that will pull you through?

1. Here she expresses her ambivalence about being told by her parents instead of the doctor.

Well, I don't know. They say that I might not pull through, but if He wants me to be well, I've got to get well.

Student: Has your personality changed, have you noticed any changes each day?

Yes, because I get along with more people. I usually do, though. I go around and visit a few of the patients and help them. I get along with the other roommates, so I get someone else to talk to. You know, when you feel depressed it helps to talk to someone else.

Doctor: Do you get depressed often? Two of you were in this room before, now you are all alone?

I think it was because I was worn out. I haven't been outdoors for a week now.

Doctor: Are you getting tired now? Tell me when you get too tired, then we will finish this session.

No, not at all.

Student: Have you noticed any change in your family or friends, in their attitude toward you?

I've been a lot closer to my family. We get along well, my brother and I were always close when we were small. You know he's eighteen and I'm seventeen, just fourteen months apart. And my sister and I were always real close. So now they and my parents are a lot closer. You know, I can talk to them more and they, oh, I don't know, it's just a feeling of more closeness.

Student: It's deepened, enriched your relationship with your parents?

Uh huh, and with other kids, too.

Student: Is this a sense of support for you during this illness?

Yes, I don't think I could go through it now without my family and all the friends.

Student: They want to help you in every way possible. How about you, do you help them, too, in some way?

Well, I try to. . .whenever they come I try to make them feel at home and make them go home feeling better and things like that.

Student: Do you feel very depressed when you're alone?

Yes, I kind of panic because I like people and I like to be around people and being with someone. . .I don't know, when I'm alone all the problems come up. Sometimes you do feel more depressed when there's nobody there to talk to.

Student: Is there anything in particular that you feel when you're alone, anything that sort of scares you about being alone?

No, I just get to feeling that there's nobody there and nobody to talk to.

Doctor: Before you were sick, what kind of girl were you? Were you very outgoing or did you like to be alone?

Well, I was pretty outgoing. I liked to do sporty things, go places, go to games and to a lot of meetings.

Doctor: Have you ever been alone for any length of time before you were sick?

No.

Student: If you had to do it over again, would you rather your parents had waited before telling you?

No, I'm glad I knew right from the start. I

mean I'd rather know right at the beginning and know that I have to die and they can face me.

Student: What is it that you do have to face, what's your vision of what death is like?

Well, I think it's wonderful because you go to your home, your other one, near to God, and I'm not afraid to die.

Doctor: Do you have a visual picture of this "other home," realizing, you know, all of us have some fantasies about it though we never talk about it? Do you mind talking about it?

Well, I just kind of think it's like a reunion where everybody is there and it is real nice and where there's someone else there—special, you know. Kind of makes the whole thing different.

Doctor: Is there anything else you can say about it, how it feels?

Oh, you would say you have a wonderful feeling, no more needs and just being there and never again alone.

Doctor: Everything just right?

Just right, uh huh.

Doctor: No need for food to stay strong?

No, I don't think so. You'll have a strength within you.

Doctor: You don't need all these earthly things?

No.

Doctor: I see. Well, how did you get this strength, all this courage to face it right from the beginning? You know many people have a religion, but very few at the time will just face it like you. Have you always been that way?

Uh huh.

Doctor: You never had any real deep hostile—

No.

Doctor: Or got angry at people who weren't sick.

No, I think I got along with my parents because they were missionaries for two years in S.

Doctor: I see.

And they've both been wonderful workers of the church. They just brought us all up in a Christian home and that has helped a great deal.

Doctor: Do you think we, as physicians, should speak to people who face a fatal illness about their future? Can you tell us what you would teach us if your mission was to teach us what we should do for other people?

Well, a doctor will just come in and look you over and tell you "How are you today" or something like that, a real phoney. It just kind of makes you resent being sick because they never speak to you. Or they come in like they are a different kind of people. Most of the ones I know do that. Well, they come down and talk with me for a little while and ask me how I feel and visit with me. They say things about my hair and that I'm looking better. They just talk to you and then they'll ask you how you feel and some get into explaining things as much as they can. It's kind of hard for them because I'm underage and they aren't supposed to tell me anything, because they are supposed to tell my parents. I think that's so important to talk to a patient because if there's a cold feeling between the doctors you kind of dread to have them come in if he's going to be cold and businesslike. When he comes in and is warm and human that means a great deal.

Doctor: Did you have a feeling of discomfort or unpleasantness about coming here and talking about it to us?

No, I don't mind talking about it.

Student: How have the nurses handled this problem?

Most of them have been real wonderful and talk a great deal and I know most of them pretty well.

Doctor: You have the feeling that the nurses are able to handle it better than the physicians in a way?

Well, yes, because they are there more and they do more than the doctors.

Doctor: Uh huh, they just may be less uncomfortable.

I'm sure of that.

Student: May I ask, has anybody in your family ever died since you grew up?

Yes, my dad's brother, my uncle died. I went to his funeral.

Student: How did you feel?

Well, I don't know. He looked kind of funny, he looked different. But, you know that's the first person that I'd ever seen dead.

Doctor: How old were you?

I'd say about twelve or thirteen.

Doctor: You said, "he looked funny" and you smiled.

Well, he did look different, you know, his hands didn't have any color and they did look so still. And then my grandmother died but I wasn't there. My grandfather died on my mother's side, but I wasn't there either, I just went on, you know. Oh, then my aunt died and I couldn't go to the funeral because it was not too long ago and I was sick and we didn't go.

Doctor: It comes in different forms and ways, doesn't it?

Yes, he was my favorite uncle. You don't really have to cry when somebody dies because you know they're going to heaven and it's kind of a happy feeling for them, to know that they're going to be in paradise.

Doctor: Did any of them talk about it to you at all?

A real, close friend of mine just died, over a month ago and his wife and I went to his funeral. That meant a lot to me because he had been so wonderful and had done so much for me when I got sick. He left you feeling so comfortable and everything.

Doctor: So what you say is to be a little more understanding and take a little time and talk with the patients.

Stay of Execution

Stewart Alsop's autobiographical account of his hospitalization for incurable cancer reveals some of the problems of dying in a hospital setting. In addition to facing the cessation of his life, Alsop must contend with the physical discomfort that is symptomatic of his disease, as well as with the diminishment of his sense of personal identity in a technological setting. He sees himself as a guinea pig, used primarily to generate research data. He does not want his children to visit and witness him in such a "demeaning" predicament. He muses on the realization that death loses some of its terrors for a miserable sick person and that "A dying man needs to die." The medicalization of death appears to be a mixed blessing. On the one hand, advances in medical technologies and treatments have saved many lives and relieved much misery. On the other hand, they have created the wherewithal to prolong the dying process to the point where dying is feared more than death itself.

One thing I discovered in those first ten days at NIH: A man can't be afraid all the time. No doubt if you were told that you were to die in three hours, you would spend those three hours being afraid of death. But when death is due to occur at some time in the fairly near but indefinite future—in a few months, or a year, or two years, or maybe even later—it is possible to forget about death for many hours at a time.

I suppose I first read the Latin tag scribbled in my notebook—"*Horribilis mors perturbat me*"—in about Third Form year at Groton, where I went to school in the Endicott Peabody era, when much Latin was compulsory. I remember thinking that "perturbed" seemed a rather mild reaction to "horrible death." But it turned out to be, as I also scribbled, "the right word." Not that I wasn't afraid. I was, and I hated the idea of dying soon. But after the initial shock of being told that I had a lethal and inoperable cancer, the protective mechanism took over, so that for the most part I was perturbed—upset, worried—rather than terrified.

"God tempers the wind to the shorn lamb" was another phrase I scribbled in my notebook. I thought the words were from the Bible, until I looked up the phrase in Bartlett's and found it was Laurence Sterne's. I had a "sudden visual picture"—of myself as the shorn lamb, naked to the cold wind, and the wind dying down as a mysterious protective mechanism took over, rendering the intolerable tolerable.

"Amazing how nice almost everybody is." A lot of the nurses wore on their shirt fronts those yellow plastic buttons with the outline of a fatuous grin, and almost all of them tried hard to cheer up their sure-to-die patients. Ward 13E, I discovered later, is not a popular ward with the nurses, and it is hard to keep it fully staffed. Taking care of leukemics is a lot of work. They have needles in their arms a good deal of the time, for chemotherapy or anti-biotics or transfusions, and the needles are always getting clogged up or coming unstuck. They require a lot of care in other ways, especially the patients in the laminar flow rooms. But there is another reason 13E was unpopular. As one young nurse remarked to me, "Gee, this ward is just so *depressing*." So it is, but almost all the nurses did their very best to seem briskly cheerful.

The patients, for the most part, felt too horrible to be very genial. Some had just completed chemotherapy and were in the early stages of "remission." They looked deathly ill, with yellow-bronze parchment faces and wispy hair. But they too made an effort at cheerfulness, or at least at concealing despair. The word *cancer* was hardly ever mentioned, and the word *death*, never.

"Remission of sins"—the phrase tantalized my memory for several days. The phrase was suggested, of course, by the "remission," alas temporary, that with luck followed a session of chemotherapy. I couldn't remember the rest of it, or where it came from. Finally, my wife, Tish, supplied the rest: "remission of sins, resurrection of the dead, and the life everlasting." From the Credo, of course. . . .

Tish, thank God, could spend a lot of time with me. She asked me whether I wanted Nicky and Andrew, the youngest of our six children, to visit me in the hospital, and I said I didn't. There is something demeaning about being in pajamas in daylight, in a hospital bed, hooked up to an IV [intravenous feeding apparatus], surrounded by nurses and sick people, and I didn't want my children to see me demeaned.

At NIH, saving the individual patient is not the essential mission. Enormous efforts are made to do so, or at least to prolong the patient's life to the last possible moment. But the basic purpose is not to save that particular patient's life but to find means of saving the lives of others, in other hospitals in this country and throughout the world. In this sense, although the NIH doctors hate the phrase, the leukemic patients are guinea pigs, and the emotions of the guinea pigs are not the first consideration. (I have been proud of being, so far, so unusual and instructive a guinea pig; presumably the government made a good investment in my case.)

How much should a patient be told? My own view is that a patient should be told the truth and nothing but the truth—but not the whole truth. I find scribbled in my notebook: "A man who must die will die more easily if he is left a little spark of hope that he may not die after all. My rule would be: Never tell a victim of terminal cancer the whole truth—tell him that he *may* die, even that he will *probably* die, but do not tell him that he *will* die."

During my second go-round at NIH, my anorexia [loss of appetite] was almost total; it was all I could do to get down one boiled egg in the morning, and liquor, to my dismay, continued to disgust me almost as much as food. Except for Tish and John Glick [chief NIH doctor on Alsop's case], people disgusted me, too. When [brother] Joe and Susan Mary [Joe's wife] paid a visit—I had passed the word that I wanted to see no one else—it was a major effort to be polite, though I love them both.

It wasn't that I felt desperately ill physically, or even desperately depressed. I felt, instead, a kind of weariness, a vast indifference. In my head during this time there was a sort of continual background music—or, rather, background cacophony—not exactly a headache but a kind of murmuring unpleasantness. And a very bad thing happened: I could hardly read at all. After half an hour, the page would blur, and the cacophony in my head would mount from a murmur to a shout. For want of anything better to do, I watched television. It was the first time I have ever watched television for more than a few minutes at a time and, I hope, the last.

The chief danger was, of course, a lethal infection; that was why I was alone in a double room. At one point John told me that my granulocyte count [granulocytes are white blood cells important in fending off infection] was down to forty—less than one-tenth of what is regarded as the minimum safety level. "One envisages them," I wrote in my notebook, "the grizzled, battle-hardened survivors of a once mighty army, now reduced to little more than a platoon, marching out once again to do battle against the foe, well knowing that their cause is hopeless."

I was pretty sure by this time that my cause was hopeless, too, but it didn't bother me half as much as it had during my first stay at NIH, when I still enjoyed picnics in the waiting room, and drinking martinis, and reading, and laughing, and seeing my friends. The second time I was in NIH, I enjoyed nothing. I didn't want to die, but I didn't want desperately *not* to die. Who would fardels bear, to grunt and sweat under a weary life, if the weary life consisted of seeing no friends, and being unable to enjoy food or drink, and sweating like a pig every night, and, *faute de mieux,* watching a mixture of tedium and vulgarity that is so much of television?

Before I got sick I hardly ever thought about death, because the subject is an unpleasant one. Since John Glick quoted the odds to me,

THE SECOND COMING

Turning and turning in the widening gyre
The falcon cannot hear the falconer;
Things fall apart; the centre cannot hold;
Mere anarchy is loosed upon the world,
The blood-dimmed tide is loosed and
    everywhere
The ceremony of innocence is drowned;
The best lack all conviction, while
    the worst
Are full of passionate intensity.

Surely some revelation is at hand;
Surely the Second Coming is at hand.
The Second Coming! Hardly are those words out
When a vast image out of *Spiritus Mundi*
Troubles my sight: somewhere in sands of the desert
A shape with lion body and the head of a man,
A gaze blank and pitiless as the sun,
Is moving its slow thighs, while all about it
Reel shadows of the indignant desert birds.
The darkness drops again; but now I know
That twenty centuries of stony sleep
Were vexed to nightmare by a rocking cradle,
And what rough beast, its hour come round at last,
Slouches towards Bethlehem to be born?

William Butler Yeats

I have had to think a lot about death, and I have learned something from the thinking. I learned something especially from a stretch of twenty days of unexplained viremia, or whatever it was (John Glick still does not know for sure). What I learned is something that most healthy people do not understand when they think about their own death.

If you are young and in good spirits and full of health, the thought of dying is not utterly abhorrent but inherently incredible. The inherent incredibility of death to a healthy young man acts as a protective mechanism and helps to keep a combat soldier sane.

But the fear of death in battle is quite different from the fear of death on a hospital bed. It is, for one thing, much rarer. Most people do not die a violent death, whether on the battlefield or in the streets. Most people die in bed, because they are very sick or because they are very old or both. But their sickness or their oldness also acts as a protective mechanism. Sickness and age do not make death at all incredible. They do make death less than utterly abhorrent.

In short, for people who are sick, to be a bit sicker—sick unto death itself—holds far fewer terrors than for people who feel well. Both Cy Sulzberger [*New York Times* columnist] and Bill Atwood [publisher of *Newsday*] wrote me letters in which they referred to death as the Greek god Thanatos. When I felt sick enough, I even felt a certain affection for Thanatos, and much less fear of him than I had before.

I was never "half in love with easeful Death," and I suspect John Keats wasn't either. Only a psychotic really wants to die. But at least the thought of death was more easeful, and far less terrible, than it had been. Afterward, when I felt well again and believed I was cured, the thought again became very terrible.

The readings on the "counts" came in, and they were low—low enough so that John decided I needed both a hemoglobin and a platelet transfusion. I lunched with Rowly Evans and a cofounder of New York's Conservative party, Kieran O'Doherty, an amusing, fast-talking fellow. I was rather appalled to find myself agreeing with some of the things he said—not many, but enough to make me nervous. Am I rapidly slipping to the right as my blood rapidly turns to water?

I used to joke with John Glick about what it would do to the reputation of the august NIH if I died and the fact came out that NIH had done nothing at all to treat my disease. He laughed, but I think it was not entirely a laughing matter to some of the other NIH doctors.

My new diagnosis, "smoldering," or "aleukemic," leukemia, was, I suspect, a way of saying that the doctors really didn't know just what was wrong. Doctors are unwilling to admit that they are puzzled—almost as unwilling as political writers. I enjoy irritating John Glick by pointing out that even the best doctors don't really know as much about the human body as a good political journalist knows about the body politic.

In May 1973, after six months outside the hospital, Alsop again entered "one of NIH's drearily familiar rooms" with his second attack of pneumonia—a likely exit for leukemics. Looking back over almost two years of living with the specter of death, he wrote the following.

John Glick can make no prognosis about what may happen next. Perhaps I shall drift back into the fever-and-night-sweats routine.

Perhaps, as after my October bout with pneumonia, I shall make a halfway comeback, with no fever and feeling reasonably well as long as I get my hemoglobin and platelet transfusions. And just perhaps, although miracles, like lightning, rarely strike twice in the same place, I shall have another remission, as I had after my bout with flu in the autumn of 1971.

In any case, one contrast strikes me. At the beginning of this book, I described the trapped and desperate feeling that came over me after I had been told that I would die quite soon. Last Saturday night, when I felt so sick, I felt rather sure that I would die quite soon, and perhaps very soon, within the next day or so. I did not at all welcome the prospect, but it filled me with no sense of panic. I kissed Tish a fond good night at ten, took some Benadryl, and went easily off to sleep. Why the difference?

Perhaps the state of the nation has something—a very little something—to do with the difference. For weeks now I have been haunted and depressed by a sense that the American system, in which I have always believed in an unquestioning sort of way, the way a boy believes in his family, really is falling apart—by the sense that we are a failed nation, a failed people. And Watergate is surely a peculiarly depressing way to say farewell to all our greatness. It is a whimper—a sleazy little whimper, a grubby little whimper—rather than a bang. . . .

I have lived what John Glick calls a "normal life." But it has not been altogether normal. It is not normal to wake up every night just before dawn, with a fever of 101 or so, take a couple of pills, and settle down to sweat like a hog for four or five hours. It is not normal to feel so weak you can't play tennis or go trout fishing. And it is not normal either to feel a sort of creeping weariness and a sense of being terribly dependent, like a vampire, on the blood of others. After eight weeks of this kind of "normal life," the thought of death loses some of its terrors.

But the most important reason why I felt no panic last Saturday was, I think, the strange, unconscious, indescribable process that I have tried to describe in this book—the process of adjustment whereby one comes to terms with death. A dying man needs to die, as a sleepy man needs to sleep, and there comes a time when it is wrong, as well as useless, to resist.

There was a time, after I first got sick, when I liked to recall one of my small collection of Churchillisms, the familiar story of how Churchill visited his old school, Harrow, in his extreme old age, and the headmaster asked him to say a few words to the boys.

"Never give up," Churchill said. "Never. Never. Never. Never." There is no doubt that the old man lived beyond his allotted span by a tremendous effort of a tremendous will. He lived so long because he never gave up. But to what good end?

I saw Churchill a year or so before he died. I was in the visitors' gallery of the House of Commons on a reporting trip to London when Sir Winston unexpectedly appeared on the floor. There was a hush as the old man waddled feebly toward his accustomed seat, hunched over and uncertain of every step. He sat down heavily and looked around the House, owlishly, unseeing, as if for some long-vanished familiar face, and then, as the debate resumed, his big head slumped forward grotesquely on his chest. He was an empty husk of a man, all the wit and elegance and greatness drained out of him by age. Like my mother, he should have died herebefore. There is a time to live, but there is also a time to die.

[Alsop died on May 26, 1974.]

An Appropriate Death

Avery Weisman, professor of psychiatry at Massachusetts General Hospital and Harvard Medical School, provides a simple, yet profound, manifesto of the needs and rights of the dying person. His concept of an "appropriate death" can serve as a guide both for those facing death and for those trying to help the dying person.

Someone who dies an appropriate death must be helped in the following ways: He should be relatively pain-free, his suffering reduced, and emotional and social impoverishments kept to a minimum. Within the limits of disability, he should operate on as high and effective a level as possible, even though only tokens of former fulfillments can be offered. He should also recognize and resolve residual conflicts, and satisfy whatever remaining wishes are consistent with his present plight and with his ego ideal. Finally, among his choices, he should be able to yield control to others in whom he has confidence. He also has the option of seeking or relinquishing significant key people.

Obviously, these conditions of an appropriate death are like the highest aspirations of mankind! Few people are ever fortunate enough to realize these goals. Consequently, it may seem most unlikely that people about to die could reach or even care about appropriate death, if the requirements are so unrealistic.

On the other hand, our preconception that death can *never* be appropriate may be a self-fulfilling idea. If we believe that death is bad, and dying people, by a magical contagion, are tainted, then appropriate deaths are never possible. By discouraging therapeutic intercessions, therefore, we may contribute deep alienation, hopelessness, and loneliness.

Given a measure of consciousness, control and competence to work with, we can encourage appropriate death, or at least a purposeful death. Patients can, for example, be protected from needless procedures that only dehumanize and demean, without offering suitable compensation. We can, moreover, ask people how much consciousness is desirable. Some patients prefer solitude toward the end in order to collect their thoughts. Others, more gregarious, need family and friends. As life ebbs away, some patients want to doze, while others prefer to be alert, and to simulate the regular periods of sleep and wakefulness that healthy people enjoy.

If we refuse to think of appropriate death as a quixotic vision beyond reach, we will protect the patient's autonomy and personal dignity. Much, of course, depends upon the concern of the key participants. Although most people tremble at the notion of dying, it is wholly practical that they can offer a substantial contribution to the mutual task. An appropriate death, in brief, is a death that someone might choose for himself—had he a choice. The central idea, of course, is that to foster an appropriate death, one must realize that death is not an ironic choice without an option, but a way of living as long as possible. Our task is therefore to separate death and its prejudices from each other.

OLD MAN 3

Tonight
May I sleep in peace
May my dreams of the day's events
not interrupt that sleep
May my family and friends
be well when I awake
May the aches the hurts I daily face
be within a range
my soul can tolerate
May my mind be clear
My memories of the past
less insistent than
the callings of today
My motives less impure
My strivings forever
just beyond my strength
The recounting of my former deeds
more modest than the events themselves
My appetites within bounds
My presence with some grace
The men I see
be acceptable to me

And if this be the night
I fail to wake
May I sleep in peace
without break
till the end of time.

Morton Leeds

8.

Death and the Child

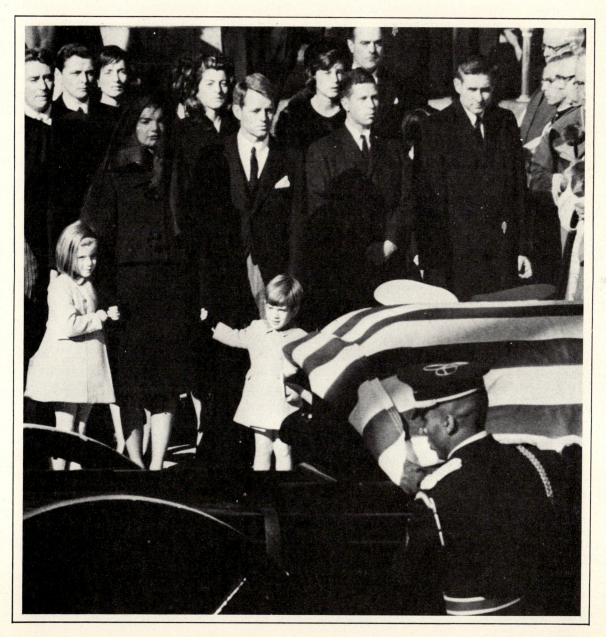

The encounter with loss and death is an essential part of the child's growth from an uncultured infant to a functioning member of society. As discussed in Section 3 on "Death in Popular Culture," each new generation must learn the meanings of life and death that prevail in its culture. In this section, we shall examine the child's confrontation with death from two perspectives: learning about death and reacting to the deaths of others.

Both the Kastenbaum and Jackson articles explore the child's growing ability to conceptualize death. The child learns about the fact of death and its cultural meanings from many sources, including direct experience, that is, witnessing the death of a pet or seeing dead animals on the road; play and games with other children like peek-a-boo; discussion of death at home, church, and school; and the mass media—especially television. Studies of children's understanding of death indicate that it develops through progressive stages, although such stages are at best only approximations or guidelines. The meanings of death, moreover, are extremely diverse and subtle—the death of a pet has much in common with the death of a person, but at the same time, there are important differences. Learning the meanings of death is a process that continues throughout life.

In earlier historical eras, young children encountered death as an integral part of life; pets and other animals died or were slaughtered; baby brothers and sisters often succumbed to communicable diseases; family members usually died at home; and wakes were held at home.

In contemporary society, however, children are less likely to have such "practical" education. As we have seen in earlier sections of this Reader, death tends to be denied or avoided in everyday life, and the dying are frequently segregated in institutions. Death is a popular subject in the mass media, however, where it is usually portrayed as violent and impersonal. As discussed in Section 3, the mass media have become extremely powerful sources of cultural learning for children. One wonders at the implications of ten-year-old children witnessing thousands of murders on television. What does it mean to a twelve-year-old to view "Holocaust" on television? How is a high school student's conception of the meaning of life affected by news stories on the neutron bomb and the potential consequences of worldwide nuclear war? These and other questions demand our attention as we endeavor to understand how children learn about death in contemporary society.

Children, no less than adults, are vulnerable to the loss of others through death and are capable of experiencing grief. When real death, as opposed to the impersonal death of the mass media, does intrude upon family life, it is apt to come as a surprise or shock to the children, if not also to the parents. Moreover, the parents are often uncomfortable in talking directly about death because of their own confusion and denial. Yet, if the child's natural concern and curiosity is met with anxious silence or evasion, recovery from the loss may be hampered. On the other hand, if the encounter with death is experienced in a context of parental caring and honesty, the child will not only be more likely to make a satisfactory adjustment, but will also have a deeper understanding of the meanings of life and death, attachment and loss. Children, moreover, are doubly vulnerable: not only must they adjust to their own loss and the complex feelings engendered by it, they are also susceptible to the effects of others' grief.

Grollman's selection in this section identifies and discusses several aspects of the child's grief responses. He underscores the fact that children need patient, caring communication when their young lives are confronted with death.

Different deaths are likely to have differing impacts upon children. The death of a pet, for example, can precipitate deep grieving but also become a valuable death-education experience. The child can realize the difference between one's own death and that of another being and gain confidence in parents who provide security and comfort. Eventually, another pet may be obtained, and the child learns about re-investing emotional attachment in another relationship. On the other hand, the death of a parent can be one of the most traumatic experiences imaginable. Not only does the child lose a vital relationship at a vulnerable point in life, but the intense grief of the surviving spouse as well as the risk of financial insecurity intensify the impact significantly. The death of a sibling has its unique risks. The child may have occasionally "wished the brother or sister were dead" in an outburst of anger or jealousy. If the brother or sister then does die, the surviving sibling may be tormented by feelings of guilt that are hard to comprehend and even harder to communicate.

Children may show signs of disturbed or unresolved grief. Symptoms may appear shortly after the death, or they may be delayed. It is difficult to generalize about what is "normal" or "abnormal" grief in either adults or children. However, experts generally concur that a virtual absence of grief, especially when all indications are that the deceased person was significant to the child, may be a sign of underlying trouble. It is fairly common for bereaved children to revert to immature behavior, that is, a toddler may "forget" toilet training, or a gradeschooler may start thumbsucking again. When a child seems unable to resume more appropriate age-level behavior for weeks and months on end, there may be some troubling feelings which are impeding resolution of the grief. Where there is a question that the child's grief may be problematic, consultation with teachers, family physicians, or knowledgeable family friends may be of value. There is no substitute, however, for the availability of sensitive communication and comfort from someone who knows the child.

Children, like all of us, must sooner or later face the reality of death as an important concept, as a source of loss of others, and, ultimately as a personal fate.

Edgar Jackson

When to Talk about Death

Edgar Jackson, a minister and psychologist who has written extensively on death and dying, provides some useful guidelines for talking about death with children. He emphasizes that children are seriously interested in the meaning and implications of death and urges adults to respond to their questions with openness and honesty. Of course, this implies that adults have themselves arrived at acceptable understandings of what death means. If adults, however, are frightened of death, they will be quite at a loss to help children understand it. If adults relegate death education to the mass media, moreover, there is the danger that children will learn distorted images of death and dying. Today's children are tomorrow's adults and will in turn be responsible for teaching their children the meanings of life and death. Today's children will be also responsible for caring for tomorrow's elderly citizens as they live and die.

Often parents ask, "When should you talk about death with a child?" Although it may seem to oversimplify the matter, the answer is, "When the child wants to talk about it." The events that can raise the question are happening regularly. Sometimes the child seems unaware of them and at other times appears to have a morbid curiosity concerning them. Children differ widely in their ability to form questions. They react differently to question-raising events. Often their approach to any given question is conditioned by the way previous questions have been met.

If you are apprehensive you may show your emotion by trying to overanswer a question, as well as by trying to divert or ignore it. Sooner or later, in one way or another, directly or indirectly, the question about death is inevitable. Like most important questions, it grows out of the experience of daily living.

An airliner crashes and the newscaster says, "One hundred and six persons perished in a jet crash." The child asks, "What is 'perish'?" The principal comes into the first grade and asks to speak to the teacher alone. She comes back into the room a few minutes later with tears in her eyes and tells her class, "I have just received word that my father is very sick and may die. I must go home for a few days." The first-grade teacher is an important figure in her pupils' lives. They identify with her feelings. They will take the emotion they saw in their teacher's eyes and attach it to the event of dying. Questions will inevitably be raised, and answers will be needed. An automobile accident, the death of an aged relative or a neighbor, will bring the fact of death into the child's world. It will need to be met at the point where it arises.

The questions will vary. They may show the limited understanding of the child but they will also show the quality of his feelings. It is this quality of feeling that is the important starting point in approaching an answer.

As your child works to tie the unusual event to his past experience, he may ask, "Why did my teacher cry?" "What do you do when you die?" "Where do dead people go?" "How do you go to the bathroom when you are dead?" Or he may show that he has made the experience more personal by asking, "When are you going to die?" or saying, "I don't want to be dead."

Usually the inevitable question is related to an inevitable event. We may be prepared for it, or we may be surprised. However it is, it is important to make sure we know what the child has in mind before giving an answer. There is little purpose in answering questions that aren't asked. We must guard against confusing our adult meanings for words with those the child has in mind.

Workmen come to cut down a dead tree. The child, very much interested in the whole process, asks, "Why are those men cutting down my tree?" You would naturally answer, "That tree is dead." This invites the further question, "When is a tree dead?" It gives an opportunity to point out to the child that the dead tree has no leaves and its bark is falling off. This fact is compared with facts about other trees whose leaves are blowing in the breeze. There is a factual difference between being dead and being alive. This simple fact may be all that is needed for an answer. It becomes part of the basic equipment for understanding why death is different from life. It is honest, it is related to the simple events, and it has met the child's question where it was raised.

Your child may come in from play carrying a dead bird. With no special feeling of the state of the bird, he may say, "Look, I caught a bird." When he had chased birds before they had flown away. This one was different. He has it in his hand. You may casually examine the bird and say, "This little bird is dead. It won't fly any more."

The child may then say, "Why won't it?" This question shows that he does not understand all that is meant by the first explanation. He wants to know more. Then you may say, "A dead bird is not like a bird that is alive. A live bird can fly, and eat the bird seed we put out for it. A dead bird can't fly or eat ever again." The answer is honest and adequate for the question asked. The next question will show whether or not it is all he wants to know. He may then say, "What shall I do with it?" It follows naturally to say, "I'll get a little box, you dig a hole over there, and we'll bury it." This may bring another question. "Why should we bury it?" The answer may well be, "When little birds die they don't need their bodies any more, so we bury them where they are safe from harm." With the activity of the burial the event will probably be closed and play will be resumed. When another event involving death and burial occurs, he has had some preparation at his level of comprehension, and he approaches the new experience without fear because no fear was engendered in the event now past.

Sometimes the stories we tell children raise the question of death. Traditional stories do not hesitate to mention it, but it is usually a type of death that does not make the child feel uncomfortable. Generations of children were told of Jack, the Giant Killer, without suffering emotional injury, because they felt as if they were Jack rather than the giant. Not every event that depicts death has an equal emotional impact upon a child. It is important to be sensitive to the child's feelings as he uses the words and tries to develop a meaning for them.

For most children the first encounter with death in the family comes through the death of a grandparent. Grandparents have a special place in the emotional life of their grand-children, for they represent affection and an indulgence that is treasured. How can the death of so important a person in the child's life be explained and made acceptable to a child? No two family situations are quite the same, but the following experiences show a constructive and a destructive way of explaining an event to a grandchild.

Susan lived in a large city. Her grand-parents lived on a farm. For Susan nothing was more interesting than a trip to the farm. Everything was alive and moving, and her grandfather was in charge of it all. He enjoyed his granddaughter so much that he spent hours with her watching the little pigs, riding a pony, and feeding baby chicks. She basked in the excitement of the farm and her grand-father's love. When word came that her grand-

father was seriously ill with a kidney infection, Susan, her parents, and her little brother went at once to the farm. For several days she was aware of the critical condition of her grand-father. She saw him a few times, and even to an eight-year-old child it was obvious that he was very sick. When he died, the simple and open honesty of rural people dealt with his death sorrowfully but candidly. Neighbors talked to Susan about her grandfather. No limits were placed on conversation or ques-tions. Susan asked to go to the funeral in the little village church. She did not understand all that was said, but she felt a part of it.

The meaning of the sad days and their events were summed up in a conversation her father overheard when Susan was explaining to four-year-old Richard the changes that had taken place. As they watched the little pigs eating their supper, she said, "Your grandpa is dead. That means he won't be here any more. He won't milk the cows. He won't feed the pigs. So if there is anything you want to know, you'll have to ask me." She accepted the fact, she accepted its meaning, and she accepted her responsibility in the new state of affairs death had caused. The circumstances were honest and open, and her reaction was direct and uncomplicated. While she would not forget her grandfather, she was not emotional-ly damaged by his death.

In the same community lived another girl named Susan, but we will call her Sue for short. She was eight also, and within a year had an experience of death quite different from our other Susan. Sue's grandfather had lived with the family for several years. He did not hear well, so people yelled at him to make him hear. Sue always thought people were angry when they yelled. Her grandfather died unex-pectedly and at night. His body was removed before Sue awoke in the morning. Her parents decided that the less said about his death the better. They thought Sue was too young to understand such things. Because most of his friends were either dead or far away, a private service was planned. When Sue asked at breakfast where her grandfather was, her father said he had a sick spell but she shouldn't worry, because everything would be all right. Sue went to school as usual. A couple of days later a private service was conducted while Sue was at school. She had felt that something strange was going on, but when her questions were dodged, she stopped asking. She was hardly prepared for the encounter that took place at school.

John, a classmate, said, "I'm sorry your grandfather died."

Sue, baffled and uncertain, said sharply, "He did not."

John, somewhat uncertain, said, "He did too. My mother said so."

Sue only repeated, "He did not. I guess I know."

John replied, "Who're you kidding? They don't have funerals for live people."

Sue couldn't face John or his disclosure. She ran into the school and blurted out her story to the teacher. The teacher wisely tried to calm Sue, and called her mother on the telephone. When her mother came for Sue, she explained, "Yes, your grandfather died, but we didn't want to tell you. We didn't want to upset you. John should have kept his mouth shut. Now what can I say?"

Sue had no questions she felt she could ask. But she wondered if her grandfather had died because they yelled at him. She wondered why they did not tell her, when Johnny knew. She never thought about her grandfather or about dying without getting an uncomfortable feeling inside. Something had happened to Sue that would take a long time to heal.

Sue couldn't tell her parents that she felt threatened by what had happened, because she could not explain her own feelings. But if she had been able to put them into words, her vague apprehension might have sounded like this: "How could they take Grandpa out and bury him without telling me about it? Didn't they know I loved him? I wonder if they really love me. If I died, would they just take me out and bury me without telling me? Doesn't love mean anything to my father and mother? How can I trust their love if they thought my love for my grandfather didn't mean anything to me?"

It is important for us to realize that the rites and rituals that we use to mark the end of life are our efforts to say a significant and appropriate "good-bye." We don't just dispose quickly of the bodies of those we love as if they were worthless. Some remnants of our love are still attached to them, whether we want to admit it or not. We cannot treat what we have loved without loving care without doing damage to all of the other loving relationships in life. If Sue's parents had understood this, they would have shown more respect for Sue's love, and in return Sue would have had more confidence in the quality of their love for her.

So, the appropriate time to talk about death is when it is part of the child's experience. The proper mood is one of openness and honesty. The important consideration for the adult is that the child's feelings and experiences are quite different from his own and have to be judged accordingly. Then he can share life as far as it can be shared in understanding, and give answers that can be built on as understanding grows. The important relationships that give security to life and love will be protected and nourished then, even in times of emotional stress and painful events.

Robert Kastenbaum

The Kingdom Where Nobody Dies

Robert Kastenbaum, professor of psychology at the University of Massachusetts and co-author of *The Psychology of Death,* states in this article that death "is an integral part of growing up." All children must eventually develop the realizations that other people must die and that they themselves will someday die, too. Kastenbaum discusses several sources for death education in the child's environment and emphasizes the importance of the child's awareness of death in the development of conceptual thinking abilities.

Children are playing and shouting in the early morning sunshine near the end of Alban Berg's opera *Wozzeck.* They are chanting one variant of a very familiar rhyme: "Ring-a-ring-a-roses, all fall down! Ring-a-ring-a-roses, all. . . ." The game is interrupted by the excited entry of other children, one of whom shouts to Marie's child, "Hey, your Mother is dead!" But Marie's child responds only by continuing to ride his hobby-horse, "Hop, hop! Hop, hop! Hop, hop!" The other children exchange a few words about "what is out there, on the path by the pool," and race off to see for themselves. The newly orphaned child hesitates for an instant and then rides off in the direction of his playmates. End of opera.

What begins for Marie's child? Without knowing the details of his fate, we can sense the confusion, vulnerability, and terror that mark this child's entry into the realm of grief and calamity. Adult protection has failed. The reality of death has shattered the make-believe of childhood.

Children are exposed to death on occasions much less dramatic than the sudden demise of a parent. A funeral procession passes by. A pet dies. An innocent question is raised at the dinner table: "Was this meat once a real live cow?" In a society such as ours that has labored so diligently to put mortality out of sight and out of mind, most of the questions children ask about death make parents uncomfortable. It is often thought that there is no appropriate answer that would not be alarming or threatening to children. Therefore, the subject of death is mostly evaded entirely or fantasized.

The intrusion of death places typical parents in an awkward position. They are not able to relax and observe—much less *appreciate*—how the child orients himself toward death. Yet much can be learned by indulging this curiosity. By dropping the adult guard that directs us to protect children from morbid thoughts and threatening events and by concentrating instead upon how children themselves react to death, surprising insights begin to emerge. We find from psychological research, clinical experience, folkways, and incidents shared with children in and around home that, despite the lack of explicit references, death is an integral part of growing up.

A child's fascination with death occurs almost any time, almost any place. Mortality is a theme that wends its way into many of the child's activities, whether solitary or social. Consider games for example. Ring-around-the-rosy is a popular childhood play theme in both this country and Europe. Our own parents and grandparents delighted in "all fall down," as did their ancestors all the way back to the fifteenth century. . . .

Death has been ritualized in many other children's games as well. In the playful romping of tag, what is the hidden agenda or mystery that makes the chaser "It"? Could "It" be the disguise for death? We may be reluctant even to speculate that the touch of death is at the symbolic root of the tag games that have flourished for so many centuries throughout so much of the world. Yet Death (or the Dead Man) certainly is central to at least some of the chase games beloved to children. In the English game "Dead Man Arise" the central player lies prostrate on the ground while other children either mourn over him or seek to bring him back to life. When least expected, up jumps John Brown, the Dead Man, the Water Sprite, Death himself, or whatever name local custom prefers. The children flee or freeze in surprise as the chaser whirls toward them for a tag that will bestow Dead Man status upon the victim.

Although children today continue to participate in rituals that can be traced centuries back, other death-attuned merriments such as "bang, bang, you're dead!" are of more recent origin, and the repertoire is constantly freshened. When everyday group games do not provide a sufficient outlet for death-oriented play, children are likely to express their own special thoughts and feelings individually through inventive play. Suffocating and burying a doll is an instance of fulfilling a death fantasy. Similarly, a game of repeatedly crashing toy cars into each other or a model plane into the ground effectively permits a youngster to test out feelings that are evoked in certain real situations. Should an adult happen to interrupt this brutal type of play, the youngster may offer some reassuring comment, such as "Nobody gets killed bad" or "All the people come home for supper.". . .

There are two different, although related, realizations that children must eventually develop. The first is that other people die, and the second is that they themselves will die. . . .

Death registers in the minds of young children whether or not adults are fully cognizant of the phenomenon. It need not be either a sibling death or a miscarriage. The death of a playmate, the man across the street, a distant relative, a pet, a sports hero, or a national political figure all make an impression somewhere in the child's mind. Real death is not a rare event in the child's world.

There is no precise way of knowing which death will make the greatest impact upon which child. The death of a pet, especially if it is the first death exposure or occurs in a striking manner, sometimes affects a youngster more than the subsequent death of a person. There is nothing automatic about the different responses to death, even in childhood. Nor can the seemingly inconsequential or remote death be disregarded if we wish to understand the child's thoughts and feelings on mortality.

Whatever the impact of other deaths, however, the loss of a parent has the most signal and longest-lasting influence on children. Bereavement in early childhood has been implicated as the underlying cause of depression and suicide attempts in later life. In one British study, for example, it was found that boys age four or younger who had lost their fathers were especially vulnerable to severe depression in adulthood. Many of the fathers died in combat. Perhaps some of the psychiatric and physical casualties of our involvement in Vietnam eventually will include the suicide committed in 1990 by the son whose father did not return. The death of a young father, however, does not automatically determine his son's fate. There is no way to predict the surviving child's response. In fact, the responses themselves cannot be explained entirely on the basis of parental death alone. What registered in the child's mind when his parent died? By what process did this first response develop into a way of life or into a sort of psychological time bomb set for later detonation? How might the child have been protected or guided? These questions have been raised only sporadically, and the answers are still elusive. . . .

Of all the methods used to piece together the meaning of death during childhood, none can replace the sharing of a direct death experience with a young child. It is only in such moments of fortunate sharing that we have a clear glimpse into the child's face-to-face encounter with death. There is something indescribably poignant about the way in which the young child attempts to attune himself to threat, limitations, and mortality at a time when he would appear to be innocent of dark concerns. In a journal that I have kept for each of my children, I recorded my son's first encounter with death.

David, at eighteen months, was toddling around the back yard. He pointed at something on the ground. I looked and saw a dead bird, which he immediately labeled "buh . . .buh." But he appeared uncertain and

puzzled. Furthermore, he made no effort to touch the bird. This was unusual caution for a child who characteristically tried to touch or pick up everything he could reach. David then crouched over and moved slightly closer to the bird. His face changed expression. From its initial expression of excited discovery and later of puzzlement, now it took on a different aspect: to my astonishment, his face was set in a frozen, ritualized expression resembling nothing so much as the stylized Greek dramatic mask of tragedy. I said only, "Yes, bird. . .dead bird." In typically adult conflict, I thought of adding, "Don't touch," but then decided against this injunction. In any event, David made no effort to touch.

Every morning for the next few days he would begin his morning explorations by toddling over to the dead-bird-place. He no longer assumed the ritual-mask expression but still restrained himself from touching. The bird was allowed to remain there until greatly reduced by decomposition. I reasoned that he might as well have the opportunity of seeing the natural processes at work. This was, to the best of my knowledge, David's first exposure to death. No general change in his behavior was noted, nor had any been expected. The small first chapter had concluded.

But a few weeks later a second dead bird was discovered. David had quite a different reaction this time. He picked up the bird and gestured with it. He was "speaking" with insistence. When he realized that I did not comprehend his wishes, he reached up toward a tree, holding the bird above his head. He repeated the gesture several times. I tried to explain that being placed back on the tree would not help the bird. David continued to insist, accompanying his command now with gestures that could be interpreted as a bird flying. All too predictably, the bird did not fly when I returned it to the tree. He insisted that the effort be repeated several times; then he lost interest altogether.

There was a sequel a few weeks later—by now autumn. David and I were walking in the woods, sharing many small discoveries. After a while, however, his attention became thoroughly engaged by a single fallen leaf. He tried to place it back on the tree himself. Failure. He gave the leaf to me with "instructions" that the leaf be restored to its rightful place. Failure again. When I started to try once more, he shook his head no, looking both sober and convinced. Although leaves were repeatedly seen to fall and dead animals were found every now and then, he made no further efforts to reverse their fortunes.

David's look of puzzlement and his repeated efforts to reverse death suggest that even the very young child recognizes a problem when he sees one. Indeed, the problem of death very well might be the prime challenge that sets into motion the child's curiosity and mental questing. Instead of constituting only an odd corner of the young child's mental life, death and its related problems may, in fact, provide much of the motivation for his intellectual development. Children obviously do not possess the conceptual structures of the adult; nevertheless, they do try to understand. Curiosity about death and "where things go" is part of a child's early motivation for exploring his environment. While many developmentalists have observed how the young child comes to an appreciation of object constancy, few have noted that this mental achievement is not possible unless there is also an appreciation of inconstancy. In other words, the young child must be aware of changes, losses, and disappearances if he is eventually to comprehend what "stays," what "goes," and what "comes and goes." Even very young children en-

counter losses, ends, and limits. Without an ability to fathom these experiences, they could not form protoconcepts of constancies, beginnings, and possibilities.

The death of animals, relatives, or friends undoubtedly has some relationship to the child's discovery of his own mortality, but there are other observations that are more germane. Adah Maurer, a school psychologist in California, suggests that an infant as young as three months old has the glimmerings of death awareness. For a while the baby alternates between sleeping and waking states, with biological imperatives having the upper hand. Soon, Maurer says, "the healthy baby is ready to experiment with these contrasting states. In the game of peek-a-boo, he replays in safe circumstances the alternate terror and delight, confirming his sense of self by risking and regaining complete consciousness. A light cloth spread over his face and body will elicit an immediate and forceful reaction. Short, sharp intakes of breath, vigorous thrashing of arms and legs removes the erstwhile shroud to reveal widely staring eyes that scan the scene with frantic alertness until they lock glances with the smiling mother, whereupon he will wriggle and laugh with joy. . . . To the empathetic observer, it is obvious that he enjoyed the temporary dimming of the light, the blotting out of the reassuring face and the suggestion of a lack of air which his own efforts enabled him to restore, his aliveness additionally confirmed by the glad greeting implicit in the eye-to-eye oneness with another human."

Babies a few months older begin to delight in disappearance-and-return games. Overboard goes a toy, somebody fetches it, then overboard again. The questions "When is something gone?" and "When is it gone forever?" seem very important to the young explorer. He devises many experiments for determining under what conditions something is "all gone." Maurer suggests that we "offer a two-year-old a lighted match and watch his face light up with demonic glee as he blows it out. Notice the willingness with which he helps his mother if the errand is to step on the pedal and bury his banana peel in the covered garbage can. The toilet makes a still better sarcophagus until he must watch in awed dismay while the plumber fishes out the Tinker-toy from the overflowing bowl."

It makes sense to take these activities seriously. They provide early clues as to how children begin to grasp what "all gone" means. Once children are old enough to begin talking in sentences, part of their verbal repertoire usually includes death words. One conversation between a four-year-old girl and her eighty-four-year-old great-grandmother illustrates the preschoolage child's concept of death: "You are old. That means you will die. I am young, so I won't die, you know." This excerpt suggests that the little girl knows what it means to die, even if she has not entirely grasped the relationship between age and death. However, a moment later she adds: "But it's all right, Gran'mother. Just make sure you wear your white dress. Then, after you die, you can marry Nomo [great-grandfather] again, and have babies."

The words "dead" and "die" are fairly common in children's conversation and often are used with some sense of appropriateness. Yet an extra comment such as "you can marry Nomo again" or a little adult questioning frequently reveals that a child's understanding of death is quite different from an adult's. Psychologist Maria Nagy, studying Hungarian children in the late 1940s, discovered three phases in the child's awareness of personal mortality. Her interpretation of death ideas expressed by three- to ten-year olds in drawings and words are classic.

Stage one: present until about age five. The preschool child usually does not recognize that death is final. Being dead is like being less alive. The youngest children regard death as sleep or departure. Still, there is much curiosity about what happens to a person after he dies. The children "want to know where and how he continues to live. Most of the children connected the facts of absence and funerals. In the cemetery one lives on. Movement. . .is limited by the coffin, but for all that, the dead are still capable of growth. They take nourishment, they breathe. They know what is happening on earth. They feel it if someone thinks of them and they even feel sorry for themselves." Death disturbs the young child because it separates people from each other and because life in the grave seems dull and unpleasant.

Stage two: between the ages of five and nine. The distinguishing characteristic of this stage is that the child now tends to personify death. Death is sometimes seen as a separate person—for example, an angel or a frightening clown. For other children death is represented by a dead person. Death usually makes his rounds in the night. The big shift in the child's thinking from stage one is that death now seems to be understood as final: it is not just a reduced form of life. But there is still an important protective feature here: personal death can be avoided. Run faster than the Death Man, lock the door, trick him, and you will not die, unless you have bad luck. As Nagy puts it, "Death is still outside us and is also not general."

Stage three: ages nine to ten and thereafter: The oldest children in Nagy's study recognized that death was not only final but also inevitable. It will happen to them, too, no matter how fast they run or how cleverly they hide. "It is like the withering of flowers," a ten-year-old girl explained to the psychologist.

Nagy's stages offer a useful guide to the development of the child's conception of death, but not all observations fit neatly into these three categories. There are instances in which children as young as five realize their own inevitable mortality. A six-year-old boy worked out by himself the certainty of death. In a shocked voice he revealed, "But I had been planning to live forever, you know." A five-year-old reasoned aloud: "One day you [father] will be died. And one day Mommy will be died. . . . And one day even Cynthia [little sister], she will be died, I mean dead, too. . . . [pause] And one day *I* will be dead. . . . [long pause] *Everybody* there is will be dead. . . . [long, long pause] That's sad, isn't it?" This insight is several years ahead of schedule and is even farther ahead of what one would expect from most theories of mental growth.

Apparently, it is possible to grasp the central facts of death at a surprisingly early age. Children probably tend to retreat from this realization when it comes so early and for several years fluctuate between two states of belief: that death is final and inevitable, and that death is partial, reversible, and perhaps avoidable.

My research indicates that the orientation many adolescents have toward death also fluctuates between a sense of invulnerability and a sense of impending, catastrophic wipeout. Some adults reveal a similar tendency to function at two levels of thought: they "know" that death is final and inevitable, of course, but most of their daily attitudes and actions are more consistent with the belief that personal mortality is an unfounded rumor.

Sooner or later most children come to understand that death is final, universal, and inevitable. Parents might prefer that children remain innocent of what is happening in their lives and sheltered from emotional stress, shock, and anguish. But it is our own make-believe, not theirs, if we persist in behaving as though children are not attuned to the prospect of mortality. It is important to remember that in this century millions of children around the world have grown up literally in the midst of death and the threat of death. They have fewer illusions on the subject than do many adults.

The kingdom where nobody dies," as Edna St. Vincent Millay once described childhood, is the fantasy of grownups. We want our children to be immortal—at least temporarily. We can be more useful to children if we can share with them realities as well as fantasies about death. This means some uncomfortable moments. Part of each child's adventure into life is his discovery of loss, separation, non-being, death. No one can have this adventure for him, nor can death be locked in another room until a child comes of age. At the beginning the child does not know that he is supposed to be scared of death, that he is supposed to develop a fabric of evasions to protect himself, and that his parents are not to be relied upon for support when it really counts. He is ready to share his discoveries with us. Are we?

How Does a Child Experience Grief?

Earl Grollman, a rabbi and editor of *Explaining Death to Children,* examines the child's grief responses in this selection. Children, argues Grollman, can feel grief very deeply, and require patience, understanding, and support if they are to adjust satisfactorily to the death of an important person. They need, in particular, to be encouraged to express their feelings and emotions, both verbally and through tears. Grollman also examines several ways in which children can react to grief, including denial, bodily distress, anger, anxiety, and guilt. Guilt is an especially problematic feeling, as its very nature makes it difficult for the child to recognize and communicate.

Do children experience grief?

Of course, the child experiences a sense of loss and with it, sorrow. His grief is a complicated mechanism. He feels remorseful that a loved one is dead. On the other hand, he feels sorry for himself because he was picked out for personal pain. He is faced with many problems about which he is helplessly confused. He may believe that the departed has run out on him. His fears often give rise to anger with hostile feelings toward those who are closest to him. The knowledge that from now on there is nothing the child can do to "make up" to the deceased can be a very heavy burden. Yet, the parents who understand that a variety of reactions may possibly occur are well on their way to helping the child toward a more positive and more mature approach in dealing with the loss.

According to Dr. John Bowlby of Tavistock Clinic, London, each child experiences three phases in the natural grieving process. The first is protest when the child cannot quite believe the person is dead, and he attempts, sometimes angrily, to regain him. The next is pain, despair, and disorganization when the youngster begins to accept the fact that the loved one is really gone. Finally there is hope, when the youngster begins to organize his life without the lost person.

How does the child face the loss of a pet?

When a pet dies, the child is brought face to face with some of the implications of death—its complete finality and the grief and loss it inflicts. The youngster may experience some guilt because he feels he had not cared well enough for the pet and was in some way responsible for its fate. He may conduct in greatest secrecy an elaborate burial. To the adult, the ceremony may seem to be a thoughtless mockery of a very sacred religious ritual, but to children these burial rites are far from prank or ridicule. The youngsters engage in them with as much zest and enthusiasm as a mock wedding ceremony or secret initiation. This kind of "game" has profound meaning. Here is their real opportunity to work things out for themselves and play out their feelings and fears. Sometimes the "play" is accompanied by real sadness and tears which afford an opportunity to help them put the experience somewhat behind them. Parents may well suggest such a ceremony to a child whose pet has died.

There is the example of a small boy whose pet dog was killed by an automobile. His first reaction was one of shock and dismay. This mood was followed by outrage against his parents who he felt were guilty of the death because they did not take proper care of the pet. The boy behaved like the adult who rages against God for neglecting His charges. Yet, the anger against the parents was but a substitute for his own guilt, for the youngster had on occasion expressed the wish to be rid of "that awful pest." The child then insisted that as part of the burial service one of his favorite toys be buried with the dog. The toy served as a kind of peace offering to the offended pet. Now, the lad was freed of his own anxiety and could continue to function effectively in his everyday activities. Thus the ritual combined the dynamics of guilt, assuagement, and reparation which possess a similarity in the mourning behavior of adults.

Usually the child accepts the loss of a pet, constituting a step in accordance of one of the many unpleasant realities of everyday living. More often than not, a new pet replaces the dead one, and life goes on much as it did before.

[What of] the child's loss of a brother or sister?

Although deprived of a sibling who had played an important role as caretaker or playmate, the child still has the security of the parents' presence. Yet it would be an error to assume that the death of a brother or sister is relatively unimportant, even though few conscious and readily discernible reactions may be detected. For the death of a child invariably affects the parents. Whether they turn more closely and protectively to the surviving child, or are so disturbed by their grief that they are unable to maintain a healthy parent relationship to him, the child will experience some modification of his life situation.

An older child's reaction to such a death may be the frightening realization that this could happen to him! Would it occur tomorrow, or next week, or next year? If the cause of death of an older sibling is not made clear, the younger child may take on babyish behavior to prevent himself from growing to that age when he, too, might die.

The youngster may try to replace the deceased person. He sees his parents grieving and he wants to make everything all right again. He may suddenly try to act like the lost brother in ways not suited to his own capacities and well-being. He may be burdened by the feeling that he must take the other child's place.

If he and his brother or sister were close, death may bring a long-lasting feeling of loss. His parents' grief, the many reminders around the house, and the abrupt cessation of a relationship that had been an important part of his life, all combine to make readjustment slow and painful. The situation may be further complicated by strong feelings of guilt because of past anger or jealousy toward the dead person, or because of failure to make the brother or sister happier while he or she was still alive.

What are some reactions to the death of a parent?

One of the greatest crises in the life of a child is the death of a parent. Never again will the world be as secure a place as it was before. The familiar design of family life is completely disrupted. The child suffers not only the loss of a parent, but is deprived of the attention he needs at a time when he craves that extra reassurance that he is loved and will be cared for. Here, too, the child's reactions are complicated by guilt feelings. Sometimes guilt evolves from earlier hostility toward the dead person, and from the feeling that the survivor bears some responsibility for his death.

Anna Freud points out that a child's first love for his mother becomes the pattern for all later loves. "The ability to love, like all other human faculties, has to be learned and practiced." If this relationship is interrupted, through death or absence, the child may do one of four things: remain attached to a fantasy of the dead person; invest his love in things (or work); be frightened to love anyone but himself; or, hopefully, accept his loss and find another real person to love.

If the boy loses a mother, he may regress to an earlier stage of development. His speech becomes more babyish. He begins to suck his thumb. He whines a great deal and demands the attention of adults. He says in effect: "Dear Mother, see, I am only a very little baby. Please love me and stay with me." Later on in life, because he was injured by his mother, the prototype of all women, he may believe that all women have a tendency to hurt men. To avoid being wounded by them, he loves them and leaves them before the girls can do what his mother did to him: hurt and abandon him. However, it cannot be overemphasized that these dynamics need *not* occur. For example, in a home where there is no mother, there are almost always mother substitutes—a housekeeper, an aunt, or an older sister. Even in time of death there can be an exposure to intimate relationship with some significant person.

The small boy whose father dies will feel the loss of a male person to imitate, a masculine foil with whom he can learn to temper his feelings of aggression and love. The mother, however, may contribute to the boy's difficulty. Deprived of a husband, she may try to make up for her own deprivation by trying to obtain gratification from her son. The boy feels he now possesses his mother and she will continue to gratify him completely. Therefore he need not look for pleasure elsewhere. From observations, one can cite many examples and consequences of doting mothers and spoiled sons. (The reverse may be observed in girls who lose their father or mother.)

In general, if a child allows himself to find someone else whom he can come to love and trust, it is a good indication that he has worked out his grief. If he has not, he may spend the rest of his years searching, consciously or unconsciously, for an exact replica of his childlike relationship with the lost person and be disappointed over and over again that someone else cannot fulfill his original needs. . . .

In times of death, should parents discourage the child from crying?

Too often, well-meaning people say: "Be brave! Don't cry! Don't take it so hard!" But why not? Tears are the first and most natural tribute that can be paid to the one who is gone.

The child misses the deceased. He wishes the loved one were still with him.

The son and daughter whose father dies should express their grief. It is natural. They loved him. They miss him. To say, "Be brave!" and especially to the son, "Be a man!" sounds as if one were minimizing their loss and places an impossible burden upon the boy. Be realistic enough to say, "Yes, it's tough!" Make them feel free to express themselves. Otherwise the adult deprives them of the natural emotion of grief.

Don't be afraid of causing tears. It is like a safety valve. So often parents and friends deliberately attempt to veer the conversation away from the deceased. They are apprehensive of the tears that might start to flow. They do not understand that expressing grief through tears is natural and normal.

Tears are the tender tribute of yearning affection for those who have died but can never be forgotten. The worst thing possible is for the child to repress them. The child who stoically keeps his grief bottled up inside may later find a release in a more serious explosion to his inner makeup.

Crying is the sound of anguish at losing a part of oneself in the death of one whom he loves. Everywhere and always, grief is the human expression of the need for love and the love of life.

Just as the parents should not deny the child the opportunity to cry, they should not urge him to display unfelt sorrow. He is likely to feel confused and hypocritical when told he ought to express a regret he does not honestly feel. There are many outlets for grief and the child must utilize those openings that most naturally meet his needs.

What are other possible reactions to death?

Death is an outstanding example of a traumatic event which threatens the safety of all the surviving members of the family. It could bring in its train these well-marked symptoms:

Denial. "I don't believe it. It didn't happen. It is just a dream. Daddy will come back. He will! He will!"

The child may frequently look as if he were unaffected because he is trying to defend himself against the terrible loss by pretending that it has not really happened. The adult may even feel that the youngster's apparent unconcern is heartless. Or the parent may be relieved and feel, "Isn't it lucky! I am sure he misses his father, but he does not seem to be really bothered by it." Usually, this signifies that the child has found the loss too great to accept, and goes on pretending secretly that the person is still alive. That is why it is so necessary to help the child accept reality by not conjuring up fairy tales and compounding the problem with: "He went away on a long journey."

Bodily Distress. "I have a tightness in my throat!" "I can't breathe." "I have no appetite at all." "I have no strength." "I am exhausted." "I can't do my homework." "I can't sleep." "I had a nightmare."

The anxiety has expressed itself in physical and emotional symptoms and is often brought on by visits from friends or the mention of the deceased loved one.

Hostile Reactions to the Deceased. "How could Daddy do this to me?" "Didn't he care enough for me to stay alive?" "Why did he leave me?"

The child feels deserted and abandoned. "Bad Mommy—she's gone away!" There may yet be another aspect. Think of a child's anger after he has been left by his mother for a day or two. Although he may not show much reaction just after her return, later he may turn on her angrily saying: "Where were you, Mommy? Where were you?" Similarly, the child uses this protest to recover the lost person and ensure that she never deserts him again. Although no amount of anger will make the loved one return, the youngster may still use it simply because the protest worked successfully in the past.

Guilt. "He got sick because I was naughty. I killed him!"

Guilt is often coupled with the expectations of punishment.

Hostile Reactions to Others. "It is the doctor's fault. He didn't treat him right." "Maybe he was murdered." "It is God's fault. How could He do this to me?" "The minister doesn't know anything—he keeps saying God is good."

The noisy anger is turned outward usually in the attempt to cope with guilt. The youngster may even be angry at sympathetic friends simply because they are not the deceased. He doesn't want any substitutes—even as the very young child does not want anyone but his mommy.

Replacement. "Uncle Ben, do you love me, really love me?"

The child makes a fast play for the affection of others as a substitute for the parent who had died.

Assumption of Mannerisms of Deceased. Do I look like Daddy?"

He attempts to take on the characteristic traits of the father by walking and talking like him. He tries to carry out the wishes of the deceased. Or the boy tries to become the father as the head of the family and the mate of the mother.

Idealization. "How dare you say anything against Daddy! He was perfect."

In the attempt to fight off his own unhappy thoughts, the child becomes obsessed with the father's good qualities. The falsification is out of keeping with the father's real life and character.

Anxiety. "I feel like Daddy when he died. I have a pain in my chest."

The child becomes preoccupied with the physical symptoms that terminated the life of the father. He transfers the symptoms to himself by a process of identification.

Panic. "Who will take care of me now?" "Suppose something happens to Mommy?" "Daddy used to bring home money for food and toys. Who will get these things for us?"

This state of confusion and shock needs the parent's supportive love: "My health is fine. I will take care of you. There is enough money for food and toys."

These are some of the reactions of children as well as adults. Some may never appear. Some come at the time of crises. Others may be delayed, since so often the child represses his emotions and attempts to appear calm in the face of tragedy. At one moment he may express his sense of helplessness by acting indifferent. A moment later the feeling of loss will take the form of boisterous play. The parents may detect what the child is thinking from some superficially unrelated questions that he may later ask: "Mommy and Daddy, where did the light go when I blew out the candles on my cake?". . .

I've come for no bad reason.
Just that you and I were inseparable
and went everywhere without any trouble.
But it was God's will
that this morning
people should say you were dead.
But you and I
used to walk together
and all men knew it.
Then God came to take you.
So I said to myself
I would bring
that pot of beer.
Thus we used to do
for everyone to see.
So I brought along
this beer to give you
to drink.
Have a good journey
and may nothing trouble you.
And this cock,
take it
along with you.
If you want to go anywhere,
the cock will aways get up at dawn,
and crow,
and you'll get up too
and set off again.

Look after the fowl well
as you go on your way.
If it crows, get up.
Every man who sets off
takes a cock with him.
And when you reach your house,
greet all your people warmly.
May there be nothing wrong there
and may they look after the place well.
Whether it was that somebody
killed you
because you and I went together
and people were angry,
whether it was because of this you were killed,
or because you yourself wanted (to eat) somebody
and God took you away,
go ahead
and I will follow you.
And these twenty cowries I give you
so you may pay
at the River
and get across.
Have a good journey
and go to see your people.
And this arrow,
take it along
and shoot the witch.
As for the beer,
and the fowl,
if there is anyone
who will be to me
as my friend was,
let him take the beer and fowl.
But if there's no one,
let me drink and weep,
and know that the friendship dies today.

A speech made by a Losaala youth
from Lawra at his friend's funeral

Does a child really feel guilt?

There is a degree of guilt involved in every death. It is human to blame oneself for the person's death. Even if the adult knows he did everything in his power to prevent the death and to make the loved one happy, he is still apt to search his mind for ways that he could have done more. After the Cocoanut Grove fire in Boston, one woman could not stop blaming herself for having quarreled with her husband just before his death. Often, the recrimination is an attempt to turn the clock back, undo the quarrel, and magically prevent the loss.

Children more than adults are apt to feel guilty since, in their experience, bad things happen to them because they were naughty. The desertion of the parent must be a retribution for their wrongdoing. Therefore, they search their minds for the "bad deed" that caused it.

Often guilt is induced by the child's misconceptions of reality. One youngster was told that to live you must eat. Since she did not eat her cereal the morning her father died, she concluded that it was she who brought about his death.

Young children believe in magic. That is, if one wishes someone harm, the belief will bring results. When the little boy said in anger, "I hope you die, Mom," and the mother did die, the lad felt responsible and guilty.

Painful thoughts are recalled. "I was terrible to her." "I kicked her." "Why did I call her those awful names?" "What will happen to me?" "Will God punish me?" Any normal child has feelings of intense hostility toward another child or an adult. If this person dies, the youngster may feel that in some way his thoughts contributed to the person's death.

The living sometimes feel guilt simply because they are alive. They may feel they should be censured for wishing that the sick person hurry up and die. Or they feel they should be blamed because they secretly hope that their friends' mommies would die, so they won't be the only one without a mother.

The resultant behavior varies. There may be aggressiveness, with or without excessive excitability. There may be unsociability and obvious despondence. There may be a lack of interest and attention in class, or a degree of forgetfulness of ordinary concerns. It must be underscored that guilt is a normal reaction to the experience of death.

[How can one help] the child to relieve the guilt?

From a commonsense point of view, the child's guilt is usually unreasonable. Therefore, it is important for the parents to help the child give vent to his anxieties. In his childish mind he may remember times when he may not have been so good to this person as he should have been. Let him know that all people try to be good and loving but do not always succeed. Nor does one have to. One does the best he can. Tell the child: "You did the best you could. You had nothing to do with his death. All people die." By all means possible, parents should avoid linking suffering and death with sin and punishment.

Explain to him that "wishing does *not* make it so." Try to recall those happy moments when the child did make the deceased very happy. For the youngster who is too young to give shape to his thoughts or to find the words which might relieve his guilt, the best therapy is through relationships with other people. Children learn self-acceptance by being accepted by others. They learn to trust through living with trustworthy parents and teachers. They learn to love by being loved....

Survivors of Death

Part Three, "Survivors of Death," is organized around three foci of concern that have received increasing attention in the past few years: (1) Grief, (2) Widowhood, and (3) The Funeral. As *Macbeth* instructs us to "give sorrow words; the grief that does not speak whispers the o'er fraught heart and bids it break," so, too, in Section 9 we pursue through the printed word a better understanding and deeper appreciation of this profound emotion—the better to give it a voice and a respite.

Section 10, "Widowhood," addresses itself not only to the ten million widows who presently have survived their husbands'

deaths, but also to all of us who will at some time or other be touched directly or indirectly by that most difficult event, the death of a spouse.

Section 11, "Funerals," takes us from the far reaches of a sixty-thousand-year-old paleolithic grave site to the Federal Trade Commission's investigation of contemporary American funeral practices. In the process, funeral customs and practices ancient and modern are described and debated. As a rite to which none are invited but all may come, the funeral not only declares that a death has occurred, but it acknowledges also the life that has been lived.

9.

Grief

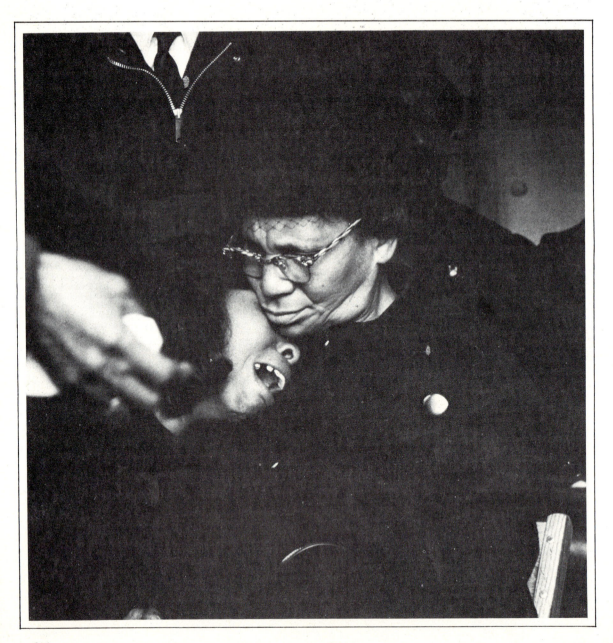

The objective study of grief is less than four decades old. Sigmund Freud, of course, had long since advanced his theory on the difference between the so-called normal depression of ordinary grief and the psychotic disorder of melancholia, and theologians discussed death and dying within the parameters of their different views of the universe, but little was known in an empirical and systematic way about reactions to loss. Anthropologists had examined burial rites and funeral practices, but mainly with reference to cultures other than our own. With few exceptions, medical and behavioral scientists in this country were virtually silent on the subject of grief. The social-psychological crisis of bereavement was not a recognized subject of scientific research.

With Erich Lindemann's investigation into the grief reactions of the survivors of the Cocoanut Grove fire that occurred in Boston in 1942, the situation began to change. His now classic article, "Symptomatology and Management of Acute Grief," (excerpted below) dramatically highlighted the medical, psychological, and sociological significance of loss. Research into grief and loss, moreover, was brought into sharper focus at that time by Anna Freud's study of English school children separated from their families during the Second World War and by the stark accounts of concentration camp life.

Systematic research into grief and bereavement began to burgeon, however, after the appearance in 1959 of Feifel's book, *The Meaning of Death.* Grief, once a private concern, became in the 1960s a public concern. This is not to say, however, that we have not attended to the problems associated with separation and loss throughout the history of Western society. To the contrary, both sacred and profane literature is replete with references to the meaning and significance of dying and death, as well as to the sorrow of bereavement. Cicero, for instance, instructs us that "there is no grief that time does not lessen or soften." And in John 11:35 we learn that "Jesus wept" upon hearing of the death of his friend Lazarus. Shakespeare has Othello cry, "My particular grief is of so flood-gate and o'er bearing nature that it engluts and swallows other sorrows," and in *Macbeth* he instructs us to "Give sorrow words; the grief that does not speak whispers the o'er fraught heart and bids it break." Victor Hugo in *Les Miserables,* observed that "Great grief is a divine and terrible radiance which transfigures the wretched," while Daniel wrote that "light cares speak, the huge are dumb." Hugo also observed that "It is the peculiarity of grief to bring out the childish side of man." But it is Shakespeare who has the last word when he reminds us, knowingly, that "every one can master a grief but he that has it."

Yet it must be said that these literary observations regarding grief, to say nothing of the extensive literature concerning *ars moriendi* (the art of dying), have not provided us with any positive, systematic knowledge regarding the behavior of bereaved persons, nor, despite this ancient and revered literature, have we actually known very much until recently about the psychological, social, and physical consequences associated with the experience of loss.

One of the early pioneers in America to deal empirically with the question of bereavement, whose work for the most part has been neglected, is David Fulcomer, a student of Thomas Eliot, who first argued the need for the study of grief in the late 1920s. In 1942, under Eliot's guidance, he undertook a study of seventy-two bereaved spouses and collected data concerning their behavior and their reactions to their loss. Available to him in addition to his own personal observations were written and oral reports prepared by the subjects themselves, and observations of persons close to the bereaved subjects. With Fulcomer's study we have one of the earliest attempts to systematically study, observe, and categorize in an empirical and scientific fashion humankind's response to loss.

It was Lindemann, at Massachusetts General Hospital, however, who brought the subject of grief to the forefront of our awareness and who in doing so expanded Fulcomer's observations to include medical and physiological reactions to loss as well.

Coming from a background in psychiatry with an interest in the emotional reactions to body disfigurement and plastic surgery, Lindemann was struck by the similarity of responses between the reaction of a patient to facial disfigurement or the loss of a body part and the reaction of the survivors of the Cocoanut Grove fire to the loss of their spouses, sweethearts, and friends. He found that all of the 101 patients he interviewed experienced a uniform reaction including (1) sensations of somatic distress, such as tightness in the throat, choking, shortness of breath, and so on; (2) intense preoccupation with the image of the deceased; (3) strong feelings of guilt; (4) a loss of warmth toward others with a tendency to respond with irritability and anger; and finally (5) disoriented behavior patterns.

The duration of the grief reaction and the manner in which a person finally adjusts to his new social environment depends, Lindemann said, upon the success of what is called the "grief work." Lindemann noted considerable resistance on the part of his patients to accept the discomfort and distress of bereavement. The patients chose instead, in many instances, to avoid the intense pain connected with the grief experience and to avoid also the expression of emotion necessary for it. Such a distortion of normal grief may well be the prelude to a morbid grief reaction that Lindemann and others have documented, and which may run the gamut of response from such psychosomatic conditions as asthma, ulcerative colitis, and rheumatoid arthritis, to anti-social behavior and possibly even psychosis.

That there is an intimate relationship between grief and emotionally-related bodily ailments was proposed in an early study by psychiatrist Karl Stern and his collaborators. They studied the grief reaction of twenty-five subjects attending an old-age counseling service. These investigators found that while there was a relative paucity of overt grief and of conscious guilt feelings, the subjects did manifest a preponderance of somatic illnesses. They reported, moreover, that the subjects tended to isolate themselves and to be hostile toward some living person.

The relationship between grief and a person's subsequent psychoneurosis was suggested by another research psychiatrist, Herbert Barry, Jr. His study of commitment to a mental hospital caused him to conclude that the death of a mother before a child is eight years old might well be a contributing factor in the development of a psychoneurotic illness.

Evidence supporting the relationship between anti-social behavior and unresolved grief is provided in a study by Dr. Mervin Shoor and Mary Speed. They interviewed fourteen adolescents in the care of a juvenile probation department in California. All fourteen came to the attention of the authorities because of their extreme delinquent behavior. In each case there had been a recent death of a close family member. Prior to the time of the death, none of the children had shown behavioral problems. Operating on the premise that these fourteen boys and girls were acting out their grief and were the unhappy victims of pathological mourning, Shoor and Speed were able to effect normal mourning processes with some of the children and to achieve their return to more acceptable modes of behavior.

Geoffrey Gorer, the English research sociologist whose essay on the "Pornography of Death" appeared in the popular culture section, concludes that certain expressions of adolescent vandalism may be a function of the refusal or the inability of some youths to mourn. In a study of recently bereaved individuals in contemporary Britain, he found that there was both an individual repudiation and a social denial of grief and mourning—a repudiation and denial that motivated him to write the moving account of his brother's death that is included in this section of the Reader.

His reminiscenses concerning his brother's illness, decline, and death and the general reactions of their relatives and mutual friends to that death serve to dramatize in a most personal and poignant way Philippe Ariès' contribution to the Reader, "The Denial of Mourning." Ariès traces the history of mourning from the fourteenth century to the present along what he calls a "mourning curve" and concludes that what was from the fourteenth century onward a necessity—if not a social obligation—to mourn publicly is now forbidden. Death has become, in the twentieth century, what sex had been for the Victorians— the great taboo.

This development in our attitudes toward death is also something of a paradox. According to Fulton in his article "Anticipatory Grief, Stress, and the Surrogate Griever," death is expanding its categories. That is, the consideration of who is alive today and who is dead is not what it once was.

"Viability," he says, "has been foreshortened by recent developments in American society and 'life' has had to pull in its belt." So, too, the notion of who grieves today and for whom has also experienced a reversal. Fulton draws attention to the phenomenon of the "surrogate griever," that is, an unrelated caregiver who, upon the death, or during the process, of his or her patient's dying, experiences grief. This phenomenon is made possible in part, he says, by placing the dying in public institutions as well as by the fact that survivors lose the ability to grieve or grieve prior to the death of their loved ones. It is important for us to recognize, Fulton cautions, that a new phenomenon is among us—one that has the capacity to reverse the roles between survivors and health care personnel. To the extent that this is so, it has important implications for the levels of stress that may be experienced by all concerned.

The importance of stress in relation to loss is also the subject of the final article in this section, "The Broken Heart," by Colin Murray Parkes. Taking up an issue that is as old as the human heart itself, Parkes asks, "Can one die from a broken heart?" The question is not an empty one—either romantically or medically.

His brief survey of the "mortality of bereavement literature" shows that while bereavement is associated with higher mortality rates among the survivors, that association still has not been explained. Nevertheless, the stress of bereavement for many is real and, as Selye, the originator of the medical concept of stress, and others have shown, stress can foreshorten one's life. It is to be hoped that knowledge, understanding, and concern can go far in allowing us to respond to Isaiah's ancient injunction to "Bind up the broken-hearted."

I felt a Funeral, in my Brain,
And Mourners to and fro
Kept treading—treading—till it seemed
That Sense was breaking through—

And when they all were seated,
A Service, like a Drum—
Kept beating—beating—till I thought
My Mind was going numb—

And then I heard them lift a Box
And creak across my Soul
With those same Boots of Lead, again,
Then Space—began to toll,

As all the Heavens were a Bell,
And Being, but an Ear,
And I, and Silence, some strange Race
Wrecked, solitary, here—

And then a Plank in Reason, broke,
And I dropped down, and down—
And hit a World, at every plunge,
And Finished knowing—then—

Emily Dickinson

Erich Lindemann

Symptomatology and Management of Acute Grief

At the time of his writing this now classic statement on grief, Erich Lindemann was a psychiatrist attached to the unit for reconstructive surgery at Massachusetts General Hospital. It was a fortuitous circumstance that allowed this sensitive and insightful physician to be in residence at the time that the victims from the tragic Cocoanut Grove fire were brought to the hospital for treatment. As a result of this profoundly moving experience, Lindemann dedicated the remainder of his professional career to exploring the management of grief and the care of the bereaved.

I NTRODUCTION   At first glance, acute grief would not seem to be a medical or psychiatric disorder in the strict sense of the word but rather a normal reaction to a distressing situation. However, the understanding of reactions to traumatic experiences whether or not they represent clear-cut neuroses has become of ever-increasing importance to the psychiatrist. Bereavement or the sudden cessation of social interaction seems to be of special interest because it is often cited among the alleged psychogenic[1] factors in psychosomatic disorders....

The points to be made in this paper are as follows:

1. Editor's note: Originating in the mind.

1. Acute grief is a definite syndrome with psychological and somatic symptomatology.

2. This syndrome may appear immediately after a crisis; it may be delayed; it may be exaggerated or apparently absent.

3. In place of the typical syndrome there may appear distorted pictures, each of which represents one special aspect of the grief syndrome.

4. By appropriate techniques these distorted pictures can be successfully transformed into a normal grief reaction with resolution.

Our observations comprise 101 patients. Included are (1) psychoneurotic patients who lost a relative during the course of treatment, (2) relatives of patients who died in the hospital, (3) bereaved disaster victims (Cocoanut Grove fire) and their close relatives, (4) relatives of members of the armed forces.

The investigation consisted of a series of psychiatric interviews. Both the timing and the content of the discussions were recorded. These records were subsequently analyzed in terms of the symptoms reported and of the changes in mental status observed progressively through a series of interviews. The psychiatrist avoided all suggestions and interpretations until the picture of symptomatology and spontaneous reaction tendencies of the patients had become clear from the records. The somatic complaints offered important leads for objective study....

SYMPTOMATOLOGY OF NORMAL GRIEF

The picture shown by persons in acute grief is remarkably uniform. Common to all is the following syndrome: sensations of somatic distress occurring in waves lasting from twenty minutes to an hour at a time, a feeling of tightness in the throat, choking with shortness of breath, need for sighing, and an empty feeling in the abdomen, lack of muscular power, and an intense subjective distress described as tension or mental pain. The patient soon learns that these waves of discomfort can be precipitated by visits, by mentioning the deceased, and by receiving sympathy. There is a tendency to avoid the syndrome at any cost, to refuse visits lest they should precipitate the reaction, and to keep deliberately from thought all references to the deceased.

The striking features are (1) the marked tendency to sighing respiration; this respiratory disturbance was most conspicuous when the patient was made to discuss his grief. (2) The complaint about lack of strength and exhaustion is universal and is described as follows: "It is almost impossible to climb up a stairway." "Everything I lift seems so heavy." "The slightest effort makes me feel exhausted." "I can't walk to the corner without feeling exhausted." (3) Digestive symptoms are described as follows: "The food tastes like sand." "I have no appetite at all." "I stuff the food down because I have to eat." "My saliva won't flow." "My abdomen feels hollow." "Everything seems slowed up in my stomach."

The sensorium is generally somewhat altered. There is commonly a slight sense of unreality, a feeling of increased emotional distance from other people (sometimes they appear shadowy or small), and there is intense preoccupation with the image of the deceased. A patient who lost his daughter in the Cocoa-nut Grove disaster visualized his girl in the telephone booth calling for him and was much troubled by the loudness with which his name was called by her and was so vividly preoccupied with the scene that he became oblivious of his surroundings. A young navy pilot lost a close friend; he remained a vivid part of his imagery, not in terms of a religious survival but in terms of an imaginary companion. He ate with him and talked over problems with him, for instance, discussing with him his plan of joining the Air Corps. Up to the time of the study, six months later, he denied the fact that the boy was no longer with him. Some patients are much concerned about this aspect of their grief reaction because they feel it indicates approaching insanity.

Another strong preoccupation is with feelings of guilt. The bereaved searches the time before the death for evidence of failure to do right by the lost one. He accuses himself of negligence and exaggerates minor omissions. After the fire disaster the central topic of discussion for a young married woman was the fact that her husband died after he left her following a quarrel, and of a young man whose wife died, that he fainted too soon to save her.

In addition, there is often disconcerting loss of warmth in relationship to other people, a tendency to respond with irritability and anger, a wish not to be bothered by others at a time when friends and relatives make a special effort to keep up friendly relationships.

These feelings of hostility, surprising and quite inexplicable to the patients, disturbed them and again were often taken as signs of approaching insanity. Great efforts are made to handle them, and the result is often a formalized, stiff manner of social interaction.

The activity throughout the day of the severely bereaved person shows remarkable changes. There is no retardation of action and speech; quite to the contrary, there is a push of speech, especially when talking about the deceased. There is restlessness, inability to sit still, moving about in an aimless fashion, continually searching for something to do. There is, however, at the same time, a painful lack of capacity to initiate and maintain organized patterns of activity. What is done is done with lack of zest, as though one were going through the motions. The bereaved clings to the daily routine of prescribed activities; but these activities do not proceed in the automatic, self-sustaining fashion which characterizes normal work but have to be carried on with effort, as though each fragment of the activity became a special task. The bereaved is surprised to find how large a part of his customary activity was done in some meaningful relationship to the deceased and has now lost its significance. Especially the habits of social interaction—meeting friends, making conversation, sharing enterprises with others—seem to have been lost. This loss leads to a strong dependency on anyone who will stimulate the bereaved to activity and serve as the initiating agent....

COURSE OF NORMAL GRIEF REACTIONS   The duration of a grief reaction seems to depend upon the success with which a person does the *grief work,* namely, emancipation from the bondage to the deceased, readjustment to the environment in which the deceased is missing, and the formation of new relationships. One of the big obstacles to this work seems to be the fact that many patients try to avoid the intense distress connected with the grief experience and to avoid the expression of emotion necessary for it. The men victims after the Cocoanut Grove fire appeared in the early psychiatric interviews to be in a state of tension with tightened facial musculature, unable to relax for fear they might "break down." It required considerable persuasion to yield to the grief process before they were willing to accept the discomfort of bereavement. One assumed a hostile attitude toward the psychiatrist, refusing to allow any references to the deceased and rather rudely asking him to leave. This attitude remained throughout his stay on the ward, and the prognosis for his condition is not good in the light of other observations. Hostility of this sort was encountered on only occasional visits with the other patients. They became willing to accept the grief process and to embark on a program of dealing in memory with the deceased person. As soon as this became possible there seemed to be a rapid relief of tension and the subsequent interviews were rather animated conversations in which the deceased was idealized and in which misgivings about the future adjustment were worked through.

An example of the psychiatrist's role in assisting patients in their readjustment after bereavement is contained in the following case history....

A man of fifty-two, successful in business, lost his wife with whom he had lived in happy marriage. The information given him about his wife's death confirmed his suspicions of several days. He responded with a severe grief reaction, with which he was unable to cope. He did not want to see visitors, was ashamed of breaking down, and asked to be permitted to stay in the hospital on the psychiatric service, when his physical condition would have permitted his discharge, because he wanted further assistance. Any mention of his wife produced a severe wave of depressive reaction, but with psychiatric assistance he gradually became willing to go through this painful process, and after three days on the psychiatric service he seemed well enough to go home.

He showed a high rate of verbal activity, was restless, needed to be occupied continually, and felt that the experience had whipped him into a state of restless overactivity.

As soon as he returned home he took an active part in his business, assuming a post in which he had a great many telephone calls. He also took over the role of amateur psychiatrist to another bereaved person, spending time with him and comforting him for his loss. In his eagerness to start anew, he developed a plan to sell his former holdings, including his house, his furniture, and giving away anything which could remind him of his wife. Only after considerable discussion was he able to see that this would mean avoiding immediate grief at the price of an act of poor judgment. Again he had to be encouraged to deal with his grief reactions in a more direct manner. He has made a good adjustment....

MORBID GRIEF REACTIONS

DELAY OF REACTION   The most striking and most frequent reaction of this sort is *delay* or *postponement*. If the bereavement occurs at a time when the patient is confronted with important tasks and where there is necessity for maintaining the morale of others, he may show little or no reaction for weeks or even much longer. A brief delay is described in the following example.

A girl of sixteen lost both parents and her boy friend in the fire and was herself burned severely, with marked involvement of the lungs. Throughout her stay in the hospital her attitude was that of cheerful acceptance without any sign of adequate distress. When she was discharged at the end of three weeks she appeared cheerful, talked rapidly, with a considerable flow of ideas, seemed eager to return home to assume the role of parent for her two younger siblings. Except for slight feelings of "lonesomeness" she complained of no distress.

This period of griefless acceptance continued for the next two months, even when the household was dispersed and her younger siblings were placed in other homes. Not until the end of the tenth week did she begin to show a true state of grief with marked feelings of depression, intestinal emptiness, tightness in her throat, frequent crying, and vivid preoccupation with her deceased parents.

That this delay may involve years became obvious first by the fact that patients in acute bereavement about a recent death may soon upon exploration be found preoccupied with grief about a person who died many years ago. In this manner a woman of thirty-eight, whose mother had died recently and who had responded to the mother's death with a surprisingly severe reaction, was found to be but mildly concerned with her mother's death but deeply engrossed with unhappy and perplexing fantasies concerning the death of her brother, who died twenty years ago under dramatic circumstances from metastasizing carcinoma after amputation of his arm had been postponed too long. The discovery that a former unresolved grief reaction may be precipitated in the course of the discussion of another recent event was soon demonstrated in psychiatric interviews by patients who showed all the traits of a true grief reaction when the topic of a former loss arose.

The precipitating factor for the delayed reaction may be a deliberate recall of circumstances surrounding the death or may be a spontaneous occurrence in the patient's life. A peculiar form of this is the circumstance that a patient develops the grief reaction at the time when he himself is as old as the person who died. For instance, a railroad worker, aged forty-two, appeared in the psychiatric clinic with a picture which was undoubtedly a grief reaction for which he had no explanation. It turned out that when he was twenty-two, his mother, then forty-two, had committed suicide.

DISTORTED REACTIONS The delayed reactions may occur after an interval which was not marked by any abnormal behavior or distress, but in which there developed an *alteration* in the patient's *conduct* perhaps not conspicuous or serious enough to lead him to a psychiatrist. These alterations may be considered as the surface manifestations of an unresolved grief reaction, which may be classified as follows: (1) *overactivity without a sense of loss,* rather with a sense of well-being and zest, the activities being of an expansive and

... You must bare your heart and expect
    nothing in return.
You must respond totally to nature.
You must return to your simple self.
I do not fool you. There lies no other path.
I have not forsaken you, but I cannot be
    among you all.
You are not alone
so long as you love your own true simple
    selves.
your natural hair, your skin, your
    graceful bodies,
your knowing eyes and your tears and
    tongues. . . .

Roll among the wet daisies. Blow out
    your lungs
among the dead dandelion fields.
But don't delay, time is not on your side.
Soon you will be crying for the hurt,
    make speed.
Splash in the Ocean,
leap in the snow.

Come on everybody! Love your neighbor
Love your mother, love your lover,
love the man who just stands there staring.
But first, that's alright, go ahead and cry.
Cry, cry, cry your heart out.
It's love. It's your only path.

O people, I am so sorry.
Nothing can be hid.
It's a circle in the round.
It's group theater,
no wings, no backstage, no leading act.
O, I am weeping, but it's stage center
    for all of us.
Hide in the weeds but come out naked.
Dance in the sand while lightning bands
    all around us.

Step lightly, we're walking home now.
The clouds take every shape.
We climb up the boulders; there is
    no plateau.
We cross the stream and walk up the slope.
See, the hawk is diving.
The plain stretches out ahead,
then the hills, the valleys, the meadows.
Keep moving people. How could I not
    be among you?

Ted Rosenthal
How Could I Not Be among You?

adventurous nature and bearing semblance to the activities formerly carried out by the deceased, as described above; (2) *the acquisition of symptoms belonging to the last illness of the deceased.* This type of patient appears in medical clinics and is often labeled hypochondriacal or hysterical. To what extent actual alterations of physiological functions occur under these circumstances will have to be a field of further careful inquiry. I owe to Dr. Chester Jones a report about a patient whose electrocardiogram showed a definite change during a period of three weeks, which started two weeks after the time her father died of heart disease.

While this sort of symptom formation "by identification" may still be considered as conversion symptoms such as we know from hysteria, there is another type of disorder doubtlessly presenting (3) a recognized *medical disease,* namely, a group of psychosomatic conditions, predominantly ulcerative colitis, rheumatoid arthritis, and asthma. Extensive studies in ulcerative colitis have produced evidence that thirty-three out of forty-one patients with ulcerative colitis developed their disease in close time relationship to the loss of an important person. Indeed, it was this observation which first gave the impetus for the present detailed study of grief. Two of the patients developed bloody diarrhea at funerals. In the others it developed within a few weeks after the loss. The course of the ulcerative colitis was strikingly benefited when this grief reaction was resolved by psychiatric technique.

At the level of social adjustment there often occurs a conspicuous (4) *alteration in relationship to friends and relatives.* The patient feels irritable, does not want to be bothered, avoids former social activities, and is afraid he might antagonize his friends by his lack of interest and his critical attitudes. Progressive social isolation follows, and the patient needs considerable encouragement in reestablishing his social relationships.

While overflowing hostility appears to be spread out over all relationships, it may also occur as (5) *furious hostility against specific persons;* the doctor or the surgeon is accused bitterly for neglect of duty and the patient may assume that foul play has led to the death. It is characteristic that while patients talk a good deal about their suspicions and their bitter feelings, they are not likely to take any action against the accused, as a truly paranoid person might do.

(6) Many bereaved persons struggled with much effort against these feelings of hostility, which to them seem absurd, representing a vicious change in their characters and to be hidden as much as possible. Some patients succeed in hiding their hostility but become wooden and formal, with affectivity and conduct *resembling schizophrenic pictures.* A typical report is this, "I go through all the motions of living. I look after my children. I do my errands. I go to social functions, but it is like being in a play; it doesn't really concern me. I can't have any warm feelings. If I were to have any feelings at all I would be angry with everybody...."

(7) Closely related to this picture is a *lasting loss of patterns of social interaction.* The patient cannot initiate any activity, is full of eagerness to be active—restless, can't sleep—but throughout the day he will not start any activity unless "primed" by somebody else. He will be grateful at sharing activities with others but will not be able to make up his mind to do anything alone. The picture is one of lack of decision and initiative. Organized activities along social lines occur only if a friend takes the patient along and shares the activity with him. Nothing seems to promise reward; only the ordinary activities of the day are carried

on, and these in a routine manner, falling apart into small steps, each of which has to be carried out with much effort and without zest.

(8) There is, in addition, a picture in which a patient is active but in which most of his activities attain a coloring which is *detrimental to his own social and economic existence.* Such patients with uncalled-for generosity, give away their belongings, are easily lured into foolish economic dealings, lose their friends and professional standing by a series of "stupid acts," and find themselves finally without family, friends, social status, or money. This protracted self-punitive behavior seems to take place without any awareness of excessive feelings of guilt. It is a particularly distressing grief picture because it is likely to hurt other members of the family and drag down friends and business associates.

(9) This leads finally to the picture in which the grief reaction takes the form of a straight *agitated depression* with tension, agitation, insomnia, feelings of worthlessness, bitter self-accusation, and obvious need for punishment. Such patients may be dangerously suicidal.

A young man aged thirty-two had received only minor burns and left the hospital apparently well on the road to recovery just before the psychiatric survey of the disaster victims took place. On the fifth day he had learned that his wife had died. He seemed somewhat relieved of his worry about her fate; impressed the surgeon as being unusually well controlled during the following short period of his stay in the hospital.

On January 1 he was returned to the hospital by his family. Shortly after his return home he had become restless, did not want to stay at home, had taken a trip to relatives trying to find rest, had not succeeded, and returned home in a state of marked agitation, appearing preoccupied, frightened, and unable to concentrate on any organized activity. The mental status presented a somewhat unusual picture. He was restless, could not sit still or participate in any activity on the ward. He would try to read, drop it after a few minutes, or try to play pingpong, give it up after a short time. He would try to start conversations, break them off abruptly, and then fall into repeated murmured utterances: "Nobody can help me. When is it going to happen? I am doomed, am I not?" With great effort it was possible to establish enough rapport to carry on interviews. He complained about his feeling of extreme tension, inability to breathe, generalized weakness and exhaustion, and his frantic fear that something terrible was going to happen. "I'm destined to live in insanity or I must die. I know that it is God's will. I have this awful feeling of guilt." With intense morbid guilt feelings, he reviewed incessantly the events of the fire. His wife had stayed behind. When he tried to pull her out, he had fainted and was shoved out by the crowd. She was burned while he was saved. "I should have saved her or I should have died too." He complained about being filled with an incredible violence and did not know what to do about it. The rapport established with him lasted for only brief periods of time. He then would fall back into his state of intense agitation and muttering. He slept poorly even with large sedation. In the course of four days he became somewhat more composed, had longer periods of contact with the psychiatrist, and seemed to feel that he was being understood and might be able to cope with his morbid feelings of guilt and violent impulses. On the sixth day of his hospital stay, however, after skillfully distracting the attention of his special nurse, he jumped through a closed window to a violent death....

PROGNOSTIC EVALUATION Our observations indicate that to a certain extent the type and severity of the grief reaction can be predicted. Patients with obsessive personality make-up and with a history of former depressions are likely to develop an agitated depression. Severe reactions seem to occur in mothers who have lost young children. The intensity of interaction with the deceased before his death seems to be significant. It is important to realize that such interaction does not have to be of the affectionate type; on the contrary, the death of a person who invited much hostility, especially hostility which could not be well-expressed because of his status and claim to loyalty, may be followed by a severe grief reaction in which hostile impulses are the most conspicuous feature. Not infrequently the person who passed away represented a key person in a social system, his death being followed by disintegration of this social system and by a profound alteration of the living and social conditions for the bereaved. In such cases readjustment presents a severe task quite apart from the reaction to the loss incurred. All these factors seem to be more important than a tendency to react with neurotic symptoms in previous life. In this way the most conspicuous forms of morbid identification were found in persons who had no former history of a tendency to psychoneurotic reactions.

MANAGEMENT   Proper psychiatric management of grief reactions may prevent prolonged and serious alterations in the patient's social adjustment, as well as potential medical disease. The essential task facing the psychiatrist is that of sharing the patient's grief work, namely, his efforts at extricating himself from the bondage to the deceased and at finding new patterns of rewarding interaction. It is of the greatest importance to notice that not only over-reaction but under-reaction of the bereaved must be given attention, because delayed responses may occur at unpredictable moments and the dangerous distortions of the grief reaction, not conspicuous at first, may be quite destructive later and these may be prevented.

Religious agencies have led in dealing with the bereaved. They have provided comfort by giving the backing of dogma to the patient's wish for continued interaction with the deceased, have developed rituals which maintain the patient's interaction with others, and have counteracted the morbid guilt feelings of the patient by Divine Grace and by promising an opportunity for "making up" to the deceased at the time of a later reunion. While these measures have helped countless mourners, comfort alone does not provide adequate assistance in the patient's grief work. He has to review his relationships with the deceased, and has to become acquainted with the alterations in his own modes of emotional reaction. His fear of insanity, his fear of accepting the surprising changes in his feelings, especially the overflow of hostility, have to be worked through. He will have to express his sorrow and sense of loss. He will have to find an acceptable formulation of his future relationship to the deceased. He will have to verbalize his feelings of guilt, and he will have to find persons around him whom he can use as "primers" for the acquisition of new patterns of conduct. All this can be done in eight to ten interviews.

Special techniques are needed if hostility is the most marked feature of the grief reaction. The hostility may be directed against the psychiatrist, and the patient will have such guilt over his hostility that he will avoid further interviews. The help of a social worker or a minister, or if these are not available, a member of the family, to urge the patient to continue coming to see the psychiatrist may be indispensable....

Since it is obvious that not all bereaved persons, especially those suffering because of war casualties, can have the benefit of expert psychiatric help, much of this knowledge will have to be passed on to auxiliary workers. Social workers and ministers will have to be on the lookout for the more ominous pictures, referring these to the psychiatrist while assisting the more normal reactions themselves....

Philippe Ariès

The Denial of Mourning

In this brief but substantive article, the distinguished French historian, Philippe Ariès, takes us across five centuries of European mourning customs: from the spasms and fainting fits of such great warriors as Charlemagne to the lugubrious rituals of the Middle Ages to our present time when grief is frequently neither displayed nor felt. The "mourning curve" that Ariès describes for us illustrates as few other statements have how intimate the connection is between one's private grief and one's public conduct. It raises anew the troublesome question: is grief natural to humankind or is it learned—a function of cultural conditioning? Perhaps the present day interest that has been engendered in the subject of grief will lead to an answer.

We have seen how modern society deprives man of his death, and how it allows him this privilege only if he does not use it to upset the living. In a reciprocal way, society forbids the living to appear moved by the death of others; it does not allow them either to weep for the deceased or to seem to miss them.

Mourning was, nevertheless, until our time the supreme form of grief, and it was both right and necessary to express it. The old word for grief (in French *douleur*), *dol* or *doel,* has remained in our language, but with the restricted meaning of mourning (in French *deuil*). But even before it had been given a name, grief over the death of a loved one was the most violent expression of the most spontaneous feelings. During the height of the Middle Ages, the most hardened warriors or the most illustrious sovereigns broke down before the bodies of their friends or relatives, like—as we would say today—women, and hysterical women at that. Here we see King Arthur swoon several times in succession, beat his chest, claw at his face "so that the blood gushed forth." There, on the battlefield, we see the same king who "fell from his horse in a faint" before the body of his nephew, "then, crying all the while he began to search for the bodies of his friends," like Charlemagne at Roncevaux. Finding one of them, "he struck his palms against one another, crying that he had lived enough.... Removing the helmet from the dead man, and looking at him for a long time, he then kissed his eyes and his frozen mouth." So many spasms and fainting fits! So many passionate embraces of already cold cadavers! So many desparate clawings, so many torn clothes! But aside from a very few inconsolable spirits who retreated into monasteries, once the great demonstrations of grief were over, the survivors took up their lives where they had left off.

Beginning in the thirteenth century, the demonstrations of mourning lost their spontaneity and became ritualized. The great displays of the early Middle Ages were from then on simulated by professional mourners. Such mourning is still carried on today in the southern and Mediterranean areas of France. Romancero's Le Cid demands in his will that there be no mourners at his funeral, as was the custom, nor flowers nor wreaths. The iconography of tombs from the fourteenth and fifteenth centuries shows processions of mourners in black robes around the exposed body, their heads hidden under cowls and penitents' hoods. Later, we can learn from last wills and testaments in the sixteenth and seventeenth centuries that the funeral cortèges were mainly composed of a crowd similar to the professional mourners: mendicant friars, paupers, children from the almshouses, all of whom were dressed for the occasion in black robes supplied by the inheritors, and who received some bread and a small amount of money following the ceremony.

One might wonder whether the closest relatives took part in the obsequies. Friends were given a banquet—an occasion for carousing and overindulgence, which the Church tried to abolish; in time these banquets became mentioned less often in the wills, except in cases where they were specifically forbidden. One notices in the last wills and testaments that sometimes the testator insisted on the presence of a brother or a son—usually a child—in his funeral procession. He would offer a special legacy as a reward for this much sought after attendance. Would this have been the case if the family always followed the procession? We know without doubt that women never attended funerals in the ancien régime. It seems most likely that, beginning with the late Middle Ages and the ritualization of mourning, society imposed a period of seclusion on the family, even keeping it away from the funeral, and replacing it by numerous priests and by professional mourners, monks and nuns, members of guilds, or ordinary people attracted by the distribution of alms.

This seclusion had two purposes: first, to allow the truly unhappy survivors to shelter their grief from the world, to allow them to wait, like a sick man who rests, for their pain to be alleviated. Henri de Campion mentions this in his Mémoires. In June 1659, de Campion's wife "gave up . . . the ghost, having delivered to the world a daughter who died five or six days after her. I was heart-broken and fell into a pitiable state. My brother . . . and my sister . . . brought me to Conches; I stayed there for seventeen days and then returned to Baxferei to put my affairs in order. . . . Being unable to remain in my house, which constantly reminded me of my sorrows, I took a house in Conches where I remained until 2 June 1660 [that is to say, until the bout de l'an, until the first anniversary of his wife's death], at which time, seeing that my sorrow would not leave me, I returned to my home in Baxferei with my children and lived there in great sadness."

The second reason for the seclusion was to prevent the survivors from forgetting the departed too soon; it excluded them, during a period of penitence, from the social relations and pleasures of secular life. This precaution was helpful in defending the unfortunate dead from being replaced too hastily. Nicolas Versoris, a Parisian bourgeois, lost his wife from the plague "the third day of September [1522] one hour after midnight." The next-to-last day of December in the same year, he was betrothed to a doctor's widow, whom he married as soon as he was able, on January 13, 1523, "the first festal day after Christmas."

The nineteenth century brought no softening in the severity of seclusion. In houses where there was a death, men, women, servants, and even horses and bees were separated from the outside world by a screen of crapes, veils, and black cloth. However, this seclusion was more voluntary than forced and no longer were close friends and family forbidden to take part in the dramatic obsequies, to make pilgrimages to the graves, or to take part in the cult of remembrance so characteristic of the Romantic era. It was no longer obligatory for women to be excluded from the funeral services. They were accepted first by the bourgeoisie; the nobility remained faithful to the customs of exclusion for a longer period of time, and it was many years before the well-bred wife could participate in her husband's death. Nevertheless, even among the nobility, the women began attending their husband's, son's, or father's burial, at first in secret, hidden in a corner of the church or in the gallery, with the approval of the Church. The traditional customs of seclusion were forced to come to terms with the new feelings of glorifying the dead and worshipping their tombs. The woman's presence, nonetheless, did not in any way alter the concept of seclusion in mourning: entirely veiled in black—a *mater dolorosa*—in the eyes of the world she was merely a symbol of inconsolable sorrow. However, seclusion was transferred from the physical level to the moral level. It served less to protect the dead from oblivion than to emphasize how impossible it was for the living to forget them and to live as they had before. The dead no longer required society's protection against the indifference of their close ones, any more than, as we saw earlier, the dying needed last wills and testaments to enforce their final wishes.

So we see that the increase in family feeling had, by the end of the eighteenth and beginning of the nineteenth centuries, combined with the traditional concept of seclusion to make mourning not so much an enforced

quarantine as a right to demonstrate extreme grief, in defiance of conventional proprieties. This was, then, a return to the spontaneity of the high Middle Ages while maintaining the ritual constraints that followed in the twelfth century. If one were to draw a "mourning curve," there would first be a peak stage of frank, violent spontaneity until somewhere around the thirteenth century, then a long phase of ritualization until the eighteenth century, and then in the nineteenth century a period of impassioned, self-indulgent grief, dramatic demonstration and funereal mythology. It is not inconceivable that the paroxysm of mourning in the nineteenth century is connected to its prohibition in the twentieth, in the same way that in the postwar years the *mort sale* of Remarque, Sartre and Genet seems to be a reaction against the extremely noble death of the Romantic era. This is the meaning of Sartre's gesture, more ridiculous than scandalous, of "passing water" on Chateaubriand's tomb. There had to be a Chateaubriand in order for there to be a Sartre. It is the same kind of relationship that links contemporary eroticism to Victorian sexual taboos.

In the mid-twentieth century the ancient necessity for mourning—more or less spontaneous, or enforced, depending on the century—has been succeeded by its prohibition. During the course of one generation the situation has been reversed: what had always been required by individual conscience or social obligation is now forbidden; what had always been forbidden is now required. It is no longer correct to display one's grief, nor even to appear to feel any.

The British sociologist Geoffrey Gorer deserves the credit for having unearthed this unwritten law of our civilization. He was the first to understand that certain facts which had been neglected or misinterpreted by humanists were in fact part of an overall attitude toward death that was characteristic of industrial societies. In the autobiographical introduction to his book, Gorer tells of the personal way he discovered that death had become the principal taboo of the modern world. The sociological investigation that he organized in 1963 on the subject of attitudes toward death and mourning in England only confirmed, clarified, and enriched the ideas he had already outlined in his noteworthy article, based on personal experience, "The Pornography of Death."

Gorer was born in 1910. He recalls that his entire family went into mourning at the death of Edward VII. He was taught to take off his hat when funeral processions passed by in the street, and to treat people in mourning with special consideration. Such practices seem very strange to British people today! But when in 1915 his father perished in the wreck of the *Lusitania,* he in his turn was treated like a special person, with unusual gentleness. People spoke to him softly, or became silent in his presence as though they were dealing with an invalid. However, when, encouraged by the feeling of importance this mourning gave him, he told his schoolteacher that he would never be able to play again nor to look at flowers, she shook him and ordered him to stop being "morbid." The war permitted his mother to take a job where she found relief from her sorrow. Before the war, social convention would not have allowed her to work, "but later," remarks Gorer, "she would not have had the support of the ritual of mourning," which she had respected and which protected her. So Gorer came into contact with the traditional manifestations of mourning in his childhood, and they must have made an impact on him for he was to remember them later. After the war, when he was a young man, he had no fur-

ther experiences of death. Once only, and then by chance, he saw a corpse in a Russian hospital he was visiting in 1931, and this unusual sight made an impression on him. This lack of familiarity with death is very definitely a general phenomenon, a long-unnoticed result of increased longevity;...the youth of today can reach adulthood without ever seeing anyone die. Nevertheless, Gorer was surprised to find that, among the subjects of his investigation, more people than he would have suspected had in fact seen a dead person. Those who had already seen a corpse hastened to forget the fact and spontaneously adopted the behavior of those who had never seen one.

After the death of his sister-in-law, he was surprised that his brother, a noted physician, sank into such a state of depression. At that time intellectuals were already beginning to abandon the traditional funeral ceremonies and outward manifestations of mourning, which they considered superstitious, archaic practices. However, Gorer did not then see the connection between his brother's pathological despair and the absence of ritual mourning. This was to change in 1948, when he lost a friend, who left behind a wife and three children. "When I went to see her, two months after John's death, she told me, with tears of gratitude, that I was the first man to stay in the house since she had become a widow...she had been almost completely abandoned to loneliness, although the town was full of acquaintances who considered themselves friends." Gorer then understood that the changes that had taken place in the ritual of mourning were not insignificant, anecdotal occurrences. He realized the importance of the phenomenon and its serious effects. It was a few years later, in 1955, that he wrote his well-known article....

Geoffrey Gorer

Death, Grief, and Mourning

Geoffrey Gorer, an English sociologist, has written a touching account of his brother's death from cancer at age fifty-four. Taken from a longer auto-biographical statement that details his experiences with loss and mourning from the death of Edward VII in 1910 to that of his brother Peter in 1961, these brief memoirs forcefully remind us how profound the loss of another can be. Moreover this vignette from his life reminds us too of the part that others play in our lives and of the opportunities to share one's humanity with others that are realized or lost at such critical junctures. In this regard he sees the decline and diminution of mourning customs and the denial of death in Western culture not only as an assault upon our emotions but also as a grievous attack upon our humanity as well.

In April, 1961, Dr. X, who had been a friend and colleague of my brother since they were medical students together, telephoned me the appalling news that Peter, who had gone for a medical check-up because of slight pains in his right shoulder, had been diagnosed as suffering from irremediable cancer; not only were his lungs affected (from a child he had suffered much from bronchitis and asthma) but also his spine; the prognosis was absolutely hopeless, a probable twelve months of increasing debility and pain before an agonized death. He asked me to decide whether his wife, Elizabeth, should be informed; he had already decided to hide the truth from Peter; and he and his colleagues engaged in the most elaborate and successful medical mystification to hide from Peter's expert knowledge the facts of their diagnosis.

I was emotionally completely unprepared. I had (have) long believed that I was likely to die of cancer, since my father's parents and his brother and sister had all died of cancer and a brother of my mother of leukemia; I had accepted that I carried a diseased inheritance. But, quite illogically, I had never intellectually considered that my brothers had the same inheritance as myself, perhaps in part because I resemble my father in features and coloring, whereas Peter and Richard took much more after my mother's family. It is probable too that, in the same way that I intellectually accepted responsibility for my mother and brothers after my father's death, I had unconsciously thought that I would take the burden of our cancerous heredity away from the others.

Peter was at the happiest and most successful period of his life, blissfully married and enjoying his two children, innocently delighted with his election as a Fellow of the Royal Society and the growing international recognition of his scientific work, and looking forward to having his own department created for him. In the 1930s, when I had a certain success as a writer, he was frequently asked whether he was related to me; in the last years of his life I was being asked whether I was related to him.

The fact that he was engaged in very original scientific work added extra qualms to my collusion in the kindly meant deception that his colleagues at Guy's Hospital were practicing on him. I felt sure that, under similar circumstances, I should wish to be informed so that, if at all possible, the scientific ideas and unrealized projects could be transmitted to others to carry through; we shared a respect for the values of scientific knowledge which I felt were being transgressed. Further, I foresaw (for my wartime work had taught me the burden of secrets) that my relationship to him, and that of anybody else so informed, would be progressively falsified by the inevitable continuous dissimulation. I fully intended to argue about the ethics of such deception with Dr. X at a slightly later date; but he and his colleagues had persuaded Peter that he was run down and slightly arthritic and needed a

At fifteen I went to war.
At eighty now I made it home.
Meeting one from my village:
"Who now is at home?"
"Over there is your house."
Pines, cypresses, tombs in clusters.
Rabbits come in from dog-holes.
Pheasants fly upon the beams.
Middle of court: wild grains rise.
Well's edge: wild mallows grow.
Grind grains to make rice.
Pick mallows to make soup.
Rice and soup soon ready.
But for whom?
Go to the east gate to look out:
Tears drench my clothes.

          The Yüeh-Fu

good holiday; and I was willing that he should have this relatively carefree period.

Whether Elizabeth should be informed was a much more pressing and perplexing problem. The knowledge would, I knew, reduce her to despair, for she was completely devoted to Peter; apart from her garden she had no interests which were not also his, her English friends and acquaintances were almost all his colleagues and their spouses.

In my perplexity I consulted Dr. Y. He is the wisest British man I know concerning human relations (our mutual friend and my former collaborator, the late Dr. John Rickman, was such another), and I thought that he would see the situation more clearly than I could in my deep distress; by good fortune he and his wife were coming to see me some four days after I had spoken to Dr. X. His advice was that Elizabeth should be told; one of the arguments he advanced was that, if she were ignorant, she might show impatience or lack of understanding with his probably increasing weakness, for which she would reproach herself later; she could use the final months of their marriage better if she knew them for what they were. That night, and for many months afterwards, I cried myself to sleep, rather noisy sobs.

Elizabeth was told by Dr. X, and took the terrible news with magnificent courage and common sense. Her role in the deception was infinitely harder than mine, for she could never let up, never safely abandon herself to grief; I doubt if she could have supported the continuous pretense for long.

It was arranged that, on his discharge from Guy's, Peter and Elizabeth should come and spend a week with me in the country, and then go on to Blagdon for some fishing, a pastime to which Peter was passionately addicted. He breakfasted in bed, and rose late, but other-

wise he seemed in the highest of spirits, indeed rather euphoric; he was continuously elaborating plans for a future that Elizabeth and I knew he would never see. I thought the euphoria might in part be due to the analgesics of which Dr. X had given him a considerable supply; but Elizabeth did not think so.

In the evening of May 10th, 1961, I had a dinner engagement in London which I kept; when I returned home a little before midnight Peter and Elizabeth were still up, happy and mellow. We went to bed rather late. In the morning when their breakfast was brought to them Elizabeth rushed into my room, saying Peter was either in a coma or dead. He was very clearly dead, his face cyanosed and his body cooling. Elizabeth collapsed into my bed.

The rest of the day was a busy nightmare, though I could find at least intellectual comfort in the knowledge that Peter had been spared the increasing pain and weakness which the prognosis had foreseen; he had died in his sleep, without any signs of pain, from what the autopsy showed to have been edema of the lung. An autopsy was necessary, since he had died away from home and was to be cremated; my doctor, kind Dr. Z, whom I had summoned immediately, gave all the help he could; but a cremation certificate could not be granted without the presence of Dr. X, and he was unable to come down.

Dr. Z got in touch with the undertakers for me, and it was arranged for a pair of ex-nurses to come by to lay out the body. They imparted a somewhat Dickensian tone; they were fat and jolly, and asked in a respectful but cheerful tone, "Where is the patient?" One of them was out a couple of minutes later to ask if he had a fresh pair of pajamas; I could not bring myself to go through his clothes, and showed them his suitcase. Some half-hour later their work was done, and they came out saying,

"The patient looks lovely now. Come and have a look!" I did not wish to, at which they expressed surprise. I gave them a pound for their pains; the leader, pure Sarah Gamp, said, "That for us, duck? Cheers!" and went through the motions of raising a bottle and emptying it into her mouth. I sat with Elizabeth when, shortly afterwards, the undertaker's men came to take the body away; the noise of their feet on the uncarpeted stairs was slow and sinister. Later, I had to go to the mortuary to make a formal identification of the corpse, before the autopsy could be made. I was frightened of fainting, for I felt nearly exhausted; I did not, however, though I slumped into a chair as I confirmed that it was my dear brother. The layers-out had done a good job; he was composed, colorless and waxen. The two pictures of his corpse remain completely vivid in my memory.

Besides all the problems connected with the disposal of the body, there were many people to be informed of his death, and complicated arrangements to be made to tell the children of their father's death and arrange for them to come to me. These arrangements Elizabeth thought out with great clarity; she was completely prostrate—it was hours before she felt strong enough to walk across the hall to another room I had had prepared for her; and I also had to tidy up their previous room and pack away Peter's clothes and belongings into a suitcase, lest their sight distress Elizabeth, or the children who would occupy the room on the morrow. Although I was crying much of the time while I performed these tasks, it was only in the evening, when Elizabeth was hopefully sleeping under sedation, that the full extent of our loss overwhelmed me. The situation was damnably redintegrative; here I was again, responsible for a widow and two young children.

Owing to the necessity of an autopsy, there was a longer delay than customary between Peter's death and his cremation; the interval passed in a daze, interrupted with bouts of busyness for me. The weather was wonderful, and nearly all the daylight hours were spent out of doors, with picnics in the garden or the fields. Elizabeth decided not to come to the cremation herself—she could not bear the thought that she might lose control and other people observe her grief; and she wished to spare the children the distressing experience. As a consequence, their father's death was quite unmarked for them by any ritual of any kind, and was even nearly treated as a secret, for it was very many months before Elizabeth could bear to mention him or have him mentioned in her presence.

In his will, Peter had requested a Church of England service for his cremation, I presume because this would cause the least trouble; none of us had any sort of religious belief. Neither of the clergymen who were personal friends was available to conduct the service; the crematorium supplied a handsome cleric, dressed in a sky-blue robe, with dramatic, even theatrical, gestures. The moment in a cremation service, when the coffin disappears through the folding doors still seems (despite frequent exposure) a moment of the most poignant finality. Many of Peter's friends and nearly all our surviving relatives were present.

The only time that I felt near to collapsing was on the return from the cremation (it involved a two-hour motor drive each way); I had to go to bed, to be by myself, for a few hours. With enormous courage, Elizabeth assured me that she and the children had had a good day; they had taken a picnic to the fields where the grass was being cut for silage. All the people who worked for me treated us all with the greatest thoughtfulness and consideration, a gentle kindness which was really comforting.

We all went for a few days to friends in Frome; and then life had to be resumed. It was the experience of the following months which suggested to me that our treatment of grief and mourning made bereavement very difficult to be lived through.

In my own case, I was able to mourn freely, to indulge in passionate bouts of weeking without self-reproach. I lost about twenty pounds in weight over the following three months, and my sleep tended to be disturbed. I had frequent dreams of Peter, many of them about our early childhood; waking from them was very distressing. I did all the routine work necessary, but felt disinclined for anything which demanded prolonged concentration. I wore a black tie for about three months. I had great pleasure in seeing real friends, but was unwilling to meet strangers. A couple of times I refused invitations to cocktail parties, explaining that I was mourning; the people who invited me responded to this statement with shocked embarrassment, as if I had voiced some appalling obscenity. Indeed, I got the impression that, had I stated that the invitation clashed with some esoteric debauchery I had arranged, I would have had understanding and jocular encouragement; as it was, the people whose invitations I had refused, educated and sophisticated though they were, mumbled and hurried away. They clearly no longer had any guidance from ritual as to the way to treat a self-confessed mourner; and, I suspect, they were frightened lest I give way to my grief, and involve them in a distasteful upsurge of emotion.

This would certainly seem to be the explanation of the way in which Elizabeth was avoided by her and Peter's friends; they treated her, she said, as though she were a leper. Only if she acted as though nothing of consequence had happened was she again socially acceptable.

This fear of the expression of grief on the part of the English professional classes unfortunately matched Elizabeth's New England fear of giving way to grief, of losing self-control. She did not wear black clothes nor ritualize her mourning in any way; she let herself be, almost literally, eaten up with grief, sinking into a deep and long-lasting depression. At the period when she most needed help and comfort from society she was left alone.

As an anthropologist, I knew that the vast majority of recorded human societies have developed formal rituals for mourning. Typically there are communal ceremonies from the period immediately after the death until the disposal of the body; typically, the bereaved are distinguished by a change in their physical appearance, such as special clothes, shaving the hair or letting it grow and so on, so that all who come in contact with them know they are mourners and treat them in a specified ritualistic fashion; and, typically, a mourner goes through what van Gennep call a *rite de passage*—a formal withdrawal from society, a period of seclusion, and a formal re-entry into society.

If a custom, such as this, is very widespread throughout human societies at all stages of development, it seems reasonable to assume that the custom is congruent with species-characteristic human psychology; and, as a corollary, those aberrant societies which lack such a custom are failing to provide their members with the support which most societies make available. The absence of such support in the professional middle classes in southern England was, as I have described, brought forcibly to my attention in the months following Peter's death....

The Broken Heart

Colin Murray Parkes is an English research psychiatrist and a consulting physician to St. Christopher's Hospice, London. His article on "The Broken Heart" derives from his long-standing investigations into the problems of loss and survivorship in England and the United States. As a physician committed to the practical solution of public problems, he believes that the reduction of stress in our lives is not only a task for the self-concerned citizen, but it is also an issue deserving of the attention of public health authorities and the medical fraternity.

He only without framing word, or closing his eyes, but earnestly viewing the dead body of his son, stood still upright, till the vehemence of his sad sorrow, having suppressed and choked his vitall spirits, fell'd him starke dead to the ground.

Montaigne's description of the
death of John, King of Hungaria

Is grief a cause of death? You will not find grief on a death certificate, not today. But the notion that one may die of grief is a popular theme among novelists and it is not long ago that it was a recognized cause of death.

Thus, in Dr. Heberden's Bill classifying the causes of death in London during the year 1657 we find:

Flox and Small Pox	835
Found dead in the streets, etc.	9
French Pox	25
Gout	8
Griefe	10
Griping and Plague in the Guts	446
Hang'd and made away 'emselves	24

Such figures would today be dismissed as examples of medical mythology, but is there in fact any evidence that grief is sometimes a cause of death?

There is, of course, no doubt that psychological factors play a part in many illlnesses, but it is only in rare cases of "vagal inhibition" and in so-called voodoo deaths that they appear to be the sole cause. Vagal inhibition is a pseudo-scientific term sometimes used by doctors for the cause of death following a sudden emotional shock. A classic example is provided in the story of some students who held a mock trial and sentenced a man to death. He was led to the place of execution, blindfolded, and hit on the back of the neck with a towel—whereupon he died. Not dissimilar are the numerous well-authenticated cases of death from witchcraft. Although the witchcraft can take many different forms, such deaths seem to follow a general pattern. The "victim" is told that the appropriate ritual curse has been carried out; if he has faith he at once becomes deeply depressed, stops eating, and within a few days is dead. In neither the vagal inhibition type of death nor death from witchcraft is there any post-mortem finding that explains the phenomenon.

Such occurrences are fortunately very rare, but there is other evidence of the effect of psychological factors on mortality among the unhealthy and aging. [Researchers] Aldrich and Mendkoff, for instance, discovered a major increase in mortality among chronically sick patients when a Chicago Home for Incurables was closed for administrative reasons. Of 182 patients who were relocated in other homes, thirty were dead within three months— a mortality rate five times greater than expectation. Mortality was highest among those patients whose grasp on reality was most tenuous, particularly among the thirty-eight whom Aldrich rated as "psychotic" before relocation, of whom twenty-four died within a year.

Apart from a few isolated cases of doubtful authenticity, I have come across no evidence that phenomena such as these are responsible for death following bereavement. The examples have been quoted simply to remind the reader that psychological factors can have profound effects even on healthy people.

For many years it has been known that widows and widowers have a higher mortality rate than married men and women of the same age. But then so have bachelors and spinsters, and it is not unreasonable to suspect that some of the fitter widows and widowers remarry, thereby ensuring that those who remain will have a relatively high mortality rate.

This explanation might certainly account for an increased mortality rate among the widowed population as a whole but it would not explain the peak of mortality in widowers during the first year of bereavement, as discovered by Michael Young and his colleagues (Young, Benjamin and Wallis, 1963). They found an increase in the death rate among 4,486 widowers over the age of 54 of almost 40 percent during the first six months of bereavement. This dropped off rapidly thereafter to around the mortality rate for married men of the same age....

Independent confirmation of this observation has more recently come from a study of a semi-rural community in Wales [by Rees and Lutkins, 1967]. A survey of 903 close relatives of 371 residents who died during 1960–65 showed that 4.8 percent of them died within one year of bereavement compared with only 0.7 percent of a comparable group of non-bereaved people of the same age, living in the same area. The mortality rate was particularly high for widows and widowers, 12 percent of whom died during the same period....

These two studies established a statistical relationship between bereavement and an increase in the death rate, but they did not explain this association, and it is still not known why bereaved people tend to die more readily than the nonbereaved.

Several diseases seem to contribute to the higher mortality but recent work has indicated that the most frequent cause of death is heart disease. The paper by Young *et al.* on the death rate among widowers was used as the basis of a further study (carried out by Parkes, Benjamin, and Fitzgerald, 1969) of the causes of death among these same widowers as revealed on their death certificates. It was soon apparent that three-quarters of the increased death rate during the first six months of bereavement was attributable to heart disease, in particular to coronary thrombosis and arteriosclerotic heart disease....

The origin of the term "broken heart" goes back to Biblical times. "Bind up the broken hearted," says Isaiah, and the idea seems to have persisted ever since that severe grief can somehow damage the heart. Benjamin Rush, the American physician and signatory of the Declaration of Independence, wrote in his *Medical Inquiries and Observations upon the Diseases of the Mind* (1835): "Dissection of persons who have died of grief, show congestion in, and inflammation of the heart, with rupture of its auricles and ventricles." Rupture of the heart is, of course, a rare condition, but when it does occur it is usually caused by coronary thrombosis. All of which leads us to suspect that the old physicians may not have been as foolish as we suppose. (In case any bereaved reader is now clutching his chest and preparing to call an ambulance may I hasten to point out that palpitations and a feeling of fullness in the chest are normal concomitants of anxiety and that bereaved people often experience them without developing heart disease.)

The fact that bereavement may be followed by death from heart disease does not prove that grief is itself a cause of death. We do not even know whether bereavement causes the illness or simply aggravates a condition that would have occurred anyway. Perhaps bereaved people tend to smoke more or to alter their diet in a way that increases their liability to coronary thrombosis. Even if emotional factors are directly implicated we still have to explain how they affect the heart. Stress is known to produce changes in the blood pressure and heart rate, in the flow of blood through the coronary arteries and in the chemical constituents of the blood. Any of these changes could play a part in precipitating clotting within a diseased coronary artery and thereby produce a coronary thrombosis, but without further research we can only speculate.

It may be that measures aimed at reducing the stress of bereavement will help to prevent such consequences. If so, then giving help to the bereaved is a practical contribution to public health....

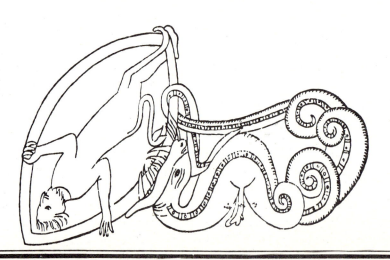

Robert L. Fulton

Anticipatory Grief, Stress, and the Surrogate Griever

Robert Fulton, sociologist and director of the Center for Death Education and Social Research, University of Minnesota, addresses several related issues in this article: the emergent definition of death, the institutionalization of the dying, and the interplay between the phenomenon of "anticipatory" grief and the professional caregiver.

It is, he says, a matter of importance that in the latter half of the twentieth century the majority of elderly persons in our society go to public hospitals to die. Separated frequently by time and distance from family members and friends, the dying often find themselves in peculiar circumstances. They are emotionally accepted by professional caregivers who are virtual strangers at the same time that they are socially or psychologically abandoned by family and friends.

The contradiction in this situation, Fulton points out, has important consequences for the surviving participants not only during the time of the dying of the patient but also following his or her death.

The categories of death are expanding in our society. The conception of death— or more correctly—the conception of life has changed. That is, in contrast to the recent past, the conception of life has contracted while death has extended its parameters over life. Who is considered alive and who is considered dead today is not the same. Viability has been foreshortened.

Formerly life began with conception. With the Supreme Court's ruling recently that a fetus is not "alive" until after the twenty-first week of gestation, "life" has had to pull in its belt. Our societal attitudes toward death, it would appear, are beginning to parallel the views of life and death found among some non-Western societies, in which not only are the dead, dead, but the elderly and the very ill are dead also, while the unborn are not considered to be of this world.

Moreover, the definition of death itself has undergone a change and has a different meaning from what it had only a decade ago. Until quite recently death was something you could put your finger on, so to speak. You could check a patient's eye for a light reaction, feel his pulse, test for respiration, prick his skin, and, failing a response, you could reasonably conclude that the patient was dead. Today, however, there are organ transplant programs and other medical science procedures that frequently make it necessary to run an EEG to be certain that a patient is "brain dead."

The circumstance of increased complexity in the area of death is reflected also in the new issues and dilemmas surrounding grief and bereavement. One of the most fruitful approaches to our understanding of human response to loss was initiated by Lindemann at Massachusetts General Hospital in the 1940s. His studies, simple as they were, were profound in their implications and illuminating in terms of our systematic understanding of the nature of grief. It was he who in fact first coined the expression "anticipatory grief." Because of him, we can talk not only about normal grief in a new light but also about pathologic grief, chronic grief, and surrogate grief, as well as anticipatory grief.

The domain of bereavement is well worth exploring, especially in view of the unanswered question of whether grief is natural to humankind or whether it is a function of cultural conditioning. The question was raised over thirty years ago by Melford Spiro, the anthropologist who worked among the Ifaluk. He observed that while women of the tribe would grieve for their fathers, uncles, and sons, they did not appear to grieve for their husbands. Neither did they show any other signs of loss when the husband died. Spiro's work flies in the face of what common sense would tell us about grief, and it challenges, as well, those studies of both humans and animals that weigh in favor of a genetically determined grief response. At best we can only say at this time that the issue of nature versus nurture with regard to the grief reaction remains unresolved. What we do know, however, is that when it comes to an immediate response to separation or loss by death, people tend to react in a variety of ways.

Observed variations in the response, for instance, permit us to make a distinction between what can be termed a "high grief" death and a "low grief" death. If the expression "low grief" be allowed to describe the reaction to the death of many elderly persons today, "high grief" might describe the impact of the sudden or unexpected death of a person on whom others depend heavily for their social and psychological wellbeing. This latter death usually precipitates a series of intense emotional and physical reactions that we know as the "normal grief" syndrome.

Experience with death, grief, and bereavement in modern urban societies has changed significantly over the past few decades. At the turn of the century, for example, over half of all deaths in the United States were those of children under fifteen years of age. Today death is increasingly an experience of the aged. A graph of the present mortality of American society would be much like a J-curve. Under one year of age there is an appreciable rate of mortality, but this flattens out until nearly the fifth decade of life when a sharp rise begins. Separation and loss experiences follow a similar pattern. What needs to be noted is that the greatest number of those who die in our society today are the elderly. Most of us in the middle years are, in a sense, death-insulated. The chances are only one in twenty that young people in our society will have any direct immediate experience with death within their nuclear families before they attain their twenty-first year.

Because most deaths today are among the elderly, causes of death have changed since 1900, when child mortality was higher. The elderly die from heart disease, stroke, cancer, and other degenerative diseases associated with the aging process. In this sense death today is different from any death that has ever been experienced by any prior society. We have a unique phenomenon. Men and women die under the care of highly skilled medical functionaries in segregated hospital communities. And they die for reasons that, by and large, were statistically speaking unknown two or three generations ago. At the turn of the century, for instance, only 4 percent of the population was over sixty-five years of age; they represented 17 percent of all deaths. Today, the elderly represent 11 percent of the population but contribute over 70 percent of the deaths. Moreover, in the majority of cases, they die in the hospital or in a setting other than their own homes.

It is important to note, also, that the contemporary setting within which the majority of people die has brought about profound changes in the level of emotional reaction to loss, as well as a change in who, in fact, shares in the loss. Research has shown that frequently professional care-givers experience grief at the loss of a patient and in many other ways react as bereaved survivors themselves. As the traditional kinship network falters or as family members disengage from their relationship with the dying patient, the attending nurses and other caregivers frequently find themselves participating in the social and emotional support of patients under their care. Such involvement, albeit at times inadvertent, brings with it a new responsibility as it involves new emotional risks. In fact, Mary Vachon, and her colleagues at the Clark Institute in Toronto have found that the stress level of critical care nurses is often as high as the stress levels of the patients for whom they care.

This occurs not only because of the circumstances of modern life in which a whole new health industry for the care of the elderly has evolved, but also because of a phenomenon called "anticipatory grief." The term refers to the fact that the patient's death is anticipated prior to the event, and there is an accomodation that goes on among the survivors and health-care personnel in expectation of what is to occur. Studies have shown that in some instances where family members were observed to withdraw physically and emotionally from a patient, health care personnel became caught up in the patient's life. New emotional bonds were established, with the result that the health care team found themselves grieved persons when the patient died. The phenomenon of anticipatory grief, thus, helps turn pro-

fessional caregivers into grievers, or what I have termed "surrogate grievers."

With what result? I believe the phenomenon gives rise to the potential for role discrepancy and role reversal on the part of the caregiver and the survivor. The caregiver grieves but is not bereaved, while the bereft survivor may be beyond experiencing his or her grief. Thus, the role of the surrogate griever not only has the capacity of complicating the dying process, but it also has the potential for casting into a bad light the muted responses or misunderstood reactions of the immediate survivor. For example, I remember an incident some years ago at Wayne State University, where a group of physicians, nurses, and paramedical personnel were meeting to discuss this issue, when a nurse jumped up and said with great emotion that "if family survivors can't behave the way they should following a death, they should stay away from the hospital and from the funeral!"

To repeat: it can happen that by the time the death of the patient occurs, the staff will experience the loss of the patient more deeply than expected, while a confused mother, not understanding her lack of affect and frequently her inability to cry or express her grief, will attempt to act out the role of hostess! Thus, it happens that her behavior is misinterpreted by the staff and she is perceived as being heartless.

A case in point is the physician's wife who lost her husband through cancer of the abdomen. He had originally experimented on himself at medical school. He had ingested some radioactive fats as part of his work towards a Ph.D. thesis on carcinogenic substances. Two and a half years later, as he was about to graduate, he became ill, and his cancer was subsequently discovered. A university medical team decided to film his dying for educational purposes, recording those events that occurred between him and his wife as well as video-taping a series of interviews with a psychiatrist friend and colleague.

Over the four to five month period that the interviews were conducted, the wife's appearance changed dramatically. Initially, she wore her long hair severely pulled back, dark horn rimmed glasses, long skirts, and "sensible" shoes. By the end of the interviews she had become *"Vogue*-like" in appearance—just the opposite of the image she first presented the viewer. Neither she nor the psychiatrist acknowledged this change, nor were they conscious of talking about her husband in the *past tense* (even though at the time he was very much alive). They never realized the mental shift that had occurred in them both. I would argue that the phenomenon of anticipatory grief played a very important part in the change in the wife's physical appearance, as well as in her emotional transformation. One is left to imagine how she thought of herself or what others who knew them both thought of her appearance or behavior at the time of her husband's death.

Increasingly, studies have investigated the role of the caregiver in relationship to dying patients. Let me mention one that deals not with the dying of an elderly patient, but rather with the death of children from leukemia. The Natterson-Knudson study was conducted fifteen years ago at City of Hope, Duarte, California. A scenario that was repeated in different cases went something as follows: A mother would bring a child into the hospital after having sought out one physician after another to reassure her that the child did *not* have leukemia. Finally, on recognizing that the child *had* to be hospitalized, the mother would come into the hospital clinging to the child. She would insist on remaining with the child. She would become consumed by the child's illness. She would leave her husband, and other children if there were any, in favor of the sick child. Over a period of months, however, as the child and mother settled into the hospital routine, she would begin to yield. Slowly she would remove herself from the child and the hospital and return to her family. She would visit her child less frequently, and often when she did return to the hospital, she would come with an article from a medical journal or an account of a new treatment or procedure and discuss the contents with the child's physician. Her preoccupation with her child's illness became a preoccupation with leukemia wherever it appeared throughout the world. She began to transcend or sublimate her experience. Finally, there was an observable decline in her involvement, emotional expressions of affection, and time spent with the child. There were fewer tears shed but more abstract discussions on the nature of the disease. She initiated contact with other children in the ward. New areas of interest opened up for her. Ultimately, when she lost all hope, she questioned the value of continuing the treatments. Surprising for all, it was now the attending physician who argued for the treatment to be continued or new procedures to be initiated! A reversal in roles had taken place. Suddenly the physician had taken on the role of mother, as she first appeared to him, while the mother had assumed the role of the physician.

Anticipatory grief may be either a personal or collective response to stress. Given the peculiarities of illnesses among the elderly—like cancer, especially with its potential for prolonging dying—anticipatory grief introduces a whole new dimension of stress for family members and care-givers alike. For family members who have to deal with the separation and loss of their loved one, the stressful event can be muted and possibly sublimated. On the other hand, professional caregivers may find an *increase* in the amount of stress they must bear.

In summary, it is important to recognize that a new phenomenon is among us. It results from human beings dying in segregated institutions attended by specialized care-givers. Such a situation has the potential to reverse the role between surviving family members and health care personnel. This reversal has major implications for the level of stress that may be experienced by all concerned.

HOW THE RABBI OF SASOV LEARNED HOW TO LOVE

Rabbi Moshe Leib told this story, "How to love men is something I learned from a peasant. He was sitting in an inn along with other peasants, drinking. For a long time he was as silent as all the rest, but when he was moved by the wine, he asked one of the men seated beside him: 'Tell me, do you love me or don't you love me?' The other replied: 'I love you very much.' But the first peasant replied: 'You say that you love me, but you do not know what I need. If you really loved me, you would know.' The other had not a word to say to this, and the peasant who had put the question fell silent again.

"But I understood. To know the needs of men to and to bear the burden of their sorrow—that is the true love of men."

Martin Buber
Tales of the Hasidim: Early Masters

10.

Widowhood

What would be the most difficult event for you to face in your life? When researchers Thomas Holmes and Richard Rahe asked this question of thousands of respondents in diverse cultural settings, the answer was nearly unanimous: "The death of my spouse." When we consider the fact that one in six women over the age of twenty-one is currently a widow, the significance of this status change becomes clear.

It seems that when life is shared with another person over a long period of time, specific individual identities are often displaced in favor of a "couple" identity. This means that husband and wife act *together* in the world. They have joint responsibilities and concerns, and are thought of as a couple by other persons.

Death shatters this identity. It tears apart the social and emotional world that has become so comfortable, and it leaves the survivors empty and alone. Widows are, of course, subject to grief responses similar to those described in the preceding chapter, but their difficulty is compounded by the potential loss of identity. In a society that places as much emphasis on the couple relationship as ours does, the loss of a spouse means the loss of a part of oneself. Often, as some of the authors point out, the widow's sense of who she is revolves intimately around her husband's occupation and social position. In his absence, she may feel that her life has lost much, if not all, of its meaning. Occasionally, in an effort to recapture this meaning, a surviving partner will begin to behave or think more like the deceased spouse. One woman, interviewed in Colin Murray Parkes' study of widowhood in London, reported the following:

> I enjoy the things my husband used to do....It's like a thought in my head—what he would say or do. I quite enjoy watching the races on televison because he liked it. It's a most queer feeling....My young sister said, "You're getting like Fred in all your ways."...There's lots of things I do that I wouldn't think of doing....I suppose he's guiding me the whole time.

In contrast to this, widowhood may come as a great relief, as Helena Lopata makes clear in her discussion. One woman, interviewed in a bereavement study at the University of Minnesota, said that the first social gathering held after her husband's death was a party. When asked why this was so, she told the interviewer that her husband had been an alcoholic for seventeen years and that her life had been a living hell. His death brought to her the first sense of peace she had known for many years. While such a response is an exceptional one, it is nonetheless important to remember that survivorship may have many dimensions.

Another important aspect of widowhood is the public reaction it elicits. In earlier cultures the widow was most often an object of scorn and disparagement. She might be held responsible for the death of her husband and consequently isolated from other members of the community. Freud describes these practices in *Totem and Taboo* where he writes:

> Among the Shuswap of British Columbia widows and widowers in mourning are secluded and forbidden to touch their own head or body; the cups and cooking vessels which they use may be used by no one else....No hunter would

come near such mourners, for their presence is unlucky. If their shadow were to fall on anyone, he would be taken ill at once. They employ thorn bushes for bed and pillow...and thorn bushes are also laid around their beds.

The nineteenth-century anthropologist Blumentritt describes a similar circumstance among the Agutainos of the Philippine Islands. He recounts:

> ...a widow may not leave her hut for seven or eight days, after the death; and even then she may only go out at an hour when she is not likely to meet anybody, for whoever looks upon her dies a sudden death. To prevent this fatal catastrophe, the widow knocks with a wooden peg on the trees as she goes along, thus warning people of her dangerous proximity; and the very trees on which she knocks soon die.

These practices reveal the spoiled identity that often accompanies widowhood. A widower, on the other hand, is seldom thought to be culpable for his wife's death. When the nineteenth-century philosopher, Herbert Spencer, examined bereavement patterns in a variety of primitive cultures, he could find almost no evidence to indicate that widowers were subjected to the same shame and indignity that accompanied widowhood. Instead, they were encouraged to remarry and typically retained their place and status within the community.

In America, the conditions of widowhood have been altered by changing national circumstances. The severe proscriptions and prohibitions of earlier cultures have for the most part disappeared as specified mourning customs have been lifted.

But the decline in rituals associated with death is only a small part of this change.

Financial insecurity still poses a major problem for many widows and reflects the accepted posture of economic dependence with which many women have grown up. Younger widows, however, have frequently been employed outside of the home prior to their husband's death. This has resulted in greater financial independence for them and an increased ability to pick up the economic burden following the death of their mates. In addition, the stigma associated with being a single woman has declined in recent years, removing one more source of frustration and anger from the path of the younger widow.

As new generations of young women grow and mature, they come to accept new ethics regarding such matters as work, social equality, and sexual behavior. As they grow older and survive their spouses, one would expect major changes in the way in which widowhood is experienced.

The articles that follow explore not only the pain and anguish associated with widowhood, but also the many changes that widowhood brings about.

The first selection by Helena Lopata brings into focus how social class differences affect a woman's response to widowhood. She shows how the working class widow, with limited education and work skills, is often seriously disadvantaged both financially and socially. Typically, however, she shared less of her husband's world than did her middle class counterpart and may therefore find it easier to recover from her loss. The middle class widow, on the other hand, was typically much involved in her husband's activities and may find the immediate effects of the loss more difficult to bear. At the same time, armed with a better education and some work skills, she is often able to reconstruct a new and somewhat different life based on her own resources.

The second article by Lynn Caine is an intimate and personal reflection following the death of her husband. Her responses are of significance to many because she represents a new kind of widow: one who has considered many of the ethics of the woman's movement and who finds her new social status particularly painful. She is a middle-class widow in the modern world, and her essay makes us feel uncomfortable and vulnerable. At the same time, however, she encourages the strongest commitment to a hopeful future.

The final selection by Arnold Toynbee calls us to examine the meaning of our love for another person. Is it better, he asks, to wish to suffer the pain of bereavement or the horror of dying oneself? Professor Toynbee's answer may challenge us as it calls forth a provocative new ethic of love and commitment.

Helena Znaniecki Lopata

Living through Widowhood

Helena Znaniecki Lopata, a Polish survivor of a Nazi concentration camp, teaches sociology at Loyola University in Chicago, where she conducted extensive research on widowhood. In this selection based on her Chicago research, she describes the invisible minority: the impoverished, poorly educated widow who must struggle for survival and renewed meaning in life. She also specifies the factors related to a widow's disposition toward recovery: the role played by enforced social isolation and limited educational resources. But there is another image as well. There are the widows who recover and grow—women who find life easier, who feel more independent and self-sufficient and are able to form new relationships. The observations contained here are both enlightening and disturbing, but above all, they reflect the changed context in which widowhood is experienced.

The main character in the cartoon strip, "Momma," is a little old widow who constantly harps at her children. She complains that they never visit her, and when they do, she complains that they don't visit her enough. She worries about her children who aren't married, and she worries about the son who is.

"Momma" takes a lighthearted look at a stereotype that often evokes more hostile reactions. Both the grouchy widow who imposes on her offspring and the well-meaning meddler who spoils her grandchildren are common images in our folklore.

Social scientists have contributed their share of false impressions about widowhood. In 1961 Elaine Cumming and William Henry argued in *Growing Old* that widowhood was less difficult for women than retirement was for men. The widow's status in a society increases, they said, but the retired man's status decreases. Women can look forward to sharing prestigious leisure-time activities with each other, they concluded. If widows choose to isolate themselves from others, society shouldn't be concerned. The separation is a normal phase in which they are happily disengaging from their prior active lives in anticipation of death. Cumming and Henry's thesis is wrong; the women they describe, I believe, currently are the exception rather than the rule.

To remedy some of the ignorance and misinformation about American widows, I conducted a lengthy survey with the help of a grant from the Administration on Aging. The National Opinion Research Center drew a probability sample and interviewed 301 such women (244 whites, 52 blacks and 5 unidentified), fifty years of age and over, who live in metropolitan Chicago. The survey asked these women many questions about their attitudes, experiences as widows, complaints, and lifestyles.

The respondents, like older people nationally, have had less education than younger generations: 69 percent never finished high school, 20 percent stopped after graduation from high school, and only 11 percent had further schooling. Almost all of the blacks were migrants from the rural South and had significantly less education than the whites. Most of these women married men of comparable education, and thus never lived at a high economic or status level. Currently they are subsisting on incomes that range from poverty to moderate levels: 15 percent live on less than $1,000 a year; 45 percent have $1,000 to $3,000. Only 10 percent live on more than $7,000 a year.

LIVING ALONE AND LIKING IT   Contrary to the stereotype, the overwhelming proportion of these widows (90 percent) do not live with their married children, partly because of anticipated conflicts, but partly because they derive satisfaction from living alone. These factors are strong enough to offset their loneliness and economic hardships.

About half of the respondents live entirely alone; the proportion drops among younger widows, who still have unmarried children at home, and the very old, who are physically incapacitated, or educationally too incompetent to live alone.

Even among widows who live with others, 69 percent tend to be heads of the household, not peripheral members. In truth, others, including unmarried children, roomers, friends or relatives whom they take in, live with them. Over half share a home with only one other person. Only 10 percent of the sample live with their married children and their families.

One reason this figure is so low may be the question of who rules the roost. One woman explained the difficulty: "I suppose it's the widow trying to get accustomed to not being in her own home after so many years of doing as she pleased and running her own home."

The widow who wishes to live in an extended family must give up her home and move into an unfamiliar network of relations. Only 16 percent of the women we interviewed saw life with their married offspring as trouble free. The problems, the rest agreed, are considerable.

There is the difficulty of leaving a familiar and comfortable style of life for a new one. Such a change is particularly hard for the older widows in this sample, who believe that women should be passive and unwilling to experiment with new roles.

There is a drop in status when one moves from head of the house to guest. While many young women are unhappy to be "just a housewife," their older counterparts found status in that role. When a widow can no longer run her own house, she feels psychologically useless. One respondent moved out of her son's home because "you can't call your soul your own; they took too good care of me—they really did too much. They thought they were nice; they would bring my food up on a tray. But I wanted to be independent. We like to feel needed and useful."

Widows anticipate problems in being mothers of grown-up children. They feel that it is easier to keep the position of the wise authority if they live in their own territory than if they live in their children's homes. If they cannot criticize or comment, they feel inhibited. But if they do speak up, their children are upset. One woman, asked to explain why she wanted to live alone, said she had a "compulsion to give advice. Advice is always resented, and I thought the resentments would build."

Another widow made her feelings plain: "Lock up your mouth and don't mix in. I wouldn't want to live with them. All my life I lived alone, that's the way it should be...no matter what you see or what they do, say nothing. The problem comes in knowing when to meddle."

THE MEDDLING MOTHER PROBLEM
The temptation to meddle often is hard to resist for mothers who watch their offspring struggle through life experiences. "My daughter says everything would be all right if I just keep my mouth shut, and I tell her, 'That's just it, I don't want to keep my mouth shut! What's the fun of living if you can't open your mouth?'"

Grandchildren present related problems. The widow is likely to disagree with her son or daughter on child-rearing, coming to the rescue of her grandchildren too often. Frequently the situation turns into a painful game, with grandmother, parents, and grandchildren taking the roles of rescuer, attacker, and victim. "My grandson is three. He's so brilliant...my son yells I'm spoiling him. My son spanked the child and the boy ran to me and I could not help but wrap my arms around him."

Widows also give positive reasons for living alone; 56 percent of all respondents, and 70 percent of those who live alone agreed with the statement, "I like living alone." This means that some women who live with others would prefer to live alone and that some would prefer to share a residence with others but are not able to make such arrangements. As one respondent explained, "I couldn't be as independent as I am, living with my children. I've become very independent since I'm a widow and wouldn't give that up for anything. If you lived with one of your kids, you'd be subject to their wills and whims. No sir, that's not for me." Another was even more vehement: "I never took orders from my husband and I sure as hell couldn't take orders from my children."

In fact, when we asked respondents about the advantages of widowhood, some listed "freedom to do as I please," "being independent," "not having a schedule," and "being my own boss." Forty-two percent of the sample (57 percent of the blacks) agreed that *I feel more independent and free now than before I became a widow;* and in spite of financial and health problems, over one-third agreed that *this time of my life is actually easier than any other time.*

Indeed, many of the respondents contrast their present independence with hard life in the past. Living alone frees them from extensive housework as well as from problems with children.

None of the widows thought she was an "unnatural mother" because she valued her independence. Many justify their desire and freedom with cultural generalizations: "two women in the kitchen don't work out"; "the generation gap"; "young people have their own ways." Only one woman in the entire sample stated that widows don't live with children because the children don't want them.

We asked our Chicago women whether they felt they had changed in any specific ways as a result of widowhood. Over half, 54 percent, reported at least one change, and most of these said that the change was beneficial. For instance, they believe themselves to be more independent or competent now than they were as wives, or they feel that they are freer and more active. Only 20 percent of the sample described their first change in negative terms. They find themselves worrying more than they used to; or feel that they are now more suspicious of other persons.

THE LONELY FREE   The fact that the majority of the widows now feel more competent and complete does not mean that they had unhappy marriages. They are the same women who list loneliness, rather than money or other worries, as the worst problem of widowhood. And they are the same women who miss their husbands most as objects of love who treated them as important people and partners, rather than as breadwinners or bodies in the house.

Nor does their positive outlook mean that the interim period was easy. Some listed increased worries; some reported serious conflicts with married friends. Often a respondent, particularly one from the middle class, expressed feelings of unworthiness after her husband's death, a sense that others would not like her now that her alter ego was gone; a sense that a vital part of her self, the personality and presence of the husband, was missing.

I was curious about the remaining 46 percent who claimed no changes as a result of widowhood, even as they admitted the need to develop new skills, make new friends, go to work, sell their homes, and so on. At first I thought that they denied personality change because they believed that healthy adults should possess stable personality traits; perhaps that they believed that staying the same preserves the husband's memory.

But this was not the case. The critical—and related—factors in whether a woman perceived herself as having changed toward increased competence and independence appear to be (1) the kind of relationship the woman had with her husband, (2) her educational level and social skills, and (3) the ease with which she can shift identities. Respondents who reported no changes were the least educated, had been less dependent on their husbands for a social life, and were more socially isolated than the women who reported positive changes.

I constructed a social-isolation scale, which consisted of forty-five questions and expressed the degree of contact a widow has with other persons. A respondent got one point each time she said she *lacked* a specific contact—for example, not seeing her child more than several times a year, not belonging to any organizations, not having a car, not having overnight guests, and so on. Among the respondents, 13 percent were highly isolated (scoring between fifty-five and eighty points, the maximum; 17 percent scored very low (up to twenty-five points); the rest were intermediate (between twenty-six and fifty-four points).

The women who did not report change in themselves as a result of widowhood were the most apt to feel alone and isolated. They listed "being shunned by other people" as the major problem of widowhood. However, it is unlikely that they actually have been shunned. For these respondents, loneliness and social isolation are chronic states, not a result of their husbands' deaths. Fully 97 percent of the highly-isolated widows reported that they have the same type, quality, and quantity of social life now as they did when their husbands were alive. This was true of only 43 percent of the medium-isolated and 41 percent of the low scorers.

WHICH WIDOWS CHANGE   I had suspected that other factors would be significant in distinguishing women who reported change from those who did not—the number of children a woman has and whether she sees them; the length of widowhood; the number of persons with whom she is living; the age at which she was widowed. But none of these factors made a difference. Education and degree of

	No change (n = 138)	Change (n = 162)
Education		
Less than 8 years	33%	18%
Eight to 12 years	43	44
High school graduate	17	24
More than 12 years	7	24
Level of social isolation		
Low	10	24
Medium	71	69
High	19	7

social isolation were the principal factors.

Education and degree of isolation also related to each other. Women who have gone beyond high school see more friends and relatives, go out more, and are more active socially than women with grade-school educations. The better-educated respondents dropped many of their activities when their husbands died, but after a while they picked them up again. They seem to have emerged from that interim period feeling more independent.

Education and social class have a major role in the way a woman views herself and her world, and in the way she puts herself and the world back together after her husband's death. For instance, we found that the lower a woman's education, the less likely she is to rank the role of wife in first place in the hierarchy of roles for women. Instead, she places the role of mother first. The less-educated woman feels that she has no share in her husband's world. She believes that she has little influence on him, or else that her main contribution is to feed him, "service" him, and encourage him to get a better job. As a result of a strong traditional sex-role pattern in the family, the less-educated woman fails to develop an identity dependent on her husband. In many ways she

is not as affected by his presence, or absence, as is the more educated woman.

The woman with higher levels of schooling ranks the wife role as the most important. She feels her performance as a wife has a direct impact on her husband—on his happiness, on his success at work, on his health. She feels that she influences his career, both directly, such as by entertaining for him, or indirectly, by understanding his problems and being able to discuss them. The middle-class woman shares many activities with her husband and socializes with him more often than her lower-class counterpart does. As a result, she is much more likely to be influenced by the man's definition of the world, to shape her identity around his, to build up a universe of shared symbols. She comes to think in terms of "we" rather than "I."

Such different styles of marriage and personal identity result in a paradox. The husband's death disrupts the better-educated woman's life more than it disrupts the life of the less-educated woman. At the same time, education provides a woman with more skills for reentering society and reconstructing her life, thereby protecting her from complete social isolation. In other words, the middle-class suffers more at an identity level, but simultaneously has more opportunities to establish a new identity and social relations than the lower-class woman.

BLACKS AND WHITES   The black respondents consistently lagged behind the white women in idealizing their marriages and their husbands. They were less likely to agree, for example, that *my husband was an unusually good man* (76 percent to 94 percent), that *my marriage was above average and no second marriage could match it* (62 percent to 76 percent), and that *my sex relations with my husband were very good until his last illness* (57 percent to 80 percent). In fact, the black women apparently had been fairly independent of their husbands. There were twice as likely as white widows to say that they had shared only a few activities with their husbands, 48 percent to 24 percent. And they are more used to making decisions on their own. While 61 percent of the whites said that decision-making is the hardest thing for a widow to learn, this was true for only 37 percent of the black women.

Indeed, blacks are more skeptical than whites of marriage altogether. Half of them feel sorry for married friends, who have, in their opinion, little freedom, compared to 28 percent of the whites. And fully 72 percent agree that many widows who remarry are very unhappy in that marriage compared to 49 percent of the whites. Whether a result of experience or assumption, more blacks than whites believe that *widows are constantly sexually propositioned, even by the husbands of their friends* (45 percent to only 18 percent) and that *other women are jealous of a widow when their husbands are around* (59 percent to 39 percent).

There are three possible levels at which a woman can return to society after her husband's death. She can go back to the medium or high levels of activity that she had prior to widowhood. Whether she does so depends on the availability of social groups that do not require the presence of a mate: relatives, long-time friends, neighbors, work associates, voluntary organizations. Second, a widow may choose to enter completely new roles and make a new set of friends. Third, she may live in isolation.

The first two solutions, or a combination of them, would appear to be the most ideal from the widow's point of view. But many circumstances make such a desirable readjustment difficult, if not impossible. We explored the problems that our respondents have had in various relationships and found that widows rarely *choose* to be isolated, whether "in preparation for death" or not. To the contrary, isolation often follows from their inability to rescue former relationships and develop new ones.

UNFRIENDLY FRIENDS   Many of the respondents reported strain with friends in early stages of widowhood. This is particularly true of the middle-class ones who later made adjustments. Friends unintentionally may add to the widow's grief rather than alleviate it. Many of our respondents reported that their friends avoided them, feeling uncomfortable about what to say and fearing that the widows would express their grief, despair, and loneliness. This "grief-work" is precisely what psychiatrists and sociologists believe is essential for a person to get through the mourning period. But many Americans are reluctant to help their friends in a crisis. They ignore the situation, using the rationale that "it is better for them to work it out alone."

Friends, in short, seem to view the woman as *widow,* not as *friend* or *wife,* which is how she still thinks of herself. By ignoring her, they can try to escape the way her experience reminds them of their own mortality.

Half of the respondents agreed that *one problem of being a widow is feeling like a "fifth wheel."* This belief was especially prevalent among women who had shared many couple-friendships with their husbands, a social pattern that has become more commonplace, replacing the pattern of same-sex friendships. Middle-class couples often get together as couples. Thus when a pair separates through death or divorce, the resulting asymmetry causes strain. Some younger respondents feel that their women friends now regard them as threats, out to get their husbands as sexual partners or mates. Others feel uncomfortable going places without a male escort, so they don't go.

If the middle-class woman encounters strains in her friendships, the lower-class woman must cope with having fewer friends to begin with. Among the respondents, those who reported no friends tended to be the minimally educated, who had had husbands of similar background, and who had moved out of their old neighborhoods. They had come to divide the world into persons whom they know and trust, generally relatives, and persons who are suspicious strangers. The less-educated widows were significantly more likely to agree that *relatives are your only true friends,* a statement that immediately shuts out a group of possible intimates.

Relatives are your only true friends

Less than 8 years education	49%
Eight through 12 years education	21
More than 12 years education	7

But relatives do not provide much comfort and support for widows either. A minority of the respondents rebuild their lives around family members, even siblings. Only 31 percent agreed that *my brothers and/or sisters became much more important to me after I became a widow.* This response did not vary by educational level.

MYTHS OF THE ETHNIC FAMILY   In spite of the persistent stereotypes about extended families and kin solidarity in black and ethnic ghettos, our lower-class respondents, black or white, do not have many relatives or long-time friends to help them. Only one black

woman has siblings whom she sees daily or even weekly; thirty-three women (63 percent) have no siblings or see all their siblings on an average of less than a few times a year. These less-educated women use brothers and sisters as an emergency contact only. Relatives pitch in to share housing, health care, or child care during a crisis, but such occasions are interspersed with long periods of noncontact. The more-educated women see siblings at regular intervals, usually around holidays, but just as infrequently.

Nor do the widows in this sample spend much time with their children; they do not have children or they see all their children on an average of less than monthly. The less-educated mothers tend to see one child more often than others, largely because it is financially and physically difficult for them to see offspring who have moved any distance away. The more-educated mothers try to see all of their children on a regular basis, and generally can afford to do so.

In spite of the fact that less-educated women put a primary emphasis on the role of mother, many of them seem to be annoyed with their children. Half of the widows with less than eight years of school, for example, agreed that *one problem with adult children is that they always want you to do favors for them—babysit or sew or things like that.* But only 11 percent of those who had graduated from high school agreed with this statement.

Finally, widows tend to receive little support from their in-laws. Once the connecting link is gone, the husband's family withdraws. Almost two-thirds of the Chicago widows (64 percent) said that in-laws did not even help with funeral arrangements. Half of the widows said that their children no longer see their father's relatives at all, and only 12 percent reported that such contacts were frequent.

Fewer than one respondent in four said that she had visited or had been visited by in-laws after the funeral. This abrupt cessation of contact with the husband's family means that the widow has freedom from control by the male line, unlike widows in fiercely patriarchal cultures, but it also means that she is isolated from yet another source of help and comfort.

THE INVISIBLE MINORITY   American society prescribes no single, predictable pattern of behavior for the widow, as many traditional societies do. Some cultures, for example, provide automatic remarriage within the same community or even family. Others isolate the widows and require them to live in special huts or wear distinctive clothing. Modern women have many alternatives but, unhappily, the majority of today's older widows lack the skills and resources to take advantage of these alternatives. Rapid social and technological changes have left older people feeling isolated and inadequate.

Of course, there are middle-class widows who enjoy lives of relative independence and leisure. They require no societal help, because they have the ability and the money to live comfortably, make friends, and enter new roles.

But that leaves many other widows—the majority of our sample—who have an almost invisible status. Indeed, most of America's nine and a half million widows share the characteristics of other minority groups that are targets of discrimination. They are women in a male-dominated society. They are old in a society that venerates youth. Many are grieving and lonely in a country that would deny and ignore such unhappy emotions. They are without mates in a social network of couples. Many are members of ethnic or racial minority groups and already face prejudice on that basis. (For example, about one and a half million of our female elderly are foreign-born.) They are poor in a wealthy land, and they tend to be ignorant and uneducated in a society that increasingly demands knowledge and skills. They are a far cry from being cartoon "Mommas."

LAMENT

Listen, children:
Your father is dead.
From his old coats
I'll make you little jackets;
I'll make you little trousers
From his old pants.
There'll be in his pockets
Things he used to put there,
Keys and pennies
Covered with tobacco;
Dan shall have the pennies
To save in his bank;
Anne shall have the keys
To make a pretty noise with.
Life must go on,
And the dead be forgotten;
Life must go on,
Though good men die;
Anne, eat your breakfast;
Dan, take your medicine;
Life must go on;
I forget just why.

Edna St. Vincent Millay

Widow

Lynn Caine, in this intimate and personal portrait from her bestselling book, *Widow,* describes the events and experiences following the untimely death of her husband, Martin. Successful as a wife and working mother, she details the surprising degree to which her own identity was shattered following her husband's death. She found that her need for financial security, emotional reassurance, and sexual fulfillment after his death necessitated major alterations in her attitudes and behaviors. It is in her exceptionally clear understanding of grief and its necessity, however, that she expresses for the benefit of thousands of readers the impact of death and the struggle that recovery requires.

BREAKING THE SILENCE   Through all the months of nightmares and anxiety attacks, the woman I presented to the world was calm, coping, cool. Part of it was pride. But more of it was fear. I felt very insecure in a world that could allow Martin to die. What did fate have in store for *me?* I feared the worst. I had a dread of letting people sense my vulnerability. Like an animal, I feared that if anyone were to smell blood, it would be all over with me. No one should suspect how tormented I was, how worried, how very shaky. For if that became apparent, I was lost. I carefully concealed my terrors....

"The widow is the center of a drama," explains sociologist Helena Lopata. "She needs to talk, to work it out." But I couldn't. I dared

not talk about my feelings. Was this how Martin had felt? Had he been as frightened then as I was now? Was this why he had refused to talk about his feelings during all those months of dying?

One of the chores of grief involves going over and over in one's mind the circumstances that led to the death, the details of the death itself. Endless dwelling on the dead person. Memories are taken out and sifted. Finally the widow accepts that fact that her husband is dead. This is the reality. And talking about it helps make it real....

Sociologist Robert Fulton raised this problem in a conference on widowhood. "Whom can you turn to when you are touched by death?" he asked. His discomforting answer was, "There aren't very many people who are prepared to come to your assistance either socially or emotionally. In fact, it is sometimes hard to find anyone who will even talk to you about your loss.".…

Talking helps us absorb less tragic situations, but even then, listeners tend to resist. People scoff at the woman who says, "Let me tell you about my operation." Why? Because it makes them feel uncomfortable. Vulnerable. Such intimations of mortality are frightening to most of us. Our fear outweighs our desire to help.

So from within and without, there are pressures on the widow not to talk. It takes strength to disregard them. Some women have such emotional sturdiness that they immediately set about the work of defining their loss and repeating its circumstances until the cruel edge is blunted enough for them to handle its reality. Other women require months before they can bring themselves to talk about their husbands, about their deaths. And until they can talk, they have not really started on the road to recovery.

There came a day when I knew that if I didn't have someone to talk to, I could not go on. But who? Who was there? Not only could I not talk about my grief, I had no one to talk about it to.

Family? I couldn't. The nuclear family is too small for talking. Our intimate world is so concentrated that when a member dies, our world contracts—sometimes to just one person. Other women have told me that they did not feel close enough or live close enough to the family members outside the nuclear group for those relatives to provide the support and comfort of the extended family of yesteryear.

Friends? Who wants to burden friends with sorrow? Who dares? The most truly helpful service a friend can perform is to listen patiently and sympathetically while the widow works through the various stages of grief. Too often, this is the one thing friends cannot do. It is too much for them. Too painful. They have not been educated to the widow's need to talk....

Other widows? There are widow-to-widow organizations, a relatively new development, formed to give recent widows the benefit of the experience of other widows. Dr. Phyllis R. Silverman, director of a program under the auspices of the Harvard University Medical School, says that most of the women who have benefited from the program emphasize the importance of being able to talk about their feelings. "The volunteer widows are comfortable talking to the new widow about her grief," she says. "They are able to listen, to be empathic and to understand the turmoil of grief."

But independent women, inhibited women, women who prize their privacy may resent this kind of help and regard it as an intrusion. The time was to come when I found tremendous comfort in talking to a widow whom I greatly admired. But she was an old friend. I don't believe I would ever have been able to confide my distress to a stranger who came ringing my doorbell stretching out the hand of widowhood, no matter how warm, how sympathetic she might have been. And in some instances I think this kind of interaction can be dangerous. It is perilously easy for a volunteer widow to be tempted to make a career of widowhood, to find her identity as "widow." And the newly bereaved woman, frantically clutching at any stability, might also be drawn into "professional" widowhood. But this is just my own reaction. The only guide I can offer is that if you think it would be helpful to talk with another widow, then probably it will be.

Religious leaders? I belong to no organized religion. But for those women who are truly religious, yes, their ministers, priests and rabbis may offer sympathy and good counsel and a patient ear. But then again, they may not. Too few have had training or experience in the needs of grief; too many offer the standard sympathetic clichés and fidget when confronted by the raw emotions of the bereaved. In one study of widows, the researchers were startled when woman after woman reported that the least helpful person had been her religious leader. So, by all means, seek consolation and support in religion. But if it is not to be found there, do not blame yourself as being lacking or unworthy. And do not lose hope....

Fortunately, we can turn to the helping professions. And they are aptly named. I would recommend that a widow who, like myself, finds she has difficulty in expressing her feelings and is suffering from this inability to talk, search out a trained therapist. Psychologist, psychiatrist, mental health worker—there are many choices and fees can range from moderate to high. However, women who live in cities with community mental health centers can usually arrange for professional help at minimal cost. The emphasis is on *trained*. Knowledge and objectivity as well as warmth are needed. Professionals will not inject their own unresolved hostilities or anxieties into your life as untrained friends, religious leaders, volunteer widows may do without meaning to....

THE LONELY GOOSE   "From the moment a goose realizes that the partner is missing, it loses all courage and flees even from the youngest and weakest geese. As its condition quickly becomes known to all the members of the colony, the lonely goose rapidly sinks to the lowest step in the ranking order. The goose can become extremely shy, reluctant to approach human beings and to come to the feeding place; the bird also develops a tendency to panic...."

When I read this description of how the greylag goose responds to the loss of its mate in Konrad Lorenz's remarkable book *On Aggression,* I was unpleasantly startled. I didn't want to have that much in common with a goose. One sentence struck me on a particularly raw nerve: "The lonely goose rapidly sinks to the lowest step in the ranking order." That is exactly where I was. I had become a second-class citizen, a member of the invisible minority of widows. And like all members of minority groups, I was deprived—sexually, emotionally, socially, and financially. My very identity was

shaky. At times I felt practically nonexistent.

A male psychiatrist, full of puzzlement, wrote that the "loss of self reported by many widows" was mystifying to him. He quoted one widow as saying, "I feel as if half of myself is missing." Another woman told him of the "great emptiness" she felt.

"What do these statements mean?" the psychiatrist asked. "How can a person be full or empty?"

Only a man could ask these questions. A woman knows the answers. A widow feels empty and incomplete because, like most women, she gained her identity through marriage. And when her husband died, there she was. A widow. Empty. Without her husband to validate her existence. Without an identity of her own. Like geese, widows sink to the lowest step of the "ranking order."

Being a widow is like living in a country where nobody speaks your language. A country that considers you an untouchable. The ten million widows of the United States, despite their numbers, "share the characteristics of other minority groups that are targets of discrimination," says sociologist Helena Lopata. "They are women in a male-dominated society...without mates in a social network of couples."

One woman who was a source of comfort to me had been through a particularly tumultuous widowhood a decade before. I was very touched by her kindness and one day I remarked, "It must be hard for you. This must reopen all your old wounds."

She smiled. "Oh, no, dear. We are a sisterhood. Only women who have been through this can understand."

She was right. And one needs that understanding. Needs it desperately. But it can become addictive. This sisterhood can be dangerously seductive. It needn't be, but a widow must recognize the possibility—in order to avoid it.

I became aware of this through the experience of another widow, a psychiatrist who had always felt that she was very much in touch with her feelings because of her professional training. Nevertheless, when her husband died, she went through the same stages of grief with its denial and anger and craziness that other widows do. And discovered that seductive underground of widows.

"I found a whole new community of women," she told me. "Like an underground current. All the women who are alone. Swirling below the surface. I was never aware of them before. And now, even though I know I should be getting out into the world, that I should build a new life for myself beyond my work, I find that I am relaxing into this community—comfortable, comforted, content."

Her report on sinking into the world of lonely women was like an emotional trigger. It set off a jangle of alarm systems. All kinds of energy came pouring back into me. Like the extra charge of energy that danger unleashes.

A memory flashed through my head. A scene at an airport. I was waiting for my flight to be announced. A woman sat down beside me. Small, well-dressed, somehow birdlike. "Good morning," she said, "I'm Mrs. Wendell Willkie." Even then I was horrified. Her husband had died years before. But he was still providing her identity!

It was a chilling flashback. I thought to myself, "I'm not Mrs. Martin Caine. I'm Lynn Caine. Goddammit. I'm no wounded bird. No goose!"

LIKE A PENIS IN THE BANK   One of the first things I had to set to rights was money. Money matters. It really does. It is right up there with love and security and identity....

Freud is supposed to have said that money is like having a penis in the bank. If so, he knew what he was talking about. Money is power. Strength. Life. It is sexual. I care more about money than I do about sex right now....

Money can't compensate two children for the loss of a father. Money can't reach out in the night and caress you. Money can't come home at night with a briefcase, a twinkle, and a hug. But money can give you ease. And peace of mind.

And I had no peace of mind. Martin had left no insurance....

I can't stress enough how important my job was to me. It was not simply that it was interesting and paid a salary that enabled me to get along. More than that, it gave structure to my life. I had to get up in the morning, get dressed and get to work. Even at my lowest times, when I was torn apart by anxieties and fears, the very fact of having a job gave me emotional security. I belonged somewhere. No matter how alone I was in the world, I had a place where I belonged. Work to do.

The best single bit of advice I can give to other widows may be—keep your job if you have one, and find one if you don't. Even if you have children that need you, get a job. A part-time job, a volunteer job, anything that will provide you with a routine and stability. A paid job, of course, is preferable, both in terms of the money and of one's attitude toward it. I realize that this may be out of the question for some women, but it is the *regularity* of the job that I want to stress. I am convinced that having to go to work every day and act as if I were fine and on an even emotional keel helped me back to normality. When I was working, I had a respite from my fears, whether real or fantasy.

Slowly I began to develop confidence in myself and get my financial affairs in somewhat better order. I had done so many stupid things—partly because I hadn't known any better, but mostly because of the craziness of widowhood—that it was a slow process....

I know I am better off than most widows. But why should any woman face deprivation and anxiety and financial terror because her husband dies? Women must learn to protect themselves and their children. We must stop playing child wife. That role hasn't been valid for a long time.

"YOU'LL GET MARRIED AGAIN"   [The] pressure to remarry, with its implications that I could not manage on my own and that I would not be acceptable unless I did remarry, was the cruelest "consolation" of all—and the most commonly proffered one. "Don't worry, Lynn. You're bound to remarry." I heard it over and over. What right did these eager advice-givers have to tell me what to do? I was a grown woman, nobody's ward. It hurt me. It made me feel unfaithful. I didn't need this meddling. More than anything else, however, it brought home to me the fact that married women regard widows as a threat, just as they regard divorcées as a threat....

There comes a time, as the widow's numbness leaves her, when she discovers that she is ostracized by our couple-oriented society. When she is yearning for comfort, for companionship, to be included in the world of families where she used to belong so naturally, then she finds that she has been excluded from most of the intimacies of her old friends, the social life she used to take for granted. The little dinner parties, the friendly get-togethers on Sundays, the impulsive "why don't we pack up the kids and go for a picnic" call from old friends.

This is not paranoia on my part. Or on any widow's part. It is "customary" for married women to drop widows socially even if they have been good friends, says Dr. Richard Conroy, a psychiatrist at St. Luke's Hospital in New York City. The widow becomes a competitor, a possible thief of the husband's love.

And so the widow is left in her exile, in that ghetto of unwanted lonely women, the one that I recoiled from so abruptly when I realized how easy it was to sink into this world apart, to live among a community of rejects....

Widows have to face up to the fact that they have what sociologist Robert Fulton calls a "spoiled identity." Widows, Fulton explains, "are stigmatized by the death of the ones they loved." It is true. The widow is stigmatized and she has to fight against society's automatic tendency to consider her taboo because her husband is dead. The progression from wife to widow and back to woman is a hard one. It is impossible for some widows and they sink into that lonely ghetto of widowhood until they, too, die.

It is sad that the progression of grief is so much more difficult for widows than for widowers. But there is a reason for it. Men do not think of themselves primarily as husbands and fathers. They have been encouraged to develop their full potential as unique human beings. So when a man becomes a widower it is a truly heartbreaking blow, but it does not spell an end to his whole way of life. He still has his identity, one that has developed through work, through play, through living. Of course men suffer when they lose a beloved wife. From loss of comfort, loss of coddling, loss of companionship. Above all, just as women do, they suffer from loss of love.

But it is easier for men to find love again. It's a matter of statistics. By the time women reach sixty, roughly a third of them are widows, but only a quarter of the men who are sixty are widowed. Not only do men usually marry women who are younger than they are, but women live longer than men. And the older women become, the fewer men there are to go around.

What is the "moral" of all this? I'm afraid the lesson is that women must learn to be more self-sufficient, more whole. Women must prepare themselves to be able to live alone. Because the majority of women will have to, eventually....

SONNET 64

When I have seen by Time's fell hand defaced
The rich proud cost of outworn buried age;
When sometimes lofty towers I see down-razed
And brass eternal slave to mortal rage;
When I have seen the hungry ocean gain
Advantage on the kingdom of the shore,
And the firm soil win of the watery main,
Increasing store with loss and loss with store;
When I have seen such interchange of state,
Or state itself confounded to decay;
Ruin hath taught me thus to ruminate,
That Time will come and take my love away.
   This thought is as a death, which cannot choose
   But weep to have that which it fears to lose.

William Shakespeare

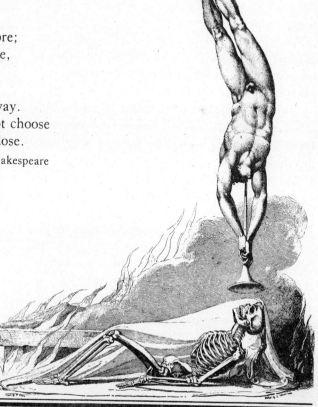

Widow" is a harsh and hurtful word. It comes from the Sanskrit and it means "empty." I have been empty too long. I do not want to be pigeon-holed as a widow. I am a woman whose husband has died, yes. But not a second-class citizen, not a lonely goose. I am a mother and a working woman and a friend and a sexual woman and a laughing woman and a concerned woman and a vital woman. I am a person. I resent what the term widow has come to mean. I am alive. I am part of the world.

If fate had reversed its whim and taken me instead of Martin, I would expect him to be very much part of the world. I cannot see him with the good gray tag of "widower." He would not stand for it for one moment. And neither will I. Not anymore.

But what of love? The warmth, the tenderness, the passion I had for Martin? Am I rejecting that, too?

Ah, that is the very definition of bereavement. The love object is lost. And love without its object shrivels like a flower betrayed by an early frost. How can we live without it? Without love? Without its total commitment? This explains the passionate grief of widowhood. Grief is as much a lament for the end of love as anything else.

Acceptance finally comes. And with it comes peace. Today I carry the scars of my bitter grief. In a way I look upon them as battle stripes, marks of my fight to attain an identity of my own. I owe the person I am today to Martin's death. If he had not died, I am sure I would have lived happily ever after as a twentieth-century child wife never knowing what I was missing. . . .

But today I am someone else. I am stronger, more independent. I have more understanding, more sympathy. A different perspective. I have a quiet love for Martin. I have passionate, poignant memories of him. He will always be part of me. But—

If I were to meet Martin today . . . ?

Would I love him?

I ask myself. Startled. What brought the question to my mind? I know. I ask it because I am a different woman.

Yes. Of course I would. I love him now. But Martin is dead. And I am a different woman. And the next time I love, if ever I do, it will be a different man, a different love.

Frightening.

But so is life. And wonderful.

Martin J. Caine
1920–1971

Martin's obituary never appeared in *The New York Times*. I was not able to pull myself together enough to write it, and I refused to let anyone else do it. Many of Martin's old friends were hurt; some were indignant. And I don't blame them. But most of all, I feel that I let Martin down. I'm sorry. It should have been in the paper for all the people who loved him.

Here it is. For Martin.

Baltimore, Md., May 13, 1971. Martin J. Caine, 50, a New York attorney, died today of cancer in the Marine Hospital (National Institutes of Health). He lived at 239 Central Park West. Mr. Caine, a graduate of New York University Law School, served with the Fifteenth Division of the United States Army Air Force during World War II and was decorated with the Silver Star for gallantry in action. An expert bridge player, he was a runner-up for the Reisinger Cup in 1959 and was a director of the Cavendish Club. He was a member of the New York State Bar Association and served on the Board of Governors of the Bankruptcy Bar Association. He leaves a son, Jonathan, 9, a daughter, Elizabeth, 5, and Lynn, his widow.

Arnold Toynbee

Man's Concern with Death

Epilogue

In this brief excerpt from *Man's Concern with Death,* world renowned historian and social theorist Arnold Toynbee provides a rare glimpse of the challenge engendered by the death of one's mate. For Toynbee, the issue is one of courage and exceptional love. Is it more loving to wish for survivorship or to wish for one's own death? The question is difficult, but in Toynbee's opinion the survivor bears the greatest pain.

When, therefore, I ask myself whether I am reconciled to death, I have to distinguish, in each variant of the situation, between being reconciled to death on my own account and being reconciled to it on the account of the other party. Supposing that I am really reconciled to the prospect of my own death at a ripe old age, am I also reconciled to the prospect of the sorrow and the loneliness that death is going to bring upon my wife if she survives me? Supposing that I feel that people who have risked and suffered premature death deliberately for the sake of fellow human beings have found a satisfactory fulfillment of the possibility of life for themselves, am I reconciled to the loss that their premature deaths have inflicted on mankind, including me? (This question is the theme of George Meredith's novel *Beauchamp's Career.*) Supposing that I feel that the oblivion conferred by senility or insanity has been a boon for someone

who was suffering spiritual agony so long as he was in full possession of his mental and spiritual faculties, am I reconciled to my loss of this friend through his lapse into a death-in-life? And, apart from my personal loss, am I reconciled to the brutal affront to human dignity that nature has committed in choosing this humiliating way of releasing a human being from spiritual suffering?

Finally, am I reconciled to the prospect that I may survive my wife, even supposing that she lives to a ripe old age in full possession of her faculties and without suffering more than the minimum of physical pain that is the normal accompaniment of death even in its easiest forms, with the exception of instantaneous deaths and deaths in sleep? The hard fact is that the ways of dying that impose the lightest ordeal on the person who dies are, by their very nature, the ways that inevitably make the shock for the survivors the severest. I have mentioned an old friend of mine whose unbearable grief for the death of her husband was eventually obliterated by the oblivion of senility. The shock that she had suffered had been extreme. She had found her husband lying dead in his bed one morning. He had appeared to be in normal health the day before; but for some years his heart had been weak, and he had died from heart failure in his sleep—peacefully and almost certainly painlessly; I myself recently had the experience of receiving a severe shock from learning of the sudden death of someone with whom my life had once been intimately bound up, though, in this case too, the death had not been a lingering one or been physically very painful, and had come at an age—six months younger than mine—at which death is to be expected.

If one truly loves a fellow human being, one ought to wish that as little as possible of the pain of his or her death shall be suffered by him or by her, and that as much of it as possible shall be borne by oneself. One ought to wish this, and one can, perhaps, succeed in willing it with one's mind. But can one genuinely desire it in one's heart? Can one genuinely long to be the survivor at the coming time when death will terminate a companionship that is more precious to one than one's own life is—a companionship without which one's own life would be a burden, not a boon? Is it possible for love to raise human nature to this height of unselfishness? I cannot answer this question for anyone except myself, and, in my own case, before the time comes, I can only guess what my reaction is likely to be. I have already avowed a boastful guess that I shall be able to meet my own death with equanimity. I have now to avow another guess that puts me to shame. I guess that if, one day, I am told by my doctor that I am going to die before my wife, I shall receive the news not only with equanimity but with relief. This relief, if I do feel it, will be involuntary. I shall be ashamed of myself for feeling it, and my relief will, no doubt, be tempered by concern and sorrow for my wife's future after I have been taken from her. All the same, I do guess that, if I am informed that I am going to die before her, a shameful sense of relief will be one element in my reaction.

My own conclusion is evident. My answer to Saint Paul's question "O death, where is thy sting?" is Saint Paul's own answer: "The sting of death is sin." The sin that I mean is the sin of selfishly failing to wish to survive the death of someone with whose life my own is bound up. This is selfish because the sting of death is less sharp for the person who dies than it is for the bereaved survivor.

This is, as I see it, the capital fact about the relation between living and dying. There are two parties to the suffering that death inflicts; and, in the apportionment of this suffering, the survivor takes the brunt.

I feel a sudden chill—
In our bedroom, my dead wife's comb,
Underfoot.

Yosa Buson (1715–83)

11.

The Funeral

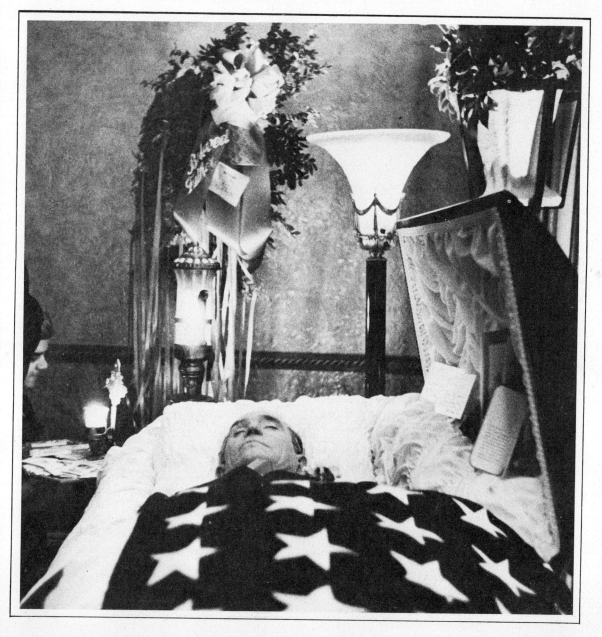

Why a funeral? What is it about this historic ritual for the dead that entails so much time and effort and expense on the one hand while attracting so much resistance, anger, and suspicion on the other? What is a funeral? What does it do? Is it worth the expense? These questions have frequently been raised today not only by a critical minority bent on funeral reform, but also in recent Federal Trade Commission hearings investigating funeral practices in the United States as well as in Senate Subcommittee hearings on small business.

Burial of the dead is, as Pine points out in his article, "The Care of the Dead: An Historical Portrait," an ancient practice among humankind. Recent archeological discoveries at Shanidar, Iraq, show that humans buried their dead ceremoniously sixty thousand years ago. The graves contained tools, weapons, and evidence of flowers. As is well known, the ancient Egyptians, Chinese, and other early peoples also placed food, jewels, and other goods in tombs. Such provisions demonstrated the belief that a person continued to exist after death and was presumed to have the same needs as in life.

While entombment is not a universal practice, it has served in many different societies to express the idea of immortality through the symbolism of the funeral as a rite of incorporation. The concept of immortality implies another world, a world in which the "dead" live. As van Gennep, the Swiss anthropologist, has observed, this corollary belief has meant that historically a primary focus of the funeral has been the "physical" incorporation of the dead with all their attributes, possessions and effects into the "next world." And as a consequence, funeral rituals have been characteristically the most extensively elaborate and expensive of all human customs short of war.

Today such beliefs and practices are contrary to the philosophical and ideological commitment of many people in American society. Many do not believe in a life after death or a world of the dead. Even if they do hold such beliefs, they do not necessarily believe that it is obligatory or felicitous to consume the resources of the living for the doubtful benefit they may have for the dead. For many, the most desirable procedure is also the simplest—one that involves as little material expense and public display as necessary. For a growing number of persons, this means immediate disposition of the body with no public ceremony.

This is essentially the burden of Ruth Mulvey Harmer's discussion in her article "Funerals, Fantasy, and Flight." For her, the Judaic-Christian conception of afterlife was a genuinely spiritual one and early funerals bore testimony to that conception: a simple shroud, no display or public lamentation, and an anonymous burial.

As she records the progress of the Christian funeral, however, she observes that it was not too long before Christian funeral practices embraced many of the features of pagan Rome: elaborate coffins and ostentatious tombs, set against a dramaturgical blaze of pomp, piety, and pageantry.

It is her view that once mortuary management became a vocation and the monopoly of a few, the exploitation of the public at the time of death became the *sine qua non* of the funeral industry.

Testimony to the shared nature of this belief is seen in the Staff Memorandum of the Federal Trade Commission released in 1975, that lists what it considers the general marketing strategy of much of the funeral industry.

The alleged strategy precepts are:

1. Eliminating low-cost funeral alternatives through control of laws, regulations, and codes of ethics
2. Inhibiting the development of memorial societies
3. Refusing to give price information over the telephone
4. Selling the customer unneeded items
5. Confusing the customer

While the ethicality of the funeral industry in the United States is still being debated and the industry has still to have its "day in court," there is no doubt that the belief is widespread that the American funeral director exploits the dead at the expense of the living.

In his article in this section, "The Place of the Funeral: The Role of the Funeral Director in Contemporary America," Howard C. Raether, executive director of the National Funeral Directors Association, takes strong exception to these charges of cupidity and venality—charges that, Pine reminds us in an earlier article, have been leveled against the funeral director, and indeed even his Roman predecessor, the *libitinarius,* since before the beginning of the Christian era. In fact, rites for the dead have been criticized for their lavishness and display since Herodotus, the Greek historian, recorded his visit to Egypt in the fourth century B.C. It has only been in the present century that we have seen concerted efforts to rid society not only of the funeral but also of evidence of death itself by the immediate disposition of the corpse.

Raether believes that the consistent criticism levelled against funerals and funeral directors is due in part to the fact that both the person and the practice represent the unacceptable reality of death. He cites the contradiction inherent in the news media's extensive coverage of a funeral for a President Kennedy or a Dr. King or a Pope and their persistent criticism and denigration of the very ceremonies and rituals they eagerly publicize.

Raether has a point that deserves consideration. In an early study Fulton found that, while almost half of a sample of clergymen believed that a funeral director exploits or takes advantage of a family's grief, less than half reported their opinion as being unqualified. Furthermore, when the clergymen were asked whether they knew personally of such an incident, the proportions were reduced even further, with two out of three respondents indicating that they believed such incidents were isolated rather than general in nature. Moreover, in a report of the hearings of the Senate Subcommittee on Small Business (1976), it was stated that the initial investigation of the funeral industry by the Federal Trade Commission in 1972 began with "less than a dozen" consumer complaints, and that after five years of investigation, in the course of which ten million persons died in the United States, one thousand complaints were registered against the funeral industry. This is a .0001 level of consumer complaint and as the report stated, "This is not only not substantial, it raises questions of even the significance involved."

Raether concedes that some funeral directors are responsible for some of the negative attitudes expressed in the media and elsewhere. Nevertheless, he staunchly defends the necessity and the propriety of the funeral on psychological as well as on sociological grounds.

Raether stresses in his article that there are important aspects of the funeral that we should recognize other than the symbolic expressions of the theological belief in immortality or the dramaturgical incorporation of the dead into an afterlife. The funeral, he argues, is also a rite of social integration and a rite of personal separation. The funerals of President Kennedy and Dr. Martin Luther King, for example, were rites of political integration. The dramatizing of these funerals declared that despite death the world goes on, that the survivors must live, that the social order prevails, and that as a nation we continue in our faith.

But the drama of the funeral tells us more: it proclaims that we have lost someone through death. As such it focuses attention upon the immediate survivors, and to the degree that it does so, it is a rite of separation as well. The loss of a significant other person is a crisis. Medical and behavioral science experts have taught us in recent years that such loss evokes powerful emotions that need to be given proper expression.

Erich Lindemann, Elisabeth Kübler-Ross, Avery Weisman, and other investigators inform us, however, that the acceptance of separation or permanent loss is exceedingly

difficult. Many persons never do recover from permanent loss or ever wholly accept, or indeed ever admit to, the death of a loved one. "How do we get people to accept permanent loss?" is the question.

Two leading British psychiatrists, John Bowlby and Colin Murray Parkes, have pointed out that a major element in acute grief is the denial that the death or the separation has occurred. As they describe it:

> There is a restless searching for the lost person, a constant wandering from room to room as if seeking for the loved individual, often calling his or her name. The necessary tasks and rituals, whether they are religious or not, which surround death serve, however, to bring home gradually to the bereaved person the reality of the loss they have sustained and the knowledge that life will never be quite the same again. Drawing the blinds, viewing the body, attending the funeral service, lowering the coffin into the grave all serve to emphasize the finality and the absoluteness of death, and make denial more difficult.

When it is responsive to the psychological needs of the survivors, the ritual of the funeral can be of aid in ventilating profound emotions and in helping to facilitate the normal dissolution of grief.

Viewing the dead body can be helpful. It is true, as certain critics charge, that there are elements of disguise in the preparation of the body for the funeral. But such disguise is no more the basis of the funeral ceremony than the use of cosmetics or a veil is the basis for the wedding. Rather, the superficial disguise of death can be functional if it helps to move the grieving survivors along from a shocked denial of the death to a recognition and possible final acceptance of it.

The events leading up to the actual interment or cremation of the body are those in which the survivors are invited to gather together, acknowledge the death, share in the grief, participate in the mourning rites, and witness the final disposition of the body. The funeral must be understood in terms of this dramaturgical denouement: the deceased has been removed forever from the living community.

But a word of caution is in order. Funeral rituals can be dysfunctional. In separate studies, two anthropologists, Geertz and Mandelbaum, cite instances in which the insistence on traditional mortuary rites served to disrupt rather than restore the sense of community. Moreover, the editors of this reader have recently concluded a survey of 563 survivors of death: spouses, parents, and children in the Minneapolis–St. Paul area of Minnesota. In brief, the study showed that funeral ceremonies and rituals may be differently perceived and received in the death-grief constellation. Care must be taken not to define too narrowly what funeral rites or behaviors are appropriate for the bereaved. The question is:

is the funeral, as a rite of integration or separation, beneficial? Ultimately, the answer depends upon the individual survivor and the circumstances surrounding a death. For some survivors, the study showed the loss of an elderly relative is an occasion for the barest acknowledgment of the death and the most expeditious disposal of the body. In such an instance of what could be described as a "low grief" death, loss can be slight and grief muted. The sudden unexpected death of a child or of a young husband, on the other hand, may be perceived as premature and unjust and/or denied or resented by the survivors. Such a death could be termed a "high grief" loss. The social and emotional needs of family, friends, and community in such instances are infinitely greater and the potential problems of the survivors more extensive than in the case of a "low grief" loss. On the other hand, "no grief" may be felt by a relative who is privately relieved or pleased at the death while "improper grief" may be experienced by a person who is not allowed to mourn publicly. Insensitivity to the nuances of grief and loss—to the intensity or absence of grief and the social expectations of the bereaved—can only intensify the difficulties of the survivors.

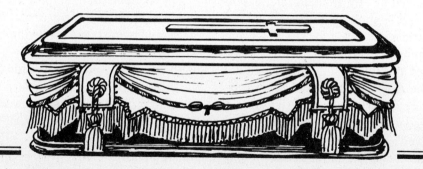

The Care of the Dead

A Historical Portrait

Dr. Vanderlyn Pine is chairman and associate professor of sociology at the State University of New York, New Paltz. In addition to his academic training and many studies in the area of death and dying, Dr. Pine brings to his topic more than a century of family traditions of caring for the dead as community funeral directors.

Little is known about the origin of the care of the dead except that it appears to have come about very early in man's history. An anthropological investigation in Iraq reports apparent funeral practices of the Neanderthal man. This discovery dates man's concern about caring for the dead to at least sixty thousand years ago. We need not go back so far in our past to discuss the care of the dead, for we have well documented reports from numerous early civilizations.

ANCIENT TIMES   Ancient Egyptian society had an intricate system of care for the dead which was carried out by an elaborate, extensive division of labor. Undertaking and embalming specialists cared for the dead and carried out many of the funeral arrangements. A well-defined division of labor emerged for the care of the dead and their surviving relatives; however, its primary concern was the dead. It is generally claimed that the Egyptians preserved the dead by embalming because of their belief that after death the soul left the body to travel through "time" and eventually came back to reinhabit the dead body. Thus, for the Egyptians, the emergence of embalming reflected the practice or the belief. In any case, the care of the dead was provided in an essentially bureaucratic fashion.

The preparations of the ancient Greek dead were made by the family, and although embalming was not practiced, perfumes and spices were used to mask the odor of putrefying flesh. Friends and relatives provided flowers for the dead, and special clothing marked the mourning of the bereaved. The Greeks viewed the dead body largely to ensure that death actually had occurred and that the body had not been molested. Later in Greek history, cremation was practiced because of the belief that flames set the soul free. Throughout their history, the Greeks dealt with death in a personal way, with certain experienced family members and friends acting as funeral experts.

The ancient Romans practiced both burial and cremation at various times; in either case, the body lay in state for viewing by the public. The wealthy were cared for by a professional undertaker or *libitinarius*. This specialist was the direct ancestor of the modern funeral director, and in the large cities his work was essentially bureaucratic. The *libitinarius* took care of annointing or embalming, supplied professional mourners and mourning clothes, and arranged for the details of the funeral procession. The practices of the ancient Romans have had a direct impact on the funeral practices of the contemporary Western world, especially our notions of splendor, pomp, and ceremony. The care of the dead was the direct responsibility of an expert server who carried out the many facets of his work as a service occupation practioner. Habenstein and Lamers sum up the impact of the Romans as follows:

> Roman influence upon modern funeral practices is to be regarded in the last instance not so much for the *content* of those death beliefs which might have been transmitted to the Western world, but for the *occupational models* useful to mass societies exhibiting an urban way of life. Most important from the point of view of this study is the secular functionary, the Roman undertaker, who as arranger, manager, and director of funeral affairs, as well as supplier of mortuary paraphernalia, sets a pattern of occupational behavior meaningful to the funeral director of mid-twentieth century. Additionally, the administrative measures of the Romans have stood as a source of suggestion to modern societies in which a body of mortuary law has been felt necessary to insure adequate public protection in the matter of the disposal of the dead.[1]

The early Hebrews believed that man was composed of two elements, flesh and breath, and that upon death the flesh returned to dust while the breath persisted. To the Hebrews, cremation was considered an indignity to the body. . . . Burial either with or without a coffin was practiced and perfuming of the dead, and, for hygienic reasons, burial on the evening of the day of death. These tasks were carried out by experienced members of the family, and the level of experience was determined largely by

the number of times such people provided this care. After the dead were prepared, professional mourners helped carry out the funeral. Funerary details and the care of the dead were largely the responsibility and duty of the deceased's family, and expertise was determined primarily by personal experience.

Early Christian burial practices were unpretentious. Friends and relatives commonly viewed the dead and practiced the longstanding Jewish custom of watching or "waking" the dead which had arisen largely from the fear of burying someone alive. An important belief among the early Christians was that death does not end all human relationships, but merely represents a transition from one type of relationship to another.

In about the fourth century A.D., the organized church established feast days to commemorate publicly and solemnly the death anniversaries of the martyrs. From this time on the Christian funeral developed into a set of actions organized as part of the wider operation of the developing urban society. Although most of the funeral functions of the early Christians were carried out by relatives of the dead, they were generally done under the direction of the clergy. The clergy's supervision was often a bureaucratically oriented service; however, it was not provided primarily for [the] fee. The early priests were careful to give the appearance of personal involvement . . . There was a merging of personal service in a bureaucratic setting. This led to the development of minor, bureaucratically organized functionaries to tend to some of the specific needs of caring for the dead. Even though it has been suggested that such functionaries were the forerunners of the modern funeral director, the evidence indicates that this distinction belongs to the *libitinarii* and their assistants of ancient Rome.

1. Robert W. Habenstein and William M. Lamers, *Funeral Customs the World Over* (Milwaukee, 1966), pp. 45-46.

THE MIDDLE AGES   As time passed the Christian Church emerged from persecution and became increasingly institutionalized. The simple burial customs of the early Christians gave way to an imposing dignity that expressed the feeling of the importance of the Church and its members. As society dispersed and grew, and urban life began to exert more influence on specific segments of the population, local funeral customs evolved that did not necessarily conform to those practiced when Christianity was a small sect in the vicinity of the Mediterranean Sea.

During the Middle Ages the Christian version of embalming included removing some body organs, washing the body with water, alcohol, and pleasant smelling oils, chemically drying and preserving the flesh, wrapping the body in layers of cloth sealed with tar or oak sap, and mummifying in a way similar to the Egyptians. These tasks were performed by specialists who acted solely as embalmers. Apparently, there was relatively little bureaucratic handling of formal arrangements, and most funerary services were kin-provided and essentially personal in nature.

Leonardo da Vinci developed a system of venous injection for preservation of the dead body to enable him to draw anatomical plates. His method served as an inspiration to the early medical embalmers whose practices later gave rise to many modern embalming procedures. . . .

By the end of the seventeenth century the English undertaker was recognized as a tradesman, even though his was neither a well-defined nor highly specialized trade. As [the undertaker's] work become more intricate and additional tasks were shuffled into his hands, [undertaking in urban centers often] became a regular service occupation. In the eighteenth century there emerged in small towns part-time undertakers whose full-time occupations were such things as livery stable owner, carpenter, and cabinet maker.

At about this time the English funeral developed into a full-fledged performance. Mutes, mourners, and livery men were gathered and directed in an effort to provide a "proper setting" for an atmosphere of heavy gloom and despair. Thus, the role of the English undertaker became even more diversified and all-emcompassing, with a more complex set of practices. In urban centers the work began to take on a bureaucratic nature.

EARLY AMERICA   Funeral behavior in colonial America generally included church funeral services, with brief prayers said at graveside ceremonies. Early New Englanders seemed to accept death as natural and inevitable and saw no reason to disguise ceremonies, since "the grave was as familiar as the cradle." Funeral ceremonies were essentially simple, and the mourners actively participated by accompanying the coffin to the grave and filling the grave with dirt. The mourning process took on an extensive social character, and rings, scarves, gloves, purses, and needlework products were given away as tributes to the dead. The communal atmosphere emphasized the personal service aspects of the work.

American undertaking evolved by gradually adding to itself specific funeral tasks previously carried out largely by other occupational groups or by the family. For instance, certain members of the community became expert at the "laying out" of the dead after a number of such experiences. Some seemed to feel an informal responsibility to offer their knowledge and services to others in the community, and by the end of the eighteenth century the laying out of the dead in larger cities had become a specialty, with certain of the attendant bureaucratic elements, such as impersonal service in funeral firms handling many funerals.

During the nineteenth century the American undertaker became something other than a jack-of-all-trades. He brought together the functions which formerly were scattered among and performed by several trades into a single and unified occupation. An important reason for his rise to prominence was the church's un-

willingness or inability to maintain authority over all aspects of the burial process. Furthermore, largely because of urbanization and changes in the social order, families were increasingly unlikely to do such things themselves.

Nineteenth-century American funerals were intensely gloomy and distressing for the bereaved. As a result, there emerged a desire to

Because I could not stop for Death
He kindly stopped for me.
The Carriage held but just Ourselves—
And Immortality.

We slowly drove—He knew no haste
And I had put away
My labor and my leisure too,
For His Civility—

We passed the School, where Children strove
At Recess—in the Ring—
We passed the Fields of Gazing Grain—
We passed the Setting Sun—

Or rather—He passed Us—
The Dews drew quivering and chill—
For only Gossamer, my Gown—
My Tippet—only Tulle—

We paused before a House that seemed
A Swelling of the Ground—
The Roof was scarcely visible—
The Cornice—in the Ground—

Since then—'tis Centuries—and yet
Feels shorter than the Day
I first surmised the Horses' Heads
Were toward Eternity—

Emily Dickinson

provide a "beautiful" setting in which to experience loss, grief, and bereavement during the funeral. In cities, undertakers were called immediately upon someone's death. Generally, they came to the home and directed the funeral in the presence of and with the cooperation of the deceased's family. Embalming often was carried out in the home, and there were early attempts to "restore" the faces of the dead with liquid tints that had been developed by the embalming chemical fluid companies.

One of the main reasons for the growth in popularity of embalming stemmed from the Civil War, when large numbers of soldiers died far from home. Since most families wanted their dead brought to their own burial grounds for final services, medical embalmers emerged on and around the battlefields of the Civil War. At the conclusion of the war the assassination of President Abraham Lincoln brought about new public awareness of embalming. The funeral procession with Lincoln's body on display extended from Washington, D.C., to Springfield, Illinois. As it progressed through many portions of the Northeast and Midwest, people along its path became aware that it was possible to keep and view the dead for long periods of time. Although buried in 1865, Lincoln's body was so well embalmed that as late as 1899 it was viewed and was proclaimed to be in a perfect state of preservation. For such reasons, embalming became a more important aspect of the American way of death.

At the end of the nineteenth century states began to pass licensing legislation to regulate the practice of embalming. State boards of health began to be concerned about such things as burial and cremation permits, and the filing of death certificates increasingly became required by state law. Thus, in addition to the technological, occupational, and social changes through which undertaking and embalming passed, the nineteenth century brought about legislative pressures which contributed to the growth of undertaking as an occupational specialty group.

During this era, funeral services normally were conducted in the deceased's home. The undertaker would bring all the supplies and paraphernalia and set them up in the living room or parlor. A defined period of mourning restricted social activity for the bereaved surviving relatives. A basket of flowers was hung on the front door, replacing a crepe badge which had been an earlier mark of mourning.

Religious services usually were held at the home or in the church; in either case, the funeral concluded with a procession to the cemetery. An important new aspect of the undertaker's job developed at this time. Someone had to remove all signs of the funeral from the home while it was vacant for the funeral procession. Thus, when it returned home from the cemetery the family had no further tasks. The undertaker bore that burden.

Because of the need for paraphernalia and other funeral equipment, funeral establishments began to appear in urban areas, and in small towns undertakers began to use their stores' back room, their barn, or their living room to provide facilities for those families to whom the home no longer was appropriate for the laying out of the dead. Usually, undertakers used a specific (large) room in which to lay out the dead and in which the bereaved could greet callers. This room replaced the parlor formerly used in the home of the deceased; thus, the undertaker's establishment came to be called a "funeral parlor." In this homelike setting, the undertaker supplied the casket, carriages, mourning materials, memorial cards, flowers, chairs, robes, pillows, and crucifixes, and he generally was responsible for the direction of the funeral services.

The notion of the "funeral director" arose in the late nineteenth century, with several factors contributing to the development of this new occupation. First, occupational mobility and the decline of the extended family led to the development of smaller houses and other living units. This change gave rise to a need for a building large enough to house big families gathered for mourning. Funeral parlors were built or existing houses modified to take into account the new needs of the bereaved and the caretakers of the dead.

Second, as embalming became more sophisticated, the equipment to carry out this task became increasingly difficult to take into private homes. Embalming became a procedure in the laboratory or "preparation room" of the newly developed buildings housing the funeral director's equipment and supplies.

Third, transportation problems increased the difficulty of gathering the mourners for the funeral ceremonies at a church. Moreover, since the church did not encourage the development of special rooms for the care of the dead, funeral directors found an additional reason to develop facilities to house such activities.

A combination of the need for a large parlor, a special laboratory, and a chapel-like facility evolved into what has become the present-day funeral home. This provided additional impetus for a specialist to carry out the new specialized tasks in such a setting. The funeral director came to look upon himself as being useful to society rather than as merely a provider of merchandise and equipment. This feeling seems to have led to the development of notions of administrative and managerial skills and the practices of funeral counseling as well as directing. It contributed to the occupational

orientation as the provider of services, that is, as a professional personal service practitioner.

These trends in America's care of the dead have led to contemporary American patterns....

CONTEMPORARY AMERICA   There are approximately twenty-two thousand funeral establishments in the United States and approximately fifty thousand people licensed to practice funeral directing. Until the past thirty to fifty years death occurred at home in familiar surroundings in the presence of kin or close friends, and funerals were community events. Times have changed, however. Each year proportionately more people die in institutions instead of their own homes, and almost all of the dead are cared for by funeral directors in funeral homes. For present-day Americans, one of the common features of death is the employment of a funeral director.

The heterogeneity of the United States is reflected by differing funeral practices. Funeral customs in the United States vary because of geographic region, ethnic background, religious affiliation, and economic and social class. Religious and ethnic groups tend to maintain unique traditional funeral practices, thus adding to regional, economic, and social variations. There are differing state laws and regulations which to some extent govern funeral practices. For the present, commonly reported practices will be described; however, these may not be completely accurate for a particular area of the country or a specific group of people.

Depending on where, how, and when death occurs, it is common to notify a physician or the police. Then, the cause of death is medically certified, either by a physician, a coroner, or a medical examiner. Finally, the family of the deceased chooses a funeral director.

Generally, the choice is ethnically oriented, but, at times, may reflect social class, status, and geographic differences.

The dead body usually is removed from the place of death by the funeral director and taken to a funeral home. There, it is customary to embalm or otherwise sanitize through disinfection. Embalming includes dressing the body and "restoring it" (applying cosmetics) in an attempt to render the deceased lifelike and socially presentable for a public appearance.

The immediate family of the deceased generally makes the necessary arrangements for the funeral. For example, the place, time, and type of funeral service, the place of burial or cremation, and the type of casket, are a few of the choices that must be made. These and other elements of the funeral are interrelated and seem to be based on social class, ethnic, and religious attitudes.

Viewing the dead is widespread in the United States and occurs in all social class levels. Usually, it is done during specified hours at the funeral home; but it may take place at the home of the deceased, or occasionally at the church where the service is to be held. During the viewing, friends and relatives spend time with the bereaved family. Religious and ethnic differences appear to be the bases for varying attitudes about the length of viewing and the attendant mourning customs. American viewing customs constitute a period of visitation for the immediate survivors, their kin, and their friends.

Most funerals in the United States include a religious service. At times there may be a service by a fraternal or other organization, and occasionally there is no service. The religious services are held either in the funeral home, the home of the deceased, or the church. With few exceptions, there is little active participation, other than attendance, by family or friends at the funeral. This is a uniquely American custom, and in many parts of the world the family actually carries out these final acts.

Generally, at the cemetery there are religious committal rites. After the committal, it is common for the family to leave the cemetery with the casket still above ground. After the departure of the mourners, the funeral director supervises the lowering of the casket into the grave. As with other parts of the funeral, there is seldom active group participation at the cemetery except for the reciting of widely known prayers.

Earth burial is the most common means of final disposition, chosen for over 92 percent of the deaths annually. Cremation is chosen for less than 5 percent of the deaths annually. Usually cremations are handled like burials, with the exception that the procession to the crematory is often smaller and occasionally includes just the hearse.

Funeral expenditure is divided among the funeral director, crematory or cemetery, clergyman, and florist. The largest portion generally goes to the funeral director. His charges usually include the casket selected by the bereaved family, his professional services, use of the necessary equipment and facilities, motor equipment, and other related items. This is unlike many societies in which funeral expenditure goes to other sources, such as religious or social groups or governmental agencies.

An historical portrait of the care of the dead, emphasizing some of the social crosscurrents that gave rise to the occupation of funeral directing, helps clarify the occupation of funeral directing and the emergence of the funeral director as an occupational specialist in present-day society.

Ruth Mulvey Harmer

Funerals, Fantasy, and Flight

Ruth Harmer, in her vigorous contribution to this section of the Reader, astutely observes that "the beginning of wisdom comes only with the acknowledgment of death." She is professor of English literature at California Polytechnic Institute, Pomona, and one of the founders of the Continental Association. In the early 1960s, Harmer, in company with Jessica Mitford and LeRoy Bowman, spearheaded the funeral reform movement in the United States, a movement that she has continued to endorse and lead, as the following article amply testifies.

The beginning of wisdom, religious and moral philosophers say, comes only with the acknowledgment of death. Until that ultimate reality has been faced, no man can hope to achieve the good life. That acknowledgment is too fearsome for most of us to make, and the extent to which we seek refuge in fantasy and flight is stunningly revealed by our funeral practices. Consider the following accounts of final arrangements:

The first was given to me by an elderly neighbor, the wife of a man so badly afflicted with arthritis that he had been forced into early retirement from his job as a semiskilled worker. She was working as a practical nurse—an occupation not calculated to encourage conspicuous consumption—to supplement his modest social security benefit. Yet out of their poverty-level income the couple had paid fifty dollars a month for three years to a large cemetery-mortuary establishment, and the contract required payment for another two years. Mistaking my amazement for applause, as she finished her recital of their "future," she smiled: "It is wonderful, dear, isn't it? Just think! That takes care of everything—even the clothes and the flowers and the minister."

The second was called to my attention by my husband, who teaches at a high school in a predominantly Mexican-American section of Los Angeles. A student—a serious boy who was helping his grandmother care for two younger brothers and a sister—had been set upon and killed by a group of toughs who had mistaken him for a member of a rival gang. "To do something nice for Tommy," fellow students raised more than a thousand dollars at a "dance in." Down to the last penny, the money went to pay funeral expenses—to the apparent approval of everyone concerned, including the grandmother who had to send the other children to a foster home because without out Tommy's financial contribution she could no longer afford to keep them.

The third account, given to me by a nun from Denver, involved the widow of a laborer of Middle European background. Without savings, without insurance, the woman could not provide her husband with the kind of funeral that she and her neighbors believed he "deserved." The undertaker obligingly offered to keep the body until she could raise the money "to do it right." That took her eight months, working as a domestic. The widow was, Sister Loretto Madden told me, entirely pleased with the affair—even though she was unable to take time off from work to attend the funeral.

Although other far more extravagant case histories could have been selected, those three typical and unchronicled ones sum up rather tellingly the motivations responsible for the elaborate nature of American funerals: the belief, particularly of the deprived, that death is an escape from the coffin of life that warrants celebration; the desire to elevate a member of the group to heroic stature; the need of the bereaved to punish himself or herself and to avert charges of "not caring" by departing from accustomed ways.

Those attitudes, by no means peculiarly "American," have shaped the size and opulence of funerals all over the world. Although funerals in this country have been singled out for sharp criticism, it is apparent to persons even slightly familiar with other cultures that elaborate rites are and have been in vogue for centuries—millennia—in the Orient, the Middle East, Latin America, and most of Western Europe. Actually, about the only contributions American undertakers have made, have been such technological "refinements" as permanent waves for corpses, hospital beds in coffins so that bodies can be cranked up to welcome guests, and drive-in funeral homes—which now make it possible for mourners to sit in their cars while paying last respects to the "loved ones" on display in mortuary windows. It is possible, however, that the blatant association of sex with death and funerals is a distinctly American innovation—and has been since the writings of Edgar Allan Poe set the tone in the middle of the nineteenth century.

What is unique about funeral practices in this country today is their cost. The hard-sell tactics mercilessly employed have made the business of selling funeral services a $2 billion a year boom and the business of buying them a crushing financial "bust" for the survivors of most of the 1,800,000 citizens who die each year. And with funerals, as with other escape mechanisms—alcohol or drugs—there is a high price to pay the morning after.

In spite of the inevitability of death, it is very difficult to attempt a rational discussion of final rites; this is partly the result of the unwillingness to acknowledge mortality. Largely, however, it is because of the semantic confusion generated by industry public relations experts. They have created the belief that the "right sort of person" does not question costs "at a time like that." They have fostered the illusion that death is not death (in industry parlance, people "pass on" or "step out of the picture") if the magic rituals are observed. They have persuaded people to accept the notion that indulging in conspicuous consumption is not only the *spiritual* way to behave when a death occurs, but is a vote of confidence in the *American free enterprise system*. In point of fact, of course, the latter notions are also delusions.

When I was doing research into the origins of modern funerals while writing *The High Cost of Dying* (1963), I was startled and impressed by the extent to which Judaism and Christianity departed so radically from the ostentatious rituals favored by all the ancient societies which left records. The epics—those oldest and most spacious of literary forms, which served not merely as entertainment but as guides to conduct—are preoccupied with celebrations of the heroic death. Thousands of the clay tablets on which the *Gilgamesh Epic* was inscribed four thousand years ago, more than of third of the lines of the *Iliad*, an impressive portion of Vergil's *Aeneid,* the entire conclusion of the *Beowulf,* and many of the most moving *laisses* of the *Song of Roland* are concerned exclusively with the funerals and burials of heroes. All of them—Babylonian-Sumerian, Greek, Roman, Anglo-Saxon, Old French—are alike in their insistence that elaborite obsequies constitute guarantees that the shadows will possess all of the rights and privileges possessed by the substance. Upper-caste pagan ancients held this world so much more desirable than the terrifying after-world of death that they used every item that came to hand and mind—food, animals, slaves, wine, blood, clothing, hair, jewels, women, weapons—to link the two existences inseparably and to keep social status intact.

Morally more sophisticated, the Jewish and later the Christian leaders looked coldly upon the world and found it wanting. Unable to free themselves from the knowledge that hunger, sickness, poverty, misery, and injustice were inescapable facts of the universe to which their Creator had exposed them—one in which vice was often rewarded far more handsomely than virtue—they fashioned an afterward that contradicted the *status quo*—a world of perfect justice where the will of a just and perfect God would be done.

The Judaic-Christian conception of the hereafter was not merely a *spirit* world, but a genuinely spiritual one. All of the values and the triumphs of the material universe were perfectly irrelevant in it. Therefore, admittance could not be gained by material bribes, nor could status be determined by material possessions. The poorest man, if he had loved God and his fellows well, was eligible for a highest place. Consequently, lavish funerary display was not merely beside the point; it was blasphemous.

Orthodox funerals still reflect the simplicity held desirable since the burial of Moses set the pattern. A simple shroud is favored; if a coffin is used, it must contain an opening to facilitate the return of "dust to dust." So, too, the Christian funeral eschewed display. Most of the early Christians were buried anonymously and indistinguishably in the winding labyrinths under Rome that offered the living a reasonably safe place of worship. Today, evidence of that starkness is still visible. Only occasionally can it be noted that one grave is set apart from the others—by the scratching of a name or by a design pressed into the mortar. The quiet tone of the early Christian funerals contrasted sharply with the wild lamenting of pagan rites. After all, had not the "real" person—the soul—passed into a new state of glory? Neither mourners nor morticians were hired; all of the members of the community shared the responsibility of providing the funeral.

It was one thing to declare theologically that all men were equal in the sight of God. It was another—particularly for persons of high degree—to accept that there was no way of getting special preferment. And just as the Jewish funerals acquired adjuncts and overtones of those of the hated Egyptians, so those of the Christians became increasingly like those of their Roman persecutors—featuring elaborate coffins instead of shrouds, black drapery instead of white, hired mourners, elaborate tombs. As Robert W. Habenstein and William M. Lamers point out in *The History of American Funeral Directing* (1955), the final services for the Empress Theodolinda in 595 A.D. contrast remarkably with those of Christ and the early Christians. Rites for the friend of Pope Gregory the Great lasted for more than a week, centering around her richly dressed body which lay in state in the Cathedral of Monza—emphasizing pomp, pageantry, and preoccupation with the mortal remains.

As serfs and peasants moved out of feudal

darkness into the light of dawning democracy, they, too, began to discard spiritual *egalitarianism,* as kings, prelates, and barons had done. Judy O'Grady might not be able to live like the colonel's lady, but—by earth, if not heaven—she could die like her. O'Grady, whose lifestyle was modeled more by James Joyce than Homer, yearned at the end of his Odyssey for a moment of glory in the heroic style. Thus death, once the great leveler, became the lever for social elevation.

Clergymen—albeit, some reluctantly—went along with the changes: Jewish, Catholic, Protestants of all denominations. They were reluctant to press their followers' faith too far; and a good many of them seemed as eager as the most wavering of their flock to curry favor with those in the Beyond as well as to impress those in the Here and Now.

After undertaking became a vocation and the financial consequences of ostentatious display became apparent, some began to speak up boldly—urging, even insisting that believers return to original practices. The worldwide depression in the 1920s and 1930s accelerated the change in some countries— England and the northern European countries. Spurred on by their example, many clerics in this country decided to act. But by that time, the price was very high, since business pressures were combined with people's doubts and fears and vanities to "upgrade" funerals. Those who acted, found themselves being attacked as un-American as well as irreligious. An interesting indication of the violence reform measures encountered was given by Reverend Hugh Stevenson Tigner in *The Christian Century* in 1938. The year before, members of the Ministers Association in Middletown, New York decided to speak up against the moral and economic aspects of funeral practices. They would do that in con-

cert since, he said, "It would have been suicide for one of us to have done this alone." The "bitterly hostile" response was more than they had bargained for. Mr. Tigner reported that local undertakers enlisted aid from the regional trade association; out-of-town clergymen were called by undertakers to conduct services "whenever the family would allow it." The undertakers persuaded the business community of Middletown to fight the ministers' action, which was held to be "bordering on subversion."

Only the bravest among the clergymen could hold out against that sort of thing. And only the bravest did. But the groundwork that had been laid in the 1930s for a religious revolt—more properly, for a religious revival— continued to grow, as more and more clergymen began to question the "paganism" of funeral practices and to protest the tendency of businessmen to usurp their roles as spiritual guides. A study made by Dr. Robert Fulton in 1958 for the National Funeral Directors Association revealed that 51 percent of Protestant clerics and 41 percent of Catholic priests responding to his questions "believed that the funeral director exploits or takes advantage of a family's grief in selling funeral services." Moreover, Dr. Fulton (1961) noted in an article in *Social Forces,* clergymen found it "galling personally" as well as contrary to the tenets of their faith to have undertakers taking complete charge of funerals and even offering the services in their own chapels.

The exploitation by undertakers was also being strongly protested by others: consumers and persons associated with social welfare agencies, insurance companies, and other organizations with first-hand knowledge of the consequences of extravagance. For the funeral industry is no less at odds with traditional principles of economics than of religion. At the heart of our American capitalistic system is a belief in the effectiveness of competition. That belief was a major cause of the American Revolution and played an important role in bringing on the Civil War. Not long after the resolution of that, the Sherman Antitrust measure was enacted to guarantee that competition, the vital keystone of our democratic society would not be dislodged. Lamentably, the funeral industry leaders—who had discovered during the Civil War that death could be the basis of a booming business—were seeking ways to subvert the spirit of the law.

The difficulties were great. No open-ended demand could be created for funerals as could be done for other goods and services. Indeed, a rising standard of living, greater availability of medical care, new discoveries in drugs and medical science, education—all worked effectively to lower demand. Moreover, industry control was widely scattered. The typical undertaker was truly a small businessman, owning a single establishment and performing services for clients personally known to him. (Quite often his undertaking business was a sideline—an adjunct to his trade as carpenter or furniture dealer or general merchandiser.) The big businessmen in the industry were chiefly the manufacturers of caskets and hearses, who had an understandable interest in protecting their "salesmen."

Under normal circumstances, a static demand accompanied by improvements in technology and transportation results in marginal operators falling by the wayside. Not so in the funeral industry. In 1927, Elmer Davis reported that an N.F.D.A. official had told him that only ten thousand were needed to do the job; in that year, there were more than twenty-three thousand undertakers. Dr. LeRoy Bowman (1959) reported in *The American Funeral* that in 1950 W. M. Krieger

of the National Selected Morticians, Inc. told him: "There are too many firms in this business...two thousand could do all the business in America." In that year there were about twenty-five thousand undertaking establishments. Today, almost as many exist.

To maintain the marginal operator a condition perilously close to price-fixing had to be established. And it was. By setting floors below which no member of the industry might provide services, all could be guaranteed a living. The owners of chains and very large establishments would, incidentally, be assured of astronomical profits. In more concrete terms, price floors last year perpetuated in business entrepreneurs who had only twelve or fifteen cases. What they did for the profits of "giants" like Forest Lawn and Pierce Brothers in Los Angeles, both of which boasted of about seven thousand cases each, is a matter known only to themselves and the Internal Revenue Service.

Funeral directors and the trade associations deny that any such price fixing exists. However, several years ago a Senate Subcommittee headed by Philip A. Hart held "anticompetitive" such practices as the prohibition of price advertising. As a result of a suit brought by the Department of Justice, price advertising was restored. A more direct example of "anticompetitive" practices was brought to my attention in 1961 at California State Polytechnic College, where I was teaching. Months earlier, sixteen football players and the team's student manager had been killed when a plane flying them home from an Ohio game crashed on takeoff. All of the mortuaries in Toledo had received "a share of the business." Curiously enough, however, the charge for preparing the bodies and providing caskets for them to be flown back to California was almost uniform. Only three bills sent to the committee appointed to raise funds showed variations from the $1225 sum that was standard; one was for $1240, another for $1262.50; a third for $1257.22.

For some years the industry operated in flagrant violation of the antitrust laws to keep members in line—principally through the withholding of supplies. Although no instances of that have been reported in this country in recent years, it has happened in Canada. When I visited Vancouver in 1964, members of the large memorial society there told me that after local undertakers refused to provide them with services, one of the members had obtained an undertaker's license. He "found it impossible" to purchase caskets; as a result, he was forced to make them himself in his garage. Usually, in this country, more subtle pressures are applied. James C. Bleitz, president of Bleitz Funeral Home in Seattle, told me that after he agreed to provide low-cost funeral services for the People's Memorial Association in 1939, he was "ostracized" by colleagues in his trade association. He persisted, however, and his is now the largest undertaking establishment in the state.

In return for such loyalty, the industry's trade associations have worked effectively to increase demand. Special laws in some areas have made it very difficult for persons to donate their bodies to medical schools and other research institutions; special laws in various states have made embalming and caskets mandatory even when cremation is desired. As a result of the lobbying of the cemetery industry, in California and three

The Lord is my shepherd; I shall not want.
He maketh me to lie down in green pastures;
He leadeth me beside the still waters.
He restoreth my soul;
He leadeth me in the paths of righteousness for his name's sake.
Yea, though I walk through the valley of the shadow of death,
I will fear no evil: for thou art with me;
Thy rod and thy staff they comfort me,
Thou preparest a table before me in the presence of mine enemies:
Thou anointest my head with oil; my cup runneth over.
Surely goodness and mercy shall follow me all the days of my life,
And I will dwell in the house of the Lord for ever.

Psalm 23

other states ashes may not be scattered—even in accord with public health regulations. "The law was," one California cemetery owner told me frankly, "a real bonanza." As a result of lobbying activities, bodies of servicemen who die overseas are automatically shipped home—despite the protests of many of their relatives and despite the fact that the government maintains a large network of national cemeteries on foreign soil.

Supplementing the effort to increase demand has been an effort to obtain higher government subsidies for funerals. Government allowances have been increased for veterans and for persons covered by social security so that combined benefits are now more than $500 and may be expected to rise—as government benefits did recently in some parts of Canada, where the issue was the price paid for funerals of persons who died without funds. In some parts of the United States, excessive sums are taken to pay for funeral expenses when persons die intestate; for example, in Los Angeles those with estates of up to $1500 are allowed at least $500 by the public adminstrator for funerals; those with estates valued at from $1500 to $7500, $750. What is left of the money, often a small sum, goes to the state.

Very little supervision of the funeral industry is now made. The state regulatory agencies are usually made up entirely of persons from within the industry. And it is not likely that they will bear witness against one of their number—not in an industry where the ultimate "sin" is to blacken the reputation of an insider. "Always remember," as Mr. Krieger told undertakers at a state convention in California several years ago, "if we can keep a solid front in our dealings with the public we can create the finest public relations that anybody ever dreamed about." Where there is regula-

tion by public relations, there is no regulation.

In addition to all those factors working against public interest, there are others that allow consumers to be manipulated into consent. One is ignorance of the law. Funeral directors in California for several sessions of the legislature have fought very hard to prevent the enactment of Senator Anthony Beilenson's funeral reform bill which proposes, among other measures, that undertakers be required to inform persons of the legal demands. In his files, in my files, and in the files of the Continental Association of Funeral and Memorial Societies are hundreds of protests from persons asserting that they were led to believe that all kinds of unnecessary services were legally required by the country and by the state.

In any normal business transaction, buyers enjoy some advantages: there is no urgency; they are not irrational; they are free to choose and to reject. Generally speaking, they are without those advantages when they go to make funeral arrangements. Since that is done only after the undertaker has possession of the body of the deceased, purchasers are in the position of "take it or else." Occasionally some determined persons do shop around. A friend of mine and her brother, a retired police captain, did just that. Realizing that the selection room into which they had been led by a salesman was wired so that even though he had excused himself he could hear everything they said, the brother wrote a note: "Let's get out of here. This place is bugged." They went to another undertaker, where they were quoted a price they considered satisfactory and had the body of their mother transferred to his establishment.

Sometimes, persons do not have even the possibility of choice. A scandal followed the first successful heart transplant in Chicago.

The donor was a young man who had died as the result of a blow received in a brawl. His body was taken from the county morgue to a private mortuary. Cost of the funeral and burial? $3500. The amount of his insurance received by his wife? $1000. In commenting on the affair in the Chicago *Daily News,* Mike Royko said: "You have better odds in a Cicero dice game."

It was in protest against the economic exploitation and the irreligious quality of modern funerals that the funeral and memorial movement was started in the United States in 1939 at two ends of the country by church groups in Seattle and in New York. Their goals were similar: to make it possible for members of the group to have simple, dignified funerals at reasonable cost.

The procedure was simple. Interested persons would pay a small fee to become members of the society. (No other money is/was required to be paid.) This nonprofit society then sought out an undertaker willing to cooperate with the group—no easy task because of the pressures exerted by the industry associations. Members would file a declaration of their wishes with the undertaker; when death occurred, there would be no need for the survivors to experience the trauma of working out arrangements. By planning in advance, persons could spare those they left behind the emotional and financial drain of an extravagant funeral. By and large, those procedures have been followed by the 103 funeral and memorial societies that have been organized in Canada and in this country since that time, all of which are now members of the Continental Association of Funeral and Memorial Societies.

The budget of that organization is ludicrously small—about $7500 a year obtained from a portion of the membership fee paid into each of the member societies. The annual budgets of the member societies are equally modest—even more modest since almost all of the work in the societies is done by volunteers. (That they are so many and so willing is the only reason they have been able to carry out their educational goals. For example, when the *Reader's Digest* mentioned their existence favorably in an article, "Facts you should know about Funerals," in 1967, volunteers converged on Continental headquarters in Chicago to answer the more than twenty-five thousand inquiries that came in.)

Growth of the societies has not been large; for the past five years the annual rate has been about ten thousand families and individuals. Presently, more than three hundred groups in Canada and the United States are members. That relatively small figure, however, in no way reflects interest in the movement to obtain simple, dignified funerals at reasonable cost. People feel about joining funeral and memorial societies much as they feel about making a will. They wish to do it and intend to do it, but resist.

Nor does the relatively small figure in any way reflect the impact the movement has had on American and Canadian funeral practices. Members are articulate. Three of us have written books that have been widely distributed and frequently cited: Jessica Mitford's *The American Way of Death* (1963) was on the best-seller list for months; Dr. LeRoy Bowman's *The American Funeral: A Study in Guilt and Sublimity* (1959) was the first of the volumes and offers a marvelously detailed sociological study of the subject; my own *The High Cost of Dying* (1963) lays considerable stress on tracing the evolution of the funeral from literary, historical, and religious sources. Ernest Morgan's *The Manual of Simple Burial,* a booklet available through Continental and the Celo Press, provides the best current material about the movement. In addition to the many articles written for publication by various members of the societies, our work has been treated favorably in almost every magazine in the country: from the *Atlantic* to *True;* the same holds in Canada. Hundreds of radio and television programs have called public attention to our work. As a consequence, the major burden of our argument—that ostentatious and elaborate funerals violate our western religious traditions and that the subversion of competitive business practices has resulted in consumer exploitation—has been conveyed to millions of persons on both sides of the border with good effect.

All of the major denominations—Catholic, Protestant, and Jewish, have either approved or endorsed our goals. Many churches have taken steps to restore simplicity to funerals—insisting that caskets be closed, covering caskets with a pall cloth, and suggesting that various trappings be dispensed with. The funerals of President Kennedy and President Eisenhower, although public affairs, reflected some of those trends: closed caskets, absence of floral displays, caskets covered with flags. Some churches have gone further: white, rather than black vestments and draperies are used in original Christian manner; often they advocate memorial services at which the body of the deceased is not present. The National Council of Churches is represented on the Advisory Board of Continental; the United Synagogues of America has publicly approved our organization. Not long ago, the director of Catholic Cemeteries in Chicago said of the funeral societies: "You have restored freedom of choice to funerals." The response of churches is not surprising since the societies emphasize the importance of spiritual over materialistic values. Most of the societies grew out of churches; however, all must function nondenominationally in order to meet Continental Association standards.

Economically, the impact has also been great. Society members have realized great savings. A study made in 1967 by the Cleveland Memorial Society revealed that members had saved approximately $150,000—when the prices of their funerals were compared to prices for comparable funerals to nonmembers. Other societies report high savings—although not all have had cost analysis studies made. (The Cleveland Memorial Society's interest in that is not surprising considering that its vice-president for several years is a legal counsel for General Motors.) Recent figures released by the Bureau of Labor Statistics indicate that the average funeral cost is well over $900; in Los Angeles and Seattle, members may obtain basic services for as little as $145 plus a few modest service charges. Basic costs are higher in some places: in Florida and Arizona, where competition is less vigorous, the lowest price is about $350. (It should be noted, of course, that many members prefer more elaborate services than the basic plans worked out by societies with cooperating undertakers; their chief purpose in joining is not to get an inexpensive funeral but to exercise freedom of choice.)

Because of the benefits to consumers, *Consumer Reports, Changing Times, Everybody's Money, U.S. Consumer Newsletter,* and the publications of many local consumer groups have carried articles pointing out the advantages of membership in the societies.

The reaction of individual funeral directors and their trade associations has been extremely hostile. For that reason, in many places local societies have been unable to secure the cooperation of morticians. It was necessary, as has been indicated, for one of the members of the Vancouver Memorial Society to obtain an undertaking license. In Santa Barbara, California, the large society has been forced to use the services of one of the funeral directors cooperating with the Los Angeles Society. It could not find a funeral director willing to work with the society within a one-hundred-mile radius. Societies have been accused of indulging in a "Communist conspiracy" in addition to being called "atheistic and unsentimental." I, myself, have experienced what I consider an extraordinary reaction. Private detectives called on our neighbors to investigate our family life and habits; my superiors at the California state college where I work were called and ordered to get rid of "that troublemaker" and "that subversive." Forest Lawn sent a letter to ministers in Southern California warning them that if they quoted from my book they might be included in the libel suit that was supposed to have been brought against me. Even my daughter's Girl Scout troop felt the fury. A local undertaker who had offered to give the troop fifty cents for each member and parent who showed up for a tour of his establishment cancelled the offer when he learned that I was a prospective tourist. Most surprisingly, Dr. Hugh Tyner—a former college president who has served for many years as the "public member" of the board regulating the funeral industry in California—told me after I stepped down from testifying on behalf of the Beilenson Funeral Reform Bill that: "If I were the president of your college, I'd fire you."

A reason for that reaction is that the movement's influence has extended far beyond the membership. People—at least literate ones—no longer feel squeamish about discussing prices "at a time like that." Societies have worked in various parts of the two countries to prevent costs from getting out of hand. In Toronto, recently, they made a strong—but unsucccessful—case against boosting welfare funeral costs from $250 to $365. Greater success has been experienced in Wisconsin, New York, Pennsylvania, and California, where public displeasure either halted such increases or encouraged less monopolistic practices.

For the past few years the chief emphasis of members of Continental Association has been to extend the benefits of the movement to persons in the lower income groups—particularly members of racial and ethnic minorities. Some are working with church groups, others with government programs in poverty areas, others with organizations of senior citizens and with neighborhood associations. It is not easy. As Paul Jackson, a leader of the program in the Hough area of Cleveland, explained...to members of the Continental board several years ago: "All their lives, my people have been relegated to the wings—underfed, under-housed, underclothed, underprivileged in every way. This is their one chance to occupy the center of the stage." It is our hope they can be persuaded that the good life is not an elaborate funeral, and that others will be persuaded, too.

A great value of the movement is that it encourages people to think in a rational way about the practical aspects of death. From that point, it is not a long step to think about the meaning of death. When the right questions have been asked and answers found, progress will have been made toward learning the meaning of life. Then perhaps it will be possible for more to follow the example of the really great teachers of morals and ethics and come to acknowledge that it is only the body that is buried—the achievements and the goodnesses are not interred with the bones.

Howard C. Raether

The Place of the Funeral

The Role of the Funeral Director in Contemporary America

Howard C. Raether is Executive Director of the National Funeral Directors Association, Milwaukee, an affiliation of state associations representing over fourteen thousand funeral homes throughout the United States. A lawyer by profession, he welcomed the opportunity to debate with Ruth Harmer the pros and cons of the contemporary funeral in America when that offer was extended to him by Dr. Kastenbaum, editor of *Omega,* the journal in which this article and that of Harmer first appeared.

Habenstein and Lamers conclude their *Funeral Customs the World Over* with the statement,

> ...for all people everywhere, funerals and funeral ceremonies satisfy basic needs, allay suffering, and help rescue death from the horror of meaninglessness.

As the 1970s begin, the funeral and funeral director can become increasingly important facets of our society despite of or because our culture is youth oriented.... There are a growing number of persons who are death denying if not death defying.

Death is not commonplace as it once was. Sociologist Robert Fulton maintains that we in the United States have now among us the first death free generation in the world. Millions of Americans have never experienced the loss, by death, of someone close to them. Millions of Americans have never been to a funeral, or have even seen a funeral procession, except one which was televised as coverage of the funeral or for news purposes. Millions of Americans have never seen a dead body except on TV, in a movie, on a battlefield, or on a highway. And when death does come it is often as University of Michigan psychiatrist Andrew Watson says:

> The ways of dying nowadays deprive relatives and friends of the use of their sensory capacity. A loved one dies behind curtains in a hospital room. His body is quickly cremated, or his coffin is shut. There is no closing of the relationship, no opportunity to say good-bye, no way in which we can feel the death that we rationally know has come.[1]

It can be said that use of "sensory capacity" is implied in *Future Shock* by Alvin Toffler.... [According to a review in *Newsweek,* August 23, 1970] Toffler "uses the concept of future shock in a clinical sense to describe the physical and psychic damage wrought by subjecting man to too much change in too little time." Toffler deals not only with change in the sociological sense but also change in the lives of people. He says that "The death of a spouse...is almost universally regarded as the single most impactful change that can befall a person in the normal course of his life."

1. From University of Michigan News Service, April 25, 1970.

Toffler refers to ritual as "an important change-buffer." He specifies those [rituals] which have to do with birth, death, puberty, and marriage. He adds that "repetitive behavior...helps give meaning to non-repetitive events." He [observes] the breaking down...of many rituals as the pace of change accelerates. He then says:

> As we accelerate and introduce arythmic patterns into the pace of change, we need to mark off certain regularities for preservation, exactly the way we now mark off certain forests, historical monuments, or bird sanctuaries for protection. We may even need to manufacture ritual.

There is no need to manufacture ritual to meet needs which, for most people, come with death. Existing and modified or adapted funeral rites, ceremonies, and symbols do satisfy basic needs, they do allay suffering, and they do help to rescue death from the horror of meaninglessness. The funeral can be, as pastoral counsellor Paul Irion says, "an experience of value as it meets the needs of those who mourn."

THE CONTEMPORARY FUNERAL AND TRENDS AFFECTING IT   In 1966, Fulton conducted a study of contemporary American funeral practices. Reponses from 3,474 practicing funeral directors indicated that in 1966 the vast majority of deaths...[were followed by a] funeral which included a public viewing, a public service (most times religious), and a public committal. Trends away from the full period of the funeral were evidenced in the Pacific Coast states with a move toward privatization of the funeral noted in some of the New England states. There is nothing to indicate a reversal of these trends in the Pacific and New England areas. Furthermore, in all sections of the country there are...instances of abbreviated services, of private funerals, and of no viewing of the body.

There are reasons for some of the deviations from the funeral of the past as well as the need for flexibility in the funeral of the future. Before examining them it should be pointed out that few people really want to die. While funeral ceremonies have had meaning and value there have always been those who have tried to "get at" death by being critical of facets of post death activity. Limiting our comments to the United States, history records that long before there were any functionaries, (layers-out-of-the-dead, undertakers, funeral directors) there was criticism of funeral expenses. According to Habenstein and Lamers [as early as] "1721, the General Court of Massachusetts passed laws prohibiting 'Extraordinary Expense at Funerals.'"

Criticism of funeral practices is not new. Fear and anger and the wish to avoid death and all that is associated with it have not only been reflected in direct criticism and even in legislation, but also in non-direct euphemisms and synonyms for death....

DEROGATORY PUBLICITY   To criticize and be criticized seems to be inherent in the so-called American way. Yet few groups have been as consistently and often unjustifiably criticized as have funeral practices and funeral directors. A reason for this undoubtedly is the symbolization of "death" found in them.

Communications media of all sorts have publicized the criticism associated with the funeral and they have avoided or rejected the positive material on the place of the funeral and funeral director. A negative piece predicated on more half than whole truths receives interest generating headlines, a prominent place in the paper, and is picked up by other publications. A fair impartial article is junked with the editor giving as his reason that it was not sensational, it wasn't what he wanted. A television documentary edited to show a funeral service and its spokesman in bad light is made available to all who are interested. A well known magazine with national circulation listed where to write for a brochure of a group advocating the bodiless memorial service as opposed to the funeral with the body present. The caption on the paragraph was "funerals." The National Funeral Directors Association immediately requested that under the same caption in a future edition its name and address be given for those interested in some brochures it has available. Months later the request had not been granted.

Negative publicity and a lack of positive material exists in other fields and in many walks of life. But apparently not as consistently as in funeral service. The whole communications situation is of increasing importance because of a growing number of people who have had limited or no personal exposure to death or to the funeral and the funeral director. They have no experience to counteract what they read, see and hear, much of which is derogatory.

Also, a paradoxical situation confronts the public and funeral service in "publicity" of the funeral. When a Kennedy, a King, a MacArthur, a Churchill, or a Pope dies, there are telecasts, broadcasts, and newspaper coverage of the funeral. Likewise, when a prominent citizen or a murder victim or person of "news value" is buried, there is news coverage of that event.

Sometimes in the coverage by the media certain procedures are explained and related to the overall funeral. But the media rarely go beyond this. In fact some of their other articles or programs, in essence, are critical of the very ceremonies and rituals they publicized.... The contradictory and possibly even hypocritical character of this treatment cannot be overlooked. It seems to reflect, among other things, the ambivalence felt toward the need to deny death and the simultaneous need to acknowledge it—particularly with regard to a person of significance.

THE FUNERAL DIRECTOR   Some funeral directors are to an extent responsible for some existing trends. Some of the practitioners are reticent to counsel on values which a family may be avoiding when they try to take what they think is the emotionally easy way out. By the same token, some funeral directors fail to adjust facets of the funeral to meet particular needs. They sometimes recommend having for mother's funeral what was done for father's service ten years ago without ascertaining whether such a service might in part be stereotyped if not dysfunctional to the members of the immediate family.

Often the place of the casket in the over-all funeral service is unclear or undefined. Historically, U.S. funeral functionaries have been providers of goods and some services. A casket was purchased and all other services provided "free." Today on the average, the merchandise provided by a funeral director amounts to about 20 percent of his total cost in providing a funeral service. The casket is not the funeral. Nor is the funeral the casket. The failure of some funeral directors to accept this fact and explain it to those they serve is in some ways responsible for some defuneralizing trends.

FUNERAL PRACTICES: WHICH SHOULD CONTINUE AND WHY   There are modifications, adaptations and changes in the funeral that are taking place and there will be others as the years go on. Before focusing upon those practices which should continue in some manner, two factors are basic. They are: (1) Time is seldom of the essence in the urgent sense. There is a therapy in thinking things through, in acting and in proceeding at less than a demanding pace. Therefore, the period of the funeral and making arrangements for it should not be hurried. This may help, also, to alleviate the withdrawal and regrets that sometimes come with "getting it over as quickly as possible" and with trying to intellectualize emotions; (2) "There are many levels or degrees of loss rather than just one," says [Robert] Fulton. He adds:

These different responses to death can be observed in the varied and changing character of contemporary mourning rites and funeral practices. Care, therefore, must be taken not to define too narrowly what funeral rites or behaviors are appropriate for the bereaved. To do so can lead to confusion, tension, or anguish on the part of the survivors....

There must be a "stronger recognition by funeral directors and other professional caretakers...to acknowledge the important distinction between 'high grief' and 'low grief' and to take into account the changing social and intellectual environment in which death is experienced in America today."

For bereaved persons who are genuinely grieved, it is imperative, in the light of growing evidence, that they somehow find the opportunity to resolve their grief. They should be encouraged to mourn. For those who are simply bereaved but not grieved, however, it would appear to be inappropriate and perhaps emotionally harmful to insist that they express feelings they do not, in fact, have.

With these points made, a review of funeral practices that should continue with a brief explanation of why is in order.

"Visitation" or "Wake" or "Calling Hours". A "visitation" or "wake" or what some refer to as "calling hours" permits family and friends in the presence of the viewable body to express together their feelings about the deceased. This sharing experience is nearly always important to the survivors. When the survivors do not share their grief, they face their grief

alone. When they share their grief, "one touch of sorrow makes the whole world kin." They should have the opportunity to express their own emotions. At the same time the family should hear what the life of the deceased has meant to others, some of whom they may not even know. The visitation in the presence of the viewable body provides a proper setting and climate for all of this—a setting and climate which generally does not exist in any other way at any other time.

"Viewing" the Body. ...It should be made clear that for hundreds of years men of most cultures have viewed their dead and they continue to do so. Viewing is not a custom of American origin. The only basic difference between viewing in the United States and elsewhere is the circumstances under which it takes place. Also, as has been stated earlier, some persons today in our land want to deny the death that has occurred. One method of disguising this reality is failing to have the body present during the period of the funeral or not viewing the remains if they are present.

But it is essential to admit to death's presence. This can be a painful experience. It also can be a helpful and rewarding one. Some say that they wish to remember the deceased as he or she appeared alive. However, to view the body is one of the first steps of accepting the death. If the death was violent or the body wasted away, the skills of the funeral service licensee will be employed in such a fashion as to modify or erase the scars of violence or the ravages of disease....

It must be remembered that the period of the funeral, from the first announcement of the death to the committal service, is a declaration that a death has occurred. The body present and viewed, when possible, is an important part of this affirmation. The following state-ments document the value of the body present and viewed.

Irion,...[in discussing how the survivor may be assisted in his or her grief, observed:]

> There are several ways in which we give this help. One, I believe, is through a tasteful show-ing of the body. I could not bring myself to en-dorse any sensational displays or practices that are not in good taste. However, it can be very helpful for a bereaved family too see their loved one in repose. Viewing the body is another means by which the whole situation is focused on reality. Often is is helpful in relieving painful memories of a lingering illness or a terrifying accident.

Reverend James L. Kidd, Wellington Avenue Congregational Church, Chicago, Illinois,...[in] reference to the funeral of his father-in-law wrote:

> ...the presence of the dead body was an impor-tant factor in helping the mourners to accept the fact of death, to overcome the experience of denial and to enable creative grief to take place.

Dr. Charles W. Wahl—Chief, Psychoso-matic Service—UCLA [has written:]

> I was recently again reminded of how valuable and legitimate a funeral service can be. I accom-panied a friend to the funeral of his mother. She had died of a chronic and wasting illness and I had been present at her death bed. My friend ex-perienced a deep and profound consolation see-ing his mother with the lines of suffering erased from her face and lying at peace....

Reverend Clarence Bruninga at an institute on "Help to the Grief Sufferer" [commented:]

> Again, I'd like to remind you that viewing the remains and the committal service, and other forms, arose not merely through the devious thinking of some undertaker who wanted to make more money, but because of the emotional needs of people, and are perpetuated because they meet some need. This does not mean that

all rituals are positive. They may contain negative elements as well. And tragically, I think, a great many reactions against ritual arise out of situations where immature, inadequate, neurotic people reacted to death in an immature, inadequate way. This you can see at almost any wake, which can often serve exhibitionist and masochistic needs.

Some persons would rather not look at the body of a dead person. Others indicate to funeral directors that they are afraid of what they will see. They don't think a body wasted away by cancer or other ravaging disease can be restored to a likeness of the deceased before the physical deterioration began. There are those also who question whether a body can be restored where the cause of death was violence. Sometimes those who question whether the casket should be open will view the body after it has been prepared and placed in the casket. Or they will designate someone else to do this. In most such instances, the casket is left open. And the nearest of kin are forever grateful. Conversely, where the family arbitrarily keeps the casket closed, there often are regrets and doubt as to whether they did the "right" thing. And who knows when a family might be depriving some person from viewing when that person loved the deceased as much or more than the relatives did.

Writing about viewing is not justification of "prettifying" the deceased to make him look better in death than he did during the healthiest days of his life. Cosmetic restoration is not an attempt to deny death by creating an illusion of life but rather it gives the bereaved an acceptable image to recall. Most times the funeral service is a religious rite. When it is the viewing should be completed and the casket closed before the worship begins. Thoughts are transformed thereby from the temporal to the spiritual.

Committal at Graveside. It is argued by some that the committal should be at the church or in the funeral home to avoid the inconvenience of the trip to the cemetery where about 95 percent of all final dispositions are made. The problems of traffic, inclement weather and other reasons are given for suggesting that there be no procession to the cemetery. Yet the same people who are against the graveside committal because of traffic and other inconveniences often think nothing of going to shopping centers during peak periods, of traveling bumper to bumper to go to an athletic event or on a holiday weekend in all sorts of weather. And, those who feel people have the right to gather and march to express feelings must agree on the right and place of the funeral procession for those who are acting out their feelings.

Irion (1954) says, "The committal service provides, as nothing else...does so graphically, a symbolic demonstration that the kind of relationship which has existed between the mourner and the deceased is now at an end." Beyond this final farewell to help complete the grief cycle there is the support that relatives, associates, and friends give at graveside. Turning away and leaving the grave is a realistic but traumatic moment for many. It should not be avoided nor should it be faced alone.

Public Funeral and Expressions of Respect and Sympathy. A public funeral gives the community a chance to offer its support and share the sorrow of the immediate family of the deceased. A private funeral limits those who may attend. It arbitrarily shuts out relatives, friends, associates, and acquaintances who may be able to bring comfort to the bereaved....

The funeral is of the person who died and it is for those who live on. It is important that relatives, friends, and associates be permitted to express their sympathy and offer their support through a public funeral. Such expression should be freely given and freely received. It is essential also to realize that the funeral can be just as important to the family who may not be well known as it is to the family of fame and fortune.

THE FUNERAL AS A RELIGIOUS SERVICE
"Weeping may endure for the night, but joy cometh in the morning" (Psalm 30:5)....

The religious funeral is geared to meet spiritual needs. Edgar N. Jackson says in his *The Christian Funeral* that the funeral should do the following for those who share in it: (1) It should recognize that what is done is to meet social, psychological, and spiritual needs of those who are able to participate in it; (2) The service is aware of the powerful emotions that are at work and tries to fulfill the feelings rather than deny them; (3) The funeral is a time for facing reality rather than for denying it; (4) While it would not deny the fact of the event, neither would it deny the validity of the emotions that attend it; (5) The funeral should give the members of the religious community a chance to give evidence of their emotional and spiritual support of the bereaved; (6) The funeral should be a time of affirmation of faith.

For Those Who Do Not Want a Religious Service. Some people do not profess a religious belief. Some of them view as dysfunctional anything with religious overtones. However, the funeral has value for those who profess a religious orientation [as well as] for those who do not. It was with this in mind that the Rev. Irion prepared a manual on the humanistic or secular funeral....

The American funeral has been mostly a religious rite. At least there was a religious officiant whether the deceased was or was not churched. Now we find a variety in the ritual because it can be secular or humanistic... as it speaks to the special needs of those in bereavement.

With half our population under thirty years of age, and many of the balance wishing and acting like they were under thirty, it can be said that ours is a youth culture. This brings up two matters of importance. They are: (1) death and the child; and (2) youth and the funeral.

DEATH AND THE CHILD In interpreting a study he made in 1962, Fulton... [observed] that there are some persons who "strive to bring their children up in a world of reality through the discouraging of such fantasies as ghosts, hobgoblins, Santa Claus, and the bogies of sex. Nevertheless, in this setting they appear to behave contrary to form and seek to shield the ultimate truth (of death) from their children."... When John F. Kennedy was assassinated in Dallas, ...children could not be shielded [from his death or funeral.] They participated by watching television. Books and articles were written immediately. Some ortho-psychiatrists who never before were interested in children and death prepared papers on the subject.

But funeral directors through their national association had [earlier] sought and secured advice. For example in 1962 the [National Funeral Directors Association journal], *Director,* carried a piece written by Dr. Mervyn Shoor who is the psychiatrist in charge of the Santa Clara County Guidance Clinic in California. Dr. Shoor was assisted by a clinical psychologist, Mary Helen Speed. The Shoor and Speed paper said that funeral directors are in a unique...position to aid and encourage the normal mourning process.... They recommend that funeral directors talk directly to a child...about the deceased. They further recommend that any questions or comments designed to help the child openly acknowledge the reality of death will prove helpful and that the child should be included in the funeral ceremonies where appropriate, even to the extent of specific assignments such as monitoring the guest register and helping with the floral offerings.

Others have since agreed. Children, researchers have said, as early as age three have an awareness of and respond to, death. They must know the truth the funeral tells and should be allowed to attend the services if they want to. They should not be denied the experience of this significant part of their life. If they are, it could have future troublesome emotional implications because they could develop a sense of abandonment instead of one of belonging. In fact, there are those who trace juvenile delinquency and other social and psychological problems to unresolved or improperly resolved grief. However, no unwilling child should be made to participate.

YOUTH AND THE FUNERAL   The greatest percentage of participation in a funeral service by an age group is by those between fifteen and twenty-four when [one of their own age] dies or is killed. Most of these young persons are sensitive to the feelings of others. An example of that sensitivity can be found in a piece written by Louisville funeral director, William Wagner, [in 1970]. Mr. Wagner helped conduct the services for a young married couple killed in a traffic accident. In his article Mr. Wagner says:

For the next day and a half approximately a thousand people came into the funeral home to pay their respects to the deceased and their survivors. Eighty percent of these people were between fourteen and twenty-four years of age. This is the group that some say [flouts] ceremony, that belittles sentimentality, that spurns religion, that doesn't believe in anything. They came with their wide ties, their loud striped shirts, their beards, their long hair. They came on motorcycles, in cars you wouldn't know how to start, with their parents, alone, often in gangs or packs—but they were there because they cared enough to be.

And they went up to the caskets and talked with the parents. Some prayed with them. Some just stood there but their presence helped the families. Some not too familiar with prayer gave the now famous two finger peace sign and walked away.

Solace and comfort were provided by the young people even though to some their ways seemed odd, direct, and too honest. I wonder if some older people might benefit thereby—people who feel a stereotyped, syrupy message often on a card, or with a floral remembrance or a memorial gift is the best way to express sympathy....

Reports of young persons' participation in [a] funeral tell of a cordon of motorcycles as an honor guard for the procession; placing a cyclist jacket in the casket before closing it; throwing a remembrance into the grave by each person attending the committal; ordering special floral pieces symbolic of a special relationship; or, offering some "farewell" gift made by the giver. Most times the gift is of something meaningful to the giver. It is not an empty expression.

Funeral directors are becoming aware of the validity of the projections claiming that the young people are better educated, are less responsive to organized restraints, want respect as individuals, and seek fulfillment of human wants and needs. The funeral of the future must meet their wants and needs....

ALTERNATE FORMS OF THE FUNERAL

The above caption might be expanded to read "alternate forms of the funeral and/or alternate forms of the operation of a funeral establishment." There have been both without any real lasting success. There have been and are various groups that bury their own, so to speak. Most of these groups or cults use none of the services, facilities, and merchandise of those licensed to provide funeral service. They have not increased appreciably in number or in size.

Cooperative Funeral Homes. There have been and are cooperative burial associations or cooperative funeral homes. These establishments offer funeral services and their personnel are licensed as required by law. In some states these cooperative associations were and are given operational advantages as to taxation and also in being able to be engaged in certain business-getting activities which are illegal for other funeral operations. One of these is the selling of certificates of membership in the cooperative. Despite these advantages, the number of cooperative funeral homes is considerably less than it once was.

Labor Union Funeral Homes. There have been and still are labor unions which have their own funeral homes or which had a connection or an arrangement with a particular funeral home. Like the cooperatives, the personnel of these establishments are licensed as required by law. Like the cooperatives, these operations have a competitive advantage at least as to the membership of the union which owns or which is operated with the funeral home. Like the cooperatives, there are fewer union funeral homes or union-associated funeral operations than there once were.

Memorial Societies. There are about one hundred "memorial societies" in about as many cities in the United States. A purpose of the memorial society movement is to encourage immediate disposition of the body with a memorial service to be held at a later date—without the body present. These societies are not in funeral service. Their officers and staffs are not licensed to conduct funerals or to make funeral arrangements. Rather they enter into agreements with funeral directors to do the things a licensee must do where there is a memorial service and a funeral functionary is needed to perform certain tasks. They also have agreements with funeral homes to provide certain minimal funeral services with the body present. Although the movement has existed for some time and has received much publicity for almost ten years, except for a very few societies, the success of the groups has been very limited—if they have had any at all. In fact, some of the societies have ceased to exist.

There are persons who believe in something less than the funeral with the body present. Their beliefs are no doubt sincere and their needs should be served. However, one must look not only at the social and ethical philosophy behind such beliefs but one must assess the implications of them for the bereaved. Some of these persons appear to be running away from fears and conflicts they have regarding death or they may even be giving vent to some unresolved and mishandled grief of their own.

Some memorial society leaders now agree that the funeral with the body present is a way of meeting social and emotional needs which should not be ignored. Nevertheless, they seem to continue to disregard these needs and in the process, deny mourning and ritual sup-

DEAD MAN'S SONG
Dreamt by a man still living
at the time of composition

I'm filled with joy
when the day dawns quietly
over the roof of the sky,
   aji, jai ja.

I'm filled with joy
when the sun rises slowly
over the roof of the sky,
   aji, jai ja.

But other times, I choke
   with fear:
a greedy swarm of maggots
eats into the hollows
of my collar-bone and eyes,
   aji, jai ja.

I lie here dreaming
how I choked with fear
when they shut me
in an ice-hut on the lake,
   aji, jai ja.

And I could not see
my soul would ever free itself
and get up to the
   hunting-grounds
of the sky,
   aji, jai ja.

Fear grew, and grew.
Fear overwhelmed me
when the fresh-water ice
snapped in the cold,
and the booming crack
   of the frost
grew into the sky,
   aji, jai ja.

Life was wonderful
in winter.
But did winter make me
   happy?
No, I always worried
about hides for boot-soles
and for boots:
and if there'd be enough
for all of us.
Yes, I worried constantly,
   aji, jai ja.

Life was wonderful
in summer.
But did summer make me
   happy?
No, I always worried
about reindeer skins
   and rugs for the platform.
Yes, I worried constantly,
   aji, jai ja.

Life was wonderful
when you stood at your
   fishing-hole
on the ice.
But was I happy waiting
   at my fishing hole?
No, I always worried
for my little hook,
in case it never got a bite.
Yes, I worried constantly,
   aji, jai ja.

Life was wonderful
when you danced in the
   feasting-house.
But did this make me
   any happier?
No, I always worried
I'd forget my song.
Yes, I worried constantly,
   aji, jai ja.

Life was wonderful . . .
And I still feel joy
each time the day-break
whitens the dark sky,
each time the sun
climbs over the roof of
   the sky,
aji, jai ja.

Eskimo Poem

port to survivors, as well as ignore the tear that the death has caused in the fabric of the family and the community....

Two American psychiatrists who have studied death, grief, and mourning have spoken very openly against the bodiless memorial service. One, Alfred A. Messer of Emory University said [in 1970]:

Memorial services, held a couple of weeks after death, are for the birds—not for human beings...When there is a funeral there should be a body there and I think it should be an open casket...When there is death there should be a funeral. There is no association in people's minds between a memorial service and a man who died two weeks ago.

William M. Lamers, Jr., who practices psychiatry in Kentfield, California, wrote the following in *Medical Economics:*

Are there any satisfactory funeral substitutes—a memorial service, for example? In my opinion, there aren't. Though a memorial service is a response to loss and can be extremely satisfying for many, it's not ideal because it lacks several basic elements. First, a memorial service usually doesn't take place when feelings are most intense, which is shortly after the death. Second, members of the family aren't involved in communication, participation, and repeated exposure to the fact that death has occurred. These things force people to acknowledge the reality of loss. Finally, a memorial service doesn't include the presence of the body, which means people aren't given as great an opportunity to fix the fact of death in their minds.

THE FUTURE OF THE FUNERAL AND THE FUNERAL DIRECTOR   Wilbur Schramm of Stanford, writing [in 1965] on the televising of the funeral of the assassinated John F. Kennedy (*The Kennedy Assassination and the American Public*), said that those viewing the televising of the services were

given "an opportunity to experience a real catharsis of grief if they wanted to." He referred to acts of mourning and said the viewers were participating—"They were going to a funeral."...

Raymond Firth, the British anthropologist, has said, "A funeral is a social rite par excellence. Its ostensible object is the dead person, but it benefits not the dead, but the living."...

The funeral for JFK allayed fears and restored some confidence as the world stood still for two days in respect, in honor, and in remembrance. The funeral for Martin Luther King did something else. The Research Institute of America pointed out shortly thereafter that the funeral brought Negro moderates and black militants, and just people, in solemn unity. One week earlier no occasion could have done that....

The American funeral involves a funeral functionary. Most times he is called the funeral director. His role as it pertains to post-death activities, including the funeral, should be maintained and enhanced. Talcott Parsons, the Harvard sociologist, said "No one can take the place of the funeral director."

Joseph Bayly in his *The View from a Hearse* writes:

The funeral director is a man, with all the feelings and capacities of most human beings. More than other men, except for pastors or other religious advisers, and doctors in certain specialties, he lives with sorrow. He is usually able to help us in our moments of grief—moments when the burdens of decision weigh heaviest.

David Switzer [a Southern Methodist pastor and counselor] apparently agrees. He writes:

...With this understanding of the positive aspects of anxiety, it is clear that it not only plays a significant role in the process of therapy but in all interpersonal situations. This needs to be emphasized in regard to grief, because in actual fact people do not normally go to a psychotherapist in their mourning and many do not even have the potentially helpful relationship with a clergyman. In these cases, grief work needs must be met by other members of the family and friends or by other professionals, such as the physician or funeral director, who, by the particular nature of the situation, may be involved.

Successful grief work is being done by the funeral service licensee. A study of childhood leukemia, by the Langley Porter Neuropsychiatric Institute, University of California, San Francisco, reported in the *New England Journal of Medicine* (Binger et al., 1969) tells of the findings of interviews of twenty families of children who had died of the dreaded disease. In discussing the support parents received, the authors reported that fifteen families expressed positive feelings toward the mortician or funeral director for the services rendered during their bereavement. The authors conclude that the funeral directors' experience with grief reactions makes them skilled in offering solace to grieving families.

Cecile Strugnell and Phyllis R. Silverman are associated with the Laboratory of Community Psychiatry at the Harvard Medical School. Dr. Silverman has been identified with the Harvard "Widow to Widow" program. These two social scientists...[have] stated that the increasing isolation of people in our society and the fractionalization of the family often make the needs of the bereaved very acute. They urge funeral directors—and their wives—to be aware and sensitive to these needs and to play a greater role in meeting them.

Strugnell and Silverman...feel that the funeral director and his wife have an experience with grief that is invaluable and that their close cooperation with the mental health specialist could be very fruitful. This is not to say that the funeral director should practice psychiatry or psychology. He has his own knowledge and expertise founded upon the invaluable experience of day-to-day encounters. He often does what no one else can because of his unique position. Also, he should be able to recognize when a person's grief is such that the assistance of a professional should be sought.

More than ever before, the funeral must continue to be a ritual—a ceremony—a response to death which is of value as it meets the individual needs of those directly involved as mourners. It also must meet the collective needs of the community and of the nation that apparently is changing so fast that sometimes we forget to examine the destructive meanings some changes bring. Concomitantly the role of the funeral director must be adaptive. He will continue to be entrusted with the dead body which was a person who loved and was loved. He will continue to provide funeral facilities, furnishings, and merchandise. He will continue to serve people many of whom will be experiencing a major crisis in their lives.

The funeral director must become more of a caretaker—a caregiver. He must continue to develop his sensitivity to the various levels or degrees of loss that death creates in our present day society. The funeral director must always realize that when he does what he does it is at a point of no return. What is done cannot be changed. What is not done will ever remain so. Neither the funeral director nor the family he is serving will have a second chance.

The place and meaning of the funeral in contemporary America is as it has been defined—a response to death that is organized, purposeful, time-limited, flexible, and group-centered.

PART FOUR

Dilemmas of Death

Part Four, "Dilemmas of Death," takes up matters both ancient and modern. In Section 12, "Morality and Mortality in Modern Society," the questions posed by such issues as euthanasia and organ transplantation form an arc across the history of Western society that reaches from the speculations of Socrates to the technical skills of the heart transplant surgeon, Christiaan Barnard. As humans increasingly learn more about the form of existence, we are challenged equally to search out its meaning.

"Suicide" constitutes Section 13 of this part and raises anew the question posed so succinctly by Hamlet, "To be or not to be?" In a society—indeed in a world—that increasingly opts "not to be," it behooves us to examine afresh, and with vigor and urgency, what it means "to be."

Section 14, "Death, War, and the Human Condition," addresses itself to the primordial story of Cain and Abel—the killing of one human being by another. Humanity has come far. An act of passion is now a profession; and

the jaw bone of an ass, a neutron bomb. What was an allegory is now a nightmare, and only our dreams are real.

Section 15, "The Death System: Review and Prospectus," invites us to enter the looking glass, like Alice, and to envision the future of death. At present its prospects are bright; ultimately, whether life triumphs over death or over life itself is for humankind to decide. For, as Humpty Dumpty said to Alice, "The question is which is to be master—that's all."

12.

Morality and Mortality in Modern Society

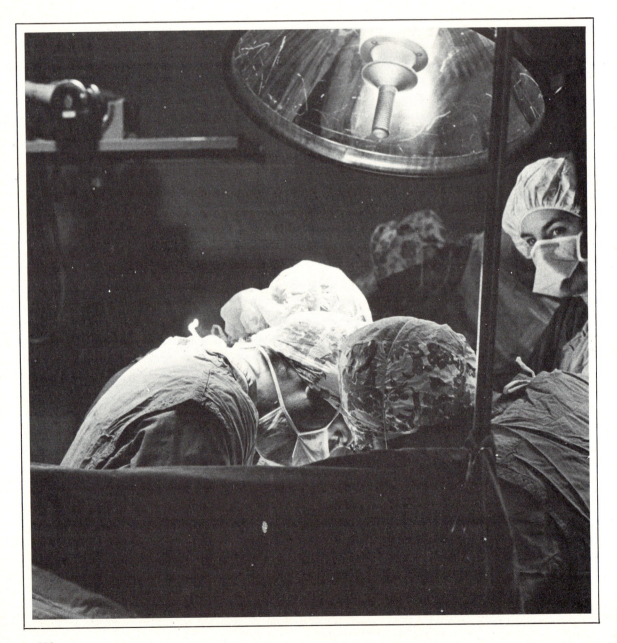

Modern technology has, to an unprecedented degree, given us control over life and death. And in so doing, it has raised new and perplexing moral and ethical issues. An examination of these issues relating to death and dying starkly reveals the interconnectedness of our concepts of death and our styles of living. Abortion, euthanasia, the right to die movement, and organ transplantation all have serious implications for the way we live as well as for the way we die. Sooner or later, many of us will confront one or more of these issues in our personal lives. Our responses can result in a variety of consequences—we may decide in a way that satisfactorily resolves the dilemma; we may be tormented by guilt; or we may we wracked by confusion and indecision.

Each of these issues involves a fundamental question: what is the meaning of human life? Is the fetus a human being or simply a product of conception? Is the comatose patient with irreversible brain damage a human being or merely a mass of tissue kept "alive" by machines?

Moreover, these issues involve the question of who has the right to decide in matters of life and death—the individual, the family, the physician, the state? As we shall see, in a problematic situation, the rights of one party often conflict with the rights of another. For example, many would argue that the unborn fetus has rights that conflict with the right of the pregnant woman to abort it. Also, the right of an individual to commit suicide may conflict with the rights of the survivors-to-be.

Such issues are as difficult as they are important. In this section, we shall examine several moral and ethical issues, although with the reservation that they are extremely complicated matters and can be only summarily considered in the space allotted.

Every society has had its moral code, its standards for right and wrong conduct, embodied in custom and/or in law. Such standards provide guidelines for what we should do, or ought to do, in a particular situation. However, as our society and culture change, so do our prevailing moral and ethical values. In our own time, for example, we have seen a growth in sexual permissiveness that tolerates premarital sex and extramarital sex as well as homosexuality, all in the name of the self-realization and self-fulfillment of the individual. This "new morality" has been embraced particularly, but by no means exclusively, by the young, while many members of the older generation regard it as no morality at all. Nor are disagreements over what constitutes moral behavior spawned only by "the generation gap"; in a society as religiously, politically, and socially diverse as ours, numerous moral beliefs coexist and clash, thus further adding to the moral confusion.

Traditionally, moral values rested on the foundation of religious dogma. The Ten Commandments or other religious proscriptions stated what was right and wrong, and theologians and clergy provided commonsense interpretations for the believers. In contemporary society, however, as we saw in Section 5 on "Death and Social Change," faith in technical expertise has in part replaced faith in religion. But we also learned that technical solutions are apt to be inappropriate for moral problems. Life-support machines can keep a brain-dead body functioning physiologically, but they cannot tell us whether the patient is "dead" or "alive," nor can they tell us whether it is right or wrong to "pull the plug." By the same token, medical research can ascertain when a fetus is capable of independent life outside the pregnant woman's body, but it cannot answer the question "when does human life begin?" Underlying the moral-ethical issues of abortion, euthanasia, the right to die, and organ transplantation is the presence of technical wherewithal and the absence of clear moral guidelines.

Abortion is a complicated and significant issue that has divided the nation—the country is rent fifty-fifty in its beliefs on the morality and legality of elective abortions. Several questions intersect in the abortion controversy. What is human life? When does it begin? Is the fetus human or simply specialized tissue? Whose rights should prevail—the mother's right to control her own body, or the alleged right of the fetus to life? The answers to these questions cannot be found in technical data. They are essentially moral questions which are ultimately answerable only in moral terms. But there is no consensus today on the "right" answers to these questions. Catholics, whose religious teaching explicitly prohibits most elective abortions, may live beside agnostics who subscribe to no religious orientation. Moreover, it is one thing to hold a strong moral position when the issue at hand is not immediately relevant, but quite another matter when one is confronted with the necessity of making a decision. Persons who are in principle against abortions on demand may see things differently when an undesired

pregnancy occurs in their lives. While we are unlikely to find easy solutions to the abortion dilemma, it is important that people have an understanding of the basic moral and ethical issues at stake.

Euthanasia, or the "good death," is the subject of the articles in this chapter by Maguire, Veatch, and Rudikoff. Modern medicine can postpone death in many cases, sometimes resulting in patients being kept alive on expensive machines and often by painful treatments long after they would have died naturally, and sometimes long after their lives have any meaning. The subject of euthanasia is haunted also by the memory of the wholesale murder of Jews and other "undesirables" by the Nazis in World War II. Proponents of euthanasia seek to avoid either undesirable extreme. They recognize that in many cases patients have the ability, and therefore should have the right, to make decisions for themselves about how long they will live and under what conditions. But what about patients who can be kept alive but who have virtually no chance of ever attaining or regaining a functioning brain? Those who favor euthanasia feel that both comatose adults like Karen Ann Quinlan and congenitally deformed infants, who are able to live only with the assistance of heroic efforts and machines, should be allowed to die. Others would argue that all life is sacred.

However, euthanasia is a complex issue. There is an important difference between active euthanasia—in which someone actually kills the patient—and passive euthanasia—in which treatments are either discontinued or not initiated. Moreover, it is important to distinguish between voluntary euthanasia—in which a competent person decides to be killed or to be allowed to die—and involuntary euthanasia—in which these decisions are made by someone else, as in the case of a comatose adult or an infant. As Maguire states, our legal structure does not currently deal in a clear and consistent manner with active euthanasia, or mercy killing, as it is often known. Veatch analyses several attempts to formulate legislative policies on mercy killing and finds the issues more complex than might appear at first glance. Rudikoff considers the matter of legislating safeguards that would protect the patient, his or her family, and the medical staff.

Some of the dilemmas involved in voluntary euthanasia and the related issue of the right to die are illustrated in the case history presented by White and analyzed by Engelhardt. The tragically burned young man demanded that doctors discontinue the treatments that were essential to his life. With clear and sound mind, he decided that he did not want to continue living with the multiple handicaps resulting from his accident. The issues involved included: did the man have a right to die? did the doctor have the right, legal and/or moral, either to kill him out of mercy or simply to allow him to die by stopping the vital treatments? And what if the burned man, as it happened, should change his mind? As it turned out, treatments were not stopped, the man lived, and he later came to accept his handicaps and make a new start in life. Had the doctors agreed to his initial demand, he would have died and been deprived of the opportunity to change his mind. But, by ignoring his refusal of treatment, they deprived him of the cherished right of self-determination. We should remember that, had this happened before the development of the technology to sustain life in severely burned persons, the entire moral dilemma would have been avoided.

An allied concern in the euthanasia–right-to-die controversy is the patient's right to know the complete details of his or her condition. As discussed in Section 7, "The Dying Patient," most patients depend on health professionals for information about their conditions, and the issue of the moral obligation of the physician to inform the patient arises in many cases. If a patient learns that he or she is certainly going to die in the near future, and that the remaining days or weeks or months are likely to be painful and demeaning, the patient may choose an early death. The question then becomes one of whose right is the more binding. What if the patient wants to die, but family and medical staff refuse? Or, what if the family wants the patient to be allowed to die, but the patient is either unable to decide or does not want to be allowed to die?

The moral quandary of who shall live and who shall die is often complicated by pragmatic considerations of the costs of keeping someone alive in intensive care units and allocating expensive medical resources to a terminally ill person—often in a comatose state—when other patients are in need.

Organ transplantation, which has saved and improved many lives, has also created or intensified moral and ethical dilemmas. The controversy surrounding the definition of death—and, therefore, of life—has been complicated by the demand for transplantable organs. Put simply, if we decide that a person is legally "dead" when the brain is irreversibly destroyed, then the body can be used as a source of transplant organs. On the other hand, if the traditional definition of death, which considers the heartbeat and breathing as primary indicators of life, is retained, then access to fresh and vital donor organs is diminished. As the article by Fulton *et al.* indicates, families who agree to donate the organs of someone who has suffered brain death are often confused regarding just what, or who, the "patient" actually is.

Of course, the debate over brain death as the criterion for legal death is not limited only to the exigencies of organ transplantation. In the case of Karen Ann Quinlan, for example, the absence of cerebral functioning was cited as a reason for discontinuing the mechanical support that apparently maintained her heartbeat and breathing. As has been repeatedly emphasized in this Reader, modern medicine has the technical power to maintain "life" in bodies under circumstances where formerly death of brain and heart would have ensued. But such technical power does not provide the basis for moral decisions. Science can show that the brain is the central organ of the body and, as Bertrand Russell asserted in Section 6, constitutes the basis for our humanness. But science cannot provide clear guidelines regarding whether we should or ought to regard the brain-dead patient as dead or alive, human or no longer human.

This summary examination of several important moral and ethical dilemmas relating to death and dying suggests that such issues are highly significant and extremely complex. Each year thousands of abortions are performed and thousands of moribund patients are "terminated" at the discretion of medical personnel. Living wills and Uniform Anatomical Gift Act donor cards are proliferating. As the success rates for various transplant procedures improves, the demand for donor organs is likely to increase. One possible resolution of this situation is presented by Gaylin, in his sardonic essay in Section 15 of this Reader.

What are the implications of the present moral-ethical confusion? Hall and Cameron, in their selection "Our Failing Reverence for Life," argue that, taken together, the developments and issues discussed above indicate that the value of human life is declining in our society. Availability of abortions, prevalence of euthanasia both as practice and as a movement, popular acceptance of the death penalty, and the growing acceptability of suicide all reflect, they suggest, the pressures of overpopulation and economic scarcity interacting with moral confusion and faith in technical solutions.

As the costs of both living and dying increase, the question of whether to eliminate unproductive or exhausted life at one end of the age spectrum and/or prevent its fruition at the other is likely to grow. In the absence of any overarching moral sanctions, and in the presence of a burgeoning technology, the dilemma of what constitutes human life—as well as death—will in all likelihood continue.

Elizabeth Hall
with Paul Cameron

Our Failing Reverence for Life

Psychologists Elizabeth Hall and Paul Cameron examine several trends that they feel indicate a decline in the value of human life. These include the availability of abortions, the practice of letting hopelessly deformed babies die, the prevalence of withdrawing or refusing treatments, the popular acceptance of euthanasia, the growing approval of capital punishment, and the increasing acceptability of suicide. The rising population of the world in the face of declining resources is precipitating, they fear, the acceptance of a "lifeboat ethics." In addition, the costs of health care are increasing, and, under the present health care system, the life-saving resources of modern medicine simply are not available to everyone. Under such conditions, the moral and ethical dilemmas of death are likely to grow ever more urgent.

On March 10, 1974, the *Washington Post* published interviews with a group of physicians at the Maryland Institute for Emergency Medicine who had participated in the killing of quadriplegics. These are patients who are paralyzed from the neck down. Often they can talk; certainly they can think, read, and watch television. The hospital gets about four of these cases each year; they are accident victims whose spinal cords have been severed just below the base of the skull.

When these patients arrive at the shock trauma unit, physicians insert breathing tubes and hook them up to respirators. After a few weeks of treatment and study, and after the doctors are sure there is no chance for improvement, the quadraplegics are killed. Without a patient's knowledge or consent, he is drugged so that he will not know what is happening and will not feel the terror of dying. Then he is unplugged. These doctors feel it would be "inhumane" to ask the patient if he wants to live or die since, as one doctor puts it, "everyone dearly loves life."

In a single generation, our society has undergone a profound change. Thirty years ago, newspapers and magazines often carried stories about Albert Schweitzer, the humanitarian who gave up successful European careers in music, medicine, and theology to heal uneducated blacks at his small African hospital near Lambaréné, Gabon. Schweitzer's philosophy of reverence for life became the credo of the American liberal. In 1949, he was the subject of a *Time* magazine cover essay, and he became virtually the patron saint of Norman Cousins' *Saturday Review*.

Since Schweitzer's death in 1965, one hears little about reverence for life. Instead, articles discuss the lifeboat ethic, in which those who have hang onto their resources and those who have not do without—even if it means starvation.

Faced with mounting populations and diminishing world resources, we have moved from talking about the value of life to talking about its worthlessness under certain conditions, from discussing the Green Revolution that would feed millions to championing the right to die. Evidence is mounting from all sectors of society that our culture no longer values human life as it once did.

From cradle to grave, decisions are going against life. By a seven-to-two majority, the U.S. Supreme Court has ruled that states may not pass laws prohibiting abortion. The Court's ruling allows women to abort freely during the first twenty-four weeks of pregnancy, permitting destruction of the fetus at a time when it has developed internal organs, hair, and sweat glands. By this time the fetus sleeps, wakes, kicks, cries, and looks disturbingly human.

Unless such late abortion is permitted, the new tool of amniocentesis, in which the amniotic fluid drawn from the womb is examined for abnormalities, will be useless. The technique cannot be used before the sixteenth week of pregnancy, and most physicians prefer to wait until the fetus is twenty weeks old.

Amniocentesis and subsequent abortion have undoubtedly prevented the births of many deformed babies. But some physicians have announced that they will abort at this stage for so slight a reason as the parents' discontent with the sex of their unborn child. In condoning the destruction of an organism that is only six weeks away from humanhood (babies born at twenty-six weeks sometimes survive), we have moved a long way from the ethics of Schweitzer, who was troubled because the antibiotics he administered killed bacteria.

LETTING BABIES DIE.   Not all couples seek amniocentesis, and defective babies continue to be born. In many cases, they need medical treatment to survive. If the parents agree, doctors commonly withhold treatment. At Yale-New Haven hospital, for instance, forty-three deformed babies were allowed to die during a period of thirty months. The doctors and parents who were involved in these terminations decided that the babies faced lives devoid of "meaningful humanhood."

Some doctors go beyond the mere withholding of treatment. In Louisville, Kentucky, a physician discovered that his black patient was about to give birth to a limbless child. Once his diagnosis was confirmed by radiologists, the physician gave the mother morphine. Morphine depresses the respiratory responses of the fetus; the baby was born dead.

Psychologist Paul Cameron, who studies American attitudes toward life, heard of the case from one of the radiologists involved. He has told this story to over thirty groups of people, and the first reaction has never been one of outrage or sympathy for the mother. Instead, he is always asked, "*Was* the infant defective?"

Life is no longer good enough for us; it must be "meaningful." Neurosurgeon Milton D. Heifetz, who wrote *The Right to Die,* says, "I treasure life, but I do not believe life is warranted if it cannot be lived with some measure of grace and dignity. The man who cannot speak, who cannot think, who would live as a vegetating mass of protoplasm without any hope of recovery should not be forced to live."

Many of us now agree with Heifetz's criteria for a meaningful life, but it has not always been so. In 1947 and again in 1950, the Gallup Poll asked Americans if doctors should be allowed to practice euthanasia. The answers were consistent; both times a majority said no. Only 36 percent were willing to grant doctors the power to end the life of a patient suffering from an incurable disease, even if both the patient and his family requested it.

A MAJORITY FOR DEATH.   Asked the same question in 1973, 53 percent replied that the doctor should end the patient's life. The majority now favored death. When death comes as a result of withholding treatment rather than by actively ending life, 72 percent are in favor of it, according to NBC-TV's poll conducted in December, [1975].

Rumor says that many physicians are already carrying out the wishes of the majority. Scattered evidence indicates that the rumor is true. When members of the American Association of Professors of Medicine responded to a questionnaire, almost 80 percent said that they had withdrawn treatment in response to the wishes of their patients.

Paul Cameron studied hospitals in Louisville, Kentucky, where his students collected reports on 125 patients in the cardiac and intensive-care units of four hospitals in which they worked. Twenty of those patients were terminated. That is, their deaths were the result of a deliberate decision by physicians. More than half died because medical treatment was withheld; the plug was pulled on the rest, either because "they had no chance of recovery," because another patient needed the life-sustaining machine, or as "an act of mercy."

At least two of the Louisville terminations were ethically questionable. In one case, an older man who kept fondling the nurses suffered a heart arrest and was allowed to lie without treatment for three minutes while the medical staff stood by. When they tried to resuscitate him, it was too late. In another case, the deformed baby girl of a sixteen-year-old black welfare recipient was denied proper care by the attending physician, who believed that the child would grow up only to produce more welfare recipients.

If the Louisville situation is typical, approximately one hundred thousand Americans die each year because someone decides not to give them medical care. The decision is usually made on humanitarian grounds, when unconscious patients with no hope for recovery have their fates decided by families or physicians. The Karen Ann Quinlan case, in which a twenty-one-year-old woman with brain damage had been in a coma for five months, differed from these patients in that her case did not end in a quiet hospital death. When doctors refused to terminate Karen, her parents took the matter to court. Although the Quinlans, both Roman Catholic, had the support of their priest, the court refused to allow the plug of her respirator to be pulled.[1]

No one knows for sure what Karen would want, even though she once told her mother that she would rather die than become a machine-supported vegetable. Most people in good health would probably give similar answers, but there is no way for anyone to be sure what decision he would make when forced to choose between life and death. A Hawaiian medical technician who had hooked up more than six-hundred patients to life-sustaining machines told Cameron that four hundred of them had been able to communicate their wishes. Not one of them asked to be allowed to die; instead, they usually asked to be attached to the machines as quickly as possible.

THE HAPPY HANDICAPPED.   In eliminating deformed children and pulling plugs on paraplegics, we believe that we are sparing them lives of misery. But the trouble is, physical or mental defects do not necessarily

1. Editor's note: The New Jersey Supreme Court subsequently overturned this decision, ruling that the "right to die" is inherent in the right to privacy. The respirator was unplugged, but as of this writing, Karen Ann Quinlan remains alive, in a coma.

mean that people are miserable. When Cameron surveyed people suffering from paralysis, muscular diseases, missing limbs, blindness and deafness, he found that they were as satisfied and optimistic as a comparable group of normal people. The handicapped were also less likely than the normal group to have contemplated suicide. In another of Cameron's surveys, mentally retarded children turned out to be happier than normal children, according to ratings by their parents and teachers.

The happiness of the patient is not always the deciding factor when physicians decide to let death come quickly. At a meeting of the Tri-State Activity Directors Association in Evansville, Indiana, on March 21, 1970, a doctor discussed death with dignity. According to Cameron, he explained a difficult decision he had made regarding a woman on whom he had planned to operate for cancer. The night before the surgery, the woman's son-in-law called, reminded the doctor that he had performed approximately the same operation on the woman several years earlier, and asked him to cancel the surgery. If the physician operated the next day, the family's savings would be wiped out and they would have to go without a color TV, a second car, and a larger home. The physician cancelled the woman's operation. He explained that "the few extra years she would gain from the operation would hardly justify the privation to which this young family would be subjected."

The son-in-law's request may seem heartless, but it points to a problem that Albert Schweitzer never had to deal with. Advances in medical technology have brought us to a place where, had we machines enough, we could keep thousands of bodies functioning that otherwise would die. The prospect of special hospitals made up of bed after bed filled with terminal patients is chilling but possible. But respirators are expensive, and so are other medical and surgical advances.

THE COST OF CARE.   Karen Ann Quinlan's medical costs had topped $100,000 at the time her case was first heard. A Long Island hospital recently insisted that Thomas Cullington, an eighteen-year-old youth who had been in a coma for more than a year, be

I COUNSEL YOU BEWARE

Good creatures, do you love your lives
   And have you ears for sense?
Here is a knife like other knives,
   That cost me eighteen pence.

I need but stick it in my heart
   And down will come the sky,
And earth's foundations will depart
   And all you folk will die.

              A. E. Housman

removed to a nursing home. His bills had passed $75,000. The Quinlan and Cullington cases are not rare. Asked how many terminal patients are kept alive by mechanical means, Robert Veatch of the Institute of Society, Ethics and the Life Sciences replied, "lots and lots."

Our power to prolong life has forced us to decide when we will refuse to prolong it. A few years ago, when dialysis machines were scarce, the Seattle Artificial Kidney Center established a committee to screen applicants. The committee, made up of two physicians, an attorney, a banker, a labor leader, a house-wife,and a minister, knew that the patients they rejected were literally condemned to death.

Now that dialysis machines are widely available, the committee has been disbanded. But the problem faced by the seven citizens of Seattle will one day be upon all of us.

In 1974, according to HEW estimates, kidney dialysis cost $240 million; by 1982, the annual cost is expected to reach one billion. Coronary-bypass surgery, an operation that is chosen by approximately thirty-five thousand patients each year, carries an annual price tag of $200 million. As new technologies develop, the cost will skyrocket. Stripped of sentiment, the problem becomes how much of our gross national product we are willing to devote to medical care.

As the financial burden gets heavier, our eroded reverence for life may wear away entirely. Its erosion already shows clearly in other areas. When the U.S. Supreme Court declared most state laws on capital punishment unconstitutional, it appeared that the fight to abolish the death penalty had been won. Today, support for capital punishment is growing, and voices that once spoke passionately against this final solution to crime re-main silent. The Gallup Poll found that in 1974, 64 percent of the American people support the death penalty, up from 47 percent in 1957.

THE CASE FOR SUICIDE.   It also appears that suicide no longer repels us. The suicide rate is climbing, especially among blacks and young people. What's more, suicide has been appearing in an increasingly favorable light in the nation's press. When Paul Cameron surveyed all articles on suicide indexed over the past fifty years in the *Readers' Guide to Periodical Literature,* he found that voluntary death, once portrayed as a brutal waste, now generally appears in a neutral light. Some recent articles even present suicide as a good thing to do and are written in a manner that might encourage the reader to take his own life under certain circumstances. Last year, a majority of Americans under thirty told Gallup pollsters that incurable disease or continual pain confer on a person the moral right to end his life.

If this trend continues, we may one day institute the euthanasia parlors portrayed in the movie *Soylent Green.* In this picture of the future, people who wish to end their lives report to a government building, where beautiful girls welcome them and administer a lethal drug. As they lie dying, the volunteers watch movies of idyllic pastoral settings and listen to Beethoven's *Ninth Symphony*.

While *Soylent Green* is only fiction, one must not forget that science-fiction writers have been on target with their forecasts of other developments in our society, from atom bombs and laser beams to communications satellites, birth-control pills, and moving side-walks. Psychologist Robert Kastenbaum, of the University of Massachusetts, agrees that suicide may win society's approval. He contends that once we recognize the right to a dignified death, suicide will become a valid ethical choice, a choice that Kastenbaum says will strengthen the social fabric.

If theologian Richard L. Rubenstein is right, no one should be surprised by these developments. Each one is an example of our application of reason to human problems. It is irrational to prolong suffering, to keep alive the malformed or the unconscious, to support murderers at public expense, or to allow unwanted babies to be born.

THE NAZI EXAMPLE.   Rubenstein, who spent years studying the Nazi massacre of six million Jews, believes that the Nazis solved their problem of a surplus population by using similar rational means. Faced with more people than their economy could support, the Nazis first instituted euthanasia for the mentally incompetent and the "incurably sick," then stripped Jews of their citizenship and applied the same solution to them. . . .

The Nazi solution, he says, was an inevitable outcome of the Judaeo-Christian tradition. From the first chapter of Genesis, the Israelites set out to show that there are no magical or mysterious forces in nature that man must appease. Although God judges humanity's actions, He does not interfere capriciously in the universe.

No earlier culture had so disenchanted the world, and, Rubenstein believes, the consequences were profound. Succeeding generations systematically secularized the world, removing ever greater areas of human life from religious domination. At the same time, reason gradually spread into every act, as humanity learned to calculate with precision just what means were required to reach a desired goal.

Only after such a development, says Rubenstein, could a system develop that would overcome the moral barrier that had always prevented the systematic elimination of surplus population. That system was not Nazism, but bureaucracy, which effectively erases love, hatred, and all emotional elements from man's dealings with his fellow man.

According to Rubenstein, the Nazis were only the first to push the Judaeo-Christian tradition to its logical conclusion. Civilization, which brings us art, literature, music, and new medical technologies, also brings us slavery, wars, exploitation, and death camps. It will, he says, bring us death camps again. . . .

Bureaucrats may already be making death-dealing decisions. One of the first cases turned up in *Prism,* a journal published by the American Medical Association. A large city hospital switched its respirators from a $299 manifold to a disposable manifold that cost less than $5. The change saved the hospital a great deal of money each year, not only in initial expense but in sterilization costs for the expensive manifold.

There was, however, one disadvantage. With the disposable manifold, the temperature of the air that flows into the patient's lungs cannot be monitored. This means that there is no way for medical personnel to know whether the air is so dry that secretions are collecting in the patient's lungs, inducing pneumonia.

When a physician pointed out this danger to the hospital purchasing agent, the agent pulled out his calculator and quickly figured the extra cost of the reusable manifold.

"You can't possibly tell me," he said, "that one small hole is worth the thousands and thousands of dollars we will save on these things every year."

The purchasing agent saw the problem clearly. It was all a matter of simple cost accounting.

Daniel C. Maguire

Death, Legal and Illegal

Daniel Maguire, a Catholic theologian, examines the concept of mercy killing in terms of existing legal definitions. He concludes that the law does not presently encompass killing for merciful motives with the permission of the "victim." As medical technology makes it possible to prolong life in patients who would formerly have died, the pressure for some kind of formal policy will continue to grow. Further pressure for policy formulation may derive from the growing proportion of old persons in our population and from the steadily rising costs of medical care. The individual's demand for a "death with dignity," moreover, confronts both the medical profession and the legal system with the challenge of developing legislation that will safeguard the rights of the patient as well as those of the physician.

A motorcycle accident in June, 1973, paralyzed George Zygmaniak, aged twenty-six, from the neck down. The indications were that the paralysis would be permanent. George begged his brother, Lester, to kill him, saying he would kill himself if he could. Lester shot and killed his brother in his hospital bed.

The case went to trial, and the jury, after deliberating for two hours and thirty-five minutes, acquitted Zygmaniak on the grounds that he was insane when he shot his brother. The jury also found that he had regained his sanity and he was freed. In this and in similar cases, what the court produces is not so much a verdict as a diagnosis. And a remarkable diagnosis it is, touching as it does on the past, present, and future mental state of the defendant. The jury judged that Zygmaniak's past insanity was such as to excuse him from what would otherwise have been an act of criminal homicide. The jury then pronounced Zygmaniak cured, and the court, by releasing the defendant without further ado, underwrote the inference that his lethal illness would not recur.

On August 9, 1967, Robert Waskins, a twenty-three-year-old college student, killed his mother by shooting her three times in the head. When the police arrived and advised him of his rights to silence, he simply replied: "It's obvious, I killed her." He was arrested and charged with murder.

Waskins' mother had been suffering from leukemia. She had at the most several more days to live. She was, however, in extreme pain and wanted to die. In fact she had begged her son to kill her. Three days previously, she had tried to commit suicide by taking an overdose of sleeping pills. Both her husband and the doctors witnessed to the fact that she was in deep pain at the time she was shot.

The case went to court. The letter of the law had little to offer Waskins. Motive, however benevolent, is no defense in cases of mercy killing. Motive can influence the judge in sentencing, but the most lenient sentence in

Waskins' case would be fourteen years in prison with no hope of probation.

On January 24, 1969, a jury deliberated for only forty minutes and with instant psychoanalysis found Waskins not guilty by reason of insanity. They further found that he was no longer insane and he was released. There is no psychiatric evidence that Waskins was ever insane, but thus the case was resolved.

In a famous case in New Hampshire in 1950, Dr. Herman Sander was charged with the murder of a cancer-stricken patient. Dr. Sander had given the patient ten cc's of air intravenously four times and she died within ten minutes. It is reported that the patient asked the doctor to put her out of her misery. The doctor noted on the patient's chart that he had given her these air injections.

The defense offered for Sander at his trial was that the patient was already dead at the time of the injections. The jury acquitted the doctor apparently on the grounds that there was no proof that his action had caused the patient's death. Thus ended what appears to be the first case in which a doctor in this country was tried on the charge of euthanasia. Jurists who had hoped that the case would set a precedent on the legality of euthanasia, however pleased they might have been for Dr. Sander, were understandably disappointed in the rationale of the verdict. The jury, it would seem, can scarcely be faulted. The judge had stated at the very outset of the trial that the question of mercy killing could not legally be an issue at the trial. One wonders what could be the issue?

Sometimes, in cases of mercy killing, the evidence is simply brushed aside. In the Illinois case of *People* v. *Werner,* the defendant pleaded guilty to a manslaughter charge for having suffocated his wife, who was a hopelessly crippled arthritic and had begged her husband to put her out of her misery. After hearing testimony from the family of the defendant regarding his devotion to his wife, and after the doctor testified to the excruciating pain and mental despair of the woman, the defendant was allowed to change his plea to not guilty. The court then acquitted him on the grounds that a jury would not be inclined to convict in such cases. The judge also observed that in this case there was no likelihood of recidivism, that is, of repeating this kind of activity.

Resorting to reasons of insanity for acquittal in mercy killing cases is a common tactic. This tactic would seem to constitute a commentary on the state of the law. What is happening in these instances is that there is a flight to psychiatry when there is no help from the law. Such cases are not rare. Carol Paight, a Connecticut college girl who had been indicted for second-degree murder for killing her hospitalized father who was dying of cancer, was acquitted by reason of temporary insanity at the time of the commission of the act. And in Michigan, Eugene Braunsdorf won the same merciful judgment after killing his crippled adult daughter, who was spastic, mute, and had required hospitalization all her life.

The wheels of justice do not grind evenly here, however. In the same year in which Paight and Braunsdorf were so acquitted, Harold Mohr in Pennsylvania was convicted of voluntary manslaughter for the killing of his blind, cancer-stricken brother. He was sentenced to from three to six years in prison and fined five hundred dollars even though he also pleaded temporary insanity, and even though, in contrast to the other two cases, there was in the Mohr case evidence that the accused had acted upon the urgent and repeated requests of his brother. Ironically, the judge in sentencing Mohr described the defendant as a martyr who must suffer the price of martyrdom! . . .

Beyond all theoretical questions of what the legal status of mercy killing ought to be, two facts are painfully obvious about the way it is. The current situation is inherently unfair by reason of the unevenness in the judgments reached. Verdicts range from murder in the first degree to acquittal. Prosecutors, judges, and juries generally approach cases of mercy killing in a way that contradicts the law as given. Devious means to circumvent the rigor of the law are the order of the day. But devious means are unregulated and in some cases the law in all of its conceptual rigor will be enforced. Thus the evenhandedness that a rule of law should ensure to create a sense of justice in society is not in evidence.

Secondly, the way in which the law has to be circumvented would appear to merit the epithet *hypocritical*. Judges and juries, sensing that the law as it stands is deficient, and being unable to do anything about it, declare the defendant deficient, that is, insane. Pleas-ing as acquittal may be to the defendant, there is some inequity in his having to get the verdict he and the jury want and believe to be just by the loss of his claim to mental health. The situation is all the more macabre since it is often clear that the defense of insanity is only a gimmick used to make it possible to slip out from under the harshness commanded by the law but not by the facts.

The present categories of the law do not encompass the realities involved in death by choice, that is, cases in which by omission or by commission one's own death or the death of another is opted for in preference to continued living. The kinds of death spoken of here are those usually referred to in popular parlance as mercy killing or euthanasia. The motives for these deaths are compassion and an unselfish desire to bring on death when continued living is unbearable for the patient due to physical and/or mental suffering. Mercy killings thus described do not fit into any of the categories of unjustifiable homicide available in American law. They are not murder in the first or second degree, nor are they a form of criminal man-slaughter.

Robert M. Veatch

The Legislative Options

Robert Veatch, a senior associate of the Institute of Society, Ethics, and the Life Sciences, analyzes several kinds of legislation dealing with the right to die and mercy killing. He notes that the rights of the patient, family, medical personnel, and community all must be clearly safeguarded. Again, we see that technical developments have created moral dilemmas for which easy solutions are unlikely to be found. It seems clear, however, that whatever legislation is eventually passed, it should reflect input not only from professional moralists, medical personnel, and legal experts, but the opinions of the general public as well.

A man in his eighties, without any relatives, was admitted to the hospital in respiratory distress from pneumonia. He had metastasized cancer and was convinced that he would eventually die from it. By the next morning he was dead. Acting on benevolent and humane motives, the medical staff had decided to let the patient die of pneumonia now rather than of cancer later. They had heard the "death-with-dignity" message. But they had not bothered to ask the patient how he felt about dying in this way.

The case illustrates the confusion that has followed upon the increasingly vigorous calls for the right to die with dignity. It also illustrates why many people, including those who are strongly committed to the right-to-life positions and to continued medical treatment for the terminally ill, are beginning to explore legislative options to clarify the individual's rights to control decisions about terminal care.

A combination of several factors has apparently led to this recent round of legislative effort. Many of the state legislators who have introduced bills say they were motivated by unnecessarily tragic deaths in their own families. Underlying these personal experiences, however, is a shift in the cultural mood, a reaction against the excessive technologizing of the dying process and its control by the professional rather than the family.

I have examined eighty-five pieces of draft legislation which address this problem. In 1977 alone bills have been introduced into forty state legislatures; eight states have passed legislation: Arkansas, California, Idaho, Nevada, New Mexico, North Carolina, Oregon, and Texas. The others are at various stages in the legislative process. Some of the bills seem to provide needed clarificaton, making relatively minor adjustments in our present public policy. Others seem to be extremely dangerous and confusing, perhaps depriving individuals of rights and responsibilities they now possess and would not want to surrender. The brief history of legislative research and development may explain why some of the bills are so inadequate.

The merits of the bills notwithstanding, it is no longer possible to take the position that there should be no policy at all. In an older and simpler day, an informal policy could suffice. The physician could decide what treatments were appropriate and when to stop treatment. We thought he was making a technical judgment. Certainly this is not the case today. There is such an obvious variation in views about what treatment is appropriate for a terminally ill patient that informal consensus is no longer adequate. Physicians, like the general public, have views ranging from "treatment at all costs to the very end," to "let the patient die even if the patient is not ready to die."

Policies regarding decisions to treat or not treat the terminally ill should be clarified publicly. The eighty-five bills I have examined fall into three basic types: (1) bills that would apparently legalize active killing, (2) bills that would clarify the rights of competent patients to accept or refuse treatment, and (3) bills that would clarify who should make medical decisions in cases where the patient is incompetent. . . .

ELEMENTS OF A MODEL BILL   A model bill should do several things. First, it should make clear that wishes expressed while [patients are] competent and never disavowed should remain valid when individuals are not able to express themselves. Mechanisms for disavowal should be spelled out. Since all competent persons have the right to refuse medical treatment even if . . . [the result is] death, it seems reasonable that their wishes should remain valid when they become incompetent. The right to have one's instructions followed should not be limited to the terminally ill no matter how defined.

A good bill will also specify the penalty for failure to follow such instructions and for forging a document. Probably the penalty for falsely making it appear someone wants treatment stopped should be different from falsely making it appear someone wants treatment to go on.

The rights of medical personnel to withdraw from a case—as long as other suitable professional support is provided—when the patient's instructions violate the professional's conscience should be spelled out, as well as the right of patients to be informed of the right to accept or refuse treatment.

The bill should clearly state that deaths resulting from treatment refusal are not suicide for legal and insurance purposes, and that medical professionals are not guilty of homicide for following such instructions.

If these guidelines are followed, ambiguous terms such as "extraordinary means" and "terminal patient" will not have to be included, but if such terms are used they should be defined.

A minimum age for execution of a treatment acceptance or refusal document should be stated. Probably the age of majority in the state [should apply] for purposes of legally accepting or refusing medical treatments in general and for executing other critical documents.

The bill should also address the problem of who should make decisions in cases where the patient is incompetent because of age or other reasons. For formerly competent patients, a person designated by the individual while competent is a reasonable first authority. For the never-competent, the next of kin is currently presumed to have the authority to consent to medical treatment. Logically the right to refuse consent is implied, but this right should be made explicit. A full statute would permit agents delegated by the individual to make treatment acceptance or refusal decisions and would make clear who has the authority in cases where no one has been so designated.

The movement to legislate "death with dignity" has gained momentum, fueled by public opinion and rising emotion. Careful analysis and attention to the consequences are essential to assure that these laws achieve their goals rather than obscuring or hindering them.

Sonya Rudikoff

The Problem of Euthanasia

Sonya Rudikoff's essay on "The Problems of Euthanasia" raises several important points. In particular, she questions whether the legalization of mercy killing would possibly create more problems than it would solve. The necessity of careful safeguards might, she suggests, create bureaucratic complexities that could interfere with the initial goal of humane care. On the other hand, the "living will," in which a person states a clear desire to be allowed to die under certain conditions, may permit the individual a measure of self-determination in an area where most decisions are made for the patient by others. Rudikoff also alludes to the fact that scarce and expensive medical resources may pressure some people to opt for early death because they fear becoming burdens on their families. Her article reminds us again that the problem of euthanasia is as complex as it is important.

Although the death of close friends and relatives may have vanished as a vivid firsthand experience for most of us, almost everyone knows, or knows of, someone who is being kept alive by machines or tubes. It is quite common to hear people say that if they themselves should arrive at such a condition, they would hope for euthanasia. Thus, membership in the Euthanasia Society of America has jumped from six hundred to over fifty thousand in four years, and the society has been filling an unprecedented number of requests for copies of its "living will," a declaration of the wish for euthanasia, which, although not legally binding, exerts a powerful demand on physician and family.

Euthanasia, from the Greek *eu* and *thanatos,* signifies a good or peaceful death. It conjures up images of dignity and repose, a calm, reconciled conclusion to a life whose meaning has been accorded its due. Euthanasia, often called "death with dignity," also implies the necessary medical efforts to reduce pain without needlessly prolonging the agony of one who is going to die. Few in the past have been fortunate enough to die such a death, and not so many in the present. It is what used to be prayed for when dying people believed that death was a significant event to be followed by other unknown developments, and when the mortally ill were surrounded by those whose convictions were equally strong. It was not thought appropriate or desirable to hasten the onset of this event, which, in any case, was independent of human will and would come in its own time. The final weeks, days, or hours of the mortally ill were almost sacred, but perhaps only believers are still mindful of what everyone used to take thought for—the deathbed scene, perhaps a confession, the reconciliations, the promises made to the dying, the revelations, the assurances, the consolations and affirmations. To think of hastening the progress of this drama would have been unusual or even unconscionable. And, it should be added, the available pharmacopeia did not offer many alternatives, even for the rich and powerful: all were to encounter what used to be called "the Last Great Adventure" or, as Henry James greeted it, "the Distinguished Thing."

Euthanasia means deliberate intervention in this process. It violates unmistakably the commandment against killing, and it is also therefore illegal. In spite of numerous attempts to introduce the idea of extenuating circumstances in what is often called "mercy killing," euthanasia remains proscribed. Individual cases—as when a doctor gives a dying patient a fatal injection or when someone kills a dying relative—may be decided in favor of the killer, as recently happened in New Jersey, but the courts are reluctant to declare euthanasia acceptable. The Hippocratic Oath has always been interpreted as forbidding euthanasia, and the opinions of religious leaders have opposed it as a general practice, if with some qualifications. It is against the law to help a dying person to die quickly, although you can legally kill a healthy person if he seems about to kill you. And if you ask for lethal drugs with the intention of taking them yourself, that is suicide. Attempts to rationalize and clarify these seeming inconsistencies have not resulted in major reforms. England's Suicide Act of 1961 removes the illegality from suicide but still forbids assisting anyone else's suicide. Switzerland permits the doctor to put poison in the hand of the patient but not actually to administer it himself.

Some of the inconsistencies result from the complex conditions of modern medicine. It would be difficult to assert that the doctor who gives a humane overdose of drugs has "murdered" his patient. Obviously, when a patient has been receiving quite a lot of potentially lethal drugs, it is not always clear which or how much was the fatal dose. Prosecutors and juries have been and will continue to be reluctant to question the good faith of such doctors, or to demand precise proof [as to] whether death was hastened, induced, or merely not actively prevented. Doctors are of course most anxious to avoid anything remotely implying malpractice suits. At the same time, there are never unlimited resources, certainly not in personnel, and in every hospital there are unwritten customs to be followed in various cases, with coded notations on patients' charts indicating whether or not "heroic efforts" should be made at resuscitation in case of approaching death. Different emergencies demand different treatment, and the needs of patients, the exigencies of medical personnel, the availability of beds or operating rooms or other facilities are all factors which must be taken into account when sudden decisions are made.

So ambiguous is the matter that interested observers have developed distinctions between negative and positive, or active and passive, euthanasia, in order to account for some of the differences in the treatment of the mortally ill. Thus, doctors distinguish between the omission of certain drugs or mechanical supports at critical times, when the patient would proceed to die without them—this is negative euthanasia—and the more specific acts of administering an overdose of drugs, injecting an air bubble in the veins, or actually withdrawing drugs or intravenous feeding or the respirator with the intention of hastening the death of an already dying patient. If a doctor administers a drug with the intention of relieving suffering, and the drug is fatal, he has not committed murder because it was not his intention. Similarly, when a doctor performs a gallbladder operation on an eighty-six-year-old man suffering from emphysema, heart trouble, and other ailments, and when the man has a stroke and dies after the operation, the operation is not murder, even though the patient died, because the doctor intended to relieve the gall-bladder condition and ease suffering. Even knowing the possibility of a patient's fatal reaction to a specific procedure does not make it murder without the explicit intention. The matter becomes more complex in the context of sophisticated medical alternatives, but euthanasia continues to mean not only the medical killing but the intent to accomplish it.

Perhaps there are really only two important questions about euthanasia, and one is the same question that might be asked about suicide, or about many more commonplace forms of self-destruction such as alcoholism or smoking: Do our bodies and our selves belong to us so entirely, as private property, that we may dispose of them in any way we wish? All sorts of developments in the history of thought and faith have led many people to think so, and current ideas of individualism and self-determination and self-realization certainly underline [this idea]. Some people, however, continue to believe that they belong to God, or that their bodies, souls, and lives are [given] as a gift or trust, rather than a private possession. Some believe that the breath of life in each of us is a part of a spirit of life, or a community of spirit over which we do not exert ultimate control; that life was given to us and we give it to others; that we may not extinguish life deliberately. Faced with the problem of balancing the two parts of that awful question, "Who shall live and who shall die?," many people find themselves willing to grant and place their trust in the power of human intervention on the one side, while insisting that the latter half remain beyond the pale of human meddling. Indeed, anyone who has seen a victim of acute coronary attack returned to life in the intensive heart-care unit of a modern hospital must be vividly aware of the degree to which it is within our power to regulate significantly the number of living and dead.

The other question involves new knowledge and possibilities for legal reform. It is the question whether *all* death nowadays is not really euthanasia, in view of recent developments in the definition of death. It may come as something of a surprise that there should be any question of defining death—surely even the untutored have known for countless millennia, and before recorded time, the difference between life and death, and have not had to be instructed in the matter by savants and researchers! The news that this certainty as well has been called into question by modern science may be greeted by impatience or even fury. Preposterous as it may seem, however, the exact determination of death has never been quite so clear-cut as might be thought, and has always implied the possibility of mysterious occurrences and inexplicable recoveries. Indeed, death, its manner of occurrence, and its precise certification, became of political and administrative importance as soon as settled civilizations developed and rulers desired to know how many people were to be taxed. Humane societies were especially interested in rudimentary methods of mouth-to-mouth resuscitation, and the growing sophistication of medical knowledge aroused an interest in the causes of death and the manner of determining them, such as by means of autopsies. The development of death certificates, of mortuaries, of special burial practices, the use of cadavers for autopsy, the registering of births and deaths, all came about along with public rolls, coroners, poor laws, and other social and economic aspects of modern life. . . .

What does death mean, when cardiac massage can make the dead live, or when heart-lung machines, electric shock, or chemicals perform easily the spontaneous recoveries witnessed in the past? Patients who "die" during operations can be instantly revived by the trained personnel in the modern operating room. If cardiac arrest and cessation of breathing no longer mean death, or if heartbeat and breathing no longer mean life, then death has become an event entirely incidental to medical technology, and always, then, an act of euthanasia. The number of patients maintained in biological life by mechanical supports has increased greatly in recent years, and the question of their survival has been raised at the same time that there has been an increased interest in the concept of "brain death" as providing more reliable criteria than heart and breathing cessation. Such patients, often called "vegetables," are alive and yet not living as human beings. The interest in brain function has become more refined, but what has provided a special urgency requiring immediate attention has been the parallel development in highly complex techniques of organ transplantation. Not only does it become a matter of concern how long biological life should be maintained artificially if the brain has died, and at what social cost, but, more specifically, in order to proceed with organ transplants there must be absolute clarity about when the donor is to be considered legally dead. These recent developments are troubling, and they provide ample warrant for wondering whether anyone can die his own death anymore.

Clinical death occurs in humans when the heart and lungs stop functioning and the brain is deprived of oxygen. Unless resuscitation begins immediately, brain death follows, because the brain cannot survive without oxygen, and brain tissues do not heal or regenerate as other tissues do. The brain dies in stages, beginning with the cerebral cortex, then the mid-brain, and the brain stem. Cellular death follows, with organs and tissues remaining alive a bit longer. It is this sequence in death which makes possible the transplantation of living organs from the newly dead and thus raises the difficult question, when does death occur and what is it? If a serious accident destroys a victim's brain, but his basic functions are maintained artificially, does he ever die? When should the respirator be turned off, and for what reason? At what point would organ transplants, often called the "gift of life," be transformed unwittingly but unmistakably into the theft of life? Dr. [Robert H.] Williams, throughout his collection [*To Live and To Die: When, Why, and How*], and especially in his own essays, emphasizes, as others do, the importance of mentation, of brain activity, as a sign of continued life. If cerebral functioning has virtually ceased, euthanasia is in a sense irrelevant. Death becomes an administrative matter: if the victim's organs are destined for use in transplants, the problem would be to synchronize the mechanically-supported life of the dying patient with the condition of the living patient awaiting a heart or kidney. Still, the question, "when?" remains.

As might be imagined, this subject has interested medical, legal, religious, and philosophical observers intensely ever since the first successful heart transplants in 1967 revealed the urgent need for immediate action, although the problem had been foreseen earlier. Legal and medical experts have been scrupulously concerned to set forth acceptable criteria for the cessation of cerebral function, and within the past five or six years, innumerable congresses and conferences have taken up the matter, legal scholars and theologians have explored it, and the courts have dealt with it. In 1968 an Ad Hoc Committee of the Harvard Medical School to Examine the Definition of Brain Death proposed four major criteria which would enable a doctor to pronounce a patient dead when the traditional signs of death—respiratory and circulatory failure—were obscured by the resuscitation machinery. The criteria would be: (1) irreversible coma; (2) complete absence of spontaneous breathing or muscular movement or response to pain; (3) complete absence of reflexes, or response to light, smells, heat, cold; fixed pupils; (4) a "flat" electroencephalogram, indicating no brain activity. Extreme care would be taken in administering such tests, and in insuring that they were not applied to patients suffering from hypothermia (temperature below 90° F.) or from central-nervous-system depressants. The tests would be repeated in twenty-four hours to ascertain any possible change, and some have suggested a longer waiting period. These tests have been used increasingly in the past five years and their usefulness has been confirmed.

The need of the medical profession for some clarity in the determination of death has become evident in a series of court cases in which the concept of "brain death" has been offered to jurors and judges. Indeed, two states have enacted statutes including "brain death" as an alternative to the traditional determination, Kansas in 1970 and Maryland in 1972, but the language of the statutes, and the attendant ambiguities, give cause for public and professional concern. An additional, perhaps a ghoulish, note is sounded by the seeming connection between new definitions of death and new techniques in organ transplantation, conjuring up an image of contemporary body-snatchers in the form of white-coated medical teams waiting to perform transplants. Are some people to be considered more dead than others if their organs are needed? All the possible abuses of this delicate situation may be imagined, when the death of a dying patient is not regarded as his own individual death but as an event contingent upon the needs of another patient with heart or kidney disease. The Uniform Anatomical Gift Act, which has been passed by fifty states in one version or another, specifies that time of death must be determined by a physician not involved in the transplant, but perhaps further efforts at separating these processes are required to allay inevitable disquiet and confusion.

In a careful examination of the problem, Alexander Morgan Capron, of the University of Pennsylvania Law School, and Leon R. Kass, of the National Research Council, have proposed refinements of the statutes and clarification of two important questions about the mortally ill, namely, "when to allow to die" and "when to declare dead."[1] (A further question, "when or whether to hasten death," explicitly evokes the intentions of the euthanasia movement, but no useful purpose is served by uniting all these questions. Euthanasia is not the same thing as donating your body for scientific research, or donating your organs for transplant, or even dying in all but your biological functions.) The exact determination of death is relevant not only to the mortally ill but in cases of suicide, accidents, and slow expiration as well; criteria must be agreed upon.

1. "A Statutory Definition of the Standards for Determining Human Death: An Appraisal and a Proposal," *University of Pennsylvania Law Review,* Volume 121, No. 1, November, 1973.

no matter what caused the death. Even in a perspective entirely different from the medical, or legal, or social, namely, the religious perspective which regards as the most important thing about death the soul's departure from the body, some explicit criteria must be employed to determine whether this has in fact occurred. Thus, the concept of brain death may be introduced for accuracy so long as the limits of its usefulness are clearly understood.

There may be some question whether mentation, cerebral activity, comprehends all that we mean by human existence, but it is clear that what really troubles us, behind the horror at becoming "vegetables," with life mechanically maintained at its most minimal, is the quite reasonable fear of the fragility of life itself. The machines that maintain life with tubes and wires, the whole impressive battery of modern medical techniques, mock the very thing that is cherished, the human person. Indeed, it is, among other things, precisely the helpless surrender to medical technology and management which the euthanasia movement attempts to counteract, with its "living will" and its deliberate confrontation with irrever-

...The regimen I adopt shall be for the benefit of my patients according to my ability and judgment, and not for their hurt or for any wrong. I will give no deadly drug to any, though it be asked of me, nor will I counsel such, and especially I will not aid a woman to procure abortion. Whatsoever house I enter, there will I go for the benefit of the sick, refraining from all wrongdoing or corruption, and especially from any act of seduction, of male or female, of bond or free. Whatsoever things I see or hear concerning the life of men, in my attendance on the sick or even apart therefrom, which ought not to be noised abroad, I will keep silence thereon, counting such things to be as sacred secrets.

The Oath of Hippocrates

sible illness. Advocates of euthanasia do not in fact urge it as public policy, but merely as a possible private alternative which should be removed from the criminal category. The Euthanasia Society believes that its "living will" insures the voluntary nature of the act. Like any other will, it is to be executed when the testator is of sound mind, and it instructs family and physician not to make extraordinary efforts to prolong his life if he should be so irreversibly ill that no recovery is possible. Obviously, the patient's initial act of consent is his visit to the doctor, and no subsequent medical procedures can be undertaken without further indications of consent. Even the sewing up of a wound in a hospital emergency room cannot be done without consent, nor can operations, transplants, autopsies, or other procedures. In the absence of a "living will," the family of the mortally ill may in effect be asking the doctor to perform euthanasia by not using all possible means of resuscitation, and the family may thus be giving its informed consent, although the patient, if comatose, does not give *his*. (In this matter—the ambiguity of consent—there is a connection with the concern of large numbers of people over the question of consent in medical and psychological research in general, and those interested in euthanasia are not unaware of it.)

Obviously, it has been the wish of many people who ponder the end of life, as people have done for centuries, that they not live beyond a certain point of disability, pain, deterioration, or unconsciousness. A calm and soberly determined and desired suicide has often seemed an appropriate alternative. Those who retain scruples about actually committing suicide might view the possibility of the "living will" as more acceptable. It is no public policy of killing the undesirables or the weaklings, but rather a stoic individual decision, as individual as wanting to leave money to a person or a cause, or wishing to be buried in a certain place, or cremation. Of course, a bureaucracy might exact consent to euthanasia from its citizens in the same cruel manner the Russians have exacted "voluntary" vows and confessions; uncontrolled bureaucracies become capable of these things when they verge on totalitarianism. And there is the other undesirable Russian practice of regarding all bodies as belonging to the state and therefore subject to autopsies or organ transplants or any other procedure without consent of the next of kin or of the patient himself. Still, there is quite a large leap from legally *permitting some* people to request that their own lives not be unnecessarily prolonged by artificial means, to a public policy *requiring all* lives to be terminated according to certain external criteria. Fears of "the entering wedge" and "the slippery slope" may blur or eliminate these significant distinctions. But does it make sense to think that we would remain unaware of all other bureaucratic encroachment on our lives and privacy until euthanasia were made mandatory? Actually, euthanasia, like abortion and contraception, might become a private matter between the patient and his doctor. Large numbers of our citizens might continue to think euthanasia a sin, as they do contraception and abortion, but they could no longer insist that it was a crime as well.

Euthanasia is not proclaimed frivolously by its advocates, or without thoughtful concern, and to speak of Nazis and ghoulish experiments in the same context is insulting. Nevertheless, instead of simplifying or clarifying a painful inevitable situation, there is reason to think that introducing euthanasia as a remedy for the travesty of death actually complicates it. To imagine euthanasia in practice, not as in a Nazi nightmare but as if it were working out in an ordinary system of medical care, is to provide more problems than cures. . . . For instance, an examination of the system of safeguards reveals how much care must be taken to establish certain qualifications for euthanasia, to have the declaration certified by witnesses, to insure that the declarer is of sound mind, and to release attending medical personnel from the violation of their Hippocratic oath and of any criminal responsibility. Then, the declaration must provide for a waiting period, for the possibility of revocation, and must include punishment for anyone willfully concealing, destroying, falsifying, or forging such a document. As the other procedural implications undergo scrutiny, so does the usual notion of euthanasia as a calm, sober act recalling Socrates nobly ending his life, or Phèdre, in grandeur, *par un chemin plus lent descendre chez les morts.*[2] The scene becomes, rather, an execution chamber, with witnesses and documents and official certification—how could it now?

What if the patient were of sound mind but had changed his mind since signing a declaration? Twenty-five percent of requests received by the Euthanasia Society are from young people; what if such a declaration were signed long ago, in another place; could it be easily revoked? One out of five Americans moves every year, and loss of documents always attends such population mobility; would a doctor in California know that his paralyzed, comatose patient had signed a "living will" in Maine? And what if the patient had forgotten? Which is the sound mind and who attests to it? Would the very doctors and nurses dedicated

to healing be the ones to perform euthanasia and if not, would a special class or caste or guild do it, and would their arrival in a ward or private room signify the approach of their dread responsibility? Is it conceivable that certain hospitals would become known as euthanasia mills? And would it be an improvement if the sense of anxiety and mistrust which many patients already feel on entering a hospital were to be confirmed by such practices and if the hospital were transformed back to what it was once thought to be, a place to die in, or rather a place in which to be made dead?

Other instances of the use of euthanasia may be beyond the reach of safeguards. Thus, if an elderly patient knows that the crowded family at home needs his room, will he be more likely to sign such a declaration, especially if family relations are not ideal, if his illness *is* a burden? How can doctors be sure that such situations are not exerting pressure on their patients, or that the nursing homes and geriatric hospitals, with their limited facilities and with an ever-increasing number of old people, do not exert such pressures? And what of the old or ill who have no relatives, who are not being cared for by a friendly family doctor, but are treated all unknown in the impersonal wards of modern hospitals? The soundness of their minds, their unknowable wishes and intentions, the unknown circumstances of their lives, all are hidden from the understanding and ministration of most medical personnel, and this very lack of knowledge might be a source of pressure.

It is often said that everyone has a right to a death with dignity, or even a right to death parallel to a right to life. Whether or not such a right can be reasonably derived is a difficult question, but as the editors of *Your Death Warrant?* point out, what it really means is a

2. Editor's note: To descend to the world of the dead by a slower route.

right to *be put to death,* and put to death by others, which in fact proposes the duty of others to kill. There are comparable difficulties with the argument that legalized euthanasia would mean an improvement in the quality of life. Clearly, the improvement is not experienced by those who are put to death, because their experience of life thereby ceases. Rather, it is the quality of *other* people's lives that may be improved when the dead forfeit their own. And there is a question whether the quality of life would in fact be improved at all. It is generally held that overcrowding, competition for scarce resources, the pollution and overpopulation and bureaucratic nightmares which face us everywhere, would all be modified if fewer resources were consumed by unproductive elderly people; more would then be available for the rest of society, for more productive purposes. The allocation of resources is indeed a problem, but those who advance theoretical arguments about the proper use of resources were themselves once unproductive as infants, and will one day become the unproductive geriatric instances they now decry. Surely it would not really improve the quality of one's life to know that others have been deliberately sacrificed for it, or that one's own life, so full of quality, would one day be readied for sacrifice. Would not the quality of life of the entire society conceivably be poisoned if it were knowingly nourished in this way.

Death in dignity, significant death, is of course what we would all desire, and in a community of care and concern. No one likes to be thought of as a patient rather than a person, no one wants his body regarded as a mine of transplantable organs, or as a statistic in the tabulated death rates, or an item in the hospital budget or the mortician's accounting.

An accumulating outrage has attended the development of modern medicine, which must reduce a person to a thing in order to return him to the status of a person once more. And yet to be treated as a thing may not be the worst that can befall a modern American patient; equally discomfiting is the pervasive habit of false personalization, such as having to endure fifteen or twenty minutes of a doctor's "relating" to you with all sorts of trivia about himself and his family in order to feel that he truly "cares" about you "as a person." This is especially painful as it affects treatment of the elderly or dying, whose condition cannot be reached by wearing a smile button and saying, "Have a nice day." When death is on the horizon there is need for a surrounding community of care, and it may be precisely the lack of such a community that as much as anything else has fostered the growing interest in euthanasia. Faced on the one hand with the antiseptic mechanical processes of efficiency which are the natural consequences of modern medical technology, and on the other with the feeble attempts to counteract these by a system of deception and false personalization, how much more acceptable becomes the wish to choose the time and circumstances of one's own death. And if one has already donated organs for transplant, one can even have a sense, not of immortality perhaps, but still of some meaning beyond one's self. . . .

Death is the most individual event in our lives, the most unique, its importance equaled only by the uniqueness of birth. Although euthanasia itself offers no solution to anything at all, the euthanasia movement may help to rouse a culture too long given over to a denial of the very reality of death, and especially in view of the new medical technologies, may illuminate a subject that most urgently needs our thought and concern.

Robert B. White
H. Tristram Engelhardt, Jr.

A Demand to Die

Hastings Center Report, June 1975

The following case study of a badly burned young man who demands to die dramatically illustrates the complexity of moral and ethical dilemmas concerning death and dying. The patient, who would have died in an earlier era before the invention of modern medical procedures, wanted to refuse treatment and to be allowed to die. Dr. White, called in for a psychiatric consultation, found the man to be in sound mind. However, Dr. White demurred from discontinuing treatment on at least two grounds: the legal status of the termination of life-saving treatment was, and is, unclear; and there was a strong possibility that the young man might change his mind at a later date. Dr. Engelhardt, a physician who teaches philosophy of medicine at the Kennedy Center for Bioethics, Georgetown University, acknowledges the difficulty of making a decision like this. However, he argues that the individual's freedom of self-determination includes the right to decide to die when life is not felt to be worth living under extreme conditions. This case raises a fundamental moral question—who "owns" our bodies and our "selves"? Does the individual have the right to end his or her own life when it is felt to be no longer worth living? Or, is this right reserved for God, the forces of nature, or the attending physician?

CASE NO. 228   Two months after being discharged from three years of military service as a jet pilot, the world of Donald C. exploded in a flash of burning gas. He was then twenty-six years old, unmarried, and a college graduate. An athlete in high school, he loved sports and the outdoors. Rodeos were his special interest, and he performed in them with skill. Upon leaving the military in May, 1973, Donald joined his father's successful real estate business. The two of them had always had a close and warm relationship. On July 25, 1973, they were together, appraising farm land. Without realizing it, they parked their car near a large propane gas transmission line; the line was leaking. Later, when they started their automobile, the ignition of the motor set off a severe and unexpected explosion. Donald, his father, and the surrounding countryside were enveloped in fire. The father died on the way to the hospital, and Donald was admitted in a critical but conscious state. He sustained second- and third-degree burns over 68 percent of his body—mostly third-degree burns. Both eyes were blinded by corneal damage, his ears were mostly destroyed, and he sustained severe burns to his face, upper extremities, body, and legs.

During the next nine months, Donald underwent repeated skin grafting, enucleation of his right eye, and amputation of the distal parts of the fingers on both hands. The left eye was surgically closed in order to protect it from the danger of infection; the cornea was badly scarred and the retina was partially detached. His hands, deformed by contractures, were useless, unsightly stubs. When admitted to the

University of Texas Medical Branch Hospitals in April, 1974, the patient had many infected areas on his body and legs. He had to be bathed daily in the Hubbard tank to control infection.

From the day of the accident onward, Donald persistently stated that he did not want to live. Nonetheless, he had continued to accept treatment. Two days after admission to the University hospital, however, he refused to give permission for further corrective surgery on his hands. He became adamant in his insistence that he be allowed to leave the hospital and return home to die—a certain consequence of leaving since only daily tanking could prevent overwhelming infection. The tankings were continued despite his protests. His mother, a thoughtful and courageous woman, was frantic; his surgeons were frustrated and perplexed.

Although calm and rational most of the time, the patient had frequent periods of childlike rage, fear, and tearfulness. He engaged his mother by the hour in arguments regarding his demand to leave the hospital—which, of course, he was physically incapable of doing unless she agreed to take him home by ambulance.

At this juncture, Dr. Robert B. White was asked to see the patient as a psychiatric consultant. Prior to seeing the patient he was given the impression that Donald was irrationally depressed and probably needed to be declared mentally incompetent so that a legal guardian could be appointed to give the necessary permission for further surgery and other treatments. The patient's mother was understandably in favor of his remaining in the hospital. She was deeply concerned about her son's welfare, and the prospect of taking him home to die from pus-covered sores on his body was more than she could bear. She was a deeply religious woman and was also concerned lest her son die without re-accepting the church which he had left some time prior to his burns.

Donald was the eldest of three children. By his family's account, he was an active, assertive, and determined person, who since childhood had tended to set his own course in life. What or whom he liked, he stuck to with loyalty and persistence; what or whom he disliked, he opposed with tenacity. His mother stated, "He always wanted to do things for himself and in his own way." Dr. White soon concluded that the mother's summary was apt. In the course of the first few interviews it was apparent that Donald was a very stubborn and determined man; he was also bright, articulate, logical, and coherent—not by any criterion mentally incompetent. He summarized his position with the statement, "I do not want to go on as a blind and crippled person." Arguments that surgery could restore some degree of useful function to his hands, and perhaps some useful vision to his remaining eye, were of no avail. His determination to leave the hospital was unshakable, and he demanded to see his attorney in order to obtain his release by court order if necessary.

Robert B. White

Donald's wish seemed in great measure logical and rational; as my psychiatric duties brought me to know him well, I could not escape the thought that if I were in his position I would feel as he did. I asked two other psychiatric colleagues to see the patient, and they came to the same conclusion. *Should his demand to die be respected?* I found myself in sympathy with his wish to put an end to his pathetic plight. On the other hand, the burden on his mother would be unthinkable if he left the hospital, and none of us who were responsible for his care could bring ourselves to say, "You're discharged; go home and die."

Another question occurred to me as I watched this blind, maimed, and totally helpless man defy and baffle everyone: could his adamant stand be the only way available for him to regain his independence after such a prolonged period of helplessness and total dependence?

Consequently, I decided to assist him in the one area where he did want help—obtaining legal assistance. He obviously had the right to legal recourse, and I told him I would help him obtain it. I also told him that I and the other doctors involved could not accede immediately to his demand to leave; we could not participate in his suicide. Furthermore, he was, I said, in no condition to leave unless his mother took him home, and that was an unfair burden to place on her. I urged him to have the surgery; then, when he was able to be up and about, he could take his own life if he wished without forcing others to arrange his death.

But Donald remained adamant, and the patient, his attorney, and I had several conferences. Finally, the attorney reluctantly agreed to represent the patient in court. The patient and I agreed that if the court ruled that he had the right to refuse further treatment, the life-sustaining daily trips to the Hubbard tank and all other life-sustaining treatment would be stopped. If he wished, he could remain in the hospital in order to be kept as free of pain as possible until he died.

Had Donald been burned a few years ago, before our increasingly exquisite medical and surgical technology became available, none of the moral, humanitarian, medical, or legal questions his case raised would have had time

to occur; he would simply have died. But Donald lived, and never lost his courage or tenacity. He has imposed upon us the responsibility to explore the questions he has asked. On one occasion Donald put the matter very bluntly: "What gives a physician the right to keep alive a patient who wants to die?"

As we increase our ability to sustain life in a wrecked body we must find ways to assess the wishes of the person in that body as accurately as we assess the viability of his organs. We can no longer blindly hold to our instinctive tendency to regard death as an adversary to be defeated at any price. Nor must we accept immediately and at face value a patient's demand to be allowed to die. That demand may often be his only way to assert his will in the face of our unyielding determination to defeat death. The problem is relatively simple when brain death has occurred or when a patient refuses surgery for cancer. But what of the patient who has entered willingly on a prolonged and difficult course of treatment, and then, at the point at which he will obviously survive if the treatment is continued, decides that he does not want further treatment because he cannot tolerate the kind of future life that his injuries or illness will impose upon him?

The outcome of Donald's case does not resolve these questions but it should add to the depth of our reflections. Having won his point, having asserted his will, having thus found a way to counteract his months of total helplessness, Donald suddenly agreed to continue the treatment and to have the surgery on his hands. He remained in the hospital for five more months until medically ready to return home. In the six months since he left, Donald has regained a considerable measure of self-sufficiency. Although still blind, he will soon have surgery on his eye, and it is hoped some degree of useful vision will be restored. He feeds himself, can walk as far as half a mile, and has become an enthusiastic operator of a Citizens' Band radio. When I told him of my wish to publish this case report, he agreed, and stated that he had been thinking of writing a paper about his remarkable experiences.

H. Tristram Engelhardt, Jr.

This case raises a fundamental moral issue: how can one treat another person as free while still looking out for his best interests (even over his objections)? The issue is one of the bounds and legitimacy of paternalism. Paternalistic interventions are fairly commonplace in society: motorcyclists are required to wear helmets, no one may sell himself into slavery, etc. In such cases society chooses to intervene to maintain the moral agency of individuals so that their agency will not be terminated in death or in slavery. Society chooses in the purported best interest (i.e., to preserve the condition of self-determination itself—freedom) of the would-be reckless motorcyclist or slave. Or, in the paradigmatic case of paternalism, the choice by parents for their children is justifiable in that at a future time as adults, the children will say that their parents chose in their best interests (as opposed to the parents simply using their children for their own interests). That is, the paternalism involved in surrogate consent can be justified if the individual himself cannot choose, and one chooses in that individual's best interest so that if that person were (or is in the future) able to choose, he or she would (will) agree with the choice that has been made in his or her behalf.

On, on I go, (open doors of time! open hospital doors!)
The crush'd head I dress, (poor crazed hand tear not the bandage
    away,)
The neck of the cavalry-man with the bullet through and through I
    examine,
Hard the breathing rattles, quite glazed already the eye, yet life
    struggles hard,
(Come sweet death! be persuaded O beautiful death!
In mercy come quickly.)

Walt Whitman
"The Wound Dresser"
Leaves of Grass

Thus, one can justify treating a burned patient when first admitted even if that person protested: one might argue that the individual was not able to choose freely because of the pain and serious impact of the circumstances, and that by treating initially one gave the individual a reasonable chance to choose freely in the future. One would interpret the patient to be temporarily incompetent and have someone decide in his behalf. But once that initial time has passed, and once the patient is reasonably able to choose, should one respect a patient's request to refuse life-saving therapy even if one has good reason to believe that later the patient might change his or her mind? This is the problem that this case presents.

Yet, what are the alternatives which are morally open: (1) to compel treatment, (2) at once to cease treatment, or (3) to try to convince the patient to persist, but if the patient does not agree, then to stop therapy. Simply to compel treatment is not to acknowledge the patient as a free agent (i.e., to vitiate the concept of *consent* itself), and simply to stop therapy at once may abandon the patient to the exigencies of unjustified despair. The third alternative recognizes the two values to be preserved in this situation: the freedom of the patient and the physician's commitment to preserve the life of persons.

But in the end, individuals, when able, must be allowed to decide their own destiny, even that of death. When the patient decides that the future quality of life open to him is not worth the investment of pain and suffering to attain that future quality of life, that is a decision proper to the patient Such is the case *even if* one had good reasons to believe that once the patient attained that future state he would be content to live; one would have unjustifiably forced an investment of pain that was not agreed to. Of course, there are no easy answers. Physicians should not abandon patients when momentary pain overwhelms them; physicians should seek to gain consent for therapy. But when the patient who is able to give free consent does not, the moral issue is over. A society that will allow persons to climb dangerous mountains or do daredevil stunts with cars has no consistent grounds for paternalistic intervention here. Further, unlike the case of the motorcyclist or the would-be slave, in this case one would force unchosen pain and suffering on another in the name of their best interests, but in circumstances where their best interests are far from clear. That is, even if such paternalistic intervention may be justifiable in some cases (an issue which is different from the paternalism of surrogate decision-making, and which I will not contest at this point), it is dubious here, for the patient's choice is not a capricious risking on the basis of free action, but a deliberate choice to avoid considerable hardship. Further, it is a uniquely intimate choice concerning the quality of life: the amount of pain which is worth suffering for a goal. Moreover, it is, unlike the would-be slave's choice, a choice which affirms freedom on a substantial point—the quality of one's life.

In short, one must be willing, as a price for recognizing the freedom of others, to live with the consequences of that freedom: some persons will make choices that they would regret were they to live longer. But humans are not only free beings, but temporal beings, and the freedom that is actual is that of the present. Competent adults should be allowed to make tragic decisions, if nowhere else, at least concerning what quality of life justifies the pain and suffering of continued living. It is not medicine's responsibility to prevent tragedies by denying freedom, for that would be the greater tragedy.

Julie Fulton
Robert Fulton
Roberta Simmons

The Cadaver Donor and the Gift of Life

This article by Julie Fulton and her colleagues at the University of Minnesota explores several issues involved in organ transplantation. They studied families who had agreed to donate organs from members who had died suddenly, usually in automobile accidents. The cadaver "donors" were "brain-dead" patients maintained on respirators. The family survivors, who were asked for permission to remove organs from the bodies of their "dead" relatives, experienced some confusion concerning the exact status of the deceased member. Was the donor fully dead, partly dead, or still alive? This dilemma underscores some of the difficulty inherent in the wide gap between medical expertise and the layperson's understanding. While physicians may have no trouble regarding the brain-dead patient as "dead," the family and friends of the patient are frequently confused. On the other hand, the term "cadaver-donor" for the physician refers to the patient, while the family knows only too well that it is they who are asked to make the decision to donate.

Stress and ethical dilemmas are elements that are present in almost all aspects of organ transplantation. In the drama of transplant surgery the stresses and ethical problems encountered by the family of the cadaver-patient are often overlooked. To illuminate this aspect of transplantation we undertook a small exploratory study of families whose relatives had served as cadaver organ donors at the University of Minnesota Hospitals.

In this preliminary research we were interested in exploring the impact of the cadaver donation experience on the family as a unit as well as its family members' perception of the decision-making process, their emotional reactions to the death and the donation, and their assessment of the problems the donation may have caused for them as well as the benefits it may have provided. . . .

THE USUAL DONATION PROCEDURE

The "usual" donation procedure is somewhat difficult to describe because during the time in which these interviews were conducted, several changes in the donation process took place. These changes were instituted either as a result of technological improvements in the storage of organs or as a result of the information obtained from our respondents in the early interviews. For example, some of the first interviews revealed that relatives were anxious to know the time of death of the cadaver-patient and time of the transplant operation, and they wished some knowledge about the person to whom the organs were given. As a result of our informing the transplant service of these concerns, a program of telephoned and written communication was established with the family of the cadaver-patient. Later interviews with other families, therefore, did not reflect the same areas of concern.

In addition, the invention of a kidney

preservation machine, which allows plasma to be circulated through the removed and stored kidney for two to three days, means that the brain-dead patient himself no longer has to perform a storage function while the transplant recipient is prepared for surgery. Most of the families interviewed in this study were interviewed before the advent of this machine, and in these cases the cadaver-patient had to be transferred from the admitting hospital to the University hospital where he/she was re-evaluated by a new team of neurologists and, if brain death were confirmed, was declared by them to be officially dead. Various machinery subsequently artificially maintained his/her circulation, respiration, and kidney function for hours or days until one or two suitable transplant recipients could be located, transported to the University hospital, and then readied for the transplant by a seven to ten hour hemodialysis. The resultant waiting period for the family members (who usually did not accompany the cadaver-patient to the University Hospital) was often extremely long and difficult.

Currently (and as was the case for some members of our sample) no such transfers are necessary. Brain death is declared at the original hospital by the local physicians and shortly thereafter a University surgeon arrives to remove the kidneys and place them in the preservation machine. The waiting period, after death is declared and before the family can claim the body, has thus been significantly shortened. In this respect, therefore, the first and last families in our sample had somewhat different experiences.

In other respects, however, their experiences were similar. In almost all cases of cadaver-patient organ donation, the cadaver-patient is a young person in otherwise good health who is the victim of a severe and ul-timately fatal accidental injury usually directly involving the head. In almost all cases the patients suffer sudden and irreversible brain damage at the time of the accident and are comatose or actually brain-dead by the time they arrive at the hospital. In most of the cases studied here the patient was taken to a local hospital, examined by a local physician, and placed on machines to maintain respiration and circulation of blood. The patient was kept on these machines for several hours or in some cases several days even though all neurological evidence indicated that the brain had ceased to function. The family frequently maintained a twenty-four hour vigil at the hospital during this uncertain time, returning home only for short periods or for brief rests. As soon as the attending physician was certain that recovery could not occur, he informed the family that the patient was essentially dead (i.e., brain-dead), although the official "declaration" and signing of the death certificate had not yet occurred.

Generally this was also the time that the physician first suggested the idea of donation to the family, although he may have mentioned it earlier as the hopeless prognosis became increasingly apparent. After having made the suggestion of donation, the physician usually left the family alone to discuss the possibility among themselves. If the family agreed to donate, another physician from the University Hospitals arrived to explain the procedure more fully and to obtain the appropriate legal forms permitting the donation.

Subsequently the declaration of death and the completion of the death certificate occurred before the organs were removed and while the machines were still maintaining circulation, respiration, and most important, kidney function. Thus in reality the "moment of death" was not physiologically different from the time that preceded or followed it: A declaration of brain death, in other words, occurs at an arbitrary moment in time and serves merely to label a situation that has occurred one or more days before and to define as permissible the cessation of the respiratory and circulation machines as well as the possible removal of organs for transplant purposes.

Once the organs were removed from the cadaver-patient, the family was notified and, subsequent to an autopsy, they or the funeral director were able to claim the body. A transplant did not relieve the family of any expenses they might otherwise incur, although once the patient was declared officially dead and permission to use the organs had been granted, the transplant service assumed all expenses for the cadaver that were incurred within the hospital. Expenses up to that point, however, were assumed by the family and the later disposition of the body was also their responsibility.

THE PERIOD PRIOR TO THE DECISION

THE SUGGESTION OF DONATION   Most of the family members interviewed were unprepared to accept the death of such young persons. The suddenness of the event as well as a refusal to relinquish hope were significant factors in the initial response of family members to the idea of donation.

In twelve of the cases the initial suggestion to donate organs was made by the physician in the local hospital to which the patient had been taken. In the other three cases the donation was brought about (1) by the suggestion of a hospital staff member who was a friend of the wife of the deceased; (2) by the parents themselves in a case in which the mother's brother had been a cadaver-donor the year before, and (3) by the cadaver-patient himself who had

written a suicide note directing that his entire body be given to the University. . . .

The decision to donate cadaver organs is a group decision made by key family members in a crisis situation. At the time of the decision these key members, both at home and in the hospital, are likely to be surrounded sporadically or continuously by other individuals who are normatively defined as having less right to make the choice but who provide emotional support—the hospital medical staff, clergymen, friends, younger children in the family, grandparents, in-laws, stepparents, and so on. Of these persons only the grandparents are likely to express an opposing view. . . .

ATTITUDE TOWARD SPECIAL BODY-PARTS: BODY-IMAGE   A decision to allow the donation of any organs at all for transplantation is the first decision that must be considered by the family, but in addition, they can decide which organs they will allow to be donated. A willingness to donate certain organs was arrived at without too much feeling of body disturbance or body mutilation, but the idea of removing certain other organs sometimes aroused great emotion. Most respondents did not have any feelings one way or another about the spleen, pancreas, liver, or

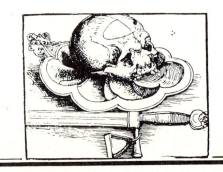

kidneys. But hearts and eyes, particularly, were organs of the body that sometimes evoked very strong images and association; these organs possess special significance even after death for many people.

Two families specified that the heart could not be taken. Because heart transplants are not being done at the University of Minnesota, no family was asked specifically to give up the heart; yet these families felt so strongly that the heart should remain with the body that they wrote in this qualification on the permission form themselves.

Unless specifically excluded, however, the permission signed by the family did allow for the removal of the eyes. Family members were not always aware of this when they signed the waiver, and two families became quite upset when they learned from their funeral director that the eyes had been used. Even though the body, if it were viewed, would have the eyes closed, it was important to them that the eyes remain with the body. . . .

WAITING FOR THE TRANSPLANT TO BE COMPLETED The time period after the signature was secured and before the body became available was especially difficult for cadaver-donor families, particularly before the institution of preservation machines. Normative and practical uncertainties made the situation stressful. Where should the family go? Should they visit the "body" in the University Hospital? Was the donor in fact "dead?" What was happening to their relative during the waiting period? Had the transplant been completed? Several funeral directors also indicated their displeasure with the uncertainty. Their questions as to when the body would be available only increased family discomfort. Transplantation had interrupted the customary accepted practices of death and had prolonged a period where the distinction between life and death was ambiguous. . . .

THE LONG-TERM REACTION TO CADAVER DONATION

OVERALL EVALUATION Although the donation was not equally salient to all family members a year or more after the death, most respondents appeared to hold a primarily positive attitude toward it at the time of the interview. . . .

Several of the respondents who maintained *very* favorable attitudes over the long-run commented on the donation as the one positive aspect of the death. The following remarks were typical:

The transplant was one of the few bright spots in the whole experience.

The death was not a total loss. There was something good that came out the whole thing.

I feel good about the transplant. I'm sure we did the right thing.

We decided to donate so he could keep living somehow.

The idea of donation helped; it gave me something tangible to hold on to.

If we can't save him, we can save someone else.

I feel good knowing that somebody got some benefit from his death, that there not only was a divine reason for it, but that there was something else, something tangible, that somebody profited in some way.

I feel like part of him lives in somebody else. I really feel that he has done well for himself, that he gave all that he could give in his life and his death. . . .

For many respondents, then, the donation seemed to give meaning to an otherwise meaningless death. . . .

EASING GRIEF   Did the respondents believe that the donation had played any role in easing their grief? Of the seventeen respondents who were asked explicitly whether they felt that the donation had helped them in their own grieving, nine indicated that it had, and two others were not sure whether it had made any difference. Of the six respondents who reported that the donation had not played such a role, two claimed that if they could have had knowledge that the transplant was a long-term success, their grief might have been eased. Without such knowledge, the donation affected their grief very little.

In sum, for various reasons, most respondents remained quite positive in their feelings about the donation. For a significant number of individuals, the donation appears as the one good thing in the death, and for several others, it served to ease their grief. In fact one father believed the donation had actually had a positive impact on the interaction of the family. He explained,

> It [donation] has probably made us more appreciative of his [the son's] memories, and I think that probably all our kids look up to us with a little bit more respect. I think they probably accept us and evaluate us more than the older generation. I think it served to bring us closer together.

For other respondents, however, the donation, while viewed positively, is seen to have little current salience in their lives and little impact on their grief. In the words of one mother who had made an instantaneous decision to donate:

> Donating hasn't made any difference. . .neither easier to accept the death nor more difficult. Nothing one way or the other. If I had not donated. . .I don't know how to say it. . .as long as she was dead I'm glad that medical science has advanced to the point where some use can be made of the organs, but that's all. . . .

CONCLUSION AND SUMMARY   A major cause of many of the difficulties that we have discussed. . .may emanate from the term *cadaver-donor* itself. While the "cadaver-patient" is labelled as the "donor," in reality it is the family who makes the donation. This mislabelling seems to have given rise to a misperception of the crucial role that the family actually plays in the donation proceedings and subsequently to the failure of the staff to be attentive to many of the psychological and social needs of the donor families. The family gives the gift of the organ and they expect information, recognition, or gratitude in return. Because the family tends to perceive the entire hospital as benefiting from the donation, they can be angered by any seeming lack of consideration even when it originates from hospital officials who have little association with the transplant service.

In conclusion, donation, whether it originates from living related donors or from the families of cadaver-patients, has many long-term psychological benefits and therefore appears to be positively regarded by the majority of donors. Yet neither type of donation is free of stress, and in a minority of cases the stress has been severe. Although there is no quantitative method to weigh the comparative psychgological costs and benefits of related and cadaver donation, these data do not establish a clear comparative advantage for cadaver donation. Katz and Capron (1975) and Brewer (1970) and many others suggest curtailing donation from living related donors. The increased reliance on cadaver donors, were there no cadaver donor shortage, would not necessarily reduce the overall level of stress or the ethical dilemmas.

13.

Suicide

Is suicide the final disposition of an insane mind, or is it a sane solution to an otherwise impossible problem? Or is it something else entirely?

Thoughts about suicide, as the authors in this section point out, are not new. Suicide has always been with us.

Literature has made much of suicide in the past, particularly as a solution to futureless romance. Romeo could not tolerate life without Juliet and found it necessary to take his own life. Aida and her lover (in the opera *Aida*) sealed themselves in a tomb so they would not have to be separated in life . . . or in death. But these romantic images of suicide mask the dimensions of this problem.

Why do people destroy themselves? No one can ever really be sure. All explanations of suicide are based on inference and there is no direct evidence that the researcher can point to with certainty and say, "This is why he did it!" But still we pose the question.

In 1881 the German scholar, Thomas G. Masaryk, published *Suicide and the Meaning of Civilization,* in which he attempted to arrive at a social explanation of suicide based on a theory of multiple causation. While Masaryk did not wholly dismiss environmental causes of suicide (that is, climate, the seasons, and so forth), he did place greater emphasis on the importance of moral decay in explaining suicide rates. Masaryk believed that modern man was more self-reflective than primitive man and consequently called into question the meaning of the moral order. He argued that "the morbid suicide tendency gradually increases among all people who have progressed in their development, and the social mass phenomena of suicide is the fruit of progress, of education, of civilization." Furthermore, he believed that the decline of Christianity was the major precipitating factor in spiraling suicide rates. He observed:

> Suicide results from the collapse of a unified world view that has consistently given Christianity its value among the masses in all civilized countries. . . . Suicides are the bloody sacrifices of the civilizing process.

This theme of moral decay and irreligion in conditioning modern orientations toward life and death is one that recurs in the writings of more recent scholars.

The famous French sociologist Émile Durkheim published his monograph, *Le Suicide,* in 1897. In this work he attempted to identify the qualities of social relationships that result in varying orientations toward suicide. He suggested that individual dispositions toward suicide cannot be explained as a function of climate, biology, or psychology, but must be conceived of as resulting from prevailing conditions within the social structure. What Durkheim called *anomic* suicide resulted from a decline in the normative regulation of social life. It was the act of an individual who had no clear sense of what was right or wrong because social life presented a multiplicity of ethics. *Egoistic* suicide resulted when an individual lacked integration into meaningful social groups and had only his own emotional resources to fall back on. *Altruistic* suicide was caused by dedication to an ideal worthy of human sacrifice. It resulted from complete identification with a cause such as wartime victory. Protest by self-inflicted death (such as occurred during the Vietnam war) would also be classified as altruistic suicide.

Today there are many explanations of suicide and many reasons to seek answers to the perpetual problems surrounding it. The suicide rates for young men and women have more than doubled in the past ten years. Increasing numbers of elderly persons are also choosing this alternative. What is the current state of our knowledge about this age-old question?

The first author in this section, Alex Pokorny, explores a number of myths associated with suicide and brings to our attention clues concerning the population at risk.

Edwin Shneidman offers a classification of suicidal intention that is helpful in understanding the subtlety of our own self-destructive acts.

Dean Schuyler points to the pressing needs of suicide survivors. The long-standing tradition of viewing suicide as a sin and the uncertainties often surrounding the circumstances of the death mean that the survivor of a suicide faces social stigma as well as the grief normally associated with loss. Furthermore, the survivor is likely to feel personal responsibility for failing to prevent the suicide. Schuyler offers suggestions about how to resolve the underlying dilemma of guilt that accompanies this kind of survivorship.

Finally, Lael Wertenbaker illuminates the meaning of death for a person dying in intense pain. She describes in personal, poignant detail her husband's suicide and the fear and courage that ultimately provided it with meaning. Together these articles yield an interesting, yet disturbing portrait of suicide in the twentieth century.

Alex D. Pokorny

Myths about Suicide

In this article by the well-known authority on suicide, Alex Pokorny, our popular beliefs about the causes and incidence of suicide are challenged. The author notes that suicide is not a simple response to a difficult situation, although this may be part of it. More likely, the act of suicide represents a complex series of social and psychological experiences that provide for each individual a unique pathway to self-destruction. The degree to which one is integrated into the social and emotional lives of other persons may be, according to Pokorny, one of the essential components in the decision to take one's own life.

The literature on suicide is well supplied with myths, superstitions, fallacies, and old wives' tales. There has been sufficient time for these to accumulate, as suicide has been with us since the beginning of history. It is a public form of behavior, readily apparent to all. Finally, death by one's own hand is one of those topics which seem simple, almost self-evident, so that almost anyone may consider himself an expert and may propose explanatory theories.

Many of the myths are not only false, but are misleading and at times positively dangerous. They may also lead us to feel that a particular facet or aspect of suicide is well understood, thus delaying or preventing the development of valid knowledge. It is therefore important to discuss such myths critically; those included have been collected from a variety of sources. All will be phrased in a positive way, so that they are all false statements.

GENERAL BELIEFS   (1) *People who talk about suicide won't commit suicide.* This is one of the most widespread and persistent false statements dealing with suicide, and one of the most dangerous. Numerous studies have shown that from 60 percent to 80 percent of persons who commit suicide have communicated their intentions beforehand. This may be by hints, such as the remark, "I might be better off dead," by more open threats or statements, and even by overt attempts or preparations. Therefore, about three-quarters of persons who commit suicide have "talked about suicide" beforehand.

It has been suggested that these communications might serve several purposes: to get help in resolving conflict about the decision to commit suicide (the person "tries it out" on associates), to warn associates, or to taunt and threaten. It may also be an inadvertent communication by an upset person, with no special effect being sought. Another suggestion is that they represent pleas to the human environment, by a person who is losing hope, for help in restoration of hope.

If three-quarters of persons who commit suicide have shown hints, threats, or attempts, what fraction of those persons who threaten or hint at suicide do eventually commit suicide? A review of a series of such studies has shown that, after a few years, from 2 to 10 percent of such suicidal individuals will have committed suicide; in one study, the percentage was 22 percent. In a follow-up extending to fourteen years, 618 patients who had shown suicidal preoccupation, suicidal threats, or suicide attempts, had a suicide rate about thirty-five times the expected rate for the general population. It can be concluded that persons who communicate suicidal intent, whether by hints or threats or by an actual attempt, present a greatly increased risk. Such behavior must be taken seriously.

(2) *Suicide happens without warning.* This has been touched upon in (1); the great majority of persons who commit suicide have given advance notification. In one well-documented series of cases, there were twenty-six different identifiable ways of communicating suicidal intent. The most frequent means (in 41 percent of the entire group) was a direct statement of intent to commit suicide. Other common modes included: statements about being better off dead, statements about a desire to die, suicide attempts, references to methods of committing suicide, dire predictions, and statements that the family would be better off if he were dead. These communications were addressed, in order of frequency, to spouse, other relatives, friends, job associates, physicians, and others. Another frequent type of warning is a discussion of depressed feelings, without specific mention of suicidal intent. It has been noted that physicians may be reluctant to ask a depressed patient about suicidal ruminations, lest they implant the suggestion; there is considerable reason to believe that such an effect does not occur, and that the usual error is in *not* asking about

suicidal ideas. At times patients who will not mention suicidal ideas to the doctor will acknowledge them if questioned. Nurses, receptionists, and orderlies often pick up such cues.

The most direct indicator is the suicide note. In Los Angeles county in the years 1945 to 1954, 12 percent to 15 percent of those who committed suicide left notes. Other acts which may be viewed as suicide communications may be the writing of a will, or giving of expensive gifts without apparent reason.

(3) *The suicide rate is rising steadily.* It is frequently stated that suicide is steadily on the increase, as if the rate per given number of persons were increasing. It is true that the total *number* of suicides will increase in ... the growing population; this is true for the country as a whole, as well as for growing communities.

Another factor which is contributing to an increase in the absolute number of suicides is the aging character of the population. Suicide is more prevalent at older ages, and the proportion of such older persons in the U.S. population is increasing.

To get a better idea about true rises or falls in suicide rates it is necessary to derive age-adjusted or standardized rates. When this is done for the United States for the years 1900 to 1960, it is found that the rate started out at 11.3 per 100,000 at the beginning of the century, then gradually rose to 17.9 by 1915, and then fell to 11.5 by 1920. From 1925 on, through prosperity years and then through the early years of the economic depression, the rate rose steadily to a peak of 18.6 in 1932. It then dropped slowly to a low point of 9.6 during World War II. Since 1945 it has remained at about 10 to 11 (all rates are per 100,000 per year). It thus appears that there are long-term shifts, with drops during wars and increases during periods of economic unrest. However the general suicide rate, after adjustment for age differences, is currently at the same level as at the beginning of the century.

(4) *Suicide and attempted suicide are the same class of behavior.* Discussion in the preceding sections, to the effect that suicide attempts are indicators of possible suicide, calls to mind the opposite fallacy—the view that suicide attempts and completed suicides are one class of behavior and should be studied and considered together. While it is true that a substantial ratio, perhaps 5 percent to 10 percent, of all persons who are seen for suicide attempts later commit suicide, this still means that perhaps 90 percent of them do not. The best opinion now is that attempted suicide and suicide represent two different, though overlapping, populations. For this reason research findings on a series of attempted suicide cases are of doubtful validity when they are applied to the topic of completed suicide.

Attempted suicides are often viewed simply as "failures" at suicide. This is not a valid view. Attempted suicide is in large part a distinct category of behavior, with its own characteristics. Three-quarters of suicide attempts are in females, most often in the age range from fifteen to forty. On the other hand, three-quarters of suicides are in males, and the rate increases in each succeeding decade of life. Attempted suicides outnumber suicides about eight to one. An attempted suicide usually signals that social circumstances and interpersonal relationships are badly disturbed; in suicide, social isolation is more typical. . . .

MYTHS ABOUT CAUSES OF SUICIDE

SOCIOLOGICAL (1) *Suicide involves only a specific class of people.* At times it is said that this is "the curse of the poor" or the "disease of the rich." Various plausible (though simple) theories are advanced to "explain" such relationships. These may refer to the deprivation and hopelessness under which the poor struggle. Or they may refer to the boredom and pointless existence of the rich. It appears, however, that all socioeconomic classes contribute members who die as suicides.

It is well documented that social factors influence suicide rates, but this is far from a simple relationship. Rather than pure socioeconomic level, the important factor seems to be the degree of integration into one's culture. Suicide risk is high in the uninvolved and in those whose involvement is decreasing.

(2) *"Good circumstances" prevent suicide.* A related and grossly oversimplified view is that only the poor, underprivileged, and deprived tend to commit suicide. Frequently the very opposite appears to be true: For example, in the military, suicide rates are higher for officers than for enlisted men. A survey of all suicides in Oregon for the years 1950 through 1961, with particular attention to professional persons, showed that the rates for physicians, dentists, and attorneys were over three times that of white-collar workers. A number of reports confirm the high suicide rate among physicians. In England and Wales more than one in fifty doctors takes his own life, and 6 percent of all deaths of doctors under sixty-five are from suicide—the same as from lung cancer. With regard to suicides of young people, it is not always the poor and neglected youngsters who attempt suicide; frequently they are children who have the "best of everything." It has been pointed out that some privileged young people at college find life futile and worthless; in one leading eastern university there were thirty-four suicides in a relatively few years. In a careful study of suicide rates in the different residential areas of Los Angeles, rates

were the highest in the most advantaged and the moderately advantaged apartment house areas; by far the lowest rate was in the least advantaged rural area. . . .

PSYCHOLOGICAL AND PSYCHIATRIC

(1) *Motives or causes of suicide are readily established.* Karl Menninger has described how quickly and glibly the public "explains" a suicide. Various superficial, seemingly adequate "reasons" are advanced and this seems to satisfy us. For example, there is a prevalent notion that loss of money is a common cause of suicide; statistics in individual cases show this to be untrue. In popular thinking suicide is not an enigma; rather, it is seen as "the simple and logical consequence of ill health, discouragement, financial reverses, humiliation, frustration, or unrequited love." Such simple and superficial explanations seem to be readily accepted.

As one goes more deeply into the individual case, however, each "cause" is found to be preceded by an earlier "cause." It appears, then, that the person who ultimately commits suicide has embarked on a self-destructive course long before the final and fatal act. Thus what initially appeared as a simple "cause" of the suicide now becomes one of the last steps in a lengthy and complex situation, many motives of which are obscure and difficult to establish.

(2) *Suicide occurs in a single disease, depression.* From the standpoint of psychiatric disease syndromes, there is a common fallacy that only the depressed commit suicide. This is shown in such remarks as, "I can't understand his doing this, he didn't act as though he were unhappy." Yet patients diagnosed by a psychiatrist as depressed account for only 10 percent to 40 percent of all suicide cases. Thus the majority are *not* cases of depression.

Depression, however, is a relatively infrequent diagnosis, as compared to neurosis, schizophrenia or passive-aggressive personality. When the actual suicides are converted to rates, using as a base the actual population at risk, depressives do have a far higher suicide rate than other psychiatric syndromes. This does not alter the fact that suicide may occur in any type of disorder.

(3) *All suicides are on the basis of the same motive.* A common fallacy is to consider all suicides as motivated by the same factor, such as the simple wish to terminate existence. In actuality, the "pathologic processes that lead to suicide travel on many roads." The act of suicide is seldom simply determined; rather, it is the final common pathway of many diverse forces and circumstances, typically a summation of predisposing and precipitating factors culminating in an act of desperation. Whenever one reviews a case of suicide ex postfactum, it is clear that there was an accumulation of factors at a rate beyond the capacity of the person to assimilate; each subsequent event, therefore, was encountered during the oppressive feeling-state lingering from previous events. Frequently, in such "hindsight" situations, it is painfully obvious that one slight change in management, a little extra interest or time, a little more consideration, might have tipped the balance favorably. . . .

(4) *A person who is in a very ill, even terminal state is not likely to commit suicide.* This fallacy is especially important to physicians and hospital staffs, who normally deal with critically ill and dying patients. It seems paradoxical that such patients should want to take their lives but it does happen; perhaps they want to end suffering, or to choose the time and place rather than face uncertainty. In this final act they retain power rather than lose it to an illness. In one study of thirty-two

cancer patients who committed suicide, fifteen were in a terminal state. Such seriously ill patients may seem too weak or helpless to commit suicide, but they may employ surprising methods, setting fire to the bed, choking themselves with bedclothes, etc.

(5) *Suicide is a "crazy" or "insane" act.* It is frequently asserted that suicide, by its very nature, is an "insane" act. This is difficult to reconcile with situations in which suicide is socially acceptable or even a socially required form of conduct under certain circumstances. There are well-known individual cases in which suicide appears to have been a carefully reasoned and seemingly rational act. Dublin points out that many of the persons who commit suicide cannot be considered psychotic in any sense. Is the act of suicide inherently irrational? Shneidman *et al.* have pointed out that schizophrenics do not ordinarily commit suicide in acute illness—as in response to severe hallucinations, delusions, or panic—but rather during the improved stage, on pass, or soon after discharge from the hospital. Depressives likewise tend to commit suicide when improving. It might be well to view the suicide act as a reasonable defensive move,

...life broke ten whipstocks
Over my back, broke faith, stole hope,
Before I denounced the covenant of courage.

Robinson Jeffers
Suicide's Stone

springing from the normal or adaptive part of the personality. Appelbaum has discussed suicide as a problem-solving technique; when alternative solutions are unavailable, the suicidal action is taken "to preserve the integrity of the psychological system despite its catastrophic effects in other respects." Farberow and Shneidman have studied over seven hundred genuine suicide notes from the standpoint of the reasoning, judgment, and logic expressed therein; in a "large minority" of instances the notes seem logical and rational and not psychotic.

This viewpoint, however, is not unanimous. Robins *et al.* studied 109 suicide attempt cases and concluded that there were no psychiatrically well patients among them (this is not to say they were all considered psychotic). In retrospective study of 134 successful suicides in St. Louis, 94 percent were considered to have been psychiatrically ill.

(6) *Suicide can be understood fully by studying suicidal individuals.* Kobler and Stotland have emphasized that suicide occurs in a social field, and that the full understanding of a suicide requires the consideration of both the individual and this social field. More specifically, they view suicide as occurring in a setting of "the end of hope"—the person cannot see his way out of a distressing situation. Suicide hints or threats are viewed as feelers or pleas to the persons in the environment to help restore hope. If hope is provided, the crisis may pass, but if the human environment does not respond, then suicide may result. These authors feel that a tabulation of characteristics of the suicide victims alone, even though it might include large numbers, will always be incomplete.

BIOLOGICAL   (1) *Suicide is inherited.* Two or more members of a family may commit suicide. This does not mean that the behavior is inherited any more than speaking the same language is. The consensus is that suicide is not inherited directly like hair color or eye color; an individual is not born with a weakness or compelling tendency to commit suicide.

It is true that there are families with a history of many suicides; one such family had eight suicides in three generations. In a period of fifty years a Connecticut family witnessed twenty-three suicides among four generations. Members of such a family may develop a *belief* that they are to commit suicide, and suicide is thereby facilitated, but the mechanism is psychological and not hereditary. In one Spanish family a direct male descendant in five consecutive generations reportedly killed himself at the age of forty-five.

Kallman and Anastasio reported on suicide in their series of twenty-five hundred twin index cases. There were eleven instances of suicide, all discordant (only one twin committed suicide). . . . The authors state that they know of no cases in which both members of a twin pair committed suicide. "For obvious reasons one cannot expect that there would be a specific combination of genetic factors determining the occurrence of suicide as such. There is no inheritance of any finished human traits, but only a transmission of potential capacities for the development of these traits under certain life conditions". . . .

METEOROLOGICAL AND COSMIC FACTORS

(1) *Suicide is related to weather phenomena.* There is a large body of literature, both technical and popular, which asserts that weather and physical environment influence suicide rates. . . .

The most widely mentioned factor is a supposed *seasonal* variation, often linked to corresponding weather changes. There is fairly general agreement that suicide rates are highest in late spring or early summer. . . . In Australia and Brazil (in the southern hemisphere) there appears to be a peak in the last quarter of the year, although there is much monthly variation. Seasonal variations have been explained by circulatory changes or changes in diet. Durkheim notes the same seasonal changes in Europe, but denies that has any connection with heat or other weather factors; he points out that there is a perfect continuity of the curve (increasing from winter to summer), which would tend to eliminate weather fluctuations as the cause. Rather, he considers the important factor to be the length of the day, increasing the time during which social factors are at work. . . .

Hot weather is stated to increase the suicide rate. Many writers advance temperature as an explanation of the observed seasonal variation. . . .

In general, most of the articles on weather, climate, and suicide are speculative and are based on crude data and coarse time intervals. This is particularly true of the older articles and even the ones which present positive findings.

The writer and co-workers have recently reported a detailed study designed to evaluate those claims. This was done by identifying all of the ninety-one suicides and four-hundred suicide attempts which occurred in Houston in 1960, and establishing the hour of occurrence in all possible cases. . . .

In summary, it appears that neither suicide nor suicide attempts are significantly related to weather phenomena. The observed seasonal variations in most parts of the world must be on some other basis.

(2) *Suicide is related to moon phases, sunspots, magnetic storms, and other cosmic*

influences. As in regard to weather, there is a variety of claims and beliefs about the effect of these more remote physical factors on suicide rates. . . .

The writer has explored the relationship of all suicides occurring in Texas in the period 1959–1961 (total of 2,497 cases) to the moon phases (full moon, first quarter, etc.) and to the apogee-perigee cycle of the moon. This was done for total suicides and also for groupings by race, sex, or both. No single significant relationship was found. . . .

In conclusion, there is no evidence that suicide rates are influenced by these remote "cosmic" factors.

MYTHS ABOUT MANAGEMENT OF SUICIDAL PERSONS

(1) *Improvement in a suicidal patient means the danger is over.* It is well known that discharged psychiatric patients who commit suicide do so within the first ninety days of leaving a hospital. This is also true for patients who have been seen for suicidal tendencies. This is related to the observation with depressed patients, that the greatest risk of suicide is during the period of improvement; at this time the patient may regain sufficient drive or energy to take his life. Also, release from the hospital means a marked increase in opportunity. . . .

(2) *Patients under a doctor's care are not a suicidal risk.* This is a fallacy of the layman. Most physicians know from painful experience that this is false. Motto and Greene have found that at least 40 percent of suicides and 60 percent of attempted suicides had been under medical care, within the six months preceding their act. All major medical specialties except pediatrics were involved. In another study of 134 completed suicides it was found that 55 percent had had medical and psychiatric care within the preceding year. In the case of manic-depressives, 73 percent had

had care within the preceding year and 53 percent within the preceding month.

(3) *Only a psychiatrist or mental hospital can prevent suicide.* Psychiatrists and mental hospitals certainly need to shoulder their part of the responsibility. The most promising new efforts, however, have come from various lay, religious, and community-based groups making up the suicide-prevention movement. The best known of these is the Suicide Prevention Center in Los Angeles, but other versions of this type of help have been in existence since at least 1906. An important feature of such centers is a telephone service which provides human contact, interest, support, and offers of more extensive help on a twenty-four-hour-a-day basis. An alternate plan is to offer such service as one aspect of a general psychiatric twenty-four-hour emergency service. Though it is hard to demonstrate the effectiveness of such services in community-wide statistics, study of individual cases makes it seem very likely that suicides are prevented by such help. . . .

(4) *Patients in hospitals, especially mental hospitals, are not a risk.* Unfortunately suicides occur in the hospital too. General hospitals may carry an increased risk because of the nature of the patients and the lack of alertness to this possibility. Even in psychiatric hospitals there is a suicide rate which usually runs three to five times that in the general population. The suicide rate in mental hospitals may even have increased following introduction of the tranquilizers, around 1954. Thus, while admission to a psychiatric ward remains one of the best steps in prevention of suicide, and while such a procedure undoubtedly reduces the toll in the high-risk group dealt with, this is not a complete solution to the problem. Admission to a hospital does not mean that concern with possible suicide should cease.

Edwin S. Shneidman

Ambivalence and Subintention

Well known for his pioneering work in suicide prevention and his research into the causes of suicide, Edwin Shneidman provides us with an interesting and rather unsettling view of ourselves in this selection from his book, *Deaths of Man*. Do we act unconsciously to hasten our own demise by taking unusual risks or misusing a variety of chemicals? When illness strikes, would we welcome its destructive power or would we make every effort to postpone or alter its effects? These and other questions are raised as Shneidman lays out a fascinating catalog of death attitudes derived from many clinical observations. He demonstrates that human beings do not always move consciously *away* from death, but instead may seek it, welcome it, taunt it, toy with it, or slowly insure its untimely occurrence through continued self-abuse.

INTENTION AND UNINTENTION When an individual plays a direct and conscious role in bringing about his own death, whether he experiences ambivalence or not, we may speak of that death as *intentioned*. Though the intention may be the same in all those who deliberately cause their own deaths, the motives behind the intention vary widely— as widely as the personalities and experiences of the individuals themselves. Let us consider some of these individuals:

First there is the *death-seeker*. A death-seeker is one who, during the time that label can properly be applied to him, wishes for an end to all conscious experience and acts in a way designed to achieve this end. The criterion for a death-seeker does not lie primarily in the method he uses—razor, barbiturates, carbon monoxide—but in the fact that *in his mind* the method will bring about cessation; and he commits the act in such a manner that rescue is realistically unlikely or impossible. During this period he is single-mindedly oriented toward death. Of course, an individual's orientations toward death shift and change over time. A person who was a death-seeker yesterday might today resist with all his strength any inducement to participate in activities that might cost him his life. It is known clinically that many individuals are suicidal for only a relatively brief period of time; if they can be given appropriate surcease and sanctuary, they will no longer seek death and will wish to continue to live.

Then there is the *death-initiator,* who believes that he will die in the fairly near future— a matter of days or weeks—or that he is failing, and, not wishing to accommodate himself to a new and less attractive image of himself, determines not to let it happen to him. If death or decline is to occur, he wants to play the dominant role himself, at his own time and on his own terms. In investigations among a number of older hospitalized persons in the terminal stages of fatal illnesses, it was found that some, with remarkable and totally unexpected energy, succeeded in taking out their tubes and needles, climbing over the bed rails, lifting heavy windows, and throwing themselves to the ground several stories below. When the occupational histories of such individuals were studied, they were typically found to have had one thing in common: they had never been fired—they had always quit. Whether one quits or is fired, he ends up unemployed, but the role he has played in the process is quite different.

Next there is the *death-ignorer*. Consider the following suicide note: "Good-by kid. You couldn't help it. Tell that brother of yours, when he gets to where I'm going, I hope I'm a foreman down there; I might be able to do something for him." Although it is true that suicide notes that contain references to a hereafter are rather rare, it is also true that some people who kill themselves believe that one can bring about termination without actually effecting cessation. These people seem to ignore the fact that, so far as we know, termination always involves cessation. One can keep in mind that even those for whom no one ever "dies," but merely "passes on," will still say of the suicide that he "killed himself." Thus the death-ignorer—or perhaps better, the death-transcender—is a person who, from his point of view, effects only his termination and continues to exist in some other manner.

The concept of death-ignoring is necessary; otherwise we put ourselves in the untenable position of equating a man who shoots himself in the head in the belief that he will soon meet his dead wife in heaven with a man who takes a trip from one city to another with the purpose and expectation of being reunited there with his wife. Obviously, these two acts are so vastly different in their effects on others that they cannot even be compared. Therefore, regardless of any individual's conviction that killing oneself does not result in cessation but is simply a transition to another life, we must accept the notion that cessation is final as far as the human personality that we can know is concerned.

Last there is the *death-darer,* a person who, to use gamblers' terms, bets his life on a relatively low objective probability that he will survive. Regardless of the outcome, a person who plays Russian roulette—in which the chances of survival are only five out of six—is a death-darer. A person with very little skill as a pilot who attempts to fly an airplane or one with unpracticed coordination who attempts to walk along the ledge of a tall building may be classified as a death-darer. Thus, such a determination is based on not what one does, but the background (the skill, or lack of it, with which he performs the feat) against which he does it.

Two young people, the first a young man of twenty-one and the second a girl of nineteen, have written statements that have the ring of an authentic, if temporary, intention to bring about their own deaths:

> During my period of depression and drinking I thought to commit suicide by throwing myself on the third rail of the subway. Luckily, I passed out before I could even make it to the subway station. My reasons were that I wanted to end a long spell of depression. After this event, my desire for suicide ended and the depression began to leave.

> I did attempt suicide when I was fourteen. It was after my father had died; my mother had had a nervous breakdown and returned from the hospital she was in before she had completely recovered because we couldn't afford to keep her there any longer. She was a little crazy (very crazy, really) then. I wanted to go out one night and my mother forbade me. I saw the mess in my house, my mindless mother, and felt disgusted and sick. I wanted desperately to be free; I wanted to die and rejoin my father (I believed

that through death we would be rejoined), so I jumped out of my bedroom window (about 25 feet up). I must have fallen correctly, because all I did was sprain my ankle. I ran (limped) off to a spot on a deserted hill to think and calm down. Then I got panicky that my mother must be worried, so I went back. She hadn't even known that I had left.

Most deaths, of course, are not suicides. They may come as a result of violence or of natural causes, but in either case, so far as the individual involved is concerned, they are unintentioned. An *unintentioned* death is any cessation, whatever its determined causes and its apparent conventional mode, in which the decedent plays no significant role in effecting his own demise. In these instances, death is due entirely to trauma from without (extrasomatic) or to biological failure from within (intrasomatic), neither of which is psychologically laden or induced. At the time of his cessation, the individual is "going about his own business" (even though he may be lying in a hospital bed) with no conscious intention of hastening cessation and with no strong conscious drive in this direction. Something from the "outside"—the outside of his mind— occurs. This "something" might be a cerebrovascular accident, a myocardial infarction, a neoplastic growth,[1] some malfunction, some catabolism, some invasion by bullet or virus; whatever it is, for him it has lethal consequences. "It" happens to "him." Inasmuch as all that anyone can do in regard to cessation is to attempt to hasten or postpone it, one might suppose that the person who knowingly faces unintentioned death must inevitably wish to postpone it; but it appears that there are other possible attitudes—welcoming, accepting, resisting, disdaining, and more—all compatible with unintentioned death.

1. Editor's note: These are commonly known as stroke, heart attack, and cancer.

The *death-welcomer* is one who, although playing no discernible (conscious or unconscious) role in . . . facilitating his own cessation, can honestly report that he welcomes the end of his life. This is common among very old people, especially after a long, painful, debilitating illness.

The *death-accepter* may be distinguished from the death-welcomer by a nuance of passivity. The death-accepter is one who has accepted the imminence of his cessation and is "resigned to his fate." He may be relatively passive, philosophical, resigned, heroic, realistic, or mature, depending on the spirit in which this enormous acceptance is made.

Most of the time, most of us are *death-postponers*. A death-postponer is one who, to the extent that he is oriented toward or concerned with cessation at all, hopes that it will not occur in anything like the foreseeable future; the event must be staved off for as long as possible. (This death-postponing orientation should not be confused with the ubiquitous human fantasies of immortality.)

The *death-disdainer* is, in a sense, supercilious toward death. During those moments when he consciously contemplates cessation, he is disdainful of death and feels that he is above any involvement in the stopping of the vital processes that it implies. Most young children in our culture, despite their usual fears about death, are typically death-disdainers, as well they may be—for a while.

The *death-fearer* is one who is fearful of death and shrinks from anything related to death. He may be phobic about death. He fights the notion of cessation, seeing death as something to be feared and hated. This position may be related to wishes for omnipotence and investment in one's social and physical potency. Hypochondriacs, fearing illnesses and assault, are perhaps also death-fearers.

Imagine five people, all elderly men on the

same ward of a hospital, all dying of cancer, none playing an active or unconscious role in his own cessation. Yet it is still possible to distinguish different orientations toward death among them: one wishes not to die and is exerting his "will to live" (death-postponer); another is resigned to his cessation (death-accepter); the third is disdainful of what is occurring to him and will not believe that death can "take him" (death-disdainer); still

A DISPUTE OVER SUICIDE

To whom should I speak today?
Brothers are evil
the friends of today love not...

To whom should I speak today?
There is no heart of man
whereon one might lean.

To whom should I speak today?
The righteous are no more
the land is given over to evil-doers.

To whom should I speak today?
There is a lack of companions
men have recourse to a stranger
  to tell their troubles.

To whom should I speak today?
I am heavy-laden with misery
& without a comforter.

Anonymous
Egypt, 1991–1786 B.C.

another, although taking no steps to hasten his end does at this point in his illness welcome it (death-welcomer); and the fifth is so fearful of death that he forbids anyone to speak of it in his presence (death-fearer).

It is, of course, possible to shout "Fire!" in the absence of a conflagration or "Stop thief!" in the absence of a crime. It is also possible, figuratively or literally, to shout "Suicide!" in the clear absence of any lethal intention. One expectation of shouting "Fire!" or "Stop thief!" is the mobilization of others. They are grab words; they give society (or certain members of society) no choice but to act in certain ways. An individual who cries "Suicide!" with a conscious absence of any lethal intention may be *death-feigner*. A death-feigner is one who simulates what appears to be an advertent movement toward cessation: he drinks from a previously emptied iodine bottle or cuts his wrist superficially with a razor blade, with no lethal possibility or intent. Such a person may use the threat of suicide to manipulate other people—usually the "significant other" person with whom the individual is involved in a neurotic relationship.

SUBINTENTION   *Subintention* is a partly mysterious concept, resting as it does on the powerful idea of unconscious motivation. Unlike ambivalence, which characterizes the dual aspect of man's behavior, subintention exists in the unconscious depths of man's being. It is what Melville pointed to in Ahab's crew as "their unconscious understandings" and what he reified as "the subterranean miner that works in us all." Subintentioned acts, whether toward death or toward the expansion of life, are essentially movements toward goals that are not consciously recognized. They are life's maneuvers that well up out of unconscious motivations, and thus are subtle in their appearance and difficult to identify. Is smoking suicidal? Drinking? Driving? Skiing? These questions cannot be answered with a simple yes or no. The answer is "It depends," and it may depend on a number of factors, including the individual's orientations toward death and toward others in his life.

Subintentioned orientations toward death are, I believe, more common than most of us would care to recognize and characteristic of a large percentage, perhaps a majority, of all deaths. The subintentioned death is one in which the person plays some partial, covert, subliminal or unconscious role in hastening his own demise. The evidence for such a role might be found in a variety of behavior patterns: poor judgment, imprudence, excessive risk-taking, neglect of self, disregard of a life-extending medical regimen, abuse of alcohol, misuse of drugs—all ways in which an individual can advance the date of his death.

Traditionally, suicidal deaths are thought to be intentioned deaths while natural, accidental, and homicidal deaths are thought to be unintentioned. This distinction is not so clear in real life—or rather, real death. What happens in fact is that there are instances of all four types of death which can be subsumed under the category of subintentioned death, depending on the particular details of each case.

Many deaths certified as natural have a participative and subintentional quality about them. Many of us know of regrettable cases in which people with diabetes, peptic ulcers, cirrhosis, Berger's disease, or pneumonia have, through psychologically laden commission, or omission, precipitated their own deaths. In addition, "voodoo deaths," inexplicable deaths in hospitals (especially in surgery), and sudden declines in health can all be considered to be of this type. There is even a notion that the speed at which some cancers grow may be related to deep psychological conflicts.

And if some natural deaths are subintentioned (and thus not entirely natural), many deaths certified as "accident" are even more so (and are thus not entirely accidental). The label "accident prone" would seem to be a contradiction in terms. Either an accident is an adventitious event or it is not an accident. If someone experiences a series of inimical events, they can hardly be thought to be "accidental." Sometimes, on the highway, we see a person drive as though he were afraid that he might be late for his own funeral; he may be hurling himself toward a subintentioned death. Many automobile fatalities are not quite accidents and not comfortably called suicides; they can be more meaningfully understood as subintentioned deaths.

Some suicides show aspects of subintention. (This is especially true of many cases of death certified as "probable suicide.") Indeed, the entire concept of subintentioned death is similar in many ways to Karl Menninger's concepts of chronic suicide, focal suicide, and organic suicide, except that Menninger's ideas have to do primarily with self-defeating ways of continuing to live, whereas subintentioned death is a way of stopping the process of living. Persons who die subintentioned deaths, may, in general, be said to have *permitted* suicide.

"Victim-precipitated homicide," a term introduced by Wolfgang, conveys to us the concept of a fatal incident certified as homicide but which might better be described as subintentioned death. It is obvious that in some cases, especially among marriage partners, lovers, or close friends, the victim "sought to run more than halfway to meet his death"—like Rodney in *Moby Dick*. To provoke someone else to kill you is not to be an unequivocally unwilling victim; it is to participate indirectly, at some level of personality functioning, in the manipulation of one's date of death, and is thus a subintentioned event.

That individuals may play unconscious roles in their own failures and act in ways that are inimical to their own welfare are facts too well documented from psychoanalytic and general clinical practice to ignore. Often death is hastened by the individual's seeming carelessness, imprudence, foolhardiness, forgetfulness, lack of judgment, or some other psychological mechanism. Many patterns of mismanagement and brink-of-death living that result in death must be recognized as subintentioned.

Among those who play largely unconscious roles in inviting or hastening death is the *death-chancer.* The death-darer, death-chancer, and death-experimenter occupy positions on a continuum of expectation and possibility of death. If a death-darer plays a game that gives him only five chances out of six of continuing to live, then a death-chancer will require odds significantly greater than that, but his game will still involve a realistic risk of cessation. The games themselves—the methods used to court death—have little if anything to do with the motivations, conscious or unconscious, of the player. Most methods (razor blades, for example) can, depending on the exact place and depth of the cut or the calculated expectation of intervention by others, legitimately be thought of as either intentioned or subintentioned. Individuals who "leave it up to chance," who "gamble with death," who "half intend to do it," are the subintentioned death-chancers.

The individual who unconsciously brings about or exacerbates a physiological disequilibrium so that his cessation (which would, in ordinary terms, be called a natural death) is expedited may realistically be termed a *death-hastener.* He may earn this label either by the style in which he lives (the abuse of his body, usually through alcohol, drugs, exposure, or malnurition) or, if he suffers from a specific physiological disorder, by the mismanagement or disregard of prescribed remedial procedures.

Closely allied to the death-hastener is the *death-facilitator,* who while he is ill and his psychic energies are low, is somehow more than passively unresisting to cessation and "makes it easy" for death to occur. Some unexpected deaths in hospitals may be of this nature. The excellent work of Weisman and Hackett explores this area.

The *death-capitulator* is a person who, by virtue of some strong emotion, usually his great fear of death itself, plays a psychological role in effecting his termination. In a sense, he gives in to death, or he scares himself to death. This type of death includes voodoo death, and the type of death by suggestion reported by hospitals in the southwestern United States and other areas where patients whose experience with medical care has been limited or nonexistent believe that people who go to hospitals always die.

The *death-experimenter* is a person of quite a different sort. Often he lives "on the brink of death," not consciously wishing extinguishment, but—usually by excessive use of alcohol or drugs—seemingly wishing a chronically altered, usually befogged state of consciousness. Death-experimenters seek to remain conscious but unaware, to "see the world as the world's not." They often experiment with increasing their self-prescribed dosages, taking some chances of extending the benumbed conscious state into a comatose state, and even taking some minimal but real risk (usually without much concern, in a kind of lackadaisical way) of extending the comatose state into cessation. When this type of death occurs, it is traditionally (but not necessarily correctly) thought of as accidental.

Dean Schuyler

Counseling Suicide Survivors

The tragedy of suicide is great, but the tragedy of being a suicide survivor may be greater. In this article by Dean Schuyler, an expert on depression, we learn that the survivors of suicide are in a special class of bereaved persons. In addition to their loss, they must also face the stigma of being consciously deserted by a loved one, deserted in a way that is irretrievable and often irreconcilable. Dr. Schuyler suggests that suicide survivors have a number of things in common, but most significantly, they share a need to reach an understanding of the death that preserves their own sense of worth and meaning. Suicide survivors are often at risk themselves, and this article calls for a humane strategy for dealing with this often neglected problem.

A suicide survivor is one who has sustained the loss of a significant person through death by suicide. It has been estimated that 50,000 people die in the United States each year as a result of suicide. If we take the conservative estimate that an average of 5 survivors are intimately affected by each loss, we can form a special-interest group with 250,000 new members added each year, although this group of survivors probably has diverse needs.

Suicide survivors have been called [by Shneidman] a vulnerable population. Follow-up studies suggest that this vulnerability extends to a varied lot of emotional problems later in life. In two studies that have been reported, overt self-destructive behavior has been noted in the surviving group. In one out of seventeen children surviving their parents' suicide, there were five suicide attempts and two suicidal deaths subsequent to the loss. In addition, subsequent depressive episodes were seen in nine of the seventeen survivors. In a second study, there were four suicide attempts and three suicidal deaths among forty-five survivors. Few studies, however, have carefully followed up significant numbers of survivors of loss by suicide. Shneidman has stated that as soon as a suicidal death occurs, the surviving group has lost an inalienable right: the right to live an unstigmatized life.

Many of us have had more contact with the suicide survivor than we realize. Perhaps our memories can be activated with a few quotations from a recent popular work:

> He had no idea why his wife had done it, and that fact made his grief more absurd and more lonely. Perhaps there was no reason, except to baffle him.
>
> He . . . decided that she must have deserted him in silence, much the same way she had lived with him. That and the fact that she left him no explanation were further twists of the knife of discontent lodged in Paul's guts.
>
> He wept for his own isolation.
>
> Paul staggered to his feet. He felt a wave of sorrow and rage and frustration break over him. She had no right to leave him like that; her departure was worse than an obscene joke, and one played at his expense.
>
> He began to sob, his body wracked by heaves. He braced himself against the chair and reached

out to touch her face. It was cold and unyielding. . . . He stepped back and looked down at her again. He felt affection, and a compelling need to explain his despair. "I don't know why you did it," he began. "I'd do it, too if I knew how. I just don't know." He paused, and considered suicide. Perhaps he was not the type, but neither was Rosa.

Someone was pounding at the front door. He turned back to look at Rosa, and he felt only affection for it seemed that he had made some tentative arrangement with his memory of her.

These are the words of a survivor of a suicidal death attempting to deal with his grief. These are the words of Paul, a focal character in [Alley's] *Last Tango in Paris,* grieving the suicidal death of his wife.

NATURAL DEATH   To understand the survivor's situation, it is necessary to look first at the usual response to natural death. When someone dies, the survivors are at once reminded of their own mortality. There is loneliness related to the concrete loss of a relationship with an individual which is no longer possible. There is a feeling of helplessness related to the irreversibility of the loss. There is often anger at being deserted. And sometimes, there is relief related to the negative feelings the survivor held for the deceased person. Anger and relief related to the deceased are personally and socially unacceptable. This unacceptability frequently evokes a large amount of guilt. With a natural death, the opportunity is often present to work through one's feelings during the period of time in which death is anticipated. Most important, society encourages grieving and lends support to the mourners. Help is often offered with the daily activities of life during the grieving period. Funeral arrangements may be made by someone other than the survivors. Child care is often provided when needed.

To grieve after a loss is healthy and many think necessary. The work of grieving involves at least three stages: breaking the bonds to the lost person, adjusting to life without the deceased, and forming new relationships. Lindemann described the symptoms of the normal patterns of grieving behavior, and made the observation that the survivor often takes on traits of the deceased person. Silverman described the mourning process in terms of three stages: *impact,* in which automatic behavior dominates; *recoil,* in which awareness of the loss impinges on the survivor; and finally, *recovery*.

SUICIDAL DEATH   With accidental or natural death, this process of grieving rarely necessitates counseling. An external cause can usually be invoked to decrease the feeling of guilt related to the deceased. Survivors of loss by suicide, however, have special problems. They are often subjected to investigations by police, coroners, and insurance agents. Up until recently those who died by suicide were, in some instances, refused burial on religious grounds. The societal stigma associated with suicide often results in a lack of support for the survivor, when that support is most urgently needed. The suddenness of the loss precludes prior working through of feelings. Finally, the deliberateness of purpose in suicidal death intensifies the feelings of involvement in the survivor.

In adults, there are a variety of reactions that have been commonly observed in survivors of loss by suicide. The first and most prominent is that of guilt. Frequently, there is no external cause (that is, a disease or vehicle) to diminish the guilt. In normal grief, guilt diminishes and the inevitability of the death can be accepted. In suicidal death, the tendency to blame oneself, especially if there was conflict, is maximized. Another common reaction is anger. With natural death, there is anger at desertion or at God for taking the person away. The deliberateness of suicide focuses anger on the deceased for his willful desertion. ("She had no right to leave me.") There is even often the feeling of the deceased having had the last word in a quarrel.

The adult survivor searches for meaning. With natural death, meaning may be dealt with spiritually ("His time had come, he led a good life"). Suicidal death, however, raises many questions.

1. Was the suicidal victim in his right mind?

2. Will my children be more likely to be suicide victims because of his suicidal death?. . .

3. Was the suicidal death a sin? And if so, is the victim relegated to eternal damnation? Finally, with suicidal death, strange hypotheses often emerge.

4. Was a murder committed? Was there a mysterious intruder who came in the night and took the victim away?

The suicide survivor often searches for a scapegoat. If the victim had been in psychotherapy, the therapist is an obvious choice. If he was in a hospital or under a doctor's care, the doctor is blamed. If he was an adolescent on drugs, the suicide was the result of the drugs. If he was an alcoholic, alcohol is implicated as the causative agent. With natural death, this reaction is usually brief. With suicide, it helps to deny the survivor's role, diminish his guilt, and helps to establish a meaning. For these reasons it may be quite persistent. In the service of seeking a meaning for the suicidal event, the survivor may engage in considerable distortion of reality. There is often identification with the deceased. This may involve the survivor assuming traits or taking on symptoms exhibited by the deceased. Tragically, it may also involve copying the suicidal behavior itself. In the course of adapting to this loss, the survivor may adopt a distorted view of himself. This may be the trigger for a clinical depression. In his preoccupation with mourning the loss, tortured relationships with others may develop. These may occur due to the survivor's suspicion of other's questions, or his withdrawal into a fantasy world to shut out all relationships with others. Paradoxically, some people will distort a relationship in an attempt to maintain it at all cost.

Social isolation is common following a suicidal death. Some survivors refuse to remarry or to have children. Some refuse to form new relationships. They feel that they are eternally scarred by the role they have played in the suicidal death of their loved one. (Quite frequently, there is incomplete mourning due to the preoccupation with the *suicidal* nature of the death to the exclusion of dealing with the *loss* that has been incurred.) And finally, suicidal thoughts and behavior are not uncommon in this group of survivors. Whether representing identification with the deceased, an attempt to rejoin a lost one, or a learned reaction to stress, it is this behavior that places the survivor at considerable risk and suggests the usefulness of a positive counseling relationship. . . . .

PSYCHOTHERAPEUTIC ISSUES   What does counseling a survivor involve? As in any psychotherapeutic endeavor, the patient or client brings to the situation his or her own unique set of psychodynamics. Although one may be tempted to stop here in attempting to identify relevant issues, I would urge that we do not. There are elements which survivors seem to bring to therapy regardless of, or in addition to, their unique patterns of thoughts, feelings, and experience. These elements seem to be an integral part of the adjustment to the suicidal death of a significant person:

1. The survivor needs to reach an understanding of the suicidal death that preserves his own self-worth and satisfies his search for meaning. Initially, the pattern of self-blame predominates along with anger at not being given an opportunity to intervene. "I know I could have stopped him," a grieving patient told me recently, "if he had only cared enough about me to call me. I should have called him. I was calling him every month. Why did I stop? I'm sure I could have saved him."

Sometimes the suicidal nature of the death is denied. ("It was an accident. It must be certified an accident. The gun was loaded because there had been prowlers.")

Earlier life is searched for a clue to explain the death. Some patients will not rest until blame can be appropriately assigned. "My husband should have spent more time with the boy," a surviving mother told me. "I guess he was going crazy and we didn't notice." Initially, the therapist does best to listen uncritically to the hypotheses presented. Once the patient is effectively engaged in the therapeutic process, reality evaluations can be suggested by the counselor. The patient can be encouraged to follow his hypotheses to their conclusions— thus discarding those least defensible. In the process, distortions, both interpersonal and interfamilial can be pointed out.

2. The survivor needs an opportunity to express his feelings in a non-rejecting atmosphere. These emotions often include sadness, anger, grief, loneliness, anxiety, abandonment. Once the patient feels that the expression of feelings can be tolerated by the counselor, the therapist can begin the task of helping the survivor "order" his feelings. Irra-tional fear, guilt, or shame can then be dealt with openly and pointed out to the patient.

3. The survivor should be encouraged to mourn the loss, consider life without the deceased, in addition to dealing with the suicidal nature of the death. Often, preoccupation with the suicide can be employed as a defensive measure to avoid the awareness of emotional pain related to the loss.

4. In the same way that a counselor must inquire about suicidal thoughts and plans in a patient felt to be at risk, the survivor should be monitored by the therapist. The response to being told of a suicidal plan must be active in terms of the therapist making himself available to the patient and encouraging him to consider the consequences of his proposed actions.

5. Since the social response to a survivor is often dominated by the stigma attached to suicide, the counselor must make special efforts to identify and encourage support from others in the patient's environment. This he must do in addition to the support and reassurance he will provide for the patient. At this time of cognitive confusion and emotional turmoil, it is critical to reinforce the coping strengths possessed by the patient. . . .

In conclusion, it is important for mental health professionals to be *alert* to the needs of this neglected group of suicide survivors. Be *aware* of the issues that seem to transcend individual considerations in these persons. And finally, be *available* to provide counseling to these people made patients by no action of their own.

Lael Wertenbaker

Death of a Man

In this chapter from *Death of a Man,* Lael Werten-baker touches us. She makes us feel the quiet despair of cancer and the strength required to live in spite of it. But the severity of her husband's pain can be managed only with increasing doses of morphine, and the horror of continued life outweighs his fear of death. He must take his own life, but this is not easy. In the end it is love and not fear that determines the outcome of his struggle.

Bad to worse to worst" read the note in the *carnet* almost illegibly on December 26th, and at five o'clock Wert said what I had known with interior tension he would say: "Time's come."

"Are you afraid?" I asked him.

"Mmmm hum," he admitted.

I wanted to plead with him for one more day, but I did not. A brief *crise* in the early evening made me glad I had not. We went upstairs at ten. It was very cold, but there was no wind. I had kept the electric heaters on all day in both the bathroom and the bedroom and the rooms were quite warm. Ama had given over protesting my extravagance and no longer pulled the plugs out to save me money when I was not looking. She had put boiling-hot-water bottles in our two beds. We undressed and waited until the house was deeply quiet except for Ama's audible snoring in the room above ours, where she slept with Timberlake. They slept like rocks. Chris, who was easier to awaken, had his room on the other side of the hall and stairwell on the third floor. Wert read over the pamphlet on morphine again while I went down and boiled water and all the hypodermics we had.

"Silly, when we are sterile and when we aren't," Wert remarked. On the ship we had not bothered. Later we did.

Carefully he refigured his possible tolerance of morphine acquired from the doses he had allowed himself when no other drugs were effective. First, he gave himself a small shot; I believe this was designed to avoid the danger of nausea. While he was waiting twenty minutes, he took his copy of Montaigne, with old bullfight tickets stuck in it for markers where he had particularly responded to certain pages, and dated it and wrote in it a message for John Hersey, to whom I was to send it. Then he took the white pills he had counted out and we made a solution of them which, as he stirred it, turned perfectly clear and looked like water.

"Here goes," he said, and began pumping the big doses into his leg. His hand shook. He bent and broke one needle, but rescued the liquid, saying, "Damn it! Don't let me make a mess of this."

With twelve grains of morphine, he was theoretically sure, but for good measure he gave himself three more. Then he lay back on the pillow and I sat beside him and held his hands. "I love you and I've had a damned fine life," he said, and closed his eyes in an exhaustion like death.

In a minute he opened one eye. "Purple haze coming as promised," he said, "but 'we cain't do nothin' till Martin gits here!'. . ."

In another minute the eye opened again and then the other one and he said, "A gentleman should know when to take his leave." A long, deep look . . . and then he seemed to go out.

Sometimes it seemed to me his heart beat fast and sometimes very slowly, but it continued to beat strongly. His breathing varied from very slow and gasping to quick and shallow. His hands seemed still conscious of holding mine. I don't know how long it was

SUICIDE OFF EGG ROCK

Behind him the hotdogs split and drizzled
On the public grills, and the ochreous salt flats,
Gas tanks, factory stacks—that landscape
Of imperfections his bowels were part of—
Rippled and pulsed in the glassy updraught.
Sun struck the water like a damnation.
No pit of shadow to crawl into,
And his blood beating the old tattoo
I am, I am, I am. Children
Were squealing where combers broke and the spindrift
Ravelled wind-ripped from the crest of the wave.
A mongrel working his legs to a gallop
Hustled a gull flock to flap off the sandspit.

He smouldered, as if stone-deaf, blindfold,
His body beached with the sea's garbage,
A machine to breathe and beat forever.
Flies filing in through a dead skate's eyehole
Buzzed and assailed the vaulted brainchamber.
The words in his book wormed off the pages.
Everything glittered like blank paper.

Everything shrank in the sun's corrosive
Ray but Egg Rock on the blue wastage.
He heard when he walked into the water

The forgetful surf creaming on those ledges.

Sylvia Plath

until he opened both eyes and said, sounding indignant, "I'm not going to die. I feel sheepish."

A little later I brought him a red casserole and he staggered to his feet, weaving. For some reason, he had taken the hot-water bottle which had been behind his shoulderblades and put it on his head. Holding the red casserole in both hands made the stance of the male performing this office even more exaggerated. He looked at my expression and began to laugh and I laughed too. It was not hysterical, but real laughter.

"It's funny," agreed Wert, "but damn it all, woman, do you realize that what I am peeing away contains valuable morphine?"

He was wholly free of pain, clear-headed and wakeful. Settling himself comfortably, for he'd had the most trouble getting comfortable lying down for days, he told me to pull up the armchair in place of my backless footstool. We stayed thus and talked until five in the morning, when he went to sleep. It was a lovely night.

The next day he could not get down the stairs. I telephoned Steve in Paris. "He took enough to kill an elephant," I said to Steve, "and all it did was make him feel good. What a man." It was foolish but I felt proud as well as intensely worried. "But today's rough, and we used a big hunk of our American supply last night, and this thing's getting unbearable, you know. The other kind of morphine works better for pain, so he wants to try it tonight. But, Steve, if we use too much, and it doesn't work, we may run into terrible trouble. Can you find out what went wrong? Can you get and send down some more? I've some French friends who can get a little in Bordeaux, but. . ." "He's got to be able to kill himself when he wants to," said Steve. "My God. I'll find out everything I can, get everything I can. What

about sleeping pills?" "He says they're for dames," I said. "He wouldn't want to use them even if he could, but he can't anyway because he can't keep anything down he swallows. Solves that problem." "I'll call you back," said Steve, who had seen Wert for a few minutes when a *crise* just bypassed him, and whose heart was in his voice.

Wert tried again the night of the 27th with vials of French morphine solution. We had a feeling this morphine was more effective and might work. We proceeded as before, and the moments were equally intense. If I quote him jesting it is not to offer, or because he offered it as, comedy relief. We were a long way beyond any self-consciousness and if he thought of something for his or our amusement, he said it. Such things are isolated in memory from the rest, being separate and sharp.

In the small hours of the night before, after he did not die, he had said, "Lo, the poor idiom." I had promised to send it on to his son Bill, and to Suzie and Frances Ann, all admirers of his puns.

"I'm running out of last words," he said before this second try. "Make a list and take your choice. But *don't* forget my last pun."

As he passed out, into a deep, slow-breathing unconsciousness, he murmured, "I love you," and I thought they were truly his last.

After an hour or so his breathing, though still slow and very heavy, no longer stopped at intervals, and I knew he was not going to die this time, either. I went through an agonized half hour trying to decide whether to give him any more. That was what he wanted me to do, if it would make the difference, if he was almost and not quite out. I could not, and so I went to bed and slept myself, clutching at unconsciousness until we could be conscious together again.

Next morning he wrote in his *carnet:* "Tried again. No go. Slept." During the day, he felt "not so bad."

"I couldn't," I told him then. "I'd have done anything you said absolutely to do, but I *couldn't* decide for you by myself. I couldn't give you another dose that might have done it or might just not have and been worse. . . ."

"You shouldn't have. You were right," he said. "Entirely right not to."

"Besides, I wanted you to go out peacefully like that, but oh, I'm so glad you're here another day. I'm so grateful for having you."

"Staunch," said Wert, using with perception the one word that wiped out my feeling that I had been selfish or cowardly or somehow lacking. "Let's let it go for three days if we can. Too much emotion. New Year's Eve, now. That would be ceremonial. I'd rather like that. Lay in a bottle of the best champagne."

Better, he dressed and was downstairs by noon. He tried to eat, choosing a dry, not-too-sweet cookie, but it didn't work. We had a scare when he gave in and took two grains of morphine and it gave him no reaction, but the next dose relieved him. Steve telephoned and said he'd found an American-trained doctor who suggested, after due double-talk, that even fifteen grains of morphine might not work if the subject were insufficiently relaxed. We should combine it with soporifics. He had stuff for us and would sent it on the Sud-Express by some passenger I should meet in Bayonne at the station unless he could locate a Basque train porter whom he could trust. From the Paris station, he would telephone and tell me for whom I was to look.

A friendly young couple were hanging out the window looking for me from Steve's description of me when the train pulled in. The package in my hands, I thanked them, without ever knowing their names.

New Year's Eve midnight, with champagne in hollow-stemmed, chilled glasses we touched and drank a little from, he made his ceremonial try. Again, this time combining the morphine with four 100-mgm. Nembutal suppositories to get the relaxation the doctor we did not know had recommended, he went off into a sleep, almost before he could finish getting the shots in, his hand shaking with haste and weakness. Sometimes he stopped breathing for as long a two minutes. Next day, January 1st, 1955, he wrote "Happy New Year!" in the *carnet.*

"There is always cutting the wrists," he said wearily. "I'd like to put that off as long as I can. Messy. Hard on you."

Each day was a kind of miracle of his being there and each day claimed from him an exorbitant price. His handwriting, which had been scraggly and nearly illegible for a while, came sharp and clear again as he headed the pages left for Notes at the end of 1954s fillers with the dates in 1955 so that he could leave the new year's pages fresh for Chris to put into the cover. "Monday—3rd. Weary from no sleep. No eat. Lunch puts anyway. Bach. Good day between times." "Tuesday—4th. Getting mighty low. Bath. Music. My love." "Wed.— 5th. Terrible night. Worst day yet. Play bubbles game. No go."

The "bubbles game" was his attempt to insert an air bubble into a vein. Wert remembered a news story of a murder committed in some French province in which the murderer, a doctor, had pumped an air bubble into the vein of his victim. I remembered a Marquand novel and an old mystery story that used this means. Wert spent the 5th engrossed in trying to manage it.

During the first hour he would call to me with excitement whenever he succeeded in getting a needle into a vein, which proved to be difficult enough. Once he thought he'd actually forced in several cubic centimeters of air. We speculated wildly on what happened next if he had.

Late in the afternoon, he said, "Damn it, you don't seem to be taking this quite seriously."

"I'd be 'ever so surprised' if it worked," I admitted. "I think it takes an expert."

"Well, you wouldn't begrudge a man his limited amusements, would you?" said Wert. "Keeps me occupied, anyway."

"I feel better about every damn human being in the whole world because you are a man," I said, and he said, "What a nice thing to say."

I'd have been glad enough if the bubbles had worked. I helped all I could. The dope problem, in spite of Cartier, Steve, and what we had left from the U.S. and Bordeaux, was getting grim. The day before, Cartier had told me the only thing left to do was to give Wert a shot in the spine, which was "dangerous," but which would paralyze him from the waist down temporarily and prove sure relief. "Body in bed," said Wert to me. "No control over functions. No."

The page for the 6th, in spite of a steady heading and two careful notes on his shots, is scribbled. I can only make out the words: "We have every . . . End hoped and tried for. . ."

On the 7th, by the fire, he said: "That's the last time I can make those stairs. I can't hear music any more. I can't drink even tea. The cigarettes taste bad. I'm only staying alive to see your face."

It had to be that night, if it was to be his way, and we both knew it. We waited until very late, talking together with a kind of final serenity unmatched at any other time. He planned everything most carefully, aware that nothing was as you planned it, but with determination that however and whatever, he must die. Debating the amount in case it should make him too shaky, he took a small last shot of morphine. I brought his Rolls razor, freshly stropped, and he detached the blade.

I couldn't watch when he cut, or as he went in again—when the flow into the red casseroles, on which he rested his wrists so that the blood wouldn't spill on the bed and the floor, slowed and stopped—although I had to hold him up then. Then the cancer seemed to rouse and to fight him, as if evil were fighting for its own life, which would die with his. I started pumping morphine into him, cutting my fingers a little on the glass tubes I was breaking as fast as I could, so that our blood mingled for an instant, symbol of all love. He was afraid of crying out and waking the children and I begged him to pass out and promised him he would die whatever I had to do and he said, "Quick, a towel, I'm losing control," and I got a towel between his legs. I said, "I love you I love you please die," and he said that one first phrase, too, and went into the final struggle to die and did.

The wax and bones of him I got between clean sheets and into clean white silk pajamas, and I bound the ragged wrists in flesh-colored adhesive tape as he planned for me to do. Although only Dominique that night would see him, he lay in dignity and cleanliness. Then it was time to wake and send Ama out into the 3:00 A.M. rain for Dominique to help me dress him, which I could not do alone. In the morning, there were his children to wake, each one, and tell and comfort them. There were the doctor, the mayor, the undertaker, to see. There were the cables to send across the ocean, as he had asked me to, and the quick, traditional visits of the Basques, who said, "Life goes on, Mommy, that's how it is." Then there was time to mourn the death of a man.

14.

Death, War, and the Human Condition

War involves the socially-approved, organized killing of human beings who are defined as enemies. In war, killing and death are utilized as means of pursuing political and economic objectives; for example, the extension of national boundaries, the overthrow of political regimes, and the acquisition of natural and human resources. In other words, the lives and lifestyles of the members of one social system are protected by destroying, or threatening to destroy, the lives and lifestyles of the enemies.

The deliberate killing of large numbers of people has been practiced throughout history. Moreover, wars have grown increasingly destructive as technology has made possible more efficient weapons. During the twentieth century alone, according to one scholar, over one hundred million persons have been killed as a direct or indirect consequence of man-made violence. An estimated twenty-five million combatants and civilians have been killed in wars just since the end of World War II. With the advent of the nuclear age, inaugurated by the atomic bombings of Hiroshima and Nagasaki in 1945, we entered an era in which war is more powerful and dangerous than ever before in history. Nuclear weapons represent the most sophisticated and efficient tools for killing ever developed.

Yet the subject of war has tended to be ignored by contemporary students of death and dying and to remain the province of historians and political scientists, professional soldiers, defense analysts, weapons merchants, and diplomats. The burgeoning interest in death and dying has focused instead on home and hospital. But at the very time that scores of well-meaning individuals are struggling to redefine and delay death, and to make dying more dignified, others are zealously striving to invent better weapons and strategies for killing ever larger numbers of people. The four articles in this chapter all address the implications of death and war for the human condition —a condition, it will be seen, that is growing increasingly precarious.

Toynbee's article on "Death in War" reminds us that war is a basic institution of developed societies, past and present. As such, war is no haphazard, accidental outbreak of violence, but is instead a highly complex enterprise requiring careful planning and organization. The extent to which our own society has institutionalized war is indicated by the fact that in 1975, of a total federal budget of $324.6 billion, $86 billion, or 26.6 percent, was spent on national defense. Moreover, tens of thousands of jobs in our society are directly or indirectly related to war and militarism. But war requires more than money or workers. War requires citizens willing to sacrifice their own lives (or those of their sons or husbands) and to kill enemies. In order to achieve this, war changes the very meanings of death. What would be suicide in civilian life earns the Medal of Honor for valor and patriotism, and what would be murder within one's own social system becomes heroism when enemies are killed.

Toynbee also stresses a point that is made in each of the other articles in this section: war in the atomic age—nuclear war—is very different from, and far more dangerous than, any wars in the past. The development and proliferation of nuclear weapons capable of being rocketed by remote control across the oceans have created the threat of extinction for civilization on this planet.

Shneidman's article on "Megadeath: Children of the Nuclear Family" explores the implications for modern youth of living under the shadow of violent mass death. "Megadeath," for our purposes, refers to the deaths of vast numbers of human beings. It can result from both natural and man-made causes, e.g., plagues, famines, natural disasters, and war. The term was originally used by Herman Kahn in his book *Thinking about the Unthinkable*—a speculative analysis of possible forms and consequences of nuclear conflict. The interrelationship between death and life in the context of possible nuclear annihilation emerges with painful clarity in the writings of Shneidman's students at Harvard and UCLA: if death is meaningless, then life in turn loses much of its meaning. The realization of death has tormented and challenged thoughtful people since the dawn of history, but the nature and extent of mass death in the modern world beggars the answers to the problem of death that have given past generations comfort and meaning. We see, as a result, a generation of young adults characterized by a disillusioned pragmatism and concern with occupational and financial security on the one hand, and low birth rates, rising rates of suicide and drug usage, and confusion about identity on the other. We are left with the disturbing message that unless we are able to confront and prevent megadeath, we will witness further deterioration of personal meaning in the lives of future generations, which may in turn accelerate the momentum towards apocalypse.

Holocausts, according to Robert Jay Lifton in "Witnessing Survival," involve massive violence which results in "the physical, social, and spiritual obliteration of a human community." The human toll from holocausts extends past the large number of persons killed to include the survivors, who are overwhelmed by massive psychological trauma. Interest in holocausts, and in particular the infamous Holocaust in which more than ten million Jews and other "undesirables" were systematically exterminated by the Nazis in World War II, is growing, says Lifton, but tends to be confined to past holocausts and to be handicapped by two dilemmas. First, ordinary psychological concepts are inadequate to comprehend the human meaning of such extensive and meaningless death, and, second, the student of holocausts must tread a fine line between depersonalizing detachment and mind-numbing empathy. Such ambivalence was manifested in response to the televising of "Holocaust," which followed the plight of a Jewish family during World War II as its members were destroyed by the Nazis. Critics decried the necessarily superficial treatment of the Holocaust on television as an injustice to the memories of the millions who died, while defenders argued that such programs are essential in order to familiarize the postwar generation with the horrors of the recent past. However, our interest must not stop with historical review. Lifton and the other authors in this section alert us to the possibility of a nuclear holocaust, in which most of the life on this planet would be consumed in fire and fallout. We must build from our understanding of the causes and consequences of past holocausts, the ability to avoid future holocausts.

Lest the reader be tempted to dismiss the foregoing as unduly pessimistic, the selection by Feld on "The Consequences of Nuclear War" provides a careful analysis by a prominent scientist of the probable physical results of a large scale nuclear conflict. As we read of casualty figures in the tens of millions and permanent damage of the global biosphere, we are reminded of Lifton's discussion of the problems in studying holocausts. Such conse-

quences are so devastating as to be virtually unthinkable; the mind recoils from images of death on such a scale. Yet, ironically, only if we are willing and able to comprehend the extent and meaning of such a holocaust do we have a chance of averting it.

Previous selections in this Reader demonstrate that we have rediscovered death and dying, and are striving to understand and humanize it in home and hospital. The articles in this section, however, reveal the necessity of extending our concern with death into the realm of war and megadeath. If we do not, or cannot, there is a distinct possibility that all other issues of death and dying may be rendered meaningless.

Arnold Toynbee

Death in War

The late Arnold Toynbee was an eminent historian whose life-long study of the development of civilization provides an excellent perspective from which to analyze the nature and functions of war in society, both past and present. In this selection, Toynbee documents the historical ubiquity of warfare as a feature of society, and discusses the uniquely terrifying qualities of war in the atomic age. His message is especially germane for the post–World War II generation, whose experience with war has focused on the unpopular Vietnam conflict—a guerrilla war in a distant part of the world. With the withdrawal of troops from Southeast Asia, popular attention has tended to recoil from thoughts of war, despite the fact that wars continue to flare across the planet and the momentum towards nuclear conflict shows few signs of abating.

War is not a spontaneous vent for human nature's innate pugnacity. This pugnacity is real, and war would be impossible without it. But the most pertinent facts about war are that it is an institution and that it cannot be a very old one. War is a recent institution measured by the time-scale of the age of the human race so far or, *a fortiori,* by the length of the race's present expectation of life on this planet.

The waging of wars is impracticable unless two conditions can be met. The first condition is that the war-making communities must have at their command a surplus of time, energy, and productivity over and above what they need to spend on just keeping themselves alive. War could not be waged by ruminant animals which have to spend on eating the whole of their time that they can spare from sleeping. Human beings, too, must have lacked the resources for waging war until the turn of the fourth and third millennia B.C., when, first in what is now Iraq and then in what is now Egypt, a considerable surplus was produced, for the first time in human history, by the draining and irrigation of soils, potentially rich for cultivation, that had previously been occupied by unutilizable jungle-swamp. These two immense feats of reclamation could not have been achieved except by an autocratic and also skillful organization of the working power of large numbers of docile human beings. The creation of the fertile fields of Sumer and Egypt required mass discipline, and mass discipline is also the second of the conditions that are required for the waging of war. If a human being is to be turned into a soldier, he has to be conditioned into risking his life, and perhaps losing it, in trying to kill fellow human beings of his with whom he has no personal quarrel. For committing this perilous public crime, docility and mass discipline are as necessary as they are for carrying out large scale productive public works.

CONVENTIONS OF WAR   War, like other institutions, has its postulates and its conventions. The fundamental postulate of the institution of war is that, in war, "killing is no murder." Murder committed by private enterprise has been regarded, almost universally, as being a crime of the greatest magnitude, whether the motive has been hatred or covetousness. Murder committed under orders by public authorities in the collective interests (real or imaginary) of a community has been regarded as a virtuous and noble activity, except by a few small religious communities (for example, the Christians of the first few generations and, among modern Christians, only the Society of Friends, who hold that taking part in war is morally inadmissible in all circumstances). The moral sense of mankind in general has been obtuse enough to regard the killer in war as being righteous—at least, so long as he keeps, more or less faithfully, to the recognized rules. If he dies in battle, or if, whether dying or surviving, he shows prowess either as a combatant or as a commander, he is hailed as a hero. One of the conventions of war which was almost universal till recently, but is now being abandoned, was that women were exempt from having to serve as combatants (though not exempt, *de facto,* from being murdered or raped by male combatants). Another convention was, and still is, that a man on the war-path must dress the part. Even in the present age, when the technology of war has become sophisticated and when the soldier's equipment has become correspondingly "functional," the equivalent of the warrior's traditional war-paint and plumes survives in unobtrusive forms (stars, chevrons, buttons).

This dressing up for war looks childish, and so it is; yet it has two serious functions, one psychological and the other practical. Psychologically it symbolizes the abrogation of the normal taboo on killing fellow human beings; it replaces this taboo by a duty to kill them. Practically, the wearing of a uniform distinguishes soldiers visibly from civilians. This practical distinction has been more or less faithfully observed during two short periods of Western history: in fifteenth-century Italy before the French invasion of Italy in 1494 and in eighteenth-century and nineteenth-century Europe before the German invasion of Belgium in 1914 and the subsequent use in war of bomb-dropping airplanes. In the West between the end of the wars of religion and the outbreak of the First World War in 1914, war was, in theory at least, a killing game played between men in uniform, in which civilians were not involved. Yet, even after the opening of the nineteenth century, it was still customary for a Western army that had taken by assault a fortified and defended town to loot, rape, and murder the civilian inhabitants—and this even when the defeated defending army had been a foreign one that had occupied and had been holding the fallen town by force, against the inhabitants' will, or at any rate without their having had any power to keep the foreign occupying army out. A notorious case was the British army's conduct in the Spanish city of Badajoz after they had captured it by assault from a French occupying garrison on April 6th, 1812.

THE RELIGION OF NATIONALISM   War is not merely an institution; it is also one that is an act of religious worship. The god in whose honor this religious act is performed is the collective power of some fraction of the human race. The performance is a form of human sacrifice or ritual murder. The rulers of a state murder (by proxy) the soldiers of another state with whose rulers they are at war; and they do this at the cost of exposing their own young men, who have been turned into soldiers compulsorily if they have not volunteered, to be wounded, maimed, or killed by the soldiers of the opposing army, whom their own soldiers have been commanded to wound, maim, and kill to the utmost of their ability.

Communities consisting of fractions of the human race have been objects of worship, served by the performance of these criminal rites, ever since man got the upper hand definitively over nonhuman nature. Since then, the worship of nonhuman nature—man's main religion so long as he remained at nonhuman nature's mercy—has become virtually extinct, while man's worship of the collective power of fractions of the human race has continued to gain currency *pari passu* with the continuing increase in this power of his as a result of the progress of his technology. This idolatrous worship of collective human power, with its hideous ritual in the shape of war, has never been successfully suppressed by the relatively recent epiphany of the higher religions whose object of worship has been neither nonhuman nature nor collective human power, but has been the Ultimate Spiritual Reality behind the universe. Adherents of the higher religions have always continued actually, though not avowedly, to give a share of their allegiance to the sinister older gods.

In the modern Western world the seventeenth-century reaction against Christianity, out of revulsion from the fanatical vein in this higher religion, was followed in the eighteenth century by a spiritual lull during which "enthusiasm" (the eighteenth-century name for what we now call "fanaticism") was at a low ebb. Even then, the institution of war did not fall into abeyance. The motives of eighteenth-century Western war makers were, indeed, more cynical than those of either their predecessors or their successors, because the eighteenth-century war makers' motives were nonreligious. The stakes for which they fought were moderate, but these eighteenth-century moderate stakes were naked economic and political interests. However, spiritual nature, like physical nature, abhors a vacuum; and, since the eruption of the American and French Revolutions, the spiritual vacuum left in Western souls by the recession of Christianity has been filled by the resurgence of the older, and always latent, worship of the collective power of human communities.

This post-Christian resurgent worship of collective human power in the West (and also in those non-Western societies that have latterly been adopting the Western civilization, for evil as well as for good) has proved more virulent than the pre-Christian form of it as this was practiced by, for instance, the Romans, the Greeks, the Sumerians, and the Chinese in the period of "the Contending States." In our post-Christian age, the worship of collective human power has been keyed up to a higher pitch by the infusion of ex-Christian fanaticism into it. This post-Christian worship of collective human power is the evil religion whose name is "nationalism." It is un-Christian, except in the point of being Christianly fanatical. Unhappily, fanatical nationalism is today about 90 percent of the real religion of about 90 percent of the human race.

The increasing fanaticism of nationalism has exacted an increasing oblation of military human sacrifice. The increase can be measured by the increasing prevalence of military conscription since the *levée en masse* in France in 1792. In the modern Western world, conscription has been the twin sister of egalitarianism. The Prussian state introduced universal military service—an institution that is egalitarian, though not democratic—as its riposte to its humiliating temporary defeat by Napoleon. In the United States, whose citizens believe themselves to be the most democratic nation that there has ever been with the possible exception of the equally self-deceived Athenians, selective conscription has been imposed on two occasions: first, during the Civil War of 1861-5, on both sides, and then, in the reunited United States, from 1941 until the present moment.

ATROCITIES Another index of the increasing fanaticism of nationalism, as measured in terms of the conduct of war, has been the accelerating recrudesence of atrocities. When, in the course of the seventeenth century, Westerners had desisted, at last, from fighting their Catholic-Protestant wars of religion, they had made a serious and partially successful effort—not, of course, to abolish the institution of war, but to reduce the inevitable accompanying atrocities to a minimum for the combatants themselves and, *a fortiori,* for civilians. Since August 1914 the relatively humanitarian standard that had been set by Westerners for their conduct of war since the close of the seventeenth century has been falling sharply—particularly as regards the exemption of civilians. When German troops shot batches of Belgian civilians in the course of their invasion of Belgium in August 1914, Western public opinion was deeply shocked. When the little Basque town of Guernica was destroyed by bombing from the air on April 26, 1937, with the inevitable indiscriminate slaughter of civilians of both sexes and all ages, a fresh wave of horror swept across the Western world. The bombing of Guernica was rightly felt to portend future bombings on a vaster scale. But, in the Second World War, atrocities that dwarfed those of the First World War in both scale and cruelty caused less perturbation. For producing a shock, atrociousness, by itself, is not enough; there must also be novelty. Human hearts become hardened to anything that has become familiar; and atrocities of the wars-of-religion degree had become familiar events again by 1939. . . .

The scale of the slaughter of European combatants in the First World War did appall all the belligerent peoples. It was a scale that they had not intended and not expected when they had gone to war with each other in 1914. All European peoples who had been belligerents in the First World War had to be whipped up into engaging in the Second. However, the degree of reluctance to go to war again differed markedly as between different peoples.

The French and the British were the most reluctant of all, and the Italians would, no doubt, have been equally reluctant if they had not then been living under a regime that would have inflicted extreme penalties on any outspokenly antibelligerent individual Italian subject. The Germans were less reluctant than the French and the British, though, in the First World War, their casualties had been still heavier. Some Germans were stimulated by a thirst for revenge, but they were also willing to sacrifice their young men to a lust for conquest. Of the European peoples, the French and the Italians broke down; only the Russians, Germans, and British endured the Second World War to the end. Of the non-European belligerents in the Second World War, the Americans were stimulated, like the Germans, by a thirst for revenge—revenge, in the American case, for the Japanese attack on Pearl Harbour. In the First World War the American casualties had been relatively light, compared to those of the European belligerents. Japanese casualties had been lighter still in that war; but the Japanese spirit in the Russo-Japanese war of 1904 suggests that, even if the Japanese casualties in the First World War had been as heavy as the German had been, the Japanese people would still have made war in 1941 unhesitatingly.

The Second World War ended with the dropping of two American atomic bombs on the Japanese cities of Hiroshima and Nagasaki. No weapon ever previously forged by man had had anything approaching this amount of death-dealing capacity. The invention of the atomic weapon produced an instantaneous change in the nature of war. A five-thousand-years-old wicked institution that had always been cruel and devastating had now become suicidal. It was evident that, in any future war in which the belligerents on both sides possessed and used the atomic weapon, the distinction between victor and vanquished—a distinction that had made vic-

AFTER AUSCHWITZ

Anger,
as black as a hook,
overtakes me.
Each day,
each Nazi
took, at 8:00 A.M., a baby
and sautéed him for breakfast
in his frying pan.

And death looks on with a casual eye
and picks at the dirt under his fingernail.

Man is evil,
I say aloud.
Man is a flower
that should be burnt,
I say aloud.
Man
is a bird full of mud,
I say aloud.

And death looks on with a casual eye
and scratches his anus.

Man with his small pink toes,
with his miraculous fingers
is not a temple
but an outhouse,
I say aloud.
Let man never again raise his teacup.
Let man never again write a book.
Let man never again put on his shoe.
Let man never again raise his eyes,
on a soft July night.
Never. Never. Never. Never. Never.
I say these things aloud.

I beg the Lord not to hear.

Ann Sexton
The Awful Rowing toward God

tory so desirable—would be obliterated. Both sides would be prostrated; no victor would emerge.

ATTITUDES TO WAR IN THE ATOMIC AGE   The intellectual understanding of this revolutionary change in the character and consequence of war spread with remarkable rapidity all over the world among people who were conscious of public affairs. Such people, though no doubt they are a minority, are the minority that decides what turn the conduct of public affairs shall take. It might therefore have been expected, on first thoughts, that the understanding of the revolutionary significance of the invention of the atomic weapon would have been followed by a revolutionary change of policy—for the sake of self-preservation, if not in virtue of a change of heart of the kind that was so potent a factor in bringing about the abolition of slavery, and is still so potent a factor today in the current struggle against racial discrimination in Southern Africa, the United States, and Britain. Yet, so far, mankind has, on the whole, been behaving since 1945 as if we were still living in the pre-atomic age.

The two post-Second-World-War superpowers, the United States and the Soviet Union, are still playing the dangerous game of power politics—a game that has wrecked one civilization after another since it was started by the Sumerian city-states in the third millennium b.c. Meanwhile, many of the minor states of the present-day world—and there are now about 125 local sovereign states on the surface of this small planet—are following suit to the two superpowers in continuing to use war—and this, in some cases, with most unfortunate success—as an instrument of national policy. The danger of the game of international power politics is that it leads, inevitably, to "confrontations." There have been at least four of these between the Soviet Union and the United States between 1945 and 1967—over Berlin, over Korea, over Cuba, and over the Middle East. . . .

Since 1945, the human race has been living under a threat of extinction that had not hung over it since man definitively got the upper hand over all other large beasts of prey on this planet. This happened perhaps about thirty thousand years ago, and, at that date, human beings can hardly have been conscious of the danger of extinction from which they were liberating themselves. Today, on the other hand, they are fully aware of the threat; they know that it comes now from themselves; and they also know that it is a far more formidable threat than the previous threat of extinction by saber-toothed tigers, and even than the recently eliminated threat of extinction by bacteria (a threat that man may be going to revive in the form of bacteriological warfare).

In the United States since 1945 a new pseudo-science has sprung up which purports to prognosticate what the effects of an atomic war would be. It expresses its findings in statistics toting up the number of human lives that would be lost and the amount of human productions of all kinds that would be destroyed. These statistics may be near the mark or may be wide of it; but, when the practitioners of this pseudo-science go on to discuss how many millions of deaths would be "acceptable," they are betraying the falsity of their claim to be scientific by trespassing on the field of the unknown and the unknowable. There is no precedent in past human experience for even a guess at the intensity of the feelings of horror, grief, fear, and, above all, guilt that ritual murder on the atomic scale would bring to the surface of a human being's consciousness from the dark and deep abyss which the progress of the genuine science of psychology is revealing to us.

Edwin S. Shneidman

Megadeath

Children of the Nuclear Family

How does the threat of violent, mass death affect the lives of modern youth? This difficult but essential question is explored by Edwin Shneidman in the following selection. As a professor at both Harvard and UCLA, he has had the opportunity of questioning members of a generation which attended grade school during the era of fallout-shelter mania and air-raid drills, was in high school when the Bay of Pigs confrontation nearly provoked a nuclear war and when President Kennedy was assassinated, and was in college when the country was wracked with civil discord and enmeshed in a disillusioning war in a far-off corner of the world. This is a generation that has grown up during a time when escalating conflicts have presaged progressively darker images of doom. The reactions of these educated, articulate students reveal some of the vital dilemmas concerning life and death, living and dying, in contemporary society.

Death is in the air. Fear of personal and mass annihilation pervades thought and emotion, touches the conscience, and influences behavior. There is persuasive evidence that this thanatological aura of our time can be traced to an evil that is "visibly personified and made practically assailable" in the omnipresent threat of nuclear destruction. The Bomb has at last made it impossible for us to deny or ignore man's irrationality and capacity for evil.

It would be surprising if the existence of the Bomb were not deeply inimical to the minds of men. The very threat posed by the historical precedent of Hiroshima and Nagasaki is enough to distort many lives. The psychological fallout from yet unexploded bombs has created a chronic low-grade psychic infection throughout the world. And every day the fear of sudden mass death is exacerbated by new tests of "improved" models in the arms race.

Death appears to be discussed more openly now than at any time since the days of the Black Death in the fourteenth century, when a giant fear cast its shadow over men's lives—but with this difference: the plague was a "natural" catastrophe and thought of as the "will of God"; the Bomb is the will of man. Today, man is the enemy. It is man who threatens his own destruction. We are afraid of our own power for evil and our seeming inability to control it in others. We talk about the nuclear death with which we are threatened, we are impelled to talk about it. Yet at the same time, as we have seen, the subject of death is taboo. How are we to account for this? And how do young people feel about these issues? Some commentators have said that the threat of sudden mass death matters little to youth; others have said that they cannot escape this specter. My own belief, one reinforced by my students' responses to the questions I put to them, is that much of this new dual attitude toward death is either directly or indirectly related to the Bomb. . . .

One cannot fail to include this overhanging threat of violent mass death as one of the vitally important items in the total array of forces that, consciously or unconsciously, have shaped our current views of life and death. Moreover, the intellectual and philosophical climate of this century has undoubtedly served both to stimulate and to reflect the dysphoric spirit of our time—the century of World Wars I and II, the German death camps, Coventry, Dresden, Hiroshima. Whether for good or for ill, some substantial portion of our current concerns with death must be attributed to Kierkegaard, Jaspers, Heidegger, Marcel, Sartre, and Camus, those existential philosophers for whom the topic of death has often occupied a central place—what Jaspers described as the "awareness of the fragility of being." For Heidegger, being-in-the-world was, in its essence, a being-toward-death. Sartre wrote that "death became for us the habitual object of our concern." And Camus began his *Myth of Sisyphus* with the declaration that *the* central problem for all philosophy was no less than that of death by self-destruction: "Judging whether life is or is not worth living amounts to answering the fundamental question of philosophy."

Sartre's words encompass the central point: death is now the habitual topic of our concern. If death is not the focus of our conscious anxieties, it is, at the hauntingly least, the omnipresent threat that mobilizes our deepest fears.

The step from thoughts of death to thoughts of war is a short one. War is heinous and wasteful. We all know that. But [was] the war in Indochina more shameful and immoral than others we have waged? What is most painfully shameful is that it [was] only one more variation on a theme. Our atrocities in Vietnam [were] bloody repetitions of similar ferocities

against Mexicans in 1846 and 1847, against Indians a hundred years ago, and against Filipinos at the turn of the century: entering territories not our own, burning villages to get at native insurrectionists, slaughtering old men, women, and children for revenge or sport, changing and perverting the indigenous culture. Familiar too are the postwar dysphoria and ennui: recall the jaded expatriates after World War I, with their disillusionment, fear, anger, despair, and fitful productivity.

Among the current young generation, many perceive the threat of mass death as very real; they cannot be assured of a future. Having lost this hope, they lack the essential future-tied perspective, that optimism which spurs people to productivity, to goal-directed actions, and, in the end, to life. It is what Alfred Kazin speaks of as the "obstinate hopes of mankind." One needs these hopes to keep going. To lose hope is to become frightened and embittered, then angry and desperate.

Nowadays the prospect of sudden death—by nuclear devices, counterinsurgency, police action, and war—is everywhere. Such notions as megadeath, overkill, and global annihilation have created an urgency to grapple with the topic of death. With nuclear bombs, man now has the capacity to literally erase both the past and the future in one flash of lethal heat. The potential enormity of the superbombs is not only that they are capable of killing practically everyone who is alive and thus jeopardizing the future, but that in doing so they would also "murder" history: all previous ages would be simultaneously erased.

Elliott, in his extraordinary book, *Twentieth Century Book of the Dead* (1972), states: "Since the atom bomb and its successors in death technology, the new possibility of total death for the species has become a reality." He continues to explicate this haunting notion of total death:

> Violence in the twentieth century has produced the new phenomenon of total death. As an *idea,* total death has existed—in mental pictures of the day of judgment, doomsday, the end of the world—at least since the formulation of the great religions. As a *reality* attainable by human means, the science of which is a permanent unalterable part of knowledge, it originates in the notorious half-century from which we are just emerging. *Can* we emerge from the nightmare of reality and vision created in that period? We cannot create a retrospective order for the chaos of the actual events. Can we escape from the chaos of the idea that is left to us? Total death could mean the obliteration of particular cities or countries or religions; it could mean the collapse of world civilization or the death of the species; or it could mean the total death of the mind within a variety of physical parameters. Total death might be brought about by a wide range of means: by the carefully considered destruction of selected millions; by the direct and secondary effects of pollution or overcrowding; by a death-breeding mixture of every kind of human motivation acting on machineries and systems which are beyond the control of living creatures. Total death has a timespan overwhelming the convenient human notion of time. It can "happen" in an instant, in a few days; it can have the monthly, yearly rhythms of traditional warfare or it could create a chronic long-term disruption of the seasons of nature and the years of human life. Its possibility is tomorrow, or in the next two hundred years, or at any "time" in the future. Total death is a hard, scientific and immediate reality at the same time as being a speculative idea in search of a philosophy. No existing mental structures, of science, philosophy, or religion, are adequate to contain it.

Robert Lifton, in the first chapter of his remarkable and searing book about the survivors of Hiroshima, *Death in Life* (1967), says:

> With Hiroshima (and her neglected historical sister, Nagasaki) something more is involved: a dimension of totality, a sense of ultimate annihilation—of cities, nations, the world. The feeling may be vague, but it is of the greatest psychological importance. What I am suggesting is that our perceptions of Hiroshima are the beginnings of new dimensions of thought about death and life.

Just as "the nuclear weapons left a powerful imprint upon the Japanese which continues to be transmitted, historically and psychologically, through the generations," those same detonations created in some of my college students (born about that time) a preprint that influenced their lives through a fallout of apprehension and fear. An interesting question is whether many of the current generation might not be termed psychological *Hibakusha* ("explosion-affected persons"). At the least, they are Atomic Bomb Age children. Their comments, then, are not to be lightly dismissed as adolescent nonsense. Here are some of them, contributed by students in my death classes at Harvard and UCLA.

> I think my whole generation has grown up and been tremendously influenced by the imminent threat of death. Perhaps this has promoted somewhat of an attitude of abandon. It certainly contributed to the aura of violence and so has the war. I think that the cloud of destruction has made many people feel the urgency of the need for reform in our own society. Things move more quickly toward change because life could be ended tomorrow. [Female, nineteen]

> When I was quite young I was afraid to stay in New York because I knew that in the event of a nuclear war it would be destroyed. [Male, eighteen]

> I'm sure a week doesn't go by when I don't seriously consider the possibility of nuclear catastrophe. You can't read the paper or *Time* magazine without getting it drummed into your head. I used as a child to be struck dumb with the thought of being killed by an atomic bomb, but as I grew I realized that if I remained in cities like New York, Boston, or London I

would hardly have the time to realize I was going to be dead before I would be. [Male, twenty-one]

At this point, in order to orient ourselves temporally, we need to interpose some chronology, remembering that the atomic bombs were dropped on Hiroshima and Nagasaki in August 1945 and the era of bomb shelters and air-raid drills was around 1950 to 1958. These students were writing during the 1969–1972 academic years.

When I was about fifteen I would dream about the world ending or having to run to our fallout shelter, but this was a time when everyone was talking about building family shelters. It was only with recent ABM discussion that the threat of nuclear destruction has become real to me once more. [Female, twenty-one]

As a child of eight or nine, I sometimes had bad dreams of bombing raids and running to shelters, something you would not expect of a child who had never had any sort of war experience. But at that age I read newspapers and I listened to newsbroadcasts, so I realized with a fair amount of sophistication the transitory nature of any security. [Male, twenty-one]

A theoretical issue: What effect does the temper of the times play on attitudes toward death? We all know that the content and degree of religious fervor, beliefs, and superstitions, together with generally accepted ideas, all directly influence basic attitudes toward death at any given time. For contemporary youth, the lifelong spirit of the time has been the spirit of war.

I fear war. I despise, for the most part, those who fight. I see absolutely no justification for starting or continuing a war. Nuclear war scares the shit out of me. I don't think it makes me, personally, more afraid of death, but it does make me worry about the death of a massive number of people. I think the greatest influence the nuclear bomb has had on me is to shock me. I can't believe that man can be so stupid as to

want to kill himself three times over. [Female, eighteen]

The bomb has made me conscientiously opposed to all forms of war. It has put a value on the now, the me, the feelings, not the job, the money, the nice life. [Male, twenty]

We live in a fulcrum time. Youth sees the current world scene as a life-and-death seesaw, with life teetering in the balance. But this is not the view of youth alone. In a [1969] article John Platt of the University of Michigan spells out in a dramatic and terrifying manner the root problems of our age, and, in the absence of their solution—a subject on which he is not resoundingly optimistic—the fifty-fifty chance

What grass not yellowed?
Which day, no march?
What man not taken
To guard the four frontiers?

What grass not blackened?
What man not sick?
Sorrow to the soldiers:
We, alone, not human?

Not oxen, not tigers
Moving along wild fields
Sorrow to the soldiers
Morning till dark, no rest.

Foxes up their tail
Moving along tall dark grass
We move war-carts
Moving along our own trek.

The Shih Ching

of our surviving until 1990. "As long as we continue to have no adequate stabilizing peacekeeping structures for the world, we continue to live under the daily threat not only of local wars but of nuclear escalation with overkill and megatonnage enough to destroy all life on earth." For both the United States and the world as a whole, "the one crisis that must be ranked at the top in total danger and imminence is, of course, the danger of large-scale or total annihilation by nuclear escalation or by radiological-chemical-biological warfare."

We are at such a fulcrum time in the psychological history of man, "vibrating in mid-deep," debating (nuclear destruction, overpopulation, environmental pollution) whether to sink into "the speechless profound of the sea" or to bound up into the blessed air, whether to respond to the imperious call of life or to succumb to the constant invitation that death seductively puts forth. In Platt's survival chart, in the grid where "total annihilation" intersects "twenty years from now," he has put a black German iron cross, and in his text this comment: "The peace-keeping stabilization problem will either be solved by that time or we will probably be dead."

Death was put in the air by the older generation. It is they who have created the shameful state of affairs for which they are accounted morally responsible. It is the older generation that threatens the life of today's youth. Authority's mistakes are youth's burdens. The unfairness of it all makes youth angry and disrespectful. Civility to authority goes out the window because approbation is not sought. And with the collapse of civility, all degrees of hostility are then psychologically possible. It depends only on the provocation, the devised occasion.

If the young people do not identify with their elders' causes, where then are their cathexes?

Their psychological investments are in their own acts, their fight, the youth crusade. What keeps it going is a very basic emotion: excitement. Excitement gives a keen edge to their sense of vitality, bravado, and exploration. This generally heightened derring-do leads to heightened risk-taking behavior; with motorcycles, confrontations with police, suicide attempts, promiscuity, drugs. And so for current youth the specter of death now hovers at two doors: the first unbeckoned with its nuclear armload; but the second, teased and flirted with. The paradox is that in youth's concern to forget that death is in the air, some have put death in their actions. . . .

For this generation there is a heightened sense of the uncertainty of the future, of the survival of the world itself. No other generation in memory has grown up with this particular global tenuousness. Young people today do not worry so much about the nature of tomorrow (as, for example, those who lived through the Depression had to do); they rather worry about whether or not there will be a tomorrow. For the first time in six centuries (since the great European plagues) a generation has been born and raised in a thanatological context, concerned with the imminent possibility of the death of the person, the death of humanity, the death of the universe, and, by necessary extension, the death of God. . . .

What are some of the effects of this lugubrious death consciousness on students? The effects seem to be varied and even contradictory: a heightened emphasis on the present (the "now generation"); hopelessness and resignation, a waiting for the end; indignation over one's impotence to control the conditions that threaten mass death; even an urge to get it over with. There is taboo and permissiveness; repression and heightened consciousness; romanticization of death and sardonic realism. . . .

Robert Jay Lifton

Witnessing Survival

Robert Jay Lifton, a professor of psychiatry at Yale University, has interviewed survivors of the atomic bombing of Hiroshima, veterans returning from the Vietnam war, and victims of the Buffalo Creek flood disaster, and has extensively studied the literature on the Nazi Holocaust. His message is clear: the study of holocausts is both vital and difficult. The study of past holocausts reveals how the meanings of life and death can become twisted in the hands of governments that have at their disposal increasingly effective means of killing. Lifton points out, moreover, that the survivors of holocausts suffer grievous trauma, both physically and mentally; in particular, survivors are susceptible to psychic numbing, in which the ability to feel and think is drastically diminished as a defense against meaninglessness and horror. Lifton's study of past holocausts underscores the importance of understanding and preventing future ones: a nuclear holocaust is likely to be unimaginably more pervasive and lethal, for both direct victims and survivors, than any holocaust in history.

O ne approaches the study of holocaust knowing that it is virtually impossible to convey the experience, to find words or concepts for the extremity of its horror. And we are faced with the paradox of making an effort to understand, in terms of human feeling, the most antihuman event in human history. The European Holocaust, after all, was invented by, and consumed, human beings. And its very extremity has something to teach us about our more ordinary confrontations with death and violence.

INVESTIGATORS' DILEMMAS   The word "holocaust," from Greek origins, means total consumption by fire. That definition applies, with literal grotesqueness, to Auschwitz and Buchenwald, and also to Nagasaki and Hiroshima. In Old Testament usage there is the added meaning of the sacrificial, of a burnt offering. That meaning tends to be specifically retained for the deliberate, selective Nazi genocide of six million Jews—retained with both bitterness and irony (sacrifice to whom and for what?) I will thus speak of the Holocaust *and* of holocausts—the first to convey the uniqueness of the Nazi project of genocide, the second to suggest certain general principles around the totality of destruction as it affects survivors. From that perspective holocaust means total disaster: the physical, social, and spiritual obliteration of a human community. To observe common psychological responses of survivors, however, in no way suggests that the historical events themselves can be equated [to these responses].

Those of us who undertake this task face two additional problems. One is the inadequacy of ordinary psychological concepts, and yet the necessity to find connections between the extreme and the ordinary in our experience. Another is the nature of the investigator's own involvement—that combination which Buber called distance and relation.

On the part of psychological investigators there has been too much distance and not enough relation, a tendency to negate or minimize survivors' experiences, largely in response to our own psychic numbing. Yet there is also the danger of the kind of uneasiness before survivors that causes the investigator to romanticize or glorify their ordeal and thereby to divest it of its unsavory dimensions. Either stance—spurious neutrality or compensatory glorification—diminishes the survivor and interferes with our understanding both of what is particular to his ordeal, and what insight it may reveal about our own psychological and historical condition.

What follows draws upon my experience, direct and indirect, with survivors of four different holocausts: Hiroshima, where I lived and interviewed survivors over a period of six months in 1962; the Nazi death camps, mostly through others' studies and the writings of survivors; the Vietnam War, through intensive work with returning veterans from 1970 through 1973; and the Buffalo Creek flood disaster of 1972, through work with survivors in West Virginia from 1973 through 1975. Precisely because these four events differ so greatly—the last in particular is of a separate order from the other three in terms of size and historical significance—the fact that survivors share certain psychological responses takes on added importance. . . .

DEFINING SURVIVORS   Who is a survivor? A survivor is one who has encountered, been exposed to, or witnessed death, and has himself or herself remained alive. Albert Camus, in his Nobel Prize acceptance speech of 1957, spoke of "twenty years of absolutely insane history." Elsewhere he asks a terrible rhetorical question: "Do you know that over a period of twenty-five years, between 1922 and 1947, seventy million Europeans—men, women and children—have been uprooted, deported, killed?" (The "Do you know" means, do we let ourselves remember—do we permit ourselves to feel!) One might well repeat the question for the ensuing three decades, in relationship to Asians, Africans, and Latin Americans, who have suffered similarly. Camus viewed such things, in the words of one of his biographers, "as a scandal that he himself finds impossible to evade." We can say that he referred to our landscape of holocaust, from which literature must emerge and life must be lived. On that basis (and without in any way equating ordinary life to the experience of holocaust) we can say that we all have in us something of the survivor and witness.

Here, as in his other work, Camus expressed the survivor's potential for confronting the death immersion and for seeking from it a measure of insight. But a contrasting response is also possible—one of cessation of feeling or sustained psychic numbing. This is the response of most ordinary people to the death immersions of their time. And this numbed response can be viewed as a second scandal of our time, the scandal of our failure to be scandalized by manmade holocausts, by mass murder.

A few more distinctions. An actual survivor of holocaust undergoes a totality of psychological responses which cannot be duplicated in ordinary experience. Yet separate elements of that death immersion do make contact with general psychological principles. If there is one thing Freud taught us, it is that no single psychological tendency, however extreme or disturbed, is totally alien from "normal" pyschic function. So we must study survivor experience both in its uniqueness and in its connection with the rest of human life. It follows that survivors vary enormously in their capacities and inclinations—many extraordinary in their life-power, others capable of destructive behavior, each bringing a particular mixture of virtues and faults to a shared ordeal.

PSYCHOLOGICAL THEMES   In previous writings I have described five psychological themes in survivors. The first of these is the *death imprint* with its related *death anxiety*. Involved here are *indelible images* not just of death but of grotesque and absurd (that is, totally unacceptable) forms of death. In Hiroshima the indelible image was likely to include grotesque shapes of the dead and the dying, as immediately encountered after the bomb fell—scenes described to me seventeen years later and yet so immediate in tone that I felt myself virtually in the midst of them. With Nazi death camp survivors, the imagery can include many forms of cruel memory—the smoke or smell of the gas chambers, the brutal killing of a single individual, or simply separation from a family member never seen again. Vietnam veterans' images were of the bodies of close buddies blown apart and of the slaughter of Vietnamese civilians. In Buffalo Creek survivors described the terrifying advance of the "black water" and people disappearing in it. In all four cases imagery included something close to the end of the world, the "end of time," the destruction of everything. There can be a thralldom to this death imagery, the sense of being bound by it and of seeing all subsequent experience through its prism. The survivor may feel himself stuck in time, unable to move beyond that imagery, or he may find it a source of death-haunted knowledge—even

creative energy—that has considerable value for his life.

The second category is that of *death guilt*—frequently termed survivor guilt, and much misunderstood. Death guilt is epitomized by the survivor's questions, "Why did I survive while he, she, or they died?" Even before he can ask this question, the beginnings of the process take shape around the indelible imagery mentioned earlier. Part of the survivor's sense of horror is his memory of his own inactivation—his helplessness—within the death imagery, of his inability to act in a way he would ordinarily have thought appropriate (save people, resist the victimizers, etc.) or even to feel the appropriate emotions (overwhelming rage toward victimizers, profound compassion for victims). Death guilt begins, then, in the gap between that physical and psychic inactivation and what one felt called upon (by that beginning image formation) to do and feel. That is one reason why the imagery keeps recurring, in dreams and in waking life. One could in fact define the survivor as one who is haunted by images of extremity that can neither be enacted (in the sense of a satisfactory original response) nor cast aside. Contained in this imagery is the survivor's sense of debt to the dead and responsibility toward them. One must be careful to distinguish these feelings of psychological guilt from moral and legal guilt, which involves ethical and social judgments concerning wrongdoing. Nowhere is the distinction more important than in the case of survivors of holocaust. Their paradoxical guilt is one of many undeserved residua of their experience, and perhaps the most ironic.

The third category is one I have emphasized in much of my work, that of *psychic numbing* or the diminished capacity to feel. In Hiroshima I was impressed by survivors'

THE BEAUTIFUL CAPTIVE

It is curious I cannot feel it yet.
To pile up weapons on both sides of a ditch makes war
  certain as sunrise
Yet I can't feel its approach.
There have been two, there will be a third, to be fought with
  what weapons? These that we test and stockpile.
And every test makes the earth
At such and such a place uninhabitable. We must not
  test them too much, they are too deadly,
We store them. If ours and theirs
Went off at once they'd probably infect the elements and blight
  the whole earth. We have general death on our hands,
But wait ten years of peace we'll have more.
Do you think we'll not use them? When a great nation is in
  trouble—when a great nation is in danger of being conquered
It will use the whole arsenal.
So—be prepared to die. Those whom the blasts miss, the
  air and water will poison them. Those who survive,
Their children will be dying monsters.
I have thought for a long time that we are too many—
  three thousand million is it?—this will adjust us.
I have pitied the beautiful earth
Ridden by such a master as the human race. Now, if we
  die like the dinosaurs, the beautiful
Planet will be the happier.
She is not domesticated, she weeps in her service, the
lovely forehead bowed down to the sleek knees—
Or is she laughing? Good luck to her.
But this fantastic third world-war and self-destruction:
  curious I cannot feel them yet. The idea is logical
But not intuitive: distrust it.
However—if not thus—God will find other means. The
troublesome race of man, Oh beautiful planet, is not immortal.

                                        Robinson Jeffers

repeated statements to the effect that, after the bomb fell, they could see that people were dying, and understand that something dreadful had happened, but, very quickly, found themselves *feeling* almost nothing. They underwent what a Hiroshima writer described as "a paralysis of the mind," a dysfunction between perception and emotional response. I came to recognize psychic numbing as a necessary psychological defense against overwhelming images and stimuli. In such extreme situations one is simply unable to experience "ordinary" emotional responses and maintain either sanity or anything like adaptive physical and psychic function. I came to think of the process as something on the order of a temporary and partial deadening as a way of avoiding actual physical, or more or less permanent psychological, death. But psychic numbing could readily outlive its usefulness and give rise to later patterns of withdrawal, apathy, depression, and despair.

A fourth category has to do with survivors' sensitivity toward the counterfeit or *suspicion of counterfeit nurturance.* On one level the problem can be understood around questions of dependence and autonomy: the survivor feels the effects of his ordeal but frequently resents help offered because it is perceived as a sign of weakness. But perhaps more fundamentally, the issue has to do with the environment of moral inversion—the counterfeit universe—the survivor has lived through. In Vietnam, for instance, the counterfeit universe consisted of what I called an "atrocity-producing situation," which was so structured that the slaughter of civilians became close to a psychological norm. Living and dying are divested of moral structure and lose all logic. Entrapped in such a world, one is torn between the impulse to reject totally its counterfeit structure and the necessity to adapt to it, even to internalize portions of it, in order to survive.

The fifth and final category is the survivor's *struggle for meaning,* for a sense of inner form. Survivors of Nazi death camps have been called "collectors of justice." They seek something beyond economic or social restitution—something closer to acknowledgment of crimes committed against them, and punishment of those responsible, in order to reestablish at least the semblance of a moral universe. The impulse to bear witness, beginning with a sense of responsibility to the dead, can readily extend into a "survivor mission"—a lasting commitment to a project that extracts significance from absurdity, vitality from massive death. For many Jewish survivors of Nazi Holocaust, the survivor mission took the form of involvement in the creation of the State of Israel.

Survivor emotions can be very important in the midst of war as well. It is not generally realized that the night before the My Lai massacre, the "combat briefing" was combined with a funeral ceremony for members of the company who had died grotesquely in mine explosions, and especially for a much admired, fatherly, older sergeant. The men were exhorted to get back at the enemy for the sake of (to bear witness to) those dead buddies, and so great was their need for the enemy that he had to be created from available Vietnamese civilians. For these reasons, and because the whole process was manipulated from above partly around competition for high "body counts," we can speak of this process as "false witness."

Whether witness is false or true, it involves such struggles around grief and mourning. Where death occurs on the scale of Nazi genocide or atomic bombings, survivors are denied not only the physical arrangements of mourning (the grave, the remains, place of worship), but also the psychic capacity to absorb and feel these deaths, to do the work of mourning. Hence the extent to which the survivor's existence can turn into a "life of grief." Impaired mourning becomes equated with a more general inability to give inner form— again significance—to the death immersion, and therefore to the remainder of one's life. The survivor may then be especially vulnerable to various kinds of psychic and bodily disturbance, as well as to formulations of his experience around scapegoating and other kinds of false witness. Survivors require expressions of grief and mourning if they are to begin to derive from their experience its potential for some form of illumination.

FAILURE AND HOPE   Those of us who approach survivors and seek to understand holocaust have a part in this process as well. The professions have a dismal record in relationship to holocaust. More often than not they have lent themselves to a denial of its brutalizing effects. In psychiatry, organically minded practitioners have tried to ignore the effects of massive psychic trauma by insisting that psychiatric disturbance stems primarily from biological inheritance. And a few psychoanalysts have contributed to this charade by similarly limiting significant trauma to the first few years of life. Fortunately, sensitive and concerned psychiatric and psychoanalytic voices have strongly contested those assumptions. But the healing professions as a whole maintain a moral distance from these issues that keeps them in considerable ignorance.

My work in Hiroshima convinced me of the immorality of claiming professional neutrality in the face of ultimate forms of destruction. I was further troubled during my Vietnam work by the extent to which American professionals, notably psychiatrists and chaplains, could inadvertently employ their spiritual counseling in ways that reinforced the atrocity-producing process. In reexamining the history of the concept of the professions, I was struck by the extent to which its early religious connotations (the profession of faith or of membership in a particular religious order) were transformed almost totally into a matter of technique (or professional skill). Overall the shift was from advocacy based on faith to technique devoid of advocacy. What we require is not a return to a mere "profession of faith," but rather a fundamental critique of the technicism, the deification of technique, within the professions.

We need a new model of the professional that balances technique with advocacy, skill with ethical commitments. That kind of model would serve us well in approaching extreme forms of inhumanity. For psychiatric work in particular we require a shift in theoretical paradigm from Freud's model of instinct and defense to one of death and the continuity of life. The latter model can sensitize us to the kinds of struggles we witness in survivors around threats to physical and psychological existence and symbolization of vitality, and also around connections beyond the self—an area Tillich called "ultimate concern" and one I speak of as symbolic modes of immortality. We need such a model if we are to gain a better grasp of the psychological universe created by holocaust, including our own reactions to that universe.

We may be limited in our capacity to do so. But as professionals of any kind, as feeling human beings, we had better try. For only by understanding more of what happens to victims and survivors, and of what motivates victimizers, can we begin to imagine the future holocausts that threaten us, and thereby take steps to avoid them.

Bernard T. Feld

The Consequences of Nuclear War

One of the problems in thinking about and preventing a nuclear holocaust is the incomprehensible scale of the consequences—the mind grows numb contemplating hundreds of millions of deaths and unprecedented destruction of the environment. Yet such thinking is absolutely essential if such a cataclysm is to be avoided. In this selection, Bernard T. Feld, a professor of physics at M.I.T. and editor of the *Bulletin of the Atomic Scientists,* examines the probable physical consequences of a large scale nuclear exchange. As horrifying as such projections are, they are only the beginning. In addition to death and destruction of lives and the biosphere, the disruption of patterns of social interaction are likely to be even more devastating. The rise of terrorism in recent years has demonstrated how vulnerable our modern societies—with high degrees of specialization and increasing interdependence—can be to the attacks of isolated terrorist activities. The survivors of a nuclear holocaust are likely to be more traumatized and demoralized than the survivors of past holocausts, described by Lifton. Furthermore, the urgency of the problem of the escalating likelihood of nuclear conflict is underscored by three current developments: the increasing danger of the proliferation of nuclear weapons, recent debates about deploying the neutron bomb in a European theater of war, and ongoing research in satellite surveillance and weaponry—all destabilizing developments.

Most people recognize what an unmitigated tragedy a nuclear war would be. The release of even a relatively small proportion of the fission and fusion energy now stored in nuclear weapons would take a fantastic toll in destruction and death, extending far beyond the borders of the nations involved. Indeed, the effects of a full scale nuclear war would be global, posing a threat to the survival of humankind.

The realization of these consequences has undoubtedly played a role in deterring nuclear war—in inhibiting the introduction of nuclear weapons into the many conflicts that have beset the world in the thirty years since the end of World War II. But it would be foolish to be sanguine about the future.

Six nations have now publicly demonstrated their capability to produce nuclear weapons. Many others are already capable of independently producing and detonating nuclear weapons on the relatively short time scale of six months to two years, once they make the decision to to so. This situation will inevitably become even more serious in the coming decades, as peaceful nuclear power technology, and the associated fissionable materials, are ever more widely proliferated throughout the world. It is estimated that by the year 2000, nuclear power reactors will be producing enough plutonium to permit the fabrication of some two hundred thousand bombs per year—a frightening perspective. Even assuming the same degree of responsibility and stability (or lack thereof) on the part of future nuclear weapons nations as has characterized the present members, the number of opportunities for nuclear conflict (and therefore, in some crude sense, its probability) increases in geometric proportion to the number of nations possessing nuclear bombs.

Even a single nuclear weapon of the strength of those dropped on Hiroshima and Nagasaki can result in hundreds of thousands of casualties. It is conceivable, as its proponents would have us believe, that the extent of some future nuclear war could remain "limited," that is, confined mainly to military targets. But the lessons of history, and the preponderance of opinion among those who have studied the problems of limiting nuclear war once the "firebreak" of no-first-use has been breached, belie any prospect that a nuclear war could be confined in its scope and extent. Once begun, the likelihood of limitation is extremely low; besides, the contemporary definition of "military targets" does not exclude the civilian population centers of the adversary—as witness the consequences of strategic bombing in World War II.

Nevertheless, current U.S. and NATO doctrine is based on this dubious hypothesis. Furthermore, U.S. military planners now profess to believe that the most likely scenario for the outbreak of nuclear war between the United States and the Soviet Union would be an attempt by the Russians to eliminate American nuclear land-based missiles in a preemptive attack on Minuteman missile silos and U.S. strategic air bases.

The U.S. response to this "threat" has been to substitute for the previously accepted doctrine of mutual deterrence (that is, the mutual threat of retaliation against population centers in response to the initiation of nuclear war by either side) the "option" of a preemptive U.S. "counterforce" threat against Soviet nuclear missile installations, coupled with the assertion that this kind of conflict would be "acceptable" in terms of the number of casualties involved and that a nuclear war, limited to a counterforce exchange between the parties, could be "won" in some military sense of the word.

SOBERING FIGURES   However, when forced by a skeptical United States Senate to quantify its assertions concerning the "acceptably small" number of civilian casualties that would result from such an exchange, the Pentagon's estimates, which many would still regard as well on the low side, turn out to be sobering. A missile attack on the Minuteman missile complex (150 silos) at Whiteman Air Force Base, located between Kansas City and St. Louis, Missouri, is estimated to result in between two and ten million deaths; and an attack on all 1,054 land-based missiles located on continental U.S. territory would lead to from three and one-half to twenty-two million American, plus more than one million Canadian, fatalities.

The wide range of these estimates arises from different assumptions concerning the size of the nuclear bombs employed in the postulated attack, and the altitude at which they are detonated. The higher figures correspond to the use of multimegaton weapons exploded near ground level—by far the most likely scenario for a counterforce attack employing currently deployed weapons.

The vast majority of the casualties would, of course, be civilian, resulting from the fallout of lethal radioactivity spread by the normally prevailing winds over vast areas of the North American continent. But these disquieting figures, which even assume an appreciable degree of protection of civilian populations through shelters, evacuation of threatened areas, and other "reasonable protective measures," do not take into account the massive social disruptions that would occur, or the breakdown of medical facilities for caring for the wounded and those suffering from radiation illness, or the vast areas of the world's most productive food-producing regions that would be rendered useless.

But if these Pentagon estimates represent an "acceptable," limited counterforce war, what would happen in the case of an exchange aimed directly at civilian populations—by far the most likely outcome of a failure of deterrence?

There was a time, around a decade ago, when deterrence was postulated to require the ability of both sides to "absorb" any kind of first-strike by the other, and still to be able to retaliate with approximately two-hundred nuclear weapons (each in the low megaton range) against the industrial and population centers of the attacker. Then, according to official U.S. sources and a committee of experts in a 1967 report to the U.N. Secretary-General, it was estimated that the result would be the elimination of around one-third of the population and two-thirds of the industrial capacity of the nation subjected to such retaliation. These estimates, however, were only for the immediate consequences of nuclear explosions, that is, blast, heat, and prompt radiation. They did not include the lethal effects of radioactive fallout or other side effects.

Over a wide range of meteorological conditions, such as generally prevail in temperate zones, an explosion involving around one megaton of fission yield at an altitude such that the fireball extends to the ground will result in a lethal level of fallout (greater than 500 rad[1]) over an area of approximately 1,000 square miles (2,500 square kilometers).

Thus, two-hundred weapons of around five megatons each, assumed to obtain half their explosive yield from fission,[2] distributed over the population centers of either of the possible protagonists, would cover with inescapably lethal fallout an area of five hundred thousand square miles and a vastly larger area with levels sufficient to cause damaging illness in a large fraction of the population. Half a million square miles may only be one-tenth the area of the United States; but the regions involved, because of the nature of the attack postulated,

1. The rad or radiation unit is the intensity of radiation which produces an energy release in the form of ionization of 100 ergs per gram of tissue. Different types of radiation (that is, alpha particles, neutrons, electrons, x-rays, or gamma rays) have differing relative biological effectiveness (RBE), but we shall not here be cncerned with such niceties. Suffice it to note that doses of 100 rad or greater result in radiation sickness or death. For such large doses, administered over the whole body in short periods (days or weeks), the survival probability follows a "sigmoid" curve, with the 50 percent survival probability for people at around 500 rad.

2. It may seem strange to some that a hydrogen bomb, triggered by an ordinary atom bomb, could have fission energy yields some five times or greater than what the maximum atom bomb can deliver. (The total explosive power contained in ten kilograms of uranium-235 or plutonium, the nominal critical mass for an atom bomb, is only around two hundred thousand tons or two hundred kilotons of TNT equivalent.) However, in assembling a hydrogen bomb, it is useful to surround it with a heavy envelope for containment during the process of detonation. A shell of some dense metal serves best for this purpose and uranium, being among the densest, can be used with the added "bonus" that escaping fast neutrons will cause further fission in the envelope, developing additional explosive energy and increasing (roughly doubling) the total explosive yield. Such devices are sometimes referred to as fission-fusion-fission bombs; they make up a preponderant portion of American and Soviet hydrogen bomb arsenals.

would include the most densely populated parts of the country. The same would be the case for a comparable attack on the Soviet Union.

But nuclear weapons deployed by both sides have increased more than tenfold since 1965. The Vladivostok accords. . .(with the political pressures all in the direction of increasing the limits), provide for SALT-II ceilings of 2,400 strategic delivery vehicles on each side, with 1,320 permitted to be multiple independently-targetable reentry vehicles (MIRV) carrying up to ten warheads each.

Even if these ceilings prevail, the amount of explosive power deployed in 1978, in strategic nuclear weapons alone, will amount to some 15 billion tons of TNT (fifteen thousand megatons).[3] An exchange involving some

substantial fraction of these could promptly destroy some 75 and 60 percent, respectively, of the populations (the urban fractions) of the United States and the Soviet Union, and upwards of 50 percent of the remaining rural inhabitants through the subsequent fallout.

Fallout is, of course, not confined by national boundaries. Nations bordering on the antagonists would be profoundly damaged as well, although they might escape the total annihilation that would be the lot of the superpowers in the case of a full-scale strategic nuclear exchange. But the rest of the world would not escape either. There would be worldwide contamination of the atmosphere in the event of such an exchange, as a conse-

3. Around 3,000 megatons in 15,000 warheads for the United States, and some 10,000 to 15,000 megatons in 8,000 to 10,000 warheads for the Soviet Union. This does not include some 10,000 tactical nuclear weapons deployed by the superpowers in Europe or the materials for hundreds of thousands of additional bombs in their arsenals.

quence of the fission products and induced radioactivity that would be distributed both in the elemental form and on dust carried aloft in the expanding fireball and which would be widely dispersed by normal atmospheric circulation.

The accurate prediction of the worldwide consequences of full scale nuclear war is extremely difficult and uncertain, not only because the scenarios on which it must be based are so insanely implausible (though not so improbable), but also because many of the physical effects and mechanisms are insufficiently or imperfeclty understood. A recent study has considered the most important effects, and the remainder of this article draws heavily on this study.[4] Generally speaking, the results of the study agree with some earlier, crude estimates by this author, based on the data accumulated from the atmospheric testing of nuclear weapons (with a total fission energy yield of approximately two hundred megatons) prior to the Partial Test-Ban Treaty of 1963.

LONG-TERM EFFECTS   The study postulated an exchange involving ten thousand megatons of explosive power, half in fission energy, in a plausible mix of low-and high-yield weapons and a variety of altitudes of detonation. On the basis of currently available knowledge, the most important consequences would include:

1. A worldwide climatological change, manifested by a probable global reduction of the average temperature by a few tenths of a degree centigrade for one to three years. This would be due mainly to a worldwide dispersal of particulate matter in the upper atmosphere roughly equivalent to the amount of dust disseminated as a result of the volcanic explosion of the island of Krakatoa in 1883. However, the size of the effect could be greatly influenced by other associated phenomena, including the large increase in the penetration of ultraviolet radiation through the atmosphere (see below).

Although this may not seem to be a very large effect, it must be borne in mind that the global meteorological equilibrium represents a balance of many interacting mechanisms, with important feedbacks from one to the other, and that massive macrochanges amounting to as little as one-half to one degree centigrade could trigger major readjustments in this balance.[5]

2. A rise in the stratospheric content of nitrogen oxide (NO) between 5 and 50 percent. This would have the effect of reducing the ozone content by 30 to 70 percent in the northern hemisphere and by 20 to 40 percent in the southern hemisphere.

The time required for restoration of the ozone to its normal atmospheric content by natural processes would be from two to four years. During this period the intensity of ultraviolet radiation from the Sun (UV-B) penetrating to the Earth's surface would increase by a factor of around six. There would be, correspondingly, a vast increase in ultraviolet induced skin cancer, sunburn, and blindness in mammals as well as drastically detrimental damage to the viability and reproducibility of other forms of plant and animal life on land and in the oceans.

The problem of ozone depletion in the atmosphere is a significant example of the kind

4. National Research Council-National Academy of Sciences, "Long-Term Worldwide Effects of Multiple Nuclear-Weapons Detonations" (Washington, D.C.: The Academy, 1975).

5. For example, the initiation of a new ice age, significant alterations of global rainfall patterns with attendant redistribution of deserts, etc.

of unexpected phenomena that can result from the introduction into our environment of significant alterations arising from new technological "advances." As little as five years ago, the importance of atmospheric ozone to the earth's ecological balance, though known in principle, had not been taken into consideration in attempts to understand the impacts of human activities on the biosphere. The problem first came to public attention in connection with the discussion in the United States relating to the development of supersonic aircraft. It was then pointed out that the combustion products of such aircraft could result in a significant depletion of the stratospheric ozone content, with attendant consequences such as those mentioned above.

More recently, a slow depletion of the atmospheric ozone content due to the widespread use of freon as the propellant in a great variety of aerosol sprays has been noted. And it now emerges that the ozone depletion effect is among the most serious consequences of nuclear explosions in the atmosphere. One is led to wonder about how many other seriously damaging effects, still lying beyond the horizon of our consciousness, are unknowingly being introduced into our environment through humankind's unconsidered march toward technological "progress."

3. Radioactive contamination of the biosphere is, of course, the most obvious and widely discussed global consequence of nuclear war. Its well publicized detrimental effects provided the major impetus for the Partial Test-Ban Treaty of 1963 (which prohibits nuclear explosions in the atmosphere, in the oceans, and in outer space—but not underground).

A great variety of radioactive nuclei, with lifetimes ranging from seconds to thousands of years, result from the explosion of a nuclear weapon. These give rise to an assortment of biological effects on living organisms—all detrimental. Among the most significant consequences, in the case of the levels of radioactive contamination here under consideration, is the increase in the burden of debilitating or lethal genetic mutations borne by living matter and passed on to future generations.

The nuclear exchange postulated in the study (ten thousand megatons) is estimated to result in a worldwide average of about 5 to 10 rad per individual (spread over the entire organism), essentially all accumulated over a period of between one week and thirty years. The main consequences of this level of radiation, according to the study, would be:

> In the first generation, an increase above the spontaneous cancer death rate due to exposure to low levels of ionizing radiation (of) about 2 percent, . . . an increase in the incidence of skin carcinoma and melanoma (due to the ozone reduction) of 3 to 30 percent, with a geometric mean of 10 percent for about forty years, at midlatitudes . . . and prompt incapacitating cases of sunburn in the temperate zones and snow blindness in northern countries would result from a large increase in UV-B.[6]

Generally speaking, while acknowledging the devastating consequences of a nuclear war of the magnitude considered in their study, the authors conclude that such an event would not threaten the survival of the human race. There are, I believe, good reasons to consider such a conclusion to be much too sanguine.

In the first place, there is no firm assurance that other effects, not yet recognized, would not be even more significant, and deadly, than those considered. Besides, the uncertainties in

6. National Research Council, "Long-Term Worldwide Effects," p. 15.

the estimates are great enough so that the upper limits estimated—particularly for the effects of ozone depletion and possible macro-meteorological phenomena—could still turn out to be too low.

Furthermore, considering the level of nuclear arms already available throughout the world, and the rate at which the number of weapons has been growing, a full-scale nuclear war in this century could well exceed—by a factor of five or ten in magnitude—the one postulated in the study. This would become a much more likely possibility if the present ban on antiballistic missile defense systems (ABM) were to be abrogated—a course openly advocated by many influential military proponents on both sides.

A nuclear war involving some fifty to one hundred thousand megatons of fission, mostly detonated near ground level, would be a different story. Global climatological changes—exceedingly difficult for human adjustment—would ensure that

> the atmospheric ozone would be effectively depleted,
>
> individuals throughout the world, even in the remotest regions, would receive a cumulative radiation dose of between 25 and 100 rad.

The survival of humankind, and of many other forms of life as well, would be seriously jeopardized.

Mr. Nevil Shute, not too long ago, attempted to describe the aftermath of such a nuclear war through a prescient work of fiction [*On the Beach*]. Unhappily, the possibilities of this sort of human catastrophe have grown rather than diminished in recent years. It is becoming frighteningly plausible to consider the level of nuclear war that would represent the end of humankind: the detonation of one million megatons of nuclear explosives (which may be defined as one "Beach") would result in a global irradiation of around 500 rad. It is very difficult, in the present anarchic world, to be sanguine about the fact that we are now about one-tenth of the way toward the possibility of this ultimate insult (used also in its medical sense) that would certainly spell the end of humankind on planet Earth.

THE MAN HE KILLED

Had he and I but met
By some old ancient inn,
We should have sat us down to wet
Right many a nipperkin!

But ranged as infantry,
And staring face to face,
I shot at him as he at me,
And killed him in his place.

I shot him dead because—
Because he was my foe
Just so: my foe of course he was;
That's clear enough; although

He thought he'd 'list, perhaps,
Off-hand like—just as I—
Was out of work—had sold his traps—
No other reason why.

Yes; quaint and curious war is!
You shoot a fellow down
You'd treat if met where any bar is,
Or help to half-a-crown.

Thomas Hardy

15.

The Death System
Review and Prospectus

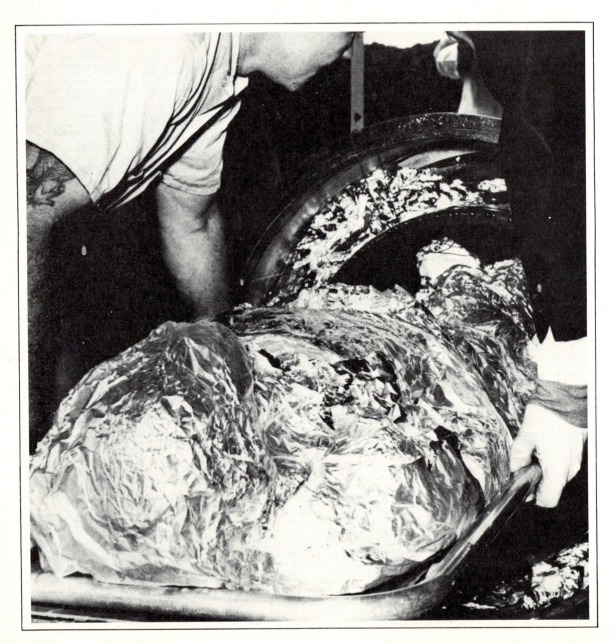

In the preceding sections of this Reader, we have seen that the meanings of death and dying are indeed characterized by change and challenge. The pace of social and cultural change has been accelerating at an ever increasing rate and shows no signs of abating. Hence, it is virtually impossible to forecast with any precision the ways we shall define and experience death in the future. The articles in this final section, however, do provide ideas and projections that can at least guide our speculation and anticipation.

Gaylin's essay on "Harvesting the Dead" offers a satirical vision of the possible future. Extrapolating from present developments in medicine, he presents a plausible scenario in which brain death is the accepted legal criterion for death—and warm, breathing corpses are maintained on machines in order to be systematically harvested for a variety of valuable purposes. This pragmatically efficient use of human tissue, he warns, may have the unintended side-effect of exacerbating our present moral dilemmas. The medical benefits of such practices are quite clear—many lives would be saved and prolonged—but the moral consequences are far more difficult to evaluate. Could such practices precipitate dehumanization or devaluation of human beings? It is of interest to note that, while Gaylin originally intended this essay as a provocative satire, its publication in *Harper's Magazine* stimulated a flood of reader responses: many were outraged at the possibilities he had envisioned, but others were seriously interested in implementing such utilization of human tissue.

Despite the satirical style, Gaylin is serious in reminding us once again of the inherent tradeoffs of expanding technical powers in a society characterized by moral confusion. Each invention or technique can create new problems. Breakthroughs in recombinant DNA research, for example, promise life-saving medical applications, but can also expand the terrifying possibility of bacteriological warfare. The recent birth of the world's first "test tube baby" creates controversy among moralists and theologians at the same time that it fosters hope for childless couples.

In his prophetic essay on "Death in the Nuclear Age," Morgenthau argues that the nuclear age has given death a new meaning— it has threatened the meanings and sources of immortality that have traditionally enabled human beings to transcend their individual deaths. A large scale nuclear war would not only kill tens of millions of individual human beings, but would in all probability destroy our very civilization and, consequently, our heritage and posterity.

Morgenthau states that "It is the saving grace of our age that it has not become aware of its condition." He may be right, insofar as popular ignorance of the probability and consequences of a nuclear holocaust may permit people to lead sane lives with relative peace of mind. But such ignorance, however blissful, could also increase the likelihood of such a catastrophe, as the populace passively permits the continuing proliferation of increasingly dangerous nuclear weapons.

Lepp, in "The Experience of Death," concludes that, regardless of modern scientific achievements, we are still unable to experience death directly. Our knowledge about death comes from observing and responding to the deaths of others. The death of a close friend or family member confronts us with our mortality—it reminds us that we, too, shall die someday, and it reveals our vulnerability to the loss of those whose lives are significant to us. However, the deaths of strangers tell us little about our own death and its personal meaning, and we tend to be indifferent to them, according to Lepp. We hear of mass deaths from war and famine in distant parts of the world and feel only a passing qualm.

Such indifference may reflect a numbing process that protects us from the emotional and intellectual shock we would experience were we to feel deeply the human meaning of such annihilation. It may also be that the impersonal deaths of large numbers of anonymous and irrelevant persons remains somehow "unreal" in our hearts and minds. However, such indifference may become deliberate. Other people can be redefined and depersonalized into either "subhumans" or "enemies." The former redefinition can then be used to justify genocide, and the latter is an integral element of war.

GRASS

Pile the bodies high at Austerlitz and Waterloo.
Shovel them under and let me work—
    I am the grass; I cover all.

And pile them high at Gettysburg
And pile them high at Ypres and Verdun.
Shovel them under and let me work.
Two years, ten years, and passengers ask the conductor:
    What place is this?
    Where are we now?

    I am the grass.
    Let me work.

                       Carl Sandburg

Willard Gaylin

Harvesting the Dead

Willard Gaylin, a past president of the Institute of Society, Ethics, and the Life Sciences, stretches our imaginations in this thought-provoking essay on the possible uses of bodies that have suffered brain death but are kept breathing and functioning viscerally by modern machines. Yesterday's science fiction often surprises us by becoming tomorrow's fact. A major breakthrough in immunosuppressive research that would eliminate the problem of one body rejecting tissue transplanted from another would dramatically increase the usefulness, as well as the problems, of organ transplantation. The recent movie *Coma* explored the grim possibility of illicit body-banking to satisfy the demand for donor organs. How will such organs be distributed among possible recipients? By lottery? By presumed social worth of the recipients? According to ability to pay?

Nothing in life is simple anymore, not even the leaving of it. At one time there was no medical need for the physician to consider the concept of death; the fact of death was sufficient. The difference between life and death was an infinite chasm [bridged] in an infinitesimal moment. Life and death were ultimate, self-evident opposites.

With the advent of new techniques in medicine, those opposites have begun to converge. We are now capable of maintaining visceral functions without any semblance of the higher functions that define a person. We are, therefore, faced with the task of deciding whether that which we have kept alive is still a human being, or, to put it another way, whether that human being that we are maintaining should be considered "alive."

Until now we have avoided the problems of definition and reached the solutions in silence and secret. When the life sustained was unrewarding—by the standards of the physician in charge—it was discontinued. Over the years, physicians have practiced euthanasia on an ad hoc, casual, and perhaps irresponsible basis. They have withheld antibiotics or other simple treatments when it was felt that a life did not warrant sustaining, or pulled the plug on the respirator when they were convinced that what was being sustained no longer warranted the definition of life. Some of these acts are illegal and, if one wished to prosecute, could constitute a form of manslaughter, even though it is unlikely that any jury would convict. We prefer to handle all problems connected with death by denying their existence. But death and its dilemmas persist.

New urgencies for recognition of the problem arise from two conditions: the continuing march of technology, making the sustaining of vital processes possible for longer periods of time; and the increasing use of parts of the newly dead to sustain life for the truly living. The problem is well on its way to being resolved by what must have seemed a relatively simple and ingenious method. As it turned out, the difficult issues of euthanasia could be evaded by redefining death.

In an earlier time, death was defined as the cessation of breathing. Any movie buff recalls at least one scene in which a mirror is held to the mouth of a dying man. The lack of fogging indicated that indeed he was dead. The spirit of man resided in his *spiritus* (breath). With increased knowledge of human physiology and the potential for reviving a nonbreathing man, the circulation, the pulsating heart, became the focus of the definition of life. This is the tradition with which most of us have been raised.

There is of course a relationship between circulation and respiration, and the linkage, not irrelevantly, is the brain. All body parts require the nourishment, including oxygen, carried by the circulating blood. Lack of blood supply leads to the death of an organ; the higher functions of the brain are particularly vulnerable. But if there is no respiration, there is no adequate exchange of oxygen, and this essential ingredient of the blood is no longer available for distribution. If a part of the heart loses its vascular supply, we may lose that part and still survive. If a part of the brain is deprived of oxygen, we may, depending on its location, lose it and survive. But here we pay a special price, for the functions lost are those we identify with the self, the soul, or humanness, i.e., memory, knowledge, feeling, thinking, perceiving, sensing, knowing, learning, and loving.

Most people are prepared to say that when all of the brain is destroyed the "person" no longer exists; with all due respect for the complexities of the mind/brain debate, the "person" (and personhood) is generally associated with the functioning part of the head—the brain. The higher functions of the brain that have been described are placed, for the most part, in the cortex. The brain stem (in many ways more closely allied to the spinal cord) controls primarily visceral functions. When the total brain is damaged, death in all forms will ensue because the lower brain centers that control the circulation and respiration are destroyed. With the development of modern respirators, however, it is possible to artificially maintain respiration and with it, often, the circulation with which it is linked. It is this situation that has allowed for the redefinition of death—a redefinition that is being precipitously embraced by both scientific and theological groups.

The movement toward redefining death received considerable impetus with the publication of a report sponsored by the Ad Hoc Committee of the Harvard Medical School in 1968. The committee offered an alternative definition of death based on the functioning of the brain. Its criteria stated that if an individual is unreceptive and unresponsive, i.e., in a state of irreversible coma; if he has no movements or breathing when the mechanical respirator is turned off; if he demonstrates no reflexes; and if he has a flat electroencephalogram for at least twenty-four hours, indicating no electrical brain activity (assuming that he has not been subjected to hypothermia or central nervous system depressants), he may then be declared dead.

What was originally offered as an optional definition of death is, however, progressively becoming *the* definition of death. In most states there is no specific legislation defining death;[1] the ultimate responsibility here is assumed to reside in the general medical com-

1. Kansas and Maryland have recently legislated approval for a brain definition of death.

munity. Recently, however, there has been a series of legal cases which seem to be establishing brain death as a judicial standard. In California in May of [1974] an ingenious lawyer, John Cruikshank, offered as a defense of his client, Andrew D. Lyons, who had shot a man in the head, the argument that the cause of death was not the bullet but the removal of his heart by a transplant surgeon, Dr. Norman Shumway. Cruikshank's argument notwithstanding, the jury found his client guilty of voluntary manslaughter. In the course of that trial. Dr. Shumway said: "The brain in the 1970s and in the light of modern day medical technology is the sine qua non—the criterion for death. I'm saying anyone whose brain is dead is dead. It is the one determinant that would be universally applicable, because the brain is the one organ that can't be transplanted."

This new definition, independent of the desire for transplant, now permits the physician to "pull the plug" without even committing an act of passive euthanasia. The patient will first be defined as dead; pulling the plug will merely be the harmless act of halting useless treatment on a cadaver. But while the new definition of death avoids one complex problem, euthanasia, it may create others equally difficult which have never been fully defined or visualized. For if it grants the right to pull the plug, it also implicitly grants the privilege *not* to pull the plug, and the potential and meaning of this has not at all been adequately examined.

These cadavers would have the legal status of the dead with none of the qualities one now associates with death. They would be warm, respiring, pulsating, evacuating, and excreting bodies requiring nursing, dietary, and general grooming attention—*and could probably be maintained so for a period of years.* If we chose to, we could, with the technology already at hand, legally avail ourselves of these new cadavers to serve science and mankind in dramatically useful ways. The autopsy, that most respectable of medical traditions, that last gift of the dying person to the living future, could be extended in principle beyond our current recognition. To save lives and relieve suffering—traditional motives for violating tradition—we could develop hospitals (an inappropriate word because it suggests the presence of living human beings), banks, or farms of cadavers which require feeding and maintenance, in order to be harvested. To the uninitiated the "new cadavers" in their rows of respirators would seem indistinguishable from comatose patients now residing in wards of chronic neurological hospitals.

PRECEDENTS   The idea of wholesale and systematic salvage of useful body parts may seem startling, but it is not without precedent. It is simply magnified by the technology of modern medicine. Within the confines of one individual, we have always felt free to transfer body parts to places where they are needed more urgently, felt free to reorder the priorities of the naturally endowed structure. We will borrow skin from the less visible parts of the body to salvage a face. If a muscle is paralyzed, we will often substitute a muscle that subserves a less crucial function. This was common surgery at the time that paralytic polio was more prevalent.

It soon becomes apparent, however, that there is a limitation to this procedure. The person in want does not always have a second-best substitute. He may then be forced to borrow from a person with a surplus. The prototype, of course, is blood donation. Blood may be seen as a regeneratable organ, and we have a long-standing tradition of blood donation. What may be more important, and perhaps dangerous, we have established the precedent in blood of commercialization—not only are we free to borrow, we are forced to buy and, indeed, in our country at least, permitted to sell. Similarly, we allow the buying or selling of sperm for artificial insemination. It is most likely that in the near future we will allow the buying and selling of ripened ova so that a sterile woman may conceive her baby if she has a functioning uterus. Of course, once *in vitro* fertilization becomes a reality (an imminent possibility), we may even permit the rental of womb space for gestation for a woman who does manufacture her own ova but has no uterus.

Getting closer to our current problem, there is the relatively long-standing tradition of banking body parts (arteries, eyes, skin) for short periods of time for future transplants. Controversy has arisen with recent progress in the transplanting of major organs. Kidney transplants from a near relative or distant donor are becoming more common. As heart transplants become more successful, the issue will certainly be heightened, for while the heart may have been reduced by the new definition of death to merely another organ, it will always have a core position in the popular thinking about life and death. It has the capacity to generate the passion that transforms medical decisions into political issues.

The ability to use organs from cadavers has been severely limited in the past by the reluctance of heirs to donate the body of an individual for distribution. One might well have willed one's body for scientific purposes, but such legacies had no legal standing. Until recently, the individual lost control over his body once he died. This has been changed by the Uniform Anatomical Gift Act. This model piece of legislation, adopted by all fifty states in an incredibly short period of time, grants anyone over eighteen (twenty-one in some states) the right to donate en masse all "necessary organs and tissues" simply by filling out and mailing a small card.

Beyond the postmortem, there has been a longer-range use of human bodies that is accepted procedure—the exploitation of cadavers as teaching material in medical schools. This is a long step removed from the rationale of the transplant—a dramatic gift of life from the dying to the near dead; while it is true that medical education will inevitably save lives the clear and immediate purpose of the donation is to facilitate training.

It is not unnatural for a person facing death to want his usefulness to extend beyond his mortality; the same biases and values that influence our life persist in our leaving of it. It has been reported that the Harvard Medical School has no difficulty in receiving as many donations of cadavers as they need, while Tufts and Boston Universities are usually in short supply. In Boston, evidently, the cachet of getting into Harvard extends even to the dissecting table.

The way is now clear for an ever-increasing pool of usable body parts, but the current practice minimizes efficiency and maximizes waste. Only a short period exists between the time of death of the patient and the time of death of his major parts.

USES OF THE NEOMORT   In the ensuing discussion, the word *cadaver* will retain its usual meaning, as opposed to the new cadaver, which will be referred to as a *neomort*. The "ward" or "hospital" in which it is maintained will be called a *bioemporium* (purists may prefer *bioemporion*).

Whatever is possible with the old embalmed cadaver is extended to an incredible degree with the neomort. What follows, therefore, is not a definitive list but merely the briefest of suggestions as to the spectrum of possibilities.

Training. Uneasy medical students could practice routine physical examinations—auscultation, percussion of the chest, examination of the retina, rectal and vaginal examinations, et cetera—indeed, everything except neurological examinations, since the neomort by definition has no functioning central nervous system.

Both the student and his patient could be spared the pain, fumbling, and embarrassment of the "first time."

Interns also could practice standard and more difficult diagnostic procedures, from spinal taps to pneumoencephalography and the making of arteriograms, and residents could practice almost all of their surgical skills—in other words, most of the procedures that are now normally taught with the indigent in wards of major city hospitals could be taught with neomorts. Further, students could practice more exotic procedures often not available in a typical residency—eye operations, skin grafts, plastic facial surgery, amputation of useless limbs, coronary surgery, etc.; they could also practice the actual removal of organs, whether they be kidneys, testicles, or what have you, for delivery to the transplant teams.

Testing. The neomort could be used for much of the testing of drugs and surgical procedures that we now normally perform on prisoners, mentally retarded children, and volunteers. The efficacy of a drug as well as its toxicity could be determined beyond limits we might not have dared approach when we were concerned about permanent damage to the testing vehicle, a living person. For example, operations for increased vascularization of the heart could be tested to determine whether they truly do reduce the incidence of future heart attack before we perform them on patients. Experimental procedures that proved useless or harmful could be avoided; those that succeed could be available years before they might otherwise have been. Similarly, we could avoid the massive delays that keep some drugs from the marketplace while the dying clamor for them.

Neomorts would give us access to other forms of testing that are inconceivable with the living human being. We might test diagnostic instruments such as sophisticated electrocardiography by selectively damaging various parts of the heart to see how or whether the instrument could detect the damage.

Experimentation. Every new medical procedure demands a leap of faith. It is often referred to as an "act of courage," which seems to me an inappropriate terminology now that organized medicine rarely uses itself as the experimental body. Whenever a surgeon attempts a procedure for the first time, he is at best generalizing from experimentation with lower animals. Now we can protect the patient from too large a leap by using the neomort as an experimental bridge.

Obvious forms of experimentation would be cures for illnesses which would first be induced in the neomort. We could test antidotes by injecting poison, induce cancer or virus infections to validate and compare developing therapies.

Because they have an active hematopoietic system, neomorts would be particularly valuable for studying diseases of the blood. Many of the examples that I draw from that field were offered to me by Dr. John F. Bertles, a hematologist at St. Luke's Hospital Center in New York. One which interests him is the utilization of marrow transplants. Few

---

DULCE ET DECORUM EST

Bent double, like old beggars under sacks,
Knock-kneed, coughing like hags, we cursed through sludge,
Till on the haunting flares we turned our backs,
And towards our distant rest began to trudge.
Men marched asleep. Many had lost their boots,
But limped on, blood-shod. All went lame, all blind;
Drunk with fatigue; dead even to the hoots
Of gas-shells dropping softly behind.

Gas! Gas! Quick, boys!—An ecstasy of fumbling,
Fitting the clumsy helmets just in time,
But someone still was yelling out and stumbling
And flound'ring like a man in fire or lime.
Dim through the misty panes and thick green light,
As under a green sea, I saw him drowning.

In all my dreams before my helpless sight
He plunges at me, guttering, choking, drowning.
If in some smothering dreams, you too could pace
Behind the wagon that we flung him in,
And watch the white eyes wilting in his face,
His hanging face, like a devil's sick of sin,
If you could hear, at every jolt, the blood
Come gargling from the froth-corrupted lungs
Bitten as the cud
Of vile, incurable sores on innocent tongues,—
My friend, you would not tell with such high zest
To children ardent for some desparate glory,
The old lie: *Dulce et decorum est*
Pro patria mori.

Wilfred Owen

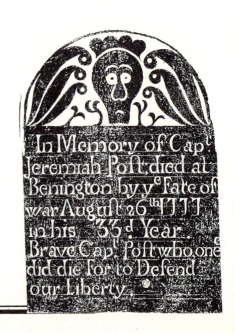

In Memory of Capt Jeremiah Post died at Bennington by ye Fate of war August 26th 1777 in his 33d Year. Brave Capt Post who one did die For to Defend our Liberty.

human-to-human marrow transplants have been successful, . . . the kind of immunosuppression techniques that require research could most safely be performed on neomorts. Even such research as the recent experimentation at Willowbrook—where mentally retarded children were infected with hepatitis virus (which was not yet culturable outside of the human body) in an attempt to find a cure for this pernicious disease—could be done without risking the health of the subjects.

Banking. While certain essential blood antigens are readily storable (e.g., red cells can now be preserved in a frozen state), others are not, and there is increasing need for potential means of storage. Research on storage of platelets to be used in transfusion requires human recipients, and the data are only slowly and tediously gathered at great expense. Use of neomorts would permit intensive testing of platelet survival and probably would lead to a rapid development of a better storage technique. The same would be true for white cells.

As has been suggested, there is great wastage in the present system of using kidney donors from cadavers. Major organs are difficult to store. A population of neomorts maintained with body parts computerized and catalogued for compatability would yield a much more efficient system. Just as we now have blood banks, . . . we could have banks for all the major organs that may someday be transplantable—lungs, kidney, heart, ovaries. Beyond the obvious storage uses of the neomort, there are others not previously thought of because there was no adequate storage facility. Dr. Marc Lappe of the Hastings Center has suggested that a neomort whose own immunity system had first been severely repressed might be an ideal "culture" for growing and storing our lymphoid components. When we are threatened by malignancy or viral disease, we can go to the "bank" and withdraw our stored white cells to help defend us.

Harvesting. Obviously, a sizable population of neomorts will provide a steady supply of blood, since they can be drained periodically. When we consider the cost-benefit analysis of this system, we would have to evaluate it in the same way as the lumber industry evaluates sawdust—a product which in itself is not commercially feasible but which supplies a profitable dividend as a waste from a more useful harvest.

The blood would be a simultaneous source of platelets, leukocytes, and red cells. By attaching a neomort to an IBM cell separator, we could isolate cell types at relatively low cost. The neomort could also be tested for the presence of hepatitis in a way that would be impossible with commercial donors. Hepatitis as a transfusion scourge would be virtually eliminated.

Beyond the blood are rarer harvests. Neomorts offer a great potential source of bone marrow for transplant procedures, and I am assured that a bioemporium of modest size could be assembled to fit most transplantation antigen requirements. And skin would, of course, be harvested—similarly bone, corneas, cartilage, and so on.

Manufacturing. In addition to supplying components of the human body, some of which will be continually regenerated, the neomort can also serve as a manufacturing unit. Hormones are one obvious product, but there are others. By the injection of toxins, we have a source of antitoxin that does not have the complication of coming from another animal form. Antibodies for most of the major diseases can be manufactured merely by injecting the neomort with the viral or bacterial offenders.

Perhaps the most encouraging extension of the manufacturing process emerges from the new cancer research, in which immunology is coming to the fore. With certain blood cancers, great hope attaches to the use of anti-bodies. To take just one example, it is conceivable that leukemia could be generated in individual neomorts—not just to provide for *in vivo* (so to speak) testing of anti-leukemic modes of therapy but also to generate antibody immunity responses which could then be used in the living.

COST-BENEFIT ANALYSIS   If seen only as the harvesting of products, the entire feasibility of such research would depend on intelligent cost-benefit analysis. Although certain products would not warrant the expense of maintaining a community of neomorts, the enormous expense of other products, such as red cells with unusual antigens, would certainly warrant it. Then, of course, the equation is shifted. As soon as one economically sound reason is found for the maintenance of the community, all of the other ingredients become gratuitous by-products, a familiar problem in manufacturing. There is no current research to indicate the maintenance cost of a bioemporium or even the potential duration of an average neomort. Since we do not at this point encourage sustaining life in the brain-dead, we do not know the limits to which it could be extended. This is the kind of technology, however, in which we have previously been quite successful.

Meantime, a further refinement of death might be proposed. At present we use total brain function to define brain death. The source of electroencephalogram activity is not known and cannot be used to distinguish between the activity of higher and lower brain centers. If, however, we are prepared to separate the concept of "aliveness" from "personhood" in the adult, as we have in the fetus, a good argument can be made that death should be defined not as cessation of total brain function but merely as cessation of cortical function. New tests may soon determine when cortical function is dead. With this proposed extension, one could then maintain neomorts without even the complication and expense of respirators. The entire population of decorticates residing in chronic hospitals and now classified among the incurably ill could be redefined as dead.

But even if we maintained the more rigid limitations of total brain death it would seem that a reasonable population could be maintained if the purposes warranted it. It is difficult to assess how many new neomorts would be available each year to satisfy the demand. There are roughly 2 million deaths a year in the United States. The most likely sources of intact bodies with destroyed brains would be accidents (about 113,000 per year), suicides (around 24,000 per year), homicides (18,000), and cerebrovascular accidents (some 210,000 per year). Obviously, in each of these categories a great many of the individuals would be useless—their bodies either shattered or scattered beyond value or repair.

And yet, after all the benefits are outlined, with the lifesaving potential clear, the humanitarian purposes obvious, the technology ready, the motives pure, and the material costs justified—how are we to reconcile our emotions? Where in this debit-credit ledger of limbs and livers and kidneys and costs are we to weigh and enter the repugnance generated by the entire philanthropic endeavor?

Cost-benefit analysis is always least satisfactory when the costs must be measured in one realm and the benefits in another. The analysis is particularly skewed when the benefits are specific, material, apparent, and immediate, and the price to be paid is general, spiritual, abstract, and of the future. It is that which induces people to abandon freedom for security, pride for comfort, dignity for dollars.

William May, in a perceptive article,[2] defended the careful distinctions that have traditionally been drawn between the newly dead and the long dead. "While the body retains its recognizable form, even in death, it commands a certain respect. No longer a human presence, it still reminds us of that presence which once was utterly inseparable from it." But those distinctions become obscured when, years later, a neomort will retain the appearance of the newly dead, indeed, more the appearance of that which was formerly described as living.

Philosophers tend to be particularly sensitive to the abstract needs of civilized man; it is they who have often been the guardians of values whose abandonment produces pains that are real, if not always quantifiable. Hans Jonas, in his *Philosophical Essays,* anticipated some of the possibilities outlined here, and defended what he felt to be the sanctity of the human body and the unknowability of the borderline between life and death when he insisted that "Nothing less than the maximum definition of death will do—brain death plus heart death plus any other indication that may be pertinent—before final violence is allowed to be done." And even then Jonas was only contemplating *temporary* maintenance of life for the collection of organs.

2. "Attitudes Toward the Newly Dead," *The Hastings Center Studies,* volume 1, number 1, 1973.

The argument can be made on both sides. The unquestionable benefits to be gained are the promise of cures for leukemia and other diseases, the reduction of suffering, and the maintenance of life. The proponents of this view will be mobilized with a force that may seem irresistible.

They will interpret our revulsion at the thought of a bioemporium as a bias of our education and experience, just as earlier societies were probably revolted by the startling notion of abdominal surgery, which we now take for granted. The proponents will argue that the revulsion, not the technology, is inappropriate.

Still there will be those, like May, who will defend that revulsion as a quintessentially human factor whose removal would diminish us all, and extract a price we cannot anticipate in ways yet unknown and times not yet determined. May feels that there is "a tinge of the inhuman in the humanitarianism of those who believe that the perception of social need easily overrides all other considerations and reduces the acts of implementation to the everyday, routine, and casual."

This is the kind of weighing of values for which the computer offers little help. Is the revulsion to the new technology simply the fear and horror of the ignorant in the face of the new, or is it one of those components of humanness that barely sustain us at the limited level of civility and decency that now exists, and whose removal is one more step in erasing the distinction between man and the lesser creatures—beyond that, the distinction between man and matter?

Sustaining life is an urgent argument for any measure, but not if that measure destroys those very qualities that make life worth living.

Hans Morgenthau

Death in the Nuclear Age

In the following article, Hans Morgenthau, an eminent political scientist and foreign policy analyst, argues that a large scale nuclear war would probably destroy our civilization. When the nuclear age was inaugurated on August 6, 1945, by the dropping of the first atomic bomb on Hiroshima, Japan, the meanings of life, death, and immortality were drastically changed. This essay was written in 1961. Since that time, the arms race has increased dangerously—nuclear weapons have proliferated to several countries, the destructive power and accuracy of weapons systems has tremendously increased, and the international political situation is no less volatile. Of all the problems and dilemmas concerning death and dying, none is more vital than the problem of preventing a nuclear war.

It is obvious that the nuclear age has radically changed man's relations to nature and to his fellow men. It has enormously increased man's ability to use the forces of nature for his purposes and has thus concentrated unprecedented destructive powers in the hands of governments. That concentration of power has fundamentally altered the relations which have existed throughout history between government and people and among governments themselves. It has made popular revolution impossible, and it has made war an absurdity. Yet, less obvious and more important, the nuclear age has changed man's relations to himself. It has done so by giving death a new meaning.

Death is the great scandal in the experience of man; for death—as the destruction of the human person after a finite span of time—is the very negation of all man experiences as specifically human in his existence: the consciousness of himself and of his world, the remembrance of things past and the anticipation of things to come, a creativeness in thought and action which aspires to, and approximates, the eternal. Thus man has been compelled, for the sake of his existence as man, to bridge the gap between death and his specifically human attributes by transcending death. He has done so in three different ways: by making himself, within narrow limits, the master of death; by denying the reality of death through the belief in the immortality of his person; by conquering the reality of death through the immortality of the world he leaves behind.

Man can make himself the master of death by putting an end to his biological existence whenever he wishes. While he cannot live as long as he wants to, he can stop living whenever he wants to. While he cannot choose life over death when his life has reached its biological limits, he can choose death over life regardless of these limits. He can commit suicide; or he can commit what Nietzsche has called "suicide with a good conscience" by seeking out death, especially at the hand of someone else. He is capable of sacrificial death. In his self-chosen death for a cause in particular, on the battlefield or elsewhere, man triumphs over death, however incompletely. He triumphs because he does not wait until his body is ready to die, but he offers his life to death when his chosen purpose demands it. Yet that triumph is incomplete because it cannot overcome the inevitability of death but only controls its coming.

Man also denies the reality of death by believing in the immortality of his person. This belief can take two different forms. It may take the form of the assumption that the finiteness of man's biological existence is but apparent and that his body will live on in another world. It can also take the form of the assumption that what is specifically human in man will survive the destruction of his body and that man's soul will live on forever, either separated from any body or reincarnated in someone else's. This belief in personal immortality, in defiance of the empirical evidence of the finiteness of man's biological existence, is of course peculiar to the religious realm. It presupposes the existence of a world which is not only inaccessible to the senses but also superior to the world of the senses in that what is truly human in man is there preserved forever.

It is a distinctive characteristic of our secular age that it has replaced the belief in the immortality of the human person with the attempt to assure the immortality of the world he leaves behind. Man can transcend the finiteness of his biological existence either in his consciousness or in objective reality by adding to that existence four different dimensions which are in one way or another independent of that finiteness. They are different dimensions of immortality. He can extend his consciousness into the past by remembering it. He can extend his consciousness into the future by anticipating it. As *homo faber,* he embeds his biological existence within technological and social artifacts which survive that existence. His imagination creates new worlds of religion, art, and reason that live after their creator. . . .

The significance of the possibility of nuclear death is that it radically affects the meaning of death, of immortality, of life itself. It affects that meaning by destroying most of it. Nuclear destruction is mass destruction, both of persons and of things. It signifies the simultaneous destruction of tens of millions of people, of whole families, generations, and societies, of all the things that they have inherited and created. It signifies the total destruction of whole societies by killing their members, destroying their visible achievements, and therefore reducing the survivors to barbarism. Thus nuclear destruction destroys the meaning of death by depriving it of its individuality. It destroys the meaning of immortality by making both society and history impossible. It destroys the meaning of life by throwing life back upon itself.

Sacrificial death has meaning only as the outgrowth of an individual decision which chooses death over life. The hero who risks his life or dies for a cause is bound to be one man, an identifiable individual. There is meaning in Leonidas falling at Thermopylae, in Socrates drinking the cup of hemlock, in Jesus nailed to the cross. There can be no meaning in the slaughter of the innocent, the murder of six million Jews, the prospective nuclear destruction of, say, fifty million Americans and an equal number of Russians. There is, then, a radical difference in meaning between a man risking death by an act of will and fifty million people simultaneously reduced—by somebody switching a key thousands of miles away—to radioactive ashes, indistinguishable from the ashes of their houses, books, and animals. Horace could say, thinking of the individual soldier ready to die, "It is sweet and honorable to die for one's country." Yet Wilfred Owen, describing the effects of a gas attack in the First World War, could call Horace's famous phrase "The old Lie," and beholding a victim of modern mass destruction, could only bewail the futility of such a death and ask in despair, "Was it for this the clay grew tall? O what made fatuous sunbeams toil to break earth's sleep at all?" The death of the Horatian soldier is the assertion of man's freedom from biological necessity, a limited triumph over death. The death of Owen's soldier and of his prospective successors in the nuclear age is the negation not only of man's freedom but of his life's meaning as well.

Man gives his life and death meaning by his ability to make himself and his works remembered after his death. Patroclus dies to be avenged by Achilles. Hector dies to be mourned by Priam. Yet if Patroclus, Hector, and all those who could remember them were killed simultaneously, what would become of the meaning of Patroclus's and Hector's death? Their lives and deaths would lose their meaning. They would die, not like men but like beasts, killed in the mass, and what would be remembered would be the quantity of the killed—six million, twenty million, fifty million—not the quality of one man's death as over against another's.

Of their deeds, nothing would remain but the faint hope of remembrance in distant places. The very concept of fame would disappear, and the historians, the professional immortalizers, would have nothing to report. What had been preserved and created through the mind, will, and hands of man would be dissolved like man himself. Civilization itself would perish. Perhaps in some faraway place some evidence would be preserved of the perished civilization and of the men who created it. Nothing more than that would be left of the immortality man had once been able to achieve through the persistence of his fame and the permanence of his works.

And what would become of life itself? If our age had not replaced the belief in the immortality of the individual person with the immortality of humanity and its civilization, we could take the prospect of nuclear death in our stride. We could even afford to look forward to the day of the great slaughter as a day on which the preparatory and vain life on this earth would come to an end for most of us and the true, eternal life in another world begin. Yet a secular age, which has lost faith in individual immortality in another world and is aware of the impending doom of the world through which it tries to perpetuate itself here and now, is left without a remedy. Once it has become aware of its condition, it must despair. It is the saving grace of our age that it has not yet become aware of its condition.

We think and act as though the possibility of nuclear death had no bearing upon the meaning of life and death. In spite of what some of us know in our reason, we continue to think and act as though the possibility of nuclear death portended only a quantitative extension of the mass destruction of the past and not a qualitative transformation of the meaning of our existence. Thus we talk about defending the freedom of West Berlin as we used to talk about defending the freedom of the American colonies. Thus we talk about defending Western civilization against Communism as the ancient Greeks used to talk about defending their civilization against the Persians.

Thus we propose to die with honor rather than to live in shame.

Yet the possibility of nuclear death, by destroying the meaning of life and death, has reduced to absurd clichés the noble words of yesterday. To defend freedom and civilization is absurd when to defend them amounts to destroying them. To die with honor is absurd if nobody is left to honor the dead. The very conceptions of honor and shame require a society that knows what honor and shame mean.

It is this contrast between our consciousness and the objective conditions in which we live, the backwardness of our consciousness in view of the possibility of nuclear death, that threatens us with the actuality of nuclear death. It would indeed be the height of thoughtless optimism to assume that something so absurd as a nuclear war cannot happen because it is so absurd. An age whose objective conditions of existence have been radically transformed by the possibility of nuclear death evades the need for a radical transformation of its thought and action by thinking and acting as though nothing of radical import had happened. This refusal to adapt thought and action to radically new conditions has spelled the doom of men and civilizations before. It is likely to do so again.

The Experience of Death

This selection by the late priest-psychotherapist Ignace Lepp, from his book *Death and Its Mysteries,* explores the ancient and timeless question of how we learn about death. His comments on indifference to the deaths of strangers are particularly relevant in an age that has witnessed several holocausts in recent years and is presently under the shadow of the threat of nuclear holocaust.

Strictly speaking, we can have no immediate experience of death, either our own or that of others. The loss of consciousness is one of the signs of individual death even though we do not die each time we lose consciousness. Even those who have experienced prolonged comas during which they seemed to be dead cannot tell us anything about the experience of death for the simple reason that they did not die. . . .

Our experience of death can only be indirect. It is in the presence of another's death that man normally becomes aware that all men are mortal and concludes that he too must die. According to [the German philosopher] Heidegger we are only capable of communicating our more banal experiences. The deep experiences of life are by nature incommunicable. Since death is one of those basic experiences the spectacle of another's death, no matter how close to us he may have been, would not constitute a genuine psychological experience. In seeing others die we become convinced of our own mortality, but as long as we are alive it is merely "someone else" who dies, always another with whom we have no possibility of communicating in depth. My own experience, both direct and indirect, of interhuman relations prohibits my sharing Heidegger's pessimism concerning the radical incommunicability of basic experiences. But I admit that such communication is difficult. As a rule we can only communicate with those to whom we are bound by deep emotional bonds. The death of strangers is impersonal and tells us nothing essential about our own death. This perhaps explains the frightening indifference of individuals and peoples confronted with the death of others as a result of war, famine, or other catastrophes. For the Germans contaminated by Hitler's racism, it was the impersonal "other" who died in the crematory ovens of Dachau. The Americans, however humanitarian and compassionate they may otherwise be, also looked upon the victims of Hiroshima impersonally. This is also true of the attitude of the majority of Frenchmen toward the atrocities committed in Algeria and other colonies but a short time ago. As I write these lines the news media carry reports of the mass murder of noncombatants in Vietnam by American soldiers convinced that they are serving the cause of freedom and democracy. We are also informed by the same media about the ravages of famine in India while the Western nations are concerned about overeating. If the death of the Vietnamese and Indians scarcely disturbs most of us, and does not afford even an indirect experience of death, it is again because as far as we are concerned it is the anonymous "other" who dies.

But those close to us die too, those with whom our communication is not limited to banalties but touches upon the essèntial. Their death constitutes an authentic experience of death for us; a part of us dies with them. This is illustrated by a famous passage in St. Augustine's *Confessions* where he speaks of the death of his closest friend:

During those years, when I first began to teach— it was in the town in which I was born—I gained a friend, my equal in age, flowering like me with youth, and very dear to me because of a community of interests. As a boy, he had grown up with me, we had gone to school together, and had played games together. . . . This man was now wandering with me in spirit, and my soul could not endure to be without him. But behold, You were close at the back of those fleeing from You, You Who are at once the God of vengeance and the font of mercy, Who in a marvelous manner convert us to Yourself. Behold, You took the man from this life when he had scarce completed a year in my friendship, sweet to me above every sweetness of that life of mine. . . .

Tormented by fever, he lay for a long time senseless in a deadly sweat, and when his life was despaired of, he was baptized while unconscious. . . . After a few days, while I was absent, he was attacked again by the fever and died.

My heart was made dark by sorrow, and whatever I looked upon was death. My native place was a torment to me, and my father's house was a strange unhappiness. Whatsoever I had done together with him was, apart from him, turned into cruel torture. My eyes sought for him on every side, and he was not given to

them. I hated all things, because they no longer held him. Nor could they now say to me, "Here he comes," as they did in his absence from them when he lived. To myself I became a great riddle, and I questioned my soul as to why it was sad and why it afflicted me so grievously, and it could answer me nothing. If I said to it, "Hope in God," it did right not to obey me, for the man, that most dear one whom [it] had lost, was more real and more good to [it] than the fantasy in which [it] was bade to hope. Only weeping was sweet to me, and it was my friend's successor in my soul's delights. . . .

I marvelled that other men should live, because he, whom I had loved as if he would never die, was dead. I marveled more that I, his second self, could live when he was dead. Well has someone said of his friend that he is half his soul. For I thought that my soul and his soul were but one soul in two bodies. Therefore, my life was a horror to me, because I would not live as but a half. Perhaps because of this I feared to die, lest he whom I had loved so much should wholly die.

There is no doubt that St. Augustine had a real experience of death in the death of his friend. By identifying with him, he experienced, as it were, his own death. He also proved himself extremely capable of the kind of communication that Heidegger says is impossible. Similar testimonies can be found in the works of such writers as Goethe, Montaigne, and others who knew the painful experience of death through the loss of a dear friend. Perhaps someday, when human solidarity and our capacity to love all men as we love ourselves are more highly developed, we will not be so indifferent to the death of black people in Africa or yellow people in Asia; perhaps then the wars and famines that victimize them will affect us as the death of Augustine's friend affected him.

The German philosopher, Max Scheler, says that every human being possesses in one form or another an intuitive certainty of his own death. Psychologists and philosophers have tried to show that some of the higher forms of animal life also have some knowledge of their impending death. They note the case of cats and dogs who hide themselves in order to die privately; other animals flee when death is imminent. . . .

I obviously do not accept the Cartesian theory which holds that animals are mere machines and have no real psychic life. Today no psychologist or philosopher would doubt the existence of psychic activity in animals. In fact that activity is highly developed in some of the higher forms of animal life. But we should avoid the opposite error of interpreting animal behavior in terms of what we know about human psychology. The psychic life of animals constitutes a vast domain that deserves study in its own right. When this autonomy is observed, we discover that the so-called presentiment of death in animals is nothing of the sort, that the behavior involved must be interpreted in other terms. Specialists in animal psychology are agreed that even the most psychically developed animals are only aware of the present, that a sense of the future and the possible is completely lacking in them. They have no abstractive ability at all. An animal is instinctively aware of an immediate danger but it cannot conclude from the death of another animal that death is common to the species as such. In reality the animal is only species; to claim awareness of the individual for him is an anthropomorphic projection. Those who compare animal death to human death have an anthropomorphic vision of animals and an animalistic vision of man. Animals, it is true, show signs of distress somewhat similar to human mourning in the presence of the death of other members of their species. But they are still unaware of their own deaths or death in general. And there is no

evidence that even such highly psychic animals as monkeys and elephants bury their dead. Death is neither a problem nor a mystery for animals.

Of all the living species in our universe, only man knows that he is mortal. It seems that self-consciousness emerged almost simultaneously with his consciousness of death. Nor do we have any evidence that he has ever considered death to be a banal event. Only in our time, and in the materially prosperous West, do men see death as a simple biological fact. But it should be noted that they usually consider the death of others in this perspective rather than their own. I know many materialists who are much concerned with dying and being buried in proper style.

It is well known that paleontologists can determine that the remains of centuries ago are human on the basis of evidence furnished by funeral rites and honors rendered to the deceased. From the earliest beginnings of time man has been characterized by a minimal sense of individuality, by a certain capacity to project into the future, from the actual to the possible, and to infer his own fate from the fate of others. In this sense we can say that only man's death is an actual going away, a departure. And it leaves a profound impression upon those who survive.

EPILOGUE

Our examination of death and dying has shed a bright, often harsh, light on life and living. About the fact of death—what it is like to die whether there is continued existence after death—we have learned little. Death keeps its silence and remains a tantalizing and often frightening mystery. Science has given us far greater powers both to create and destroy than our most visionary forebears could have imagined. But science has not revealed the nature of death.

In this epilogue, we shall examine some themes which emerged in the preparation of this Reader that have, in our opinions, profound implications for our lives.

We have observed rapid and extensive changes in the very nature of society and culture. Religion has become less central to many of us as a source of meaning in life as well as in death. Science, both as a method for obtaining knowledge and as a perspective on life, has increasingly come to dominate our thoughts and lives. As a result of these two interrelated trends, our age can be characterized as one of moral confusion and technical power. An important manifestation of this dual trend has been the medicalization of death. Scientific medicine has enabled us to lead longer and healthier lives than any generation in history. By relegating the dying and the dead to trained professionals, we have largely managed to banish death from our daily lives. Yet, we have seen that such changes have been a mixed blessing for dying patients, their families and those who minister to their needs. New solutions to old problems contain the seeds of further challenges. Machines that are used to save lives have precipitated the question of when human life begins and ends.

There have also been changes in the sources from which we learn our culture's meanings for death and life. Traditionally, the basic institutions of family, church, and school have been the primary transmitters of the cultural heritage from one generation to the next. However, these institutions are undergoing important changes in contemporary society. Families are smaller, more mobile, and, as manifested in rising divorce rates, increasingly fragile. Churches are considerably less relevant to the lives of many modern people. Schools are burdened by declining enrollments, dwindling budgets, low performance scores, and troublesome violence and vandalism.

At the same time as families, churches, and schools have been beleaguered with stresses and problems, the pervasiveness and power of the mass media have grown immense. Children spend as much time watching television as they do in school; some critics worry that television is replacing both parents and clergy as guides to living in the modern world. However, we have observed that the depiction of death and dying in the mass media tends to be pornographic, violent, and impersonal. While we deny and avoid actual death in our daily lives, we eagerly seek to be entertained by media death. The implications of this disjunction—especially for children—while very complex and difficult to pinpoint, are nevertheless of extreme significance and concern.

Our study of the social inequality of death reminds us of the inequalities of life. We have seen that, within our own society, there are variations among people with respect to life expectancy, causes of death, and availability of health care. Our zealous concern to provide dignified care for dying patients, however, noble, must be complemented by continuing efforts to facilitate life with dignity among all of our citizens. The growing scarcity and cost of vital societal resources and services—from oil to health care—are likely to aggravate both moral dilemmas and social conflicts.

Another important theme in this Reader is the ageless yearning for continued existence after the death of the body. This yearning is expressed nowadays in a characteristically modern manner. Rather than theologians, physicians like Kübler-Ross and Moody are our guides to the afterlife. Scientific "evidence" has replaced faith as the foundation for our beliefs. We must remember, however, that the paradisiacal visions described by Kübler-Ross and Moody are not derived from reports of people who died, but instead from reports following resuscitation. They tell us nothing about either death or its aftermath. Perhaps our need for comforting visions of afterlife, combined with our uncritical acceptance of anyone or anything "scientific," explains the burgeoning popularity of such accounts. However, there is the possibility that indulgence in pseudoscientific stories of "cities of light" may have hidden hazards. If such promises render us incapable of confronting the harsh realities of death in this life, we may be doing ourselves and our children a fatal disservice.

The contemporary death education movement may be both a symptom and a solution to our problems with mortality. To the extent that the rediscovery of death in our homes, hospitals, and schools can lead to a more honest and authentic confrontation with one of life's basic facts, both our lives and our deaths will be more meaningful. On the other hand, superficial and simplistic death education can do more harm than good. Death and dying cannot be separated from life and living and as we have seen, the study of death reveals much that is unpleasant about life. We learn how vulnerable we are—both as individuals and as

a nation—to the ravages of death. We learn that much of our progress has entailed serious tradeoffs: our longer lives are often less meaningful and secure; our higher standard of living has been purchased with the development of a technology that can be turned against us; our peace is maintained by the threat of nuclear war that could destroy our civilization. The lessons of death are frequently painful.

The confrontation with death has always been one of humankind's most important challenges. This confrontation must continue. We must study death, not as detached, "objective" scientists, but as scientifically trained, self-aware, compassionate human beings. We must learn and teach the facts of death in order to understand and improve our lives.

The personal experience of death has been complicated by changes in society and culture. Further complicating the age-old challenge of death is the prospect of annihilation in a nuclear war. We moderns must not only face the inevitability of our own demise, but must also live under the shadow of the destruction of our pasts and futures.

We must apply our skills, energy, and courage to preventing a nuclear holocaust and apply the lessons from our prior studies of death to the overwhelming problem of megadeath.

Death has always been difficult to confront, and the difficulty has probably never been greater than at the present time. Ironically, the very generation that has managed largely to eliminate death from everyday life has created the wherewithal to obliterate itself. Those of us who have endeavored to avoid and deny the reality of death must regain our abilities to confront it, and we must confront it in more horrifying forms than ever before. We must allow neither our fear nor apathy nor the false promise of paradise to blind us to the actual prospect of hell.

FURTHER READING

1.
Death and Dying: The Issues Today

Choron, Jacques. *Death and Modern Man*. New York: Collier Books, 1971. Originally published with the title *Modern Man and Mortality* (New York: Macmillan, 1964). A thoughtful, philosophical discussion of our age-old confrontation with death by a wise student of the subject.

Feifel, Herman. *New Meanings of Death*. New York: McGraw-Hill, Inc., 1977. Original essays on old as well as new topics. Articles range from death as a recent taboo subject to hospice care and the emerging role of the grief counselor.

Fulton, Robert with Robert Bendiksen, eds. *Death and Identity* (2d ed.). (Bowie, Md.: Robert J. Brady Co., 1977). Reviews the recent research on attitudes and reactions to dying and death in American society.

Glaser, Barney G. and Anselm L. Strauss. *Awareness of Dying*. Chicago: Aldine Publishing Co., 1965. A pioneer study by two sociologists of systems of care and communication in modern hospitals.

Gorer, Geoffrey. *Death, Grief, and Mourning*. New York: Doubleday, 1965. Classic study of the loneliness of contemporary widowhood in modern England by an anthropologist. The book also contains his moving account of his mother's death and his important essay, "The Pornography of Death."

Kübler-Ross, Elisabeth. *On Death and Dying*. New York: Macmillan, 1969. This is the classic statement that stimulated our contemporary concern with the dying patient and heightened our present day awareness of the problems and issues surrounding both the dying and the dead in Western society.

Lifton, Robert Jay. *Death in Life: Survivors of Hiroshima*. New York: Random House, 1967. This book won the National Book Award in Science in 1969. It is an account of Lifton's poignant interviews with the survivors of the atomic bombing of Hiroshima.

Lopata, Helena Z. *Widowhood in an American City*. Morristown, N.J.: General Learning Corporation, 1972. A report based on a survey of widows of blue and white collar workers in Chicago by a leading sociologist and long-time student of the subject.

Mitford, Jessica. *The American Way of Death*. New York: Simon and Schuster, 1963. A critical and humorous diatribe against American funeral directors and funeral customs. It sparked a movement that culminated in the Federal Trade Commission investigations of how America buries the dead.

Pine, Vanderlyn R. *Caretaker of the Dead: The American Funeral Director*. New York: Irvington Publishers, Inc., 1975. A historical account of the role and rise of the American funeral director as well as a knowledgeable discussion of the funeral and its meaning.

Sudnow, David. *Passing On: The Social Organization of Dying*. Englewood Cliffs, N.J.: Prentice-Hall, 1967. An insightful study of differential treatment accorded patients and emergency cases in a public and a private hospital.

Toynbee, Arnold and others. *Man's Concern with Death*. New York: McGraw-Hill, 1968. This internationally renowned scholar together with eight colleagues reviews the issues, the problems, and the prospects of humankind's concern with death.

Warner, W. Lloyd. *The Living and the Dead: A Psychiatric Study of Terminality*. New York: Behavioral Publications, 1972. A Harvard psychiatrist and a pioneer in the care of the dying shares his observations and insights on this increasingly problematical issue.

Wolfenstein, Martha and Gilbert Kliman, eds. *Children and the Death of a President*. New York: Doubleday, 1965. A collection of nine studies, with insightful commentary by the editors, in the reactions of young children and youth to the death of President John F. Kennedy.

2.
Historical Perspectives on Death

Ariès, Philippe. *Western Attitudes toward Death from the Middle Ages to the Present*. Baltimore: The Johns Hopkins University Press, 1974. A brief and exciting overview of the treatment of death in the West during the past ten centuries.

Habenstein, Robert and William Lamers. *The History of American Funeral Directing*. Milwaukee: Bulfin, 1955. A survey of the evolution of formal funerary practices in the United States, published under the auspices of the National Funeral Directors Association.

Jackson, Charles O., ed. *Passing: The Vision of Death in America*. Westport, Conn.: Greenwood Press, 1977. A collection of previously published essays on subjects ranging from the tombstones of early New England to the modern park cemetery.

Ludwig, Allan I. *Graven Images*. Middletown, Conn.: Wesleyan University Press, 1966. A pioneering and still very valuable study of the art and iconography of early American gravestones.

Stannard, David E., ed. *Death in America*. Philadelphia: University of Pennsylvania Press, 1975. A collection of essays originally commissioned by the editor for a special issue of *American Quarterly;* the subjects range from Puritanism and Mormonism to the rural cemetery and Mexican folk culture.

Stannard, David E. *The Puritan Way of Death*. New York: Oxford University Press, 1977. A book that focuses on the attitudes and behavior of the earliest large-scale American settlers, and then traces the subsequent developments of these themes down to the present.

Tashjian, Ann and Dickran Tashjian. *Memorials For Children of Change*. Middletown, Conn.: Wesleyan University Press, 1974. Another study of early American gravestones, linking some of the imagery to other art forms, and taking issue with some of Ludwig's earlier findings (see above).

3.
Death in Popular Culture

Arlen, Michael J. *The Livingroom War*. New York: Viking Press, 1969. The role of TV in the Vietnam war.

Drucker, Peter. *The Unseen Revolution*. New York: Harper & Row, 1976. An account of the hidden environment of security services and pensions.

Fromm, Erich. *The Anatomy of Human Destructiveness*. Greenwich, Conn.: Fawcett Publications, 1975. The best book on the mystery of Hitler's death programs.

Giedion, Siegfried. *Mechanization Takes Command*. New York: Oxford University Press, 1948. A classic study of technology as an art form.

Moody, Raymond A. *Life After Life*. New York: Bantam, 1976. A study of reports of people who died and were brought back to life.

McLuhan, H. M. *Understanding Media*. New York: McGraw-Hill, 1964. Concerned with the psychic and social consequences of the media.

McLuhan, Marshall. *From Cliche to Archetype*. New York: Viking Press, 1970. The behavior of language when pushed to an extreme.

McLuhan, Marshall. *The Mechanical Bride*. New York: Vanguard Press, 1951. Comic account of the Love Goddess Assembly Line.

Waugh, Evelyn. *The Loved One*. Boston: Little, Brown, 1948. A classic on the mortuary industry.

White, David Manning and John Pendleton, eds. *Popular Culture: Mirror of American Life*. Del Mar, Calif.: Publisher's Inc., 1977. The Reader for the eighth in the *Courses by Newspaper* series provides an excellent overview with over fifty selections dealing with American life and the mass media.

4.
Demography of Death

Fuchs, Victor R. "Who Shall Live?" Chapter 2 of *Who Shall Live? Health, Economics, and Social Choice*. New York: Basic Books, 1974. This classic chapter dramatically illustrates large health differentials unrelated to income or to the availability of medical care. It suggests that rising income is no longer significantly associated with better health, that more physicians and hospitals would not improve our general health, and that the greatest potential for improved health resides in sound decisions about our habits and environment.

Lerner, Monroe and Richard N. Stutz. "Have We Narrowed the Gaps Between the Poor and the Non-Poor? Part II. Narrowing the Gaps, 1959–61 to 1969–71: Mortality." *Medical Care* 15, 8:620-635. This report analyzes socioeconomic differentials in mortality in the United States during 1959–1961 and 1969–1971 and life expectancy for the ten highest and ten lowest states ranked by income, (and for three geographic divisions.)

Retherford, Robert D. *The Changing Sex Differential in Mortality*. Westport, Conn.: Greenwood Press, 1975. This monograph comprehensively reviews the literature on sex differentials in mortality, points out that in the West this differential has increased markedly during the 20th Century, and attributes the increase to environmental factors such as diet, working conditions, health technology, stress, and others.

Stolnitz, George J. "A Century of International Mortality Trends." *Population Studies* 9(1955): 24–55 and 10(1956)17–42. This paper discusses long-term trends in world and regional mortality, and the determinants and consequences of these trends.

U.S., Department of Health, Education, and Welfare; National Center for Health Statistics, *Health: United States, 1975*. Washington, D.C.: U.S. Government Printing Office, 1976. DHEW Publication No. (HRA) 76-1232. This publication reveals some of the more important trends and current differentials within overall mortality and for life expectancy at birth. These include differentials by color, sex, and state in life expectancy for 1969–71, and trends in life expectancy and mortality by color and sex for selected years form 1900 to 1974.

5.
Death and Social Change

Bakan, David. *Disease, Pain, and Sacrifice—Toward a Psychology of Human Suffering*. Boston: Beacon Press, 1968. A philosophical discussion that draws upon recent biological and psychiatric research, as well as Biblical sources, in an effort to understand the conditions of human mortality.

Becker, Ernest. *The Denial of Death*. New York: The Free Press/MacMillan, 1973. A reflective treatise on the meaning of death, synthesizing theological and psychological insights on the nature of man.

Cassell, E. J. *The Healer's Art*. New York: Lippincott, 1976. The last chapter deals with a physician's view, drawn from personal clinical experience, of how the dying can and should be cared for.

Hillman, James. *Suicide and the Soul*. Zurich: Spring Publications, 1976. A discussion of death, medicine, individuation, and the meaning of death within the symbolic context of human life.

Krant, Melvin J. *Dying and Dignity*. Springfield: Charles C. Thomas, 1974. The personal view of a physician with wide experience; a practical manual for families and health care staff.

Kübler-Ross, Elisabeth. *On Death and Dying*. New York: MacMillan and Co., 1969. Classic research in the field.

Mack, Arien, ed. *Death In American Experience*. New York: Schocken Books, 1974. A series of essays embracing a wide range of disciplines, including sociological, anthropological, psychiatric, theological, medical, and literary approaches to death.

Pattison, E. Mansell, ed. *The Experience of Dying*. Englewood Cliffs, N.J.: Prentice-Hall, 1977. Interviews with and individual accounts of the dying that provide the reader with a framework in which to understand the dying process.

van den Berg, J. H. *The Psychology of the Sickbed*. New York: The Humanities Press, 1972. A physician's description of the psychological changes in sick persons that arise from the state of being ill.

Veatch, Robert M. and P. Steinfels. *Death Inside Out—The Hastings Center Report*. New York: Harper and Row, 1975. A series of essays by social scientists exploring the meaning of death and dying.

6.
Life after Death:
Old and New Meanings

Bucke, Richard M. *Cosmic Consciousness*. New York: Dutton, 1968. A Canadian psychiatrist who has a mystical experience that changes his life tries to discover from others who have had similar experiences what it means and how it affects assumptions about life, death, and the survival of consciousness after bodily death.

Huxley, Aldous. *The Perennial Philosophy*. New York: Harper Colphon Books, 1970. A philosopher who explored the boundaries of human experience looks at the assumptions of the human mind as it confronts survival after death and the rational attitudes one can take.

Koestler, Arthur. *The Roots of Coincidence*. New York: Random House, 1972. A scientifically-oriented exploration of the paranormal: phenomena of experience that cannot be approached through limited perspectives but call for a broader scientific perception.

LeShan, Lawrence. *Alternative Realities*. New York: Evans, 1976. A philosophical extension of his earlier book. The basis for a belief in survival after death is founded on the development of the inventive-creative capacity of the human mind and consciousness.

LeShan, Lawrence. *The Medium, the Mystic and the Physicist*. New York: Viking, 1974. A clinical psychologist compares three approaches to reality in an effort to understand life experiences whose nature cannot be determined by the usual scientific methods. Probably the best contemporary study.

Myers, Frederick W. H. *Human Personality and Its Survival of Bodily Death*. rev. ed. London: Longmans Green, 1954. A professor of logic at Oxford makes a searching examination of the experience, phenomena, and theories related to survival after death in his massive two-volume classic. Definitive and basic.

Spraggett, Allan. *The Case for Immortality*. New York: New American Library, 1974. In a crisp, readable style marked by scientific curiosity, cool logic, and an open mind, a newsman comments on phenomena he has had reported to him.

Toynbee, Arnold. *Man's Concern with Death*. St. Louis: McGraw-Hill, 1968. An eminent historian explores contemporary attitudes toward death and survival after death and their relation to life attitudes and historical perspectives.

7.
The Dying Patient

Choron, Jacques. *Death and Western Thought*. New York: Collier Books, 1963. A philosophical evaluation of what famous philosophers have written about death. A useful reference for scholars.

Edel, Leon. "Portrait of the Artist as an Old Man." *American Scholar,* Winter, 1977–78. How a literary man sees age affecting several creative writers.

Feifel, Herman, ed. *The Meaning of Death*. New York: McGraw-Hill, 1959, and

Feifel, Herman, ed. *New Meanings of Death*. New York: McGraw-Hill, 1977. These works provide an excellent background in the current thinking of various thanatologists.

Fulton, Robert. *Death and Identity*. rev. ed. Bowie, Md.: Charles Press, 1976. This is the most comprehensive collection of essays available on the subject. Fulton has surveyed the field and made judicious choices.

Garfield, Charles, ed. *Psychological Care of the Dying Patient*. New York: McGraw-Hill, 1978. A fine selection of essays about caring for the dying.

Grollman, Earl A. *Explaining Death to Children*. Boston: Beacon, 1967. The content is concise and, although somewhat dated, still valuable.

Jackson, Edgar. *Coping With Crises in Your Life*. New York: Hawthorn Books, 1974. A practical book about dealing with bereavement.

Kastenbaum, Robert and Bruce B. Aisenberg. *The Psychology of Death*. New York: Springer, 1972. This is the closest one can come to an encyclopedia of death. While lacking a central theme, the book reviews most aspects of death and dying.

Kent, D., R. Kastenbaum, and S. Sherwood, eds. *Research Planning and Action for the Elderly*. New York: Behavioral Publications, 1972. Many suggestions for students of the elderly. Excellent compilation of references.

Knopf, O. *Successful Aging*. New York: Viking Press, 1975. A well known psychoanalyst offers personal experience with the aging process.

Menninger, Karl. *Man Against Himself*. New York: Harcourt Brace, 1938. A classic book on self-destructiveness by an outstanding psychiatrist.

Pattison, E. M., ed. *The Experience of Dying*. Englewood Cliffs, N.J.: Prentice-Hall, 1977. The theme is attitudes towards death as a function of age and type of illness.

Schoenberg, A., and others, eds. *Psychosocial Aspects of Terminal Care*. New York: Columbia University Press, 1972. Brief presentations by clinical specialists with a focus on practical considerations.

Shur, M. *Freud: Living and Dying*. New York: International Universities Press, 1972. The father of psychoanalysis thought deeply about death but did not synthesize his observations.

The book offers insight into Sigmund Freud not found elsewhere.

Shneidman, Edwin. *Deaths of Man.* New York: Quadrangle/New York Times, 1973. An analysis of society from the standpoint of its deaths.

Veatch, Robert M. *Death, Dying and the Biological Revolution: Our Last Quest for Responsibility.* New Haven: Yale University Press, 1976. An up-to-date consideration of euthanasia, informed consent, organ transplant, and other contemporary controversies.

Weinberg, J. "Geriatric Psychiatry," in *Comprehensive Textbook of Psychiatry,* vol. 2, edited by A. Freedman and others. Baltimore: Williams and Wikins, 1975, pp. 2405-2420. Psychiatric disorders found among the aged.

Weisman, Avery. *On Dying and Denying: A Psychiatric Study of Terminality.* New York: Behavioral Publications, 1972. Practical psychiatric aspects of terminality.

Worden, J. W. *PDA—Personal Death Awareness.* New Jersey: Prentice-Hall, 1976. Exercises in becoming more aware of death.

8.
Death and the Child
About Children

Furman, Erma. *A Child's Parent Dies.* New Haven: Yale University Press, 1974. Studies the psychological impact of bereavement on the young and offers concrete suggestions for helping children cope with their losses.

Jackson, Edgar. *Telling a Child about Death.* New York: Channel Press, 1965. Discusses the impact of death on the life and experience of the child from several different angles.

Mitchell, Marjorie. *The Child's attitude Toward Death.* New York: Schocken Press, 1967. Offers assistance to parents in dealing with the child's interest in death from the earliest years into adolescence, in order to prevent the growth of morbid fears and misconceptions about death.

Wolf, Anna. *Helping Your Child to Understand Death.* rev. ed. New York: Child Study Press, 1973. Discusses questions of children and parents regarding death and gives specific answers in an understanding and compassionate manner.

For Children or to Be Read to Them
(suggest careful perusal first)

Fassler, Jean. *My Grandpa Died Today.* New York: Behavioral Publications, 1971. Story of a little boy whose grandfather dies and the difficulty he has accepting this death.

Lee, Virginia. *The Magic Moth.* Greenwich, Conn.: Seabury Press, 1972. Story of the death of a ten year old girl—its sensitive presentation will reach children of all ages.

Mills, Miska. *Annie and the Old One.* Boston: Little, Brown and Co., 1971. Story of a Navajo girl who has difficulty understanding her grandmother's impending death—discusses the concept that there is a time for all things to return to the earth.

Tresselt, Alvin. *The Dead Tree.* New York: Parents' Magazine Press, 1972. Story following the life span of an oak tree—explains death in a way that a child can relate to his/her environment.

Viorst, Judith. *The Tenth Good Thing about Barney.* New York: Athenson, 1971. Story of a little boy who loses his pet cat and how his mother helps him accept the cat's death.

White. E. B. *Charlotte's Web.* New York: Dell Publishing Company, 1952. Deals with the concept of death by telling the story of a pig who loses his best friend, a spider—valuable because it explains the life/death cycle as found in nature.

9.
Grief

Agee, James. *A Death in the Family.* New York: McDowell, Obolensky, Inc., 1958. Agee's classic story of the death of a father provides many insights into the mind of his young son. Less sentimental than Louisa M. Alcott (*Little Women* and *Young Wives*), who provided generations of school children with their first confrontation with death.

Anthony, Sylvia. *The Discovery of Death in Childhood and After.* London: Allen Lane, The Penguin Press, 1971. An odd little research study which analyzes the attitudes towards death of children of various ages as revealed in story completion tests.

Bowlby, John. *Attachment and Loss.* 3 vols. vol.

1. *Attachment,* 1969. vol. 2. *Separation: Anxiety and Anger,* 1973. vol. 3. *Loss,* forthcoming. London: Hogarth. The third volume of Bowlby's *magnum opus* is eagerly awaited by all who have been impressed by his studious and scientific analysis of the nature of human attachments given in the first two volumes. Drawing on a wide range of studies of the effects of separation and loss in childhood, Bowlby develops "Attachment Theory," which bids to replace many other theories of human relationships. Not light reading but highly recommended.

Bowman, LeRoy. *The American Funeral: A Way of Death.* Washington, D.C.: Public Affairs Press, 1959. After Jessica Mitford's *The American Way of Death* and Evelyn Waugh's *The Loved One* there was a need for a more sober analysis of the funeral industry in the United States. Bowman's book provides facts and figures and a less sensational analysis of their implications. He neither glosses over the anomalies nor adopts a judgmental attitude towards them. As Rosenblatt's book also reveals, complex societies need "death specialists," whose function in part is to mitigate the painful impact of death upon the survivors. American funeral directors have been criticized for their attempts to do just that.

Caine, Lynn. *Widow.* New York: William Morrow and Co., 1974. Lynn Caine is intelligent, well educated, ruthlessly frank, and totally lacking the "invisible means of support" that sustained most of our forebears. Her description of her own widowhood is stark, bitter, and uncompromising—in the end, she survives in a kind of glory.

Freud, Sigmund. *Mourning and Melancholia.* vol. 14. In *Standard Edition of the Complete Psychological Works of Sigmund Freud.* New York: Macmillan Co., 1917. One of the best known and most influential papers Freud wrote. One cannot fail to admire the ingenuity with which he draws out and explains the differences between grief and depressive illness. His observation that ambivalence and guilt are likely to complicate the course of mourning has been amply confirmed by later and more scientific studies. But his idea that mental energy must be withdrawn from the object of love before it can be reinvested elsewhere should not be taken too literally.

Grollman, E. A. *Talking about Death: A Dialogue between Parent and Child.* Boston: Beacon Press, 1976. A useful book for parents who find it hard to talk about death to their children. Contains much of the wisdom distilled from the author's earlier multicontributed volume, *Explaining Death to Children.*

Lewis, C. S. *A Grief Observed.* London: Faber, 1961. "Don't speak to me of the consolations of religion" wrote C. S. Lewis after the death of his wife. Despite, or perhaps because of his strong religious faith, Lewis expresses his grief in terms of a battle with God. He shares Lynn Caine's openness and vulnerability and, like her, begins gradually to rebuild the world which has fallen around him.

Lindemann, Erich. "Symptomatology and Management of Acute Grief." *American Journal of Psychiatry* 101(1944): 141–148. This short, classic paper remains the best descriptive account of acute grief. In it Lindemann first distinguished between normal and pathological grief and suggested a straightforward method of correcting repressed or delayed grief. Unfortunately he failed to recognize that one of the commonest conditions requiring psychiatric help is "chronic grief," and this is not cured by Lindemann's therapy.

Marris, P. *Loss and Change.* London: Routledge and Kegan Paul, 1974. In his earlier work *Widows and Their Families,* Marris described the way London widows cope with the stress of bereavement. Drawing on his experience as a sociologist studying life change experiences, he develops in this book a theory of loss and change. Situations as diverse as the effects of urbanization on African tribal societies, the effects of slum clearance, and the changes facing American students entering universities reveal a common pattern of response and have practical relevance for the planning of change.

Parkes, C. M. *Bereavement: Studies of Grief in Adult Life.* New York: International Universities Press, 1972. A concise, readable review of the psychology of grief that deals mainly with the loss of a spouse but touches on many wider issues. Aimed originally at doctors, clergy, social workers, nurses and other members of the caregiving professions, it has also proved to be a source of reassurance to many bereaved people who have found that it helps them to understand the nature of their own reactions to bereavement.

Pincus, Lily. *Death and the Family: The Importance of Mourning.* New York: Pantheon Books, 1974. After working for many years as a marital therapist in London's Tavistock Clinic, and after the death of her own husband, Lily Pincus diverted her attention to the task of helping family members face problems of death and bereavement. In a book that is rich with case material from her own practice, she shows how different types of marriage give rise to different types of grief and indicates the clinical approaches which she has found useful.

Rochlin, G. *Griefs and Discontents: The Forces of Change.* Boston: Little, Brown and Co., 1965. Rochlin is another psychoanalyst who has recognized in the process of grieving a fundamental concept influencing much human behavior. He discusses how the developing child learns to cope with fears of loss and death and suggests that these remain important problems throughout adult life. Far from taking a pessimistic view, however, Rochlin believes that many of the springs of creativity and spiritual development arise as a consequence of man's attempts to mourn for losses, including the threatened loss of his own life.

Rosenblatt, R. C., R. P. Walsh, and D. A. Jackson. *Grief and Mourning In Cross-cultural Perspective.* New York: H.R.A.F. Press, 1976. Funeral and mourning customs have always proved fascinating to anthropologists who have regularly described them as they exist in the diverse cultures which they have studied. To the non-anthropologist the sheer number and variety of different customs is confusing; even anthropologists themselves have been reluctant to generalize beyond the particular cultures that they have studied. This book is an exception. Adopting systematic and scientific methods of analysis, the authors of this short volume have extracted their data from detailed reports of seventy-eight representative societies from all parts of the world. Consequently they are able to demonstrate and explain the main patterns of mourning that exist.

Volkan, Vamik., A. F. Cilluffo, and T. L. Sarvay. "Re-Grief Therapy and the Function of the Linking Object as a Key to Stimulate Emotionality." In *Emotional Flooding,* edited by Paul Olson and others. New York: Human Sciences Press, 1975. Two important ideas propounded in this paper are Vamik's concept of "linking objects" and their use in therapy to promote "re-grief therapy." Firmly rooted in the psychoanalytic tradition, Volkan's intriguing ideas have wider implications than one would at first imagine.

10.
Widowhood

Berardo, Felix. "Social Adaption to Widowhood among a Rural-urban Aged Population." *Agricultural Experiment Station Bulletin* 689 (December). Washington State University, 1967. A comparison of widows and widowers in rural and urban areas of the state of Washington, with the conclusion that rural widowers were the most isolated because of their lack of social skills.

Berardo, Felix. "Widowhood Status in the United States: Perspective on a Neglected Aspect of the Family Life-cycle." *The Family Coordinator* 17 (1968): 191–203. A call for research into the problems and life styles of the widowed in America, published about the time that Lopata began her study of older widows in metropolitan Chicago.

Caine, Lynne. *Widow.* New York: William Morrow and Company, 1974. A personal and dramatic autobiography of a woman, starting from the time she and her husband found out that he was dying until she started to "feel normal" again, that is, when she completed her grief work. Caine is very atypical, but many widows of middle class and above report similar emotions and actions which they later regretted.

Glick, Ira, Robert Weiss and C. Murray Parkes. *The First Years of Bereavement.* New York: John Wiley and Sons, 1974. Written by a combination of psychiatrists and sociologists, this book is a result of several years of counseling and studying mainly younger widows and widowers by the staff of the Harvard Medical School. The authors discuss some of the problems and phases of the grief following the death of a spouse, as well as some of the ways the bereaved are helped by others. The importance of being able to grieve, to complete "grief work," is emphasized.

Lopata, Helena Z. *Women as Widows: Support Systems.* New York: Elsevier Press, 1978. A sociological analysis of interviews with 1,169 widows living in metropolitan Chicago who are or who have been beneficiaries of social security as survivors of an eligible worker. The book explores the economic, service, and social support systems of these women and the network of people who provide these supports or are recipients of her action. The contributions to the support systems by the late husband's memory, a new husband, boyfriends and other friends, children, brothers and sisters, other relatives, friends and neighbors, co-workers, and members of the "helping professions" are discussed in detail.

Lopata, Helena Z. "Couple-companionate Relations: Wives and Widows." In *Old Family/New Family,* edited by Nona Glazer-Malbin. New York: D. Van Nostrand Company, 1975. An analysis of the type of friendships couples develop with others during marriage, mainly at the initiative of the wife, and what happens to these friendships in widowhood.

Lopata, Helena Z. "Contributions of Extended Families to the Support Systems of Metropolitan Area Widows: Limitations of the Modified Kin Network." *Journal of Marriage and the Family,* 1978. The author argues that the extended family of widows living in a metropolitan area, composed of brothers and sisters, nieces and nephews and even grandchildren, does not very frequently contribute to a widow's economic, service, social and emotional support systems. Most widows are mainly involved in exchanges of supports with their children (usually daughters), with friends, and with other people entering the systems in selected activities. Parents are usually dead, siblings scattered and involved in their own lives, and grandchildren unavailable for frequent contact.

Lopata, Helena Z. "The Effect of Schooling on Social Contacts of Urban Women." *American Journal of Sociology* 7(1973): 604–609. This article documents the importance of formal education in providing widows with personal resources for developing support systems and for utilizing societal resources for a full life. Minimally educated widows tend to be socially isolated or heavily dependent on their children.

Lopata, Helena Z. "Living through Widowhood. *Psychology Today* 7(1973): 86–92. A general discussion of problems and long range adjustments of older widows, based mainly on a study, with a historial and cross-cultural perspective, of 301 such women.

Lopata, Helena Z. "Role Changes in Widowhood: A World Perspective." In *Aging and Modernization,* edited by Donald Cogwill and Lowell Holmes. New York: Appleton-Century-Crofts, 1972. A look at the situation of widows in other countries and at other times. Uses the degree of disorganization experienced because of the death of the husband as a theoretical framework.

Lopata, Helena Z. "Widows and Widowers." *The Humanist* 36(1977). July–August, 1977. An overview of the situation of American widows and widowers, including contrasts with the situations of people who lose their spouses in other parts of the world or in our own history.

Marris, Peter. *Widows and Their Families.* London: Routledge and Kegan Paul, Ltd., 1958. A look at London widows in the 1950s whose husbands had been no older than fifty-four at the time of death. The widows are quite independent and have little contact with their in-laws.

Peterson, James A. and Michael L. Briley. *Widows and Widowhood: A Creative Approach to Being Alone.* New York: Associated Press, 1977. An analysis of what happens in widowhood. Based on research and discussions by other authors, this work also has some very good counsel on how to solve some of the most common emotional, social, and economic problems.

Silverman, Phyllis, Dorothy MacKenzie, Mary Pettipas and Elizabeth Wilson. *Helping Each Other in Widowhood.* New York: Health Sciences Publishing Corp., 1974. A collection of papers from several workshops organized by Dr. Phyllis Silverman and the staff of the Widow-to-Widow program affiliated with the Harvard Medical School. The book contains explanations of how the program started and worked, as well as reports from numerous similar groups. These papers can be very useful to widows or widowers wishing to start such self-help organizations in their own communities.

Weiss, Robert A. *Loneliness: The Experience of Emotional and Social Isolation.* Cambridge, Mass.: MIT Press. Weiss brings together several articles and develops a theoretical analysis of social and emotional loneliness. Included is a Lopata article based on the study of widows in the Chicago area.

11.
The Funeral

Bowman, LeRoy. *The American Funeral.* Washington, D.C.: Public Affairs Press, 1959. A critical treatment of American funeral practices, including an analysis of attitudes toward death, funeral behavior, interaction between funeral directors and bereaved people, and the influence of social change on the funeral service field.

Feifel, Herman. *New Meanings of Death.* New York: McGraw-Hill Book Company, 1977. A collection of essays by authorities in the field of dying and death, which focuses on clinical and empirical findings, approaches of professional practice, existing conceptual frameworks, and public policy.

Fulton, Robert. *Death, Grief, and Bereavement: A Chronological Bibliography, 1843-1970.* University of Minnesota: Center for Thanatological Studies. A complete, chronological bibliography of books, articles, and speeches written from an empirical perspective in the area of death, grief, and bereavement.

Fulton, Robert. *Death and Identity.* Bowie, Md.: Charles Press Publishers, Inc., 1976. A multi-disciplinary compilation of essays that blends the work of leading scholars in the field of thanatology. Material includes treatments of theoretical, attitudinal, psychological, and societal aspects of dying, death, and bereavement.

Glick, Ira O., Robert S. Weiss, and C. Murray Parkes. *The First Year of Bereavement.* New York: John Wiley and Sons, 1974. A social-psychological analysis of the dynamics of bereavement, especially as experienced by widows and widowers. Discusses how various stages can lead to the resolution of grief, and emphasizes the need for less stringent time constraints on the grief and mourning process.

Gorer, Geoffrey. *Death, Grief and Mourning.* Garden City, N.Y.: Doubleday and Co., Inc., 1965. A treatment of the social and individual denial of grief and mourning, and an anthropological view of mourning practices primarily in Great Britain and the United States.

Grollman, Earl A. *Concerning Death: A Practical Guide for the Living.* Boston: Beacon Press, 1974. An edited collection of questions and answers dealing with various aspects of dying, death, funerals, mourning, grief, and bereavement. Provides a useful handbook of practical considerations for those preparing for death and coping with its aftermath.

Habenstein, Robert W. and William M. Lamers. *Funeral Customs the World Over.* Milwaukee: Bulfin Printers, Inc., 1960. A comprehensive crosscultural study of the meaning of death, funeral customs, and burial practices.

Habenstein, Robert W. and William M. Lamers. *The History of American Funeral Directing.* Milwaukee: Bulfin Printers, Inc., 1962. A detailed historical treatment of the development of American funeral customs and the rise of American funeral directing. Their evolution is traced to their roots in early Western civilization.

Harrah, Barbara K. and David F. Harrah. *Funeral Service: A Bibliography of Literature on Its Past, Present, and Future, The Various Means of Disposition, and Memorialization.* Metuchen, N.J.: The Scarecrow Press, Inc., 1976. A detailed reference book to literature on the subjects of funeral service, disposition, and memorialization. Incldues entries for books, articles, brochures, pamphlets, and audio-visual material. Some entries are annotated.

Irion, Paul E. *The Funeral: Vestige or Value?* Nashville: Abingdon Press, 1966. An analysis of contemporiary funeral pracitces and their relevance to modern American society. Describes the functions of a funeral, and proposes possible adaptations to prevailing customs. These adaptations would help to fulfill social and psychological needs which arise at the time of death.

Irion, Paul E. *A Manual and Guide for Those Who Conduct a Humanist Funeral Service.* Baltimore, Md.: Waverly Press, Inc., 1971. A collection of resources that can be of value in conducting a humanistic funeral. Includes a discussion of the social and emotional needs that arise at the time of death, and offers general and specific recommendations for a non-religious funeral service.

Kastenbaum, Robert J. *Death, Society and Human Experience.* St. Louis, Mo.: C. V. Mosby Company, 1977. A comprehensive textbook focusing on the interplay of life and death throughout all levels of American society. Suggests that the structure of society can be understood by exploring the way individuals come to terms with mortality.

Manchester, William. *The Death of a President.* New York: Harper and Row, 1963. A chronological account of the assassination of President John F. Kennedy, including a detailed description of the funeral, private and public reactions to it, and its social aspects.

Mitford, Jessica. *The American Way of Death.* Greenwich, Conn.: Fawcett Publications, Inc., 1963. Presents a critical account of the American funeral, focusing on the economic aspects and satirizing the practices of funeral directors.

Pine, Vanderlyn R. *Caretaker of the Dead: The American Funeral Director.* New York: Halsted Press, 1975. A case study of funeral directors and their funerary activities in the occupational setting of their funeral homes. Utilizes participant observation, archival data, and survey research to examine funeral directors as service practitioners.

Pine, Vanderlyn R. and others, eds. *Acute Grief and the Funeral.* Springfield, Ill.: Charles C. Thomas, 1976. A collection of essays providing a multidisciplinary approach to grief and to the funeral as a therapeutic expression of that grief in contemporary society. Contributors include physicians, psychologists, ministers, sociologists, nurses, gerontologists, philosophers, educators, attorneys, and funeral directors.

Schoenberg, Bernard and others, eds. *Bereavement, Its Psychosocial Aspects.* New York: Columbia Unversity Press, 1975. A multidisciplinary collection of essays that examines the psychosocial aspects of bereavement and includes some practical and theoretical suggestions for meeting the needs of the bereaved.

VanGennep, Arnold. *The Rites of Passage.* Chicago, University of Chicago Press, 1960. An anthropological and sociological study of the transitional stages in man's life as marked by universal ceremonies. Focuses specifically on birth, puberty, marriage, and death.

Weisman, Avery D. *On Dying and Denying: A Psychiatric Study of Terminality.* New York: Behavioral Publications, 1972. An empirical and scholarly monograph reporting on the author's experience as a psychiatrist working with dying people. Focuses specifically on the role of denial as it relates to dying and death.

Worden, J. William and William Proctor. *PDA— Personal Death Awareness.* Englewood Cliffs, N.J.: Prentice-Hall, 1976. A workbook-type approach to personal death awareness and understanding of individual mortality through the use of tests and exercises. Underlying view is that increased personal death awareness will lead to a healthier, happier life and a better ability to cope with death on a personal level.

12.
Morality and Mortality in Modern Society

Annas, George J. "In re Quinlan: Legal Comfort for Doctors." *Hastings Center Report* 6 (1976): 29–31. An analysis of the legal issues raised by the Quinlan opinion.

Capron, Alexander M., and Leon R. Kass. "A Statutory Definition of the Standards for Determining Human Death: An Appraisal and a Proposal." *University of Pennsylvania Law Review* 121 (1972): 87–118. Introduces a model statutory definition of death preceded by an examination of the problems of other legislative proposals and a list of criteria for good legislation on the definition of death.

Choron, Jacques. *Death and Western Thought.* rev. ed. New York: Collier Books, 1973. New edition of a survey of what the great philosophers of the Western world, from Socrates to the existentialists, have thought about death.

Duff, Raymond S., and A. G. M. Campbell. "Moral and Ethical Dilemmas in the Special-Care Nursery." *New England Journal of Medicine* 289 (1973): 890–94. The authors reviewed patient records in the special-care nursery and found that 14 percent of the deaths occurring over a two-and-a-half-year period were related to withholding treatment. Thus, forty-three infants, most of whom suffered from multiple anomalies, were permitted to die.

Engelhardt, H. Tristram, Jr. "The Counsels of Finitude." *Hastings Center Report* 5 (1975): 29–36. A critical examination of the effort to extend the human life span and the philosophical reasons why such efforts may be misguided.

Fletcher, Joseph. "Medical Diagnosis: Our Right to Know the Truth." In *Morals and Medicine.* Boston: Beacon Press, 1964. An early, but still important discussion of an ethicist's defense of disclosing diagnoses.

Foot, Philippa. "Euthanasia." *Philosophy and Public Affairs* 6 (1977): 85–112. A critical philosophical examination of the presumed difference between killing and letting die.

Garland, Michael. "The Right to Die in California —Politics, Legislation, and Natural Death." *Hastings Center Report* 6 (1976): 5–6. An analysis of the California Natural Death Act.

Gruman, Gerald J. "An Historical Introduction to Ideas About Voluntary Euthanasia: With a Bibliographical Survey and Guides for Interdisciplinary Studies." *Omega* 4 (1973): 87–138. A thorough, scholarly examination of the duty to prolong life. Includes rich bibliographical suggestions.

Harvard Medical School, Ad Hoc Committee of the Harvard Medical School to Examine the Definition of Brain Death. "A Definition of Irreversible Coma." *Journal of the American Medical Association* 205 (1968): 337–40. The definitive article outlining a set of empirical measures found to correlate with irreversible coma. The article does not take on the philosophical argument that people in irreversible coma ought to be considered dead, but presumes they ought to be.

Heymann, Philip B., and Sara Holtz. "The Severely Defective Newborn: The Dilemma and the Decision Process." *Public Policy* 23 (1975): 381–418. A carefully reasoned review of current legal status of decisions not to treat severely afflicted newborns together with an examination of a possible legal basis for justifying such decisions.

Institute of Society, Ethics and the Life Sciences, Task Force on Death and Dying. "Refinements in Criteria for the Determination of Death." *Journal of the American Medical Association* 221 (1972): 48–53. The Task Force establishes a set of principles by which to judge criteria for determining that death has occurred. They caution that criteria for the determination of death neither solve the problem of defining death, nor do they solve many of the other issues which death and dying pose.

Kelly, W. D., and S. R. Friesen. "Do Cancer Patients Want to be Told?" *Surgery* 27 (1950): 822–6. A study revealing that patients, in general, report they prefer to be told the truth about their diagnoses.

Oken, Donald. "What to Tell Cancer Patients." *Journal of the American Medical Association* 175 (1961): 1120–28. A dated, but provocative study of medical attitudes about truth-telling, indicating a preference among physicians for not telling: a valuable contrast to the data about patients' views on the same question. (see Kelly and Friesen).

Sigeler, Mark. "Pascal's Wager and the Hanging of Crepe." *New England Journal of Medicine* 293 (1975): 853–57. Author discusses the form of physician-to-family communication in which the bleakest, most pessimistic prediction of a critically ill patient's outcome is made in order to lessen the family's suffering if the patient dies. He describes advantages and disadvantages, offering an alternative strategy whereby the physician attempts to predict accurately the outcome of the disease. An interesting contrast to the stereotype that physicians tend not to disclose bad news.

Society for the Right to Die, Inc., *Legislative Manual, 1977.* 250 W. 57th St., New York. This year's volume covers the major legislative events of 1977 with respect to Right to Die legislation, and includes the text and analysis of the eight bills that have passed.

University Publications of America, *In the Matter*

of Karen Quinlan. vol. 2. Arlington, Va.: University Publications of America, 1976. A published collection of all the court records for the Supreme Court review of the Quinlan decision. The court opinion itself is much more brief and is available in the published court record.

Veatch, Robert M. *Death, Dying, and the Biological Revolution.* New Haven: Yale University Press, 1976. A critical appraisal of the medical, ethical, and legal issues arising from the relationship between the public policy commitment to use all available technology to extend life, and patients' rights and responsibilities to make decisions about their own dying. Veatch considers possible definitions of death, whether to keep the terminally ill alive, what to tell dying patients, and whether efforts to extend the life span ought to be pursued. Contains full bibliography.

Veatch, Robert M. "The Whole-Brain-Oriented Concept of Death: An Outmoded Philosophical Formulation." *Journal of Thanatology* 3 (1975): 13–30. Attempts to push the definition of death debate beyond the general conflict between heart and brain-oriented definitions. Asks what parts of the brain must be destroyed before the person as a whole should be considered dead.

Veith, Frank J. and others. "Brain Death:" part 1, "A Status Report of Medical and Ethical Considerations," and part 2, "A Status Report of Legal Considerations." *Journal of the American Medical Association* 238 (1977): 1651–55 and 1744–48. The first part of this two-part series tries to mediate the brain death dilemma by summarizing the scientific evidence acknowledging the certainty of determining the destruction of the brain, arguing that total destruction of the brain is a legitimate determinant of death and is in accord with secular philosophy and major Western religions. Part two argues for the need for statutory recognition of brain death, reviews the present status of laws relating to the determination of death in the United States, and examines model laws.

13.
Suicide

Alvarez, A. *The Savage God: A Study of Suicide.* New York: Random House, 1972. A beautifully written book by an English critic and poet who himself made a serious suicide attempt. The prologue relates Alvarez' relationship with poet Sylvia Plath; the bulk of the book is an artist's view of the fallacies, theories, and feelings of the suicidal state. More than a survey, it is a critic's attempt to relate various styles of literature to suicide.

Choron, Jacques. *Suicide.* New York: Scribners, 1972. Choron's book is easy to read; one might say that it is written in a charming style. There are many references to philosophers, historical figures, and literary people. There are also chapters on rational suicide and the meaning of life. A comprehensive book, extremely interesting and clearly worthwhile.

Dublin, Louis I. *Suicide: A Sociological and Statistical Study.* New York: Ronald Press, 1963. Louis Dublin was chief statistician of the Metropolitan Life Insurance Company; his book on suicide became a standard reference work for statisticians. Its closing section entitled "Toward the Conquest of Suicide" pointed the way to the establishment of suicide prevention centers.

Durkheim, Emile. *Suicide.* Glencoe, Ill.: Free Press, 1951. Durkheim's book was first published in 1897 (*Le Suicide*). A sociological classic on the topic of suicide that has no rival. Using the statistics on suicide in various countries in western Europe, Durkheim demonstrated the effectiveness of the sociological and statistical approach in understanding enigmatic social problems. From his analysis of the statistical data, Durkheim posited essentially three kinds of suicide: egoistic, altruistic, and anomic. Durkheim explained suicide in sociological terms so brilliantly that practically all subsequent sociological discussions of suicide have been variations on his original theme.

Farberow, Norman L. *Bibliography on Suicide and Suicide Prevention: 1897–1967.* Washington, D.C.: U.S. Government Printing Office, 1969. (PHS Publication No. 1979). Farberow's bibliography on suicide is an indispensable reference. He reproduces and supplements the almost 3800 items which appeared in a bibliography by R. Rost from 1897 to 1927 and continues with a bibliography from 1928 to 1967. Farberow's bibliography lists both American and foreign references.

Friedman, Paul, ed. *On Suicide*. New York: International Universities Press, 1967. Essentially an edited translation of the proceedings of the Psychoanalytic Society's 1910 symposium on suicide in Vienna. Participants included Sigmund Freud, Alfred Adler, and Wilhelm Stekel. At this symposium, Stekel said: "No one kills himself who has not wanted to kill another, or at least wished the death of another."— for many years, the standard psychoanalytic position on suicide.

Menninger, Karl A. *Man against Himself*. New York: Harcourt, Brace, 1957. In a comprehensible, fluid style, America's best-known living psychiatrist interprets complex psychoanalytic theory for the layman in this widely-read book. Two main ideas dominate the book: first, that there are three components to any suicidal act: the wish to kill; the wish to be killed; and the wish to die; second, the idea that man's behavior against himself includes many behaviors in addition to overt suicide. For Menninger, "chronic suicide" includes asceticism, martyrdom, neurotic invalidism, alcohol addiction, antisocial behavior, and psychosis. "Focal suicide" includes mutilation, malingering, poly-surgery, purposeful accidents, impotence, and frigidity. A "must" for anyone attempting to understand suicide.

Shneidman, Edwin S., ed. *Essays in Self-Destruction*. New York: Science House, 1967. This volume consists of essays by fellows or guests at the Los Angeles Suicide Prevention Center. Shneidman includes philosophical essays by Henry Murray, Jacques Choron, Steven Pepper; sociological essays by Talcott Parsons, Harold Garfinckel, Louis Dublin; psychological essays by Avery Weisman, Robert Litman, Norman Farberow, Paul Friedman; and speculative essays by Lawrence Kubie and Theodore Curphey. The book deals with self-destruction rather than just suicide.

Shneidman, Edwin S., Norman L. Farberow, and Robert E. Litman. *The Psychology of Suicide*. New York: Science House, 1970. This substantial volume represents the writing of the three principal investigators of the Los Angeles Suicide Prevention Center over an eleven year period, 1955–1966. It covers theories and taxonomy, administration and organization, diagnosis and evaluation, therapy and treatment, and forensic and professional issues. An especially outstanding contribution is Litman's "Sigmund Freud on Suicide."

Shneidman, Edwin S., ed. *Suicidology: Contemporary Developments*. New York: Grune and Stratton, 1976. This recent volume gives a comprehensive over-view of suicidology: demography, methodologial developments, logical and cognitive aspects, clinical correlates, philosophic and legal aspects, and responses to suicide.

Stengel, Erwin. *Suicide and Attempted Suicide*. Baltimore: Penguin Books, 1964. Stengel's brief book is the classic work on the overlap between committed suicide and attempted suicide. Treating statistics, motives, causes, underlying psychodynamics, and the prevention of suicide, it is the best inexpensive book on suicide.

World Health Organization. *Prevention of Suicide*. Geneva: WHO, 1968. Available from the Columbia University Press, this pamphlet provides international data on suicide prevention service, methods of committing suicide, percentages of repeat attempts, previous psychiatric contacts, mental disorders and alcoholism among suicides, and death rates from suicide for twenty-one countries, 1952–54 and 1961–63.

14.
Death, War, and the Human Condition

Becker, Ernest. *The Denial of Death*. Glencoe: Free Press, 1973. Becker outlines the pervasive attempts by twentieth century man to ward off the terrifying knowledge of death. Recent history and psychological themes in art and literature are shown to be related to this flight from the confrontation with death.

Hachiya, Michihiko. *Hiroshima Diary*. Chapel Hill: University of North Carolina Press, 1955. A first person account of the bombing of Hiroshima by a history professor who survived it.

Lifton, Robert Jay. *Death in Life*. New York: Simon and Schuster, 1967. The definitive study of the psychological experience of the survivors of the bombings of Nagasaki and Hiroshima. The book provides detailed, vivid reports of personal interviews with survivors and carefully explores the psychological meaning of being a survivor of holocaust.

Lifton, Robert J. *The Life of the Self*. New York: Simon and Schuster, 1976. This book traces a sequence of change from Freud's instinctual model of mental function to one which stresses the significance of images of death and life and their effect upon the individual's growth and behavior. The *Life of the Self* approaches our confrontation with death and death imagery as the means by which we liberate ourselves and transform our lives.

Lifton, Robert Jay. *Boundaries*. New York: Random House, 1967. These five lectures explore many of the complexities around destruction, death, revolution, and man's changing perceptions of himself in relationship to the massive historical, social, and cultural changes of the twentieth century. Lifton outlines the shifting boundaries between self and other, between past and present in a world totally transformed by the requirement to come to terms with death in new and untried ways.

15.
The Death System:
Review and Prospectus

Death Education 2 (1978): nos. 1 and 2. Washington, D.C.: Hemisphere Publishing Corporation. This special issue presents reports from six hospice-type services in the United States and Canada as well as commentaries and observations on such topics as the ethics of terminal care and the legal dimensions of "death with dignity." It is a convenient and up-to-date source for those who want to know what is happening, from the people who are directly involved, in our first generation of hospices.

Feifel, Herman, ed. *New Meanings of Death*. New York: McGraw-Hill, 1977. The original essays in this volume are far ranging and offer new information and insight—a worthy follow-up to Feifel's earlier groundbreaking collection, *The Meaning of Death* (McGraw-Hill, 1959). Major sections are devoted to developmental orientation toward death, clinical management, and the survivors.

Garfield, Charles A., ed. *Psycho-Social Care of the Dying Patient*. New York: McGraw-Hill, 1978. These essays were written by many of the pioneering and influential individuals concerned with death and with the improved care of the dying patient. Although intended chiefly for physicians, the contributions will be of interest to anyone who shares this concern. Sections are devoted to guidelines, terminal patient care, patients and families facing life-threating illness, doctor-patient relationships, psychological needs, counseling the patient's family, and recent developments in the care of the dying patient.

Kastenbaum, Robert. *Death, Society, and Human Experience*. St. Louis: C. V. Mosby Co., 1977. This relatively small book presents an encompassing and up-to-date view of our society's "death system" and its relationship to the individual. We see how social and political forces influence life and death, but we also learn of the most recent clinical and research developments, including the author's own continuing studies. It has become a popular death education book because it does not read like one.

Kastenbaum, Robert and Bruce B. Aisenberg. *The Psychology of Death*. rev. ed. New York: Springer Publishing Company, 1976. When this book first appeared (1972), it provided the first integrated view of death-related phenomena from the psychological standpoint. The concise 1976 edition is slightly updated and has shed some material that is no longer as relevant. Although a completely revised edition is needed because of subsequent developments in the field, this remains a foundation volume for those with serious education and research interests related to death.

Stannard, David, ed. *Death in America*. Philadelphia: University of Pennsylvania Press, 1975. A collection of essays that add a valuable historical dimension to our understanding of death in our own time. Contributions include "Death and the Puritan Child," "Death in the Popular Mind of Pre-Civil War America," and "The Cemetary as Cultural Institution." Recommended for those who are curious about where some of our current ideas and practices have come from.

Stoddard, Sandol. *The Hospice Movement*. Briarcliff Manor, N.Y.: Stein and Day, 1978. This is the best general introduction to the hospice movement. It answers many of the most common questions about what a hospice is and does. Information is conveyed in appropriate context, so the reader is able to understand the emotional climate in which hospices have developed and the needs they are intended to serve. It is a warm, involved, informed, and well-written book. One would have to look elsewhere, however, for a critical examination of problems that could affect the eventual success or failure of the hospice movement.

Veatch, Robert M. *Death, Dying, and the Biological Revolution*. New Haven: Yale University Press, 1976. Here is a clear and much needed guide to the increasingly complex legal and ethical issues that surround dying and death today. The author knows his topic very well and communicates admirably. The book is additionally valuable for its willingness to take positions on certain issues instead of assuming a neutral stance. So much is happening in this area that even a good recent book does not stay completely up to date, but this is one of the better places to begin one's inquiry.

NOTES ABOUT THE AUTHORS

Stewart Alsop was a magazine columnist for *Newsweek* from 1968 until his death in 1974, and worked for the *Saturday Evening Post* as national affairs contributing editor and then Washington editor, from 1958 to 1968. He wrote *The Center* and *Stay of Execution,* as well as collaborating with his brother, Joseph Alsop, on *We Accuse* and *The Reporter's Trade: Nixon and Rockefeller.*

Philippe Ariès, French historian, is the author of *Western Attitudes toward Death* and *Centuries of Childhood,* and contributor to *Death in America.*

Michael J. Arlen was born in England and has been a reporter for *Life* and a contributor and TV critic for *The New Yorker.* He received the award for television criticism from the Screen Directors Guild in 1968 and the National Book Award for contemporary affairs and Le Prix Bremond in 1976. He is the author of *Living-Room War, Exiles, An American Verdict, Passage to Ararat,* and *The View from Highway 1.*

Robert Blauner is professor of sociology at the University of California, Berkeley, California, and author of *Alienation and Freedom: The Factory Worker and His Industry.*

Lynn Caine is an editor for a New York publishing house and author of the best selling book *Widow.*

Paul Cameron is associate professor of human development at St. Mary's College of Maryland.

Eric Cassell is a physician, clinical professor of public health at Cornell University Medical College, fellow at the Hastings Center, Institute for Society, Ethics, and the Life Sciences, and author of *The Healer's Art.*

Ronald Jay Cohen is senior psychologist at the Department of Psychiatry, New York University, Bellevue Medical Center.

H. Tristram Engelhardt, Jr. is professor of philosophy of medicine at the Kennedy Center for Bioethics, Georgetown University, Washington, D.C.

Bernard T. Feld is professor of physics at the Massachusetts Institute of Technology and editor-in-chief of *The Bulletin of the Atomic Scientist.*

Stanley French is associate professor of American History at California State University at Northridge, and a specialist in American intellectual and social history of the nineteenth century.

Julie Fulton is a Ph.D. candidate at the University of Minnesota and co-author with Robert Fulton of *"A Psychosocial Aspect of Terminal Care: Anticipatory Grief."*

Robert Fulton is professor of sociology and director of the Center for Death Education and Research at the University of Minnesota, editor of *Death and Identity,* and academic coordinator of the tenth Course by Newspaper, "Death and Dying: Challenge and Change."

Willard Gaylin is a psychiatrist and president of the Institute of Society, Ethics, and the Life Sciences in Hastings-on-Hudson, New York. He is the author of *Partial Justice: A Study of Bias in Sentencing.*

Calvin Goldscheider is professor of sociology at the Hebrew University in Jerusalem and the author of *Population, Modernization, and Social Structure.*

Geoffrey Gorer is the British author of *The American People, Africa Dances, Sex and Marriage in England Today,* and *Death, Grief, and Mourning,* among other books.

Earl Grollman is rabbi of Beth El Temple Center in Belmont, Massachusetts, and editor of *Explaining Death to Children.*

Stanislav Grof is affiliated with the Maryland Psychiatric Research Center. He was formerly head of the Psychiatric Research Institute in Prague, Czechoslovakia, and is a prime researcher on psychedelic therapy with dying patients. He is co-author of *The Human Encounter with Death.*

Elizabeth Hall is managing editor of *Psychology Today* and author of *From Pigeons to People: A Look at Behavior Modification.*

Ruth Mulvey Harmer is on the faculty of the English department at California State Polytechnical College near Los Angeles and is author of *The High Cost of Dying.*

Rosalind Heywood is a member of the Council of the Society for Psychical Research, author of *The Sixth Sense* and *The Infinite Hive,* and contributor to *Science and E.S.P.*

Ivan Illich served as assistant pastor in an Irish-Puerto Rican parish in New York City in 1951 and as vice-rector of the Catholic University of Puerto Rico from 1956 to 1960. He is co-founder of the Center for Intercultural Documentation in Cuernavaca, Mexico, and since 1964 has directed research seminars on "Institutional Alternatives in a Technological Society," focusing especially on Latin America. He is the author of *Celebration of Awareness, Deschooling Society, Tools for Conviviality,* and *Energy and Equity,* and has contributed articles to *The New York Times, The New York Review of Books, The Saturday Review, Commonweal,* and *Le Monde.*

Edgar Jackson is a theologian and crisis psychologist and the author of many books including *You and Your Grief.*

Robert Kastenbaum is superintendent of Cushing Hospital in Boston, and is author of *Death, Society, and Human Experience,* and, with Bruce B. Aisenberg, *The Psychology of Death.*

Elisabeth Kübler-Ross is a physician and an international consultant on the care of dying patients and their families. She is the author of *On Death and Dying* as well as numerous journal articles.

Ignace Lepp was a French priest-psychotherapist as well as journalist and professor, and the author of more than 25 books, including *Atheism in Our Time, The Faith of Men,* and *Death and Its Mysteries.* He died in 1966.

Monroe Lerner is professor of medical care at Johns Hopkins University, co-author of *Health Progress in the United States, 1900–1960,* and a noted authority on life expectancy and population trends.

Robert Jay Lifton is professor of psychiatry at Yale University, and author of *Living and Dying* and *Death in Life.*

Erich Lindemann was professor emeritus of psychiatry at Harvard University and visiting professor of psychiatry at the Stanford Medical Center in Palo Alto, California, until his death in 1974.

Jane Finkbiner Looney is a registered nurse and a clinical specialist with the hospice project at St. Luke's Hospital Center in New York City.

Helena Lopata is professor of sociology at Loyola University in Chicago, and author of *Widowhood in an American City.*

Melvin Maddocks is a journalist who has contributed to *The Christian Science Monitor, Time, The Atlantic,* and *Encounter.*

Daniel Maguire is professor of theology at Marquette University in Milwaukee, Wisconsin, and the author of *Death by Choice.*

Eric Markusen is a research and clinical associate at the Center for Death Education at the University of Minnesota and intake director of the Wolf Lake Refuge Program for Delinquent Youths.

Raymond Moody is a physician and author of *Life after Life.*

Hans J. Morgenthau is the director of the Center for the Study of American Foreign Policy at the University of Chicago and author of *The H-Bomb.*

Roberta Lyder Paige is a registered nurse and clinical specialist with the hospice project at St. Luke's Hospital Center in New York City.

Colin Murray Parkes is professor of psychiatry at The London Hospital Medical College, University of London, and author of *Bereavement.*

Vanderlyn Pine is professor of sociology at the State University of New York at New Paltz, and author of *Caretaker of the Dead.*

Alex D. Pokorny is clinical professor of psychiatry at Baylor University College of Medicine, and is on the staff of the Psychiatry and Neurology Service at Veterans Administration Hospital,

Houston. His research interest focuses on suicide, violence, and chemical addiction.

Thomas Powers, a former reporter for United Press International and winner of the Pulitzer Prize for national reporting in 1971, has written *Diana: The Making of a Terrorist* and *The War at Home: Vietnam and the American People.*

Howard C. Raether is executive director of the National Funeral Directors Association, a member of the National Council on Tissue Transplantation and Utilization, and author of *Organ and Tissue Transplantation and Body Donation.*

Diane M. Ross was an intern at the Office of Long Term Care, Public Health Service, Rockville, Maryland, and is working toward her master of public health degree at the University of California, Los Angeles.

Sonya Rudikoff is a frequent contributor to *Commentary* magazine and author of "Marriage and Household."

Bertrand Russell, the British philosopher, mathematician, historian, political and social scientist, and man of letters, was the author of over forty books, including *History of Western Philosophy, The Principles of Mathematics, Marriage and Morals, Conquest of Happiness,* and *Why I Am Not a Christian.* He received the Nobel Prize for Literature in 1950 and died in 1970 at the age of 97.

Claire F. Ryder is director of the Division of Policy Development, Office of Long Term Care, Public Health Service, Rockville, Maryland.

Cicely Saunders is the founder and director of St. Christopher's Hospice in London, and author of numerous articles on patient care.

Dean Schuyler is director of Continuing Education in Psychiatry at Georgetown University in Washington, D.C.

Edwin Shneidman is professor of thanatology, University of California, Los Angeles, and author of *Deaths of Man.*

Roberta Simmons is associate professor of sociology at the University of Minnesota and co-author of *The Gift of Life: The Social and Psychological Impact of Organ Transplantation.*

David E. Stannard is on the American Studies and History faculties of Yale University. He is the author of *Death in America* and *The Puritan Way of Death.*

Arnold Toynbee, the British historian, authored dozens of books, including his twelve volume masterpiece, *A Study of History,* and *Man's Concern with Death.* He was director of studies at the Royal Institute of International Affairs, London, from 1924 to 1956; a member of the British delegation to the Paris Peace Conferneces in 1919 and 1946; and professor emeritus of international history at the University of London from 1955 until his death in 1975.

Samuel Vaisrub is senior editor of the *Journal of the American Medical Association.*

Robert M. Veatch is a physician; an associate for medical ethics at the Hastings Center, Institute of Society, Ethics, and the Life Sciences; and author of *Case Studies in Medical Ethics.*

Alexander Walker is a British film critic and author of *The Celluloid Sacrifice; Doubletakes; Hollywood, England; Rudolph Valentino; Stanley Kubrick Directs;* and *Stardom.*

Avery Weisman is professor of psychiatry at Massachusetts General Hospital and Harvard Medical School; the author of several books including *On Dying and Denying: A Psychiatric Study in Terminality;* and principal investigator for Project Omega, a research group studying coping and vulnerability in cancer patients.

Lael Wertenbaker was a war correspondent for *Time* magazine during World War II, and is the author of *Lament for Four Virgins, The Eyes of the Lion, The Afternoon Women,* and *Death of a Man,* among other books. Her husband, Charles, was associate editor and foreign correspondent to *Time* and associate editor of *Fortune* during the 1930s, and was the author of several books, including *A New Doctrine for the Americas.* He died on January 8, 1955.

Robert B. White is professor of psychiatry at the University of Texas Medical Branch at Galveston.

Death and Dying
Challenge and Change

Greg Owen

Courses by Newspaper
A project of University Extension
University of California, San Diego
funded by The National Endowment for the Humanities

Addison-Wesley Publishing Company
Reading, Massachusetts • Menlo Park, California
London • Amsterdam • Don Mills, Ontario • Sydney

Courses by Newspaper
Death and Dying: Challenge and Change

Copyright © 1978 by the Regents
of the University of California.
All rights reserved.
Printed in the United States of America.

Library of Congress Catalog Card No. 78-59488

Addison-Wesley Publishing Company
Reading, Massachusetts 01867

ISBN 0-201-07725-6
ABCDEFGHIJK-AL-798

Study Guide / Contents

This study guide has but one purpose: to assist both the general reader of, and the student enrolled for credit in, the Course by Newspaper entitled "Death and Dying: Challenge and Change."

The materials for this Course by Newspaper consist of a series of fifteen newspaper *articles* that may be thought of as "lectures" by a distinguished faculty; a *Reader* of articles and poems that supplement the newspaper articles; and this *study guide,* which is intended to integrate and highlight the themes of the newspaper and Reader articles.

The study guide is organized into four major parts to correspond to the four major topics of the course: (1) Changing Meanings of Death and Dying, (2) The Experience of Death, (3) Survivors of Death, and (4) Dilemmas of Death. These parts, in turn, are divided into sections that correspond to the weekly newspaper articles and the supplemental readings that accompany them.

Each section of the study guide begins with a brief discussion of major points (highlights) raised in the newspaper article and the accompanying Reader articles. This essay is followed by a short explanation of key concepts that will provide quick reference to words and expressions that may be difficult or unfamiliar to the reader. Key concepts will further emphasize some of the most important ideas. Following this we have included a few factual review questions and essay and discussion questions to provide a ready check on important points and to stimulate further thought about the topics.

Although each student will discover for himself/herself how best to use the course materials, we suggest the following approach:

1. Read the newspaper article each week; clip it and carefully save it for future review.
2. Glance over the highlights and the key concepts in the corresponding section of the study guide. These will call attention to some of the more important points in the readings, and will help you to read more critically and with a better understanding.
3. Read the appropriate selections in the Reader.
4. Reread the key concepts and highlights more thoroughly, considering the issues raised. (You may wish to reread the articles as well.)
5. Check your comprehension of key points in the articles by answering the factual review questions. If necessary, go back to the appropriate articles to check your answers.
6. Proceed to the essay and discussion questions. While there is no single "correct answer," there are a number of issues to be considered before reaching a conclusion on any question, and we have provided some suggested guidelines.
7. Turn to the bibliographies in the Reader for suggestions of further reading on topics of interest.

Throughout the study guide we have sought to avoid definitive conclusions and dogmatic interpretations. Instead, we have endeavored to stimulate more questions than we have answered. The measure of good teaching, after all, whether by newspaper or otherwise, is the extent to which each student continues to think independently and critically once the teaching *per se* has been concluded.

The text of the study guide was written by Greg Owen, with the assistance of Jane L. Scheiber, Robert Fulton, and Eric Markusen.

We gratefully acknowledge the support of the National Endowment for the Humanities, which provided the funding for this project. The views presented in this study guide are those of the author only, however, and do not necessarily reflect the views of the Endowment or of the University of California.

Study Guide/Course Outline

PART ONE
Changing Meanings of Death and Dying

1. Death and Dying: The Issues Today   *Robert Fulton*
2. Historical Perspectives on Death   *David E. Stannard*
3. Death in Popular Culture   *Robert Fulton* and *Eric Markusen*
4. Demography of Death   *Monroe Lerner*
5. Death and Social Change   *Eric Cassell*
6. Life after Death: Old and New Meanings   *Edgar Jackson*

PART TWO
The Experience of Death

7. The Dying Patient   *Avery D. Weisman*
8. Death and the Child   *George Williams*

PART THREE
Survivors of Death

9. Grief   *Colin Murray Parkes*
10. Widowhood   *Helena Lopata*
11. The Funeral   *Vanderlyn Pine*

PART FOUR
Dilemmas of Death

12. Morality and Mortality in Modern Society   *Robert M. Veatch*
13. Suicide   *Edwin S. Shneidman*
14. Death, War, and the Human Condition   *Robert Jay Lifton*
15. The Death System: Review and Prospectus   *Robert Kastenbaum*

Changing Meanings of Death and Dying

Learning Objectives
   TO UNDERSTAND the nature and extent of current interest in the topic of death and dying.

the way in which the event of death has been experienced previously in our history.

the significance of the modern mass media in shaping our views of death.

the changes that have occurred in our experience with death as a result of population shifts and disease control.

the effect of technological advances on the way in which we define death and care for the dying.

the history and significance of beliefs in life after death and the current investigations into their validity.

Newspaper Articles
   AND READER SELECTIONS

our deaths. It is this theme, played in multi-variations, that runs through the readings in Part One. If the meaning of death and dying has changed in the twentieth century—and it is the overwhelming opinion of these authors that it has—it is necessary to examine the changes in our social and physical worlds that have given rise to this fact.

In the first six newspaper articles and the selected readings that accompany them, we are invited to explore these changes and investigate their consequences. Has the medical control over death sanitized our emotions and removed not only the sting of death but the solace of others as well? Is death the last "pornographic frontier"? Must our children be educated in a special way so that thoughts of death and finitude are painless when they appear in life's experience? Is modern death unfair, striking some groups more than others? Do we survive death, and is it possible to be more certain of the answer to this question now than it was in the previous sixty thousand years of human existence?

The one unalterable fact about death is this: in the end it claims every living thing. In the face of such a fact all others pale except one—the continuity of life itself. But the continuity of life on our planet is established and proved only for the past. In the opinion of some authors in later sections of this course, the future casts dark shadows.

INTRODUCTION

As the context of human existence is reorganized and transformed by science, technology, and modern belief systems, so, too, must the context of our dying be altered. It is not possible to live in a world of highly refined medical technology and instant global communication without being subject to the circumstances they create for our lives—and for

1.
Death and Dying: The Issues Today

HIGHLIGHTS

This section examines the many changes in modern life that are thought to affect our attitudes toward death and our perceptions of it. In the newspaper article by Robert Fulton and his Reader article "On the Dying of Death," the author notes that modern medicine has brought about a shift, both in the likely causes of death as well as in its expected timing. Fast-acting infectious diseases have been replaced by chronic and degenerative ailments. These strike less at random and tend to concentrate in the older age groups. Increased life expectancy makes modern death "increasingly an experience of the aged."

Other shifts are noted as well. Our society has moved from a predominantly rural, agricultural base to an urban, industrial base. In the process, much of the naturalness of death is left behind. We are no longer exposed to the death of animals and the aging and dying of locally residing kin. The organization of our family life around the nuclear family—a couple and their children—and geographical separation of family members once the children are grown, also serve to change our response to death both by insulating children from its occurrence and by removing the emotional support of previously close kin.

Even our definition of death has been transformed with the advent of organ transplantation and the legalization of abortion. Our grief, moreover, is no longer represented in traditional mourning customs and our beliefs no longer center on a world beyond death. Later articles in other sections will elaborate on these themes.

Melvin Maddocks; article examines the metamorphosis of American attitudes toward death as they have shifted from avoidance and distaste to a point bordering on preoccupation. In citing the growth of death courses, death specialists, and death politics, he points out that the present view of death is quite pragmatic; we must "do something about it!" Moreover, death has been reevaluated,

according to Maddocks, and our past fear and loathing has been replaced by a willingness to embrace the beautiful death—a death with "gusto."

Shneidman's discussion of the *Psychology Today* survey demonstrates the heightened interest in problems associated with death. While we are warned the sample used in this survey is in no way representative of the general population, the survey is interesting, nonetheless, in the attitudes it reveals among youthful readers: their inexperience with death, their general skepticism about an afterlife, their primarily secular orientation, and their dislike of traditional funerary ceremonies.

The final two articles by Vaisrub and Cohen debate the significance and utility of the current growth in death literature. Whereas Vaisrub concludes that there is little more to be said, Cohen finds this modern genre of death literature to be both educational and beneficial. The reader is left to arrive at his or her own position.

Overall these articles point to rapid changes in the nature of death and the way in which it is experienced in our culture.

KEY CONCEPTS

Denial of death. As used in this section, this term refers to the tendency in modern Western society, at least until the last few years, to avoid direct confrontation with the idea of our own mortality. Death is treated as a "taboo" subject and we try to shield ourselves from its reality. Increasing secularism and the fact that death today occurs mainly among our elderly, who die in institutions rather than in the home, are major factors contributing to this attitude.

Nuclear family system. A unit of family organization consisting of a couple and their children. This is the typical organization of modern urban families, and its central position has affected our attitudes toward the aging and toward death.

Extended family system. A family unit that consists of a nuclear family plus one or more relatives (e.g., grandparents, niece, cousin) living together. This organization, with some modifications, typified much of early rural life in America.

Mortality rate. The number of deaths per 1,000 persons in the population in any given year. In 1900 the mortality rate was 17.2. In 1977 the mortality rate was 8.7. Modern disease control has accounted for much of this change.

Existential world view. A philosophical point of view that each person exists as an individual in a purposeless universe, one in which good and evil are relative to time and circumstance.

Secularism. A system of doctrines or practices that rejects the validity and meaning of religious faith and worship. This has become a prevalant mode of thought in contemporary life. Doctrines of immortality also decline in secular societies.

Memorial society. A group advocating the simplification of funerary practices and the elimination of the deceased's body from any service of memorialization. (See Key Concepts in Section 11.)

Euthanasia. Literally, a good death, one that is easy, painless and devoid of prolonged suffering. (See Key Concepts in Section 12 for extended discussion.)

FACTUAL REVIEW

1. According to Fulton, what has been our basic attitude toward death until the last few years?
2. Within what framework were questions related to death traditionally answered in Western society? What outlook has changed this traditional orientation?
3. Approximately how many persons die each year in the United States, and what percentage of these die in institutions? (See newspaper article by Fulton.)
4. What is the total number of persons in the United States now over the age of sixty-five?
5. According to Fulton, what has been the impact of the nuclear family on our attitudes toward the elderly and toward death?
6. According to Fulton, what percentage of these persons who died in the United States in 1976 were children under the age of fifteen?
7. Who said "we owe God a death," and what did he mean?
8. What are the indicators of humanhood suggested by Joseph Fletcher? (Cited in Maddocks, "Life and Death in the USA.")
9. How does Maddocks distinguish between the death pragmatist, the death optimist, and the death existentialist?
10. What three scenarios does Maddocks describe?
11. According to Shneidman's survey, what event most influenced people's attitudes toward death?
12. At what age were respondents in the Shneidman survey most afraid of death?
13. What does Samuel Vaisrub suggest is responsible for the current growth of essays, editorials, etc., on death?
14. Vaisrub says that fear of death is not confined to the dying. When (why) else does he say people have a feeling of death hanging over their shoulders?
15. How many "approaches" to the subject of death does Cohen distinguish?
16. Does Cohen believe that dying is being "worked to death?" Why?

ESSAY AND DISCUSSION

Discuss the way in which death and dying has changed from a taboo topic to a virtual preoccupation in our culture.

Suggested guidelines: A. Consider Fulton's discussion of the denial of death in his newspaper article.

B. Consider the significance of changes in the age and place of death. What does Fulton say about the effect of these changes?

C. Review Maddocks' discussion of the rise in death literature and death courses.

D. Consider Vaisrub's mention of the fear of death. What does this have to do with the threat of nuclear weaponry described by Fulton?

E. How does Cohen react to Vaisrub's conclusions?

2.
Historical Perspectives on Death

HIGHLIGHTS
In David Stannard's newspaper article on "Death in American History" and the Reader articles in Section 2, we are introduced to the experience of, and response to, death in America's past. Most significantly, we learn that death in early America was a familiar event—familiar not only to the older person, but to persons of all ages. Death was much more unpredictable then than today, and thus it was closely tied to "the natural order of things." In early pioneer society, for example, burial laws were sometimes required to insure the proper disposal of bodies. Funeral ceremonies, when utilized, were simple affairs and graves were seldom permanently marked. In contrast to this, the Puritans made much of death. Their community life was of great importance and the death of a family member occasioned much activity and ceremony. It is to these circumstances that Stannard applies the idea of "social loss." Stannard points out that the nineteenth and twentieth centuries did much to alter the connectedness of an individual to his or her community. Specializa-tion and compartmentalization served not only to isolate tasks, but personalities as well. The sense of community that prevailed in early America was lost to the twentieth century bureaucrat and specialist and death was handed over to the professsional.

Ideas about life after death were also transformed during this time. No longer was death romantically embraced as a heavenly and sacred garden. Instead, these nineteenth-century beliefs gave way to a sense of distrust in anything eternal. Earthly gratifications became paramount and thoughts of death were avoided. The twentieth century made death an "illogical, meaningless affront."

The Reader article on "The Puritan Way of Death" provides us with additional historical data, particularly as they pertain to the socialization of children. The Puritan child was constantly reminded of the nearness of death as well as its often terrible consequences. For the Romantics and Victorians, however, death could be beautiful and the child of this era was instructed accordingly. Even the Victorian cemetery, as Stanley French describes it, was a place of pastoral retreat were mourners could be comforted and instructed.

Philippe Ariès, in his article on "The Reversal of Death," addresses the twentieth-century taboo on death: the taboo that prevents us from mastering our own death or even speaking of it. Ariès describes the death bed scene typical of seventeenth- and eighteenth-century Europe in which the dying person is seen to preside over his own public death. Even strangers were sometimes found here, acting out of a sense of custom and piety and providing the dying person with an audience for his parting words. The modern hospital scene is in sharp contrast to this, according to Ariès, for it is here that concealment of information about impending death is a primary objective. Death has become secret and banal while dignity has taken on a new and stylized form—discretion.

These articles, taken together, provide a vivid portrayal of the changes already effected in American attitudes toward death.

KEY CONCEPTS

Social loss. The sense of grief and tragedy that is experienced by a tightly-knit community when one of its members dies. Individuals in such societies have important and irreplaceable functions, and their death causes community-wide grief.

Romanticism. The Romantic period in art and literature, which began in the late eighteenth century, was characterized by an emphasis on feelings, imagery, and sympathy. Art during this period broke away from formal traditions and emphasized creative expression. Death in this tradition was a transition to a heavenly state. Death could be celebrated and the dying could expect great joy in the world to come, where they would be reunited with loved ones.

Rural cemetery movement. A movement that began in the 1930s to establish garden-like cemeteries that were, in the Romantic tradition, regarded as perpetual, peaceful homes for the community's dead. This movement marked a shift in attitude toward graveyards, which had earlier been regarded as necessary evils.

Pastoralism. This tradition romanticized and idealized rural life. It celebrated its peaceful, simple, and natural beauties. The rural cemetery movement was one expression of pastoralism. The markers in pastoral cemeteries indicated an acceptance of the fate of death and often encouraged a certain light-heartedness in the survivors.

Funeral elegy. A poem of lament and praise for the dead.

FACTUAL REVIEW

1. What were the major characteristics of early pioneer society?
2. Why were laws requiring burial sometimes necessary in Colonial America?
3. How did Puritan attitudes toward death differ from those of other colonists?
4. What was the purpose of Puritan funeral laws?
5. Where is the fear of death rooted in young children?
6. What was the purpose of James Janeway's "A Token for Children," and other children's literature of the period?
7. What was the prevailing attitude toward death in the Romantic period?
8. When was the Mount Auburn cemetery opened?
9. According to French, what is the lesson of the rural cemetery?
10. What had been the standard burying grounds during the eighteenth century?
11. When did the modern sociology of death begin in the Western world?
12. What had been the relationship of the dying person to the circumstances surrounding his death prior to the "modern" period?
13. According to Ariès, what is the primary duty of the family and the doctor in caring for the person who is about to die?

ESSAY AND DISCUSSION

How has our view of death changed over the preceding four centuries?

Suggested guidelines: A. Consider David E. Stannard's description of seventeenth-century sermons.

B. What images of death are presented in the literature of the seventeenth and eighteenth centuries, poetry and school texts in particular?

C. How did these images change in the late eighteenth and early nineteenth centuries?

D. Review Stannard's Reader selection for possible social and economic causes for these changed attitudes.

E. Review French's discussion of the significance of the Mount Auburn Cemetery in Boston and the proximity of death to ordinary experience at this time.

F. What does Ariès say about the way in which Europeans of the fifteenth and sixteenth centuries were able to experience their own deaths?

G. Contrast these accounts with the discussion by Fulton in Section 1 about the institutionalization of the dying and the dead, and with Ariès's discussion of how the dying man is deprived of his own death.

3.
Death in Popular Culture

HIGHLIGHTS
How does popular culture in North America reflect our attitudes and experiences with death? Do the modern media present us with death as it touches us—or death as it titillates us?

These and other questions are raised by the authors in Section 3, and their answers are disquieting. Fulton and Markusen, in their newspaper article, argue that death as portrayed by our mass media is violent and impersonal, seldom revealing the significance or emotion connected to individual deaths in real life. Furthermore, while we attempt to avoid actual death, we find media death entertaining. The authors view this paradox with concern.

"The Air," Michael Arlen's analysis in the Reader of a week of American television viewing, documents the contention made by Fulton and Markusen. Arlen concentrates on the depiction of death and concludes that "we are a violent people—seemingly entranced by violence and have no serious regard for death." Even the news, according to Arlen, provides a sterile treatment of death with an avoidance of grief and sorrow.

In "The Case of the Vanishing Bloodstains," Alexander Walker describes the new cinematic anatomy lessons that have come to represent death in modern film. Slow motion provides the complete and gory details of death down to the last exploding fragment of flesh. He suggests that this form of cinema does not even invite our pity and may predispose us to tolerate increasing levels of violence.

In his Reader selection, Geoffrey Gorer interprets this treatment of death as pornographic. It is intended to delude us by creating a fantasy world where death has no natural meaning. He further suggests that changes in our religious beliefs are partly responsible for this shift. Without a doctrine of immortality and a belief in future life, "natural death and physical decomposition have become too horrible to contemplate or discuss." Natural death, with its processes of corruption and decay, is all but absent in our daily media fare. Instead, it is replaced by violent death, which has as its object the "complete hallucination of the reader or viewer." According to Gorer, the continuation of death pornography is insured as long as natural death is excluded from polite society.

KEY CONCEPTS
Popular culture. This is a somewhat controversial and imprecise term that refers to the culture of the people rather than of just an educated elite. As used in this section, it refers primarily to the culture that is transmitted by the mass media, particularly television and movies.

"Real" death. This term is used by Arlen and others in this section to distinguish death in real life, which is personal and fraught with meaning and emotions, from death as usually portrayed on television and in the other media, which is impersonal, meaningless, devoid of emotion, and often synonymous with violence.

Medical materialism. Vivid and explicit depiction of violent death showing detail of bodily mutilation. This is thought by some to dominate the imagery of death in contemporary films.

Pornography. The description of tabooed activities to produce hallucination or delusion. Death can be pornographically displayed when it is separated from humane emotions and ordinary circumstances for the sake of stimulation and amusement. Gorer argues that death has replaced sex as the primary topic of pornography in the twentieth century.

Subliminal. Lying below the threshold of conscious awareness. Much of death imagery is thought to take this form.

FACTUAL REVIEW

1. How does the film *The Loved One* depict the departing of the human soul after death?
2. What do Fulton and Markusen say about our emotions in the face of real death?
3. According to Fulton and Markusen, how does "media" death differ from real death?
4. Approximately what percentage of homes in America have television sets?
5. According to Arlen, what attention did Jack Benny's death receive on television?
6. According to Arlen, do Americans have a serious regard for death?
7. What cinematic technique allows death to be depicted with exceptional vividness and gore? (See Walker's article.)
8. According to Walker, where does the world's escalating violence find its most vivid expression?
9. What standard death depiction of the Victorian writers has disappeared from the modern novel? (See Gorer's article.)
10. How effective has the censorship of pornography been according to Gorer?

ESSAY AND DISCUSSION

How is death depicted in popular culture?

Suggested guidelines: A. Review Gorer's discussion of the function of pornography.
B. Consider Arlen's description of television programming. Are there other programs that depict

death differently that are not considered?
C. How does Walker describe recent cinema depictions of death? Is he ignoring the effect of other kinds of film?
D. Consider the newspaper discussion of other forms of popular culture. How significant are they in shaping our conceptions of death?
E. Drawing on your own experience, consider how children's literature portrays death. How does this compare with the treatment of death on children's television programs?

4.
Demography of Death

HIGHLIGHTS

In his newspaper article, Monroe Lerner points out that human beings in the modern world are in a unique position: They can expect, on the average, to live longer than their ancestors did at any previous time in history. Moreover, the greatest increase in life expectancy has occurred in just the past seventy-five years—hardly more than a moment in human history. These gains, however, have not been uniform for the population as a whole, Lerner notes. Mortality rates are higher for men than for women, for blacks than for whites, for urban poor than for others. Lerner also discusses the changing causes of death, with degenerative diseases replacing communicable diseases as major factors. He notes the implications of these changing demographic facts for our society, including a greater proportion of aged people and increased institutionalization of the dying.

Lerner's Reader selection, "When, Where, and Why People Die," expands on his newspaper article, comparing the United States' life expectancy to that in other countries and providing further data on mortality rates.

Robert Blauner, in his Reader selection, further discusses the consequences of removing the ill and the dying from the family setting. Not only does institutionalization of the dying remove families from exposure to death, it also increases the routinization of the handling of death while isolating the dying from the rest of society. The bureaucratization of death, according to Blauner, decreases the disruptiveness of death but at the same time increases the depersonalization of the dying patient. At a time when the average life expectancy has exceeded all expectations, it appears that our longevity may have a high price. The cost is not calculated in dollars, but in the experience of meaninglessness in the face of efficient routine.

In the final selection in this section, Calvin Goldscheider comments on the inverse relationship between social class and mortality, noted by Lerner. Citing studies in several countries, he shows that persons in the upper social classes have, on the average, a greater life expectancy than those in the lower social classes. Thus the social inequalities in life persist into death.

KEY CONCEPTS

Demography. The study of such characteristics of human population as size, growth, age, sex ratios, and vital statistics. The demography of death refers to who dies, when, where, and of what causes.

Mortality rate. See Section 1.

Life expectancy. Refers to the number of years a person of a given age and sex is expected to live, assuming mortality rates remain constant. Average life expectancy is equivalent to the average duration of life in any given society.

Neonatal mortality. Death of the newborn within the first twenty-eight days of life.

Infant mortality. Death of an infant prior to the age of one year.

Post neonatal mortality. Death of an infant after the first twenty-eight days of life but prior to one year.

Maternal mortality. Death of the mother resulting from pregnancy or childbirth complications.

Degenerative diseases. These are diseases such as heart disease, cancer, and stroke that generally occur later in life and are thought to be associated with the aging process. They have replaced the communicable diseases, such as tuberculosis and intestinal illnesses, which often struck hardest at the young, as leading causes of death in our society. Degenerative diseases often entail a prolonged dying process and expensive institutionalization of the dying person.

Social disruptiveness of death. The impact of mortality differs from one society to another. In general, the death of an individual causes greater losses in a small, preindustrial society than in a large, industrialized society. Much depends on how involved the deceased has been in the society's activities. In our own society, death occurs mainly among the aged, who have often already been excluded from an active social and economic role. The death of an elderly person, therefore, often has little effect outside the immediate family.

Bureaucratization. A method of social organization in which a trained administrative staff is responsible for devising, overseeing and coordinating the activities of other participants in an organization. The bureaucratization of death means that the same kind of specializaiton and division of labor used to run offices and factories is applied to the care of the dying and the dis-posal of the dead. This also involves some degree of impersonality in the activities of the specialists. The bureaucratization of death is seen as one way of controlling the social disrup-tiveness of death.

Socioeconomic strata. A class of persons in a society distinguished by similarities in income, education, and occupational prestige. In this section we see that the position one occupies in this structure affects one's life expectancy.

FACTUAL REVIEW

1. What was the average life expectancy in ancient Greece and Rome?
2. What was the death rate in the United States in 1900? In 1977?
3. What are the major causes of death in the United States today? What were they at the beginning of the century?
4. The development of what two drugs led to a rapid increase in life expectancy following World War II?
5. What is average life expectancy today, for men and for women?
6. How does death disrupt the "dynamic equilibrium" of society?
7. How is the effect of infant and child mortality lessened in some primitive societies?
8. How often does mortality disrupt business life in modern societies?
9. Is there a common pattern in the age composition of death in preindustrial societies?
10. What is the relationship between socioeconomic class and life expectancy?

ESSAY AND DISCUSSION

What demographic changes have altered our experience with death in the last half century, and what are some of the implications for our society?

Suggested guidelines: A. Consider Lerner's discussion of the change from infectious to degenerative disease as a cause of death. What does this mean in terms of institutionalization and health care cost?

B. Review Blauner's description of the new and growing elderly population, and of the "bureaucratization" of death.

C. Consider Goldscheider's discussion of the effects of social class on mortality statistics.

D. In light of Fulton's discussion in Section 1, review the effect of death on a highly mobile nuclear family with diffuse kinship ties.

5.
Death and Social Change

HIGHLIGHTS

While caring for the dying person in the midst of modern technology and institutions may provide us with greater control over the time and place of death, it also brings with it moral and ethical difficulties. As will be shown in more detail in Section 12, both the caring and the cared for may raise questions about the quality of terminal life, the dependence on drugs and life-support devices, the responsibility of the family and the physician, and the rights and autonomy of the seriously ill person. Eric Cassell argues in his newspaper article that these questions and others have revolutionized the treatment of the terminally ill. New drugs and diagnostic tools are not only able to relieve most of the major symptoms of the dying patient's illness, but are also able to provide him or her with greater certainty about the progress of the disease. When the patient has this kind of accurate knowledge and feels that medical personnel are being honest in their dealings, then the patient assumes some degree of autonomy and independence despite the institutional context of treatment and care.

Stanislav Grof's Reader article on "The Changing Face of Death" examines the situation of the dying person in contemporary Western civilization by comparing it with that of individuals in ancient cultures or from preindustrial countries. He notes that earlier cultures did not view death as the absolute termination of existence. Instead, they believed that life or consciousness existed in some form after physical death and that certain rituals were necessary to assure the deceased a safe journey into the spirit world. Importantly,

Grof notes, a belief in some form of consciousness or life beyond biological existence "can alter the experience of aging, the concept of death, and the experience of dying itself." Clearly, Grof does not agree with Cassell's opinion that the plight of the dying is improving. In fact, he suggests that the dying person in our culture is "facing a profound crisis that is basic and total." The modern world view that denies religion, places all faith in science, and believes only in the experience of the material world is at the root of this crisis, according to Grof.

Ivan Illich's "Death against Death" elaborates on the role of religion and medical care from the fourteenth century to the present. In chronicling changes in the meaning of death during this time period, he suggests that "the image of natural death has...increasingly acquired a medical character." From what Illich describes as "a constant awareness of the gaping grave" in the fourteenth century, we have now turned to "death under intensive care." This new death places the physician in the center of the battle and gives to modern medicine the aura of religion. Not only do we fail to preside over our own death, but we also fail to be responsible for our own health.

This theme is counterpointed by Eric Cassell's "Dying in a Technological Society." Here the author suggests that death has lost all moral meaning in the modern hospital and has been replaced by a technical concern for the disease itself. While it does not seem possible to return to technological innocence, there is a call for balance between technical expediency and moral concern.

KEY CONCEPTS

Expectations of omnipotence. The phrase used by Cassell to describe the faith placed in modern medical techniques and the resulting belief that we might be able to overcome death altogether.

Hospice. A care facility for terminally ill patients distinguished by its objective of humanizing the dying process. (See Section 7 for further discussion.)

Necropolis. City of the dead.

Posthumous journey. The travels of a deceased person into the world of the dead.

Reincarnation. The doctrine that the soul reappears after death in another and different bodily form.

Rite of passage. Any ritual designed to mark the transfer of an individual from one state to another, e.g., marriage. (See Section 11 for further discussion.)

Ecstatic religion. Religions that emphasize the rapture and joy of divine experience.

Cosmology. Theory or philosophy of the nature and principles of the universe.

Anthropomorphic. Attributing human qualities to nonhuman entities such as gods, animals, objects, or events. The event of death is often given such qualities.

"Natural death". A death that comes without previous sickness, violence, or mechanical and chronic disturbances.

FACTUAL REVIEW

1. How much literature of the nineteenth century was devoted to techniques for caring for the dying?
2. What is the result of faith in the power of technical solutions to medical problems?
3. What dual purpose do post-death rituals play?
4. What produces consciousness, according to materialistic philosophies?
5. How was death depicted in fifteenth-century woodcuts?
6. What was the "danse macabre"?

7. By what criteria was heaven compartmentalized during the Baroque period?

8. What is meant by the depersonalization of care?

9. What does Illich mean by the "medicalization" of death?

10. What has replaced the moral order, according to Cassell?

ESSAY AND DISCUSSION

Discuss how the changing nature of religious beliefs, medical care, and institutional treatment of the dying affects our modern experience with death.

Suggested guidelines: A. What does Grof say about changing religious beliefs as they affect the experience of death and our perception of it?

B. What does Illich mean by the medicalization of death, and how has the role of the physician changed with respect to care of the dying?

C. Consider Cassell's discussion of the shift from a moral to a technical order in transforming our experience with death. Is this in line with Grof's analysis?

6.
Life after Death
Old and New Meanings

HIGHLIGHTS

Is death the end... or a new beginning? Is it possible to take leave of one's body for a time and then *decide* to return? The posing of such questions, according to Edgar Jackson, in his newspaper article, is not a new human activity. In fact, the archeological evidence suggests that such questions have been a part of the response to death since the dawn of human life. There is, however, one thing that distinguishes the modern inquiry into these questions from the speculations of the past, and that is their basis in the un-

answered questions of science. What is the nature of consciousness? Does the energy of consciousness survive change? If modern energy physics extends beyond space and time, is death an illusion measured by the limits of our sensory apparatus? How do we explain out-of-body experiences and how can we justify the selective avoidance of certain bits of evidence?

The first Reader article by Eric Markusen examines "Religious Conceptions of Afterlife." He notes that for a number of early civilizations, including the Mesopotamians and Homeric Greeks, the hereafter was a bleak underground place to which everyone was consigned following death. The Muslims and Christians, however, distinguished between those who were saved and those who were damned, believing that conformity to sacred doctrine was rewarded by salvation in the afterlife. Hinduism and Buddhism represented a departure from these traditions, with their belief that followers were subject to a series of reincarnations.

In the next Reader selection, Rosalind Heywood analyzes psychical research into such phenomena as extrasensory perception and concludes that the only comfortable position to occupy with respect to such questions is "on the fence." Belief in survival must still be "an act of faith."

In the Reader article by Raymond Moody and the interview with Elisabeth Kübler-Ross, the authors discuss their numerous interviews with the near-dead and the resuscitated. Their respondents provide a wide array of afterlife visions. Common threads in these visions include unusual sounds, bright lights, the experience of being drawn into a tunnel, moments of enlightenment, heavenly visions, and then a forgetting of newly acquired knowledge. Such episodes are not, of course, subject to verification by other observers, but the similarity of experiences is compelling. Kübler-Ross also notes that her own out-of-body experiences have convinced her that there is some spiritual "essence" that is distinct from the physical body and that probably survives the event of physical death.

The brief article by Samuel Vaisrub expresses reservations about such statements as those made by Moody and Kübler-Ross. In examining the testimony of persons supposed to be dead and later resuscitated, he reminds us:

> Their hearts may have stopped beating for a minute or more, but their brains remained alive. There is nothing extraordinary, let alone supernatural, in seeing dream-like visions as consciousness returns to normal.

For Vaisrub, the search for proof diminishes the meaning of this "awesome mystery."

The final article in this section by Bertrand Russell is another call to skepticism. He states, "It is not rational arguments but emotions that cause belief in a future life. Moreover, Russell suggests that an attitude of complete and and total belief in eternal existence would have consequences that might be upsetting. Indifference to the event of physical death could encourage indifference to life itself.

KEY CONCEPTS

Life after death, Afterlife, Life after life, Survival, Future life, Post mortem existence. These concepts all convey the same essential meaning. It is the idea that there is a world or existence following death in which some form of human spirit or consciousness survives. Such thoughts, as we have seen in the Reader selection by Eric Markusen, have been common to a wide variety of religious belief systems and have provided individuals with a sense of future beyond death.

Paranormal. Things, ideas, or events that lie beyond the realm of ordinary experience. Phenomena of this kind are typically difficult to establish on the basis of multiple independent observations. Jackson argues that paranormal experiences are related to immortality.

Psychical research. Refers to research into the processes of the human mind, especially the extrasensory and nonphysical mental processes such as extrasensory perception.

Psi component. An element of consciousness described by C. D. Broad that is thought to exist after the event of physical death.

E.S.P. Extra Sensory Perception, or perception through means other than the normal senses.

Precognition. Previous knowledge of an event or circumstance.

Clairvoyance. A power, attributed to persons in a mesmeric trance, of discerning objects that are not present to the normal senses.

Psychosomatic. A physical disorder of the body originating in, or aggravated by, the psychic or emotional state of the individual.

Out-of-body experience. The sensation of departing from the physical body and existing in consciousness outside of it. This is regarded by some observers as evidence for survival beyond death.

FACTUAL REVIEW

1. What are the three major religious themes for belief in life after death? Which major religions have subscribed to each?
2. What are paranormal phenomena?
3. Does the brain die at the same instant the heart stops beating?
4. What kinds of scientific research are being conducted into life after death?
5. What is a "city of light," according to Moody?
6. According to Moody's respondents, what happens to visionary knowledge when one is

resuscitated from cardiac arrest?
7. What is an out-of-body experience?
8. According to Vaisrub, why can't testimony of resuscitated patients be taken as proof of an afterlife?

ESSAY AND DISCUSSION

What evidence has been brought forward to support the belief in life after death, and how does this evidence differ from the ideas supporting earlier beliefs in an afterlife?

Suggested guidelines: A. Consider Edgar Jackson's and Eric Markusen's discussion of religious beliefs.

B. Jackson suggests that scientific investigation of phenomena related to continued consciousness permits the possible enhancement of traditional religious views. How does this contrast with Vaisrub's observations on this point?
C. Consider the conclusion that Heywood arrives at and her basis for this conclusion from her personal paranormal experiences.
D. Consider the evidence cited by Moody and Kübler-Ross for their belief in survival after death. How does Vaisrub assess this information?
E. Take into account also the conclusion reached by Bertrand Russell. Does this statement in fact negate the possibility of life after death? Does Jackson's discussion anticipate Russell's objections to the likelihood of survival after death?

The Experience of Death

L EARNING OBJECTIVES
TO UNDERSTAND current methods in the treatment and care of dying persons.

the nature of the dying process and the controversy that surrounds it.

institutional death and the role of the family in providing support.

new approaches to terminal care and pain relief as practiced in the hospice movement.

the way in which children experience death in our culture.

the way in which children respond to the death of a family member.

how one can approach a child's questions about death.

N EWSPAPER ARTICLES
AND READER SELECTIONS

7.
The Dying Patient
Avery D. Weisman

from the Reader:

Terminal Care: Issues and Alternatives
Claire F. Ryder and Diane M. Ross

Hospice Care for the Adult
Roberta Lyder Paige and Jane Finkbiner Looney

Should a Patient Know?
Cicely Saunders

Learning to Die
Thomas Powers

Death Work and the Stages of Dying
Edwin S. Shneidman

Interview with a Seventeen-Year-Old Girl
Elisabeth Kübler-Ross

Stay of Execution
Stewart Alsop

An Appropriate Death
Avery D. Weisman

8.
Death and the Child
George Williams

from the Reader:

When to Talk about Death
Edgar Jackson

The Kingdom Where Nobody Dies
Robert Kastenbaum

How Does a Child Experience Grief?
Earl Grollman

I NTRODUCTION
As we have already seen in Section 5, the situation of the seriously ill person in a modern medical facility is one of mixed blessings. At one level the patient is afforded technically advanced diagnostic and treatment methods under the supervision of highly trained medical personnel. At another level, however, the patient may come to feel isolated, powerless, and reduced to a statistic by a seemingly endless series of tests. This problem is compounded by the changed character of modern disease. The now predominant degenerative illnesses require, for many persons, extended periods of care. Such lengthy hospital stays

not only are financially burdensome, but they may also carry with them a high cost in terms of diminished family interaction and support. The situation of the dying patient is, of course, infinitely more distressing because the ultimate result, regardless of the excellence of care, is death itself.

The authors in the following two sections, "The Dying Patient" and "Death and the Child," address this complex set of problems by posing a number of questions. For example: how may care of the dying patient be humanized? How may the family participate in this care? What feelings and emotions is the dying patient subject to? What are the special complexities of treating a dying child? How will friends and relatives respond to the last few weeks of life? What are the special difficulties facing the elderly patient when death is not only expected, but timely? And how can we best teach children about death?

There are no simple answers to these questions, as there are no easy alternatives to the present system of institutionalized care. But as increasing numbers of persons turn to hospital and nursing home facilities, the search for humane options becomes more pressing.

7.
The Dying Patient

HIGHLIGHTS
The inevitability of death for all living things means that we will all die *someday*. But *someday* is distant, abstract, and less threatening than *next month, next week,* or *tomorrow.* When death finally comes, the sense of complete powerlessness in the face of such an event is staggering. Loneliness, anger, depression, and fear are all to be found in the emotional repertoire of the dying person.

Avery Weisman, in the newspaper discussion of "The Dying Patient," focuses on how we can help the dying patient to achieve a decent death when death is inevitable. He points out that doctors sometimes make it difficult to die a good death because of their attempts to prolong life. Weisman stresses the needs of the dying patient for relief from pain, for control over at least part of their situation, for reflection, for honesty, and for communication—above all, for someone to share and care.

Ryder and Ross, in their Reader selection, suggest that the physician and nurse may have become desensitized to death. Supportive compassion may give way to preoccupation with "diagnostic tests, technological gadgetry, and heroic therapy." Fear of legal reprisals may result in the prolongation of life beyond its natural course. The situation of the dying patient is additionally complicated by the high cost of extended care. Considerations of such costs may cause severe guilt as the patient contemates other needs of his or her family. The authors conclude that home care for the terminally ill is the "most desired goal for patients and concerned health professionals."

Another important alternative to traditional hospital care is the hospice. This type of facility aims at providing both relief from distress as well as an individualized and meaningful death, going beyond the limits of traditional pain relief and involving the family in the day-to-day activities of the patient. While such care may require a "willingness to do the unlovely," as Paige and Looney suggest, it also may have great rewards for both the patient and the caregiver. Cicely Saunders, the founder of St. Christopher's Hospice, writes, "The most important principle is love; not sentimentality, but compassion and understanding." Religion is also important if it is treated in the context of the patient's beliefs and aspirations.

In the process of dying, the patient may go

through a series of stages, a model first set forth by Elisabeth Kübler-Ross and summarized in Powers' Reader selection. These stages are (1) denial, (2) anger, (3) bargaining, (4) depression and (5) acceptance. Hope is thought to persist throughout. Recently, this stage theory of dying has been challenged by Edwin Shneidman and others. Shneidman argues that "One does not find a unidirectional movement through progressive stages so much as an alternation between acceptance and denial." He maintains that the emotional mix is complex and transitory and difficult to express in a single formula.

Elisabeth Kübler-Ross's "Interview with a Seventeen-Year-Old Girl" and Stewart Alsop's "Stay of Execution" provide us with personal glimpses of the experience of dying. The interview with the young girl reveals no signs of anger and appears to indicate that not everyone goes through Kübler-Ross's "stages." Lest we think that death is a tragedy beyond what is natural, Alsop reminds us that "A dying man needs to die, as a sleepy man needs to sleep, and there comes a time when it is wrong, as well as useless, to resist."

Avery Weisman's discussion of "An Appropriate Death" provides the dying person and his caregivers with a set of humane expectations that may make death more acceptable. He suggests that the dying person should be relatively free of pain with minimal emotional and social stresses. Furthermore, the dying person should be encouraged to operate on as high and effective a level as possible while resolving residual conflicts and satisfying, to whatever degree possible, remaining wishes. Finally, the patient should be free to relinquish control over his or her affairs and relationships. Dying, according to this formula, is a way of living as long as possible, not an abandonment of all that is human and satisfying.

KEY CONCEPTS

"Death denying". This phrase is used in a variety of ways and is applied to both individual attitudes and cultural dispositions. It often contains the ideas that (1) death is an unnecessary failure of medicine, (2) death happens to others but not to me, or (3) the emotional response one feels following the death of another need not be recognized. This is to be distinguished from denial which is a normal and not necessarily unhealthy individual response to the news of a fatal diagnosis.

Prolongation of life. Keeping a person alive, through the use of new medical techniques, beyond the point when death would naturally have occurred. Many doctors regard this as their duty; others—doctors, lay persons, and dying patients—emphasize the need to consider the quality of the life that is being prolonged.

Preterminal. The period prior to immediately expected death in which the patient is still alive as a person and deserving of privilege. Most importantly, this period is distinguished from the *terminal* period in which death is expected within a few days. One of the difficulties experienced by a dying person is the stigma associated with the "terminal" label. This often creates a barrier between the patient and his or her friends and relatives such that all interaction is based on expected death rather than remaining life.

Death with dignity. This has become a controversial term because of the moral dilemmas surrounding questions of prolonging life. For some, the term means acceptance of death by the dying patient, but as used by Ryder and Ross—and generally today—it refers to retaining one's individuality and not being subjected to dehumanizing treatment that prolongs meaningless life.

Hospice. Originally the name of a resting place for travelers, this term now refers to special care facilities for the terminally ill. Important aspects of these facilities include extensive and continuous pain relief, family involvement, and the individualization of death.

Individualization of death. The recognition of the dying person as an individual with special needs, who must be helped to live until he or she actually dies. It is a primary goal of the hospice movement, and is designed to counteract the tendency toward depersonalization of death, routinization of care, and social death that prevails in many hospitals.

Social death. A process of mutal disengagement of the dying person from society. It usually takes the form of avoidance by persons attending a dying patient. It refers to the fact that a terminally ill patient may be considered dead for all intents and purposes and would thus not be deserving of any special consideration or attention. It precedes biological death.

Stages of death. These are the sequential reactions that a dying person may have after learning of a fatal diagnosis. As outlined by Elisabeth Kübler-Ross, they include denial, anger, bargaining, depression, and acceptance, with hope persisting throughout all of the stages.

Anticipatory pain relief. Refers to the administration of drugs in the expectation that greater pain will come. This is done to avoid the fear that often results from a patient's experience of increasing levels of pain, and it is an important component of hospice-type care.

Appropriate death. Weisman uses this term to refer to the kind of death a person would choose for himself. It includes relative freedom from pain, control over procedures and degree of consciousness desired, and resolution of personal conflicts. Elsewhere in the literature on death and dying, the term is used to mean the death of an elderly person who has led a full life, as opposed to the death of a child, for example.

"Death watch". The careful monitoring of vital signs when death is soon expected.

FACTUAL REVIEW

1. What percent of terminally ill persons are institutionalized in general hospitals?
2. What is the most desirable care goal for terminally ill patients?
3. For what purpose does medicine exist?
4. What does Weisman believe causes the greatest amount of suffering—personal death or the grief that accompanies it?
5. What is the function of empathy in caring for the dying patient?
6. How does hospice care differ from traditional hospital care of the dying patient?
7. Does Cicely Saunders believe that it is essential for every terminally ill patient to know that he or she is dying?
8. List Kübler-Ross's five stages of dying, as described by Powers.
9. What emotion is thought to exist throughout all five stages?
10. Does Shneidman feel that there is a unidirectional movement through progressive stages of dying?
11. What attitudes toward death did the seventeen-year-old girl express in her interview with Elisabeth Kübler-Ross?
12. What are the major characteristics of an "appropriate death," according to Weisman?
13. Did Stewart Alsop think much about death before the onset of his illness?

ESSAY AND DISCUSSION

What are the major problems facing the dying person in our culture? How has the modern health care system both aggravated and alleviated these difficulties?

Suggested guidelines: A. Review Weisman's newspaper discussion of the status of the dying patient. What does he say about the patient's needs?
B. Consider professional attitudes toward the dying person as discussed by Ryder and Ross. Also note what they say about specialization and the fragmentation of care.
C. Evaluate the hospice concept as discussed by Paige and Looney and Ryder and Ross. What advantages does the hospice offer over and above general hospital care?
D. What does Weisman say is an "appropriate death"? What obstacles sometimes preclude the possibility of such a death for some patients?

What are the stages of dying and what controversy surrounds them? Should the information that is given to a terminally ill patient be truthful in all respects? Does this affect the patient's sense of hope?

Suggested guidelines.   A. Review the stages of dying discussed by Powers and Shneidman. What aspects of this trajectory are in dispute?
B. Consider the comments of Alsop and the young girl interviewed by Kübler-Ross. What concerns do they reflect? Do they seem to confirm or refute the idea of "stages" of dying?
C. What does Saunders say about the information that a patient should receive? How does this compare with Weisman's position about telling the truth? How does Alsop respond to this question?

8.
Death and the Child

HIGHLIGHTS
    Both the newspaper article in this section by George Williams and the Reader articles by Jackson, Kastenbaum, and Grollman deal with a child's awareness of death and the various ways children deal—or can be helped to deal—with death and loss.

Williams challenges the notion that a child (presumably over the age of three years) is too young to understand the meaning of death and loss. Parents, however, because of their own discomfort with death, often try to keep children from confronting death or even asking questions about it. Williams goes on to say that children have various ways of their own of dealing with grief and that there are five rather distinct facets to this process of coping: (1) denial and isolation, (2) expressing anger, (3) bargaining, (4) depression, and (5) resolution in which the child finally accepts the death. Williams emphasizes that there is no set order to these stages, and often a successful resolu-

tion will take a great deal of time.

Jackson's Reader selection expands upon some of the notions set forth by Williams. He concurs that death is part of a child's life experience even at a young age and that questions about death are inevitable. Jackson cautions, however, that adults must listen carefully to the child's questions because they provide the clue to the child's level of understanding. Often simple fact, not philosophies, will suffice as answers to children's questions about death. Jackson feels that the appropriate time to talk about death in greater detail is when death is part of the child's experiences. At these times, he feels, adults have a chance to include children in the funeral rites and to enhance their sense of security by showing respect for the child as well as for the deceased.

Kastenbaum agrees that adults, because of their own discomfort with the subject, often avoid dealing with children's questions about death. As a result, children are left to their own devices in explaining death-related events in their lives. Childhood games are often the means by which children deal with their concerns of dying ("all fall down") and nothingness ("all gone"). Kastenbaum points out that children must come to an understanding of death on two levels: that people, in general, die and that they, in particular, will also die. Citing the work of other scholars, he argues that children are aware of death at a very young age—younger than Williams suggests— and they learn by stages about their own mortality.

Grollman's article describes some specific ways in which a child may experience loss and grief. He urges parents to take seriously the child's funeral and burial attempts when a pet dies and to realize that the child is trying to work through some of his or her own feelings and fears rather than trying to mock adult rituals.

KEY CONCEPTS

Denial. In this context, denial is the child's *refusal* to believe that a death has actually occurred. It is a psychological defense to avoid the pain of separation. (See also "death denying" in Section 7.)

Isolation. The state of being detached or set apart from others; this can be as a result of the action of others (as in the isolation of a patient with an infectious disease or the isolation of a child for purposes of punishment) or as a result of an individual's conscious or unconscious decision to keep him/herself apart from other people for personal reasons. In this context, it is a self-imposed isolation so that the child will not have to hear upsetting comments about the death of a loved one.

Process of identification. A process by which an emotional tie causes a person to think, feel, and act as he imagines the person with whom he had the tie did. Symptoms of illness may occur in this way. (See Erich Lindemann's article in Section 9.)

Autopsy. An examination and dissection of the body after death to discover the cause of death or to view the extent of the disease. An autopsy is performed in a hospital or medical facility by physicians who have specialized in the medical study of diseases, their causes and their symptoms.

Magical thinking. Children's expectations that by wishing or hoping they may cause something to happen; this may be particularly important to recognize if a child feels he is responsible for the death of someone else because he has wished injury upon that person.

Guilt. The feeling of having done something wrong. A child often feels guilty in the face of a bereavement because of past angry feelings toward the deceased, or for failure to make the deceased happier, or, in some cases, because he or she feels responsible for the death.

FACTUAL REVIEW

1. What are the five stages in the child's grief reaction as described by Williams?
2. When does the child typically have his or her first experience with the death of a close relative?
3. According to Jackson, when is it appropriate to talk about death with a child?
4. The death of what person or persons has the most signal and longest lasting impact on children?
5. What is meant by "the sharing of direct death experience"?
6. What characterizes the third stage in a child's realization of death?
7. Should parents discourage a bereft child from crying?
8. What emotion complicates a child's reaction to the death of a parent? Of a sibling?
9. What symptoms are typically shown by a bereaved child?

ESSAY AND DISCUSSION

How do children react to the idea of death and how do they respond to it when it separates them from someone they care about?

Suggested guidelines: A. Consider Kastenbaum's discussion of Maria Nagy's work. Why is it important to keep a child's age in mind when discussing death?
B. When does Jackson suggest that we talk about death with children? How does he consider age and the receptiveness of the child?
C. What do Williams and Grollman say about the death of a pet? Is grief to be acknowledged at such a time?
D. Consider the grief reaction of the child as described by Williams.
E. Review Grollman's discussion of reactions to parental and sibling death.

Survivors of Death

L EARNING OBJECTIVES
TO UNDERSTAND the symptoms of
normal and abnormal grief.

the nature of anticipatory grief and its significance in prolonged illness.

the emotional response to death and its cultural expression in mourning.

the problems associated with widowhood in
particular and survivorship in general.

the historical significance of funerary rites.

the meaning of the modern funeral and the
controversy that surrounds it.

the alternatives to traditional funeral practices and the value and difficulties that
they pose.

N EWSPAPER ARTICLES
AND READER SELECTIONS

9. Grief
Colin Murray Parkes

from the Reader:

Symptomatology and Management of Acute Grief
Erich Lindemann

The Denial of Mourning
Philippe Ariès

Death, Grief, and Mourning
Geoffrey Gorer

The Broken Heart
Colin Murray Parkes

Anticipatory Grief, Stress, and the Surrogate
Griever
Robert Fulton

10.
Widowhood
Helena Lopata

from the Reader:

Living through Widowhood
Helena Lopata

Widow
Lynn Caine

Man's Concern with Death: Epilogue
Arnold Toynbee

11.
The Funeral
Vanderlyn Pine

from the Reader:

The Care of the Dead: A Historical Portrait
Vanderlyn Pine

Funerals, Fantasy, and Flight
Ruth Mulvey Harmer

The Place of the Funeral: The Role of the Funeral
Director in Contemporary America
Howard C. Raether

I NTRODUCTION
There are few areas of social behavior
more confusing or complex than the human
reaction to loss. The response of any individual to the death of another must be seen
first and most clearly in its uniqueness. However, no person escapes the circumstances of
his or her time and place in the world. As a
result, the social conditions that prevail at any
given time result in certain uniformities in the
response to death.

In the study of contemporary bereavement patterns, numerous social changes must be considered in order that the universal as well as the unique aspects of survivorship may be properly understood. Significant changes relevant to the event of death in our culture would include a transformed medical technology, a bureaucratized system of health care, an institutionalization of the ill and aged, a decline in the use of religious solutions for dealing with crisis, a widely separated and fragmented kinship structure, and major advances in life expectancy. It is within the milieu imposed by such social and cultural conditions that modern bereavement patterns must be analyzed.

The authors in this part examine a wide variety of issues related to survivorship including the symptoms of normal and abnormal grief, the consequences of unresolved grief, culturally defined mourning practices, the anticipation of loss, the experience of widowhood, the history of ritualized mourning, and the significance of the modern funeral. It is in these discussions that we learn the price of commitment in human relationships.

9.
Grief and Loss

HIGHLIGHTS
All human relationships end in separation. There are no exceptions to this fact. Regardless of how much energy or emotional commitment we invest in a relationship, it cannot last forever. While there are, of course, many ways in which it is possible for a relationship to end, our interest in this section is in the termination of relationships by death, called bereavement. The emotional reaction to such a loss is known as grief.

In the newspaper article "Grief," by Colin Murray Parkes, we learn that this response is normal, often painful, and potentially harmful if avoided. The fundamental goal of grief is the internal realization and recognition of death. Grief, according to Parkes, can be seen to follow a predictable pattern beginning with shock and *numbness,* proceeding to *pining* and feelings of *dejection,* and finally, when successful, resulting in *recovery.* Recovery, however, does not mean that all emotional significance of death has ended. Rather, it signifies the ability of the griever to form new relationships and make new commitments.

Parkes suggests a number of ways in which we can help persons suffering from grief. Most importantly, we can encourage them to express their feelings of distress, anger, shame, and bewilderment that usually accompany human loss. Later we may wish to assure them that it is permissible to stop grieving and begin life anew. The pain of grief matures us, according to Parkes, and provides us with a new perspective on life and its significance.

In Erich Lindemann's Reader article, "Symptomatology and Management of Acute Grief," we are introduced to the idea of a grief syndrome with both normal and abnormal manifestations. Normal grief is reflected in the following symptoms:

> sensations of somatic distress..., a feeling of tightness in the throat, choking with shortness of breath, need for sighing, an empty feeling in the abdomen, lack of muscular power, and an intense subjective distress...or mental pain.

When these symptoms of bodily distress become pronounced and include a preoccupation with the image of the deceased, feelings of guilt and hostility, and a loss of ordinary patterns of conduct, there is the potential that the grief may become pathological. In addition, there is the possibility that feelings of grief may be so painful that the bereaved may find it necessary to postpone their suffering. The expected emotional responses may instead take the form of psychosomatic illness, overactivity without purpose, or a lasting withdrawal from usual social interaction. Agitated depression without real grief work (that is, the recognition and readjustment to what has been lost) may give way to suicidal impulses. At this point some kind of intervention by trained personnel is essential.

Philippe Ariès' article on "The Denial of Mourning" describes how contemporary society has come to prohibit bereaved persons from socially expressing their loss. According to Ariès, we have lost the spontaneity of our emotional response to the death of a loved person. Moreover, we no longer have many ritualized procedures for the expression of our grief. Judging by Lindemann's discussion, this situation may prove to be unhealthy for those deeply affected by a death.

Geoffrey Gorer's article, "Death, Grief, and Mourning," is a personal account of what Ariès describes as the "reversal of death." When Gorer's brother died of cancer in midlife, neither his widow, children, nor other family members were provided with an opportunity to grieve in an open fashion. Friends did not acknowledge their loss and were not prepared to offer consolation. Gorer concludes that there is "no longer...any guidance from ritual as to the way to treat a self-confessed mourner."

"The Broken Heart," by Colin Murray Parkes, brings to our attention another important aspect of bereavement: the mortality rate for recently bereaved persons is much higher than it is in the general population. Significantly, the major causes of death in these cases are coronary thrombosis and arteriosclerotic heart disease. While the author recognizes that death from heart disease does not prove that grief is the cause of death, he suggests that aid to the bereaved may still be an important contribution to public health.

In the final selection in this section, "Anticipatory Grief, Stress, and the Surrogate Griever," sociologist Robert Fulton provides some observations about the nature of modern grief. He notes, for example, that degenerative disease processes in which dying takes place over an extended period of time makes "anticipatory grief" more frequent. This phenomenon occurs when individuals have an opportunity to anticipate and prepare for the death of a loved person before its actual occurrence. In addition, the families often begin to withdraw from the bedside of a dying person and professional caregivers become more emotionally attached and supportive of the patient. This reversal of roles is termed surrogate grief and is manifested in the increased stress levels of health care personnel. Professor Fulton suggests that this has important implications for the institutionalized care of the terminally ill person.

KEY CONCEPTS

Bereavement. The experience of having lost something or someone; here it refers to a loss resulting from death. It is important to keep in mind that this is not synonymous with grief, because it is possible to be bereaved and not grieve. In fact, bereavement may engender feelings of relief and happiness, depending on the nature of the relationship that has been ended.

Grief. The emotional pain one experiences as a result of having lost someone of value. Parkes describes a number of stages of grief, including numbness, pining, dejection, and recovery.

Grief work. The emotionally painful process of facing the reality of a death, acknowledging its significance in memory, and preparing for new emotional attachments.

Normal grief. The primary components of normal grief are a willingness to face the reality of death, sort out the many memories associated with the relationship, and give vent to the many feelings associated with the loss. Normal grief, according to Lindemann, has definite symptoms that result in being freed from the emotional bondage to the deceased and a readjustment to the environment in which the deceased is missing. The ability to form new relationships is a sign that grief is proceeding normally.

Morbid, abnormal, or pathological grief. The most general characteristic of the abnormal or morbid grief response is a failure to face the reality of death and acknowledge all of one's feelings associated with the loss. It may manifest itself as a delayed or postponed response and include expectations of the deceased's return. In addition, it may present itself as some form of physical illness, such as ulcerative colitis, rheumatoid arthritis, or asthma. Feelings of extreme anger, restlessness, overactivity, and depression are common, with a tendency toward withdrawal from most social interaction.

Mourning. Culturally defined patterns for the expression of grief. Mourning customs can include specified styles of dress, withdrawal from social activities for a specified period of time, and so on. One of the peculiarities of our culture, as Ariès points out, is that there are no longer any mourning behaviors that enjoy wide usage.

Anticipatory grief. The feelings of loss and pain that one may experience in the anticipation of a death that has not yet occurred. This may be the time in which most of the grief work is done and can result in an emotional void in the survivor when the death actually occurs. This is most common in prolonged illness.

Surrogate grief. A term used to describe the emotional attachment and subsequent feelings of loss experienced by professional caregivers when confronted by the death of a patient. It is surrogate in the sense that the emotional commitment of the caregiver may substitute for the family's support when, in the course of terminal illness, much of the family's grief is worked through before the death.

FACTUAL REVIEW

1. Describe three symptoms of normal grief.
2. What are the four phases of grief described by Colin Murray Parkes?
3. What are the main objectives of "grief work"?
4. When did demonstrations of mourning first lose their spontaneity and become ritualized?
5. During what time period were professional mourners in vogue?
6. How does Gorer characterize his emotional state when he first learns of his brother's illness?
7. How did Gorer interpret the public reaction to his own grief?
8. Does death following bereavement prove that grief is a cause of death?
9. What did Melford Spiro find when he studied the grief response of Ifaluk widows?
10. What is anticipatory grief and under what conditions is it likely to occur?

ESSAY AND DISCUSSION

What responses characterize the normal grief reaction, and how may this reaction become complicated and distorted? What significance does the suddenness of death have in the grief response?

Suggested guidelines: A. Review Lindemann's and Parkes' discussion of normal grief. Do their descriptions agree?
B. Consider Ariès' and Gorer's discussion of the suppression of mourning and its recognition.
C. Recall Lindemann's discussion of the distorted grief reaction and consider how the denial of mourning might contribute to a distorted response.
D. Note Parkes' discussion of increased mortality rates for widows and widowers.
E. Finally, review the grief response described by Fulton in the case of lengthy terminal illnesses.

10.
Widowhood

HIGHLIGHTS Widowhood is a unique constellation of experiences in technologically advanced societies. Increased life expectancy means that the majority of the more than ten million widows in the U.S. are over age sixty-five. The fact that men typically marry women younger than themselves and usually predecease them means that widows outnumber widowers by more than five to one. Additionally, the experience of widowhood has been changed both by changes in family structure (widows today typically live alone), and by changes in community structure (the widow's circle of friends is typically smaller and more isolated than in the past). In such a setting, the loss of a life-long companion and helpmate can be difficult and often traumatic.

In Helena Lopata's newspaper article, "Widowhood," we learn of the many situations that can weigh heavily upon the shoulders of a woman following the death of her husband. For example, the loss of one's partner in a world of partners places the widow in a distinctly disadvantaged position when she begins to reenter the social world. The loss of income and the disruption of financial affairs also requires much adjustment. The younger widow with growing children has the additional burden of not only helping her children adjust to their father's death, but also filling in the emotional void that the children are likely to feel in his absence. Lopata points out that women who are most successful at coping with the role of widow are those "who have developed their own personal resources rather than depending fully on resources provided by the husband." Lopata's Reader article, "Living through Widowhood," extends the newspaper discussion by reporting on a study of widows conducted in metropolitan Chicago. Lopata notes that there are, for some women, advantages to widowhood, including " 'freedom to do as I please,' 'being independent,' 'not having a schedule,' and 'being my own boss.' " In fact, 42 percent of the sample said that they currently felt more independent than they did at any time prior to widowhood. The author warns us, however, that this should not be interpreted as a response to a previously unhappy marriage. Loneliness is still the number one problem, and these respondents still missed their husbands. But the events following widowhood required some changes, and not all of these changes were perceived as being adverse. Of additional importance are the social class differences reported by Lopata. The higher income, better educated women were hardest hit by the emotional trauma of widowhood, but at the same time, they possessed the social and educational resources necessary to build a new and satisfying life.

The second Reader article, "Widow," by Lynn Caine, is a personal portrait of a middle-class woman's struggle to put her life in order following the death of her husband. She describes the attitude of proper calm that she managed for the sake of others and the internal torment that revealed her own vulnerability. She found it difficult to resist the lure of "professional" widowhood: the temptation to find one's entire identity as a widow. Importantly, she notes that the need for money and the desire for sexual fulfillment do not end with a husband's death. Her job provided much satisfaction, and she recommends work to other widows. But in the face of much well-intended advice about romantic affairs, she found it necessary to make her own way in the world at her own pace. "Women," she suggests, "must prepare themselves to be able to live alone. Because the majority of women will have to, eventually."

In the final selection in this section, the epilogue to *Man's Concern with Death,* Arnold Toynbee suggests that there are two separate ways in which one becomes reconciled to death: one is in the anticipation of one's own death, and the other is in the anticipation or experience of the death of another. According to Toynbee:

> If one truly loves a fellow human being, one ought to wish that as little as possible of the pain of his or her death shall be suffered by him or her, and that as much of it as possible shall be borne by oneself.

The survivor of death is apportioned the greater amount of suffering, and this is the price of survival.

KEY CONCEPTS

"Urban Villagers." This refers to people living on the edge of the urban world but not really feeling a part of it. The sense of community is hard to find in urban areas because friendship networks are diffuse and family ties often fragmented, making it difficult for the widow seeking the support of local peers.

Status change. This refers to a general alteration of an individual's sense of self as a result of changing circumstances. The death of one's spouse is only part of the status change for a widow. Alterations in financial affairs, social behavior, and living conditions also affect the way a widow will view herself and the way others will view her.

Levir or levirate system. A custom of the ancient Jews by which a dead man's brother was obligated to marry the widow if there were no sons.

"Couple" identity. The identification of a person as part of a couple rather than as an individual. This can present major problems for a widow, who often feels a severe loss of identity when her spouse dies; she is no longer sure of who she is or of her

place in the social and economic world. In addition, she often feels like a "fifth wheel" when she attempts to renew acquaintanceships with couples whom she has seen previously only with her spouse. Other women may see the widow as a threat to the stability of their own marriage. The same may also be true for divorced men and women.

Invisible minority. Lopata's term to describe widows, particularly older widows with few financial resources, who are targets of discrimination. They are discriminated against in part because they are women, old, single, and poor in a male-dominated, youth- and couple-oriented, wealthy society.

Widow-to-widow programs. Designed to give recent widows the benefit of the experience of other widows and the companionship and support that are sometimes difficult for a widow to find.

FACTUAL REVIEW

1. Approximately how many widows and widowers are there in the U.S. today? What is the average age of these widows?
2. Why is a widow's status particularly difficult in our society?
3. What is the significance of jealousy in a widow's interaction with married friends?
4. What are three of the "practical problems" a widow must attend to in the period following her husband's death?
5. What percentage of widows in Lopata's sample lived with their married children?
6. What percent of the respondents said they liked living alone?
7. What are some of the advantages of widowhood cited by Lopata's respondents?
8. How does social class and economic status seem to affect the experience of widows?
9. What are the "chores of grief" described by Lynn Caine?
10. Of what significance is a job for the widow?

11. What does Lynn Caine mean by the lure of professional widowhood?
12. What does Toynbee consider to be the most loving desire one can express toward another human being?

ESSAY AND DISCUSSION

Describe the different conditions that affect a woman when she faces widowhood. What resources can she mobilize in her behalf? What outcomes can be expected?

Suggested guidelines: A. Review Helena Lopata's newspaper discussion of the disruptions of widowhood. What generational differences exist between younger and older widows?
B. Consider the discussion of social class in Lopata's Reader article. Note the significance of education, race, job skills, and living arrangements.
C. Compare Lynn Caine's description of the help she received from friends to Lopata's discussion. Are they consistent?
D. Recall Lopata's Reader discussion of the widows who change. How are these changes evaluated?
E. Do you agree with Toynbee?

11.
The Funeral

HIGHLIGHTS

When individuals die, they must be disposed of in some way. It is of course possible simply to bury them or burn them without regard for any of their personal qualities, as the Nazis treated the Jewish dead during World War II. But for the most part, throughout human history, we have taken time to recount the worthwhile attributes of the deceased, recognize their absence from the community, and encourage their safe journey into some other place or time. This recognition at the time of death is known in our culture as a funeral.

In Vanderlyn Pine's newspaper article, "The Funeral and Its Meaning," we learn that funeral practices serve both as a means of disposal for the dead and as an aid to the recovery of survivors. Pine describes three distinct functions performed by the funeral including the rites of (1) separation, (2) transition, and (3) incorporation. *Separation* refers to the separation of the living from the dead. *Transition* is the rite designed to aid survivors in their transition from a position of active association with a person to a world in which that person is absent. *Incorporation* refers to the incorporation of the deceased into another-worldly existence. The author also notes that funeral practices tend to vary according to ethnic, religious, and socioeconomic lines and include some form of material expenditure. This expenditure, Vanderlyn Pine suggests, communicates the loss felt by the survivors to the rest of society.

In his Reader article, "The Care of the Dead: A Historical Portrait," Pine provides a historical overview of funeral customs, tracing them from the ancient Romans to the present day. He notes the development of professionalization and embalming, and discusses the evolution of the professional American funeral director.

Ruth Harmer's article, "Funerals, Fantasy, and Flight," calls the modern funeral director to account. She suggests that the practice of funeral directing in the United States is plagued by price fixing, repressive laws, consumer manipulation, economic exploitation, and extravagant ceremony and merchandise. She supports the memorial society movement in its efforts to reduce the cost of funerals and to spare survivors the burden of arrangements. She suggests that the "great value of the movement is that it encourages people to think in a rational way about the practical aspects of death."

The final Reader selection, "The Place of the Funeral: The Role of the Funeral Director in Contemporary Society," by Howard Raether, is a rebuttal to Harmer's "Funerals, Fantasy, and Flight." Raether, the executive secretary of the National Funeral Directors Association, suggests that modern funeral directors are consistently and often unjustifiably criticized, partly because they are a symbol of death in a society that finds death distasteful. He notes, however, that there is much to be said for the funeral service as it is traditionally practiced in the United States. The visitation, for example, provides the survivors with an opportunity to share their grief with others. The viewing of the body allows the survivors an opportunity to face the reality of death and begin their grief work. The public nature of the funeral provides the community an opportunity to acknowledge its loss. Furthermore, he argues that funeral directors are in a unique position "to aid and encourage the normal mourning process." He urges the funeral director to become a "caregiver" and "to continue to develop his sensitivity to the various levels...of loss that death creates in our present day society."

KEY CONCEPTS

Rite of separation. This is the aspect of the funeral ceremony that emphasizes the distinction between the world of the living and the world of the dead; committal of the body to a separate place away from the living is an example of such a rite.

Rite of transition. This aspect of a funeral ceremony aids the survivors in their accommodation to a social world in which the deceased is absent; visiting the bereaved, public mourning, and the funeral procession are thought to encourage this transition.

Memorial service. A memorial service is a service of commemoration for a deceased person that occurs *following* the disposition of the body. Such services are usually organized through memorial societies that encourage the immediate disposition of the body and dispense with many of the traditional funeral rituals.

Traditional funeral. The primary elements of a traditional funeral include the viewing of the body of the deceased person and a public ceremony in recognition of the death. Some persons feel that the viewing of the body is a significant aspect of the funeral, in that it encourages survivors to face the reality of death and begin their grief work.

Adaptive funeral. Any modified funeral ceremony in which the survivors may choose special readings, symbols, and behaviors to mark the death in an individualized way is called an adaptive funeral service. The service may be devoid of any religious symbolism, such as in a humanistic funeral ceremony, or it may include more than one ceremony with different emphasis in each.

Conspicuous consumption. In the discussion of funeral service, this refers to any extravagant show of wealth over and above what is necessary for ceremonialization and disposition of the body.

Embalming. The modern practice of embalming a dead body involves the removal of blood and the substitution of some kind of chemical preservative; it may also include cosmetic treatment to restore lifelike qualities to the corpse. In the past, it could involve the removal of all internal organs and subsequent treatment of the body with oils and spices, such as was practiced by the ancient Egyptians.

High grief. The potential impact of an unexpected, sudden, or untimely death upon those with close emotional ties to the deceased. A young child's death would be a high grief death to his or her family.

Low grief. The potential impact of an expected or timely death upon those who no longer depend on the deceased for emotional well-being and support. An elderly parent's death might be a low grief death for his or her adult children.

Libitinarius. The specialist of ancient Rome responsible for anointing, embalming, and ceremonializing the event of death for upper class citizens; considered to be the direct ancestor of the modern funeral director.

Wake. The watch or vigil kept over a corpse before burial, often involving festivities or ritual.

FACTUAL REVIEW

1. What three rites of passage can occur during a funeral?
2. What is an adaptive funeral?
3. How far back in human history can funeral practices be traced?
4. Describe early Christian burial practices.
5. What functions did the American undertaker of the nineteenth century serve?
6. What distinguishes a memorial service from a funeral service?
7. According to Harmer, when did funeral directors discover that "death could be the basis of a booming business"?
8. What did researchers Shoor and Speed recommend to funeral directors?
9. What is a cooperative funeral home?

ESSAY AND DISCUSSION

Discuss the historical and contemporary significance of the funeral ritual. What controversy surrounds the modern funeral and what alternatives are possible?

Suggested guidelines: A. Review Vanderlyn Pine's Reader discussion of the funeral with particular attention to the functions it has served.
B. Consider Pine's newspaper discussion of the separate rites performed during the funeral. Of what significance are these rites today?
C. Examine Ruth Harmer's discussion of funeral extravagance and waste. Review her major criticisms.
D. Recall Howard Raether's discussion of the various functions served by the funeral. Does he address Harmer's criticisms?
E. Return to Harmer's discussion of alternatives to the traditional funeral and evaluate them in light of Raether's defense.
F. Consider the section introduction in the Reader. What does it say in relation to low grief and high grief deaths and the function of the funeral?

Dilemmas of Death

L EARNING OBJECTIVES
TO UNDERSTAND the issues raised by changing technology and extended life expectancy.

the meaning and significance of euthanasia as it is currently practiced.

the dilemma of the physician and caregiver in treating patients that do not wish to live.

the problems in the definition of life and death and how they bear upon abortion and euthanasia legislation.

the significance of organ donation as it affects the families of the donor and the recipient of the organ.

the current issues and problems associated with suicide and its possible prevention.

the difficulties faced by the families of those who commit suicide.

how war has changed the meanings of death throughout history.

the threat imposed by modern nuclear weapons and how it affects our thinking.

the potential trends in death-related issues during our lifetimes.

N EWSPAPER ARTICLES
AND READER SELECTIONS

12.
Morality and Mortality
in Modern Society
Robert M. Veatch

from the Reader:

Our Failing Reverence for Life
Elizabeth Hall and *Paul Cameron*

Death, Legal and Illegal
Daniel C. Maguire

The Legislative Options
Robert M. Veatch

The Problem of Euthanasia
Sonya Rudikoff

A Demand to Die
Robert White and *H. Tristram Engelhardt, Jr.*

The Cadaver Donor and the Gift of Life
Julie Fulton, Robert Fulton, and
Roberta Simmons

13.
Suicide
Edwin S. Shneidman

from the Reader:

Myths about Suicide
Alex D. Pokorny

Ambivalence and Subintention
Edwin S. Shneidman

Counseling Suicide Survivors
Dean Schuyler

Death of a Man
Lael Wertenbaker

14.
Death, War, and the Human Condition
Robert Jay Lifton

from the Reader:

Death in War
Arnold Toynbee

15.
The Death System:
Review and Prospectus
Robert Kastenbaum

INTRODUCTION

In the ordinary view of things, it might seem that death poses few dilemmas. After all, living has become a habit with us, and death is simply an event that we wish to postpone for as long as possible. On the other hand, if we look beyond our ordinary experiences we see that the prospect of death yields a number of choices, none of which is easy.

The authors in Part Four provide us with a challenging view of many of the contemporary problems associated with death. For example, is it reasonable to terminate prematurely the life of a dying patient because of intense pain and suffering? And if so, who should be responsible for this decision? Is suicide a justifiable form of behavior, and under what circumstances would it be a reasonable choice? Are there alternatives to nuclear proliferation for the maintenance of world peace, or must we forever live under the shadow of nuclear holocaust? Should we think of the artificially maintained human body as an organ bank from which we may make withdrawals in order to preserve the lives of others? If so, how might this affect the grief response of survivors?

These and other questions are highlighted in Part Four, and the answers are not simple. In fact, the complexity of each question typically requires careful scrutiny of individual cases rather than general procedures to be followed in specified situations. One of the key issues is whether or not the individual has the freedom to control his own life and death and whether or not society has the right or the responsibility to interfere with this decision. Whatever answers we may come to, it is important to recognize that the ultimate decisions cannot be based on scientific "evidence" or philosophical "truths." These issues of right and wrong must be based on our religious and philosophical beliefs. This fact, above all, brings the dilemmas of death into close range for ourselves and for those who follow us.

12.
Morality and Mortality in Modern Society

HIGHLIGHTS

Human beings have created an amazingly sophisticated technology in their efforts to preserve life. At the same time, the technology thus created requires us to make choices that we have never before had to make. Robert Veatch, in the newspaper article "Morality and Mortality in Modern Society," identifies a number of problems posed by this technology, including when to withdraw treatment, when to administer death-inducing drugs, and how to decide when death has occurred. The difficulties of when to withdraw treatment and when to refrain from providing it, particularly when the patient cannot speak for himself or herself, remain as a major dilemma.

In the Reader article "Our Failing Reverence for Life," Elizabeth Hall and Paul Cameron survey various instances in American culture that appear to demonstrate a devaluation of life. They cite as evidence (1) the Supreme Court's legitimization of abortion during the first twenty-four weeks of life, (2) the "mercy-killing" of quadraplegics without their consent, and (3) the increasing public acceptance of "mercy-killing" and suicide as alternatives that are sometimes permissible. The authors suggest that bureaucracy, which has the power to eliminate the emotional component from human relationships, allows us to deal with excess population "efficiently." According to them, "Bureaucrats may already be making death-dealing decisions."

Daniel Maguire, in his article, "Death, Legal and Illegal," cites a number of recent court cases in which, under present laws, an act of mercy-killing could only be seen as manslaughter. In a number of the cases, however, by use of a judgment of temporary insanity, the defendant was acquitted. Maguire notes that when the letter of the law has not seemed fair, "there is a flight to psychiatry." This solution is not satisfactory, however, because justice dealt in this fashion is uneven. Maguire concludes that "The present categories of the law do not encompass the realities involved in death by choice . . . the motives for these deaths are compassion . . . they are not murder."

In "The Legislative Options," Robert Veatch reports on his analysis of eighty-five pieces of draft legislation that address the problems with which Maguire was concerned: mercy-killing, patients' rights, and the process of medical decision making. His analysis results in a design of a model bill that, among other things, would make clear that wishes expressed while patients were competent should remain valid when individuals are not able to express themselves, and would specify the penalty for failure to follow the patients' instructions. The author concludes that careful analysis of the objectives and consequences of this kind of legislation are necessary if new laws are to achieve their goals rather than hinder them.

Sonya Rudikoff's article, "The Problem of Euthanasia," begins by describing the growing interest in the issue as demonstrated by fast-increasing membership in the Euthanasia Society of America. She explains that "Euthanasia, often called 'death with dignity,' also implies the necessary medical efforts to reduce pain without needlessly prolonging the agony of one who is going to die." She distinguishes between negative or passive euthanasia, the omission of procedures without which the patient will die, and positive or active euthanasia, in which a specific act, like drug overdose, results in death. The two important questions about euthanasia, she suggests, are: (1) Do our bodies and ourselves belong to us in a way that allows us to specify the means of our own disposition? and (2) Is not all death nowadays really some form of euthanasia? The difficulty in the definition of death complicates these questions, but even more disturbing is the fact that in the absence of a small close-knit community of persons who care about a dying person, the pressure for euthanasia may increase, causing the potential for a dignified death to slip away into a meaningless death.

"A Demand to Die," by Robert White and H. Tristram Engelhardt, is a case study of some of the moral dilemmas surrounding death and dying. They discuss the ethics of caring for a person who requests the discontinuation of treatment. Robert White, the psychiatrist in the case, asks if such a demand might be the only way for the patient to regain his independence. While he agrees to help the patient obtain legal assistance in securing the termination of his treatment, the patient, once having won his point, consents to continued treatment and is able to survive and leave the hospital. Philosopher of medicine H. Tristram Englehardt views the case differently. He suggests that when the patient who is able to give free consent does not, the moral issue is over. Paternalistic intervention has no place beyond the wishes of the competent patient. According to Engelhardt, the competent adult patient should be allowed to make tragic decisions.

In the final selection in Section 12, Julie Fulton, Robert Fulton, and Roberta Simmons discuss their study of families who have donated organs from the body of a deceased family member. They found that this decision was often difficult to make and that there were problems in knowing how to respond to the brain-dead, artificially maintained, cadaver. For the most part family members were satisfied with their decision and felt they had done the right thing. The authors point out, however, that the family, in giving the gift of the organ, expect and are entitled to accurate information, recognition, and gratitude in return.

KEY CONCEPTS

Euthanasia. Literally translated from the Greek, this means the good or peaceful death, but this meaning has been altered in recent years by a variety of usages. *Mercy-killing* is also represented as a form of euthanasia in that it seeks actively to end life in the face of great suffering. The refusal of extraordinary measures, so that a person may experience "death with dignity," also falls under this rubric. Issues raised with regard to

euthanasia include the "quality of life" remaining and the idea of "meaningful humanhood." Both phrases signify an evaluation of the conditions under which life is experienced and a judgment as to whether or not life under such conditions is worth living. Under any circumstances it is important to specify who is making the judgment and what actions are to be followed as a result of it.

Active or positive euthanasia. The administration of some toxic agent or the withdrawal of some treatment from a terminally ill person in order to cause the death of that person. Examples would include a medication overdose or the removal of a respirator.

Passive or negative euthanasia. Failure to provide a treatment or medication to a terminally ill person at a critical time in order to bring about death. A physician's DNR (Do Not Resuscitate) order on a patient's chart would be an example of passive euthanasia.

Voluntary euthanasia. Euthanasia in which the patient consents to be killed or to be allowed to die; in *involuntary euthanasia* this decision is made by others.

Self-determination. The principle that an individual has the right to determine what course of action should be pursued in regard to himself or herself. Under this principle, doctors should not prolong treatment when the patient wishes it discontinued, regardless of the needs of others or of society. It is closely related to the idea of *the right to die,* which maintains that an individual has a right to bring his or her own life to an end.

Brain death criteria. Defined as the cessation of all electrochemical activity in the brain as typified by a flat electroencephalograph tracing. It is possible artificially to maintain the physical functioning of a human body in the absence of brain activity, so that organs may be kept alive for transplantation purposes.

Uniform Anatomical Gift Act. This is a piece of legislation that has been passed, in one form or another, in all fifty states; it specifies not only the rules to be followed in the case of transplant surgery but also allows an individual (and not his kin) to specify the way in which his or her body can be utilized or disposed of following death. This is a great departure from past traditions in that the survivors no longer have control over the disposition of a loved person's body.

Donor card. An outgrowth of the Uniform Anatomical Gift Act. It allows a person to specify the way in which his or her body may be utilized for medical purposes following death.

Living will. A document that is made out by a person of sound mind in the event that he or she should suffer a serious illness or accident; it typically requests that all extraordinary measures of care be withdrawn if the person's condition appears hopeless and the person is unable to communicate his or her wishes.

Cadaver-donor. Specifically, the cadaver-donor is the body from which an organ is removed for purposes of transplantation. The term is misleading, however, because it is not the deceased person that donates the organ; the donation is made by the family of the deceased at the time of death. Donation under such circumstances is difficult because the family members are not only shocked by the death but are also confused about how to think of the deceased. Maintenance of bodily functions with the use of a respirator gives the impression that life still exists, and refusal to give up hope at this time may make donation a very painful experience.

Abortion. The termination of pregnancy is in great dispute because of disagreements about the nature of what is being aborted. Advocates of the "right to life" position say that the unborn fetus is a human being with the same rights as other human beings; in this sense abortion is murder. Persons believing that an individual has the freedom to decide about all things concerning his or her own body and its treatment suggest that women have the right to abort an unborn fetus, particularly if there are compelling social, psychological, or medical reasons for doing so. Advocates of this position do not consider abortion murder.

FACTUAL REVIEW

1. What technological and medical developments account for new moral dilem-

mas surrounding death?

2. What does England's Suicide Act of 1961 permit?

3. What does *euthanasia* mean, and what does Veatch suggest that we do with the term?

4. What is meant by *passive euthanasia?* By *active euthanasia?*

5. What is a lifeboat ethic?

6. What did Paul Cameron find when he surveyed articles on suicide?

7. What tactic is assumed to obtain acquittal in mercy-killing cases?

8. What are the three basic types of euthanasia legislation currently under consideration in various states?

9. What is paternalistic intervention?

10. Who made the suggestion for organ donation in the case studies by Fulton, Fulton, and Simmons?

11. Who is involved in the decision to donate cadaver organs?

12. What is meant by *brain death,* and what is its significance?

ESSAY AND DISCUSSION

What are the problems of euthanasia? Why have these problems arisen and whom do they concern? What are the legislative prospects for the legalization of euthanasia?

Suggested guidelines: A. Review Sonya Rudikoff's article, paying particular attention to the distinction between positive and negative euthanasia.

B. Consider Veatch's discussion of the religious considerations involved.

C. Evaluate Hall and Cameron's discussion of the costs of care.

D. Review Maguire's study of judicial outcomes in euthanasia cases. Contrast these outcomes with the case presented by White and Engelhardt.

E. Weigh Veatch's suggestions for a model bill

against the issues raised previously. What problems still remain?

What is meant by a "failing reverence for life"? How do the families of cadaver-donors sometimes experience a sense of irreverence in the face of rapid hospital procedure?

Suggested guidelines: A. Consider Hall and Cameron's discussion of the possibility of unlimited machines that would keep thousands of bodies functioning. What examples do they cite as evidence of our "failing reverence for life"?
B. Review the criteria for "meaningful humanhood."
C. What does Rudikoff say about the "gift of life" and the "theft of life" in organ transplantation?
D. Consider Fulton, Fulton, and Simmons' discussion of the difficulty a family experiences in making an organ donation.

13.
Suicide

HIGHLIGHTS

Every individual in every society has had at least one alternative to continued existence. That alternative has been, and continues to be, suicide. What does the act of suicide mean to the person who chooses such an alternative or considers it? What does it mean to the survivors who must live with it? These and other questions form the center of our concern in Section 13.

In his newspaper article, Edwin Shneidman notes that suicide has meant different things in different cultures. The ancient Greeks and Romans, for example, did not condemn the act and apparently did not respond to it with great alarm. Suicide was not sin. Several hundred years later, however, persons who committed suicide were excommunicated from the Catholic Church because these people had taken from God the power over life and death. Later, during the Enlightenment, the idea that suicide was sinful was rejected, and

suicide was not considered a transgression against God or one's fellow citizens.

This fluctuation in the reaction to suicide has been accompanied by similar fluctuation in explanations of self-destructive behavior. Sociologists found that the relationship of an individual to his or her society was amiss. Psychologists, particularly the psychoanalysts, felt that suicide represented an individual's hostility toward another turned inward. The existential philosophers found it to be a response to life's apparent meaninglessness. Professor Shneidman, however, feels that the most important concepts in understanding suicide are those of hopelessness, helplessness, and ambivalence. Ambivalence means that the suicidal individual not only has the wish to die, but also the wish to be saved. The best way to help such persons, according to the author, is to help them communicate with others, break a fatal secret, and provide other alternatives to action.

In Alex Pokorny's article, "Myths about Suicide," we find that many of the ideas typically held by persons with respect to suicide are inaccurate. Contrary to popular belief, people who talk about suicide *will* often commit the act. In addition, those who commit suicide have typically given advance notification to someone. Suicide is not a single disease, but most often the result of a series of mental processes that are different for different people. Terminally ill persons will commit suicide as will persons recovering from severe depression or other mental illnesses. Finally, while suicide is not inherited, it may occur more frequently in a family with a history of many suicides because of beliefs among family members that suicide is their fate.

Edwin Shneidman's article, "Ambivalence and Subintention," discusses the subtleties involved in suicide. He provides us with a classification scheme for understanding not only the active death seeker, intending to bring about his or her own death, but also the more common "subintentioned" orientations toward death. The author states that:

> The evidence for such a role might be found in a variety of behavior patterns—poor judgment, imprudence, excessive risk-taking, neglect of self, disregard of a life-extending medical regimen, abuse of alcohol, misuse of drugs—all ways in which an individual can advance the date of his death.

Dean Schuyler's article, "Counseling Suicide Survivors: Issues and Answers," highlights the problems associated with being a survivor of a person who has committed suicide. The main problems appear to be stigma, guilt, and the need for a satisfactory explanation of the act. The author suggests that:

1. The survivor needs to reach an understanding of the suicidal death that preserves his or her own self-worth while satisfying the search for meaning in the death.
2. The survivor needs an opportunity to express feelings in a non-rejecting atmosphere.
3. The survivor needs to be encouraged to mourn the loss.
4. The survivor should be monitored for possible suicidal thoughts and behaviors.

The final article in this section is a personal view of suicide committed by a terminally ill man in great pain. It demonstrates not only the complexity of emotion involved in the act of suicide, but also the compassion that it may represent toward the survivors.

KEY CONCEPTS

Survivor stigma. This refers to the social and psychological burden suffered by the survivors of suicide as a result of being abandoned in such a hurtful way. It represents negative judgments by others regarding the survivors' qualities as human beings (e.g., "what kind of life did they cause the suicide victim to lead") and self-reflective feelings of guilt and a search for meaning.

Ambivalence. Shneidman suggests that ambivalence is the key concept in understanding the suicide act. Ambivalence refers to the suicidal individual's mixed desire to end his or her life and, at the same time, plead for help or recognition. Suicide is not a simple act of willful self-destruction; it involves different and often conflicting attitudes toward the ending of life.

Suicide prevention centers. Organizations dedicated to the prevention of suicide by the offering of help at a critical juncture in a person's life. While there have been a variety of such organizations since the Save-A-Life League founded in 1907, the National Institute of Mental Health provided funds for the establishment of such centers in the mid 1960s. They usually offer social, psychological, and/or religious help to the person contemplating suicide and the family members of potentially suicidal persons.

Intentional suicide. In intentional suicide, the individual plays a direct and conscious role in bringing about his own death. Shneidman suggests that there are four categories of persons that might be described as death intenders: persons who wish in some way to bring about their own deaths. *Death seekers* actively pursue their death with a commitment to the cessation of their lives. *Death initiators* choose to bring about their own death rather than have illness take life away. *Death ignorers* feel that it is possible to commit suicide and still survive in some form. *Death darers* are persons who bet their lives in games with difficult odds, such as Russian Roulette. They taunt death by placing themselves in vulnerable positions.

Unintentional death. Any death in which the decedent plays no significant role in bringing about his own demise. There are, however, different ways of acting upon the prospect of death and Shneidman uses the following categories: the *death welcomer*, the *death accepter*, the *death postponer*, the *death disdainer*, the *death fearer*, and the *death feigner* who threatens suicide for the purpose of manipulating others.

Subintentioned death. Shneidman suggests that death is not always sought consciously but the desire may be acted upon below the level of consciousness. He cites poor judgment, self-abuse, imprudence, and neglect of medical regimen as examples of unconscious behaviors that encourage early death.

FACTUAL REVIEW

1. How did Christians traditionally view suicide?
2. What did David Hume say in the eighteenth century to change the meaning of the suicidal act?
3. What are the psychological, sociological, and philosophic interpretations of death?
4. What does Shneidman mean when he says ambivalence is the key to understanding suicide?
5. Were rates of suicide during the depression years in the United States higher or lower than rates during the war years?
6. Is there any relationship between class background and rates of suicide?
7. What is a death-feigner?
8. What is subintentioned death, and what acts are associated with it?
9. What people are likely to investigate the survivors of suicide?
10. What is incomplete mourning, and why does it occur among suicide survivors?
11. What method did Lael Wertenbaker's husband finally resort to for the purpose of ending his suffering?
12. Why must we view suicide statistics with caution?

ESSAY AND DISCUSSION

What are the major factors associated with a person's decision to commit suicide? How is it possible to recognize a suicidal person, and what can be done to try to prevent suicide? What can be done to help survivors of suicide?

Suggested guidelines: A. Review Shneidman's newspaper article and his discussion of the key elements in the suicidal act and how it is possible to intervene.

B. Consider Shneidman's categories of intentioned death in the Reader.
C. Review Lael Wertenbaker's description of her husband's decision.
D. What does Pokorny say about depression and terminal illness? Does this correspond to "Wert's" decision?
E. Evaluate Schuyler's discussion of aiding survivors.

14.
Death, War, and the Human Condition

HIGHLIGHTS

It seems strange indeed that, at the very time when human beings have come to manage death so successfully and control disease in a way unimagined prior to the twentieth century, we have simultaneously lost control over another crucial and frightening mode of death: death in war. The ordinary person in the world today has little control over this aspect of life and there is no place on earth where he or she can feel entirely safe from the threat of a nuclear holocaust. The authors in this unit discuss the implications of such a threat and the human responsibility that falls to us and future generations in the face of it.

In Robert Jay Lifton's newspaper article, "Death, War, and the Human Condition," we are introduced to the concept of *psychic numbing,* which refers to our response to the potential for massive and meaningless death. The Hiroshima survivors suffered this when thousands of their fellow citizens were annihilated on August 6, 1945. Its essential ingredients are disorientation, a sort of paralysis of the mind, and inability to feel. Most threatening, however, is the fact that "numbing is perhaps greatest in those who create and anticipate using the weapon." Lifton goes on to describe how nuclear war threatens to destroy our past and our future, and thus our symbolic forms of immortality. Nuclearism, he argues, is both a pseudo-religion and a disease. By recognizing it as such, we can begin to overcome it.

Arnold Toynbee's insightful essay "Death in War," reprinted in the Reader, provides us with an analysis of war as a basic institution of society. In war, "killing is no murder"; it is redefined as noble and glorious. Moreover, war is an act of religious worship designed to satisfy the national community on whose behalf it is waged.

Furthermore, the higher religions have had little effect on the fanatic nationalism that has developed in this century. The use of nuclear weapons in defense of national interests is, according to Toynbee, one of the great atrocities of our time and results in the obliteration of the distinction between victor and vanquished.

Edwin Shneidman's article, "Megadeath: Children of the Nuclear Family," discusses the way in which the present generation of young persons is affected by the threat of mass violence and destruction. He argues that

> ...many perceive the threat of mass death as very real; they cannot be assured of a future. Having lost this hope, they lack...that optimism which spurs people to productivity, to goal-directed actions, and in the end, to life.

In addition, Shneidman feels that this loss of future beckons youth to another specter of death, one that is flirted with in the form of greater risk-taking behavior, police confrontations, suicide attempts, promiscuity, and drug abuse.

Turning from the impact of possible annihilation to the impact of actual annihilation,

Robert Lifton's article, "Witnessing Survival," provides a close look at the survivors of a holocaust. He describes five psychological themes that appear to be common to anyone "who has encountered, been exposed to, or witnessed death and has himself or herself remained alive." These include (1) *death imprinting,* in which the images of death are indelibly etched upon the mind, (2) *death guilt,* in which the survivors feel responsible for their helplessness during the holocaust, (3) *psychic numbing,* described previously as a paralysis of the mind in which ordinary feelings are abandoned, (4) *moral inversion,* or a *suspicion of counterfeit nurturance,* in which living and dying lose all moral structure, and (5) the *struggle for meaning,* in which the survivor desperately tries to reestablish the semblance of a "moral universe." Lifton suggests that when death occurs on such a massive scale, not only are survivors denied the opportunity of mourning, but they also lose the psychic capacity to absorb such tragedy.

In the final article in this section, "Consequences of Nuclear War," Bernard Feld, a physicist, introduces some "sobering figures" of what a nuclear holocaust would be like. What the U.S. Pentagon believes would be an "acceptably small" number of casualties resulting from a "counterforce" exchange with the Soviets turns out to be a rather large figure. An attack on all land-based missiles located only on continental U.S. territory would result in the deaths of from 3.5 to 22 million Americans and more than one million Canadians. The vast majority of these casualties would be civilians. Moreover, it is impossible to predict with any certainty the longterm effects of massive nuclear exchange. There is the potential for major climatological shifts, a reduction of the ozone layer, and a consequent increase in the amount of harmful ultraviolet radiation reaching the earth's surface. Additionally, there are the cancer-producing radioactive nuclei to be considered. These nuclei could affect not only surviving generations, but their offspring as well. Feld concludes that warfare of this type, given continued sophistication of weaponry, could "spell the end of humankind on planet Earth."

KEY CONCEPTS

Psychic numbing. This is the phrase coined by Lifton to represent the way in which our minds react to actual or potential holocaust. The survivors of Hiroshima are said to have experienced this in their reactions of hopelessness or helplessness. It results in a diminished capacity to feel; a "paralysis of the mind." Such a reaction, in muted form, is also thought to obtain in contemporary culture under the threat of nuclear warfare.

Moral universe. This refers to a set of ethical principles by which life is somehow ordered. In the event of a disaster of some kind it is difficult to feel that such a universe is intact or possible to restore. This is related to the "struggle for meaning" that follows great tragedy when the survivors attempt to make sense out of what must appear senseless.

Nuclearism. A pseudo-religion, according to Shneidman, in which "the bomb" becomes a deity—the source of creation, destruction, and salvation.

Death guilt or Survivor guilt. The illogical feeling that survivors often have as a result of living through an experience that killed many others. Part of the difficulty is the sense of complete helplessness that one feels when surrounded by massive death and horror.

Megadeath, Overkill, Global annihilation. These are all terms referring to the potential devastation of our planet through nuclear warfare. They signify a new dimension of death that has been made possible only with increasing amounts of nuclear weaponry.

Hibakusha. "Explosion-affected persons" refers to the survivors of atomic bombing in Japan.

There is great stigma associated with being a survivor because the effects of radiation distorted physical appearance and these persons were often felt to be cursed in some way. Shneidman asks if the present generation of young persons might not be psychological Hibakusha, affected by the many bombs that are unexploded.

Global tenuousness. A phrase used by Shneidman to indicate the limited sense of future experienced by younger persons in the face of potential nuclear catastrophe. It results in a heightened emphasis on the present.

Religion of nationalism. Toynbee uses this phrase to describe current commitments to national ideals. He suggests that this is the worship of collective power and results in the ritual of war.

Global village. A symbolic description of the modern world in which we can have instantaneous communications between any two points but still retain physical distance and detachment. It emphasizes our shared vulnerability to nuclear destruction.

Preemptive attack. An offensive strike with nuclear weapons in which there is no warning and no specific reason for suspecting an attack.

Mutual deterrence. A strategy involving the mutual threat of retaliation against population centers in response to the initiation of nuclear war by either side. This strategy has been replaced by the threat of "counter force" in which nuclear missile installations in the Soviet Union could be preemptively attacked by American missiles.

"Experiential transcendence." A psychic state thought to arise out of the vision of nuclear death in which people attempt to escape mystically from the world through intensified experience.

Immortality. The belief that somehow we survive death. According to Lifton, there are five kinds of symbolic immortality we pursue: biologic, through our children; creative, through our works; religious, through spiritually conquering death; natural, through rebirth in eternal nature; and transcendental, through mysticism. The first four, he argues, are threatened by nuclear destruction.

FACTUAL REVIEW

1. What is the *global village?*
2. What does Lifton mean by *nuclearism?*
3. What is *"psychic numbing,"* and what is its significance?
4. Through what kinds of symbolic immortality have we tried to transcend death?
5. How does "experiential transcendence" solve the threat of death?
6. When did war begin on this planet?
7. What conditions must be met to make war possible?
8. What is *megadeath?*
9. What is the effect of the threat of nuclear holocaust on young people, according to Shneidman?
10. What does the word *holocaust* mean?
11. What are the five psychological themes of survivorship?
12. What would be the effect on our environment of a massive nuclear exchange?
13. What kinds of nuclear testing were still permitted following the Partial Test-Ban Treaty of 1963?

ESSAY AND DISCUSSION

Discuss the prospects of nuclear war, the impact of these prospects on the current population, and the potential consequences of such a holocaust.

Suggested guidelines: A. Reread Toynbee's discussion of the religion of nationalism.
B. Consider Lifton's newspaper account of the "death-haunted global village" and the disease of nuclearism.
C. Review Shneidman's discussion of children of the nuclear family.
D. Review Feld's discussion of the consequences of nuclear war.
E. Compare Feld's account to the description of survivors provided by Lifton in "witnessing survival."

15.
The Death System: Review and Prospectus

HIGHLIGHTS

Death is a single event in the life of every person. It happens every hour of every day, but never to the same person twice. This course has had as its object the understanding of this event as we contemplate it, observe it, avoid it, and prepare for it. Needless to say, it is difficult to obtain closure on such an event, whether it is discussed in a course such as this or experienced in a hospital bed. Nevertheless, there are some final points worth making, and the authors in Section 15 have taken this on as their task.

Robert Kastenbaum, in his newspaper article "Review and Prospectus," notes that we are a self-critical people. When we feel our failings in the face of death we address them in the form of social criticism. In fact, much of this course has taken just such a form. Unfortunately, the atmosphere that is sometimes generated by this activity "is not," according to Kastenbaum, "conducive to serenity, balanced judgment, and acting from one's own deepest impulses." But Kastenbaum is hopeful. He notes that whenever we improve the quality of life for terminally ill persons or their survivors, we improve and enrich the lives of us all. If we agree that the situation of the dying patient is inhumane or worse, we cannot continue to tolerate the status quo unless we are thoughtless of our own future. Kastenbaum points out that, although death is a personal event, it also takes place within a public death system. Our death system today has unprecedented powers both to cure and to kill, and we must be wary lest they overshadow the other functions of the death system.

In the Reader article "Harvesting the Dead," author Willard Gaylin presents a "modest proposal." He suggests that we make full utilization of brain death criteria by maintaining a laboratory (bioemporium) of artificially maintained corpses (neomorts) for use as organ donors. He suggests that we could not only make regular harvests of blood and other tissues, but we could also use the corpses for the training of young medical practitioners. He applies a cost benefit analysis to this proposal and falls short on only one criterion: "how are we to reconcile our emotions?" More than anything this article warns us that in the age of remarkable technology, we must not forget that such technology is produced for service to humanity. If the technology destroys the qualities that we regard as human, it should be difficult to accept its benefits.

Hans Morgenthau's article, "Death in the Nuclear Age," suggests that human beings have attempted to transcend death in three ways: (1) by making ourselves the masters of death (e.g., by an act of suicide), (2) by denying the reality of death (e.g., through the belief in immortality), or (3) by conquering the reality of death through the immortality of the world we leave behind (e.g., through the social organizations and physical artifacts that survive individual existence). As Lifton pointed out in his newspaper article, these different methods of transcending death are, however, in danger of extinction in the nuclear age. According to Morgenthau:

> nuclear destruction destroys the meaning of death by depriving it of its individuality. It destroys the meaning of immortality by making both society and history impossible. It destroys

the meaning of life by throwing life back upon itself.

He warns us that we must not refuse to believe in the potential for nuclear war simply because it seems so absurd. The greatest absurdity is our refusal to adapt our thinking about the meaning of life and death to a radically transformed social world, one in which nuclear devastation is a real possibility.

The final selection in Section 15 is "The Experience of Death," by Ignace Lepp. He notes that our experiences with death are always indirect. We learn of what death means in our social existence, not in the event of our own death. Significantly, human beings appear to be the only living things that know ahead of time of our own destiny in death. All evidence suggests that, until recently, this information has never been taken lightly. But now, when individuals view the death of another, it appears as a simple biological event. It is only our own deaths we find troublesome.

KEY CONCEPTS

Death system. Refers to the way in which events associated with death are organized in a particular culture. The idea of a system reflects the fact that there are relatively stable practices and expectations with regard to what *people* are involved, what *places, objects,* and *symbols* are to be utilized, and what *functions* are to be fulfilled. *Body disposal, reintegration, memorialization,* and *killing* are all functions of the death system.

Neomort. The term used by Willard Gaylin to describe newly "brain dead" cadavers that are maintained on respirators to be used as a source of human parts for transplantation.

Bioemporium. This is the term Gaylin uses to describe the housing facilities for neomorts. Gaylin's "modest proposal" is that these facilities could be used for the training of medical students, the testing of new drugs and procedures, biological experimentation, the storage of usable organs, the harvesting of renewable resources (like blood), and the manufacturing of substances like hormones.

Homo faber. This refers to the human being as he or she creates original cultural artifacts. This is thought to represent a striving toward immortality in that what is created lives on beyond the life of the creator.

Immortality. See Section 14: Key Concepts.

FACTUAL REVIEW

1. What is the death system?
2. What are the functions of the death system?
3. What would be harvested in a harvest of the dead, according to Gaylin?
4. What technology is required for maintenance of the neomort?
5. In what three ways have human beings attempted to transcend death?
6. How does nuclear destruction destroy the meaning of death?
7. What creatures of the earth know of their own mortality?
8. How did St. Augustine come to give meaning to death?

ESSAY AND DISCUSSION

What are some of the potential forms of death in the last quarter of the twentieth century? Are these forms more or less humane than the forms of death we have seen in this century?

Suggested guidelines: (This is a speculative question and requires individual judgments about what constitutes a humane death.)

A. Consider Kastenbaum's discussion of America's self-criticism. Does this coincide with Morgenthau's assessment, that we are not aware of our own condition?
B. How does Morgenthau regard the future prospects of death?
C. Review what Lepp says about our indifference to the deaths of strangers.
D. Evaluate Willard Gaylin's proposal for harvesting the dead. How is it possible to retain our humanity under the conditions he describes?